W9-BRZ-882

The Social Media Revolution

The Social Media Revolution

An Economic Encyclopedia of Friending, Following, Texting, and Connecting

Jarice Hanson

GREENWOOD™

An Imprint of ABC-CLIO, LLC
Santa Barbara, California • Denver, Colorado

Library of Congress Cataloging-in-Publication Data

Names: Hanson, Jarice, author.
Title: The social media revolution : an economic encyclopedia of friending, following, texting, and connecting / Jarice Hanson.
Description: Santa Barbara : Greenwood, 2016. | Includes bibliographical references and index.
Identifiers: LCCN 2015045802 | ISBN 9781610697675 (print : alk. paper) | ISBN 9781610697682 (ebook)
Subjects: LCSH: Social media—Encyclopedias. | Online social networks—Encyclopedias. | Communication—Technological innovations—Encyclopedias.
Classification: LCC HM742 .H3756 2016 | DDC 302.23/1—dc23 LC record available at http://lccn.loc.gov/2015045802

ISBN: 978-1-61069-767-5
EISBN: 978-1-61069-768-2

20 19 18 17 16   1 2 3 4 5

This book is also available as an eBook.
Visit www.abc-clio.com for details.

Greenwood
An Imprint of ABC-CLIO, LLC

ABC-CLIO, LLC
130 Cremona Drive, P.O. Box 1911
Santa Barbara, California 93116-1911
www.abc-clio.com

This book is printed on acid-free paper (∞)

Manufactured in the United States of America

Contents

Alphabetical List of Entries

Preface

Social media present us with a fascinating context in which to examine technology, economics, behavior, and social change. Our ability to obtain information and become a publisher of our own content online has never been so accessible or so easy. Whether we hope to connect with one person or with many, social media have allowed us to think about participating in a *global village* in a number of different ways. Our information processing ability is faster, cheaper, and easier to operate than at any time in history and the changes seem to have occurred so seamlessly that we often take new technologies and their information processing power for granted, and we often forget that social media are currently only in their adolescence.

When Web 2.0 (the *interactive* nature of communications over the Internet) opened the 'Net to two-way information flow in the early 2000s, the media industries that controlled much of the content of the former communications technologies began to compete with user-generated messages. Very quickly new services began to be introduced that challenged the former economic models that supported legacy media. But, like traditional media, most of them could not operate without funding and creating a sustainable flow of financial support. Free models competed with advertising-supported models, and *venture capital* became a buzzword for predicting the likely success of dot-com start-ups.

At the same time, the number of digital technologies that allowed us to access media content and produce our own blogs, websites, gaming opportunities, and businesses began to open new opportunities for people to collaborate with others or participate in communities online. The technical capacity of mobile phones began to challenge the information processing ability of personal computers. Today's smartphone has the information processing power of a mainframe computer of 20 years ago. This mobility and the ubiquity of the Internet allowed many people who began to rely on these digital tools to feel they could not live without Internet connectivity anywhere, anytime.

All of the new devices and ways of communicating have important consequences for the way we think of the world and our sense of self in that world.

Though mobile phones and Internet connections are better than they've ever been before for many people, vast disparities in global access exist. Even within the United States, the ability to afford the simplest of mobile phones still eludes many, and Internet connections are not always available or affordable. So who does benefit from these changes in communication and information? What companies are responsible for these new ideas and the implementation of social networking? Most important, how do social media and social networking affect our lives?

This book begins to examine these issues from a very simple starting point. By examining what is happening to legacy industries and evaluating the new models and forms of communication, this book provides a "snapshot" in time of what many people have called "the social media revolution." By looking at the individuals, the companies, the policies, and the practices of those involved with technologies and uses of social media and social networks, we will have a better sense of the forces that shape our future.

There are many people who contributed to the writing of this encyclopedia. First and foremost, Hilary Claggett of ABC-CLIO deserves credit for her vision of the project, and I owe a personal debt of thanks to her for thinking about me as the author of this book. Frank Aronson has been, and continues to be, the Computer Mensch who makes me laugh and poses the nerd-questions that make me stop to think about the impact of technology from the user's point of view. My students at the University of Massachusetts have often been my first audience, and therefore have explored with me and challenged me to see the world through their eyes. Together we have pondered the future by examining the past and present through our own type of microscope. I thank them for their interest, optimism, and quest for a better life.

Introduction

The fabric of civilization is being rewoven around us. The very nature of life, work, and society is changing so profoundly that we are approaching a moment at which our old ways of thinking about the structures that sustain us may be seen as obsolete.

—David Rothkopf (2014, 79–80)

Especially for the younger generation, the Internet is not some standalone, separate domain where a few of life's functions are carried out. It is not merely our post office and our telephone. Rather, it is the epicenter of our world, the place where virtually everything is done.

—Glenn Greenwald (2014, 5)

This encyclopedia includes facts and examples to help understand the way in which individuals, technologies, industries, companies, governments, and policies dealing with social media have intersected to create new contexts for communication. All of these contexts influence the way individuals, groups, and nations adopt, reject, or change, due to new ways of communicating. As David Rothkopf, author and editor of the magazine *Foreign Policy,* has observed, the ways we do things are changing all around us, and those changes are coming fast. He titled his essay "Disconnected," and many people have agreed that rapid changes in the way we do things makes us sometimes feel insecure or pushes us into a situation where we *re*act, rather than *act* thoughtfully or logically.

But, at the same time, there are generations of people whose worldview is conditioned and mediated by the technologies they use for everyday purposes. Investigative journalist Glenn Greenwald's comment reflects that the younger generation, like all "younger generations," perceives their world in a very different way than their parents, teachers, bosses, and politicians did. For this reason, this encyclopedia bridges the gap between older forms of media that influenced the way people have become used to doing things, and the important economic, social, and cultural changes that are becoming a greater part of our daily lives today.

Many of the changes we're experiencing affect a number of aspects in our lives. For example, the subtitle of this book includes the words "friending," "following," "texting," and "connecting." Social media have changed the way we think of friends by allowing us to "friend" people we may never have personally met. What makes a friend? Is it someone who agrees to accept a Facebook invitation? Is it possible to have virtual friends? How do you really know if what people tell you or the pictures they post online are real? Using social media forces us to consider what "friends" are and we should be reminded that not everything on the Internet is authentic.

Similarly, the concept of *following* can have many meanings. Do you follow all of your online friends? Do you follow political news, and, if so, do you choose only the news sources that express a political view that confirms your values? Do you follow your favorite celebrities on Twitter? And, without being facetious, if social media allow you to follow news, information, and others, what does it mean for someone to lead? The new vocabulary makes us especially critical of how we use these terms (or, at least, the new vocabulary should make us critical about what those terms mean).

Texting is an excellent example of a social practice that has changed the way we communicate and ultimately has changed speech patterns. In the early days of texting it took effort to type capital letters, so many texts were sent in all lowercase form, often making me think that someday, civilization will uncover early tweets and instant messages and wonder how the poet e. e. cummings had such a powerful impact on culture. Text shorthand, like lol, omg, and cu have now crossed over into forms of literature and other print and graphic-based technologies, as well as daily speech.

What type of *connections* do we make with other people and to information? Sure, there are physical technological connections that can be made with others and with service providers, but, in social media, do we connect with others as meaningfully as we would in face-to-face communication? Without a doubt our behaviors change as we adapt to new technologies and new ways of communicating, but, ultimately, are we sure that the messages we send are accurately received by others? And, likewise, are we communicating in the way we want to communicate for the best expression of our feelings, thoughts, and emotions? One of the biggest questions we should be asking in terms of the "connections" we make is, "When we use social media, are we communicating *more*, or *less*?"

This encyclopedia is intended to be a reference for the many actors and actions that are influencing the way we communicate through social networking. For many, the experience can be rewarding at times, but also disconnecting in many ways.

Throughout each of the entries, the economic, social, and political aspects of the topic are identified to help explain the way in which social media and social networking in general are creating situations that divorce us from prior ways of thinking and doing, and sometimes propel us into behaving and thinking in entirely new ways. As we leave some of the old ways behind, we should be mindful of the way the new contexts suggest change.

An important question we should ask is, "Are social media really social?" Some forms may be, but other forms may well have the capacity to limit or restrict actual "connection" to someone else, or meaning. Some forms of social media have been found to create alienation and contribute to loneliness. Bullying and harassment affects people of all ages, and with social networking, how can you defend yourself from unwanted attacks? You may find that at times in your life, the question can be answered in a number of different ways. What is most important now, however, is that you think broadly, with an open mind, about the many ways in which social media and social networking change our relationships to the past, to others, and how they may possibly contribute to how we think of the future.

One thing that will undoubtedly occur to you as you peruse the various entries in this encyclopedia is that every form of media and every mode of communication inevitably changes over time. In the case of social media and social networking, are these changes revolutionary, or evolutionary? It's my perspective that they are revolutionary in the sense that they are evolving quickly and creating massive change on a global scale—in fact, so quickly that it's hard to keep up with the constant changes, new products, and marketing hype. But at the same time I would agree that some of the changes are indeed evolutionary. New business models evolve, thanks to the forces that create new business opportunities, and often in reaction to previous models. Current controversies about the *agency model* for the delivery of electronic books are a particularly good example for bringing together traditional copyright issues, legacy print publishers, and the distribution of books without paper. Amazon, as a leading online retailer, has revolutionized purchasing, but the shift to digital forms is also evolutionary.

And having mentioned Amazon, the organization created the "one-click" purchasing process for Amazon. Does that new opportunity to make purchases easily change the consideration we've given to making a purchase? Do we sometimes buy on impulse, or buy what we really don't need? The more we buy online, the less we need brick-and-mortar stores, resulting in fewer job opportunities, a shift in the way we think about goods, and in the act of shopping itself. But does it also change our relationship to the goods we purchase, or contribute to a different way of thinking?

Social media is intricately tied to many of the new ways we conduct business and the way we think about what's important in our daily lives. We can react to a host of different forms of advertising over social media, and we can make purchases, play games, and possibly even vote using the same networks we use to keep up with "friends," gossip, and cat videos.

At the same time, every legacy industry has had to cope with an evolution to digital forms. The recording industry has undergone major changes in marketing and revenue, while companies like Blockbuster have gone out of business as videotapes and DVDs (once the new technologies sweeping the nation) have shifted to streaming platforms, Netflix, and a variety of different entertainment delivery options. How will this type of content be paid for? Will the future involve a different type of currency, such as cybercurrency? If so, how will our economy change to incorporate digital distribution of exchange, or, will new ways of trading goods and services emerge?

So, as Rothkopf and Greenwald remind us, old media industries are bound to change, and different generations may perceive these changes in different ways. What each of us has to consider is what those changes mean for us, and how they affect the quality of our lives.

References

Greenwald, Glenn. 2014. *No Place to Hide: Edward Snowden, the NSA, and the U.S. Surveillance State.* New York: Henry Holt.

Rothkopf, David. 2014. "Disconnected." *Foreign Policy,* 94: 79–80.

Timeline

19th Century: Early Wired Communication

1844 Samuel F. B. Morse develops language for effective use of the telegraph.

1871 Western Union handles 90 percent of the telegraphic traffic.

1876 Alexander Graham Bell receives patent for what became the telephone.

1888 Heinrich Hertz demonstrates use of electromagnetic waves.

1898 Guglielmo Marconi demonstrates wireless communication (radio).

20th Century: Early Wireless Communication and Development of Digital Technology

1926 NBC Red, NBC Blue radio networks founded.

1927 CBS radio network founded.
Federal Radio Commission (FRC) established.

1934 Communications Act of 1934 passed; establishes Federal Communications Commission (FCC).

1946 Television begins regular broadcasts.

1947 97 percent of the U.S. radio stations are affiliated with one of the four networks (NBC Blue, NBC Red, CBS, and Mutual).

1955 Bell Labs develops the transistor, allowing radio receivers to become portable. Also introduces its first transistor computer.

1956 Russia launches their first satellite (Sputnik).
In the United States the silicon wafer is invented.

1957 U.S. launches their first satellite (Early Bird).

1959 First commercial radio phone for cars developed.

1963 MCI challenges AT&T's monopoly over wired telephony by using satellite distribution of telephone signals.

1966 First ARPANET plan discussed.

1968 Microwave Communications of America Inc. (MICOM) is started; this is the first serious challenge to AT&T's monopoly of telephony in the United States (becomes MCI in 1969), and it is allowed to operate wireless telephony.

1969 First two research labs (UCLA and the Stanford Research Institute) link up to Internet.

1971 First e-mail transmitted.

1972 First mobile phone demonstrated in London.

1974 The name "Internet" is given to describe "Internetworking."

1975 Bill Gates and Paul Allen form Microsoft.

1976 Steve Jobs and Steve Wozniak start Apple (incorporated in 1977); Apple I home computer invented.

1978 Electronic Bulletin Board System starts (BBS).
Project Gutenberg begins with the goal of digitizing all books.
First mention of spam.

1979 Usenet developed at Duke University and University of North Carolina.

1981 NSF develops Computer Science Network (CSNET).
BITNET (because it's there network) is developed.

1982 Internet Protocol Suite (TCP/IP) standardized.

1983 In the United States, the first analog-based mobile phone developed.
Time Magazine names the computer "Man of the Year."

1984 First digital phone developed.
Prodigy ISP developed.
First smartphone developed.
AT&T's monopoly over U.S. telephony ends, along with deregulation of media industries.

1985 Whole Earth "Lectronic Link" started (WELL).

1988 The first transatlantic fiber optic cable is completed.

1989 CERN releases World Wide Web (WWW).

1990 BITNET ceases; term "Internet" more widely used.
Electronic Frontier Foundation (EFF) is founded.

1993 More than 200 web servers online.
MOSAIC developed.
U.S. White House goes online (www.whitehouse.gov/).
Linux developed.

1994 Jeff Bezos introduces Amazon.
Jerry Yang and David Filo start Yahoo!
Marc Andreessen develops Netscape.
Al Gore begins to use the term "information superhighway."
First Virtual, the first cyberbank opens.
MOSAIC introduces Netscape web browser.

1995 GeoCities developed.
Amazon launches online bookstore.
RealAudio, the first audio streaming service begins.
The term "Internet" is first used by the public.

1996 Communications Decency Act (CDA) passed by Supreme Court.
Telecommunications Act of 1996 passed January 3, 1996, and signed into
law on February 8, 1996.
Internet Explorer web browser introduced by Microsoft.

1997 Start of what became known as the "dot-com bubble" (until 2000).
Blogging begins.
AOL Instant Messenger introduces chat feature.
Blackboard, the online course management system is introduced.
Hotmail developed.
eBay started.
Digital Video Discs (DVDs) go on the market.

1998 Google founded.
ICANN created.
Children's Online Protection Act (COPA) passed.
Children's Online Privacy Protection Act of 1998 (COPPA) passed.
Dot-com boom starts.
Apple introduces the iMac, a consumer grade all-in-one desktop computer.
Netscape is acquired by AOL.

1999 Amazon gets patent for 1-click.
Original Napster cofounded by Shawn Fanning, John Fanning, and Sean
Parker (peer-to-peer file sharing program shut down by courts in 2001;

continues to operate with the name "Napster" by other companies that purchased the protocol).

Mozilla web browser introduced.

2000 Dot-com bubble bursts (March): at this time 70 million computers are connected to the Internet.

AOL merges with Time Warner.

21st Century: Interactive Technologies Boom

2001 Wikipedia starts.

Apple introduces iPod.

2002 Friendster, the first social network for friends starts.

Chimera and Phoenix web browsers introduced.

Microsoft Internet Explorer becomes largest browser, worldwide.

2003 Mark Zuckerberg releases Facemash at Harvard.

MySpace, LinkedIn, and Skype all begin.

Apple introduces iTunes.

Firebird, Safari, and My Internet Explorer 2 web browsers available.

25 percent of U.S. home users have broadband.

2004 Mark Zuckerberg registers thefacebook.com domain.

Facebook launched February 4.

Facebook expands to other colleges in the Northeast United States.

Facebook incorporates and moves to Palo Alto, CA.

Podcasting starts.

Flickr starts.

Digg starts.

Camino, Safari, Firefox, and Maxthon web browsers introduced.

2005 News Corp. acquires MySpace.

YouTube started.

Facebook starts branching out into high schools.

Etsy, an online commercial site starts.

Apple introduces Mac Mini and iPod nano.

Lunascape web browser introduced.

2006 MySpace is the most popular social network service.

Twitter launched.

WikiLeaks becomes known as an organization based in Iceland.

Apple introduces MacBook Pro.

2007 Microsoft buys stake in Facebook.
Facebook launches Beacon advertising system.
Tumblr starts.
Apple releases first iPhone.
Apple TV is demonstrated (discontinued in 2009).
Netsurf web browser introduced.

2008 Facebook surpasses MySpace in terms of subscribers.
Facebook attempts to buy Twitter, but is unsuccessful.
Brian Chesney and Joe Gebbie start Airbnb.
Apple introduces the MacBook Air, an ultraportable notebook.
Iron web browser introduced.
Google introduced Chrome web browser.

2009 Bing starts.
Term "unfriend" becomes popular.
Megan Meier Cyberbullying Prevention Act proposed to Congress.
Google introduced Android operating system.
Uber, the car sharing service, is founded in San Francisco.
Pinterest launched.

2010 Google launches Buzz to compete with Facebook and Twitter.
Apple releases iPad tablet.
Internet surpasses newspapers as primary news source in United States.
First prototype of Google Glass.
"Apps" becomes the word of the year.

2011 Google launches Google+ (pronounced Google Plus), its own social network.
Apple introduces iPad2.

2012 Facebook acquires Instagram for $1 billion; the largest acquisition to date.
Facebook goes public with stock options.
Facebook reaches one billion users worldwide.
Internet advertising gains more revenue than print advertising.
Department of Justice files complaint about e-publishers use of Agency Model for paying authors.
Apple introduces "new iPad."

2013 Edward Snowden leaks classified information from the National Security Agency (NSA).
Google Glass is launched.
Apple introduces iPad Air.

2014   Apple releases iWatch, iPhone 6, and iPadAir2.
Apple Pay is introduced; canceled days after implementation for security breach. Would later be reinstated in different countries at different times.
European Union's Court of Justice rules on "The Right to Be Forgotten."
Amazon wins first awards for original programming with the series, "Transparent."

2015   New point-of-purchase terminals for debit and credit cards with computer chips used in the United States.
PlayStation begins developing original scripted programming.

Historical Overview

What's *Social* about *Social Media*?

Many people complain that technological changes occur faster than they can keep up with them these days and there is plenty of anecdotal evidence to indicate they may be right, but there haven't been many social movements that advocate for slowing technological growth or returning to earlier, "simpler" times. What makes understanding the subtle social and economic changes related to technological growth so difficult is that technology changes on so many levels and affects individuals so differently, it is sometimes inadequate to think of change as something that has a cause and effect. It is also hard to really grasp the consequences of new technologies or new ways of doing things until we've lived with those consequences for some time and we have the perspective necessary to see what those changes are, and whom they effect.

Technological change is steeped in the myth of creating more efficient, convenient ways of doing things, despite some evidence to the contrary. For example, hybrid cars are considered far preferable than others for environmental reasons and because of the benefit of less gasoline consumption, but the cost of a hybrid car is much greater than the nonhybrid type. Giving up your wired phone in the home in favor of using a cell phones is obviously an economical alternative to maintaining two phones and paying two bills, but what happens when the wireless system is affected by a power outage, storm, or dead battery?

While these examples may seem like obvious trade-offs, there are many more examples of contexts that show us that communication technology may be mired in a host of potentially conflicting issues, and, for that reason, this book approaches the problems under the rubric of friending, texting, and connecting. The term *friending* connotes social relationships, *texting* references different modes of communicating, and *connecting* suggests not only the physical connections necessary to communicate over the tools of media and communication and information technologies but also the way we make sense of what we do when we use these tools.

The reason for approaching the topic of *social media* as the unit of analysis in this collection is that with the development of Web 2.0, the interactive nature of using tools of communication over the Internet has contributed to the rapid acceleration of change in many ways: socially, economically, technologically, and culturally. As a result, if we look at the way other media forms evolved and the spirals of influence they had, and were subject to, we might better understand that all media are inherently social in some way—but the questions are better asked if we consider who uses these technologies, how they use them, for what purposes, and, ultimately, with what impact or effect?

Lessons from History

The major technological changes in history have provided contexts for examining the social, economic, and cultural changes we, as humans, experience as our modes of communication change. For example, every major new medium for communication that was referred to as "big media" changed multiple ways of doing things; newspapers put a heavier emphasis on the need for literacy and contributed to a linear way of thinking, but at the same time they contributed to the field of journalism and the role of the press in a democratic government. In Western cultures we read from left to right—giving an implied meaning that print is a linear medium and that logic can be charted linearly. We start at the beginning and move sequentially toward the end. The telegraph allowed people to send news and information over wired communication forms that actually contributed to the United States (as one example) becoming a nation and to the growth of industries that relied on transnational communication as well as organizing the continental United States into four time zones. Radio enhanced the imagination with its use of images it supplied in the minds of listeners, spurred the development of the advertising industry, and created expectations of important information coming to the public within minutes. Film, on the large screen, became an industry that provided a special place for audiences to see images that were larger than life, contributed to celebrity culture, and led American domination of global entertainment media. Television, of course, brought visual entertainment into the home, changed the way families communicated, and provided a form of mass popular culture that has defined generations of viewers. What each of these forms of media have in common, though, is that they emerged and evolved in the late nineteenth and early twentieth centuries, when "mass" communication and "mass audiences" were the most efficient and effective ways of allowing the medium to grow and survive. Economic forces grew to support the profitability of each of these forms of media and laws and policies to regulate or deregulate them emerged within historical circumstances that were influenced by current events, political dominance of ideas, and legal frameworks.

Now, streaming technologies deliver sound, images, and text to us without the burden of cable or wires on small, portable technologies that we can use anywhere, anytime (as long as you are in the footprint of reception and have the software to function within that geographic region). Small start-ups in the forms of app developers, or one-time video producers who post something on YouTube, show that the economic scale of technological change has evolved. The initial cost of producing something for distribution over the Internet has challenged the prominence of the former legacy media and has created new sets of relationships among users of these "small" media. Laws and regulations, like copyright, may no longer be adequate to address the realities of these new media forms, and the idea of "free" forms of media content have revolutionized earlier media industries.

The recording industry was the first to undergo massive reorganization due to the ability to stream audio; the film and print industries were the next ones to have to deal with the idea of electronic delivery of their products. Today, television is the newest "old" form of media undergoing a massive change as appointment viewing shifts to binge watching, and every content provider is in the business of creating original content. As I write this historical overview, HBO and CBS have announced plans to deliver their services to viewers through streaming services, effectively starting the crumble of the traditional television industry and organization into one of à la carte pricing for content.

The growth of any industry is subject to the social and economic realities of the time, but social networking is unique in that it combines the speed of Internet connections with the content of the World Wide Web, and, in so doing, has shifted the issues related to changes in the way we do thing into warp speed. Never before was it so easy to get information from across the globe with only a few key strokes or the push of a button. With our myriad changes occurring even faster than we can comprehend—the impact of social networking can be easily overlooked. But in reality, just like every other major form of communication technology, if we examine the tools and how they are used, we can see how our lives our changing and how our beliefs and attitudes are being conditioned by those technological changes.

Some readers would stop at this moment and think "oh, this author is a technological determinist"—one who sees technology inevitably changing everything and forcing readers to take the perspective that technological change is inevitable and unstoppable. But to those readers I say "wait a minute!" In the topics and issues developed in this encyclopedia, there is also a more liberal philosophy at play that addresses the chance of *change* and reflects how business cycles reflect, reinforce, and challenge laws and policies, and how human beings make sense of the cycles of social relations and economic realities. This ecological approach toward understanding social change reflects competing elements, each of which can be prominent at some times, and recessive at others. The categories of social, economic, technological, and cultural dimensions introduce some flexibility into the picture of what impact communication technologies have, and, in the case of social media, the first examination should be whether or not the name of the phenomenon is an oxymoron. Is there something social about the way we use social media? The answer depends upon how you frame that question.

One way is to look at social media from the perspective of thinking that nothing is really radically new; we still communicate through talk, writing, gestures, and body language—but in social media we introduce a layer of filters that mediate and moderate our social interaction. Social networking just adds another way of communicating and becomes one more choice, for those who live in a place where social networking is available and affordable. But another perspective to consider is that every new form of communication alters the terrain upon which we communicate, or in the phrase commonly attributed to Marshall McLuhan, "We become what we behold. We shape our tools and then our tools shape us" (McLuhan 1994, xxi).

For the person who uses social networking to reduce the amount of social anxiety they may have in face-to-face situations, perhaps the social network is a layer of protection that keeps them from the real vicissitudes of interpersonal face-to-face communication. At the same time, the privacy and "aloneness" of using social networks to communicate can mean that we say hurtful or painful things that we don't intend to say. We may expand the number of friends in number on a social network like LinkedIn or Facebook, but we may limit our real experiences with others by staying online longer than necessary to maintain a healthy social life in the real world.

There are four primary differences between traditional media and social networking. First and foremost, much of our use of text-based social networking is *asynchronous*, meaning that we communicate, but not in real time. Online chats might be immediate through "instant messaging" but even then there is a short lag time. Text-based social network communication is often done at the convenience of one participant to be read and commented upon later by the recipient, or readers of the messages. Even the lag in time of text-based instant messaging calls attention to the time passage in sending and receiving messages.

Second, social networking seldom gives us social cues to really help explain the subtleties of communication. For this reason, humor is often less successful when used in social networking, something that might be meant as ironic can be read as an insult, or yelling is textually shifted to capital letters that have a cultural reference that can impede the intended message within the communication process.

Third, social networking is subject to where people use their technology. Often public and private "appropriate" forms of communication can become confused when one person uses their smartphone or computer in an intimate way, while the receiver is "reading" the message or playing the message in a public place.

The fourth element is really the most important. Not everyone can afford the technologies of social networking, nor do all people react similarly to social networking and what participating in social networks does to and for people. Not everyone can afford cell phones, computers, or Internet access, and even when there are subsidized programs to help people have access to information, there is a steep learning curve in how to use social networking. Additionally, the companies behind social networks, just like other forms of media, are in the business of making a profit. How they create that profit has much to do with the control over the social network; are profits necessary to please shareholders if the company is supported by the sale of stock? How can "free" services continue to be supported when every business requires some money just to operate? This leads to the economic component of social networking, which has contributed to many new forms of business models and economic realities.

Economic Imperatives and Social Realities

While the four issues mentioned above, time, intention, place, and access to technology all influence how social networks can be used and abused, there is one important economic shift from traditional media industries to the world of social networking, and that deals with whether the service (or social network) must make a profit to continue to operate, and, if so, how its maintenance is structured. In the United States, advertising was the primary, most dominant form of funding the maintenance of traditional media. While there might have been exceptions to the rule, such as the original establishment of nonprofit media like Public Television or Public Radio, or the revenue of ticket sales at movies, or the sale of records for the recording industry—advertising always made up some part of the equation of the maintenance of these industries. Even newspapers and magazines had a purchase price, but most of the cost of underwriting the production of the newspaper or magazine came through running ads.

When the cost of producing media content becomes low enough that someone can shoot a video on a cell phone and post it on the Internet, the issue of the cost of content takes a dramatic turn. Furthermore, we may believe that the Internet is "free" for us to use—but is that factually true? Everyone who uses the Internet (or the company or school that provides the Internet) has to go through an Internet service provider (ISP). These firms must operate on a profit motive to survive. The Internet is supported in a variety of ways, but we should question whether this economic model is sustainable. It is not surprising then, that bloggers, and a host of social networks, rely on advertising in some form to underwrite the cost of their operation—explored in each section of this encyclopedia—and that big businesses who do their work over the Internet have a different economy of scale to fulfill the objectives of their business operations.

What is new, however, is the mind-set that as our media and use of media is in transition, we may expect new models of economic support to evolve. Ideas of "freeware" are not just idealistic terms. Today's copyright law could change dramatically as digital communications make it easier for us to duplicate original content with the same quality as the original. With extreme shifts in what it costs to send messages over social networks or the Internet, we can expect to see the economic realities of communication shifting rapidly as we live with new forms of distribution that do not have the same exorbitant costs that traditional media forms incurred.

As a result, this encyclopedia reflects economic realities of the time in history in which it has been written. Twenty years from now we might expect to see a number of changes in how we use social networking, and how we pay for new communication forms. But is it likely we will fall into the same old models, and move away from the promise of "free" exchange of information toward one that is underwritten by advertising, subscriptions, or some other form of paying for content?

Permanence and Change

One of the most intriguing, but potentially problematic issues related to using social networks has to do with how we pay for the services, or how we will continue to pay for the services in the future. Money and our economic transfer of goods for services is dramatically changing, as the technologies of producer/consumer content generation and distribution also change. In this case, the social network is the determinant of many of these changes.

Consider for a moment, the problem of identity theft and the Internet. As more of our personal information is stored on computers and in cell phones (including passwords and identifying information), the business of hacking, phishing, and cybercrime becomes more prominent. If transfer of traditional cash or electronic bank information is vulnerable, might we come up with a better way of paying for goods in the future? Credit cards and debit cards were inventions of the twentieth century, but are they too vulnerable to use in online financial transactions?

Many companies are attempting to shift consumers toward a more secure form of cybercurrency that can be safer than traditional cash or the exchange of financial goods online. Bitcoin is only one of many cybercurrencies that are in the experimental stages. In 2014, Apple introduced the Apple wallet, which is a way of digitally exchanging money for goods by tapping your Apple smartphone against a special receiving unit in a store. Already, game players have become used to using cybercurrency of some form, like Linden Dollars (for *Second Life*) and Amazon offers Amazon coins for purchasing apps from the company, but, as yet, the forms of alternative currencies are not universal. The big question is whether any form of cybercurrency will challenge the prominence of a cash-based economy.

The Dot-Com Bubble and Dot-Com Bust

As in any new industry shift, we can expect peaks and valleys in the evolution of social networking. In what was called the "dot-com bubble," or the "dot-com boom" from 1997 to 1999, speculators flocked to the Internet to engage in e-commerce. Some of those entrepreneurs made millions of dollars, while others faded away or seemed to disappear. The excitement of the Internet, as it became available to the public and contained the mystique of an exciting online future, saw the birth of many start-ups.

Some of those new companies did quite well, and experienced meteoric growth in their number of users and in their profits, while others crashed in the "dot-com bust" in 1999–2000. With fortunes made and lost sometimes within days, the period of wild speculation came to a crashing halt. While this short period of history bore witness to excitement about the potential uses of the Internet, they also cautioned many to realize that the Internet was not (and is not) the wild new frontier of change and opportunity.

In their early days, most social networks did not make a profit, nor did they promise great opportunities for entrepreneurs and speculators. Now that some social networks have survived and some have failed, we have learned much more about the shifting social dynamics of using social networks, and we have a better understanding of the impact of social networks over time. Undoubtedly some of the social networks we now know will survive, but some will fail, and we can expect many others to emerge over time.

As we march toward the future, let us be mindful of the successes and failures that have paved the way for technological and social change, and let us understand the implications for new ways of communicating and exchanging messages. Like everything, those who understand some of the history are less likely to repeat the mistakes of the past. But, at the same time, those who understand the breadth of the issues are most likely going to be able to envision a future with clearer vision.

Guide to Related Topics

Agencies
Cyber Crime Center (C3)
Federal Communications Commission
    (FCC)
Federal Trade Commission (FTC)
International Telecommunications
    Union (ITU)
Internet Corporation for Assigned
    Names and Numbers (ICANN)
World Wide Web Consortium (W3C)

Changing Industries
Advertising
E-Publishing
Gaming
Legacy Media
Pornography
Social Media
Social Networking

Companies
Amazon
America Online (AOL)
Apple
AT&T
Bitcoin
Comcast
European Council for Nuclear
    Research (CERN)

Google
Microsoft
Netflix
PayPal
Samsung
Yahoo!
YouTube

Concepts and Social Practices
Addiction
Anonymity
Blogs
Censorship
Collective Intelligence
Convergence
Cyberbullying
Cybernetics
Dating
Digital
Digital Divide
E-Mail
Friending
Hacker
Hyperconnectivity
Information Superhighway
Meme
Network Theory
Piracy
Podcast

Larry Page
Edward Snowden
Norbert Wiener
Steve Wozniak
Mark Zuckerberg

Places
Cyberspace
European Council for Nuclear
    Research (CERN)
Silicon Valley

Political Activities
Arab Spring
Occupy Movement
Political Fund-Raising
Smart Mob

Security and Surveillance
Anonymous
Bots
Cookies
Cyberattack
Cybercrime
Cyber Crime Center (C3)
Cyberwar
Data Mining
Malware
Phishing
Spam
Spyware
Surveillance
WikiLeaks

Social Networks and Services
Airbnb
BuzzFeed
Craigslist

Digg
eBay
Etsy
Expedia
Facebook
Flickr
Foursquare
Friendster
Instagram
LinkedIn
MySpace
Netscape
Pandora
Pinterest
Reddit
Tumblr
Twitter
Uber
Wikipedia
Yelp

Technologies
Android
App
Apple iOS
BlackBerry
Browser
Cloud
E-Reader
Mobile Phone
Mobile Phone Cameras
MP3
Smartphone
Streaming Media
Tablet
3D Printing
Wearable Technology
Web 2.0

A

Addiction

Relying on any form of technology for gratification can lead a person to develop habits, compulsions, or, in extreme situations, addictions. Though the three behaviors may overlap, each one is increasingly hard to change. As behaviors slip from a person's conscious actions to those that occur subconsciously, or unconsciously, it becomes much harder for a person to realize that they are becoming addicted to certain stimuli and that their behavior is no longer controlled by their will. Habits are behaviors that a person develops over time, while at the same time behaviors can become habitual. Habits may become compulsions, and compulsions can often develop into addictions. Some habits can be positive, like good hygiene, politeness, or even a strong work ethic, but, when habits interfere with the person's healthy behavior, they may be negative.

Compulsions are irresistible urges to engage in an activity that often interferes with other activities, like work or other responsibilities. They may produce anxiety when a person can't engage in an activity that reduces the compulsion, like constantly checking Facebook or a mobile phone. Addictions, however, are those behaviors that are difficult for an individual to control, and they occur when the compulsions become overwhelming. Addictions often result in psychological or physiological dependency on something—such as extreme reliance on social networks to tell you what your friends are doing or what topics are "trending." When people become unable to stop using a technology or are no longer aware of their reliance on technology, they may be said to have developed an addiction to that technology. When it comes to social media and social networking, we've learned that both the tools and the content of these forms of technology can influence habits, compulsions, and addictions to connecting to others or to types of content.

Continually checking social network status pages, tweeting, reading celebrity gossip or celebrity tweets, shopping online, gaming, or relying on pornography are some of the typical forms of social media or social network addiction. In recent years, online shopping, pornography, and gaming—especially gambling—have received the most attention with regard to the industries that benefit when people become addicted to these forms of content. The rise of uncontrolled use of, or addictive behaviors because of, social networks or personal communications technologies (like the use of mobile phones) has resulted in what some psychologists now refer to as *social network addiction* as a recognized new clinical disorder.

Some parents fear that their children are becoming so addicted to social networks and personal technologies that they send their children to rehabilitation camps to break the addictive cycle of constantly checking their devices. Internet addiction has also been the cause of some court cases concerning child neglect, when a parent is addicted to using the Internet and social networks so much that they no longer care for their children. In general, most social network–related addictions have to do with the availability of access to the Internet and the immediate connectivity to others or to social networks afforded by mobile phones.

The problem of addiction to any form of technology use or accessing content over the Internet has become so great that there are now a number of self-help groups that have formed to help individuals break, or at least control, their addictions. Internet addiction has become a serious problem for people of all ages, but often it strikes individuals who may be away from home for the first time (like college or university freshmen), people who may be housebound, or those with other compulsions that can be served by using social networking, such as playing games (especially gambling) and accessing pornography.

The field of economics dedicated to examining social media or technology addictions is called *behavioral economics*. This can refer to the amount of money a person spends gaming, shopping, or accessing pornography, for example, but another way of measuring behavior has to do with the amount of time a person spends on social media or social networks. Consistently checking Facebook, using a mobile phone, or spending an inordinate amount of time gaming or checking the status of friends, or other extreme compulsions, does not always translate into dollars lost or gained, but the amount of *time* spent engaging with these forms of media certainly can be quantified and constitutes a measurement of addiction.

On January 12, 2015, National Public Radio station WNYC in New York City launched a challenge to listeners to monitor the conscious use of mobile phones. Using an app called Moment, more than 18,000 listeners to the podcast *New Tech City* tracked their smartphone usage for a week and were challenged to cut down their smartphone use in the following week. The idea behind the project was to make people aware of how often they consulted their mobile phones and for what purpose. Everything from constantly checking to see if any messages arrived to playing games and checking the time counted as a point of interaction with the phone. Initial data from Moment showed that, before the study, most people checked their mobile phones for a total of two hours a day, though data from the research company Flurry, a firm that monitors social media analytics, indicated that most people consult their mobile phones even more—for a total of 2 hours and 57 minutes per day (Graslie 2015). After the study, the respondents' awareness of their behavior resulted in an average decline of mobile phone use of only about four minutes a day, signifying that awareness of one's behavior may help them make more conscious decisions, but that awareness may not be enough to radically alter one's reliance on social media or one's choices about the reliance on personal media consumption.

In terms of industry economics, it is also important to keep in mind that some industries try to get people addicted to content so that they return again and again to the same experience. The industries can exploit the addicted person and make money through cultivating a relationship in which they know some people will become active audience members for some type of content. The contemporary online advertising industry measures people's behaviors and social media use and often targets these types of consumers. The effectiveness of online advertising geared to niche audiences has streamlined the types of appeals and the measurement of audience involvement with products and brands. Online gaming industries also know that the amount of time someone spends online increases the opportunities for selling games and software. And, of course, entertainment industries like film, television, and music have all migrated to online platforms and the services that provide this type of content seek the returning consumer who is part of the growing online audience for their content.

Though it is hard to determine whether the addictions people exhibit with social media reflect a long-term pattern of change for communications tools, or a need to feel connected to someone or something over those tools, social media statistics show us that some people rely on social media for a number of reasons. In the case of people with uncontrollable desire to use their technologies as tools to access content over social networks, the balance of what is meant by "connectivity" becomes tenuous. In some cases, people substitute online relationships, either personal or para-social, creating an *illusion* of intimacy. The addiction may occur because of social anxiety caused by discomfort with real-world interactions and negative experiences. Addiction often occurs because of a fear of face-to-face interactions, resulting in problems related to one's socialization and sense of self, or identity. Among the many problems with online interactions with others and addictions is the problem of a lack of social cues (Baym 2010, 6–9) that provide adequate feedback for the user, therefore the online experience is often unfulfilling, driving the addict to even more technology use to try to accomplish a social balance with the person(s) with whom they interact or the gratification they expect to receive from the behavior.

See also: Advertising; Anonymity; E-Commerce; Identity; Niche Marketing

Further Reading

Baym, Nancy K. 2010. *Personal Connections in the Digital Age*. Malden, MA: Polity Press.

Graslie, Serri. 2015. "Pick Up Your Smartphone Less Often. You Might Think Better." NPR's *All Tech Considered*. Accessed February 10, 2015: http://www.npr.org/blogs /alltechconsidered/2015/02/09/384945981/pick-up-your-smartphone-less-often-you -might-think-better.

Young, Kimberly. 2010. *Internet Addiction: A Handbook and Guide to Evaluation and Treatment*. Hoboken, NJ: John Wiley and Sons.

Advertising

Though the word *advertising* is a noun that refers to both the activity and the profession of producing ads for commercial purposes, *what* can be advertised and *how* it is advertised has always relied on social values that are accepted in any society as well as the available media that could present those ideas to the public at the time. Print and word-of-mouth advertising was already a part of American culture by the late 1900s when the start of the modern advertising industry began. Advertising forms and campaigns evolved as print media industries expanded using newspapers, magazines, and direct mail to reach the mass audience. Radio, film, and television introduced new ways of reaching consumers throughout the twentieth century, and cable television and subscription channels presented a greater number of opportunities to use the techniques learned during the era of *legacy media*, but while methods and opportunities for advertising have changed over the years, some of the basic principles behind promoting goods and services have remained rooted in understanding human behavior and enticing audience members to pay attention. Since the use of the Internet for advertising purposes began, and with the addition of social media, the advertising industry has had to think about how advertising budgets are spent (on what forms of media) and how advertising's effectiveness can be measured. From earlier models that saw advertising messages designed and distributed to a *mass* audience, we now see how advertising over the Internet, mobile phones, and through social networks has resulted in models that emphasize reaching individuals and niche audiences.

In the early part of the twentieth century advertising grew into an industry, largely because of the efforts of Edward Bernays, who became known as the "father" of modern advertising. In his 1928 book *Propaganda*, Bernays wrote that irrational forces drive human behavior and that using the techniques of propaganda, it would be possible to manipulate people's behavior without their conscious knowledge. This approach toward understanding the psychology of the consumer dominated twentieth century advertising and influenced models that were taught in business schools, such as an emphasis on the "four P's: product, price, place, and promotion." The advertising and media delivery industries developed their own system of accounting for effectiveness through ratings systems based on the cost of reaching 1,000 individuals, called CPM (cost per thousand), and ratings became a form of "currency" for the ad industry. While the cost of trying to reach those consumers would be tied to specific campaigns and products, a general rule was that it would cost an advertiser approximately $1–$18 to reach 1,000 listeners in radio, and $5 to $20 for a traditional 30-second network television ad.

As the industry developed, a number of new approaches were tried, but what shifted the advertising industry from some of the old, established models was the growth of e-commerce over the Internet, in which advertising campaigns switched from using mass media to directly reaching potential consumers through their personal technologies. This shift has involved four stages: first, the early stages of using the Internet for advertising; second, the rise of online advertising after the Internet became more widely available to the public; third, the techniques and development of online advertising as e-commerce grew (including the role of social networking in spreading advertising); and, finally, the impact of mobile phones and an advertising shift to mobile platforms. And, of course, the fact that online retailers can do business nonstop, 24 hours a day, 7 days a week, from any location, over the Internet, increases the likelihood that someone using a computer or mobile technology can make purchasing decisions anywhere, anytime.

Early Online Advertising

It may be worthwhile to remember that the Internet was never intended to be a platform for advertising. Instead, the developers of the Internet and the World Wide Web who focused on the military and educational uses of the Internet advocated for the network and information distribution system to be open to anyone to facilitate communication and information exchange freely and without censorship.

The advertising industry was slow to explore online advertising because it took several years for a number of home users to adopt computers, and for Internet Service Providers to accommodate the type of bandwidth necessary for graphics, audio, and full-motion images. Until the public began accessing the World Wide Web in 1991, and the interoperability of user-generated content became possible with Web 2.0 around 2004, advertising companies were wary of whether or not this new distribution form—the Internet—could be effective as an advertising medium. The dot-com bubble that seemed to be expanding between 1997 and 1999 saw a great amount of speculation, but when the bubble burst (the dot-com crash) in 2000, advertisers remained uncertain about the potential of the Internet to become a major advertising medium. For people in the advertising industry, it was just a matter of waiting until the platform and payment systems were reliable enough, and it became ubiquitous enough, to engage in techniques that would become part of the online strategy for reaching consumers.

There were some attempts at trying to use the Internet for promotional or advertising purposes that predated the dot-com bubble, though. As the Internet was still developing, researchers had attempted to send different types of content over the system. Even though advertising was prohibited in the early days of the emerging Internet, the first commercial junk mail message was reputedly sent over the Usenet e-mail forum in 1994 by attorneys Laurence Canter and Martha Siegel advertising their immigration services. Canter and Siegel sent a bulk message to their clients over Usenet, an early form discussion service on the Internet that relied on dial-up services to connect computers. People on discussion boards began to refer to the unwanted information as "spam" based upon a popular British comedy group's sketch in which the product Spam (a canned meat) was on every item of a diner menu, thereby offering customers only spam, whether they wanted it or not. When the prohibition on promotional messages was lifted in 1991, the era of experimentation in Internet advertising began.

By 1994, banner ads were introduced to run along the edges of the computer screen. One of the leaders in placing banner ads was DoubleClick, a company formed in 1996 that researched analytics to help customers learn what type of information was being seen and recognized on the computer screen. DoubleClick initially worked with a wide variety of companies, like Yahoo!, that usually paid somewhere between $30 to $100 per banner ad, depending on the size and colors used in the ad. Between 1995 and 2000 the number of Internet start-up companies grew exponentially, and the focus of those companies on the potential of the Internet to deliver advertising messages was a part of the growth. Companies like JavaScript and Flash made it possible to catch the computer user's eye with pop-up ads and animated features. In 1994, Netscape devised a way to insert code into a web browser that would use a cookie to report a computer user's actions back to a host company. Suddenly, it became possible to see if a computer user would click on a prompt on the screen that had been enabled by the cookie, and the pay-per-click model (also called cost-per-click model) became a new way to measure online ad effectiveness. The cookie, in effect, directed website traffic, and the website advertiser could receive remuneration every time a user clicked on an ad. For a long time, the pay-per-click model dominated the emerging online advertising field and it is still an effective measurement of online activity using computers and purchases made over smartphones. Soon, *advergames* were introduced to online advertising as a way to learn even more about consumers who seemed to be oblivious to the information that passed over the Internet concerning their behaviors and Internet history. If a person clicked on an advergame, the amount of time a person played the game and the level of involvement could tell marketers a lot about the user's online habits. Advergames have been found to be particularly effective for heavy Internet users who spend a lot of time online.

Throughout this period, advertisers began to use what has become known as *behavioral targeting* to use information collected from a person's web-browsing behavior. The application of techniques to entice consumers to click ads is called *behavioral advertising*, though sometimes it is called *targeted advertising*. But, whatever your preference for what the term is, it means that a consumer's behavior is being monitored through a record of the pages they have browsed, the time spent on the site, the number of clicks made to other sites, the timing of the site access, and any other types of interaction someone might have with a site (like forwarding it to friends).

On March 10, 2000, the dot-com bubble had reached its pinnacle, but suddenly, the bubble burst. Almost overnight, a number of companies began to fail and many were forced to declare bankruptcy. Before the start of the year 2000, and in part because of the dot-com bubble, the Internet advertising business had become an $8.2 billion industry, but there was still little evidence to show that these ads were working. In retrospect, it seems that the speculation of what might be done online was not being carried out, and, by October 2002, online advertising dollars fell by 32 percent. While advertising companies seemed to withdraw and regroup, one company that seemed to have found the right combination for online advertising was Google, which was moving from being a search engine to being an online advertising leader. While Google did not start the pay-per-click advertising model, they perfected it. Much of the company's success in advertising comes from the knowledge they have about how to link content from one site to another, and while other companies have followed the Google model, Google has been the most successful in deriving revenue from online advertising. Google alone accounts for almost half of all advertising spending in the United States.

Learning from Experimenting: The Growth of Online Advertising

While Google did not become the only company to experiment with online advertising, it did become the leader in online analytics. A part of the success had to do with the PageRank system that Google had initially developed, and the approach they had toward linking content from one site to another. At the same time, social networking became an excellent way to reach audiences that had similar interests. The logic seems simple: If you like a product and tell a friend or mention it to friends on your social network, the chance is that that friend/those friends might like the same product. Social media became a major platform for advertising and introduced a host of new terms, such as *viral* marketing and *engagement* advertising.

In 2000, Google started a division of the company called AdWords. Instead of using banner ads that were the dominant form of advertising at the time, Google's AdWords would use the search engine characteristics to find similar products that matched the words for which the user was searching and presented them on screen. In 2003, it acquired a company called AdSense that allows advertisers to present text, images, videos, or interactive media advertisements that are targeted to match specifically with site content and audience. Google then managed the records of who clicks on what and developed a consumer profile that could specify who was interested in what. When Google first used AdSense the only way the service paid for ads was on a per-click basis, but soon after the program was implemented, Google realized that some people were inflating the value of their advertising messages by repeatedly clicking on their own content.

In 2008, Google acquired DoubleClick, a New York–based company, for $3.1 billion. The DoubleClick technology inserts HTTP cookies into a user's computer and tracks their behavior as they move from one website to another. Some people have criticized this technique as being tantamount to spyware, and many more have criticized DoubleClick for having an ineffective "opt-out" option that is required by the FCC. It absorbed the DoubleClick technology into the AdSense business and continued to use the AdSense name and icon. In the first quarter of 2014, Google reported that 22 percent of its total revenue came through Google AdSense, using DoubleClick protocols.

By 2009, Google acquired the AdWords system that allowed advertisers to create text ads for placement on the Google search engine and would relate to AdSense. As Google describes the differences, AdWords enables the creation of ads that appear "on relevant Google search results pages" and on "network partner sites." AdSense is targeted to individuals' websites and pays web publishers for the ads that a user clicks on. The financial arrangements are somewhat tied to the client, but in general about 68 percent of the advertising message is received by the content provider, and the remainder goes to Google for hosting the space.

Online advertising is so lucrative that Google earned $3.4 billion dollars in ad revenue in the first three months of 2014. The Interactive Advertising Bureau (IAB) compiles data for the effectiveness of online advertising and monitors the revenue of the more than 600 leading media and technology companies that sell 86 percent of online advertising in the United States. According to the IAB, Internet revenues reached $11.6 billion in the first quarter of 2014, which was an increase of 19 percent over the same period in 2013 (IAB 2014).

Following Google, the social network Facebook accounts for 5 percent of all online advertising. The analyst *eMarketer* forecasts advertising revenues for a handful of the top U.S. digital ad-selling companies and predicts that Google and Facebook will continue to lead in social media advertising, especially with the use of mobile apps. With combined online and mobile audiences, Google and Facebook are likely to control a $200 billion total media advertising market by 2016 (IAB 2014).

Social media and social networks spread messages faster and more inexpensively than any form of traditional advertising, and they do so by exploiting the relationships that exist through those media and over those networks. For example, viral marketing is now more popular than ever. The concept behind viral marketing is that certain ideas replicate themselves in nature and spread throughout society. Like a virus, an idea spreads quickly when it goes from person to person (see Meme).

Viral marketing is getting the audience to distribute your messages for you. Engagement advertising is directly involving consumers to participate in the spread of messages. One of the most successful viral marketing campaigns that also exemplifies the engagement strategy to date has been the Old Spice campaign featuring Isaiah Mustafa, an actor whose success in the Old Spice series of commercials has made him highly recognizable, even if he's described as "the Old Spice Guy." The campaign titled "Smell Like a Man, Man" debuted in 2010 and was the product of the advertising firm Wieden+Kennedy. Originally, the 30-second commercial that was created was intended to feature Old Spice's "Red Zone After Hours Body Wash," but the campaign was so successful, it was expanded to include other Old Spice products. What Wieden+Kennedy did was post the series of commercials on YouTube featuring the handsome, often shirtless actor directly addressing the camera and asking the audience about what they think, or what they would do with the question he poses. Then, influential viewers who are known well by social media users and regular viewers were asked to contribute questions and address them to Mustafa, in the form of another video or social media form. Those messages then spread through the responders' own social media channels and drove attention back to the original set of commercials. The result is a set of relationships between the actor and the commenters, the commenters and their social network consumers, and the advertising agency. Added to this is the recognition of the name "Old Spice" in a number of outlets.

Criticism of Social Media Advertising

Without a doubt, part of the success of social media advertising is the active involvement of people to help spread a message, but how can that type of sharing of information turn into the type of numbers that social media advertisers need to do their business?

As discussed above, cookies are controversial in the sense that they provide data to create an in-depth profile of the person that is very attractive to other advertisers.

The information gathered and sold to third parties is sometimes seemingly benign. For example, Facebook uses third-party cookies often, and if you click on a "like" button for some site, additional information may be shifted to Facebook, where this information contributes to an even larger data pool about your own behavior. The ad technique of transmitting an ad to a specific user because of the personal profile they have developed is called a *contextual ad* that runs alongside search results for certain key words. So, for example, if someone has been browsing websites looking for a new coffeemaker, a contextual ad sponsored by a coffeemaker manufacturer or retailer might emerge in the margins of the computer user's screen.

The methods used for social media advertising are legal, and sometimes very creative, but they all lead us to bigger questions concerning the right of the individual to privacy, and the right to know what information about you is being sold to someone else for a profit. The sheer number of ads to which we are exposed daily may well lead us to complacency about the growing power of online communication, but the number of ads sent along with even the most personal of messages often leads us to the question of whether data mining for personal information should be legal or not. Like all eras in advertising, advertisers attempt to cut through the clutter of information on a screen, but how much is too much?

In his excellent overview of advertising and American culture, Arthur Asa Berger compiled data from several reports and concluded that "we spend around $536 per person on advertising" in the United States (Berger 2015, 140) and the average person probably sees somewhere around 5,000 to 15,000 ads on a typical day (Berger 2015, 139). It seems logical to assume that there is a rationality to the amount of money we spend on, and the amount of money invested in, advertising, ethical or not. For this reason, many scholars have critiqued the impact of the *consumer culture* in which we, the audience, are subject to increasing commodification of goods and services. One of the tenets of consumer culture ideology is that the goods become separated from the meanings they convey to us and that advertising functions as a distraction from what is important and even necessary in our daily lives. With these important concepts in mind, we turn to the next wave of advertising with social media, the growth potential of using mobile technologies to continue to reach us with messages anywhere, anytime.

Mobile Advertising

If the old business school model using the "4 P's"—product, price, place, and promotion—is changing, it could be said that today's model could be described as SoLoMo: social, local, and mobile. A number of analytics firms have predicted that mobile advertising was becoming the next "big thing" in advertising. With an average adult in the United States spending about 2 hours and 51 minutes on mobile devices each day, the global analytics firm Statistica predicted that mobile ad spending in the United States would reach $35.55 billion in 2015, and that globally $59.67 billion would be spent on mobile advertising in 2017 ("Mobile Advertising Spending Worldwide from 2010 to 2017" 2015). Certainly a part of the reason for this increase is the growing number of mobile phones available worldwide and the developing sophistication of the analytics necessary to understand social media advertising and how to mine data for valuable information that allows advertisers and companies that sponsor advertising to profit on these techniques and consumer behavior.

See also: E-Commerce; E-Publishing; Federal Trade Commission (FTC); Google; Meme; Niche Marketing; Paywalls

Further Reading

Berger, Arthur Asa. 2015. *Ads, Fads, and Consumer Culture: Advertising's Impact on American Character and Society*, 5th ed. Lanham, MD: Rowman & Littlefield.

Bernays, Edward. 1928. *Propaganda*. New York: H. Liveright.

Google. Investor Relations. 2014. Accessed September 25, 2014: http://investor.Google.com/earnings/2014/Q1_google_earnings.html.

Interactive Advertising Bureau (IAB). 2014. "At $11.6 Billion in Q1 2014, Internet Advertising Revenues Hit All-Time First Quarter High." June 12, 2014. Accessed October 29, 2014: http://www.iab.net/about_the_iab/recent_press_releases/press_release_archive/press_release/pr-061214#sthash.pCBKfT0Q.dpuf.

Levy, Ari. 2012. "Ad-Supported Software Reaches Specialized Audience." *San Francisco Chronicle*. April 23, 2012. Accessed May 11, 2014: http://www.sfgate.com/business/article/Ad-supported-software-reaches-specialized-audience-3501806.php.

"Mobile Advertising Spending Worldwide from 2010 to 2017 (in Billion U.S. Dollars)." 2015. Statistica. Accessed April 5, 2015: http://www.statista.com/statistics/280640/mobile-advertising-spending-worldwide/.

"Total US Ad Spending See Largest Increase Since 2004." 2014. e-Marketer, July 2, 2014. Accessed March 23, 2015: http://www.emarketer.com/Article/Total-US-Ad-Spending-See-Largest-Increase-Since-2004/1010982#sthash.nJimcAYo.dpuf.

Agency Model

The traditional economic model of a publishing company is to have the publisher set the price of a book or music CD, for example, and the retailers get a percentage of the cost of the book or CD for distribution—usually 30 percent of the cost of the product. When digital forms came along and bypassed traditional business models that involved a manufacturer, distributor, and point-of-sale agent (like a bookstore or music store), the money that paid for the manufacture and distribution of the physical product shifted. Think for a moment about how electronic books (e-books) are sold. There is no need for cover art as books can be printed on demand (POD), and there is no cost of paper, printing, or binding of the book. When digital forms of media products became possible, a variety of new business models emerged. In the agency model, a fixed percentage of the price of the book goes to the distributor of the book, rather than allowing wholesalers to discount books.

Electronic publishing is a significantly less expensive mode of transmitting print materials because the cost of distribution is so much less than printing on paper and distributing through stores or direct mail. Once e-readers caught on, it became cheaper and easier to distribute printed materials electronically, though the shift created a major upheaval in the traditional printing industry. Until 2008, traditional publication houses set their own prices for e-books and they chose what books to distribute electronically, while others remained in print only for at least a designated period of time before they could be electronically distributed.

When Amazon, whose original business was an online bookstore, started marketing the Kindle and other book and print-related distributors started marketing their own e-readers, it took a bold lead in changing the pricing of e-books. Traditional publishers feared that price-fixing would occur, and their own industry irrevocably changed for the worse. At first, in 2007, Amazon took a loss on distributing those books that were on the *New York Times*' best-seller list, and all new releases, by pricing all of them at $9.99. The rationale from Amazon's point of view was that the Kindle cost $399 when it was first launched, and the money made from that transaction padded their comfort level with dropping the cost of e-books for the consumer.

Immediately critics raised questions of copyright for the author of the book. Would that author receive royalties previously agreed upon (usually a percentage of book sales), and, if so, would the author's remuneration for their labor be devalued? If the author still retained the same royalty—whether in e-book form or print— how could the publisher make any profit when they dropped the cost of the book to a fixed price, regardless of the reputation of the author, popularity of the book, and length of the book?

By 2009, the problem of e-book distribution and the use of the agency model became more pronounced when Apple began talking about acquiring a patent for e-books that would be distributed by its (then) forthcoming new product the iPad, which debuted in 2010.

Initially, John Sargent, the CEO of Macmillan, proposed new terms and, after several days, Amazon backed down and agreed to follow the agency model, but the price wars had begun to affect the publishing industry. Eventually, large trade publishing houses like Hachette, HarperCollins, Simon & Schuster, Penguin, and Random House adopted the agency model.

Finally, in November 2014, an agreement was forged between Amazon and the consortium of publishers and authors. The result was that both Amazon and the publishers' group, led by Hachette, gave some concessions, but neither group emerged entirely victorious. The two sides developed a multiyear agreement that would give the publisher control over pricing, but also offered incentives to sell at lower prices. Amazon agreed to increase co-op funds, which represent the money that creates cooperative advertising (meaning that both the publisher and Amazon will fund ad campaigns).

The agency model is still in existence, though, when it comes to print and e-print, the business model has been somewhat "adjusted" in the agreement. Most critics agree, though, that it won't be long before the agency model is in the headlines again. Two authors' groups, Authors United and the Authors Guild, the latter of which has 9,000 members, have written to the Justice Department urging an antitrust investigation into Amazon and its pricing policies.

See also: Advertising; Amazon; E-Publishing

Further Reading

Streitfeld, David. 2014. "In Latest Volley against Amazon, Hachette's Writers Target Its Board." *New York Times.* September 14, 2014. Accessed September 24, 2014: http://www.nytimes.com/2014/09/15/technology/in-latest-volley-against-amazon-hachettes-writers-target-its-board.html?_r=0.

Thompson, John B. 2010. *Merchants of Culture: The Publishing Business in the Twenty-First Century,* 2nd ed. London: Plume.

Airbnb

Two roommates who were having trouble raising money to pay the rent on their loft apartment, Brian Chesky and Joe Gebbia, were inspired to start Airbnb, an alternative to traditional motels or hotels, in San Francisco in 2007. At the time, San Francisco was hosting the Industrial Designers Society of America, and all hotel rooms were booked, so Chesky and Gebbia bought three air mattresses and rented each one for $80. They also gave their guests breakfast and acted as informal guides to the area. By 2008, they added the talents of Nathan Blecharczyk to create the online site and launched Airbnb. The company grew quickly, and, by April 2014, the company was valued at approximately $10 billion and had facilitated over 10 million connections between "hosts" and "guests." One year later, another aggressive round of fundraising from interested venture capitalists valued the company at closer to $20 billion. The headquarters are in San Francisco, though additional regional headquarters have been established elsewhere in major cities around the world.

Airbnb is a way for individuals to rent their homes, or a room or bed in their house/apartment, or other space to people who wish a different experience than staying at a traditional motel or hotel. Often these accommodations are trendy, or informal, with travelers searching from the Airbnb site to see pictures of the accommodations, check the calendar for availability, and communicate via e-mail with the hosts, asking questions or arranging for renting the facility. Airbnb uses what is known as a broker's model for facilitating financial transactions. In exchange for providing the market and services like customer support, payment handling, and $1 million in insurance for hosts, Airbnb takes a 3 percent cut from the renter and a 6 to 12 percent cut from the traveler depending on the property price. Additional costs to the guest may be a cancellation fee and/or a cleaning fee, but the host identifies the policies and costs on the site. The host also posts pictures of the rental space and provides information about the location and amenities. Some facilities are unique, like the rental of yurts, private islands, castles, and more, and the luxury accommodation market has been growing quickly.

Airbnb could not exist if it were not for the sharing of information online. Interactive web connections make it possible for hosts and guests to communicate directly, and the ability of both hosts and guests to comment on each other builds the type of trust and security that helps online consumers make decisions, and keeps online service providers (like hosts) accountable to their potential guests.

The hotel industry is understandably concerned about this challenge to their prominence in arranging accommodations for people, and local city and state tax revenues fall when people book accommodations through Airbnb. Some communities have policies against having Airbnb facilities in their towns or cities, primarily to protect the tourism industry, but the Airbnb business had continued to grow and now has available rentals in 192 countries.

There have been some personal horror stories with Airbnb rentals, including an occasional assault on a guest by a host, or vice versa, and an occasional story in which the guest refuses to vacate the premises, causing problems for the host. Airbnb has a feature on its site in which hosts review guests, and guests review their experience at the facility, and their interaction with the host. But most of the problems are confined to policy issues within communities. For example, some cities have laws that restrict rentals of less than 30 days, and most cities have health and safety regulations that are not utilized by Airbnb hosts and facilities. One of the biggest problems, though, is in the loss of taxes to communities that levy special rental fees that help bring revenue into the community.

Airbnb is an example of the sharing economy in which people who have extra accommodations make them available to others when the hosts do not need the space. At the same time, it creates an economic challenge for the traditional business and tourism industries that have specialized and created economic models to support the needs of travelers, and it affects local and state tax revenue that is collected as a part of the traditional short-term lodging economy.

See also: Creative Economy; Do-It-Yourself; Sharing Economy; Uber

Further Reading

Friedman, Thomas L. 2013. "Welcome to the Sharing Economy." *New York Times, Sunday Review*. July 20: SR1.
Geron, Tomio. 2013. "Airbnb and the Unstoppable Rise of the Share Economy." *Forbes*, 191: 58–64.

Amazon

Amazon.com Inc. is the largest Internet company in the United States and has aspirations of becoming the world's leading online retailer. The company was incorporated in 1994, and 10 months later, in July 1995, Amazon.com went online as an alternative to traditional brick-and-mortar bookstores. Jeff Bezos, president and CEO of the organization, chose Seattle, Washington, as the home of Amazon and named the company after the world's largest river—in part, because he liked the fact that the name started with an "A" and would appear early in any alphabetical listings. From the beginning, Jeff Bezos decided that he had to create an enjoyable way for people to shop online if he was going to compete with traditional brick-and-mortar stores and the human connection between salesperson and buyer. Though Amazon was not an "overnight success," many of the techniques used by the company have become markers of what a successful e-commerce retail company can achieve. The number of products Amazon carries have multiplied, and the company has developed a variety of delivery and storage options that continue to further Amazon's mission of being "customer centric."

From its roots as an online bookseller, Amazon introduced a number of improvements for online retail functions. Originally, books ordered from the site were located by a team of individuals who kept computerized databases of book inventory in large distribution areas. The book was packaged and sent to the customer through the U.S. mail. Bezos realized that the customer service problem of online retail had to be attended to and his team worked on ways to establish a better rapport with customers online. Customers could "browse," put items in their electronic shopping cart, and then edit that cart before checking out.

In 1999, Amazon bought a small online service called PlanetAll, which matched sales with customer e-mail addresses and zip codes. The service generated a set of books that customers might "like" based upon others in their groupings that also bought similar books. The company also launched a service to locate hard-to-find books through the "orphan book" program.

Perhaps the most significant improvement was the program designed by Peri Hartman that resulted in the "1-Click" purchase program, patented by Amazon. Other successful additions to the website allowed for customer reviews and discounts—especially on best-selling books. In October 2001, the "Look Inside the Book" feature was added, and, in 2003, an even more specific feature allowed customers to "Search Inside" the book. In 2008, Amazon patented another feature, as yet not implemented, that would allow kinetic movement to make purchases, resulting in a "1-Click" type of transaction that could be triggered by a nod of the head.

It may seem surprising to learn that Amazon was not profitable for many years, but finally made its first profit for stockholders at the end of 2001. In the meantime, Bezos and his team were working on plans to expand Amazon online retailing to other products, and to other countries. The business plan for expansion began in 1996, and, in 1998, Amazon started selling music CDs and video DVDs and expanded business operations to the U.K. and Germany. By 2002, Amazon was operating in Canada and included office products in their list of physical goods for sale online. From that time on, the company began to increase its income. In 2014, the net revenue was $88.99 billion (U.S. dollars; Net Sales Revenue 2015).

In 2005, Amazon launched Amazon Prime, a membership that cost a flat-rate of $79 for a year, but promised free two-day shipping anywhere in the continental United States. It has since made this program available in other select countries, too. This action has been particularly successful with Amazon's clients who use the delivery benefits to greater advantage than the casual Amazon shopper, and the delivery service helps the company overcome one of the biggest challenges for online retailers—the loss of the customer's interest when it takes too long to actually receive the purchased goods. In 2013, Jeff Bezos appeared on the weekly television show *60 Minutes* and announced that, in the future, Amazon would deliver products directly to homes by drones, small aircraft that would be used for Amazon Prime Air, a division of the company that could deliver products weighing less than five pounds to homes within 30 minutes after they were ordered online. Unfortunately for Amazon, the Federal Aviation Authority (FAA) has been blocking licenses for domestic drones because of the threat of privacy violations and safety. In the meantime, Amazon has been experimenting with drone deliveries in Canada.

Amazon received a great deal of attention when it developed the Kindle e-reader that worked seamlessly with Amazon to deliver electronic books to users in 2007. The Kindle used "e-ink," which created a readable screen that was much more readable than other e-readers. In July 2010, Amazon announced that the number of e-books exceeded sales for hardcover books. Later, the Kindle Fire tablet was developed that can store all sorts of media both in its hard drive and in cloud-based computing through Amazon Web Services.

Amazon continued to develop its list of products, which ranged in diversity from video games to works of art and original television programming. In 2011, the company launched the Amazon Appstore, and, in 2014, it released a smartphone called the Fire Phone. Its acquisition of a number of video gaming companies resulted in the establishment of the Amazon Game Studio in 2012. The company has also invested in a number of acquisitions that feed the consumer database about customers' buying or search habits. The Internet Movie Database (IMDb) was acquired by Amazon in 1998, Audible Inc. in 2008, and Zappos Shoes in 2009. Amazon also developed Amazon Coins, a form of digital currency, in 2013, to be used for other Amazon goods.

Amazon also started its own publishing service, Amazon Publishing, and, in 2008, became involved in film production by partnering with 20th Century Fox to produce the film *The Stolen Child*. This was just the first attempt at media production that grew into Amazon Studios, started in 2010. Original pilots of television programs began in 2013. The first series to be renewed was *Transparent*, which debuted in the 2014 season.

The list of product acquisitions for sale continues to grow, but, generally, Amazon reports that it has a customer base of about 30 million people around the world. Using what is referred to as a multilevel sales strategy in which Amazon retains a portion of the sale of an item, the company also carries products from other distributors through a lease-system for other retailers. Small retailers usually negotiate a small percentage of the sale to Amazon but "drop shippers" are those companies that usually specialize in selling large volumes of products from overstock or companies that have been liquidated, often pay Amazon anywhere between 50 and 100 percent of the price of a product.

In 2010, Amazon opened Amazon Studios to develop ideas for television shows, movies, and comics that the company solicits from online submissions and customer comments. Amazon Instant Video is the arm of the company that streams digital video, and the company has partnered with other film production and distribution companies to stream services to homes. Using crowdsourced comments, Amazon has developed a number of pilots, some of which have been developed and others scrapped after initially showing them to niche audiences who participate in the process.

Amazon has also developed a partnership with a number of schools to fulfill textbook orders directly from students, often with distribution facilities located on campuses for the ease of student access, and the company has been experimenting with delivery of food to homes on the same day the order is placed. While neither of these programs are distributed nationally yet, it seems only a matter of time before Amazon learns from these experiences and makes decisions about these products, too, that start with online orders and end with physical delivery of the goods ordered.

Despite its tremendous growth and the leadership it has demonstrated in retail expertise, Amazon has been criticized for a number of business practices. Like Facebook and Google, it has been accused of gathering personal information about customers and using that data to create targeted ads and market special products to those most likely to use them. In particular, the methods of direct marketing that they have pioneered through online statements that address consumers by name (i.e., "Joe, people like you have also bought") are ways to personalize the shopping experience and entice customers to buy on impulse. At the same time, Amazon wouldn't be able to use this type of service if it were not using techniques to compile a user's personal profile.

The company has also been criticized for being a major factor in driving traditional brick-and-mortar stores out of business, but it is difficult to know whether Amazon has created a consumer more willing to shop online than in a traditional store, or whether consumer habits have changed that have favored a growth in online retailing.

Amazon has also been criticized for poor working conditions for its employees, both in the corporate area and in the distribution centers that exist around the world. With over 100,000 employees located in various regions around the globe, Amazon has been criticized for making warehouse workers operate in unheated or overheated warehouses and at minimum wage. The reliance on part-time and temporary workers has also been cited as a problem for the company, and a number of reports have surfaced that allege Amazon intimidates warehouse workers and holds them responsible for meeting unrealistically high quotas.

See also: Advertising; Amazon Coins; Bezos, Jeff; E-Publishing; E-Reader; Streaming Media

Further Reading

Amazon.com Inc. 2014. "Annual Report Form 10-K." U.S. Securities and Exchange Commission, January 31. Accessed November 8, 2014: http://sec.gov/Archives/edgar/data/1018724/000101872414000006/0001018724-14-0000006-index.htm.

Brandt, Richard L. 2011. *One Click: Jeff Bezos and the Rise of Amazon.com.* New York: Penguin.

"Net Sales Revenue of Amazon from 2004 to 2014 (in Billion U.S. Dollars)." 2015. Statistica. Accessed April 6, 2015: http://www.statista.com/statistics/266282/annual-net-revenue-of-amazoncom/.

Thompson, Derek. 2013. "The Riddle of Amazon." *The Atlantic Monthly,* 312: 26–31.

Amazon Coins

Amazon coins are a form of cybercurrency, also known as digital currency. Amazon coins were introduced in 2013 in the United States and Great Britain, where the value of a coin is tied to the value of local currency. For example, one Amazon coin in the United States would be the equivalent of one penny. Five hundred Amazon coins would equal the value of $5.

As a form of *virtual* currency, Amazon sells the coins to encourage buyers to accumulate their coins up front and spend this type of cybercurrency only on Amazon products. The coins are an alternative to using a coupon or gift card, but they allow Amazon to see who buys them and how they spend them. In many ways, Amazon coins present no risk for the company because they can only be used for the purchase of items through other Amazon products, like the Kindle Fire and the Amazon Appstore. Furthermore, Amazon coins expire within one year of purchase, so if the consumer forgets about them or doesn't use them, any unspent coins result in pure profit for the company. Because the only way to purchase Amazon coins is with the 1-Click system (controlled by Amazon), the currency is known as a "closed system." Coins can only be used by the person who buys them and can't be transferred to other people.

Amazon can also offer coins as an incentive for people to buy products through the company. For example, a person can also earn promotional Amazon coins when they purchase certain items, especially in terms of apps. In this case, Amazon profits in two ways: The coins enhance customer loyalty for the service, and Amazon retains 30 percent of the profit from an app from a third-party developer, who earns 70 percent of the purchase. In this way, Amazon also drives business to its own Appstore. Though it may be impossible to measure the popularity of Amazon coins at this point, the number of apps carried by the Amazon Appstore has increased exponentially since 2011 when the Appstore for Android and iOS phones was released in over 200 countries. When the service opened in March 2011, the Appstore carried about 3,800 apps, but by February 2015 the number had grown to over 330,000 apps.

See also: Bitcoin; Cybercurrency; Gaming

Further Reading

Rosenberg, Alyssa. 2013. "Why the Federal Government Is Going after Bitcoin, but Amazon Coins Are Safe." ThinkProgress. Accessed September 19, 2014: http://thinkprogress .org/alyssa/2013/05/15/2017091/why-the-federal-government-is-going-after-bitcoin-but -amazon-coins-are-safe/.

America Online Inc. (AOL)

America Online Inc. is a multinational corporation that develops brands and websites. As a company that developed one of the first major web browsers, it has one of the longest histories and evolutions as a digital media company. AOL began as Control Video Corporation (or CVC) in 1983. The founded was Bill von Meister, an entrepreneur who founded 10 start-ups in nine years but who never stayed with any one of them for more than two years. When von Meister developed CVC, it had one product, an online service called GameLine that ran on the Atari 2600 video game console. The company quickly brought on other individuals to handle the business, and von Meister left in 1985. By that time, Jim Kimsey, an investor in the company, had taken over and become CEO. Kimsey changed the company's strategy and launched a dedicated online service for Commodore 64 and 128 computers, first called Quantum Link (or "Q-Link"). Within a couple of years, Quantum partnered with Apple to launch AppleLink as a dedicated browser for Apple computers, but, in 1989, Apple split from the partnership and Quantum changed the service's name to America Online.

When Kimsey retired in 1991, Steve Case was promoted to the role of CEO, and many of AOL's acquisitions were made under his leadership. The company also adopted the shorter name, AOL, which it retained until 2009, when it self-stylized the name to read AoL. But when Case took over, the company had become known for a wide range of video games that it carried, many of which were groundbreaking and original. Using the PlayNet software, it produced the first fully automated play by e-mail game, *Quantum Space*, from 1989 to 1991, and the first chat room–based text role-playing game, *Black Bayou*, in 1996. The first multiplayer online role-playing game that also used graphics was called *Neverwinter Nights*, which ran from 1991 to 1997 on AOL. Perhaps even more importantly, AOL became known as the leading company for personal computer browser services.

The company also became involved in supporting many educational endeavors that paved the way for other computer firms to carve niches in a number of formats. Under Steve Case, the company launched a variety of services that facilitated education. AOL developed partnerships with the National Education Association, the American Federation of Teachers, National Geographic, the Smithsonian Institution, the Library of Congress, Pearson, Scholastic, and multimedia producers of educational content like the Discovery Networks, Turner Education Services (CNN Newsroom), National Public Radio, The Princeton Review, Stanley Kaplan, Barron's, Highlights for Kids, the U.S. Department of Education, and many other education providers. For some time, AOL sponsored homework help services for students that matched them with teachers online for tutorial help, and for a while services were offered to parents and also for teachers.

Originally, AOL charged users an hourly fee, but in October 1996 the rates changed to a flat monthly rate for a subscription at $19.95. Compared to rates from other browsers like CompuServe, Prodigy, and Netscape, AOL's rates were considered modest. At the time, all connections to the Internet were through dial-up service, meaning that telephone lines were used and connections were often slow. The amount of data transmitted over telephone lines was more limited than made possible by broadband services that were offered by cable companies in the late 1990s.

In 1998, AOL announced that it would acquire Netscape in 1999, and, for several years, Netscape carried the majority of Internet traffic in the United States. The company was highly criticized for marketing their product by sending CDs to potential users, either through the mail or sometimes tucked into magazines that were delivered to homes, with the software necessary to run AOL. The company was also criticized for creating such environmental waste, but the marketing scheme seemed to work. Everyone knew about AOL, and the company was gaining users through its set of acquisitions. As the dot-com bubble began in 1998, AOL continued to grow, with major successes and some startling failures.

One of its most successful acquisitions was Mapquest, a free online web mapping service acquired by AOL for $1.1 billion—the most expensive acquisition made after Netscape. Mapquest had grown from a division of R. R. Donnelley & Sons, in Chicago, Illinois, which was a well-known publisher of telephone books and other geographic reference books and sources. Mapquest was originally known as Cartographic Services and was founded in 1967. It became an independent company in 1994 and was renamed GeoSystems Global Corporation. AOL acquired the company in 2000 and developed its app for both the Android operating system and iOS.

In one of the most highly publicized acquisitions in 2000, AOL paid approximately $182 billion in stock and by absorbing Time Warner's debt, creating a media powerhouse that could potentially reach every American through the media assets of music, publishing, news, entertainment, cable, and Internet connectivity. The result was a new company worth a total of $350 billion. Billed as "the largest deal in history" the combined firm was said to have "unrivaled" assets among other media and online companies (Johnson 2000). But the newly constituted company came with some heavy baggage.

Time Warner had been formed in 1990 when Time Inc. and Warner Communications merged. Together, the two companies controlled HBO, Turner Broadcasting, New Line Cinema, the CW Television Network, Warner Bros., Kids' WB (the Warner Bros. division for children's content), Cartoon Network, Boomerang, Adult Swim, CNN, DC Comics, Warner Bros. Animation, Cartoon Network Studios, Hanna-Barbera, and Castle Rock Entertainment. The treasure of media content seemed unparalleled, but from the time AOL announced its acquisition of the Time Warner organization, things began to fall apart.

Clashing business models and personnel squabbles had much to do with the unhappy marriage of AOL and Time Warner, but history was also about to change as the dot-com bubble burst and a host of new services flooded the Internet and World Wide Web. The growth of mobile phones during this period also affected the financial side of the company that had been developed to deliver multimedia over computers. The profits of the combined company began to drop, and investors dropped their stock in order to invest in more profitable ventures.

In 2009, the company announced that it would split into two companies officially, thus dissolving their partnership. AOL hired Tim Armstrong, a former executive at Google, to become chief executive officer, and a new business plan was announced that would see AOL acquiring different new companies, and specializing in news services. Armstrong understood the impact of online news services and began to focus on creating a partnership that would make AOL a leader in news. By 2007, the newly rebranded AoL Inc. purchased the news blog, TechCrunch, and, in 2011, the Huffington Post. In 2012, AoL Inc. announced the acquisition of Hipster, a mobile photo sharing app. But the new direction that was most highly touted was the announcement of competing against Google, Microsoft, and Yahoo! for the U.S. online advertising market.

AoL had its strongest financial year in 2013, reporting $679 million in revenue. Tim Armstrong said, "2013 was AoL's most successful year in the last decade. AoL plans to invest in our market leading strategies in 2014, while we continue to grow the company" (Ha 2014). At the beginning of 2015 there was much speculation about the possibility of AoL merging with Yahoo!, but, in May 2015, in what seemed like a surprise to many, Armstrong announced that Verizon would buy AoL for $4.4 billion. The acquisition allows Verizon to compete in the digital media business by using AoL's content over the Verizon mobile market.

See also: Browser; Dot-Com Crash; Netscape; Yahoo!

Further Reading

Arango, Tim. 2010. "How the AOL-Time Warner Merger Went so Wrong." *New York Times.* Accessed December 1, 2014: http://www.nytimes.com/2010/01/11/business/media/11merger.html?pagewanted=all&_r=.

Ha, Anthony. 2014. "AOL's Q4 Revenue Grows to $679M but Earnings per Share of $0.43 Fall Short of Estimates." TechCrunch. Accessed September 3, 2014: http://techcrunch.com/2014/02/06/aol-q4-earnings-2/.

Johnson, Tom. 2000. "That's AOL Folks: Internet Leader and Entertainment Firm to Join Forces: New Company Worth $350B." CNN Money. Accessed March 22, 2015: http://money.cnn.com/2000/01/10/deals/aol_warner/.

Klein, Alec. 2003. *Stealing Time: Steve Case, Jerry Levin, and the Collapse of AOL Time Warner.* New York: Simon & Schuster.

Steel, Emily. 2009. "AOL–Time Warner Divorce Is Official." *Wall Street Journal.* Accessed March 22, 2015: http://www.wsj.com/articles/SB10001424052748704825504574586393655471238.

"Verizon Buys AOL for $4.4 Billion." 2015. CNN Money. Accessed May 21, 2015: http://money.cnn.com/2015/05/12/investing/verizon-buys-aol/.

American Telephone and Telegraph (AT&T)

From its incorporation as the American Telephone and Telegraph Company (AT&T) in 1885 (which became a subsidiary of AT&T Inc. in 2005), AT&T has been a giant in telecommunications. The company has undergone massive changes since it was founded but has remained a leader in telecommunications in the United States and overseas. From what was once the largest company in the United States, through deregulation, to today's world in which AT&T participates in mobile telephony, social network apps, and satellite delivery of media services, AT&T has been a pioneer in communications and information technologies.

AT&T began as a traditional (wired) telephone company at a time when telephone companies throughout the United States were small, local, and independent. In the early part of the twentieth century, Congress allowed AT&T to form a monopoly for telephone service to better serve the growing market of business and home consumers. AT&T's business plan was built on growth and making the new tool (the telephone) affordable for people. The *vertical integration* that resulted in AT&T's prominence over wired telephony in the United States gave extraordinary power to the company to handle all aspects of wired communications from the manufacturing of telephones, to the laying of transmission lines, billing, and research and development. The firm eventually became known somewhat pejoratively as "Ma Bell" to indicate the power it exerted over U.S. telephony.

Alexander Graham Bell, credited with receiving the patent that made the telephone possible, was not a businessman and had no interest in anything other than improving the quality of the telephone and working on other inventions, including the helicopter and submarine. His father-in-law, Gardiner Hubbard, was a businessman who had the foresight to see that telephones could be profitable. After hiring railroad executive Theodore Vail, the plan to create four parts of the new company came into being: Bell Labs (for experimentation), Long Lines (to string the necessary cables across the country, next to railroad lines for ease of access), the Bell Companies, eventually known as the Baby Bells (for processing payments), and Western Electric (to manufacture phones). Vail also had the idea to rent telephones to consumers, thereby controlling telephony from manufacture through rental and delivery of service.

A number of innovations from Bell Labs are worthy of mention, and they all involve the initial efforts of Alexander Graham Bell, who was interested in developing many more technologies than just the telephone. When his former laboratory became known as Bell Labs, the multifaceted approach to innovation continued. Over the years, Bell Labs engineers have been credited with development of the transistor, the laser, the UNIX operating system, the programming languages C, S, and C++, and the Linux operating system, and they have provided leadership in information and network theory. The dynamic AT&T structure crafted by Vail became a world leader in telephony and wired telephone innovation for decades, until new technologies (especially wireless technologies) and entrepreneurs challenged AT&T's dominance over wired communications in the United States.

In 1963, Microwave Communications International (MCI) became the first major challenger by using a series of microwave towers to bypass AT&T's Long Lines (the wired infrastructure) between Chicago and St. Louis, Missouri. The FCC approved MCI's request for a license, and, with that act, began the trajectory to the eventual dissolution of AT&T's monopoly over telephony in the United States. In 2006, MCI (which had become MCI WorldCom) was bought by Verizon.

Another challenge to AT&T's monopoly came in 1968, when the FCC allowed Thomas Carter to hook up wireless technology similar to a radio to the AT&T closed system of landlines. Known as the Carterfone decision, the end result was that other companies could make phones and technologies that could connect to AT&T equipment. Among the first wave of new technology included the answering machine, a variety of phone styles (other than the standard AT&T wall or desk phone manufactured by Western Electric), and ultimately, the wireless phone for the home.

Both the MCI decision and the Carterphone decision contributed to the U.S. Department of Justice's 1974 antitrust lawsuit against AT&T and the breakup of the biggest corporation in U.S. history. At first, the antitrust suit required AT&T to give up the Western Electric component of its business, but, after much court wrangling, it was decided that on January 1, 1983, AT&T would divest itself of its 22 regional operating companies, resulting in AT&T's loss of about 70 percent of its revenue. The Baby Bells as they became known, were then organized into seven different regional companies: Bell Atlantic, New York New England (NYNEX), Ameritech, Southwest Bell, Pacific Telesis, US West, and Bell South. Eventually, after the deregulation of the telephone industry in 1984, these companies merged, acquired new companies, or were acquired themselves. One of the giants of telecommunications today, Verizon, was the result of the merging of Bell Atlantic and NYNEX in 1997, with and another firm, GTE, in 2000.

Today's AT&T grew from the success of Southwest Bell and South Central Bell, which became renamed as SBC Communications Inc. In 2005, SBC purchased its former parent company, AT&T Corp., for $16 billion and renamed itself as AT&T Inc. The purchase (and parentage of the company) led to the new AT&T being allowed to use the traditional AT&T logo. All that is left of the original 1885 AT&T is the long-distance phone subsidiary of the company.

The deregulation of the original AT&T occurred because the one company had become so large, it was considered to have become a monopoly. In 1984, FCC Commissioner Mark Fowler initiated "marketplace rules" in which the deregulation of media industries (and many other industries as well) were enforced so that no one company would become so large and dominant again. But technological development and market forces between 1984 and the present, with particular emphasis on the development of the Internet and the World Wide Web and the proliferation of wired and wireless technologies that comprise our telecommunications infrastructure, have changed dramatically. Still, because of the prominence the original AT&T had, regulators at the FCC and U.S. Department of Justice have always been wary of AT&T's desire to create powerful mergers with other companies.

Still, AT&T has forged powerful allies. From 2007 to 2011, AT&T was the only carrier for Apple's line of iPhones (Crawford 2013, 163). AT&T subsidized iPhone purchases and offered customers long-term contracts. This business arrangement is called a private-carriage wireless model, and ended only when it became more profitable to set up a different payment system for mobile service that eliminated long-term contracts.

In March 2011, AT&T announced that it would like to merge with T-Mobile USA, the American division of T-Mobile owned by Deutsche Telekom, a major German company. The U.S. Department of Justice immediately began antitrust proceedings and blocked the merger, and in December 2011, AT&T gave up its bid to merge with T-Mobile. Both the Department of Justice and the FCC reasoned that if the purchase had been completed, AT&T would have domination over both wired and wireless communication in the United States. If this happened, it was feared that the company could exert its influence and charge consumers higher prices, force out competition, and stifle innovation in wired and wireless communications.

Since 2005, the new AT&T has remained a major player in telecommunications through its leadership in having the greatest number of wired (fixed) phones, but also by providing broadband subscription television services. Like many other telecommunications companies, AT&T has continued to develop and manufacture mobile phones and provide service plans for wireless access. In 2009, AT&T launched Social Net, a free mobile social networking app that gives users access to social networks like Facebook, MySpace, Twitter, and others, and that can be customized for news feeds within a single application.

In 2014, AT&T petitioned the FCC and Department of Justice to request permission to acquire DirecTV for reportedly $48 billion. The acquisition was completed in July, 2015. Initially AT&T began to start merger proceedings in 2014, but the business arrangement was bogged down for over a year because of a number of regulatory hurdles (Cox 2014). When the merger was completed, AT&T had gained access to the second largest pay-TV provider in the United States (the first is Comcast). While pundits questioned whether approval of such a merger could see AT&T become an even stronger telecommunications provider with access to wired and wireless connections for the home consumer, only time will tell.

See also: Federal Communications Commission (FCC); Legacy Media

Further Reading

Coll, Steve. 1986. *The Deal of the Century: The Break-Up of AT&T.* New York: Athenaeum.
Cox, Kate. 2014. "Why Isn't America Freaking Out about AT&T/DirecTV Merger—And Should We Be?" *The Consumerist.* Accessed April 6, 2015: http://consumerist.com/2014/09/05/why-isnt-america-freaking-out-about-attdirectv-merger-and-should-we-be/.
Crawford, Susan. 2013. *Captive Audience: The Telecom Industry and Monopoly Power in the New Gilded Age.* New Haven, CT: Yale University Press.

Android

The term *Android* (with a capital "A") denotes an operating system, a mobile device, and or a type of robot (though the robotic android uses a lower case "a"). For purposes of relating to social media, only the Android operating system and Android mobile phones are discussed in this encyclopedia, and only the Android operating system is described in this entry.

In 2005, Google acquired the developer of the Android system, a company called Android Inc., which used the Linux operating system that had become so popular for desktop and laptop computers. Android Inc. was founded in Palo Alto, California, in 2003 by Andy Rubin, Rich Miner, Nick Sears, and Chris White for the purpose of making "smarter mobile devices" (Elgin 2005). All of the developers had experience in a variety of forms of digital technologies, so together, they saw the potential of an operating system that could facilitate access to a wide variety of content. From the start, the operating system was intended to be used for commercial purposes. As Andy Rubin said in the announcement of Google's acquisition: "If people are smart, that information starts getting aggregated into consumer products" (Elgin 2005).

Android has become the most used mobile operating system in the world and is the software used for Android mobile phones, tablets, personal digital assistants (PDAs), and other portable equipment. The system was introduced on the mobile platform in 2008. While there are other operating systems in existence, Apple's iOS and Android systems are currently the most popular mobile systems in the United States.

The Android mobile operating system is a free, open system that occasionally needs to be updated to maintain maximum functionality. This is in contrast to Apple's iOS that is considered to be a "closed" system since it is compatible only with other Apple products. Google named the Android updates after desserts, such as Cupcake, Donut, Gingerbread, Ice Cream Sandwich, etc., and, as of November 2014, the latest version was named Lollipop 5.0. As of 2013, the Android operating system had been activated over 1 billion times worldwide (Yarrow 2013).

The Android iOS was designed for touchscreen mobile devices like smartphones and tablets, but the operating system can also be used with Android televisions, in cars that are specially outfitted with Android interoperability, and in the growing market of wearable technology, like computerized wristwatches.

See also: Apple iOS; Apps; Google; Mobile Phone; Open Source; Smartphone; Wearable Technology

Further Reading

Elgin, Ben. 2005. "Google Buys Android for Its Mobile Arsenal." *Bloomberg Businessweek.* Accessed April 6, 2015: http://www.webcitation.org/5wk7sIvVb.

Yarrow, Jay. 2013. "Android Activations Hit 1 Billion." Business Insider. Accessed December 3, 2014: http:// www.businessinsider.com/chart-of-the-day-android-activations-hit-1 -billion-2013-9#ixzz3KqjT0wuK.

Anonymity

One of the key components, yet one of the most complex phenomena of social networking, is that people can choose to be anonymous online, though we are increasingly learning that there are ways to identify even the most careful user who attempts to be anonymous. Companies may allow a user to be anonymous through the choice of how they describe themselves or the pseudonym they use, but in the days of computer or mobile phone hacking, totally masking one's identity may not be so easy. Today we know that government intervention into private files of Internet Service Providers and the tracking of mobile phone devices can be accomplished through sophisticated means that may be legal, if the authority conducting the hack is authorized to do so. Certainly, for most casual game players, Facebook users, or shoppers, anonymity may be a choice, but when social media use becomes suspicious or violates the law, even the most "anonymous" user can be tracked.

Today, given the casual use of social media that allows a person to choose to be anonymous, the best we can say is that anonymity may be promised, but it can never be assured. IP addresses are among the ways to track people, even when they take steps to be anonymous online. People may choose to use a different name or create a different persona (digital identity), to represent themselves with avatars or images that are different from their own appearance, or to mask their identities in any number of ways. Still, with encryption methods and digital records, anonymity may be an illusion.

Increasingly we learn of situations in which information was first made public from a person who preferred to remain anonymous, like Edward Snowden or the hacktivist group that uses the name Anonymous, but not all anonymous activity online is of a high-profile nature, as these cases suggest.

There can be a number of reasons why an average person would want to remain anonymous online. Privacy is probably one of the most common reasons for a desire to remain anonymous. Sometimes information may be embarrassing to the user—such as asking a question in an online forum about health matters. Sometimes *lurking,* or reading what's online without making any comment, is a way of avoiding self-disclosure. It may be an axiom, but the more we learn about online behavior, the more we have data to support the idea that lurkers comprise about 99 percent of the people who participate in online services (Rushe and Lewis 2014).

In social networking, the number of lurkers, or those who attempt to remain anonymous are more difficult to assess. For example, the number of social networks to which someone belongs doesn't equal the number of times they choose to use those networks, and they may have a variety of screen names and personas. Many studies have attempted to learn whether people choose to represent their identities as someone of a different gender, race, or ethnicity.

But an important question to ponder is whether anyone can ever be completely anonymous online. Even websites or apps that don't ask for your name or identifying characteristics can be processed and identities determined. For most casual, personal encounters anonymity may be easier to mask, but when it comes to processing messages through large companies, or when a hacker becomes involved, anonymity is much harder to assure.

The author of *Data and Goliath*, Bruce Schneier, claims that anyone can be exposed, thanks to today's ability to track and store data. He writes: "Maintaining Internet anonymity against a ubiquitous surveillor (sic) is nearly impossible. If you forget even once to enable your protections, or click on the wrong link, or type the wrong thing, you've permanently attached your name to whatever anonymous provider you're using" (Schneier 2015). As evidence, Schneier reports that computer scientist Latanya Sweeney combed the 1990 census data and was able to identify 87 percent of the U.S. population from just their zip codes combined with their birthdays and gender. Schneier concludes: "In the age of ubiquitous surveillance, where everyone collects data on us all the time, anonymity is fragile. We either need to develop more robust techniques for preserving anonymity, or give up on the idea entirely" (Schneier 2015).

Schneier discusses many of the high-profile cases of cracking the code of anonymity in his book, including cases such as Paula Broadwell's use of a number of hotel and public networks to communicate with former CIA director David Petraeus while the two were having an affair. The FBI was able to correlate registration data from several hotels and link the use of those e-mail systems back to Ms. Broadwell to expose her identity. Similarly, a member of the hacktivist group Anonymous who used the name "wormer" was located and identified after he took a picture of a woman's bare breasts on his smartphone. The phone's GPS coordinates could be tracked to a house in Australia. "Wormer" had indicated on Facebook that he had an Australian girlfriend, and he was quickly arrested and convicted of hacking U.S. law enforcement sites.

Users should always be aware that anything that is posted can be tracked. Apps are particularly vulnerable to allowing third-party comparisons of data to profile an individual. The most secure connections to websites are through the labyrinth of "tunnels" of information on the dark net (dark web) that function as an underground version of the Internet, but even though more people are accessing the dark net for purposes of accessing illegal information, the number of dark net users are minuscule compared to those who use the Internet for their daily communication and information needs.

See also: Avatar; Cybercrime; Dark Net; Identity; Privacy

Further Reading

Baym, Nancy K. 2010. *Personal Connections in the Digital Age.* Malden, MA: Polity Press.

Rushe, Dominic, and Paul Lewis. 2014. "How the 'Safest Place on the Internet' Tracks Its Users." *The Guardian.* Accessed January 22, 2015: http://www.theguardian.com/world/2014/oct/16/-sp-whispers-secret-safest-place-internet-tracks-users.

Schneier, Bruce. 2015. *Data and Goliath: The Hidden Battles to Collect Your Data and Control Your World.* New York: W. W. Norton and Co.

Schneier, Bruce. 2015. "In Our Modern Surveillance State Everyone Can Be Exposed." *Christian Science Monitor.* Accessed March 17, 2015: http://www.csmonitor.com/World/Passcode/Passcode-Voices/2015/0311/In-our-modern-surveillance-state-everyone-can-be-exposed.

Anonymous

The members of the group calling itself *Anonymous* represent an international hacker community that engages in hacking activities for political purposes. Some people agree with the members of the group that they are more like "freedom fighters," while other people have called them "vandals." The hackers in Anonymous believe they are fighting for justice and use the Internet to call attention to those people, policies, and practices that they find problematic, or even abhorrent.

Members of the group Anonymous grew from a 2003 discussion board on a site called 4chan where fans of anime could post pictures and comments. Many of the images they posted became some of the most well-known Internet memes, such as LOLcats and Chocolate Rain. Because 4chan did not require that people post their name, all users who didn't enter a screen name were given the default identity of "Anonymous." The site became popular for its irreverence, and, by 2004, some people on the bulletin board started to refer to the "Anonymous" people as an independent group. The members of Anonymous tend to refer to themselves as "Anons."

In 2007, the group made its first public stand when it became known that the Church of Scientology edited a YouTube video featuring Tom Cruise, one of its most well-known members. The video was shared by Gawker Media but the Church sent a "cease and desist" letter to Gawker demanding that they remove the video from their site. The group of 4chan Anonymous members considered this a form of censorship and decided to mount a campaign against the Church of Scientology. At first, one of the Anons issued a press release claiming that the hackers would "take down" the official Scientology website. The group issued distributed denial of service attacks (DDos) that caused the Scientology website to crash. They also pranked the Church of Scientology members by sending hundreds of pizzas to the headquarters in Europe, and some sent black faxes (i.e., black sheets of paper sent to a fax machine in an endless loop to drain the ink and damage the machine) to the Los Angeles headquarters. Death threats were made toward the leaders of the church. The campaign to discredit Scientology was so thorough, the church requested the help of the FBI to investigate this group called "Anonymous."

Another well-known cyberattack attributed to Anonymous occurred in 2010 and became known as Operation Payback. In 2010, the online company PayPal decided not to process donations to support WikiLeaks, the hacktivist group led by Julian Assange. Members of Anonymous used a free computer program called Low Orbit Ion Cannon (LOIC) to flood PayPal with illegitimate traffic for one week, thereby shutting down the server and forcing PayPal to be temporarily shut down. According to court records, PayPal estimated that the loss of access to business cost the company $5.5 million in damages. Visa and Mastercard, companies that also refused to process donations to WikiLeaks, claimed that they lost a combined $250 million since Operation Payback was instituted. Ultimately, 14 members of Anonymous were found to be responsible and were prosecuted in court on felony charges in 2013.

The number of cyberattacks attributed to WikiLeaks are many, but a more recent action involved Anonymous's use of Twitter to disrupt what the organization perceived to be unjust activity. In a campaign called Operation KKK, Anonymous hacked the Twitter account of the Ku Klux Klan (KKK) in Missouri, shortly after the protests about a police officer's shooting of the unarmed black teenager Michael Brown. In the hack, Anonymous posted the names and addresses of the members of the KKK, a secret white supremacist organization.

See also: Assange, Julian; Dark Net; Snowden, Edward; WikiLeaks

Further Reading

"Anonymous Hacks, Outs Missouri KKK 25." 2014. *Toronto Sun.* Accessed December 3, 2014: http://www.torontosun.com/2014/11/17/anonymous-hacks-outs-missouri-kkk.

Coleman, Gabriella. 2014. *Hacker, Hoaxer, Whistleblower, Spy: The Many Faces of Anonymous.* London: Verso.

Krupnick, Matt. 2011. "Freedom Fighters or Vandals? No Consensus on Anonymous." *Oakland Tribune*, MercuryNews.com. Accessed September 23, 2014: http://www.mercury news.com/top-stories/ci_18686764.

Kushner, David. 2014. "The Masked Avengers: How Anonymous Incited Online Vigilantism from Tunisia to Ferguson." *The New Yorker* 90: 48.

Mackay, Robert. 2010. "'Operation Payback' Attacks Target MasterCard and PayPal Sites to Avenge WikiLeaks." *New York Times.* Accessed January 28, 2015: http://thelede.blogs .nytimes.com/2010/12/08/operation-payback-targets-mastercard-and-paypal-sites-to -avenge-wikileaks/.

App

The term "app" is an abbreviation of "application" meaning a self-contained program or type of software that has a particular purpose. Apps that are intended to be shown on computers are generally called "web apps" and those that are used on mobile devices are called "mobile apps." Apps are usually developed by start-up companies and then distributed through a major company (like the Apple Store or Google Apps), but some app developers control the distribution themselves for the operating systems on which their apps can run. When apps are developed that become extremely popular, or change the way we think of communicating or processing information, they are called "killer apps." For example, e-mail has been referred to as a killer app that revolutionized personal communication. In January 2011, the American Dialect Society named "app" the 2010 Word of the Year.

While apps can be useful, fun, informational, and entertaining, they can also function to provide a significant amount of information about the app user to advertising companies. Some apps can be downloaded for free and others have a modest fee (usually), while a hefty fee can be charged to users of advanced versions of apps. The idea behind making some apps free (at least until they are successful) this is that free apps are more widely adopted, but the fees that are paid for some apps underwrite the cost of distributing some apps for free.

The use of the term, "app" goes back to 1985, though it could have been used earlier by computer programmers as a shorthand way of describing an "application" (Holwerda 2011). In 2011, Apple attempted to trademark the term and received some bad press for sending "cease and desist" letters to other developers using it while they were promoting their new App Store. Apple decided to give up on their claim to the term.

When apps were first developed, they took a tremendous amount of battery power to run on social media. Over time, they have been adapted to use less power, which is offset by the development of better processors to make app use more seamless. As the costs have gone down and the technology has improved, apps have extended the use of computers, smartphones, and mobile devices to a range of consumers who have become reliant on apps for entertainment, information, and connecting to services like banking, navigation, and more. Early mobile phones could not accommodate apps because of their technological limitations, but when smartphones emerged and could play Flash video, the number of apps skyrocketed. Flash worked more efficiently on Android phones, and, in large part, the availability of apps spurred the growth of Android operating phones worldwide. During the second half of 2008, when Apple introduced the iPhone 3G, the improved app connectivity resulted in a quadrupling of profits from the previous year. The job of developing apps has become one of the fastest growing part-time jobs in the creative economy.

Apple's App Store boasts that it sells over a million different apps, and Google Apps claims that over 5 million businesses have their own apps. For the companies that sell apps, one general business model exists. For example, when Apple sells an app, they retain 30 percent of the cost, and 70 percent is returned to the app company.

Apps, like any form of media content, change over time. The first wave of apps focused primarily on games that the mobile phone user could play alone. Over time, apps became tools for more social activity. Apps like Foursquare, Meetup, okCupid, and Zoosk targeted people who wanted to meet others for socializing or dating. But the future wave of apps seems to be those that facilitate one-to-one meetings in which the users retain better control over their privacy. As Shani Hilton, executive editor for news at BuzzFeed, said, "People don't want to perform their lives publicly in the same way that they wanted to five years ago" (Madrigal 2014, 39).

To illustrate Hilton's point, two recently developed apps, discussed below, can provide a snapshot of the features we might expect to see in the near future. These representative apps demonstrate how temporality and spatiality (time and space) can be influenced by the use of apps.

App developers know that one of the most guarded features of social media users is privacy. Since the debates about Facebook's privacy settings and what major companies do with personal information, some apps have been developed to limit access to content. Snapchat, an app that emerged in 2011, allows users to set a time limit for the length of time recipients can access their images. Then, after a designated time, the images are hidden from the recipient's device and deleted from the Snapchat server. While much of the Snapchat content is meant to be funny or provocative, a small percentage of the content is often in the form of sexting, but the sender has the assurance that the image will not be able to live in a database any longer than they desire it to be available. Snapchat has a number of competitors, like Instagram and Flickr, but it appeals to users who like the short-term feature of content storage.

Yik Yak, a popular app on high school and college campuses was released early in 2014 and functions somewhat like a virtual bulletin board. People can post information anonymously, and the app functions only within a small geographic area, confining content to local spaces. Yik Yak calls itself an alternative to Facebook or Twitter, but unfortunately, it has occasionally been responsible for the spread of rumors and inaccuracies. Yik Yak has been banned in some Canadian schools because someone anonymously posted information near a high school warning of a gun hidden in the school's library (Bogart 2015). Still, Yik Yak shows that those in small geographic regions still have a need to share instant messages with people in a confined geographic area. As a result, Yik Yak is an even better monitor of contemporary peer-related values and information than Facebook or Twitter.

See also: Mobile Phone; Privacy; Smartphone

Further Reading

Bogart, Nichole. 2015. "What Is Yik Yak? The Latest App to Cause Concern at Canadian Schools." *Global News.* Accessed January 22, 2015: http://globalnews.ca/news/1785227/what-is-yik-yak-the-latest-app-to-cause-concern-at-canadian-schools/.

Holwerda, Thom. 2011. "The History of 'App' and the Demise of the Programmer." *OSNews.* Accessed October 2, 2014: http://www.osnews.com/story/24882/The_History_of_App_and_the_Demise_of_the_Programmer.

Madrigal, Alexis C. 2014b. "The Fall of Facebook." *The Atlantic Monthly* 314: 34–35, 39.

Apple

Apple Inc. is major multinational computer hardware and software firm based in Cupertino, California. The company was started by Steve Jobs and Steve Wozniak who met through a mutual friend and immediately found that they had the same interest in electronics, music, and playing pranks. One of their pranks (see below) eventually led to a successful working relationship and the founding of the Apple Computer Co. Since those early days, Apple has grown to be one of the most recognizable brands in computers, hardware devices, and new products, and its distinctive logo, of an apple with a bite taken out of it, is recognized worldwide.

One of their legendary pranks occurred in 1971 when Wozniak read an article in *Esquire* magazine about hackers and phone phreaks (people who liked to prank AT&T, the monopoly telephone company at the time) who figured out how to make long-distance phone calls at no charge. The article discussed how sounds generated at the same frequencies as the AT&T system could simulate the call-routing switches. The two immediately did the research and bought the components necessary to simulate the "Blue Box" as the hackers' machine was described, but the first attempts failed. When Wozniak figured out how to make a digital circuit, their system did work, and the two set out to make as many prank calls as they could. One call they made was to the Vatican, and Wozniak impersonated Henry Kissinger and demanded to speak to the Pope. The person who answered the call at the Vatican refused to wake the Pope, and quickly figured that the call was not authentic, but Wozniak and Jobs were ecstatic that their version of the "Blue Box" worked (Isaacson 2011, 28–29). From that point on, they became good friends. Jobs then graduated Homestead High and left to attend Reed College in Portland, Oregon, and Wozniak attended Berkeley.

By 1975, Jobs had dropped out of college and Wozniak was working at Hewlett-Packard. Both became involved with a group of computer enthusiasts who participated in "The Homebrew Computer Club," where many of the participants had been discussing the January 1975 issue of *Popular Mechanics* that introduced the Altair personal computer kit (the same issue that served as the stimulus for Bill Gates and Paul Allen to develop the program they sold to Altair). Wozniak began to tinker, and Jobs began to figure out how they could sell the improved circuit boards and components that Wozniak was making.

At that time, Wozniak was working for Hewlett-Packard and initially offered the company the improved circuit board, keyboard, monitor, and components he was developing, but HP was not interested. Members of the Homebrew Computer Club were interested, but no one had a vision about how this new machine could become profitable—except Jobs. Even Wozniak was uncertain about giving up the job he liked at Hewlett-Packard. So to convince Wozniak to devote more time to the new company, Jobs brought in Ronald Wayne, whom he had met while working at Atari, to help develop a business plan, and together, the three established the company in 1976. Their purpose was to sell the computer kits Wozniak had developed, which they had priced at $666.66. They decided to name the company Apple, and the Wozniak computer was called Apple I. In recounting how and why the name was chosen, Jobs told his biographer, Walter Isaacson, "I was on one of my fruitarian diets. I had just come back from the apple farm. It sounded fun, spirited, and not intimidating . . . Plus, it would get us ahead of Atari in the phone book" (Isaacson 2011, 63).

In 1977, Wayne sold his share of the company back to Jobs and Wozniak, and with the help of a financier, Mike Markkula, Apple was incorporated as a business that year. Wozniak also worked on the design for the Apple II, which became a far more commercially successful model of the computer.

Though Apple's consumers often demonstrate a brand loyalty, not all of Apple's products have been successful.In the early years, Apple's software designs clashed with another fledgling firm that was emerging at the same time, Microsoft. There were also smaller firms interested in developing computers and software, such as Commodore and Tandy. But Apple's business plan grew in such a way as to leave the desktop computing market to Microsoft, which was developing a superior suite of office software products, and develop products that were stylish and visually interesting and capitalized on graphical interfaces that made visual images more appealing to users. Microsoft's success in designing improvements for office and personal computers drove many of their other competitors out of business.

By 1980, Apple went public by selling stock and generated more capital through this act than any other company in history, except for the Ford Motor Company, which went public in 1956. In what seemed like an almost "overnight" event, approximately 300 of Apple's stockholders became millionaires. The company became known for product innovation in computers and in other devices that use computational hardware and software.

Starting in the 1980s, Apple continually introduced new models of computers as they considered branching out into newer products. One of its first computer successes was the Lisa model of computer (1983) named after Jobs's daughter, but which varied from other computers in that it used a handheld mouse for easy screen navigation. One of Apple's best-selling computers (at the time), called the Macintosh, was introduced in 1984 and used a graphical user interface (GUI) that, along with the mouse, allowed users to point and click commands, rather than having to negotiate keyboard controls to function. The Macintosh was debuted in a legendary television commercial aired during the Super Bowl in 1984. Directed by Ridley Scott, a movie director noted for science fiction and futuristic films, the commercial was called "1984" and cost $1.5 million to create—the most expensive commercial ever created, to that date.

In 1985, John Sculley, an Apple executive, was named chief executive officer (CEO) and a series of battles with Steve Jobs ensued. This resulted in Jobs's leaving the company for a time while pursuing other interests. He returned as an advisor to the company in 1996, but, in the meantime, Apple Inc. introduced a number of initiatives that had varying levels of success. Attempts to develop digital cameras, portable CD audio players, speakers, video consoles, and TV appliances all failed. One of the major problems for Sculley was the conflict over who "owned" the copyright on the graphical user interface that was being used by a number of other computer manufacturers. A lawsuit brought by Apple in 1988 referred to as *Apple Computer Inc. v. Microsoft Corporation* dragged on for four years before it was finally dismissed.

Despite the lawsuit, Apple continued to make new products, with varying rates of success. In 1986, Apple introduced both the Mac Plus computer and the Laser-Writer printer, which interested consumers and was sold as a package to facilitate what was then called "desktop publishing." In 1994, the Power Macintosh was introduced and sold as a high-powered personal computer. By 1998, the iMac came along, which was designed to be set up and used easily by the home consumer who was still grappling with the complexities of putting together a computer package that would work easily in the home or at the office. The Macintosh Portable was introduced in 1989, and the line of PowerBooks began in 1991.

In 1997, Apple introduced the Apple Online Store, which used a "build-to-order" manufacturing strategy that has been criticized for giving Apple the maximum amount of time to assess orders and not find themselves with overstocked items but, at the same time, provides Apple with a long publicity program that drives up interest in the new product.

In June 2011 despite being on medical leave, Steve Jobs unveiled an online storage and syncing service for music, photos, files, and software called iCloud. On October 5, 2011, Steve Jobs died of complications from cancer, but the new CEO, Tim Cook, continued the practice of public announcements of new products. Among the products that have debuted since Jobs's death in 2011, there have been many new model roll-outs and acquisitions that show where Apple's businesses are headed in the future.

Apple products have spanned the range of audio, video, and tactile technologies, but all have at the core of their existence an operating system used only by Apple. The company has claimed that their proprietary control of their operating system makes their technologies less "buggy" than others (meaning that they are less likely to get infections, viruses, and other forms of malware), but some critics claim that despite using the "closed" iOS system, even Apple products sometimes can fail. Though the closed operating system makes it possible to link different components within the Apple system, the makers of apps and additional content features sometimes find it more difficult to get their technologies to communicate with the Apple system. Apple products are also known for the design features they include in each system, the packaging, and the marketing campaigns that promote the release of each new technology.

iPods

One of Apple's early ventures was to become a leader in digital music distribution, and the success of their digital media players and digital audio players has severely influenced the recorded music industry's response to their technologies and business models. Apple introduced the iPod in 2001 and, in 2003, announced the new iTunes Music Store, which would ultimately have the effect of contributing to the death of brick-and-mortar music stores—though it should be recognized that iTunes was just one of many changes within the legacy recorded-music business that began to revolutionize that industry, too. The iTunes Music Store ultimately became the world's largest music retailer until the beginning of 2015 when the business seemed to be losing momentum. While the iTunes Music Store was still the market leader in downloads, other streaming music services like Spotify, Pandora, and YouTube were challenging its domination of the business. In 2014, sales were down by 14 percent. According to James McQuivey, an analyst at Forrester Research: "The reason iTunes was adopted so well in the beginning was really not because it was great software . . . It was because it was connected to this hardware that was unlocking your music access and letting you take it with you on the go and that was such a novel sensation" (Sydell 2015). Since then, Spotify, Pandora, and SoundCloud have been working on perfecting their streaming services and are now much easier to use than iTunes.

iPhones

Apple released the first iPhone in 2007 and in the same year the company name was changed to Apple Inc. As previously mentioned, Apple products work only with the Apple iOS operating system, and this makes it more difficult for apps and peripheral technologies to interconnect with iPhones. The competition that uses the Android operating system has become far more popular. Still, by October 2008, Apple had become the third-largest mobile handset supplier in the world, and it is eclipsed only by Samsung Electronics as the world's leader in smartphone manufacturing.

The day prior to Jobs's death, Apple announced the new iPhone 4S, which included an improved camera and a dual-core chip capable of producing graphics seven times faster than the previous model. The new phone also had an "intelligent software assistant" named Siri. In 2012, Apple unveiled the iPhone 5, and, in September 2014, two models of the iPhone 6 (varying in size) were released. The two new iPhones with improved interoperability with apps have improved Apple's market share of smartphones on the global level. The success of the iPhone 6 models has been remarkable. Apple reported that in the last three months of 2014, 74.5 million iPhones had been sold globally, far beyond what analysts had predicted. The sales of iPhone 6 (both models) allowed Apple to post the greatest three-month revenue profit in company history, fueled by the new phones ("Apple Posts the Biggest Quarterly Profit in History" 2015). China was the country that accounted for most of the growth in the sale of the iPhone 6 models.

Apple's decision to streamline its products with new technologies and content that can only be played on other Apple products has led the company to investigate exclusive relationships with distributors. For several years, AT&T was the major telecommunications company that carried wireless services for Apple, but those days may now be over as new competition threatens to marginalize any company that does not open itself to services that consumers find desirable.

iPads

Apple first released a version of a tablet computer in 1993 called the Newton MessagePad, but the early attempt was eclipsed by a range of personal desk assistants (PDAs) released by other companies, at much lower costs. For a while, Apple stopped developing the tablet until it was ready to hit the market with some strength. In the meantime, it had been focusing on iPhones, but, in 2010, Apple came out with the iPad, the first commercially viable tablet in the Apple line of products. Apple's entry into the tablet market produced a lightweight, touch-sensitive technology with an onscreen keyboard, but the features thought to be most desirable were the combined strengths as an e-reader, a gaming device, and a music and video player. But, in 2010, the public was not yet sure of whether the price of an iPad (minimally in the $800 range) was worth the cost, when prices of laptops were dropping.

David Pogue, technology writer for the *New York Times* summed up the difference between Apple's laptop computers and the new line of iPads that emerged in 2010 in a cleverly worded article in which he reviewed an Apple laptop and the iPad from the perspectives of a "techie" and the "regular people." As Pogue wrote: "The haters tend to be techies; the fans tend to be regular people." He continued to discuss the multifunctions of a laptop compared to the sleek uses, but more "passive" features, of the iPad that seemed to appeal to "regular people" because of its entertainment purpose (Pogue 2010).

Additional versions of the iPad followed: the iPad 2 (2011), the third generation iPad (2012), and the fourth generation iPad eight months later (2012). The iPad Air and iPad mini debuted in 2014. But compared to Apple's other products, the iPad has been losing popularity. In 2014, sales were 22 percent lower than they were in 2013 ("Apple Posts the Biggest Quarterly Profit in History" 2015).

Apple TV

Apple has also been active in developing a series of Apple TVs that have changed greatly from the first model released as iTV in 2006. The name of the unit was the same as a British television channel called iTV (Independent Television), and after the broadcaster threatened to take legal action, Apple shifted the name of its television sets to Apple TVs. Apple stopped making the Apple iTV in 2009, and a free upgrade turned the product into a regular, stand-alone television receiver that could stream some media content available through the iTunes Store.

The second generation Apple TV was released in 2010 with increased streaming capabilities, and, in 2012, Apple's CEO Tim Cook announced that a third version would be released in 2013. When it was released, the third generation looked very much like the second generation Apple TV, but it included a faster processor and can stream content from both the iTunes Store and Netflix.

The App Store

In July 2008, Apple launched the App Store to sell third-party applications for the iPhone and iPod Touch, and within a month the App Store was bringing in approximately $1 million. One of the newest areas for app development is in facilitating the streaming of media content that was previously exclusive to different forms. HBO, for example, started as a subscription service that was then delivered by cable companies. The service cost consumers about $15 a month, but now, Apple has developed an app that allows HBO to stream to any number of Apple devices, such as iPhones, iPads, and the Apple TV. The app is exclusive to Apple.

Retail Stores

As mentioned, Apple Inc. likes to control the distribution of its products. Apple opened its first two retail stores on May 15, 2011 (one in Tyson's Corner, Virginia, and the other in Glendale, California). Since that time the company has opened over 450 stores in urban areas around the world. But, in 2014, Apple also started selling its products in other retail establishments, too, indicating that the tight control once held over its product distribution may be changing.

New Directions

In 2012, Apple announced that it was going to be getting into the business of selling iBooks Textbooks for iOS and iBook Author for its Mac OS X computer line, indicating that the company is branching out from audio and video content and picking up the growing e-book business. But it is not stopping there. In 2013, Apple acquired PrimeSense, an Israeli 3D-sensing company, and, in 2014, along with the product launch of the iPhone 6, Apple introduced the new Apple Watch, a wearable technology with Internet connectivity that was released in 2015.

In 2013, Apple filed a patent for an augmented reality system, but the bigger news that year involved CEO Tim Cook's attendance at a summit held by President Obama that also included Google vice president, Vint Cerf, and AT&T's CEO, Randall Stephenson. The event that caused this meeting to be held was the leak of government secrets by Edward Snowden, and the resulting discussions concerning cybersecurity.

Criticism

Among the criticisms that Apple has received over the years, one outstanding problem is in the area of labor practices. A considerable amount of negative attention came to the company involving their use of the Foxconn manufacturing facility in China. The initial reports of subhuman working conditions began in 2006 with a newspaper story reporting that employees in the manufacturing plant where Apple's iPods were made were required to work more than 60 hours a week and earned only about $100 a month. Additionally, the employees were required to pay the company (Foxconn) for rent and the food they consumed, which generally represented about half of the employees' earnings.

Since the original story was released in 2006, Apple has attempted to be more vigilant, though new reports of child labor and employees' contact with toxic chemicals have continued to taint the manufacturing arm of Apple products in China. Some reports of worker depression and suicide because of the labor practices at Foxconn continue to enrage activists who advocate for worker safety and fair labor practices.

See also: Jobs, Steve; Mobile Phones; Smartphones; Wozniak, Steve

Further Reading

"Apple Posts the Biggest Quarterly Profit in History." 2015. BBC News. Accessed April 7, 2015: http://www.bbc.com/news/business-31012410.

Isaacson, Walter. 2011. *Steve Jobs*. New York: Simon & Schuster.

Pogue, David. 2010. "Looking at the iPad from Two Angles." *New York Times*. Accessed April 7, 2015: http://www.nytimes.com/2010/04/01/technology/personaltech/01pogue .html?pagewanted=all&partner=rss&emc=rss&_r=0.

Sydell, Laura. 2015. "With Downloads in Decline, Can iTunes Adapt?" NPR's *Morning Edition*. Accessed January 7, 2015: http://www.npr.org/blogs/therecord/2015/01/06/375 173595/with-downloads-in-decline-can-itunes-adapt.

Apple iOS

Operating systems are a combination of hardware and software that is necessary for the operation of compatible digital technologies. The Apple system used for all Apple-manufactured mobile technologies is called the iOS, drawing from the "i" that refers to every Apple title, followed by "operating system." The original name of the system was the iPhone OS, but with Apple's development of tablets, television sets, and wearable technology, the name was just shortened to iOS. The system was originally introduced in 2007 and was intended to operate all "i" technologies such as the iPhone, iPod Touch, iPad, and iPad mini. Considered a "closed" system, iOS does not communicate with other, non-iOS technologies. Because of Apple's name recognition and number of digital devices made by Apple, 60 percent of the technologies used in the United States have iOS systems. When it was first introduced, the iPad was the Apple technology responsible for the most downloads of the iOS system, but, since then, the Apple line of smartphones has dominated the type of device that uses the iOS system.

The most important thing about operating systems is that they are not compatible with other technologies, so Apple products work only with the Apple iOS. The primary competition for mobile operating systems is the Android, which has the largest worldwide share of smartphones, tablets, PDAs, and mobile devices. There are other operating systems that are used in the world, but Android is by far the most used in the global arena, and Apple iOS is the second most popular in the United States. When a new system is introduced, the company sends out a wireless message and a consumer can update their technology to the newest operating system by downloading the software to their device. At the beginning of 2015, the iOS generation in use was iOS 8. Apple claimed that the speed of the operating system allowed for a number of new apps to be developed and sold and new functions allowed users to have Siri control home devices and have health and fitness apps communicate directly with a person's doctor. Apple also improved connectivity with the iCloud for stored services.

But iOS 8 emerged to mixed reviews. For example, Martin Bryant, a reviewer for TheNextWeb (thenextweb.com) gave iOS 8 good reviews for improvements to the speech-activated connection using Siri, and an improved keyboard (modeled after Android phones), but faulted Apple for a system that was sometimes inconsistent. The improvements, too, according to Bryant, were in the hands of third-party developers, and not from Apple itself. In sum, he felt that the best improvements have yet to be made on future iterations of the iOS system (Bryant 2014).

See also: Android; Apple

Further Reading

Bryant, Matt. 2014. "iOS 8 Review: The Real Advances Here Are Yet to Come." The Next Web. Accessed January 8, 2015: http://thenextweb.com/apple/2014/09/17/ios-8-review/1/.

Arab Spring

The term *Arab Spring* refers to a wave of revolutionary demonstrations and protests that began in December 2010 in Tunisia when a street vendor immolated himself while protesting confiscation of the produce he sold and the mistreatment he routinely endured from civil authorities. This action enraged other individuals who felt that in their own respective countries, something needed to be done to respond to the heavy-handedness of the government and military leaders. This sparked violent protests throughout the country, primarily by young people and members of unions. Within two years, protests were also staged in Egypt, Libya, Yemen, Algeria, Iraq, Jordan, Kuwait, Morocco, Israel, and the Sudan, and civil uprisings occurred in Bahrain and Syria. The term *Arab Spring* is a reference to the Prague Spring in 1968, in which university students protested the repressive government and lack of job opportunities, and the Revolutions of 1989 that swept through Eastern Europe, all largely led by young people.

The Arab Spring is widely believed to have been instigated by problems within Arab nations that had dictatorial governments rather than elected officials, and where members of the population experienced many human rights violations and economic decline. In a good number of these countries there were a growing number of young people who had few opportunities for education or employment. The Internet and the World Wide Web may not have been widely available in all areas in these countries, but the media that existed helped spur ideas of change in these countries. Social media also spread information through a number of sources, like WikiLeaks, which leaked information that documented the greed and corruption of a Tunisian president and his family in the form of dispatches from U.S. diplomats who described lavish homes, banquets, and even wild animals that lived in the presidential compound.

Where social media were available, change seemed to be in the hands of the people using new technology. The wave of protests throughout the Middle East were often organized by people using social media like Facebook (and other social networks), and, especially, Twitter. In Egypt, for example, people were prohibited from gathering publicly in groups, and the police could arrest individuals who appeared to be organizing for antigovernment purposes. Instead of public gatherings, social media allowed people to mobilize and communicate among themselves faster, often without the knowledge of the government or military. One Tunisian protestor tweeted, "We use Facebook to schedule the protests, Twitter to coordinate, and YouTube to tell the world" (Shirky 2011, 1). In general, the social media used during the Arab Spring examines how social media can be used to inform, organize, and mobilize people for political action.

While the initial impetus for political change throughout the Arab countries seemed to rely on social media, some authors have opined that while social media certainly played a role in helping to organize and spread the word about public gatherings, their role in the political insurrections that fueled the Arab Spring may have been overstated. What most scholars and journalists agree upon, though, is that social media may have been more important at the beginning of political mobilization in these countries, but that, over time, governments also learned how to use social media to stop mobilization or "out" political leaders.

Evgeny Morozov is an author who has written about the role of the Internet and how the praises of the Internet for social and political mobilization are often overstated (2011). Instead, he cautions that the Internet can also be used by authoritarian regimes to control the public through censorship and misleading information. Likewise, Christian Fuchs has written about the role of the citizen journalist who uses alternative media like social media to tell the story of political uprisings and questions how surveillance of these media forms can be detrimental to those who try to participate in political change (2014). Fuchs acknowledges the role of social media as informational, but reminds us that the Arab revolutions were the result of significant cultural and economic factors that set the stage for a revolution and that calling Twitter and Facebook the causes of revolution are inaccurate and misleading (Fuchs 2014, 4).

The Arab Spring has taught us that social media is indeed a factor in social and political mobilization for change, but it also cautions us to be skeptical about "cause/effect" issues and encourages us to think of how social media play a role in creating change by considering a number of historical, economic, political, religious, and cultural factors relevant to a particular situation. Social media offer a new alternative to traditional media models in social and political situations, but they comprise only some factors among many.

See also: Occupy Movement; Twitter

Further Reading

Fuchs, Christian. 2014. *Social Media: A Critical Introduction*. London: Sage, 4.

Gladwell, Malcolm. 2010. "Small Change: Why the Revolution Will Not Be Tweeted." *The New Yorker*. 86: 30.

Morozov, Evgeny. 2011. *The Net Delusion: The Dark Side of Internet Freedom*. New York: Public Affairs.

Shirky, Clay. 2011. "The Political Power of Social Media." *Foreign Affairs* 90: 1.

Assange, Julian

As the controversial editor-in-chief of WikiLeaks, Julian Assange (1971–) is known not only for his creation of the WikiLeaks, but also his personal issues involving his taking political asylum in the Ecuadorean Embassy in London to avoid extradition to Sweden, where he was wanted on charges of rape.

Born in Townsville, Queensland, Australia, Assange became fascinated with computers at an early age. As a child, he and his mother (and stepfather, for a while) traveled extensively throughout the country. Julian attended about 37 different schools as a child and was often homeschooled. He began hacking the computers of major companies, and, in 1991, he got in trouble for hacking the computers of Nortel, a telecommunications company. Eventually, he was charged with more than 30 counts of hacking in Australia but managed to get away with only having to pay a fine. He studied mathematics at the University of Melbourne, but left before receiving his undergraduate degree.

He started the site WikiLeaks in 2006 as editor-in-chief and positioned the site in Sweden because of the more liberal laws regarding censorship and the protection of peoples' anonymity. Assange called WikiLeaks the first "stateless news organization" and had the goal of publishing important documents on the Internet so that people could see what different governments were doing with classified information. In 2007, the site went live and soon published a U.S. military manual with information related to the Guantanamo detention center. Then, in 2008, WikiLeaks shared communications from the Republican vice presidential candidate, Sarah Palin, that had been received from an anonymous source.

Claiming that the press must be free, WikiLeaks began to publish information from a number of countries. In 2009, WikiLeaks was publishing thousands of diplomatic cables between then secretary of state Hillary Clinton and the U.S. government every week. Though Hillary Clinton had denounced the publication as "an attack on the international community" that would "tear at the fabric" of government, WikiLeaks continued to gain the attention of the press and the wrath of the U.S. government, as well as other governments whose private messages were posted on the site (Assange 2014).

WikiLeaks' most highly publicized leak started in February 2010, when 25-year-old private first class and intelligence officer in the U.S. Army, Bradley Manning, smuggled secret documents out of his office and communicated with a person believed to be Julian Assange. WikiLeaks started to publish what became known as the "War Logs" concerning military actions in Iraq and Afghanistan. One video showed a U.S. Apache helicopter in Baghdad opening fire on a group of individuals who were believed to be insurgents, but the images proved that Iraqi children and two journalists were also killed in the fire. Manning was arrested in Iraq in May 2010 and taken to military court where he was acquitted of aiding the enemy but convicted on other counts of espionage and for leaking State Department cables and information about the detainees at Guantanamo Bay, Cuba. He was sentenced to 35 years in prison for his actions.

Not all of WikiLeaks' messages have been considered to be as potentially volatile as the high-profile leaks related to government secrets. When a number of e-mails from a company known as Stratfor were leaked, the content of those e-mails was more aligned to internal communication than many felt justified such attention. Many journalists and members of the public felt that the messages were much more related to public relations than security issues, and many dismissed this leak as making much of Stratfor's internal operations rather than anything that really involved the public (Coleman 2014). This type of attention weakened WikiLeaks claims of operating with the best intention of shining a spotlight on greed or corruption.

WikiLeaks also played a role in supporting Edward Snowden who released classified National Security Administration (NSA) information from his hotel in Hong Kong in 2014. While Snowden did not release his classified information over WikiLeaks, the organization helped pay for his lodgings in exile and sent one of their top advisors, Sarah Harrison, to help facilitate Snowden's travel to Russia where he sought asylum.

Some feel that Assange, WikiLeaks, and the whistleblowers like Snowden are traitors to their countries, but, at the same time, the many people who have been able to see the type of information flowing through WikiLeaks have supported the organization's efforts to facilitate free speech and expose governments that manipulate public opinion. The power relations that are expressed in WikiLeaks messages shift traditional information flow that starts with institutions that then send information to individuals. In defending the position of this shift from the individual to the institution, Arne Hintz suggests that actions by groups such as those involved in the Arab Spring and in WikiLeaks confirm some of the earlier predictions by cyberlibertarians who have viewed cyberspace as a place of liberation from traditional institutional restraints (Hintz 2013).

Assange was named the *Time* magazine "Person of the Year" in 2010. But in that same year, Swedish police were after Assange for two sexual assault cases that had been filed by women in Sweden. Assange turned himself in to London police, and, after two months, he was given asylum by the Ecuadorean Embassy in London to avoid extradition to Sweden. His asylum meant that he could not go anywhere without fear of being picked up by police, but he continued to work with WikiLeaks despite his being detained in the Ecuadorean Embassy for years. He has continued to pursue his belief in freedom of the press and the role of WikiLeaks in exposing what it believes is hypocrisy, and he has continued to advocate for transparency and control over corporate and government abuses of power.

Assange has written two books: *Cypherpunks: Freedom and the Future of the Internet*, with Jacob Applebaum, Andy Muller-Maguhn, and Jeremie Zimmermann (2012), about corporate and government control of the Internet, and *When Google Met WikiLeaks* (2014), based upon Assange's 2011 meeting with Google's CEO, Eric Schmidt, while Assange was living under house arrest in England.

See also: Anonymous; WikiLeaks

Further Reading

Assange, Julian. 2014. *When Google Met WikiLeaks*. O/R Press.

Coleman, Gabriella. 2014. *Hacker, Hoaxer, Whistleblower, Spy: The Many Faces of Anonymous*. London: Verso, 351.

Hastings, Michael. 2012. "Julian Assange: The Rolling Stone Interview." *Rolling Stone*, 1142: 50–60.

Hintz, Arne, 2013. "Dimensions of Modern Freedom Expression: WikiLeaks, Policy Hacking, and Digital Freedoms," In *Beyond WikiLeaks: Implications for the Future of Communications, Journalism, and Society*. Edited by Benedetta Brevini, Arne Hintz, and Patrick McCurdy. New York: Palgrave Macmillan, 146–165.

Avatar

An avatar is a graphical representation of a physical body that is often used to substitute or hide a person's real identity or physical appearance. Some people choose to create an avatar for themselves in the online world because it is a way of hiding their true identity, but sometimes creating an avatar is part of the fun of participating in a cyber-environment, like an online game. The game *Second Life* requires each player to compose an avatar to play the game and this feature is a part of participating in the immersive nature of online game playing.

The word comes from Sanskrit, and, translated, it means the "bodily incarnation of a god" in the Hindu religion. The term has been popularized in contemporary film, particularly with James Cameron's 2009 film, *Avatar,* and in many computer games that create virtual worlds where humans can take any form—or gender, ethnicity, or even species.

Many scholars have explored the avatars people create with consideration for how they represent a person's real identity (especially in issues of gender, race, and ethnicity), but avatars also allow a person to explore different representations of one's self through a different image. Early avatar creation was usually confined to a few stock images that a person could mix and match to create a new entity, but more recent avatar creation has been the result of a picture that is then manipulated to mask the real image. As a result, contemporary avatars may actually resemble the person who is extending that image to the online world. Additionally, some software programs now allow voice recordings and vocal sounds to be linked to the avatar for a form of speech that may, or may not, resemble the speech of the creator.

The software necessary to create an avatar and participate in an online virtual world is available at a wide variety of costs to the consumer. Some games include the software necessary in the license for the game, but other systems like Maya, Poser, and Avimator are relatively easy-to-use commercial software systems that can also be used to create and animate avatars.

See also: Gaming; Identity

Further Reading

Au, Wagner James. 2008. *The Making of Second Life*. New York: HarperCollins.

Turkle, Sherry. 1995. *Life on the Screen: Identity in the Age of the Internet*. New York: Simon & Schuster.

B

Berners-Lee, Tim

Sir Timothy John Berners-Lee (1955–) is a British computer scientist credited for developing the World Wide Web in 1989 when he was a computer engineer at CERN, a particle physics laboratory located near Geneva, Switzerland. He is the director of the World Wide Web Consortium (W3C), which oversees the web's continued development and holds the Founder's Chair at MIT in the Computer Science and Artificial Intelligence Laboratory. His contribution to the development and ongoing maintenance of the web has garnered him many honors, including membership in the World Wide Web Hall of Fame (1994), officer of the order of the British Empire (OBE) in 1997, and in 1999 *Time* magazine named him one of the "100 Most Important People of the 20th Century." Queen Elizabeth conferred knighthood on him in 2004, for "services to the global development of the Internet."

Berners-Lee has continued to work for social and economic equity for all persons concerning access to the Internet. Knowing that a number of people in the world still do not have easy access to the Internet because of the cost of equipment necessary to facilitate Internet connections (computers, wired or wireless connections to nodes, etc.), Berners-Lee has remained committed to creating greater access to information. At MIT he began the World Wide Web Consortium dedicated to the ongoing development of the web. He has acknowledged that the digital divide appears to be widening as access to affordable connections impacts health, education, and science. As of 2013, only 31 percent of the developing world had access to the Internet, while 77 percent of the developed world had connections. In Mozambique, for example, he claimed that 1 GB of data would cost two months of wages for an average person (Gibbs 2013).

Among his many contributions to the development of the World Wide Web and Internet infrastructure, Berners-Lee has advocated for greater access to technologies for the use of the Internet, for the maintenance of net neutrality, and for the equality of access and information to all people of the world. In 2013 he led a coalition of major Internet providers like Google, Facebook, Intel, and Microsoft to form the Alliance for Affordable Internet (A4AI) with the purpose of increasing affordable access to the Internet for people all over the world who have limited income.

See also: Digital Divide; European Council for Nuclear Research (CERN); World Wide Web Consortium (W3C)

Further Reading

Gibbs, Samuel. 2013. "Sir Tim Berners-Lee and Google Lead Coalition for Cheaper Internet." *The Guardian.* Accessed September 19, 2014: http://www.theguardian.com/technology /2013/oct/07/google-berners-lee-alliance-broadband-africa?CMP=EMCNEWEML 661912&et_cid=51918&et_rid=7107573&Linkid=http%3a%2f%2fwww.theguardian .com%2ftechnology%2f2013%2foct%2f07%2fgoogle-berners-lee-alliance-broadband -africa.

Bezos, Jeff

Jeffrey Preston Bezos (1964–) is the developer of Amazon, an online retail company founded in 1994. Bezos was born in Albuquerque, New Mexico. His biological father left when he was only 18 months old, but his mother Jacklyn married Miguel Bezos when Jeff was four years old, and Bezos legally adopted him. Miguel Bezos worked for Exxon, and the family moved to Houston, Texas, where Jeff attended fourth through sixth grade. Then, the family moved to Miami, Florida, and Jeff became the valedictorian at Miami Palmetto Senior High School. As a child and young adult, Jeff was an avid reader and computer enthusiast who was enamored with space travel.

His first entrepreneurial opportunity came after high school when he and his friend, Ursula Werner, started a two-week learning camp for children, where campers were taught about space travel and advanced thinking skills.

While at Princeton, Jeff shifted his attention from space travel and the study of physics to computer science and electrical engineering. After graduation, Jeff began working on Wall Street, and he initially focused on analyzing the banking industry. In 1990, at age 26, he was hired by the D. E. Shaw firm, which was in the vanguard of computer use on Wall Street, and aspired to excel in computerized selling. The Internet was just in its infancy, but Shaw was interested in looking at how it might be used in the future to facilitate commerce. At Shaw, he met his future wife, MacKenzie, and the two were married in 1993.

In 1994, D. E. Shaw charged Bezos with looking at the emerging Internet as an opportunity for business. Bezos recognized the amazing growth potential of the

Internet and had researched how large the consumer reliance on computers could become. Among all of the products that he believed could be marketed online, he felt books were in an excellent position to be a top seller, since there were only two major chains, Barnes and Noble and Borders, but distribution could be facilitated by an already-existing infrastructure. In 1994 he offered the suggestion to David Shaw, but the company felt that books were not an area they wished to enter, and Bezos left Shaw to start his own e-commerce company.

Bezos settled on Seattle, Washington, as the headquarters for his new company, and after some time spent searching for the best name, he settled on Amazon, after the largest river in the world, and because it started with a capital A and would therefore be high in the alphabetical list. Initially, he invested his own money and the money of family and friends.

For the first several years, Amazon made no profit, but the company focused on the buying and selling experience online, and ultimately became the world's largest bookstore. Bezos diversified Amazon's offerings with the sale of CDs and videos in 1998, and later he created retail partnerships with other manufacturers that allowed Amazon to branch out into clothing, electronics, and toys. As an early entrant during the dot-com boom, Amazon easily survived the dot-com crash. Sales rose from $510,000 in 1995 to over $17 billion in 2011.

In 2007, Amazon.com branched out into electronic readers (e-readers) with the release of the Kindle, a digital book reader that allows users to buy, download, read, and store their book selections. That same year, he announced his investment in Blue Origin, a Seattle-based aerospace company for commercial space travel. Amazon entered the tablet market in 2011 with the Kindle Fire, and, the following September, Bezos released the Kindle Fire HD to compete directly with Apple's iPad.

In 2013, Bezos purchased the *Washington Post* for $250 million, considered a risky proposition because of the decline in print newspapers. In a letter to the employees, Bezos indicated the direction he hoped to go with the company when he wrote that the Internet was transforming the news business and that the future of the *Washington Post* was in experimenting and inventing new models of journalism and communication.

Despite Amazon's first few profitless years, Amazon is widely regarded by many as the first successful dot-com business. Bezos was named Person of the Year by *Time* magazine in 1999, and, by 2008, he was selected by *U.S. News & World Report* as one of America's best leaders. In 2011, *The Economist* gave Bezos an Innovation Award for the Amazon Kindle, which was revolutionizing e-readers. In 2012, *Fortune* magazine named him "Businessperson of The Year."

See also: Amazon; E-Commerce; E-Publishing; E-Reader

Further Reading

Brandt, Richard L. 2011. *One Click: Jeff Bezos and the Rise of Amazon.com*. New York: Penguin.

Launder, William, Christopher S. Steward, and Joann S. Lublin. "Bezos Buys Washington Post for $250 Million." *Wall Street Journal*. Accessed September 18, 2014: http://online .wsj.com/news/articles/SB10001424127887324653004578650390383666794.

Bitcoin

Bitcoin is a type of cybercurrency, also known as digital currency, or cryptocurrency, created in 2009. It can be exchanged for goods and services in a similar way to traditional currencies, such as the dollar and the pound. Unlike traditional currencies, however, Bitcoin only exists in sequences of computer code transferred from one computer to another using peer-to-peer (P2P) software. Peer-to-peer software enables computer code to be shared directly among user's computers, rather than being stored on a computer server. Bitcoin, with a capital "B" is the name of the service, but the term bitcoins (with a lowercase "b") is used to describe the actual monetary units.

Bitcoin is not bought or sold through banks, and acquiring bitcoins requires a digital "wallet"—a computer program that enables secure sales and purchases over the Internet. Bitcoins may be acquired by selling goods or services. They can also be purchased through a bitcoin exchange or a special automated teller machine (ATM). The supply of bitcoins is linked to publicly distributed computer files called blocks. Each block includes a mathematical problem that people can "mine" for bitcoins by using computers to find solutions. Doing so unlocks a new block and awards the miner a certain number of bitcoins. The system makes more bitcoins available to miners approximately every 10 minutes.

The total supply of bitcoins is designed to have a natural limit, much like the supply of traditional means of exchange such as gold. The number of bitcoins awarded by new blocks will decrease over time. The total number of bitcoins in circulation can never exceed 21 million. The system also makes the math problems progressively harder to solve, based on past activity. Bitcoin miners may work in groups called mining pools and distribute any acquired bitcoins among the group members. In some cases, people have built entire data centers filled with computers designed to only mine bitcoins.

The value of bitcoins has fluctuated wildly through several boom-and-bust cycles. Initially, a bitcoin was worth a few cents, at most. Spurred by increasing adoption, media coverage, and speculation, the price of a single bitcoin briefly spiked above $1,000 in late 2013. Some critics claim that bitcoin's popularity has risen mainly through the investment of speculators hoping for a quick profit as the currency increases in value. In early 2014, Mt. Gox, then the largest bitcoin exchange in the world, claimed that its massive supply of bitcoins was stolen and suddenly declared bankruptcy, further fueling criticism of the cryptocurrency as unstable. In addition, because bitcoins do not pass through banks, they may be used with the intention of concealing illegal activity.

Supporters of the currency note that exchanges made in bitcoin generally have lower transaction fees than those made with credit cards. They have also argued that an independent currency with a limited supply is preferable to a fiat currency, such as the dollar, that can be printed by a government at will. National governments have explored various approaches for regulating and taxing bitcoins while some countries treat bitcoins as financial assets or property rather than currency. Many countries have yet to adopt official positions on cryptocurrency but on March 24, 2014, the Internal Revenue Service of the U.S. government took the official position that bitcoins and other cryptocurrencies would be evaluated as property and therefore would be treated as taxable income.

See also: Amazon Coins; Cybercurrency; Dark Net

Further Reading

Silva, Sean. 2014. "Bitcoin, Litecoin, Dogecoin and Other Cryptocurrencies Now Taxable Income." *Bloomberg.* Accessed September 20, 2014: http://www.bna.com/bitcoin-litecoin -dogecoin-b17179890404/.

Stokes, Robert. 2012. "Virtual Money Laundering: The Case of Bitcoin," *Information & Communication Technology Law,* 21 (3), October: 221–236.

BlackBerry

One of the early mobile phones to be called a smartphone, the BlackBerry focused a lot of attention on the emerging mobile phone market. The Canadian company Research in Motion (RIM), founded by Mike Lazaridis and Doug Fregin in 1984, began by producing pagers, a popular messaging device that businesspeople soon found indispensable. When a pager rang, buzzed, or vibrated, the user would check the phone number and then go to a wired phone to contact the caller. Pagers were actually a technology that bridged the traditional wired phones (and public phones that were available) and mobile phones. Perhaps because of the timing of the release of the first BlackBerry, and the time in history in which it was released, many users have compared the addictive use of the BlackBerry to the addictive nature of crack cocaine. Many jokingly refer to the unit as their "CrackBerry."

Before developing the BlackBerry, RIM had already made a name for itself by improving early pager technology. The first RIM device was the Inter@ctive Pager 800, released in 1996. IBM contracted with RIM for an improved model, and promised to buy $10 million worth of the next model, the Inter@active Pager 900, which was released in 1998. In the same year, another model, the Inter@ctive Pager 950, was released. Then, when the BlackBerry 850 was released in 1999, businesspeople started to realize how valuable a multifunctional device could be.

Though initially marketed as a personal desk assistant (PDA), the BlackBerry had a number of useful functions that had not yet been seen in other PDAs. Each device had calendar functions, an address book, a screen that could hold eight lines of text, and a track wheel for maneuvering from one function to another. The QWERTY-based keyboard introduced thumb typing and short messages could be transmitted from one BlackBerry user to another. Almost immediately, the Black-Berry became popular and RIM changed its name to BlackBerry Limited to demonstrate the shift in their marketing plan.

BlackBerry has remained a popular mobile phone device, particularly for people in business and in government, and has been very successful on the global market. Despite the popularity of Android and iOS operating systems, the Black-Berry has retained a number of loyal customers. President Obama joked about his constant use of his BlackBerry while campaigning in 2008.

All units in the BlackBerry line use proprietary software that services only BlackBerries. But with the flood of new smartphones on the market, the popularity of BlackBerry started to decline in 2011, and for the first time in 2013 another smartphone company (Nokia) sold more units globally. Still, primarily citing the user-friendliness of the keyboard, BlackBerry has remained the smartphone of choice for many people. Whether the appeal is because of user familiarity with the device, or product loyalty, BlackBerry has maintained a number of loyal users but now serves about half of the market it held in the early 2000s.

Though, initially, a number of different companies began negotiations with the company for a buy-out, the BlackBerry management turned down all offers and decided to refocus efforts on developing new BlackBerry units. The company has released a number of improved units over the years, but it has found it difficult to compete with major manufacturers of smartphones that continue to offer new services. In 2013, BlackBerry Ltd. announced that the company was downscaling its workforce and that it would seriously consider offers to be purchased by other companies.

Today's BlackBerry does what every smartphone does, but some of the services that were unique to the BlackBerry have changed. In April 2013, Black-Berry announced that it would no longer support its own streaming music service, BBM Music. Rather than go after the general consumer market, BlackBerry would specialize in some select areas. Though the appeal of the BlackBerry has waned, it has remained a popular device for specialized agencies, like the police, government, and health care providers who prefer to have the security features rather than the number of consumer features included on other smartphones.

In 2014, BlackBerry released its new BlackBerry Passport model with Black-Berry Assistant, a feature that had a more dynamic structure for helping business users remain organized and productive. In the future, BlackBerry may continue to specialize in markets that have special requirements, such as health care. In 2014, BlackBerry and NantHealth, a data provider of health care information, announced that they would be developing a program to help doctors monitor the health of cancer patients through the Passport smartphone.

See also: Addiction; Mobile Telephone; Smartphone

Further Reading

Arthur, Charles. 2012. *Digital Wars: Apple, Google, Microsoft & the Battle for the Internet*. London and Philadelphia: Kogan Page.
Woyke, Elizabeth. 2014. *The Smartphone: Anatomy of an Industry*. New York and London: The New Press: 19–23.

Blogs

Blogs are the equivalent to personal diaries published on the Internet. Part self-expression, opinion, or even rant, blogs can serve a number of purposes. Blogs grew from the characteristic of affording greater interactivity in online communication enabled by Web 2.0. Generally, credit for the first personal blog has been given to Justin Hall and his *Links from the Underground*, started in 1994 when Justin was a college student at Swarthmore. For 11 years he chronicled his life online, and though he stopped blogging at age 31, he is looked upon as one of the pioneer bloggers. His topics ranged from general to deeply personal, including romantic relationships and his father's suicide, and he attracted thousands of readers every day.

Two popular blogging services, Blogger and LiveJournal, were both launched in 1999, and soon after that, *wikis* became available to help people contribute to the web through sites that compiled opinions and information from multiple users. Wikis are websites that enable multiple people to quickly and easily edit their content. The success of *Wikipedia*, a wiki-based encyclopedia started in 2001 that quickly became one of the Internet's most popular sites, is an example of the type of program that was also instrumental in making blogging so easy for users.

Blogs have often served as a way to connect people for mutual purposes, like dealing with grief or trauma. Some blogs are short-lived, while others, like Hall's *Links from the Underground*, go on for years. A number of personal blogs were started in response to the terrorist attack on the World Trade Towers on September 11, 2001, as individuals felt compelled to speak about their reactions to the event and the medium of the Internet gave voice to those who felt the need to make public statements and responses to the event. From this point on, the content of blogs became broader, encompassing not only personal journaling activities, but also the creation of commentary on social and political events.

Though Justin Hall may have been one of the first to attract a large audience of readers, a number of bloggers have turned their blogging into full-time careers. Andrew Sullivan, a former editor of *The New Republic* magazine, started an influential blog in 2000 called *The Dish*, and contributed to creating a niche for political blogging. He eventually moved to different publishing platforms including *Time* magazine, *The Atlantic*, and *The Daily Beast*, and, in 2013, he started his own independent, subscription-based blog called *Dish*. As an openly gay writer with conservative views, Sullivan has attained cult status as one of the leaders in using blogs as a means of self-expression and self-publication that can be profitable, through either sponsored advertising or subscriptions. Similarly, Michelle Malkin started her career as a conservative political blogger and now writes regularly for conservative magazines as well as appears on Fox News. The world also learned of events in the Middle East through the blogs of Salam Pax (a pseudonym for Salam Abdulmunem), whose blog *Where Is Raed?* received a great deal of attention during the 2003 invasion of Iraq. Salam Pax started the blog as a way to communicate with his friend, Raed Jarrar, an activist who was studying in Jordan and who was a critic of the Iraqi government. For a while, *Where Is Raed?* became one of the most widely read blogs in the world.

Political blogs are only one form of blogging that attracts attention from other readers. Celebrity bloggers, like Perez Hilton, have turned celebrity information into highly profitable content through web blogs and Twitter feeds. Hilton has been so successful in cultivating a large number of readers that he earns thousands of dollars through advertising on his blogs, and he has become a celebrity, of sorts, himself. Likewise, many celebrities have blogs (whether they write them themselves or not) and use Twitter as a way of staying in touch with their fans—making web blogs and Twitter among some of the lowest-cost publicity media in history.

But perhaps the range of blogs from regular people shows the capacity of the Internet and social media for making connections better than focusing on celebrities or political bloggers. Reasons for why "regular people" choose to blog are many. Many people claim that the ability to share information online through blogs helps them create some type of connection to others, and whether their blogs are read by many or just a few, they are exercising self-expression that fulfills a human need to express oneself. Sometimes bloggers organize with others to share experiences and viewpoints, and for those people the act of blogging becomes similar to sharing in a community with others. While there are a number of blog communities that bill themselves as just that—a place to share ideas and resources—blog communities can often be very small and specific, such as the community that connects bloggers interested in a particular lifestyle, or they can be much larger to address ongoing problems and challenges related to parenthood, or issues concerning child care and healthy lifestyles.

For some time, blogs and their media derivatives have demonstrated how social media can be used to make private thoughts public. While there is nothing inherently wrong about this, evidence shows that sometimes blogs blur the distinctions between private and public thoughts and demean our privacy. Sometimes ethical contradictions arise, such as when people express dark emotions that then become synonymous with presumed behaviors, such as identifying a death wish, or acting out in an inappropriate, or threatening way, as did the perpetrators of the 1999 Columbine High School shooting. In these cases, blogs can be a cry for help as well as a warning of what might occur. In these cases, the responsibility for monitoring blogs becomes one that spans both ethical and moral dimensions.

For purposes of this encyclopedia, though, the cultural phenomenon of blogging reflects the way social media allow us to connect to others and follow ideas and concepts. These forms of social media have not been confined to print/text alone, or a combination of words and pictures. They have also gone the way of full motion media that incorporates a range of technologies that are attainable to many. Today, there seem to be blogs on every possible topic imaginable, and "how to" websites are available online to help people start and improve their blogs. Established companies have blogs, professional writers have blogs, and blogs are even used in schools to engage students in writing their own journals and communicating their thoughts with classmates and teachers.

For a while, blogs became so popular that a number of blog search engines began sifting through them to identify what they were and where they were located. *Technorati*, one of the leading blog search programs dominated the blogosphere and published lists of the most popular blogs for many years. Then, in May 2014, the website shut down its list of "Top 100" blogs to refocus its efforts elsewhere, on advertising. While the company didn't specifically say that they were changing their interests and moving away from blogs, many speculate that the growth in social media shifted attention from blogs to posting personal information on different types of sites like microblogs. Another reason some may have lost interest in blogs is that privacy concerns and authenticity have become more important for social media users in recent years. Changes in technology have influenced the type of content available and have pushed the boundaries of blogging into a number of different dimensions.

Vlogs are video blogs that also use low-cost cameras on mobile phones, computers, or camcorders to include pictures along with blog-like content. From 2006 to 2008, YouTube ran a vlog that appeared to be the video journal of a 15-year-old girl who talked about her feelings and her insecurities. *Lonelygirl15* gained worldwide attention but later was found to be the work of a professional company that had cast the webseries (webisode) with a 19-year-old Australian actress named Jessica Rose. The public's reaction to having been fooled was massive, and many viewers felt betrayed by a company that would use such a personal medium for its own purpose.

While it has always been difficult to assess how many blogs and vlogs exist, in large part because some have constant postings and others may exist one-time only, the number of blogs on the Internet seems to have peaked around 2006. After that time, the way people use social networks and blogs began to change, raising questions about whether blogs and vlogs had just been a passing fancy, or just activities that burned out over time. Perhaps, though, one reason that blogs and vlogs seemed to have crashed is that new forms of personal expression have found their way into different formats. Microblogs like Tumblr, Twitter, and other short-form messaging services seem to have picked up the activity lost to more long-form blogs and vlogs, but it remains to be seen whether these personal expressions maintain the interest of the public over time.

See also: E-Publishing; Webisode; YouTube

Further Reading

Gillette, Felix. 2014. "Department of Blogging Extinction; Technorati Rankings Are Dead." *Businessweek.* Accessed November 3, 2014: http://www.businessweek.com/articles/2014 -06-24/department-of-blogging-extinction-technorati-rankings-are-dead.

Wolfe, Kristin Roeschenthaler. 2014. *Blogging: How Our Private Thoughts Went Public.* Lanham, MD: Lexington Books.

Bots

A *bot* is a piece of code on a digital device that performs repetitive tasks, like counting, or inserting information into other content that is then shown on your digital device screen. The term comes from "web robot" and indicates that tasks can be accomplished faster and at a higher rate than a human could perform. Among the most common bots are web crawlers, chat room bots, spambots, and malicious bots. There are good bots and bad bots, and some bots can create content that is funny or annoying, but because bad bots can do so much harm, they often receive most of the attention. According to one study, in 2013, more than half of Internet traffic was in the form of bots (61.5%), and approximately half of those are malicious bots (Jeffers 2013). Today, even short-form messaging, like Twitter, may experience bots.

Because they are unwanted, most people think of bots as only bad pieces of technology. This is not surprising since we often hear about bots when hackers and cybercriminals send spam, or infect computers with viruses, worms, and other malware that can steal private data or launch denial of service (DoS) attacks. The most common way these bots operate is to impersonate someone else and encourage the user to click on information that releases the bot through the user's operating system. These bots are certainly illegal, but there are also a range of bots that are legal, and they have a serious effect on our daily use of social media because they signal a new way of counting users and monitoring digital media users' behavior.

The majority of bots online are for commercial purposes and as such might be considered good or bad, depending on your point of view. If you were in the business of data mining for advertising purposes, you might think of bots as useful tools, but if you value your privacy and become enraged at the thought of your behavior patterns being sold for a profit to other companies without your knowledge, you probably would think of bots as evil tools. There is no doubt, the frequency with which bots are used has much to do with adjusting the cost of advertising and using the Internet for collecting data. Advertising models, online or in legacy media forms, measure their impact and adjust their cost of operation and profit through collecting data on viewers or users, but, in the case of online advertising, bots can sometimes provide information that allows a company to inflate the number of messages transmitted by advertisers—therefore creating false reports on actual consumer behavior.

As two of the most prominent organizations accessible through social networks, Google and Facebook set some of the highest rates for online advertisers, but, even though they may try to monitor the traffic for consistency, fraudulent numbers sometimes are generated for assessing the cost of ads. Their use of bots to monitor behavior has raised many questions from consumers and the Federal Trade Commission (FTC) alike. In 2010, the FTC developed a "Cybersecurity Roadmap," to identify dangerous vulnerabilities in the Internet infrastructure, as well as threats to consumers, businesses, and governments. While the FTC has been concerned about bots from the perspective of protecting consumers from fraudulent activity, actually finding bots and prosecuting those who use bots is another matter. Some of the major Internet Service Providers and content providers use a form of bots as a way to monitor their traffic, and the FTC takes the position that these are not illegal uses of bots.

Nevertheless, some organizations have had to defend their business practice of using bots to monitor traffic. Some online app stores like the Apple App Store and Google Play have been accused of using bots to inflate their ratings or reviews and to mislead the public on their positioning of products in the market. eBay has attempted to sue a third-party company from trolling their site to search for bargains and has a stated position on what they refer to as "bid-bots" that inflate the price of an item automatically during the auction process. But perhaps one of the most egregious types of bots is the spambot, which has created chaos for companies and consumers alike, with computer in-boxes filling up with unwanted repetitive information. The hacktivist group Anonymous has often engaged in this type of activity, claiming that they do so as an act of civil disobedience.

In recent years, Twitter bots have received greater attention. Twitter bots are computer programs that seemingly send tweets of their own accord, but in reality they are very similar to spambots—though they flood a person's Twitter accounts with fake information. As the list of bots grows, we see that some bot creators are becoming even more creative. Some bots consume, remix, or change content on the Internet or on Twitter. In an article in the *New Yorker*, journalist Rob Dubbin described a number of the newest bots that have created mischief. He includes Adam Parrish's *everyword* bot that "has been chipping its way through the entire English language, tweeting one word at a time every thirty minutes since 2008" (Dubbin 2013). Additionally, *Professor Jocular* is a bot that retweets a popular message and tries to explain why it's funny. The end result, according to Dubbin, is a world of creativity, but, at the same time, he claims: "Twitter bots persevere, infusing one of our era's great time-wasters with absurdity, serendipity, and chilling reminders of omnipresent surveillance" (Dubbin 2013).

See also: Malware; Privacy; Spam; Spyware

Further Reading

Dubbin, Rob. 2013. "The Rise of Twitter Bots." *The New Yorker*. Accessed April 18, 2014: http://www.newyorker.com/tech/elements/the-rise-of-twitter-bots.

Holiday, Ryan. 2014. "Fake Traffic Means Real Paydays." *Observer.com*. Accessed October 3, 2014: https://observer.com/2014/01/fake-traffic-means-real-paydays/.

Jeffers, Dave. 2013. "Bots, Both Good and Evil, Dominate the Internet." *PC World*. Accessed October 3, 2014: http://www.pcworld.com/article/2080300/bots-both-good-and-evil-dominate-the-internet.html.

Brin, Sergei

Sergei Mikhailovich Brin (1973–) is a Russian-born American computer scientist, who cofounded the pioneering Internet company Google Inc. Brin helped develop

Google's Internet search engine, along with the company's other cofounder, Larry Page. The methods Brin and Page developed to allow the Google search engine to identify relevant websites and information based on keywords entered by a user have been among the most successful in the world. Profits from Google's search engine and other services helped make Brin one of the wealthiest people on the planet.

Brin was born in Moscow but his family immigrated to the United States when he was six years old. Brin met Page in Stanford University's PhD program in computer science and the two collaborated in 1996 to create a search engine called BackRub that counted links to each web page it found. They reasoned that pages with many incoming links were probably the most important and most relevant and based their program on the popularity factor of how many "hits" each page received. Therefore, the list of web pages are ranked according to popularity. BackRub gathered so much data from the Internet, Stanford's computer system became overwhelmed.

Brin's academic focus was on data mining, and along with one of his professors he started a group called Mining Data at Stanford (MIDAS). From that experience, he became interested in ways to analyze patterns that could be harvested by the amount of data transmitted over the World Wide Web.

Brin and Page launched Google, based on BackRub, in 1998, and it quickly became the world's most popular search engine. The database they developed had close to 518 million hyperlinks. The idea that led to the creation of Google began when the two authored a paper called "The Anatomy of a Large-Scale Hypertextual Web Search Engine" and presented the paper at a conference in Australia. It is unknown how many people heard the paper and realized what Brin and Page had developed.

Brin and Page began trying to license the software they had developed to other companies, but not even the major Internet companies at the time like Yahoo!, Excite, and AltaVista were interested in their search strategy. So, they decided to start their own company, which they called Google. They rented a garage and two spare rooms in the Menlo Park house of a friend, Susan Wojcicki, who eventually joined them in Google. On the wall of the garage, where they set up their new business, they put up a sign that said "Google Worldwide Headquarters" (Isaacson 2014, 464).

From 2001 to 2011, Brin served as copresident at Google and led technology-development strategy. Beginning in 2011, Brin directed Google's special projects that focused on Google X, the division of Google that focuses on risky projects like smart contact lenses, Google Glass, and wind turbines. While he remains active at Google, he has also become a philanthropist and has dedicated a considerable amount of money to fight Parkinson's disease. He has also invested heavily in Tesla

Motors, the development of electric automobiles, and the manufacturing of "smart" vehicles.

See also: Google; Page, Larry

Further Reading

Arthur, Charles. 2012. *Digital Wars: Apple, Google, Microsoft & the Battle for the Internet.* London: Kogan Page, Ltd., 11–14.
Isaacson, Walter. 2014. *The Innovators.* New York: Simon & Schuster, 314–343.

Broadband

The term *broadband* defines the data transmission of multiple signals and types of messages, such as voice, data, or video. The term recognizes a range of distribution forms that are all faster than traditional "dial up" service that was possible over wired telephone lines. As the speed of transmission of data over broadband increases, some engineers have advocated for classifying broadband in faster terms, but in general, broadband technologies transfer information at one million bits per second (1–2 MB) or faster. Broadband has become an umbrella term to cover a number of modes of information transfer including digital subscriber lines (DSL), cable modems (coaxial cables controlled by cable companies), fiber (meaning fiber optic lines), powerlines, wireless, and satellite forms of information transmittal.

To better understand how and why broadband has become such an important component of the telecommunications infrastructure, it may be helpful to contextualize the need for faster services. In the days prior to the Internet, most homes in the United States had a wired telephone, and that wire was provided by the telephone company. If a person also had cable television, the cable company would lay the coaxial cable that would deliver the video and audio streams that took up much more space along the "wires" than the telephone wire could handle. When home computers came along, many people were stuck with "dial up services" that required a modem to switch the electrical impulses over the telephone wire to connect to an Internet Service Provider, but the wires could not contain any more than basic text transmission. Even after cable companies began to use the coaxial cables used for television distribution for Internet home delivery, and a variety of companies began to use fiber optics as an even better and faster delivery mode, the amount of "space" available to transfer content was limited. By the time broadband (all of the delivery systems that fit under this category) came about, home technologies became faster, better, and more capable of delivering full motion video and audio services on the Internet over the broadband connections.

For people who have choices of which broadband method to use, price and availability in the area in which you live often dictates what is practical. In many communities, one telecommunications company, like Comcast or Verizon, might have a monopoly over the distribution of broadband in that region, but while this availability was once taken for granted, today, more competition has been added in some markets. According to data from the U.S. Department of Commerce, today, 88 percent of Americans have their choice of at least two wired Internet providers in their area, and 98 percent have their choice of more than two wireless Internet providers in their region (Competition among U.S. Broadband Providers 2014). Often telecommunications companies *bundle* services over broadband connections, allowing customers to pay a combined lower rate for Internet access, television, phone services, and other add-ons, like home security services or music streaming programs.

As of March 2014, 87 percent of the population of the United States had access to broadband services (United States of America Internet Usage and Broadband Usage Report 2014). Companies with traditions in telephony controlled 46 percent of those connections, and companies that had traditionally worked in cable had 54 percent of the connections. In a 2010 Pew Internet and American Life Survey, 15 percent of the U.S. population who were least likely to have broadband access in the home included senior citizens, adults with less than a high school education, and those living in households earning less than $30,000 a year (Smith 2010).

See also: Internet; Legacy Media

Further Reading

"Competition among U.S. Broadband Providers." 2014. U.S. Department of Commerce, Economic and Statistics Administration. Accessed April 8, 2015: https://www.ncta.com /sites/prod/files/BroadbandCompetition-800.png.

Smith, Aaron. 2010. "Trends in Broadband Adoption." Pew Internet Research Project. Accessed December 5, 2014: http://www.pewinternet.org/2010/08/11/trends-in-broadband -adoption/.

"United States of America Internet Usage and Broadband Usage Report." 2014. Internet World Statistics. Accessed December 5, 2014: http://www.internetworldstats.com/am /us.htm.

Browser

A web browser is a software application for exchanging information stored on the World Wide Web over the Internet. A browser can also access information on private networks. An address called a Uniform Resource Identifier/Locator (URI/URL) connects the user's technology (most often a computer or mobile phone) to the web page. Some web browsers have been offered to the public for free, and others have charged for the use of the browser. Today, there are many different browsers available around the world, and web and mobile browsers have become major gateways for effective use of social media.

Perhaps the technology that started the browser wars was the development of the World Wide Web, developed by Tim Berners-Lee at CERN, but different research agencies around the world were also working on computer systems and software that grew into a number of commercial web browsers that could communicate with the web.

In the United States, the Mosaic web browser was developed at the National Center for Supercomputing Applications (NCSA) at the University of Illinois Urbana-Champaign. The NCSA released it as a browser in 1993, but even though Mosaic eventually provided the ideas to develop Netscape Navigator, which dominated the browser market for a long time, NCSA stopped supporting the Mosaic browser in 1997. One of the authors of Mosaic was Marc Andreessen, who developed the browser with Eric Bina. Andreessen was recruited by Jim Clark, who led a team of venture capitalists to participate in a company originally named the Mosaic Communications Corporation, but proprietary concerns were raised by the University of Illinois, and the company changed their name to the Netscape Communications Corporation.

Based on Mosaic protocols, the Netscape series of browsers were developed and sold commercially. For a while in the mid-1990s Andreessen became the public face that symbolized the youthful exuberance and attitude that captured the imagination of the American public coming to terms with the emerging Internet ("Innovators under 35" 1999). As a journalist for CNN Money, a division of *Fortune* magazine wrote: "Netscape mesmerized investors and captured America's imagination. More than any other company, it set the technological, social, and financial tone of the Internet age. Its founders, Marc Andreessen and Jim Clark— a baby-faced 24-year-old programmer from the Midwest and a restless middle-aged tech pioneer who badly wanted to strike gold again—inspired a generation of entrepreneurs to try to become tech millionaires" (Lashinsky 2005).

The frenzy of tech start-ups and development companies had started. In 1998, America Online bought Netscape for $4.2 billion and Andreessen became the chief technology officer (CTO) of the organization (Junnakar and Clark 1998). A number of new versions of Netscape were released, and, at its peak in the 1990s, Netscape Navigator became one of the major browsers, used to transmit 90 percent of all Internet traffic.

One of Netscape's major competitors was Internet Explorer, a free service that came bundled with Microsoft's Windows program and was introduced to the public in 1995. It, too, was released over the years in a variety of versions and peaked in 2003 when it surpassed Netscape with 93 percent of the users. The competition between Netscape and Internet Explorer, as well as the competition from other browsers that were becoming known in the United States and around the world, set off what was called the "Browser Wars" of the late 1990s.

Netscape finally ceased operations in 2008, and Microsoft stopped supporting the Internet Explorer browser in 2015. While each had made a significant contribution to the development of consumer and business Internet connectivity, each system just had too many flaws to continue. The "bugs" were patched in different versions of the systems, but newer, better browsers had the benefit of greater security and enhanced technology.

Today there are also mobile browsers that access the Internet and web on smartphones, tablets, and other portable digital devices. Among the most popular in the United States are Opera, Safari (produced by Apple), Firefox (a part of Mozilla), and Chrome (produced by Google). By 2014, Chrome was handling 45 percent of the U.S. browser traffic. Internet Explorer, which had the majority of the U.S. web traffic in 2012, began to rapidly lose its customer base, prompting Microsoft to announce that it would cease supporting Internet Explorer in 2015.

The mobile market is also served by *microbrowsers* that are similar to the same types of computer browsers, and like web browsers, they come bundled with the smartphone or device that you purchase.

See also: Apple; Google; Internet; Netscape; World Wide Web

Further Reading

"Innovators under 35." 1999. MIT Technology Review. Accessed May 21, 2015: http://www2.technologyreview.com/tr35/profile.aspx?TRID=518.

Junnarkar, Sandeep, and Tim Clark. 1998. "AOL Buys Netscape for $4.2 Billion." CNET News. Accessed April 1, 2015: http://news.cnet.com/21http://news.cnet.com/2100-1023-218360.html00-1023-218360.html.

Lashinsky, Adam. 2005. "Remembering Netscape: The Birth of the Web." CNN Money. Accessed December 1, 2014: http://web.archive.org/web/20060427112146/http://money.cnn.com/magazines/fortune/fortune_archive/2005/07/25/8266639/index.htm.

BuzzFeed

BuzzFeed Inc. is an Internet news media company founded in 2006 in New York City by Jonah Peretti and Kenneth Lerer, both of whom also founded the *Huffington Post*. The site was originally intended to track viral content on the Internet. A typical description of BuzzFeed in the early days was that it was an aggregator of memes and popular culture.

Over the years, however, the company has grown from an entertaining online site into a major news company that has a video production studio in Los Angeles that produces original content, BuzzFeed Motion Pictures to produce feature-length films, and a YouTube channel that has over 3.3 million subscribers. More importantly, BuzzFeed has moved from being a slap-dash start-up to a full-fledged news source, with stories that are professionally vetted and copyedited before appearing online. It exemplifies how an early start-up company can change over time and how a social media organization can grow and change.

When it began it was known as BuzzFeed Labs. It quickly gained a number of loyal followers who enjoyed the quirky content and who looked to BuzzFeed to see what was going on on the web. In those days, about 75 percent of BuzzFeed's content came from Facebook and Twitter, but, by 2014, about 75 percent of the content came from a much wider variety of social media sources. Content attracted users because it was funny and immediate, but not always true. But in the early days of Internet start-ups, it found a way to survive in an environment that continually pushed the envelope of authenticity. It was quick to attract advertisers and has been successful in supporting the organization's growth, but, at the same time, it still requires venture capital to keep the organization financially stable. Now, however, with increased circulation, BuzzFeed has been hiring new personnel to help it find its legitimacy.

There are a number of conflicting reports about the economic value of BuzzFeed, but its success in tracking viral content, advertising, and the development of analytics to measure content and audience size has made the organization one of the preeminent digital distributors. In August 2014, the venture capital firm Andreessen Horowitz invested $50 million, thereby helping the company's valuation at $850 million. Chris Dixon, a partner at Andreessen Horowitz explained why the value of the company grew so steadily: "Many of today's great media companies were built on top of emerging technologies . . . We're presently in the midst of a major technological shift in which, increasingly, news and entertainment are being distributed on social networks and consumed on mobile devices. We believe BuzzFeed will emerge from this period as a preeminent media company" (Griswold 2014).

As BuzzFeed grows, it has begun to resemble more traditional news distribution companies, in addition to the original content it creates and the flow of viral videos it shares. Shani Hilton, the 28-year-old deputy editor of BuzzFeed came to the organization from NBC's Washington, D.C., affiliate. She said, "I charged myself with bringing more old-school DNA to this place" (Shontell 2012). Along with the new philosophy she and other new employees bring to the organization,

BuzzFeed journalists have been charged to fact check and consult with the people who post the online content that goes viral. This changing culture takes time, but results in a stronger product.

BuzzFeed is an example of a small start-up that grew up and gained legitimacy. In the intervening years, it blurred the new characteristics of online news companies to get content fast and find out about its accuracy later with more traditional journalistic values. BuzzFeed's early content was often criticized for hoaxes and inaccurate information, but, over time, it has become a more well-respected organization.

See also: E-Publishing; Social Media

Further Reading

Fisher, Marc. 2014. "Who Cares If It's True?" *Columbia Journalism Review* LII: 26–32.

Griswold, Alison. 2014. "What Makes BuzzFeed Worth $850 Million?" Slate, August 11, 2014. Accessed April 11, 2015: http://www.slate.com/blogs/moneybox/2014/08/11/buzzfeed_raises_50_million_jonah_peretti_is_building_a_viral_media_empire.html.

Shontell, Alyson. 2012. "Inside BuzzFeed: The Story of How Jonah Peretti Built the Web's Most Beloved New Media Brand." Business Insider. Accessed April 8, 2015: http://www.businessinsider.com/buzzfeed-jonah-peretti-interview-2012-12?page=2.

C

Cell Phone (see Mobile Phone)

Cell Phone Camera (see Mobile Phone Camera)

Censorship

Censorship, the suppression of ideas and information, has a long history. Long before the arrival of forms of media to express ideas, oral cultures experienced censorship through social pressure exerted by social groups, political entities, or religious dogma. In oral cultures, anyone daring to explore topics that were considered taboo by the group risked a number of forms of punishment or expulsion. But undoubtedly, the development of media technology made the subjects of censorship more concrete. In the United States, the founding fathers attempted to guarantee free speech and freedom of the press in the First Amendment to the Constitution. Since then, the proliferation of media forms, distribution channels, and popular content has continually reminded us that media today is very different from the print form that dominated the early days of the founding of the United States. Even more importantly, the power of the Internet to distribute information across national borders and the flow of information on the World Wide Web have presented new challenges concerned with censorship.

In some ways, censorship seemed to be a little clearer when the primary media were designed for mass distribution. The Communications Act of 1934 that established the Federal Communications Commission (FCC) specifically barred the FCC from censoring broadcast material or creating regulations that would interfere with the First Amendment's freedoms of speech and of the press. Obscene material was restricted, but what constitutes obscenity has also provided volumes of interpretations over the years. Though hate speech and child pornography fall into the categories of the most offensive content, and the FCC has exercised its right to penalize this type of questionable content, most of the FCC's interpretations over the years have reflected the recognition that social values are determined by communities that have the right to identify what is offensive to others (The FCC and Freedom of Speech 2015).

In general, media content in the United States has been most hotly debated when it comes to the question of whether content is suitable for children. Adults are assumed to have the sense to turn off content that they feel is objectionable, but children have always been considered more impressionable, and, therefore, many of the questions of censorship for children have to do with content that parents may deem appropriate. In an effort to stave off potential government involvement in the censorship of film content, the Motion Picture Association of America (MPAA) developed the MPAA ratings systems in 1968. The Recording Industry Association of America (RIAA) established its Parental Guide for the rating of music lyrics in 1985. The television ratings to guide parents to make decisions about what their children could or should watch went into effect in 1997. But when the Internet came along and young people were using computers to access information often without their parents' knowledge, the issues behind Internet censorship began to heat up.

Because the Internet is the spine of social media, the architecture of the Internet seems to provide an unprecedented way to allow individuals and groups to communicate without intermediaries monitoring or censoring content. Most of the effort to keep the Internet "free" advocates for maintaining the distribution medium as the one truly global forum for the exchange of ideas. But these grand statements, as important as they are, often interfere with some of the daily activities of the gatekeepers of the flow of information, the Internet Service Providers (ISPs).

ISPs have taken on the bulk of censorship on the Internet, especially in terms of social networks and the way social media distribute content that could be deemed "inappropriate" on a number of levels. In general, the ISPs do this to avoid discussions of government involvement in the daily flow of information on the Internet, in the same ways the film, music, and television industries adopted ratings systems to avoid government intervention. Almost every commercial website has a statement of the "Terms of Service" a user can expect, and often there are specific guidelines in the terms that discuss what appropriate content is, and what may be done if the user is found to violate these terms. But there are also professional services that many ISPs use to eliminate the most egregious content. Major social media companies like Facebook and Google, as well as content apps and corporate clients, want sites monitored to avoid offensive material. This type of censorship is called "content moderation."

The labor force of people who remove objectionable material from sites makes up about half of the workforce of social media sites. Hemanshu Nigam, a former chief security officer at MySpace who later became a safety consultant for online companies, estimates that the number of content moderators who monitor and clean-up the world's social media sites, mobile sites, and cloud services runs to "well over 100,000" people (Chen 2014, 112). The need for the scrubbing of some content has been referred to as the "Grandma Problem," because grandparents are increasingly using social networks and coming across content that is often posted by a "panoply of jerks, racists, creeps, criminals, and bullies" (Chen 2014, 112).

Almost every social network has the practice of having content moderators troll the sites for inappropriate information (pictures or text). Most of the time this type of content falls into the category of sexual solicitation, bestiality, pornography, gore, minors, racism, beheadings, and hate speech. These moderators are often people who last in their jobs for a short time, ranging from three to five months, but then become so traumatized themselves for having to see so many images that are disgusting, they develop post-traumatic stress disorder (PTSD) and have to leave the job. Content moderators are also often low-paid workers. While content moderators in the United States are paid better than in many places, a significant amount of the content for moderation is outsourced to foreign countries, and, in particular, to the Philippines. It is estimated that about half of the jobs in social media are those of the content moderators who take down offensive material on social network sites so that the companies sponsoring the networks are not brought before the law.

Though the actions of content moderators may not always be visible to social media users, there are a number of examples of censorship that go beyond the borders of nations. This type of censorship reflects the values of a nation, and, often, the political control of the nation, especially in places that have no guarantee of free speech or freedom of the press. In China, for example, the government blocks access to websites that it considers dangerous or inappropriate. The United Nations has recently focused on the problem of government censorship of the Internet within national borders, and the impact of censorship as it relates to matters of personal privacy. Additionally, the "big picture" of Internet censorship has bridged the traditional security issues of secret information that a government deems necessary for national security. Organizations like Anonymous and WikiLeaks, who use the Internet for sometimes embarrassing or possibly seditious or treasonable acts have brought larger national concerns about censorship before the public.

See also: Anonymous; Assange, Julian; Digital Millennium Copyright Act (DMCA); Net Neutrality; Pornography; Snowden, Edward

Further Reading

Abramson, Jill. 2015. "The Public Interest: Defying the White House, from the Pentagon Papers to Snowden." *Columbia Journalism Review,* 53: 14–16.

Bennett, Philip, and Moises Naim. 2015. "21st Century Censorship." *Columbia Journalism Review,* 53: 22–28.

Chen, Adrian. 2014. "Unseen." *Wired,* 22: 109–117.

"The FCC and Freedom of Speech." 2015. FCC Website. Accessed May 21, 2015: http://www.fcc.gov/guides/fcc-and-freedom-speech.

First Amendment

The First Amendment to the U.S. Constitution reads:

> Congress shall make no law respecting an establishment of religion, or prohibiting the free exercise thereof; or abridging the freedom of speech, or of the press; or the right of the people peaceably to assemble, and to petition the Government for a redress of grievances.

Source: First Amendment to the United States Constitution. U.S. Government Printing Office. http://www.gpo.gov/fdsys/pkg/GPO-CONAN-1992/pdf/GPO-CONAN-1992-10-2.pdf.

Cerf, Vint

Known as the "father of the Internet," Vint (Vinton) Cerf (1943–) is an Internet pioneer who, along with Robert Kahn, developed the Internet by defining and perfecting *packet switching.* His work focused on developing the protocol that influenced the fundamental architecture of the Internet. Cerf received a BA in mathematics from Stanford University in 1965 and then went to work for IBM before continuing his education at the University of California at Los Angeles (UCLA) where he received a master's degree in computer science in 1970. He then returned to Stanford and received a PhD in computer science in 1972.

Cerf met Kahn at UCLA while he (Cerf) was working on a communication protocol for the first network based on packet switching, called ARPANET (Advanced Research Projects Agency Network). At the time, Kahn was a senior scientist at the engineering firm Bolt Beranek and Newman (now, BBN Technologies) a defense research group in Cambridge, Massachusetts. When Kahn moved to the Defense Advanced Research Projects Agency (DARPA) in 1972, his primary task was to focus on packet switching for military radio and satellite communications. This led him to start to think about how packet switching might facilitate online communication.

He approached Cerf and asked him to help design the new network. Together, they proved to be a formidable team. They would have intense brainstorming sessions in which they would sketch different diagrams to figure out how the different computers could be linked together. In 1973, Cerf came up with a simple sketch in a San Francisco hotel that linked a number of host computers through a set of "gateway" computers that would be able to shift packets from one path to another.

The result was the establishment of an Internet Protocol (IP) address and a Transmission Control Protocol (TCP) that coded how packets would be reassembled, once transmitted. This became known as the TCP/IP address.

Cerf's work focused on making the Internet a medium that could be used by the public. He left DARPA in 1982 and became a vice president at the MCI Communications Corporation, which later became WorldCom Inc. At MCI he worked on the project that eventually contributed to making e-mail possible. In 1986 Cerf became a vice president at the Corporation for National Research Initiatives, a not-for-profit corporation located in Reston, Virginia, that Kahn formed to develop network-based information technologies for the public good.

Cerf and Kahn are both in the Internet Hall of Fame, and both have received numerous awards for their contributions to computing and the Internet. Among those awards was the United States' Medal of Technology, awarded by President Bill Clinton in 1997. In 2004 both Kahn and Cerf won the A. M. Turing Award, the highest honor in computer science.

Cerf, however, went on to become a more public figure in Internet communications. From 2000 to 2007 he was the chairman of the board of the Internet Corporation for Assigned Names and Numbers (ICANN), and since 2005 he has held the position of vice president and chief Internet evangelist at Google where he is responsible for identifying new enabling technologies to support the development of advanced, Internet-based products and services. Among his present projects, he works with NASA and the Jet Propulsion Laboratory (JPL) to envision a new set of protocols that can be used in the unique environment of space. While the space-network is still in its infancy and has few nodes, Cerf has said that we are now at "the front end of what could be an evolving and expanding interplanetary backbone" (Mann 2013).

See also: Internet; Google

Further Reading

Mann, Adam. 2013. "Google's Chief Internet Evangelist on Creating the Interplanetary Internet." *Wired.* Accessed March 2, 2015: http://www.wired.com/2013/05/vint-cerf-interplanetary-internet/.

CERN (See European Council for Nuclear Research)

Child Online Protection Act (COPA)

Pornography has always been a major problem on the Internet, but it is most problematic when children become victims of pornography, or consumers (wittingly or unwittingly) as they use the Internet. In 1998, the U.S. Congress passed the Child

Online Protection Act (COPA) with the purpose of restricting access by minors to material that was defined as potentially harmful, but three different attempts to stop the law from taking effect resulted in a permanent injunction against it in 2009.

When the act was passed, it criminalizing speech that, "taken as a whole," appeals to "the prurient interest," that depicts sexual contact, and that "lacks serious literary, artistic, political, or scientific value for minors" (Harris 2008). It also defined minors as children under the age of 16. What the law sought to punish were the content providers that tried to get the attention of children through posting content that might be deemed harmful to children. Furthermore, the law sought to restrict these content providers from making a profit by attempts to attract children to sites through nefarious means, and encouraging children to use their parents' credit cards to access information that could be harmful to them.

COPA put the emphasis on requiring commercial distributors to be responsible for transmitting any content that could be harmful to minors, and it was intended to curtail pornography that was particularly developed to be seen by children. Previously, the Communications Decency Act (CDA) had been struck down as unconstitutional and restricting freedom of speech, and the members of Congress who backed COPA hoped that shifting the emphasis onto the distributors of information would be more specific than the wording of CDA. Unfortunately, they were wrong. COPA defined inappropriate content much more narrowly than CDA and only limited commercial speech, but after lower courts adjudicated the matter, the Third Circuit Court found the act unconstitutional. In May 2002, the Supreme Court reviewed this ruling and turned it back to the Third Circuit Court, where, the second time around, the court ruled that it would potentially violate the free speech of adults and violate both the First and Fifth Amendments. Again, the matter went to the Supreme Court, in 2009, and when the court refused to hear the appeal of the lower court decision, the act was shut down.

Both CDA and COPA signaled efforts to control access to some types of material on the Internet that could have potentially deleterious effects on children, but both were found to inhibit freedom of speech, and, therefore, were deemed (by their respective courts) as violations of the First Amendment. The language of COPA in particular was considered vague, since material for younger children might or might not also be problematic for teens.

See also: Communications Decency Act (CDA); Pornography; Privacy

Further Reading

Harris, Alex. 2008. "Child Online Protection Act Still Unconstitutional." The Center for Internet and Society, Stanford Law School. Accessed March 26, 2015: http://cyberlaw .stanford.edu/blog/2008/11/child-online-protection-act-still-unconstitutional.

Children's Internet Protection Act (CIPA)

Though not just tied to social networking, the possibility of children accessing inappropriate content on the Internet has often juxtaposed regulations and restrictions that are intended to protect children with those that conflict with interpretations of the freedom of speech. The Children's Internet Protection Act (CIPA) is one such attempt to control children's access to material on public computers that gained the attention of Congress and was upheld by the Supreme Court. Unlike some other attempts at creating regulations regarding children's access to possibly questionable material on the Internet that posed questions because of the wording of the acts, CIPA was quite specific in terms of who was accountable and where that accountability could be exercised. But just because it was crafted as a more precise act doesn't mean that it has not been controversial.

In 2000, Congress held a number of hearings concerned with children's access to questionable content on the Internet. The CIPA required that schools teaching the K-12 levels and public libraries implement filters and other measures to protect children from harmful content online, in order to be eligible to receive federal funding. The act was signed into law on December 21, 2000, but was immediately challenged by a number of companies that felt that any filters or controls would impinge upon their First Amendment right of freedom of speech. However, the FCC issued rules clarifying CIPA, and the act was upheld by the U.S. Supreme Court in 2003. Unlike the Communications Decency Act (CDA) and Child Online Protection Act (COPA) that were both overturned by the Supreme Court for restricting freedom of speech, CIPA was focused more on organizations (schools and libraries) that received federal discounts for Internet access, called the E-rate program.

The act requires that the school or library (a) safeguard the safety and security of minors when using e-mail, chat rooms, or other direct electronic communications; (b) take measures to restrict hacking and other possible unlawful activity by the children using the system; (c) do what they can to restrict children providing personal information about themselves; and (d) measure the responses that suggest questionable content. Additionally, any school or library that accepted federal money under the E-rate program to support the telecommunications infrastructure was required to have an Internet safety policy, to include monitoring the online activities of minors, and a program in place to help students understand appropriate online behavior, including communicating with others over social networks and in chat rooms and dealing with cyberbullying awareness and response.

Though CIPA was controversial, especially with those who were required to activate the filters and monitor the online behavior of children (especially librarians and teachers), it was more successful than previous attempts to control children's access to potentially unwanted or questionable content because it used funding as the centerpiece of the activity, rather than requiring individuals to make judgment calls on the appropriateness of what the Internet transmitted.

See also: Child Online Protection Act (COPA); Communications Decency Act (CDA); Pornography

Further Reading

Children's Internet Protection Act. 2015. Federal Communications Commission. Accessed March 26, 2015: http://www.fcc.gov/guides/childrens-internet-protection-act.

Children's Online Privacy Protection Act (COPPA)

In 1998, Congress passed the Children's Online Privacy Protection Act (COPPA) after the Federal Trade Commission (FTC) urged passage of regulation to protect the privacy of children under the age of 13. In particular, the concern was that many websites were accessible only by installing a cookie in the computer of a user. Children are seldom aware of these cookies and the fact that cookies can track behavior and monitor a person's use of the Internet. The information from the cookie is often sold or traded to a third party, which is a concept difficult for children to understand. Even more importantly, however, is the potential for pedophiles or unauthorized individuals to extract personal information from a child that might put that child in danger.

The act applies to operators of commercial websites and online services (including mobile apps) directed to children under 13 that collect, use, or disclose personal information from children. It also applies to operators of general audience websites or online services with actual knowledge that they are collecting, using, or disclosing personal information from children under 13, whether they have parental permission to do so or not.

COPPA became effective in April 2000. It required that commercial website operators provide information that explained how data collected online would be used and by whom, including whether that information was shared by third parties or not. The language of the commercial provider had to be written in such a style that a typical 13 year old, or someone younger, would understand the meaning of the act. It also required that all users be furnished with the company's privacy policy. As can be assumed, the attempt to legislate such an action was potentially problematic.

In 2011, the Federal Trade Commission (FTC) announced amendments would be made to the act to clarify what it meant to collect information from children. The new rules also required that any data collected from children had to be deleted after a certain amount of time. Some of the most significant amendments were made in 2013, and went into effect on July 1 that year. These amendments addressed the need for parental consent to be obtained for collection of geolocation information (such as a child's use of a mobile phone).

The amended rule added categories of information to the definition of personal information. It prohibited the use of personal pictures taken of a child without the express permission of the parent and any information related to a child's activities, such as membership in organizations, sports teams on which they played, or other after school activities that could provide information about the child's location to unauthorized individuals.

See also: Child Online Protection Act (COPA); Children's Internet Protection Act (CIPA); Communications Decency Act (CDA); Federal Trade Commission (FTC)

Further Reading

"Complying with COPPA: Frequently Asked Questions." 2015. Federal Trade Commission (FTC). Accessed March 26, 2015. https://www.ftc.gov/tips-advice/business-center /guidance/complying-coppa-frequently-asked-questions#COPPAEnforcement.

Kordell, Nicole. 2011. "FTC Will Propose Broader Children's Online Privacy Safeguards." *National Law Review*. 123 (2). Accessed December 18, 2014: http://www.natlawreview .com/article/ftc-will-propose-broader-children-s-online-privacy-safeguards.

Cloud

While the term *cloud* suggests a fluffy white mass gently wafting in the breeze, cloud computing is actually a friendly term for storing information on a huge computer somewhere, though the actual location may be unknown to the user. The term *cloud* actually means that the computing tasks and processes are spread among various storage computers. Businesses that promise their customers can access information anywhere, on any device, using cloud storage actually maintain the huge computers necessary to store data.

There are a number of benefits to storing information in the cloud, such as being able to collaborate on a file with someone in real time, or not taking up storage space on your own device, but there are also some negative aspects, too. Cloud storage also means that the company can locate the user's geographic position and the device they are using, because there is a record of uploading, downloading, and accessing any information that is stored in the cloud computer database. Occasionally, the companies that offer cloud services have made decisions to stop making that information available to users, and that has resulted in individuals losing access to whatever they have stored in the cloud.

Both data and software programs that are used over the Internet can be cloud-based. For example, when you store iTunes music or a collection of pictures "in the cloud" (meaning on the company's computer), they are actually renting the storage space on a computer away from their own devices, like personal computers, mobile phones, tablets, or digital music devices.

Amazon and Apple are major retailers that use cloud-based services because it helps make their services available to a number of different user devices, but, at the same time, they can track who is using what device, for which purpose at any time. Therefore, they can develop a very complete user profile of the customer. At this point there are no laws or policies that restrict the use of cloud computing or that protect the customer's privacy, though questions have been raised about how long companies can keep records of what is stored through cloud-based services, and what the host company's rights are, in terms of the data they collect about the users.

According to the U.S. National Institute of Standards and Technology, there are different types of cloud configurations that can be used for different purposes: private, community, public, and hybrid cloud services (Mell and Grance 2011).

A *private cloud* can provide specialized services to a single organization but can be accessed by multiple customers. This is the type of cloud used by each of the companies, like Amazon or Apple.

A group of organizations that have shared purposes, like banks, medical facilities, or any type of organization that needs special security measures to protect data, is called a *community cloud* because the organizations that share the computing services usually also share highly developed systems to protect privacy and secure the data.

Public school systems, academic libraries, and local governments or organizations that have similar purposes might use public clouds.

A *hybrid cloud* would be a combination of any two or more of the other types of cloud formations. Companies or facilities that have different types of services, suggested by the other formations above, would sometimes benefit by sharing data applications or balancing services among different types of services. Local governments who might share cloud services with utilities or local police and fire departments would fit this category.

While cloud facilities centralize service functions and provide special security measures, it is important to realize that the more companies rely on cloud-based computers, the more individuals can be compromised by having large data sets of information that relates to their privacy and security managed elsewhere. Cloud services are more economical for the companies that use them, and it could be argued that greater security can be given to specialized services, but in reality, cloud services are rental facilities for information. Once that information is stored on any device, a person loses the type of immediate access they would have if they stored that information on their own devices. However, if their own devices are lost, damaged, or hacked, they have no recourse to reconstruct that data.

See also: Broadband

Further Reading

Mell, Peter, and Timothy Grance. 2011. "The NIST Definition of Cloud Computing: Recommendations of the National Institute of Standards and Technology." Special Publication 800-145. U.S. Department of Commerce. Accessed February 25, 2015: http://csrc .nist.gov/publications/nistpubs/800-145/SP800-145.pdf.

Collective Intelligence

The concept of collective intelligence has roots in the changing models of behavior that seem to evolve from rapid, digital distribution of ideas over the Internet, or through social networks. Collective intelligence is one of the many effects of the information society, where economic models and concepts reflect modes of production and lifestyles that value the quality of knowledge over manufactured goods or agricultural economics. Social media, constituting the tools of the information society, allow ideas to be shared quickly, in a variety of forums where the ideas of many people can be articulated and debated before a decision is reached. Hopefully, the final decision reflects the group's consensus.

Behavioral economics has contributed to the studies of collective intelligence, but, in the spirit of what collective intelligence tries to do, here are the opinions of individuals and the mission of a "think tank" that all collectively express the range of ideas that support collective intelligence. You will note that each perspective shares some core ideas, but that the applications and description of how they take place are influenced by the author and the audience for whom the author writes.

Pierre Lévy, author of the book *Collective Intelligence: Mankind's Emerging World in Cyberspace* defines *collective intelligence* as "a universally distributed intelligence" (Lévy 1997, 13) that bridges the worlds of technology and humanity. The concept is rooted in the idea that many people have knowledge of some kind, but not about everything. Therefore, when people pool their knowledge, skills, or talents in a variety of ways, the collective nature of those ideas will be better than if those ideas were kept to the individuals, or "siloed." The Internet and World Wide Web enable collective intelligence to flourish, and social organizations that learn how to channel energies over social media have great potential to drive social and technological change for the better.

At the Massachusetts Institute of Technology (MIT), the Center for Collective Intelligence explores the range of questions that make up the emerging study of collective intelligence. The center focuses on questions that deal with the parameters of what it means to be "intelligent"; how human beings can be organized to perform intelligently; and how the field of artificial intelligence (computers with capacities to simulate thinking processes) can influence social action. The basic question they ask is: "How can people and computers be connected so that—collectively—they act more intelligently than any person, group, or computer has ever done before?" (MIT Center for Collective Intelligence 2015).

James Surowiecki, author of *The Wisdom of Crowds: Why the Many Are Smarter Than the Few and How Collective Wisdom Shapes Business, Economies, Societies and Nations* (2004) popularized the idea of collective intelligence and provides a number of examples in his book to show that human beings make better decisions when they collectively pool their intelligence. The number of situations he addresses consistently show that over history, groups have made more accurate assessments and predictions than individual experts. Even Surowiecki's conversations with people in the heart of New York City's Time Square demonstrate that when taken together, ideas from groups are stronger and more accurate than when individuals express their own experiences or knowledge.

Collective intelligence is similar to *crowdsourcing* as people put their talents together to come up with better applications of intelligence. And, in many ways, the success of social media is based on trying to use methods of collective intelligence to produce consensus. For example, Google's search strategy is a form of producing results that have been created by collective intelligence, and reading the experiences of others on sites like TripAdvisor or Angie's List uses different types of experience/intelligence to help others make better decisions.

See also: Creative Economy; Crowdsourcing; Information Age; Sharing Economy

Further Reading

Lévy, Pierre. 1997. *Collective Intelligence: Mankind's Emerging World in Cyberspace.* Translated by Robert Bonnano. Cambridge, MA: Helix Books: 13.

MIT Center for Collective Intelligence. 2015. Accessed March 31, 2015. http://cci.mit.edu /mit.edu/.

Surowiecki, James. 2004. *The Wisdom of Crowds: Why the Many Are Smarter Than the Few and How Collective Wisdom Shapes Business, Economies, Societies and Nations.* New York: Anchor Books.

Comcast

The Comcast Corporation is the largest cable company and Internet Service Provider (ISP) in the United States, and the third largest home telephone provider. Headquartered in Philadelphia, Pennsylvania, the company provides services to 40 states and the District of Columbia. Comcast provides cable television, Internet, telephone service, and security systems to residential and business customers and sells these services under the brand name XFinity. As a major distributor of wired and wireless communications, and a content provider, Comcast has become one of the largest media companies in the areas of traditional broadcast and telephony and in the delivery of social media, because of their Internet and mobile wireless delivery customer base.

The company was founded as American Cable Systems in Tupelo, Mississippi, in 1963 by Ralph J. Roberts and two business partners, Daniel Aaron and Julian A. Brodsky. American Cable had been a small cable operator in Tupelo with only five channels and 15,000 customers ("A Look at Comcast's Changes Over the Decades" 2011). While it is not the only company that grew from humble beginnings throughout the era of media deregulation in the 1980s, it has certainly become one of the most profitable ones.

While still in Mississippi, the owners had big ideas. In 1969, the company was incorporated in Pennsylvania with the name Comcast, which combined "communication" and "broadcast" to define the new approach the company planned to take. In 1990, Brian L. Roberts, son of the earlier president, took over the company. Comcast began to invest in programming and to purchase a number of other small cable providers. The expansion made Comcast a recognizable name, and strengthened Comcast's audience base. The company began providing mobile phone service in 1988.

Some of Comcast's best investments were in niche cable programming. At one point Comcast had partial or complete ownership of the QVC home shopping channel, E! Entertainment Television, PBS KIDS Sprout, TV One (which offered lifestyle and entertainment programming for African Americans), and Comcast SportsNet. Comcast also began offering programming on demand for subscribers who wanted to see television and films over their cable connections on their home television sets.

Throughout the 1990s, the company continued to increase its subscriber base through its acquisitions, and some of the programming it had invested in began to bring in big financial rewards. In 1996, it began to deliver Internet connectivity through its broadband connections to homes. In 2002, Comcast acquired AT&T Broadband for $47.5 billion (Associated Press), which propelled it into becoming the largest cable television company in the United States with over 22 million subscribers at that time.

In 2011, Comcast purchased a majority holding in NBCUniversal from the General Electric Company (GE). At the time, the acquisition was very controversial, with many people complaining that this new configuration would give Comcast too much control over cable rates and access to content. Though the deal was initially discussed in 2009, it took two years of planning and working with the FCC and Department of Justice to consider the impact of these two major firms coming together. When the deal was finalized, Comcast gained access to some international programming services under the umbrella of NBCUniversal, like Telemundo (the Spanish language network), Universal Pictures, and Universal Parks & Resorts, with a global total of nearly 200 family entertainment locations and attractions in the United States and several other countries, including United Arab Emirates, South Korea, Russia, and China, and several additional locations reportedly planned for the future.

Comcast's relationship with NBCUniversal was not supported by all FCC commissioners, nor did public advocates think that the proposed merger was in the best interest of the public. Many feared that Comcast's control over NBCUniversal would result in their charging higher fees for customers to access NBC's television line up. Still, the FCC approved the merger on January 16, 2011, with a vote of the commissioners coming in at 4 to 1. FCC Commissioner Michael Copps cast the one dissenting vote on the merger and issued a scathing critique of the decision suggesting that the new deal was "too big, too powerful, and too lacking in benefits for American consumers and citizens" (Copps 2011, 2). The FCC did require that Comcast make a number of concessions if allowed to continue with the merger, though, including NBC's management stake in Hulu, the online television website.

In 2014, Comcast announced that it hoped to acquire Time Warner Cable for $45 billion thereby combining the two largest cable companies in the United States. If the merger were successful, it would have extended Comcast's reach to major urban areas, including New York City, Los Angeles, Dallas-Fort Worth, Cleveland, Cincinnati, Charlotte, San Diego, and San Antonio, giving the newly formed company access to more than half of the cable homes in the country. Approval for the acquisition was submitted to the Federal Communications Commission (FCC) and Department of Justice, but the acquisition was so complicated and raised so much concern, the company withdrew its proposal on April 24, 2015. One of the reasons for Comcast's decision to withdraw the application had to do with officials from the FCC and Department of Justice who made it clear that a number of changes in the application would be required, and, as part of the deal, Comcast would be required to spin off NBCUniversal into a separate company. That alone, was enough to prevent Comcast from trying to push the deal through. In a statement announcing the decision to abandon the project, FCC Chair Tom Wheeler said: "The proposed merger would have posed an unacceptable risk to competition and innovation, including to the ability of online video providers to reach and serve consumers" (Littleton 2015).

One of the biggest complaints people have is that Comcast's dominance over the market has resulted in prices for Internet access and cable television that are outrageously high. Because cable systems operate without competition in most areas, they feel that the media giant is too big and acts as a corporate "bully." Comcast was one of the most outspoken critics of net neutrality, and, along with Verizon, spent a considerable amount of money lobbying the FCC to have a "tiered system" of access for Internet Service Providers. Comcast was called "The Worst Company in America" by *The Consumerist* magazine in 2014. It had been the "Worst Company" in 2010 as well. *The Consumerist's* awards are based on the number of customer complaints each company gets within one year.

Though Comcast seeks to grow, and has participated in some of the most expensive mergers in telecommunications, the company has lost customers every year since 2007. One reason is that many consumers—particularly young consumers who are comfortable with streaming technologies and media delivery platforms—are saying "no" to Comcast's high costs for cable and other bundled services. So, while Comcast may have benefited from growth at a time in history when the deregulation of media industries resulted in a number of companies buying up smaller stations and programs, it may also be one of the first companies to experience the competition from the growing use of social media platforms to distribute entertainment and information.

See also: Broadband; Legacy Media

Further Reading

"A Look at Comcast's Changes Over the Decades." 2011. *Seattle Times.* Accessed April 2, 2015: http://www.seattletimes.com/business/a-look-at-comcasts-changes-over-the-decades/.

Copps, Michael J. 2011. "Dissenting Statement of Commissioner Michael J. Copps Re: Applications of Comcast Corporation, General Electric Company and NBC Universal, Inc. for Consent to Assign Licenses and Transfer Control of Licensees. MB Docket 10-56, FCC 11-4." FCC. Medendtenbank.db.edu: 1-3. Accessed February 28, 2015: http://www.mediadb.eu/fileadmin/downloads/PDF-Artikel/Copps_Statement.pdf.

Crawford, Susan. 2013. *Captive Audience: The Telecom Industry and Monopoly Power in the New Gilded Age.* New Haven: Yale University Press.

Littleton, Cynthia. 2015. "Comcast CEO on Ending Time Warner Cable Deal: 'Today, We Move On'" *Variety,* Accessed April 24, 2015. http://variety.com/2015/biz/news/comcast-ceo-time-warner-cable-cablevision-1201479107/.

> **Excerpts of the Dissenting Statement of FCC Commissioner Michael J. Copps on the Comcast/NBCUniversal Merger**
>
> Comcast's acquisition of NBCUniversal is a transaction like no other that has come before this Commission—ever. It reaches into virtually every corner of our media and digital landscapes and will affect every citizen in the land . . . And it confers too much power in one company's hands.
>
> In sum, this is simply too much, too big, too powerful, too lacking in benefits for American consumers and citizens . . . Our job is to determine whether the record here demonstrates that this new media giant will serve the public interest . . . It further erodes diversity, localism and competition—the three essential pillars of the public interest standard . . . I would be true to neither the statute nor to everything I have fought for here at the Commission over the past decade if I did not dissent from what I consider to be a damaging and potentially dangerous deal.
>
> *Source:* Applications of Comcast Corporation, General Electric Company, and NBCUniversal, Inc. for Consent to Assign Licenses and Transfer Control of Licensees, MB Docket 10-56, FCC 11-4.

Communications Decency Act (CDA)

As a part of the diffusion of computers and the Internet in the mid-1990s, many people became concerned about children's access to potentially harmful content on the Internet. In part, children used their computers without parental supervision, and many had computer skills that were superior to their parents, but, at the same time, questionable content was flowing over the Internet and it was easy for children to come across spam, or, in particular, pornography that was disguised to lure children to the sites, such as a domain name that would mislead children to see material that was not suitable for minors. In particular, two defunct sites, www.whitehouse.com (note the .com suffix rather than the .gov [dot gov] suffix that actually is linked to the White House) and Dinsey.com (an easily misspelled link that a child could come across while searching for Disney) were pornographic sites. What resulted from this was an attempt to amend the Telecommunications Act of 1996 with a section called the Communications Decency Act (CDA).

Parents and legislators felt that something should be done, and the first attempt to create a policy for the restriction of children's access to pornography was to amend Title V of the Telecommunications Act of 1996. The act was introduced to the Senate Committee of Commerce, Science, and Transportation by Senators

James Exon (D-NE) and Slade Gorton (R-WA) in 1995 and was passed by the Senate on June 14, 1995, in an 84–16 vote. Primarily concerned with Internet users under the age of 18, the act imposed criminal sanctions on anyone who used an interactive computer service to send anyone under the age of 18 "any comment, request, suggestion, proposal, image, or other communication that, in context, depicts or describes, in terms patently offensive as measured by contemporary community standards, sexual or excretory activities or organs" (Telecommunications Act of 1996). Title V attempted to regulate indecency (when available to children) and obscenity in cyberspace. Section 230 of the act specified that operators of Internet services were not to be considered publishers and for that reason were not legally liable for the content posted by others over their distribution systems.

As the first major attempt to control pornography on the Internet, the CDA received a lot of attention, both positive and negative. In 1997, in the landmark cyberlaw case of *Reno v. ACLU*, the U.S. Supreme Court struck down the anti-indecency provisions of the act.

See also: Child Online Protection Act (COPA); Pornography

Further Reading

Reno v. American Civil Liberties Union et al. 1997. U.S. Supreme Court No. 96-511 521 U.S. 844 1997. Argued March 19, 1997; Decided June 26, 1997. Accessed March 26, 2015: https://scholar.google.com/scholar_case?case=1557224836887427725&q=reno+v .+aclu&hl=en&as_sdt=40000006&as_vis=1.

Telecommunications Act of 1996. Federal Communications Commission (fcc.gov). Accessed September 12, 2014: http://transition.fcc.gov/telecom.

Convergence

The term *convergence* literally means "things coming together" but when defined in terms of media convergence (as is appropriate for social media) the word implies that old media and new media are coming together to form something unique. When the term first became popular, most authors discussed *technological* convergence, such as the "coming together" of wireless radio with wired telephony to result in new mobile phones, but shortly after the word became used in popular discourse the concept of "convergence" began to be applied to a wider range of topics.

In his book, *Convergence Culture: Where Old and New Media Collide*, Henry Jenkins sums up the ethos of the word "convergence" when he writes: "Convergence involves both a change in the way media is produced and a change in the way media is consumed" (Jenkins 2006, 16). What he and scholars of convergence mean is that the tools used in communicating with media today are those that allow a person to be both a producer and a consumer of information, all over the same technological forms. The content we exchange may be commercially produced, but it can also be produced by individuals, for individuals, and, therefore, *convergence* signals a new way of thinking about communication, content, and connecting with others.

As mentioned above, one way of looking at convergence is to address the phenomenon as a *technological* form. Another way of looking at convergence is through the *new practices* that new media engender, such as the impact of citizen journalism (through blogs or postings on social media, for example) on more established forms of journalism. *Industries* are often referred to as converging, as different companies merge and develop new avenues for their content. For example, AOL and Time Warner merged in 2001. The social network MySpace was bought by News Corporation, a traditional news company, in 2005. NBCUniversal merged with Comcast in 2011. Every one of these mergers resulted in converging business practices and a wider range of content that relied upon computers and communications.

Social media are, by their nature, converged technology forms that result in new practices and have resulted in a host of new industries and niche businesses. The Internet as the spine that makes social media capable of being social, and the World Wide Web that connects people to content are extreme versions of convergence at every level. Participation in social media means that people produce and consume content. Even the lurker—one who doesn't post anything but logs on to see what other friends are doing on Facebook, Pinterest, or any number of social media sites—is participating by turning their attention to the content on the site.

See also: Digital; E-Publishing

Further Reading

Jenkins, Henry. 2006. *Convergence Culture: Where Old and New Media Collide*. New York: New York University Press, 16.

Cookies

Cookies are actually text codes that reside on browsers and in software. When *cookies* are transferred to a person's computer or smartphone, they become embedded in the software and can act as a gateway between the cookie sender and the computer or smartphone user in a number of ways. Some cookies can be good, such as *authentication* (also known as *secure*) cookies that are used for security purposes to control access to specific information. Online banking, subscribing to a particular service, or using a program to transfer some kinds of information can be great beneficiaries of good cookies. But, on the other side, bad cookies can steal personal information from the computer user, install malware on your device, or block certain websites. Cookies that store passwords for you can be very helpful, but they can also become the targets of hackers who are searching through cookies to get those very important passwords.

Cookies are more readily usable in computers, while cookies on smartphones are a little more complicated. Smartphones use apps that are produced by different companies, and, sometimes, the greater number of companies there are, the more complicated it is for a cookie to do its job. As a result, cookies are used more often in computer communication because the browsers mediate the traffic from the content source to the computer.

The term *cookie* was shortened from the original "magic cookie" that was developed by programmers at Netscape Communications in 1994. The purpose of creating and using cookies was to monitor a computer user's access to certain sites, thereby giving the site host some data about the number of people who looked at the site. Though the public was first unaware of the embedding of cookies in web browsers, the existence of cookies soon raised the potential problem for invasion of privacy. In 1996 and 1997, the Federal Trade Commission held two hearings about cookies, prompted by concerns of citizens. A number of consumer advocacy groups requested that the FTC create a Do Not Track list for online advertising, which would have required the FTC to compile a list of the domain names that placed cookies or tracked consumers. The Senate Commerce Committee Chairman John Rockefeller proposed the Do-Not-Track Online Act of 2011, which would allow the FTC, at a minimum, to collect information about companies that used cookies, and empower the FTC to prosecute offenders. If a consumer asked not to be tracked, the bill would require companies to destroy any information they had gained about the user (Lee 2011). Though the bill never passed because of a number of concerns dealing with the possibility of restraint of trade, attention stayed focused on what could be done to control unwanted access to personal information.

While the initial proposal lost momentum, a new ad-on option called the opt-out cookie was developed so that consumers who wanted to block advertisers from sharing their information could enable those cookies themselves. These, in effect, do what the Do Not Track advocates proposed in 1997. The Do Not Track tools send messages to websites and advertising companies asking that the user's online activity not be tracked, but the system only works if the web companies agree to cooperate (Wingfield 2011).

Tracking cookies have become valuable for monitoring the way a person uses a computer or smartphone, and the data that they provide are valuable commodities for advertisers and those who want to develop a history of the computer or smartphone user. They often fall into the category of first-party cookies that can be good, because they share domain names with a web browser, but they can often contain third-party cookies that collects data from the user's machine and sends it to an advertiser. This is how *contextual* advertising seems to show up on a person's screen if they've been searching for a product. They may be surprised to see ads showing up that address the exact product they've been looking for, or products that fit the categories for which they've browsed.

A number of other types of cookies have been developed over the years. A *session* cookie (also known as an in-memory, or transient cookie) exists only while the user is browsing, but it expires once the user logs off of the computer or turns off the smartphone. *Persistent* cookies stay enabled for a certain length of time and can be enabled again if the user returns to a specific website. *Zombie* cookies have the ability to re-create themselves after they have been deleted. They do this by storing code in a number of locations, and if the device realizes that a cookie is not where it should be, it can locate the cookie wherever it is stored.

Another category of cookie is the *supercookie* that is inserted as a suffix in upper-level domain names. So, for example, a message coming from the United Kingdom could be addressed as .co.uk (dot co dot uk). Many of these supercookies resemble real address names (dot uk), but mask fictitious sites that are often used for phishing and identity theft.

Cookies have not been popular with the public, but, along with privacy concerns raised by social networking and especially the use of smartphones, manufacturers are now looking for alternatives to the cookie—especially in the smartphone area. Along with the iPhone launch in 2007, Apple promised a level of privacy and refused to put third-party cookies into the new phones. While their decision may seem to favor the privacy of the iPhone user, perhaps another reason they decided to eliminate third-party cookies on smartphones is that Apple can control knowledge about who is using their technologies without having to share that type of data with third-parties. Google uses third-party cookies both on its Chrome browser and on the mobile Android operating service used for tablets. Google also has other ways of tracking ads because so many of their services are interrelated, but no longer uses cookies for smartphones because apps do a better job tracking information (Reilly 2014).

There are many ways to clear your browsers of cookies, but, when attempting to do so, remember that some of the good cookies that are helpful to your navigation of subscription sites may also be lost. Directions can be found online at WikiHow's "Clear Your Browser" site: http://www.wikihow.com/Clear-Your-Browser%27s-Cookies.

See also: Advertising; Amazon; Bots; Malware; Peer-to-Peer (P2P); Privacy

Further Reading

Lee, Edmund. 2011. "Sen. Rockefeller: Get Ready for a Real Do-Not-Track Bill for Online Advertising." *Advertising Age.* Accessed April 1, 2015: http://adage.com/article/digital/sen-rockefeller-ready-a-real-track-bill/227426/.

Reilly, Richard Byrne. 2014. "The Cookie Is Dead. Here's How Facebook, Google, and Apple Are Tracking You Now." Venture Beat. Accessed April 1, 2015: http://venturebeat.com/2014/10/06/the-cookie-is-dead-heres-how-facebook-google-and-apple-are-tracking-you-now/.

Wingfield, Nick. 2011. "Apple Adds Do-Not-Track Tool to New Browser." *Wall Street Journal.* Accessed April 1, 2015: http://www.wsj.com/articles/SB10001424052748703551304576261272308358858.

Copyright

Ideas of copyright and the evolving forms of media and communications technologies go hand in hand. U.S. copyright was originally modeled on the British system that had been developed to allow the original owner to control the dissemination and distribution of that person's intellectual property. In 1787 the Constitution of the United States described copyright as the act of "promote(ing) the Progress of Science and the useful Arts." For almost 200 years copyright remained connected to the expressions of intellectual property in tangible form. Copyright laws give the creators of original content the right to be compensated for their work and the ability to control how their works are used. Then, when digital technologies began to appear in the 1970s, the older laws about copyright began to unravel.

A number of groups have been advocating for copyright change so that digital content that can be so easily remixed or become a mashup can reflect the original creator, but not penalize those who create something different from the original copy. When the media arts were in a fixed form, like film, print, recorded music, or broadcast television, copyright most often favored the distributors (usually large companies) that held those copyrights. Contracts with original authors were necessary for the large organization to pay the original author royalties for the right to distribute the content. The current law in the United States was adopted in the Copyright Act of 1976, though many amendments have been made since that time. For many years, subtle changes to copyright often dealt with terms of the extension of the copyright holder's length of time to claim rights to the content.

Today, though, there are a number of legal categories that allow some use of some content. Works either that have never been copyrighted or whose copyright has expired are said to be in the *public domain*. The works of Shakespeare, or the Bible, for example, are in the public domain. Project Gutenberg, a large-scale project that was started at the University of Illinois, has been scanning public domain works in print, and making them available online for free.

Fair use is a category of copyright law that allows works to be used without attribution or payment to an author for purposes of news and comment, parody, teaching, and noncommercial research, but many court cases have involved the fine lines between fair use and stealing intellectual property.

The First Sale Doctrine allows a person who buys a copyrighted work to make a copy for their own use. For example, a person can buy a CD and burn a copy so they can play it in their car, but they cannot sell that copy to someone else. The First Sale Doctrine also allows lending privileges to libraries that buy media but legally share that material on a loan basis.

But while all of these clauses attempt to clarify who owns the intellectual property, who may use it for specific purposes, and what type of distribution is considered "legal" in traditional copyright law, many of the principles of using social media to exchange information, connect with others, and share ideas over digital distribution forms seem to have "violation" built into their systems. The type of collaboration possible over social media, for example, blurs who an "original" owner of "intellectual property" might be. Crowdsourcing, remixes, mashups, and retweets are all examples of making connections to others with content that is created for one purpose to be shared with others. Memes, viral videos, and slash arts are all examples of content that defy traditional copyright.

A number of alternatives to traditional copyright have been presented. The Creative Commons (CC), founded by legal expert Lawrence Lessig proposes an alternative that encourages digital creativity and sharing of content to spur innovation. The CC makes free licenses available to creators who wish to be able to share their content with others, and allow others to change their original content, as long as attribution for the original work is specified. By 2014, the CC had issued 882 million licenses worldwide to encourage collaboration ("State of the Commons" 2014).

The Free Software Foundation (FSF) has advocated a concept they call *copyleft* as opposed to copyright, in which the creator of intellectual property gives the authority to change their original content. The GNU Project of the FSF advocates four freedoms for users who adopt their freeware: "The freedom to run the program as you wish; the freedom to copy the program and give it away to your friends and co-workers; the freedom to change the program as you wish, by having full access to source code; the freedom to distribute an improved version and thus help build the community" ("Overview of the GNU System" n.d.).

A number of lawyers have claimed that total abandonment of traditional copyright law might also hurt more than it helps new artists and the development of new technologies. Legal decisions, including changing laws, all rest on precedents that create models for new legislation, and in the area of copyright. There are advocates on both sides of the copyright fence. Some believe that moving slowly toward newer interpretations or modifications of the law prevents an upset to established businesses, and others argue that the current law is hopelessly outdated and needs a total revision. Depending on who makes the argument and for what reason, there is much to consider with regard to the number of implications for how any changes might affect individual rights and established industries and business models.

See also: Creative Commons; Digital Millennium Copyright Act (DMCA); Freeware; Legacy Media

Further Reading

"Duration of Copyright." United States Copyright Office. Accessed April 9, 2015: http://www.copyright.gov/circs/circ15a.pdf.
"Overview of the GNU System." Free Software Foundation. N.d. Accessed April 20, 2015: https://www.gnu.org/gnu/gnu-history.html.
"State of the Commons." 2014. Creative Commons 2014. Accessed April 9, 2015: http://creativecommons.org/.

Craigslist

craigslist (which uses a lower case "c" in its official title) is a private company developed by software engineer Craig Newmark in 1995. At first, the San Francisco company focused only on activities that were going on in the San Francisco Bay area where Newmark was a newcomer. He observed other social media and networks that were in the early stages, like The WELL, one of the earliest virtual communities started in 1985, and Usenet, an early Internet discussion site, started in 1980. Each of these online services connected like-minded individuals for a specific purpose, and Newmark reasoned that there would be interest from people who wanted to know what types of events were going on in the local community.

When he first started working on an idea to connect people, he created an e-mail distribution list for friends. Many of the things he would post interested other software developers, like himself, and who were also new to the area. His postings became popular and his list grew. Before long he realized that other people would like to post things, too. He used his own list as a model and incorporated the company as a private, for-profit company in 1999 as craigslist.org. The company now operates in over 200 cities in the United States and in over 50 different countries.

Newmark saw the value in creating a service where people could post things about jobs, including posting of resumes, housing, items that people needed (especially important for new people coming to an area), items that were no longer needed, and events that might attract like-minded individuals. All of these services, he believed, should be free to users. As he expanded to let people know about local activities, the number of items for sale or give-away started to overwhelm the site. Discussion forums helped not only newcomers to the community, but connected others to a wider range of issues. As the site continued to grow, it began to take much of the focus off of the classified advertising section of the local newspapers. Over time, craigslist has become blamed for being one of the major contributors to the death of the advertising model of supporting classified ads in newspapers.

In 2000, Jim Buckmaster was hired to be the lead programmer and chief technology officer (CTO). He was largely responsible for helping the company grow to include the multicity architecture of the site, the development of a search engine, discussion forums, personal categories, and more. Soon after he became the CEO later in that same year, craigslist started to expand rapidly to nine additional U.S. cities. By 2004, the list of cities in the United States had grown to 31. At this point, the company started charging $25 to post job openings, though low-cost and unpaid internship opportunities were posted for free. This was later expanded to apartment listings in some cities and the advertising of some personal services.

When Newmark started his project, he did not have profit as the end goal of his site. Instead, he hoped that users would form a community, and that the community would engage in practices that would sustain interest in maintaining the site. The modest cost for job postings and some apartment listings and services, supports some of the maintenance and personnel of craigslist, but the company has still not made a profit, though the revenue brought in would seemingly disprove this. According to one analytical firm, craigslist's 2012 revenue was about $126 million, and at the time it appeared that 2013 revenue would reach $153 million (Charles 2015). Most of the money taken in supports the maintenance of the site, and some employees (including Newmark and Buckmaster) are paid, but no advertising supports craigslist. Most of the money that comes in through job postings goes to support the Internet servers, electric bill, and Internet bandwidth use.

Craigslist now receives about 2 million new job listings every month, and the range of what can be advertised has continued to grow. Some of the new listings have been controversial and legally problematic. For example, while postings related to dating now have additional descriptions such as "strictly platonic," or "casual encounters," some descriptions have actually masked the use of posting solicitations for prostitution on craigslist. Some of those postings have resulted in high profile criminal cases, such as a "craigslist killer," Philip Haynes Markoff who met his victims through erotic services ads on craigslist in 2009. Markoff allegedly killed one of his victims and robbed two others. He was subsequently arraigned on murder and robbery and, while awaiting trial, killed himself while in custody. More importantly, Markoff was not the only person who used craigslist to meet potential victims. The "adult services" controversy continued until the organization blocked blatant categories in 2010.

In another situation that prompted law enforcement officials to react to the transactions that occur when people connect to others through craigslist, two Georgia residents in 2011 were robbed and killed when trying to buy a car they had seen advertised on craigslist. The seller of the car violently killed the couple, and the press seized upon the vulnerability of people who engage in transactions in private places. Since then, a number of police departments around the country have created safe places in the parking lots of the police stations so that people exchanging money and goods feel that there is reasonable surveillance if anything goes wrong when using craigslist to connect to someone else.

See also: eBay; E-Commerce

Further Reading

Charles, Aaron. 2015. "How Can Craigslist Be Free?" *Houston Chronicle.* Accessed April 9, 2015: http://smallbusiness.chron.com/can-craigslist-free-64147.html.
Lindenberger, Michael A. 2010. "Craigslist Comes Clean: No More 'Adult Services' Ever." *Time* magazine. Accessed January 8, 2015: http://content.time.com/time/nation/article /0,8599,2019499,00.html.
Weiss, Philip. 2014. "A Guy Named Craig." *New York.* Accessed February 25, 2015: http://nymag.com/nymetro/news/media/internet/15500/.

Creative Commons

The Creative Commons (CC) is a nonprofit organization founded in 2001 to explore alternatives to traditional copyright and takes into consideration the unique characteristics of today's digital technologies and the variety of distribution forms, primarily anchored by the Internet. Its founder is Lawrence Lessig, one of the most prominent and widely respected legal minds whose work is most closely aligned with new media. The Center for the Public Domain funded the establishment of the CC and a board of directors guides the organization. In addition to clarifying contemporary copyright for the exchange of content, the CC also works to facilitate the reform of outdated copyright legislation.

In part, the CC is a reaction to traditional copyright restrictions that favored legacy media. But with digital media, it is very easy to tweak content and create something new, or, at least, partially derivative of the original. Persons who take out CC licenses allow others to modify their work, but the license restricts other companies or corporations from profiting from use of the work.

The CC started issuing licenses in 2002 based upon a logic developed in part of the Free Software Foundation's GNU Public License (GNU GPL). The licenses they distribute (for free) help standardize rules that allow the public to use content that the original owner approves of modifying. One feature that CC licenses have that is different than traditional copyright is that it changes the terms of use from "all rights reserved" (as used in earlier copyright) to "some rights reserved." The organization claims that "our vision is nothing less than realizing the full potential of the Internet—universal access to research and education, full participation in culture—to drive a new era of development, growth, and productivity" (Creative Commons 2014).

CC licenses have made a significant impact on book publishing, particularly academic books that may benefit from collective wisdom and criticism, and gaming technologies that can be improved and better utilized when players have access to changing the outcome of the game. App developers have been particularly interested in CC licenses, too, because so many new uses of apps evolve from interested users applying them to new creative activities.

The 2009 Nobel Prize in Economics was awarded to Elinor Ostrom whose work in examining the economic impact of commons-based material and envisioning the future with greater attention to sharing through creative projects heralded world attention to the growth potential of this movement. Ostrom's early work emphasized the role of public choice on decisions influencing the production of public goods and services, and her career focused on how the decisions of human beings could create more efficient forms of governance than large bureaucratic structures, like government. The ideas that bridge Ostrom's work and that of the Creative Commons have much to do with the values associated with the information age and creative economy.

CC licenses have been applied globally, and have never faced legal challenges to their legitimacy.

See also: Copyright; Creative Economy; Digital Millennium Copyright Act (DMCA); Information Age

Further Reading

Creative Commons.org. 2014. Accessed October 4, 2014: https://creativecommons.org/.
Ostrom, Elinor. 1990. *Governing the Commons: The Evolution of Institutions for Collective Action.* Cambridge, UK: Cambridge University Press.

Creative Economy

The term *creative economy* has evolved to describe how work, people's labor, and wages have changed in an information-based economy, facilitated by the many means of digital information processing. Often the term refers to using computers and the Internet as a distributor of creative products and innovations. This is in contrast to the type of work and economic structure, most dominantly manufacturing and the factory assembly line, that was constitutive of the major form of labor in the nineteenth and twentieth centuries in industrialized nations. In general, the creative economy signals a shift to a different value system of what is important than in the past. Values, wage-labor, and the lifestyles that accompany people who engage in the creative economy are sometimes sharply divided from the modes of production and value systems of their parents and grandparents.

Several prominent authors have attained success in writing about the opportunities in the creative economy, including John Howkins, who used the term in 2001 to describe how value is placed on imaginative qualities rather than on the traditional labor activities. In Howkins's view, a creativity-based model is broadly conceived and encompasses creativity that spans art, innovation, and other forms of intellectual creativity.

The great leveler of opportunities in the creative economy is the Internet, and a look at the type of creative industries that are flourishing in the creative economy are often those that capitalize on the unique characteristics of Internet communication. John Hartley, author of the book, *Creative Industries,* defines the term as "the conceptual and practical convergence of the CREATIVE ARTS (individual talent) with cultural Industries (mass scale), in the context of NEW MEDIA TECHNOLOGIES (ICTs) within a NEW KNOWLEDGE ECONOMY, for the use of newly INTERACTIVE CITIZEN-CONSUMERS" (punctuation and capitalization are that of the author's; Hartley 2005, 106). Even the flexibility to break the boundaries of typical print style shows that authors who believe in the creative economy feel free to break traditional rules and norms of communication!

Richard Florida popularized the term in his book *The Rise of the Creative Class* (2011) and has become an expert on where and how the "creatives" balance the type of work they do with their desired lifestyles. The result, according to the data he cites, is that urban areas are the primary incubators of the creative economy. Among the regions he finds to be most supportive of creative work and the creative economy are the Boston, route 128 beltway, and Cambridge, Massachusetts, New York, particularly lower Manhattan and Brooklyn, and the San Jose area of California.

According to Florida, the creative class, which made up only about 10 percent of the workforce in the late nineteenth century and about 15 percent for much of the twentieth century, is now poised to make up about half of the workforce today (Florida 2011, 15). Along with this shift, people who make up the contemporary creative age have two social classes, workers in science and technology, arts, culture and entertainment, health care, law, and management, whose occupations are based on mental or creative labor, and a second, larger service class that work in administrative jobs, food service, home and personal health care, and janitorial work.

The Internet has allowed individuals greater flexibility in developing their own personal talents and entrepreneurial skills. But this raises the question of whether artistic efforts still have the same cultural value, or whether, in a creative economy where an individual assumes more roles, the end product is art, or something else. For example, an individual can sell, promote, and deliver directly to users and compete with traditional companies that previously had a market on publicity and distribution. As cultural critic William Deresiewicz has written, "Creative entrepreneurship is spawning its own institutional structure—online marketplaces, self-publishing platforms, nonprofit incubators, collaborative spaces—but the fundamental relationship remains creator-to-customer, with creators handling or superintending every aspect of the transaction" (Deresiewicz 2015, 96).

Jeremy Rifkin, author of a number of books on social, cultural, and technological change, identified several elements that describe the changing forces in the creative economy in his book, *The Age of Access* (2000). Among those features are the transformation of our economy from markets that exchange goods between buyers and sellers to networks based upon ongoing relationships between suppliers and users; a shift from wealth based on tangible assets to wealth based upon intangible assets, such as goodwill, ideas, brand identities, copyrights, patents, and expertise. He also sees elements of the shift of ownership of goods to the accessing of services; and from production of sales to customer relationship marketing, and finally, a shift from production-line manufacturing to the "Hollywood" organized model of project-based collaborative teams that are brought together for a limited period of time (Flew 2005, 350).

Related to the creative economy is the type of work that is available, often referred to as *knowledge work*. This term helps describe the shift from the manufacturing of goods and services to that of the intellectual endeavors of those who participate in the creative economy. When this description is applied, the value of what one knows, learns, and can use factors into economic terms.

Even though the creative economy is often touted as the next emerging economy, there are critics of what such a shift in economic resources could do to the status quo. Journalist Scott Timberg is not as optimistic about the success of a creative economy. In *Culture Crash: The Killing of the Creative Class,* he paints a picture that is not so rosy. Basing his evaluations on the effect of the economic crash in the United States in the 1980s, he writes: "Book editors, journalists, video store clerks, all kinds of musicians, novelists without tenure—they're among the many groups struggling through the dreary combination of economic slump and Internet reset. From their vantage point, the creative class is melting" (Timberg 2015, 15).

See also: Sharing Economy

Further Reading

Deresiewicz, William 2015. "The Death of the Artist and the Birth of the Creative Entrepreneur." *The Atlantic Monthly*, 315: 92–97.

Flew, Terry. 2005. "Creative Economy." In *Creative Industries*, edited by John Hartley. Malden, MA: Blackwell Publishing, 344–360.

Florida, Richard. 2011. *The Rise of the Creative Class Revisited*, revised and expanded. New York: Basic Books.

Hartley, John. 2005. "Creative Industries" In *Creative Industries,* edited by John Hartley. Malden, MA: Blackwell Publishing, 106–116.

Rifkin, Jeremy. 2000. *The Age of Access*. New York: Tarcher/Putnam.

Timberg, Scott. 2015. *Culture Crash: The Killing of the Creative Class*. New Haven: Yale University Press.

Community Media and Maker Spaces

Though originally a community television station, Amherst Media has become a center for creative activity and media-related projects.

Maker Spaces are workspaces intended to foster interdisciplinary and intergenerational collaborations through creative arrangements of hardware, software, and art. Universities, libraries, and community centers are increasingly adopting this model and carving out spaces for "maker" activities. Makers at Amherst Media (M@AM) in Amherst, Massachusetts, is an example of such a space where faculty and students from the college campuses in the area come together with the larger community to share expertise. In addition to instructional workshops, the makerspace at this local center has housed a university course on open source science, an after school program on electronic art, and drop-in hours for the community to use media tools and resources to work on any projects they choose. Such spaces are promising hubs of innovation while simultaneously offering alternative pedagogical approaches to multimodal literacies and education.

Christine Olson—Amherst Media

Crowdfunding

Raising money using online tools is often called *crowdfunding*. Social media and social networks make it easy to distribute appeals for fund-raising to friends and colleagues who might be interested in supporting the same causes as the creator of the fund-raising activity, and, when that happens, the term usually applied is *crowdfunding*. In this economic model, people make donations to a cause, often because they believe in supporting a person, project, or idea. Donations are usually made through the Internet, by means of a specific web appeal to potential funders. Generally, there are two major models for crowdfunding. The first is donation-based funding in which people donate toward a goal in return for products or rewards, or just because they believe in a project and want to contribute to support it. The second model involves a system in which donors receive some form of financial return, such as stock or ownership of a form of the product itself.

The origin of the term is unclear. According to WordSpy.com, an online source that attempts to track the origin of new words, the first person to use the term crowdfunding was Michael Sullivan the originator of an early crowdfunding site in 2006, called *fundavlog*. While fundavlog was intended to help raise money for videoblog-related projects and events, the project failed. A few years later, the term crowdsourcing reemerged when the Kickstarter site was launched. For the commercial service, persons who wish to contribute to a specific cause, or support an idea, make a contribution online, and the crowdfunding site takes a percentage of the donation. Crowdfunding through a bank or financial services company is usually for a different type of support that benefits an individual or cause. For example, a family that has lost a home to a fire or vandalism might be supported through a local crowdfunding site, or a person with an extreme illness might be supported by friends and community members.

As social networks began to connect more people, the ability to send one message to many facilitated a new way of asking for support. Many creative artists sent messages to their "friends" or "crowds" to help raise money for a recording, or even to support a tour. The British group Marillion collected $60,000 in 1997 by reaching out to their fans on social networks to finance a U.S. tour (Castrataro 2011). Soon after, a number of crowdfunding sites started to emerge, each of which often tended to specialize in a specific type of fund-raising.

Among one of the most well-known projects includes musician Amanda Palmer's campaign that raised $1.2 million in 2012 for her new album. Later, Palmer performed a Ted Talk called *The Art of Asking*. Filmed in February 2013, the YouTube video has already been seen by over 6 million people.

Charity sites, personal sites, niche sites, and sites that are targeted to a specific region or geographic location are among the most prominent type of sites. Kickstarter, Indiegogo, teespring, YouCaring, causes, Giveforward, crowdrise, and Fundly are among the top 10 sites, and each often specializes in a specific type of fund-raising (Barnett 2013). Other types of funding services can be set up, too, either through a special website dedicated to a cause, or through a bank or other financial service agency.

In 2013, crowdfunding raised over $5.1 billion for a variety of projects (Broderick 2014). And while we may be most familiar with those types of crowdfunding sites we see more regularly in the United States, the potential for fund-raising through crowdsourcing in emerging economies has been raising some expectations. A World Bank report from 2013 predicted that by 2025, China could be the beneficiary of $50 billion in crowdfunding projects, and other regions may not be far behind (Broderick 2014). Much of the fund-raising is not just for specific projects, and some new sites have used the crowdfunding model to raise money for a host of reasons.

Kiva is a crowdfunding site launched in 2005 that operates as a microlending platform to people in developing nations. It expands the concept of peer-to-peer lending that is an alternative to traditional bank lending. A person submits a photo (if possible) and a description of what they hope to do with the funds and individuals donating to the site can choose a specific project to which they make a contribution. Over $165 million has been raised by Kiva, and the repayment rate (to fund other projects) is an amazing 98.83 percent rate (Castrataro 2011).

Crowdfunding appeals to people on a number of levels. First, social networking makes it easy to contribute to a cause that appeals to you. Second, there is often great satisfaction in knowing you made a difference, even if one's contribution may be small. The success of Barack Obama's presidential fund-raising online came from asking for small donations from many, and it worked. Crowdfunding strategies have been so successful for relatively small projects that there is a great deal of interest in exploring whether crowdfunding could be conducted on a much larger scale, such as trying to raise several million dollars to finance a housing development, or a new school.

Crowdfunding reportedly appeals to millennials—those people born between 1980 and 2000. This type of giving may be different from earlier forms of fund-raising, but there is indeed an element of communal investment in a project through crowdfunding. The number of successful projects are a testament to this type of fund-raising activity.

See also: Cybercurrency; PayPal; Political Fund-Raising

Further Reading

Barnett, Chance. 2013. "Top 10 Crowdfunding Sites for Fundraising." *Forbes*. Accessed December 3, 2013: http://www.forbes.com/sites/chancebarnett/2013/05/08/top-10 -crowdfunding-sites-for-fundraising/.

Broderick, Daniel. 2014. "Crowdfunding's Untapped Potential in Emerging Markets." Forbes BrandVoice. Accessed March 31, 2015: http://www.forbes.com/sites/hsbc/2014 /08/05/crowdfundings-untapped-potential-in-emerging-markets/.

Castrataro, Daniela. 2011. "A Social History of Crowdfunding." Social Media Week. Accessed March 31, 2015: http://socialmediaweek.org/blog/2011/12/a-social-history-o http://socialmediaweek.org/blog/2011/12/a-social-history-of-crowdfunding/f-crowd funding/.

Crowdsourcing

Crowdsourcing is a simple idea that has major economic consequences. In general, the term is used to describe a division of labor that allows for the input of many for an end result that reflects a compilation of the best ideas. Social networking is an excellent medium for collecting these types of ideas and allowing the online space to be the place where the collection, sifting, and evaluation of ideas takes place. Where the idea becomes more complicated is when those ideas are linked to monetary exchange, and that brings into question the economic value of the intellectual capital. Whereas, in the past, a "boss" might have her salary based upon the number of people she oversees and the way she interacts with them to get a job done, it is harder to assess individual contributions when a nonhierarchical structure that pins monetary gain to status or responsibility changes the traditional organizational structure and accountability.

The term was coined in a 2005 article that was the result of the work of two *Wired* magazine editors, Jeff Howe and Mark Robinson, who discussed how the Internet was changing the nature of work, with the idea that people who participate in projects over the Internet contribute ideas that make a product or project better. They described the activity as "outsourcing to the crowd," which Howe then defined on his blog as a companion to a June 2006 *Wired* article, "The Rise of Crowdsourcing," The focus Howe and Robinson took was on the way businesses were changing their way of making decisions and expecting employees to contribute to business decisions.

Their ideas were formed by the work of academics and journalists who explored the multitude of ideas coming together in a shared fashion. Canadian Professor Pierre Lévy wrote about *collective intelligence*, in 1997, discussing how the ideas of many improved the outcome of ideas. Journalist James Surowiecki was also influential with his book *The Wisdom of Crowds* (2004) in which he echoed Lévy's ideas and provided a number of concrete examples over history that show that collective intelligence produces better results than more hierarchical decision making.

The concept of crowdsourcing has gained academic interest, and, in 2008, Daren C. Brabham published a journal article that further defined the features of crowdsourcing as a human organizational principle. Businesses continue to explore the possibility of using crowdsourcing for even larger projects, and business schools and economics departments continue to examine the emerging economic models of crowdsourcing projects.

See also: Collective Intelligence; Creative Economy; Crowdfunding

Further Reading

Brabham, Daren. 2008. "Crowdsourcing as a Model for Problem Solving: An Introduction and Cases." *Convergence: The International Journal of Research into New Media Technologies,* 14: 75–90.

Howe, Jeff. 2006. "The Rise of Crowdsourcing." *Wired.* Accessed December 3, 2014: http://archive.wired.com/wired/archive/14.06/crowds.html.

Lévy, Pierre. 1997. *Collective Intelligence: Mankind's Emerging World in Cyberspace,* Translated by Robert Bonnono. Cambridge, MA: Helix.

Surowiecki, James. 2004. *The Wisdom of Crowds: Why the Many Are Smarter Than the Few and How Collective Wisdom Shapes Business, Economies, Societies and Nations.* New York: Anchor Books.

Cyberattack

Cyberattacks come in many forms. They can be person-to-person, business-oriented, or even government-ordered. In most cases, however, major cyberattacks tend to create havoc for the receivers of the attack, either through loss of privacy and security or because of the financial cost of the attack. Cyberattacks are attempts to gain unauthorized access to a computer, computer system, or communications network, with an intent to harm whomever is affected by the attack. A cyberattack may be similar in many ways to cyberwar, cybercrime, or cyberterrorism, and scholars have debated the fine line that separates each of these categories. What may seem like a cyberattack to one person might be classified as cyberterrorism by another.

Additionally, more than one category can be applied to some cases. A hacker might attack one person's computer for personal information, and that could be judged a cybercrime as well as a cyberattack. Though it may be difficult to assess the economic cost of a cyberattack, some have ranged from simple annoyances to customers, to billions of dollars in lost revenue. An accurate assessment of money that hackers get from identity theft is unknown because so much goes undetected, and sometimes the person whose identity has been stolen is too embarrassed to report minor problems.

The IRS has estimated that identity theft cost $5.2 million in 2013, based on the number of false claims made by thieves who have stolen social security numbers (Hicks 2014). While all of these may not be the result of cyberattacks, a significant number of them are from that source.

Noted security analyst Raimund Genes has approached the problem by suggesting that the *ends* and the *means* should determine the categorization of any type of cyberinfiltration. He claims that if the intent of the hack is to steal information, the action should be considered an attack, but the term "war" should be used only when there is a political intent to destroy data or a technological infrastructure. But as Genes notes, structures, techniques and tools are all the same no matter what the outcome of a malicious invasion of secure data (Genes 2015).

Of course, sometimes it is difficult to know what the intent of an attack may be unless an organization claims that they have mounted an attack for a specific reason. After Christmas, 2014, a young hacker group calling themselves Lizard Squad issued Distributed Denial of Service (DDoS) notices for people playing games on Microsoft's Xbox Live and the Sony PlayStation Network allegedly "for the laughs" but also to force the game companies to upgrade their security (Smith 2014). In computing, a denial-of-service attack (DoS attack) or distributed denial-of-service attack (DDoS attack) is an attempt to make a machine or network resource unavailable to its intended users. Lizard Squad's actions annoyed a number of people who had received new games and gaming technologies for Christmas, but while the attack was annoying, it did not constitute a "war" or "terrorism."

Some of the most common attacks have focused on stealing credit card data, like the interruptions that occurred on the networks of major retailers, like Home Depot, Target, and Anthem Health Care. When this happens the organization loses credibility and the breach of security can result in ill will with consumers as well as a nightmare for any consumer whose data is compromised.

Some cyberattacks, however, have been found to be government-to-government actions that have created political storms. One of the most famous cyberattacks is the 2010 Stuxnet virus that was allegedly designed by the United States and Israel to hijack the industrial-control systems that destroyed centrifuges of Iran's nuclear program. More recently, the Regin malware virus in 2014 has hints of being deployed by the United States and Great Britain and primarily attacked computers in Russia, Saudi Arabia, and a group of countries including Afghanistan, Ireland, and Mexico. The vulnerability of computers has resulted in some countries attempting to use different technologies to avoid cyberattacks. It has been reported that Russia has ordered typewriters for secret correspondence, and that other governments, including the U.S. government, may be returning to using floppy discs instead of other types of digital data storage.

In 2014, the cyberattack on Sony Entertainment Pictures received worldwide attention. This attack affected Sony Pictures employees and their families, celebrities, internal communications, and copies of unreleased Sony films. While the hackers who claimed credit for the November 24 attack called themselves the "Guardians of Peace" (GOP), U.S. intelligence officials determined that the attack was sponsored by North Korea. What complicated the situation was the impending release of the film *The Interview* in which two comedic journalists were asked by the U.S. government to assassinate North Korea's leader, Kim Jong-un. The cyberattack on Sony was seen as a "warning" to those who discredited North Korea and its leadership.

Though the financial cost of the attack to Sony Pictures may not be public information, it has been rumored that the attack would cost Sony "tens of millions of dollars" in lost revenue, but the massive breach of security has also lost Sony goodwill and relationships with employees. It was reported that the hackers gained access to possibly as many as 47,000 social security numbers in the Sony files (Sanger and Perlroth 2014). Embarrassing confidential information such as private e-mails between executives and the salaries of employees and celebrities that were made public reportedly also created stress and will undoubtedly strain future relationships.

According to researchers who examined how the attack occurred, it is the notion that the attack was mounted from centers around the world, including a convention center in Singapore and Thailand. The attack bore similarities to a previous attack on South Korean banks and broadcasters by a cybercriminal gang in Seoul. In addition to the hackers uploading the films that were going to be released, including *Annie*, *Fury*, and *Still Alice*, to the Internet, the Sony hack cost Sony approximately $15 million in losses.

See also: Anonymous; Cybercrime; Cyberwar; Hacker; Privacy; Snowden, Edward; WikiLeaks

Further Reading

Genes, Raimund. 2015. "What the Next Government's Cyber-Security Policy Should Look Like." *SC Magazine*. Accessed May 21, 2015: http://www.scmagazineuk.com/what-the-next-governments-cyber-security-policy-should-look-like/article/413600/.

Hicks, Josh. 2014. "Identity Theft Cost the IRS 5 Billion Last Year. Here's What Congress Can Do about It." *Washington Post*. Accessed April 13, 2015: http://www.washingtonpost.com/blogs/federal-eye/wp/2014/09/23/identity-theft-cost-the-irs-5-billion-last-year-heres-what-congress-can-do-about-it/.

Sanger, David E., and Nicole Perlroth. 2014. "U.S. Said to Find North Korea Ordered Cyberattack on Sony." *New York Times*. Accessed January 20, 2015: ww.nytimes.com/2014/12/18/world/asia/us-links-north-korea-to-sony-hacking.html?_r=1.

Smith, Dave. 2014. "Why Hacker Gang 'Lizard Squad' Took Down Xbox Live and PlayStation Network." Business Insider. Accessed January 20, 2015: http://www.businessinsider.com/why-hacker-gang-lizard-squad-took-down-xbox-live-and-playstation-network-2014-12#ixzz3PO7Fd6xq.

Cyberbullying

The use of online communication to harass, intimidate, or otherwise harm the reputation of someone is generally referred to as cyberbullying. The act or behavior of cyberbullying is often related to the use of social media for antisocial purposes.

The problem of cyberbullying came to the attention of the public in the mid-2000s when a number of particularly problematic cases of the cyberbullying of teenagers became the focus of the press. These cases initially raised concern that social media and social networks were regularly being used to intimidate or harass individuals—particularly teens—but since that time we've learned that cyberbullying can affect every age group in a number of ways and within a number of contexts.

Among the most common forms of cyberbullying are cyberstalking (spamming someone's mobile phone or social network profile page), sexting someone without their prior agreement to accept such content, sending jokes, comics, or texts that make someone feel uncomfortable; sending gross or indecent images to someone, or, in general, saying (or writing) insulting or intimidating messages to someone or to a list of people who might read those messages about someone.

Though there are, unfortunately, many cases of cyberbullying that have been popularized in the media, one of the first to capture national attention was the story of 14-year-old Megan Meier, who hanged herself because of cyberbullying in 2006. Megan was a typical teen who just wanted to be liked. She engaged in a MySpace friendship with a boy named Josh Evans. Initially, Josh seemed kind and interested in Megan, but when his affections seemed to turn, he allegedly wrote that the world would be a better place without her. The loss of this special friend and the harm it did to Megan's self-esteem caused her to commit suicide.

After Megan's death, it became known that there was no Josh Evans and that he was the creation of the mother of a former friend in the neighborhood where Megan lived, who thought it would be a joke to create "Josh" and impersonate him on Megan's MySpace page. The mother, Lori Drew, was indicted in the death in 2008, but the case was overturned upon appeal in 2009. Megan's mother went to the press, and the story resulted in international headlines about computer fraud, impersonation, and the cyberbullying of a young girl. The reason that the Megan Meier case was so heinous was that it was an adult perpetrating the "joke" and that, prior to this time, there was no legislation to punish persons who caused such cruel acts online. Megan's mother's campaign for the creation of a law against cyberbullying resulted in a proposal to the U.S. Congress called "The Megan Meier Cyberbullying Prevention Act." After Megan's story was told in national media, the problem of cyberbullying began to become known to many.

The rash of teenage suicides due to cyberbullying has resulted in a better understanding of the vulnerability of young people and the power of social media to harm, as well as to help people connect to others. It is probably not surprising that those people who suffer from social anxiety, a problem of interacting face-to-face, often find themselves the victims of cyberbullying. For young people, especially teens who are trying to assert their own personalities, the need to be liked makes them particularly vulnerable to nasty rumors and the spread of information through social networks. The harm to reputations can be frighteningly real for someone who is bullied through online forms of communication.

The Cyberbullying Research Center is an organization that focuses specifically on the role of bullying and adolescents. The organization defines cyberbullying as: "Willful and repeated harm inflicted through the use of computers, cell phones, and other electronic devices." It is also known as "cyberbullying," "electronic bullying," "e-bullying," "sms bullying," "mobile bullying," "online bullying," "digital bullying," or "Internet bullying."

According to studies by the Pew Internet Research Project, about one in three teens reports that they have experienced a range of "annoying and potentially menacing online activities," such as receiving threatening messages, having private e-mails or text messages forwarded without their consent, having an embarrassing picture posted without permission, or having rumors about them spread online. While teen girls are more likely to be victims of cyberstalking, boys are not immune from cyberstalking as well (Lenhart, 2007).

In Britain and some parts of Europe, the problem of what Britons call "happy slapping" has become a major cyberbullying offense. In these cases, young boys are held down and forced to watch on mobile phones pornography, bestiality, or other images that could be considered humiliating to them in what the boys call happy slapping. Another form of humiliation occurs when a boy is beaten up, and the beating is recorded by mobile phone and sent to others. The phenomenon has evolved to where the happy slapping experience is not just humiliating, but there have been incidents of deaths and sexual assault as a result of what starts as something that someone does for "fun" but devolves into something far more serious.

There are many ways to conceptualize *cyberstalking*, but the most common forms are facilitated by social networks that allow others to post on walls or comment in some way so that the harassment can be either directed to the individual or posted in a way to humiliate or harm someone's reputation. Some cyberstalkers send individuals messages with viruses or worms to disrupt their own social network and computer use; some install keystroke loggers or spyware on computers or cell phones so that their whereabouts can be easily tracked. Generally, more women are cyberstalked than men, but that is not always the case. Postintimate relationships may result in acts of revenge from the person who feels harmed in the breakup, and cyberstalking often occurs under those conditions.

Cyberbullying also takes place in the workplace, with many of the same effects. When anyone feels that they are being made a target, their self-esteem drops, and they are not as productive as they would be if they worked or studied in a healthy environment. Sending risqué or embarrassing jokes through e-mail, rumors, and embarrassing pictures are among some of the most common cyberbullying techniques in the workplace.

The cost of establishing seminars, programs, and help groups for students and employees to learn about cyberbullying and becoming aware of their behaviors and their rights has become a topic of concern for helping people deal with such issues, but the harm to one's self-esteem and the loss of integrity are important values to consider.

See also: Anonymity; Identity; Privacy; Sexting

Further Reading

Cyberbullying Prevention Center. 2007. Accessed October 29, 2014. "About Us." http://cyberbullying.us/abo http://www.pewinternet.org/2007/06/27/cyberbullying/ut-us/ut-us/.

Leisring, Penny A. 2009. "Stalking Made Easy: How Information and Communication Technologies Are Influencing the Way People Monitor and Harass One Another." In *The Culture of Efficiency*, edited by Sharon Kleinman, 230–244. New York: Peter Lang.

Lenhart, Amanda. 2007. "Cyberbullying." Pew Internet Research Project. Accessed October 29, 2014. http://www.pewinternet.org/2007/06/27/cyberbullying/.

Cybercrime

Ideas and information are not the only things that spread quickly over the Internet. Cybercrime is a serious problem that can take many forms, including using viruses and worms to infect others' machines, using bots that send out countless unsolicited spam e-mails advertising questionable products, or inserting malware. Stealing identity information like passwords, social security numbers, or credit card numbers are among the most common of the major crimes. The international police agency, Interpol, also includes crimes called "sexploitation" as one of the major growing categories of cybercrime, and warns of the growing nature of crimes against children in this category ("Connecting Police for a Safer World" 2015).

In addition to the amount of cybercrime on the Internet, cybercrime also takes place on what is often referred to as the *dark web*, or *deep web*. The connections that are made over the dark web are not subject to being detected by regular search engines and therefore function almost like an underground Internet. Illegal activity often takes place in this communications area, and the points of origin are extremely hard to detect. Starting in 2011, the Silk Road, an underground narcotics source where tightly secured communications facilitated the purchase of illegal drugs, guns, and IDs, was started by Ross Ulbricht, a young Texan who operated the site until he was caught in 2013. Calling himself the Dread Pirate Roberts, he was considered a "mastermind" of the dark web. After he was caught and arrested, others took over the site, but Ulbricht was finally sentenced to life in prison without parole for his participating in the Silk Road site.

Though we know cybercrime is a serious problem, it is difficult to measure the economic impact of cybercrime for a number of reasons. One reason it's a challenge to measure the financial costs of cybercrimes is that the victims often don't know they've been attacked. Even when the breach is known, how do you measure the economic impact of a stolen social security number, a formula for a new drug, blueprints for a new car, or the proprietary information of a major utility company? Furthermore, when sensitive information is lost, some companies are reticent to provide accurate information about the financial loss of data, because they do not want the bad publicity or because they are reluctant to admit they have been hacked because they fear a loss in confidence from consumers or clients. This can lead to underreporting of the problem.

A number of figures have been tossed around, but in every case, skeptics have questioned how accurate those numbers may be. For example, McAfee, the Intel-owned company that markets security programs for computer safety's Center for Strategic and International Studies reported in June 2014 that the likely cost to the global economy from cybercrime is approximately $575 billion a year. Almost immediately after the report was published, skeptics questioned the figure and the sources of data that produced it; but still, the number was reported by major media news outlets. Therein lies part of the problem; the companies that produce high figures have products to sell that they believe will help control cybercrime.

We do, however, have a better idea of the financial impact of individual cybercrimes that have been adjudicated. In 2007 the computers of TJX, the parent company of the retail stores TJ Maxx and Marshalls in the United States, and TK Maxx in Europe, were hacked and cyber criminals obtained the credit card numbers of 45 million customers. Once the case went to court, it appeared that actually, 94 million customers were affected by the hack. TJX engineered a financial settlement of $256 million to pay Visa, Mastercard, and the customers whose personal information was stolen, but many analysts felt that the actual cost of the hack was probably closer to $1 billion (Goodman 2015, 17).

The Sony cyberattacks in 2014 were estimated to be among the most costly in history, with an estimated cost of $100 million for Sony. In this cybercrime, personal information of regular citizens was not lost, though anyone who had worked for Sony in any capacity from the security guards and lunchroom staff to the background actors and celebrities found their personal information to be vulnerable. Trade secrets were exposed and what was previously private correspondence was made available. Additionally, the loss of revenue for the films that were stolen and put up on the Internet added to the overall financial impact, and the loss of productivity while investigations were under way may reach a final total of tens of millions of dollars (Mamiit 2014).

Marc Goodman, a former cybercrime detective has written a book called *Future Crimes* in which he discusses the current situation with cybercrime, and the likelihood for growth in this area in the future. He writes that "92% of the time" cybercrime against an organization is not found by one of the employees within the organization, but, rather, by a customer or local police department investigating crime (Goodman 2015, 16–17). The cost to the company then involves money spent on detecting the security breach, investigating the matter, identifying perpetrators, and repairing and recovering the computer network. Additionally, any company found to be lacking in appropriate security measures often loses some value in the stock market from shareholders who worry about the financial viability of a company that experiences cybercrime.

See also: Cyberattack; Cyber Crime Center (C3); Cyberwar; Dark Net; Spyware

Further Reading

"Connecting Police for a Safer World." 2015. Interpol Website. Accessed April 20, 2015: http://www.interpol.int/About-INTERPOL/Structure-and-governance.

Goodman, Marc. 2015. *Future Crimes*. New York: Doubleday, 16–17.

Mamiit, Aaron. 2014. "Sony Pictures Cyber Attack May Cost $100 Million, Says Expert." Tech Times. Accessed April 20, 2015: http://www.techtimes.com/articles/21869/2014 1210/sony-pictures-cyber-attack-may-cost-100-million-says-expert.htm.

"Net Losses: Estimating the Global Cost of Cybercrime Economic Impact of Cybercrime II." 2014. McAfee Center for Strategic and International Studies. Accessed April 20, 2015: http://www.mcafee.com/us/resources/reports/rp-economic-impact-cybercrime2.pdf.

"Tech Firms Chip Away at Credit Cards' Share of Transactions." 2014. NPR Morning Edition. Accessed October 2014: http://www.npr.org/2014/10/02/353177261/tech-firms -chip-away-at-credit-cards-share-of-transactions.

Cyber Crime Center (C3)

In 2003, the U.S. Immigration and Customs Enforcement Agency, under the Department of Homeland Security, formed the Cyber Crime Center to investigate and combat Internet-related criminal acts within the United States and across borders. As one of many U.S. government centers dealing with issues of cybercrime, the C3 deals with issues most closely tied to the abuse of the Internet for crimes against children, and criminal activities. The organization trains law enforcement agencies and maintains a forensics laboratory that specializes in digital evidence recovery. The organization encompasses three units: the Cyber Crimes Unit, the Child Exploitation Investigations Unit, and the Computer Forensics Unit.

The Cyber Crimes Unit deals with issues related to identity and focuses on document fraud, money laundering, financial fraud (including e-payment fraud and Internet gambling), commercial fraud, counterproliferation investigations, narcotics trafficking, and illegal exports.

The Child Exploitation Investigations Unit investigates issues dealing with the sexual exploitation of children; production, advertising, and distribution of child pornography; and child sex tourism. Along with this unit is Operation Predator, the investigative force that deals with targeting sexual predators, child pornographers, and child sex tourists. This unit often partners with other government agencies to join forces to find missing and exploited children and deal with the use of the Internet to protect children against predatory activity by others, both in the United States and around the world. It also works with nongovernmental organizations like the National Center for Missing and Exploited Children.

The Computer Forensics Unit examines the data that agents must investigate during the course of an inquiry or investigation. Encryption methods and codes are a special concern of this unit, and agents often furnish expert computer forensic testimony in criminal trials.

See also: Cyberbullying; Pornography; Sexting

Further Reading

"Cyber Crimes Center." 2014. U.S. Immigration and Customs Enforcement, Department of Homeland Security, U.S. Government. Accessed October 29, 2014: http://www.ice .gov/cyber-crimes.

Cybercurrency (also known as digital currency, e-currency, or cryptocurrency)

Pay systems that are an alternative to traditional cash monetary exchanges have been grouped into the category of *cybercurrency*, though they are sometimes called digital currency or cryptocurrency. Some companies that want to secure their payment for goods or transactions immediately can use cybercurrency as a faster, more secure form of monetary exchange. While financial regulators do not yet agree on all terms of using cybercurrency, the number of experiments currently under way point to a future in which cybercurrency may well be one option for transferring money online.

Some video games, like *Club Penguin*, and *Second Life,* work on a system of exchange where users can "buy" services with alternative cash, and Internet retailers like Amazon have developed specific monetary units in digital form through Amazon coins that can be used for Amazon purchases. Bitcoin is another example of a monetary unit that makes it difficult to trace the origin of the sender of the bitcoin, but at present there is volatility in the value of bitcoins as a cybercurrency (the capital "B" is the name of the form of cybercurrency, but the lowercase "b" is the description of the units of exchange). At present, there are many virtual currencies being used in different parts of the world, including Bitcoin, Litecoin, Doegcoin, Darkcoin, Ripple, Digitalcoin, Worldcoin, Vertcoin, and Peercoin. Cybercurrencies are different from payment systems that transfer a traditional currency electronically, like Apple Pay, Google Wallet, or PayPal.

The term *cryptocurrency* was first described in 1998 by Wei Dai on the cypherpunks mailing list, suggesting the idea of a new form of money that uses cryptography to control its creation and transactions, rather than a central authority, but as the concept of digital monetary exchange over computer networks becomes more widely available, the term cybercurrency is becoming more popular. Cybercurrencies are not controlled by traditional banks, therefore the value of whatever unit is used is somewhat unstable, but advocates believe that the more cybercurrency is used, the more stable it will become. The benefit of using cybercurrency is that a person's anonymity is better protected than when using other forms of monetary exchange. This may be useful in purchasing goods or investing in things for which a person prefers to remain anonymous, but, at the same time, this means cybercurrency can often be used to cover up possible nefarious actions, including gambling (therefore hiding any winnings from tax authorities) or illicit trade in drugs or pornography.

In the United States, the IRS issued a position on cybercurrency that defines cybercurrency as property, for tax purposes. According to the IRS the position on cybercurrency is that all wages paid to employees in digital currencies are taxable and must be reported. Digital currency payments made to independent contractors and service providers must be reported, as income tax and profits and losses from the sale of digital currencies are subject to capital gains when they are used as a capital asset. Additionally, the IRS determined how fair market values of cybercurrency assets will be evaluated in the future, and whether penalties would be imposed on taxpayers who participated in cybercurrency transactions prior to the March 25, 2014 date of decision implementation.

Cybercurrency transactions can take place in a number of ways. The use of a credit card payment on the Internet could be described as an element of cybercurrency but usually specific technologies can be used to facilitate electronic transfer of money by use of a credit or debit card. The Square, which can be attached to a tablet, laptop, or smartphone was developed by Jack Dorsey, one of the founders of Twitter. The Square Reader and the Square Stand are both "point of sale" technologies that make digital money transfer easy, though they would not be classified specifically as cybercurrency.

Mobile payments are among the most interesting features today, and the race is on to control the flow of bits and cash across a billion smartphones and at millions of online and physical locations. The research firm Gartner estimates that mobile payments will top $720 billion a year by 2017, up from $235 billion in 2014 (Reza 2015). Researchers estimate that whoever ends up with controlling interests in mobile digital e-funds transfer will be rewarded in billions of dollars in transaction fees. They will also collect massive amounts of consumer data and make massive amounts of money from the sale of personal information to advertising companies.

See also: Amazon Coins; Bitcoin; E-Commerce; Gaming

Further Reading

Bertoni, Steve. 2014. "Can PayPal Beat Apple, Google, Amazon and Icahn in the Wallet Wars?" *Forbes.* Accessed March 4, 2015: http://www.forbes.com/sites/stevenbertoni /2014/02/12/can-paypal-beat-apple-google-amazon-and-icahn-in-the-wallet-wars/.

Reza, Pantha Rahman. 2015. "The Mobile Money Revolution Is Transforming Bangladesh." Translated by Pantha Rahman Reza. Global Voices Online. Accessed March 4, 2015: http://globalvoicesonline.org/2015/01/08/the-mobile-money-revolution-is-transforming -bangladesh/.

Cyber Monday

Cyber Monday represents the increasing reliance on online shopping during the holiday season. The term was introduced in by the National Retail Federation, an organization that tracks sales. The term was coined to describe what happens shortly after Thanksgiving in the United States, when the holiday shopping "officially" begins.

To understand Cyber Monday, it is important to get a sense of what has become known as Black Friday. The day after Thanksgiving in the United States has been called "Black Friday" and though the definition of Black Friday is somewhat disputed, one interpretation of the name is that most retailers have their best sales on that day, allowing their financial balances to go from "red" to "black" ink—meaning they make a profit. However, it is more likely that the term comes from events during the mid-1960s in Philadelphia, when city police used the term to define the crush of shoppers that would go to stores, and the chaos that resulted from the number of people on the streets, congestion, and the short temper of frustrated shoppers.

In 2014, Cyber Monday sales resulted in the spending of $2.04 billion, up 17 percent from 2013. The analytics firm, comScore reported that it was the biggest online shopping day in history, and the first to surpass $2 billion in sales (Wahaba 2014). While Black Friday 2014 was not as big as it had been the previous year, analysts determined that people where shopping over a five-day period, rather than concentrating on shopping in retail stores on Friday, and online on Monday. Among the largest online retailers, Amazon and Wal-Mart posted their highest sales ever.

See also: Advertising; E-Commerce

Further Reading

Moyer, Justin. 2014. "The Surprisingly Political Origins of 'Cyber Monday.'" *The Washington Post*. Accessed December 9, 2014: http://www.washingtonpost.com/blogs/wonkblog/wp/2014/12/01/the-surprisingly-political-origins-of-cyber-monday/.

Vasel, Kathryn. 2014. "When Did Black Friday Start?" CNN. Accessed December 9, 2014: http://money.cnn.com/2014/11/28/news/black-friday-history/.

Wahaba, Phil. 2014. "Cyber-Monday Sales Pass 2 Billion." *Fortune*. Accessed December 9, 2014: http://fortune.com/2014/12/02/cyber-monday-sales-pass-2-billion/.

Cybernetics

The term *cybernetics* has its root in the Greek word Kubernetes, which means "to steer" or "steersman." The mathematician and electrical engineer Norbert Wiener coined the term in 1948 to describe a system of control and machines; with the notion that both humans and machines exercise a level of control over the communication interaction. Wiener's work in ballistics is what came to be associated with what became known as the Palo Alto School. The problem he sought to understand dealt with World War II and the training of artillery personnel whose task was to attack enemy airplanes. Instead of trying to think of the gunner, the planes, and the maneuvers necessary as individual entities, the thought was that they could think *cybernetically*, as a total, complete system. In developing this concept, the notion of an *informational system* developed. Later, this was applied to computers, information theory, network theory, and the field of artificial intelligence.

By 1972, Gregory Bateson used the concept of cybernetics to describe human systems and the expression of meaning as people communicated, and more recently the environmental movement has used the term to describe the natural ecosystem and the balance necessary for sustainable living. His work as well as that of his wife, Margaret Mead, brought ideas of cybernetics to the social sciences.

Today, within the applications of information theory, cybernetics is a key concept. Network theory, which has emerged from information theory, also uses cybernetics to describe how humans and machines work as a system.

See also: Network Theory; Wiener, Norbert

Further Reading

Bateson, Gregory. 1972. *Steps to an Ecology of Mind: Collected Essays in Anthropology, Psychiatry, Evolution, and Epistemology.* San Francisco: Chandler Publishing.
Wiener, Norbert. 1948. *Cybernetics: Or, Control and Communication in the Animal and the Machine.* New York: Wiley.

Cyberspace

The term *cyberspace* was coined by William Gibson in his futuristic novel *Neuromancer* in 1984. The term describes the unseen "space" in which electronic communication passes and has come to be a descriptor of a place in which electronic data is transferred from users and technologies to each other. Because it is a metaphorical space, it has connotations of having special characteristics that influence time and geographic space. In a 2000 documentary called *No Maps for These Territories*, Gibson said: "All I knew about the word 'cyberspace' when I coined it, was that it seemed like an effective buzzword. It seemed evocative and essentially meaningless. It was suggestive of something, but had no real semantic meaning, even for me, as I saw it emerge on the page" (Kennedy 2013).

Gibson undoubtedly took the root word "cyber" from the work of Norbert Wiener in 1948, who wrote a book called *Cybernetics* to describe electronic communication and the science of electronic message transfer. The word "cybernetics" comes from the Ancient Greek term that means "to steer" or "steersman," In the 1990s, the concept of cyberspace became attractive to give a name to the imagined space of the Internet and the messages that were transferred over it. The prefix "cyber" relates to a number of events that occur on the Internet.

The provocative nature of cyberspace has become more pronounced in popular culture with films and futuristic novels that use the classification to indicate that space and time have a role to play in the imagination of what constitutes cyberspace. *Cyberpunk* is a genre of science fiction that has been described as combining "high tech and low culture." Films like *Blade Runner* and *Johnny Mnemonic* use ideas of cyberspace themes in film. A number of games have also capitalized on cyber ideas, like *Cyber Slots* and *Cyber Ortek Flier* that actually use "cyber" in their titles, but because so many electronic games take place online or on a mobile platform, they often integrate aspects of cyberspace, whether they use the term or not.

See also: Cybernetics; Digital; Gaming; Wiener, Norbert

Further Reading

Gibson, William. 1984. *Neuromancer.* New York: Berkley Publishing Group.
Kennedy, Pagan. 2013. "William Gibson's Future Is Now." *New York Times Book Review.* Accessed April 19, 2015: http://www.nytimes.com/2012/01/15/books/review/distrust-that -particular-flavor-by-william-gibson-book-review.html?pagewanted=all.

Cyberstalking (see Cyberbullying and Privacy)

Cyberterrorism (see Cyberwar)

Cyberwar

Like cyberattacks and cybercrime, cyberwar is a category that often blends into other forms of cybercrime. However, when the term cyberwar is used, there is generally a political motive behind the attack and the purpose of the action is to damage a company or government. As security expert Raimund Genes has written, if the goal of the attack is to destroy a company's data or infrastructure, or if there is a political intention to the attack, it may be considered an act of cyberwar, or cyberwarfare. Cyberterrorism is a particular type of cyberwar that seeks to instill fear in those who are attacked.

There is some controversy, though, about whether the term cyberwar is accurate or not. Most of the controversy is surrounded by what actually constitutes a "war." In 2012, Thomas Rid wrote an article for the influential *Journal of Strategic Studies* in which he claimed that we have never experienced a cyberwar, and never would (Rid 2012, 5). Using classic definitions of war, Rid makes the argument that cyberactivity would not result in war because there would be no way the action would be manifested in violence and casualties, which are one of the key components of traditional war. But while cyberwar might take an entirely different type of approach toward a twenty-first century version of war, there would undoubtedly be plenty of casualties. Perhaps no violence in the traditional sense, but most definitely casualties that would be the victims of a cyberattack that bridged into cyberwar.

An example of what might constitute a cyberwar in the United States (or anywhere else) could be the type of attack that attempts to harm a country's electrical power grid. Without electricity, communications are shut down, security measures that are tied into the power grid are lost, and all Internet connectivity could fail. In many ways this could cripple an entire nation, if the grid were not able to be immediately repaired or rebooted. In April 2009, national security officials reported that China and Russia had infiltrated the U.S. electrical grid and left behind software programs that could be used to disrupt the system; however, the harmful code was found and destroyed.

When U.S. Director of National Intelligence James Clapper addressed the Senate Intelligence Committee in 2013, he defined cyberwar as having two components, both espionage and cyberattacks, the latter of which he considered to be the top security threat to the United States (Gjelton 2013). Two years later, in January 2015, President Obama authorized financial sanctions against malicious overseas hackers or companies that use cyberespionage to steel U.S. trade secrets in the first major overhaul of the U.S. government's cyberstrategy. Until the announcement, most American cyberattacks on adversaries have been covert operations, but with the new directive, the Department of Homeland Security was charged with detecting more complex attacks. Obama also indicated that about 2 percent of the attacks are leveled specifically at the government, and that if and when these attacks threatened, a response would be led by the Pentagon and the military's Cyber Command, which is based at the National Security Agency in Maryland.

With the Internet so vulnerable to malware and the growing number of sophisticated hacking and cybercrime activities, every country needs to think about possible scenarios if they become victims of cyberwar. Like warfare, for centuries, an attack can have devastating consequences. The casualties may not look the same way as they did in more traditional military wars, but it seems certain to project that there will be plenty of casualties if a cyberwar does break out.

See also: Cyberattack; Cyberwar; Hacker; Privacy

Further Reading

Genes, Raimund. 2015. "What the Next Government's Cyber-Security Policy Should Look Like." *SC Magazine.* Accessed May 21, 2015: http://www.scmagazineuk.com/what-the-next-governments-cyber-security-policy-should-look-like/article/413600/.

Gjelten, Tom. 2013. "Cyberattacks, Terrorism Top U.S. Security Threat Report." NPR's *All Things Considered.* Accessed April 24, 2015: http://www.npr.org/2013/03/12/174135800/cyber-attacks-terrorism-top-u-s-security-threat-report.

Rid, Thomas. 2012. "Cyber War Will Not Take Place." *Journal of Strategic Studies*, 35: 5–32.

D

Dark Net (Dark Web)

Most of the information on the Internet can be easily accessed because search engines find keywords and easily locate that information for us within fractions of seconds. But there is an "underground" web that can only be accessed by those who know how to get to it. By using the Tor browser, information can be sent from place to place, similar to routing information through a series of tunnels. The Tor network is a group of volunteer-operated servers that function in the same way the Internet and World Wide Web process information, but, in this case, the Tor browser and network tend to operate with information that has been dubbed the dark net, or dark web. While the dark net is a marketplace for illicit information and communication, it really should not be equated with the power or reach of the regular Internet and should be thought of as a relatively small area that uses the tools of social media. Even though the profits made by those conducting business on the dark net may be huge, the dark net should always be considered as a black market for transactions.

The purpose of the Tor Project is to have a means of electronic communication that can be truly anonymous by creating a pathway for information searches and access that is too complicated to trace. While most Internet and World Wide Web information can be traced to the point of origin, Tor makes the search far more difficult by obfuscating the pathway between the information seeker and the source of information. It was founded to protect personal privacy and relies on volunteers who sponsor proxy servers and who volunteer to code information so that some sites can remain hidden.

Known as the "underground web," this mysterious place was originally developed in the mid-1990s by the U.S. Naval Research Laboratory to protect secure U.S. intelligence online. Later it was developed by the Defense Advanced Research Projects Agency (DARPA) and the U.S. Navy. Called "onion routing" because it sent information through many layers, similar to peeling an onion, it functions like a private Internet.

Like any technology, the dark net can be used for a number of reasons, both good and bad. Using the dark net is a way to keep other people from accessing your information or seeing what sites you visit. Many governments use the dark net to reach people in countries where the regular Internet may be censored or blocked, like China or Iran. Even Facebook has accessed the dark net to reach consumers in these countries.

Much more attention is given to the dark net and how it is used for illicit and questionable purposes. The Silk Road, an underground marketplace for narcotics and gun sales, is one of the most well-known sites on the dark net. When Ross Ulbricht, the mastermind behind the Silk Road, was arrested and sentenced to life in prison for his illegal activity on the dark net, the existence of the underground Internet became more familiar to many through the attention given to the story by popular media. Ulbricht started the Silk Road in 2011 and was arrested while using a public library to conduct his business in 2013. In February 2015, a federal jury in Manhattan found Ulbricht guilty of seven charges related to computer-hacking conspiracy, narcotics-trafficking conspiracy, and money laundering. On May 29, 2015, he was sentenced to life in prison with no parole. Since his arrest, a number of pseudo–Silk Road sites have begun to operate on the dark web, some of which use the name Silk Road.

Because the dark net often traffics in illegal activity, Bitcoin is often the currency of choice because it cannot be easily traced. Other cybercurrencies are often used, too, but Bitcoin is the most difficult to trace, even though there is volatility in the value of bitcoins. Perhaps surprisingly, most of the illegal businesses on the dark web resemble any typical form of e-commerce that allows users to rate transactions and satisfaction with service.

The dark net is one of the major marketplaces for pornography—and is a major distributor of child pornography and a location where individual users can post amateur pornography of themselves engaging in sexual acts or camming—meaning that they use personal cameras to perform and then upload to a site (Bartlett 2014, 175–179). In an interview on National Public Radio's "All Tech Considered," journalist Jamie Bartlett cited information from the Internet Watch Foundation, a U.K.-based Internet monitor, "about a third of child pornography images are now being produced by young people themselves, people under the age of 18 who are taking photographs or images or videos of themselves and their partners and then sharing them amongst their friends or posting them online" (Bartlett 2014, 176). This type of user-generated content makes it easy for pedophiles to collect images and share them with others, often profiting from the sale of the user-generated content.

The dark net is also a place where there are emerging subcultures, such as self-harm communities (like cutters, pro-anorexic communities), assassination sites, and more. With such uncensored content freely flowing and difficult to trace, it may seem odd that there has been no government or police attempt to curtail the activities on the dark net. The reason is really very simple. There is almost always a black market that exists in illicit trade, and the denizens of the dark net know how to resurrect the protocols that keep it safe. Therefore, if the information on the dark net is concentrated in one place, it becomes easier to monitor what goes on, even though it may be more difficult to catch perpetrators or those engaged in illegal activity.

See also: Anonymity; Anonymous; Bitcoin; Cybercrime; Pornography

Further Reading

Bartlett, Jamie. 2014. *The Dark Net.* Brooklyn, NY, and London: William Heinemann: 175–179.

Bartlett, Jamie. (Interview) 2015. "Infiltrating 'The Dark Net,' Where Criminals, Trolls and Extremists Reign." NPR's *All Tech Considered.* Accessed June 4, 2015: http://www .npr.org/sections/alltechconsidered/2015/06/03/411476653/infiltrating-the-dark-net -where-criminals-trolls-and-extremists-reign.

Criminal Acts on the Dark Web

The *dark web* is a set of Internet connections that cannot be indexed by regular search engines. In June 2011, Silk Road began to be well known after Gawker published an article about the site, and reddit perpetuated stories about the site.

Silk Road was a website for the exchange of illicit drugs, guns, and IDs. In February 2012, the administrator announced that he would be known as the Dread Pirate Roberts, a name taken from the film, *The Princess Bride.*

In October 2013, the FBI approached Ross Ulbricht as he used the free Wi-Fi in the Glen Park library of San Francisco. They seized his laptop and arrested him immediately.

On May 29, 2015, Ross Ulbricht was sentenced to life in prison without parole on charges dealing with conspiracy to sell drugs, launder money, and hack computers. He was also ordered to pay more than $183 million in restitution.

Data Mining

The term *data mining* has a positive connotation for some but strikes fear into the hearts of many because the term is often used to refer to extracting personal information from large data sets. Using the algorithmic methods of extracting information, data mining sifts through massive amounts of information online and extracts what's useful to the data miners. Pieces of information can be matched and collections of data can create patterns that tell miners about the characteristics of a population, or, sometimes, about individuals.

Since all computers, mobile phones, and electronic devices use forms of identifying users, data mining has become big business. It should also be noted that data mining is not always done for purposes of monetizing that information for other companies to use, though when we refer to social media that is usually the primary use of data from data mining. But there are many other valuable uses of data mining, such as that used for medical research, making statistical projections, collecting environmental data, and charting trending topics.

Personal profiles can be used to microtarget audiences and audience members, meaning that messages can be sent directly to individuals through a variety of methods. Think for a moment about how much information a simple "loyalty card" can generate. Loyalty cards in grocery stores, for example, are linked to the user's name, address, e-mail account, and applications for loyalty cards usually ask personal information such as gender and age. Payment for the goods purchased with a loyalty card often provides a credit or debit card number and the name and account number of the bank that issues the cards. For purchases made with loyalty cards, stores keep a record of what products a person buys in a store, how much money they spend, and how often they shop at the store. This information can also be used to generate specific ads or a direct mail campaign to send coupons to the card user, based on the knowledge of what that person is likely to buy.

With reference to social networking, though, data mining can produce valuable information for advertisers. The more we use the Internet, the more data becomes available that some company, somewhere, can turn into a profitable commodity. Smartphones are particularly good generators of data because the more apps we use, the more of a digital trail we create. As Marc Goodman, a security specialist has written: "Smart phones [sic] are turning human beings into human sensors, generating vast sums of information about us. As a result, children born today will live their entire lives in the shadow of a massive digital footprint, with some 92 percent of infants already having an online presence" (Goodman 2015, 84). That digital presence can start in the form of a sonogram posted to Facebook, a parent looking for baby names on the Internet, a birth announcement, ordering baby clothes from Amazon, or any number of social media uses that start to compile information about a new life.

Many data mining companies have been formed to be the intermediaries between personal consumers and the companies that value the information mined. The honest companies try hard to protect data, but even the most rigorous security controls are sometimes subject to hacking or human error. In 2013, Experian, a data brokerage company mistakenly sold personal data from about two-thirds of the American population to an organized crime group in Vietnam, releasing about 200 million social security numbers to criminals around the world (Goodman 2015, 89).

Sprint, Verizon, and AT&T all have programs that provide data about subscribers to marketers, advertisers, and retailers, even though each claims that they take steps to make the information "anonymous" so that it can't be directly linked to names and identities of subscribers (Woyke 2014, 206). The onus is placed on subscribers who receive small-print notifications that allow them to "opt out" of third-party information distribution, but still, this information can be compared to other databases to locate individuals and provide a wealth of information about them.

Data mining can also have some unintended effects. Shazam is a popular music app that became available in 2002. A person who wants to know information about some music that they hear somewhere (perhaps in a coffee shop, a movie, or as background sound elsewhere) can open Shazam and have the service listen to a short piece of data generated by the music. Shazam searches for the source and identifies the title of the song and the name of the artist. According to *Atlantic Monthly* writer Derek Thompson, Shazam has actually been able to predict hits and has changed the way the music industry operates. He cites Jason Titus, Shazam's former chief technologist who said: "Sometimes we can see when a song is going to break out months before most people have even heard of it" (Thompson 2014, 69). The way Shazam aggregates data is to examine the daily 20 million Shazam searches from around the world and then create an interactive map where the company can chart where the most "Shazam'd" data is generated. The map represents an analysis of where the world's most popular new music is coming from, and allows scouts to go to those locations and discover unsigned artists. In February 2014, Shazam announced that it would be working with the Warner Music Group to develop new artists.

For many, data mining brings up concerns about personal privacy. There are a number of laws on the books in the United States, but the social media revolution is occurring so quickly, it is hard to find specific laws that protect consumers from companies that mine their data, even if they are legal companies. The "terms of use" for each app and social network define what the company can legally do with information generated by users, but the onus is on the consumer to "opt out" of allowing third parties to have access to data, and that means reading the small print and taking action. Even when someone does this, breaches of security can occur through human error or because of the cyberskills of hackers.

There is one notable exception, however, and that is a law that attempts to protect information gathered from children. The Children's Online Privacy Protection Rule ("COPPA") required that websites and app developers obtain "verifiable parental consent" before any personal information was gathered from social media users under the age of 13. Passed in 2000, and subsequently amended, the law restricted collecting information such as names, addresses, contact information, photos, and videos. While this law helps create a structure for controlling data that could potentially violate privacy matters for children, the problem of authenticating parental approval is very difficult to ascertain.

See also: Advertising; Peer-to-Peer; Privacy

Further Reading

Goodman, Marc. 2015. *Future Crimes*. New York: Doubleday, 84–89.
Thompson, Derek. 2014. "The Shazam Effect." *The Atlantic Monthly*, 314: 67–69, 72.
Woyke, Elizabeth. 2014. *The Smartphone: Anatomy of an Industry*. New York and London: The New Press, 206.

Dating

Social networks get a lot of attention for the way they help people connect to each other and to a wide variety of services on the Internet, but online dating and finding romantic relationships through social networks has received more interest than many topics. As discussed in the section on Friending, exactly what, or who, becomes a "friend" on a social network can be a complicated issue, depending on the reason a person hopes to "friend" another. Using online services to connect to potential romantic partners has a history that predates social networking, and scientists have developed a number of theories about using electronic systems to introduce people with the purpose of creating a lasting emotional bond. But, at the same time, the hard science that might explain how someone is attracted to another person through an online website or mobile app is hard to pin down. But whether you are an optimist or a pessimist in terms of thinking about whether online dating services work or not, the online dating industry has been growing about 10 to 15 percent a year, and earns approximately $1.9 billion a year (Boorstin 2010).

Before the Internet, computer dating became a business that would help people "scientifically" find their best matches. In 1965 Project TACT (Technical Automated Compatibility Testing) was the brainchild of Lewis Altfest, an accountant, and Robert Ross, a computer programmer, who designed a system to allow New Yorkers to find potential partners with a computer program. Clients filled out questionnaires that had more than a hundred multiple choice questions. They then paid $5 to have their data processed by a computer and the computer made the matches based on the data. As might be expected, the computer dating scene was riddled with critics who bemoaned the technologizing of something as personal as per-sonal attraction and decried mechanized matches as a gimmick. Still, there are advocates of using available technologies and programs to meet people. In a Valen-tine's Day spot dedicated to online dating on National Public Radio, UCLA social psychologist Benjamin Karney said that "Online dating is an amazing technologi-cal advance, and it really makes it easier to find a potential partner . . . and we know that people are willing to do and say all sorts of things online that they wouldn't do face to face" (Singh 2015).

Though not well known yet, and lacking statistics to indicate the level of the problem, anecdotal evidence has emerged to blame online dating sites and social networking and "friending" as contributors to the breakup of some romantic rela-tionships and family units. As one divorce attorney wrote: "Facebook has cer-tainly created constant business for us . . . Families dissolve because of it. People will sacrifice long-term, real relationships for these on-line connections which can actually be very fleeting" (Boorstin 2010). She also cautions her clients to stop all social media interactions while a divorce is in progress, because online com-ments or pictures can contribute to suspicious relationships that can muddy divorce proceedings.

But despite the grumblings of those who doubt the efficacy of using the Internet to find love, the number of online services and social networks dedicated to helping people find a romantic partner have blossomed. According to a study conducted in 2013 by the Pew Research Center's Internet Project, 38 percent of Americans who are single and actively looking for a partner have used online dating at one point or another. The study also indicated that most of the online daters were in their mid-20s to mid-40s; 22 percent of the 25- to 34-year-old respondents and 17 percent of the 35- to 44-year-old respondents had gone on a date with someone they had met online. One-fourth of the online daters reported that they had entered into marriage or had a long-term relationship with someone they initially met through a dating site or app (Smith and Duggan 2013). The Pew Research Center's first study of online dating in 2005 identified people who are heavy Internet users as those most likely to use an online service or app for dating or romantic purposes.

There are both general sites and niche sites for people interested in using the dating sites or apps. Match.com and eHarmony.com are the largest sites and both have a global presence. Match.com was launched in 1995 and now operates in 25 countries in more than eight languages. In 2014, Match.com launched a mobile app called Stream that uses photographs and location-based pictures. eHarmony has a stated mission to match people for long-term relationships, and was launched in 2000, but now has members in more than 150 countries. It also has a division particularly for same-sex users called Compatible Couples. eHarmony also has a mobile app version. Both of the sites above use the typical membership based upon a subscription service, but there are also a number of free sites that operate on ad revenue rather than on a subscription service, like PlentyofFish and OkCupid.

And though there are a number of general sites that do much the same thing as Match.com and eHarmony, there are also a large range of niche sites for people with specific interests. The company that owns Match.com (IAC) owns Blackpeoplemeet.com, singleparentmeet.com, and seniorpeoplemeet.com. JDate.com focuses on Jewish clientele, and Christianmingle.com is geared toward people of the Christian faith. Both sites are owned by the same company, Spark Networks. Ethnic interests can also be addressed on Amigos (for Latino/a singles); Asian People Meet (obviously, for Asians), and Shaadi (for Indian singles). One of the potentially largest markets is the baby boomer generation, those born during the period of 1946–1964, for whom about 30 percent are single, either by choice, by divorce, or by becoming a widow/widower.

There are also "dating" sites that do more than introduce people for potential romantic relationships. Some sites specialize in helping people meet others for sexual encounters, those that specialize in physical types, or even fetish sites.

Though there are all types of sites and apps available, the Internet and social networks are not the only technologies that facilitate people meeting other people. In fact, as more people use online social networks for specific reasons that involve attraction and personal characteristics, *video dating* has become an important feature of some websites and apps. *Virtual dating* is another variation in which people play out their entire relationships online. *Dating assistants* can also be used to help craft a person's digital persona to make a person more appealing to someone else.

At the time of this writing, the mobile app Tinder was getting a significant amount of press. According to social psychologist Eli Finkel, "The new paradigm is a mobile app like Tinder. You quickly browse photos on your phone, swiping to the right if the photo appeals, to the left it if doesn't. If the attraction is mutual—that is, if both of you have swiped right—you might try to set up a date for, say, five minutes later" (Finkel 2015, SR9). While some have likened Tinder to a video game rather than a dating site, Tinder calls into question the element of time; can one make an immediate decision in the few microseconds it takes to register an emotion based upon a picture?

See also: Anonymity; Cyberbullying; Identity

Further Reading

Boorstin, Julia. 2010. "The Big Business of Online Dating." CNBC.com. Accessed February 27, 2015: http://www.cnbc.com/id/35370922.

Finkel, Eli. 2015. "In Defense of Tinder." *New York Times*. February 8: SR9.

Groth, Aimee. 2011. "This Is What 'Computer Dating' Looked Like in the 1960s." Business Insider. Accessed March 1, 2015: http://www.businessinsider.com/first-online-dating-site-2011-7.

Paumgarten, Nick. 2011. "Looking for Someone." *The New Yorker.* Accessed March 2, 2015: http://www.newyorker.com/magazine/2011/07/04/looking-for-someone.

Singh, Maanvi. 2015. "Apps Can Speed the Search for Love, but Nothing Beats a Real Date." National Public Radio. Accessed March 25, 2015: http://www.npr.org/blogs/health/2015/02/12/385745267/apps-can-speed-the-search-for-love-but-nothing-beats-a-real-date.

Smith, Aaron, and Maeve Duggan. 2013. "Online Dating and Relationships." The Pew Research Center. Accessed March 25, 2015: htttp://www.pewinternet.org/2013/10/21/online-dating-relationships/.

Digg

Digg is an example of an *aggregator* website that allows users to discover, share, and recommend web content. Aggregator sites collect related items of content and display them or links to them. Aggregators are also called Rich Site Summaries or Really Simple Syndication, both descriptions are often abbreviated as RSS. Fulfilling the promise that social networks could help people discover, disseminate, and mobilize people toward more political and social awareness, Digg became an example of overcoming space and time for news and information.

Digg was started in November 2004 by Kevin Rose, Owen Byrne, Ron Gorodetzky, and Jay Adelson and is an example of how social media not only challenged emerging practices in the shift from legacy media to a new platform, but it also represents a start-up that was challenged by other emerging social networks that copied its ideas and became more successful. As Kevin Rose said of Digg's evolution, "Twitter became a major place to find out what was breaking on the Internet" (and) "Facebook became a place to share links. Social media really grew up" (Ante 2012).

As one of the original news aggregators, Digg allowed people to vote on web content and charted the trending of the popularity of the stories. In its early days, Digg received about 3.8 million visits per month. It was so successful that other sites emerged, like Reddit, Prismatic, and Google Currents. But though Digg was initially successful, the site began to lose visitors to those other sites that were more user-friendly. Many early Digg users blamed the site's problems on difficulty in posting user content.

Despite Digg's initial success, including an unsuccessful offer from Google to buy the service for $200 million, Digg was forced to adapt to changing times. The site was redesigned in 2010, but, by 2012, Digg was broken up and sold in three parts. The Digg brand, website, and technology were sold to a company called

Betaworks for what was estimated to be $500,000. Some of the staff were transferred to the *Washington Post's* online division called SocialCode. And finally, a number of the patents taken out and made successful by Digg were sold to LinkedIn for approximately $4 million.

Digg emerged in a new form in 2012 with the ability to share content with other social network platforms, like Facebook and Twitter. In 2015, it was announced that the newly repurposed Digg would introduce a video feature called Digg TV that would allow users to share videos. The feature includes a button that activates Digg Video, a collection of curated videos available to viewers.

See also: BuzzFeed

Further Reading

Ante, Spencer E. 2012. "Kevin Rose: Digg Failed Because 'Social Media Grew Up.'" *Wall Street Journal.* Accessed February 26, 2015: http://blogs.wsj.com/digits/2012/07/13/kevin-roses-exit-interview-digg-failed-because-social-media-grew-up/.

Walter, Joseph, and Spencer E. Ante. 2012. "Once a Social Media Star, Digg Sells for $500,000." *Wall Street Journal.* Accessed February 26, 2015: http://www.wsj.com/articles/SB10001424052702304373804577523181002565776.

Digital

Digital technology uses a system of binary digits in ones and zeros to electronically communicate through codes, which are mathematical structures of information. The precision of a digital wave makes it possible to compress information in a very small band of the electromagnetic spectrum to send signals wirelessly, or, if compressed into a physical object like a CD, to render an excellent sound or video quality. The smallest component of a digital wave is called a bit.

The precursor to transferring or storing digital information is called *analog* information, which reflects the use of Hertzian waves to transmit the signal. For example, an old-fashioned record player would play records that were recorded in an analog form. The needle of the machine would run through the grooves and transfer the sound to audio waves so that the information could be heard. But analog methods of information transfer are not as accurate as digital signals in terms of quality, and a copy of a record might sound like an inferior product. Digital signals, however, are smaller and more precise. A compact disc (CD) is a different product than a record and uses digital sound waves. A CD can contain more information than a record, and the quality of the sound is greatly improved. If a person were to make a copy of a CD, the sound quality would be virtually as good as the original.

As different industries have shifted to digital modes of transferring or storing information, better methods of information compression have evolved that have improved the image or sound quality of the information. Unlike analog signals, digital signals can be compressed but not lose any sound or visual quality. As a result, digital transfer of information has made streaming of all forms of media possible.

However, when different media industries that relied on analog transmission of their signals (like broadcast radio or television) switch to digital modes, consumers have to have technologies capable of receiving the digital signal. The shift from analog to digital has also resulted in a shift in the need for broadcast signals. The proliferation of mobile phones has also created a demand for more frequencies to be available for mobile platform use and has prompted the FCC to try to persuade broadcasters to sell some of their frequency distribution back to the FCC so that it can be auctioned off for additional wireless use (Ruiz 2015).

Computers and social media/social networking programs all rely on the transfer of digital information, and, therefore, the term *digital* as an adjective has been extended to describe both the method of information transfer as well as the type of technologies used. The benefits are many, in particular, digital technologies can often be produced much cheaper than analog technologies and the mode of transferring the signals can be far more effective. Digital information is also subject to what is called "Moore's Law" based on the 1965 idea by Gordon Moore, cofounder of the Intel Corporation, that a computer chip's processing speed doubles every 18 months to 2 years.

Along with the benefits of transmitting or storing digital information, there are some definite drawbacks, too. One of the most significant drawbacks is that digital information can easily be erased or destroyed. Anyone who has ever had a magnet come in contact with a magnetic stripe on a credit card knows that digital information can be easily lost or destroyed by physical means, but digital information as it is used today has a related problem—that of either being stored (and potentially misused) for a long time on sites that are not updated, or, conversely, digital information that seems to live forever in cyberspace.

Journalist Jill Lepore has written on the problem of archiving information on the Internet and the pros and cons of migration of information to the digital form. There is a facility known as the Internet Archive in California, started by Brewster Kahle, a librarian and computer scientist who also developed the "Wayback Machine" to archive early web pages for posterity. Still, despite using web crawlers to search for information, the amount of information in digital form on the Internet Archive and Wayback Machine is sometimes difficult to access because they gather information based on the date saved. And if that information is not saved, it may disappear from the web by being buried by the increasingly flowing data that pushes it to the rear of the search. As Lepore reports, "The average life of a Web page is about a hundred days" (Lepore 2015, 36).

See also: Digital; Identity; Internet; Streaming

Further Reading

Burnett, Robert, and David P. Marshall. 2003. *Web Theory: An Introduction.* London: Routledge.
Lepore, Jill. 2015. "The Cobweb: Can the Internet Be Archived?" *The New Yorker,* 89: 34–41.
Ruiz, Rebecca. 2015. "Jackpots for Local TV Stations in F.C.C. Auction of Airwaves." *New York Times.* Accessed April 28, 2015: http://www.nytimes.com/2015/04/17/technology/local-broadcasters-could-reap-billions-in-airwaves-auction.html?_r=0.

The Definition of Digital Disruption

Digital disruption is a term that describes the way digital technologies change our established ways of creating values, our social interactions, the way we do business, and the way we think. While it could be said that every form of media *disrupts* the previous ways in which we do things, digital disruption seems to occur faster than any migration to a different mode of communicating than ever before. Businesses that use digital technology are increasingly using the term *disruption* to explain how digital technology changes the economy of their industry.

Digital Divide

As digital technologies became more available to a wider range of people, the concept of who had access to them, and who does not, became known as the *digital divide.* The term encompasses technological aspects of hardware, software, and electricity, but there is a strong social component to the concept, too, with much attention going to issues of equity among people to have access to information in a world that increasingly has no geographic boundaries to restrict information flow. Though it may not be obvious at the beginning of the discussion as to how social media and social networks relate to the enormous problem of the digital divide, the problems of access, skill, and know-how still affect users. Ultimately, issues relating to the digital divide influence what people know about news, world events, and the global communication infrastructure.

Issues related to the digital divide began to emerge in the late 1950s, after World War II, with greater attention to differing levels of national development that affected both the quality of life issues within a region and the cultural, economic, and social dynamics of a world that had a very unequal information flow. At the time it was felt that telephony, print, radio, television, and film could effectively be used to bridge a digital divide that existed in terms of education, but, once the Internet and World Wide Web came along, the discourse shifted to questions of information flow and equal access to news, information, and critical health, weather, and political information that affected the lives of people who previously had no access to others outside of their geographic communities.

At first, the term was used to denote *access* to technology and discourse was focused on those countries that had more access, like the industrialized West, versus those that were considered to be less developed and without the means to buy technology or supply electricity or know-how to make it work. Access issues were always at the heart of digital divide problems, because getting technologies to people who could use them was one of the first issues of equity that emerged as digital technologies (and the Internet in general) became the focus of many studies to better understand the needs of people locally, regionally, nationally, and globally.

Access issues not only reflect the cost of technology, but the electronic infra-structure necessary to make electronic technology work. For example, many of the earliest issues of the digital divide were debated in the United Nations, where access to technology in developing countries was a significant problem. Entire courses on development communications began to appear in colleges and universities, and the role of government as well as nongovernmental agencies (NGOs) focused on the problem of Information and Communication Technol-ogy (ICTs). These early debates often dealt with how ICTs could play a role in helping a poor nation become more self-reliant, with technology applications improving health, education, and the ability of people to help themselves. A range of paradigms emerged that addressed questions of access and the digi-tal divide, all examining the relationship of human beings and the way tech-nologies (of all forms) could be used to improve lives (for a brief overview, see McPhail, 2009).

Not all issues of access and the digital divide were international in scope. Many of the discussions dealt with the problems of schools in communities where children had little or no access to computers, versus schools in wealthier com-munities where children might have their own computers or mobile phones, or have access to them at home. Socioeconomic studies of children's access to digital technologies flourished in the 1990s, and the topic became a political issue for the growth of the Internet and the Information Superhighway. During the Clinton

Administration, the U.S. Department of Commerce, National Telecommunications & Information Administration (NTIA) published a number of reports about who, in the United States had access to communications technologies and who did not. The first report, "Falling through the Net: A Survey of the 'Have Nots' in Rural and Urban America," was published in 1995, the second, "Falling through the Net II: New Data on the Digital Divide," was published in 1998, and finally, "Falling through the Net: Defining the Digital Divide" was published in 1999. The final report defined the problem of access as one of America's leading economic and civil rights issues.

Political efforts, funded projects, and communities have dealt with access problems for years, but, fundamentally, the Internet and the wealth of information available over the World Wide Web have become the major focus for contemporary discussions of the digital divide. According to the Internet World Statistics, by the second quarter of 2014, the availability of Internet connections reached: 87.7 percent of the population of North America; 72.9 percent of the population of Oceana/Australia; 70.5 percent of Europe; 52.3 percent of Latin America and the Caribbean; 48.3 percent of the Middle East; 34.7 percent of Asia; and 26.5 percent of Africa. What this means is that in total, 42.3 percent of the people of the world live in an area where the Internet was available by mid-June 2014 ("Internet Users in the World by Geographical Region" 2015). These numbers reflect how many people could connect to the Internet, if they have access to the technologies through work, school, home, or other public means (like libraries and community centers).

As the Internet spread, issues related to the digital divide became more nuanced. Conversations began to include the questions of dumping technology (outdated technology in the industrialized world being "donated" or sold to those countries that were struggling to get the technologies) and also involved issues of skill level and the dominance of a way of foisting a "system" on a country that might conflict with the country's cultural, historical, of philosophical ideas.

In a series of studies about American's ability to efficiently use the web, Eszter Hargittai wrote of what she referred to as the "second level digital divide" (Hargittai 2002). Skill, in this context, is defined as the ability to efficiently and effectively find information on the web. Hargittai's ideas are important for considering how issues of access and skill affect what people know and how they know it. Without a certain form of "information literacy," the tools people use to connect to the Internet, and the way information is presented over the World Wide Web, can be misleading and paint a false picture of reality.

Other ways of thinking about the digital divide concern issues of availability in terms of what can be used; for example, 80 percent of the websites in use are in English, leading some to call the World Wide Web, the "World White Web"

(McPhail 2009, 125). Though the number of languages available on the web have continued to grow, the problem of translation and available information in languages that can be understood remains a problem. This relates to the use value of information on the web, and calls into question how accurate information can be, and whether people can discern accuracy from what is available.

Another type of digital divide is the group of people who choose not to use information technologies. These people have been called the "new minority" (Hanson 2013), because these people have chosen not to participate in using the Internet and web. If the digital divide has traditionally included the "haves" and "have nots," the new minority are the "don't wants." For this relatively small group of people who have chosen not to have the Internet or a smartphone (or mobile phone of any kind), there is a social cost to not being connected, but they increasingly run the risk of being marginalized by government policies that require some level of connectivity. Most of them claim "they don't need" computers or mobile phones, and many resent the high cost of buying and using these technologies. But, at the same time, there may be features of life that they can't easily access if they don't have the technologies necessary. For example, many forms, including IRS forms are available online, and increasingly employers want applications filed online. The "new minority" may eventually choose to participate more fully in the information society and, certainly, public computers are available in libraries and other public buildings, but they do present a new twist on the digital divide.

See also: Privacy

Further Reading

"Falling through the Net: A Survey of the 'Have Nots' in Rural and Urban America." 1995. National Telecommunications & Information Administration, U.S. Department of Commerce. Accessed April 6, 2015: http://www.ntia.doc.gov/ntiahome/fallingthru.html.

Hanson, Jarice. 2013. "The New Minority: The Willfully Unconnected." In *The Unconnected: Social Justice, Participation, and Engagement in the Information Society*, edited by Paul M. A. Baker, Jarice Hanson, and Jeremy Hunsinger. New York: Peter Lang, 223–240.

Hargittai, Ezster. 2002. "Second Level Digital Divide: Differences in People's Online Skills." First Monday. Accessed April 1, 2015: http://www.firstmonday.org/issues/issue7_4/hargittai/.

"Internet Users in the World by Geographical Region." 2015. World Internet World Statistics. Accessed April 1, 2015: http://www.internetworldstats.com/stats.htm.

McPhail, Thomas L., ed. 2009. *Development Communication: Reframing the Role of the Media*. Malden, MA: Wiley-Blackwell, 125.

Digital Millennium Copyright Act (DMCA)

In 1998, President Bill Clinton signed the Digital Millennium Copyright Act (DMCA) into law. The act criminalizes production and dissemination of technology, devices, or services that are intended to circumvent Digital Rights Management that is related to ownership of property through traditional copyright laws and is regarded as an effort to update traditional copyright law to be more in line with the characteristics of digital distribution and the Internet. The intention of the law is to protect Internet Service Providers (ISPs) from violating copyright and shifting the burden of legal posting to the individuals or organizations that input the content onto the Internet. Therefore, material that is posted online through an ISP is not the ISP's responsibility, though the ISP must take down the information if it is notified that something that has been posted by others is a copyright violation.

The DMCA was passed so that it would monitor the changing evolution of the use of the Internet and World Wide Web. The law was initially intended to stop digital piracy, but a significant amount of criticism has revolved around the way in which consumers and legitimate businesses (inventors, scientists, etc.) have been threatened by invoking the DMCA to stifle creativity and impede new businesses from offering new products and goods for the market.

In 2010, manufacturers of DVDs who protected the content from being duplicated by using legal content scrambling systems were exempted from restricting the efforts of certain individuals who were using the material for purposes other than for profit. For example, educational uses involving the showing of DVDs in classes, and the use of DVDs for students who might be studying content were exempt. Documentary filmmakers, noncommercial videos, obsolete software and video game formats, and computer programs that used wireless handsets to connect to infrastructures were all exempted from the DMCA when it was passed. Even some literary works that were distributed in e-book format were also exempted in some forms.

Some of the challenges to the DMCA show how difficult applying traditional copyright is to a situation when the technologies involved have contributed to an ease of duplicating material. While there are many cases that test this position, two specific cases outline some of the arguments. In the 2009 case of *RealNetworks Inc. v. DVD Copy Control Association Inc.,* the DVD Copy Control Association claimed that RealNetworks, an Internet streaming company, was allowing users to copy DVDs and store them on their hard drives. Even though the DVD Copy Control Association applied antipiracy measures to the DVDs they controlled and worked with other companies to scramble content so that DVDs could not be pirated RealNetworks was working around those protective measures. The courts found in favor of the DVD Copy Control Association Inc.

See also: Copyright; Creative Commons

Further Reading

Sandoval, Greg. 2009. "RealNetworks Loses Critical Ruling in RealDVD Case." CNet. Accessed December 18, 2014: http://www.cnet.com/news/realnetworks-loses-critical -ruling-in-realdvd-case/.

Von Lohmann, Fred. 2010. "Unintended Consequences: Twelve Years under the DMCA." Electronic Frontier Foundation. Accessed December 18, 2014: https://www.eff.org/files /eff-unintended-consequences-12-years_0.pdf.

Do-It-Yourself (DIY)

Because of the wealth of information available on the Internet through the World Wide Web, the do-it-yourself (DIY) ethic has become an alternative to traditional ways of getting things done by purchasing goods from other people. In many ways, the DIY ethic has been around for a very long time, but, today, social media help many people figure out how to do things themselves through a host of online sources that might include blogs, videos (YouTube and other), discussion forums, and instructional posts. Sometimes called the "Do It Yourself Movement" or even the "Maker Movement," DIY activities can span a wide range of topics.

In the late 1960s and early 1970s when a number of technology companies were forming and experimenting with processors, microchips, and the hardware necessary to make computers viable, the "hippy" movement that was part of the counterculture rejected a number of ideas that were viewed as coming from established authorities. A strong "do it yourself" ethic began to emerge as a rejection of standardized ideas and values. At the time, Stewart Brand came out with *The Whole Earth Catalog* that provided a number of ecologically friendly tools that enabled people to create their own technologies and develop new practices. Some of the early hobbyist computer kits were featured in the catalog, and, from that time on, hobbyists—many of whom would be considered "hackers"—began experimenting with technology. A number of their efforts have resulted in today's personal computers, streaming technologies, and a host of software that often was developed through open-source modes.

Self-help and DIY topics have long been a staple of book publishing, and the idea of taking charge of one's life and doing "it" themselves is not new, but do-it-yourself projects have thrived on the Internet and World Wide Web, and having access to information online has made it much easier for people who want to create something, learn about something, or share ideas with others over social media. The economic downturn of the 1980s and the long economic recession has probably contributed to the growth of DIY industries and websites, and the scope of topics seems endless. While areas of home improvement, gardening, financial services, automotive, and beauty care have anchored the growth of the movement, many sites offer much more. For example, Etsy is a site devoted to handcrafts. Crowdfunding is a type of DIY fund-raising. The growth of 3D printing also offers another form of realizing a number of DIY projects.

See also: Creative Economy; Prosumer; 3D

Further Reading

Dawson, Ashley. 2012. "DIY Academy: Cognitive Capitalism, Humanist Scholarship, and the Digital Transformation." In *The Social Media Reader*, edited by Michael Mandiberg. New York: New York University Press, 257–274.

Markoff, John. 2005. *What the Dormouse Said: How the Sixties Counterculture Shaped the Personal Computer Industry*. London: Penguin.

Dot-Com Bubble

The number of start-up businesses active on the Internet skyrocketed during the late 1990s. In many ways, the opening of the Internet to the public and the growth of e-commerce fueled experiments, and with more people having digital technologies in the home, a great deal of speculation and experimentation occurred. Some of the companies became extremely profitable, and investors in those technologies and services that became big, became wealthy. This rapid expansion of Internet businesses came to be known as the *dot-com bubble* and is generally defined as the period between 1995 and 2000. The idea of a "bubble" reflects the stock market's interest in these new companies and the amount of money invested in the new firms, often inflating the value of the company. So many people were getting home computers and broadband connections that the potential audience looked very promising. Smartphones were not yet a part of the speculation—it took a few more years before the mobile market became strong enough to be an attractive market for speculators. The designation of "dot-com" reflected the last part of the web address of each of these Internet-based start-ups.

As we look back at the dot-com bubble today, it is possible to see how innovations and practices became a part of our current culture. Creative collaboration began to emerge as one of the key concepts of this innovative period in history, and fueled a number of collaborative models that we use today, like crowdfunding, crowdsourcing, and collective intelligence. Free models emerged to compete with those that favored traditional copyright, and we still see debates about hardware and software profitability versus free models today. Perhaps most importantly, the role of venture capital in funding creative start-ups began to influence business and economic models that have continued to support technological development in the early part of the twenty-first century.

Throughout the dot-com bubble, there was enormous speculation with computer and social networking start-up companies, many of which became highly successful, like Amazon, Apple Inc., Google Inc., Facebook, Microsoft, Netflix, and Yahoo!, to name a few. Almost all of these companies have had mergers, made acquisitions, and had a number of successes and failures, but the ones that have become leaders in their fields have forged the international flow of information and technology that makes the information society possible. The technologies and services during the dot-com bubble exploited the person-to-person networking that has made the social media revolution possible.

See also: Dot-Com Crash; E-Commerce

Further Reading

Kelleher, Kevin. 2014. "5 Lessons from Survivors of the Dotcom Crash." *Fortune.* Accessed February 26, 2015: http://fortune.com/2014/01/03/5-lessons-from-survivors-of-the-dotcom-crash/.

Dot-Com Crash

With wild speculation and a flood of start-up money from venture capitalists, the inflated dot-com boom resembled the "wild west" of speculation and Internet land-grabbing. The year 2000 was the year that the "bubble" burst. On March 11, 2000, the stock market began to lose money, and when the crash hit bottom, 75 percent of the value of the dot-com stocks had been lost. Within a month, a trillion dollars was gone and people who became overnight millionaires during the dot-com bubble, had lost most, if not all, of their investments. In a *Time* magazine article on the crash, one JP Morgan analyst was quoted saying that a number of companies "were losing between $10 and $30 million a quarter—a rate that is obviously unsustainable, and was going to end with a lot of dead sites and lost investments" (Geier

2015). While it may not be possible to accurately count the number of start-ups that failed during that period, we know that it took 15 years for the stock market to rebound to what it was on March 10, 2000.

As another monitor of the sites that were vulnerable, the Super Bowl ads of 2000 featured ads for 17 different dot-coms, but, one year later, only three were advertised (Geier 2015). While the number of sites that failed span a wide range of subjects, many people wonder whether another crash could occur. The growth of the mobile market and interest in cloud-based services (both of which began in 2013) generated interest in a new aspect of the technology sector, and the growth of jobs in app development has signaled the possibility of another bubble starting to form. When it closed at $5,056.06 on March 23, 2015, the Nasdaq Composite Index hit a new high—surpassing the old record close of $5,048.62, reached March 10, 2000, at the height of the dot-com bubble.

Some people question whether another bubble is possible, since the stock market surpassed the high point of the dot-com bubble, but most analysts feel that the speculation that fueled the earlier bubble has been tempered with a number of companies that have proven over time that they are more solid investments (Arnold 2015). Whether the current technology sector continues to grow or not, lessons learned from the dot-com bubble and dot-com crash have become standard case studies in business schools.

See also: Dot-Com Bubble; E-Commerce

Further Reading

Arnold, Chris. 2015. "15 Years after the Dot-Com Bust, a Nasdaq Record." NPR's *All Things Considered*. Accessed March 24, 2015: http://www.npr.org/blogs/thetwo-way /2015/04/23/397113284/15-years-after-the-dot-com-bust-nasdaq-closes-at-new-record.

Edwards, Jim. 2013. "Where Are They Now? The Kings of the '90s Dot-Com Bubble." Business Insider. Accessed February 26, 2015: http://www.businessinsider.com/where -are-they-now-the-kings-of-the-90s-dot-com-bubble-2013-10?op=1#ixzz3SrIyY4uD.

Geier, Ben. 2015. "What Did We Learn from the Dotcom Stock Bubble of 2000?" *Time* magazine. Accessed April 19, 2015: http://time.com/3741681/2000-dotcom-stock-bust/.

E

eBay

In 1995, a French-born Iranian-American computer programmer and entrepreneur by the name of Pierre Omidyar (1967–) developed the first online auction site called AuctionWeb. Though he had worked on different Internet start-up companies and called his own business the Echo Bay Technology Group, he envisioned Auction-Web as a free service. When he first wrote the computer code for AuctionWeb, it was simple and had only three components. Users could list items, view items, and place bids. He believed that the community that would eventually use the service would accept the responsibility for fulfilling the purchases, and that any conflicts would be worked out among the members of the community. AuctionWeb had no publicity other than Omidyar's notifying people that it existed on various free list-serves and through word of mouth. But within the first month, interest in Auction-Web caught on, resulting in one of the most successful Internet start-up companies in history.

At first, he thought of AuctionWeb as a hobby rather than a business and had no business plan or intention of making any money with the project. He did, however, think that the site would be a good place for people who had similar interests to engage in a type of online community. He ran AuctionWeb off of the website he had established for his own business ventures, but then registered the name eBay. com to focus on the AuctionWeb component of the business. At the time, anyone who wanted to use the site would also have to negotiate Omidyar's other business ventures to get to AuctionWeb. With no warehouse, business office, inventory, or shipping department, eBay was a totally virtual company.

As an experiment, Omidyar decided to sell a laser pointer that no longer worked. His reasoning was that he would at least be able to see how many people read about it, and whether something this obscure would interest those who fre-quented AuctionWeb. He listed it as "Broken Laser Pointer" and wrote that the pointer was originally purchased for $30. During the second week, someone bid

$3, and then, another person raised a bid to $4. Finally, within two weeks, the bidding reached $14 and the bid was closed. Someone had just paid $14 for a broken laser pointer. At that point, Omidyar realized he was onto something big.

By 1996, the web server company supporting Omidyar's site was getting so much traffic it started charging Omidyar a fee to support the website. This necessitated charging users of the site a small percentage of the cost of their transaction. Over the years, different payment models have evolved.

At first, the typical eBay user was interested in collectibles or antiques, and, by 1997, these artifacts made up almost 80 percent of AuctionWeb's profits, and the name was formally changed to eBay. The original site that was broken down into areas defined as "antiques and collectibles," "Automotive," "books and comics," "consumer electronics," and "miscellaneous," began to have subheadings specializing on collectibles like "Beanie Babies" (a small, stuffed toy), "Barbie collectibles," and "Star Trek collectibles." eBay began to become a place where collectors could connect with other collectors, and new categories began to emerge on a weekly basis.

eBay's success attracted attention, and, in 1997, Benchmark Capital invested $6.7 million in the company. A year later, Meg Whitman was hired as the new eBay president and CEO, and, in the same year, the company went public. Under Whitman's leadership, eBay grew and began acquiring a number of companies that helped solidify its profit margins. When Whitman resigned to enter politics, she left a larger, fiscally more stable company. In her years as CEO, eBay grew from a $4 million to an $8 billion company, and the number of employees grew from 30 to 15,000. Since 2008, the CEO of eBay has been John Donahoe, who previously spent 20 years in the venture capital consultancy group, Bain & Company. Under Donahoe, the acquisitions have continued and the strength of the company has grown.

Among the many high-profile acquisitions made by eBay was the 2002 purchase of PayPal, the online payment system. eBay also acquired Skype, the online communications application in 2005 and expanded its customer base to more than 480 million registered users worldwide. In 2009, eBay sold a majority of their ownership (65%) in Skype, and, in May 2011, Skype was purchased by Microsoft for $8.5 billion (Thorpe 2015).

eBay now operates in over 30 countries. It still serves individuals who sell items to other individuals, but it also facilitates shopping services from major retailers direct to stores as well as individuals. It also facilitates online ticket event trading through StubHub and online money transfers through PayPal, and it has its own classified advertising service. In 2014, eBay announced that it would split eBay and PayPal into two different companies by the end of 2015.

The reason given for separating the two companies was that the changing landscape in both commerce and payment systems had created too many problems for effective management. While there is great speculation about whether eBay and

PayPal each, as separate entities, could be acquired by other leading Internet and retail companies, little is known at this time about what direction the companies may take.

While eBay may be one of the most successful start-up Internet companies to have evolved, the business has been controversial. Many people feel that eBay is the type of Internet company that contributed to the demise of classified advertising that supported local newspapers and radio stations. Difficult cases related to consumer fraud have also occasionally hurt the company's reputation and have made some people skittish about using online pay services for funds transfer. Some people have also complained that eBay's requirement that buyers and sellers use PayPal is unethical and at least three major antitrust actions have been taken by people who feel that the link between the two companies restricts their own businesses and trading opportunities.

See also: Cybercurrency; PayPal

Further Reading

Cohen, Adam. 2002. *The Perfect Store: Inside eBay.* Boston: Little, Brown and Co.
Thorpe, Devin. 2015. "Omidyar Network Pairs Grants with Investments to Solve Problems." *Forbes.* Accessed February 24, 2015: http://www.forbes.com/sites/devinthorpe/2015/01/22/omidyar-network-pairs-grants-with-investments-to-solve-problems/.

E-Books (See E-Publishing)

E-Cards (See E-Publishing)

E-Commerce

The technologies that facilitated the growth of the information society evolved over decades. The work of hobbyists, electrical engineers, computer scientists, and mathematicians all contributed to the development of computers and the systems we use to connect computers. Much of the funding for these developments came from governments, corporations, and research centers that all understood the value of creating technologies and distribution systems that would improve collaboration and the exchange of information. By the time the Internet was made available to the general public, entrepreneurs had figured out how to capitalize on this type of communication for business purposes, too, and so e-commerce grew as more individuals obtained personal computers and both the Internet and the World Wide Web diffused through society.

From 1993 to 2000, the years building to the dot-com bubble, e-commerce began to thrive. Venture capitalists often funded some of the most promising projects and legacy companies explored online ventures. At the same time, the Internet allowed even smaller companies to launch ideas with very little capital at hand. Some of the start-ups in that period became successful, even though many start-ups failed in the dot-com crash. Some of the survivors became major economic powers, like Google, Amazon, and Pay Pal (to name only a few). The successful companies capitalized on the Internet's ability to easily—and inexpensively—connect buyers and sellers around the world. The real impact of e-commerce has been the shift from buying and selling in physical stores to buying and selling online, along with the host of benefits and problems that come from this shift in shopping and commercial exchange of products and goods.

New economic models have emerged that challenge some of the traditional industries and their business models, most of which involve two factors: a sense of place (for the retailer or sponsor) and a shift from the advertising models that traditionally supported so many industries to transactions that take place electronically. Among emerging models are the "free" model (such as that used when a company gives away a product or service), the agency model (often used by publishers to assess the purchase price of electronic, versus physical, objects, like books), sharing economy (such as that in which crowdsourcing or crowdfunding takes place), and dynamic pricing (the adjustment of price according to demand, such as in paying more at peak times of use).

But perhaps one of the most striking features of e-commerce is the ubiquity of the retail experience. As Martin Lindstrom, an internationally renowned marketing professional has written, "The online onslaught is obliging the retail industry to redefine itself: service, delivery, customer and supplier relations, infrastructure and distribution systems and all the attitudes and assumptions that mould (sic) retail culture are under review. . . . Online shopping is available twenty-four hours a day, seven days a week, and this forces retail equivalents to be similarly accessible to the consumer" (Lindstrom 2002, 49).

Organizationally, the social shifts that occur in tandem with e-commerce have been given names like the *creative economy*, *sharable culture*, and *do-it-yourself* movement. Most of these organizational and economic engines offer alternatives to the economic models generated during the industrial revolution because they offer alternatives to the supply/demand models of the twentieth century. Without the Internet and World Wide Web, these models would not be allowed to exist side-by-side with the more traditional economic models. So in e-commerce, it is easy to see how the twentieth century ideas of business and commerce have evolved, and sometimes clash with the newer models of the twenty-first century. Personal computers, the Internet, and the World Wide Web are the technologies that have made new modes of production and consumption possible.

Don Tapscott, chairman of the Alliance for Converging Technologies, and his coauthor Anthony D. Williams have written that the big shift in business models has been the overthrow of the traditional *vertical integration* model in favor of the *horizontal integration* model that allows online companies to create business relationships with other companies that focus on related industries. For example, they cite the decision of American Airlines to start an online company called Sabre Holdings to manage reservations for the airline company. Sabre eventually developed Travelocity, which became a leader in related (horizontally integrated) travel services (Tapscott and Williams 2006, 125). This new type of business model was in stark contrast to the vertically integrated company, as represented by major companies that often had holdings related to subsidiaries in which the supply chain of products or goods fed the industry itself.

The benefits of online stores, marketplaces, and auction sites reach beyond geographic limitations of traditional stores. Before the Internet, people typically purchased largely from local stores typically referred to as "brick-and-mortar stores" that controlled inventory by selling popular items, discounting those that were less popular, and discontinuing products that did not result in store profit. Specialty items—known as niche products—could not attract enough buyers in a particular region to be sold at a profit, but when online purchases became possible over the Internet, a number of smaller products sold to a larger number of people became known as the economic model called the long tail (Anderson 2006). Using this model reduced the cost to the online retailer of having a brick-and-mortar store and enabled stock to be housed in inexpensive warehouses and delivered directly to the consumer through the mail. This fact enabled online retailers, such as Amazon.com and Apple's iTunes Store, to make great profits by selling a wide range of niche products.

Websites that sell digital media, such as music, can offer free samples of content which makes it easier for customers to discover niche works. In Apple's rollout of the new iPhone, the group U2's new album was included free—whether the consumer wanted it or not, actually spurring controversy about the power of Apple to control media content. Surprisingly, many consumers complained to Apple about including U2's music.

Some traditional stores and media companies have declined during the Internet era. In some cases, online upstarts have drawn away their business. For example, the online movie rental service Netflix was largely to blame for the decline of traditional video rental stores. Craigslist displaced many classified advertisement sections. Such sections had served as a mainstay of revenue for traditional local newspapers.

In e-commerce, the website becomes the "store" for all products. Some large companies—notably Amazon.com Inc.—exist entirely as online retailers. Other sites connect sellers with potential buyers. For example, eBay is a popular auction website. Craigslist is a nonprofit site that enables people to post classified advertisements for free.

Paying for goods can take a number of methods, including the traditional purchasing of items online with a credit card. Some services, such as PayPal, enable people to make payments from online accounts. Traditional banks also run websites on which people can pay bills and manage their accounts, and banking services have even begun to shift to online activity, with some banks specializing in online functions alone. Many businesses, such as utility services and credit card companies, offer an option called online bill pay. With online bill pay, customers can arrange to pay their bills electronically.

Paying for goods in e-commerce is technically easy, but the availability of credit card information and personal identification information (like passwords and bank routing numbers) has resulted in the growth of cybercrime. The use of cybercurrency may be one way to help curb the current rise in cybercrime related to unauthorized access to e-commerce and payment systems, but the early experiments with this type of virtual currency have not yet proven to be foolproof.

One of the current problems for e-currency's adoption of electronic wallets, or the use of alternative cash (like Bitcoin) is that the economic model of paying for goods is an old one. Merchants are charged for the swipe feature of major credit cards and must pay approximately 3 percent of the transaction to the credit card company. A significant amount of fraud can take place in these transactions because of bogus credit cards, card theft, and number theft.

In 2015, banks in the United States joined those in many other countries that embed computer chips in credit cards for security purposes. This requires that merchants invest in new card readers in brick-and-mortar stores, but the shift to a more secure payment system is easy to program for online purchases in e-commerce. Some Internet services employ cybercurrency that might possibly be safer from cybercriminals when making online transactions, but cybercurrency tends to be unstable from a value-standpoint, though efforts are being made worldwide to stabilize some of the current and future virtual currencies.

E-commerce has grown steadily throughout the twenty-first century. In 2014, U.S. e-retail sales surpassed $300 billion first time, with a posting of $304.91 billion. Industry estimates predict that by 2018, e-commerce will result in a 57.4 percent growth for an estimated $414 billion market (Enright 2015). The majority of the expected sales traffic will be built on the growth of the mobile market.

See also: Advertising; Cybercrime; Cybercurrency; Cyber Monday; Expedia; Legacy Media; Niche Marketing

Further Reading

Anderson, Chris. 2006. *The Long Tail: Why the Future of Business Is Selling Less of More.* New York: Hyperion.

Enright, Allison. 2015. "U.S. Annual E-Retail Sales Surpass $300 Billion for the First Time." Internet Retailer. Accessed April 30, 2015: https://www.internetretailer.com/2015 /02/17/us-annual-e-retail-sales-surpass-300-billion-first-time.

Lindstrom, Martin. 2002. *Clicks, Bricks & Brands*, rev. ed. South Yarra Victoria, Australia: Kogan Page, 49.

Tapscott, Don, and Anthony D. Williams. 2006. *Wikinomics: How Mass Collaboration Changes Everything.* New York: Penguin, 125.

"Tech Firms Chip Away at Credit Cards' Share of Transactions." NPR's *Morning Edition.* Accessed October 29, 2014: http://www.npr.org/2014/10/02/353177261/tech-firms -chip-away-at-credit-cards-share-of-transactions.

E-Currency (see Cybercurrency)

Electronic Communications Privacy Act (ECPA)

Though the Internet was originally intended to be free of censorship, problems related to personal or private information have always muddied the water for understanding what type of information can be put and stored online, and what cannot. The emergence of hackers and hacktivists, the unauthorized distribution of government secrets by the group Anonymous, information leaked by Edward Snowden, and cyberterrorism have brought contemporary digital reality into conflict with some of the laws that were previously written to protect electronic communications. Furthermore, law enforcement agencies that could benefit from the large amount of data held by major firms, like Google, are in a quandary about how they might get access to personal data without violating the ECPA.

In 1986, the U.S. Congress enacted the Electronic Communications Privacy Act to extend restrictions on wire taps for phone calls to the transmission of information over the Internet to a computer. The act was written as an amendment to the Omnibus Crime Control and Safe Streets Act of 1968 (also called the Wiretap Statute), Title III. The act and amendment were intended to restrict the government from accessing private electronic communications. This act, which received little attention at the time it was enacted, meant that the government could not tap into people's telephone calls without a specific warrant. While it favored the available technology of the time that was predominantly wired telephony, it soon became the component of communications law that generated a significant amount of controversy.

After the enactment of the Patriot Act, quickly signed into law after the events of 9/11 in 2001, the ECPA was amended. In subsequent reauthorization of the Patriot Act, the ECPA was extended. The ECPA generally protects any type of electronic communications while in transit (Title I), but also deals with the storage of information (Title II). The addition of Title III dealt with any technologies that would intercept electronic communications, such as circuits, pens, addresses, or other forms that provided gateways between the transmissions of data, unless court orders were filed.

But as digital information became easier to transmit and the U.S. government became concerned that government secrets as well as customer data was being hacked questions began to arise as to whether the ECPA was adequate for contemporary purposes. The concerns were not just leveled by government leaders. Many Internet companies and consumer advocates say the ECPA, which was enacted in 1986 before cellphone and e-mail use was widespread and before social networking was possible, is now outdated. Susan Freiwald, an expert in electronic surveillance law, has said; "Some people think Congress did a pretty good job in 1986 seeing the future, but that was before the World Wide Web" and "The law can't be expected to keep up without amendments" (Helft and Millerjan 2011).

Major personal information firms and search engines—as well as social networks—have been asked to comply with law enforcement officials who have asked to look at their storage of personal information about people. In 2007, Verizon told Congress that it received about 90,000 requests a year, and, in 2009, Facebook told a *Newsweek* reporter that subpoenas and other orders were coming to the company from law enforcement officials the rate of about 10 to 20 a day.

See also: Censorship; Data Mining; Privacy; WikiLeaks

Further Reading

Helft, Miguel, and Claire Cain Millerjan. 2011. "1986 Privacy Law Is Outrun by the Web." *New York Times*. Accessed March 30, 2015: http://www.nytimes.com/2011/01/10/technology/10privacy.html?hp&_r=0.

E-Mail

In the evolving history of social media it is sometimes difficult to pinpoint exactly when peoples' behaviors and communication patterns changed. But when it comes to e-mail, there is general agreement that e-mail revolutionized the way people communicate, and it did so rapidly. Even though e-mail is very much a part of our culture today and has spread to every corner of the globe where digital technologies exist, some people have foregone e-mail to opt for newer ways of communicating over social media. Still, every new form of text-based communication owes a debt to the development of e-mail that allowed for instant connection to people over the Internet.

Electronic mail is a message sent from one computer or mobile device to another using special addresses that can pass over an Internet Service Provider (ISP). Both wired and wireless forms of communication can be seamlessly processed. A message can consist of text only or text and graphics, or it may contain attached additional files containing text, illustrations, sound clips, or moving images. The first e-mail message was reputedly sent in 1971 as Ray Tomlinson, an ARPANET employee experimenting with the form. That message sent was also received by Tomlinson, because there were few computers that were set up to handle the transfer of messages until his protocol became standard. For many businesspeople, the BlackBerry introduced short e-mail forms of communication that contributed to the growth of e-mail as an instantaneous method of sending or responding to other e-mail messages.

When e-mail first became available, it was typical for a person to have to concentrate to think about how to use the system, but, very soon, sending an e-mail became easier than sending traditional mail (also called snail mail because of its slow speed) through the Post Office. E-mail addresses serve the same function that a street address does for traditional mail delivery. Individuals obtain e-mail addresses from ISPs or online services. These businesses also supply the computer software needed to compose, send, receive, and read e-mail, and route customers' e-mail messages to the intended recipient. Electronic mailboxes store delivered e-mail on networked computers or mobile devices. To read a message, a user opens the file attached to his or her address. The user can respond to the message immediately through the texting feature of the computer or mobile device.

The ability for people to build large mailing lists of the electronic addresses of their friends and business associates was one of the draws for many to participate in social networking, since most e-mail systems allow a user to send the same message to any number of addresses at one time. When people are operating their e-mail through a service that allows them to communicate with others in real time, it may be called Instant Messaging (IM, or IMing), but occasionally people make a mistake and send a message intended for one person to their entire list of addresses—sometimes with embarrassing consequences.

As e-mail became more widely used, many companies began to send unsolicited e-mail messages to long lists of users. Many of these messages became known as *spam*. Most spam consists of advertisements that direct users to an Internet site where they may purchase a product or service. ISPs and online services began seeking ways to reduce the amount of spam sent to their customers. Processing a large volume of messages sent by "spammers" slows the servers (computers that distribute information) at these companies and an increase in spam can result in slower service for subscribers as well as create a need to delete the unwanted "junk mail."

Over the years, who uses e-mail, and for what purposes, has changed. The form is still used in businesses and for official communications within industry and governments (the United States and many others) but many people in younger generations consider e-mail to be the type of communication you use with your older relatives and with teachers. Instead, the texting features of smartphones have taken over as the primary form of communication for many people who rely on their mobile phones as the dominant personal technology. But for people who are in the age group called "millennials" and those who are younger, e-mail may seem to feel like a dinosaur—dead and decomposed. Communicating over social networks and social media may seem like a more efficient and more contemporary way of sending messages, but each has a technological bias for how the message is sent and received.

But for many, e-mail is the cheapest form of communication available. As Alexis C. Madrigal wrote in the *Atlantic Monthly*, "You can't kill email! It's the cockroach of the Internet, and I mean that as a compliment. This resilience is a good thing" (Madrigal 2014a). He then enumerated the ways in which e-mail contributed to the way we accepted the new form. According to Madrigal, e-mail can be a newsfeed; it can represent one's passport and identity; and it has been the primary means of direct social communication on the Internet. "Email is actually a tremendous, decentralized, open platform on which new, innovative things can and have been built. In that way, email represents a different model from the closed ecosystems we see proliferating across our computers and devices" (Madrigal 2014a).

Even though e-mail is quick, inexpensive, and ubiquitous—especially in business—it is not always the most effective way to communicate. Not only do people tend to read e-mail messages quickly, but, in their haste to respond, they often respond incompletely, or in a misleading way. A typical complaint is that a person might ask three questions, but get an answer to only one, or a cryptic comment that doesn't really answer the message at all. For example, a message that is sent as "Do you want to go to the movies tonight? Which one? And should we ask Sarah to join us?" can elicit an answer of "Sure," which leaves a fair amount of ambiguity as to which part of the question is being answered.

E-mail is also often misread, or misunderstood. Researchers Justin Kruger, Nicholas Epley, Jason Parker and Zhi-Wen Ng have studied the way people communicate over e-mail and have found that the lack of gestures, vocal emphasis or intonation, or emotion can mislead the recipient of a messages (Kruger, Epley, Parker, and Ng 2005, 296–297). The lack of social cues can lead a message to backfire, creating confusion or a misconception rather than facilitating communication. For this reason, humor doesn't always translate well over e-mail.

But e-mail for people who use it, especially in business, can be a major source of information overload as people struggle to keep up with the rate of incoming messages. Eve Tahmincioglu, a writer for MSNBC, reported that the number of e-mails sent in 2010 totaled about 294 billion a day, compared to 50 billion in 2009. Quoting workplace productivity expert Marsha Egan, she wrote: "We are more wired than ever before, and as a result need to be more mindful of managing email or it will end up managing us" (Tahmincioglu 2011). This type of information overload often results in feelings of being overwhelmed and can result in messages that are "lost" only because as soon as another message comes in, the importance of the last message recedes.

James Fallows, writing in the *Atlantic Monthly*, reminds us that there is hope for those who feel that information overload is encroaching on their lives. He writes that even though e-mail has become indispensable, new filtering systems may help control the numbers. The spread of anticipatory intelligence, or the user-friendliness of technology, will increasingly become more transparent, causing us less stress for using systems, and greater advantages by their seemless nature. He also has written that we are on the threshold of better ways of getting information and dealing with it, and that the future is likely to have more intuitive technologies, because the systems are being improved upon (Fallows 2014, 30–32).

So with different generations having preferred forms of communication and a variety of platforms from which to choose, what is the future of e-mail? According to the Radicati Group, a market research firm, the total number of e-mail accounts worldwide is expected to grow to over 4.9 billion accounts by 2017, and, even though consumer accounts may not grow as fast as business accounts, the use of social networks for e-mail will likely grow from about 3.2 billion accounts in 2013 to over 4.8 billion by the end of 2017 (Radicati and Levenstein 2013).

See also: BlackBerry; E-Publishing; Mobile Phone; Spam; Texting

Further Reading

Fallows, James. 2014. "How You'll Get Organized." *Atlantic Monthly,* 314: 30–32.

Kruger, Justin, Nicholas Epley, Jason Parker, and Zhi-Wen Ng. 2005. "Egocentrism Over E-mail: Can We Communicate as Well as We Think?" *Journal of Personality and Social Psychology,* 89: 925–936.

Madrigal, Alexis C. 2014a. "Email Is Still the Best Thing on the Internet." *Atlantic Monthly,* August 14, 2014. Accessed April 30, 2015: http://www.theatlantic.com/technology/archive /2014/08/why-email-will-never-die/375973/.

Radicati, Sara, and Justin Levenstein. 2013. "Email Statistics Report, 2013–2017." The Radicati Group Inc. Accessed April 30, 2015: http://www.radicati.com/wp/wp-content /uploads/2013/04/Email-Statistics-Report-2013-2017-Executive-Summary.pdf.

Tahmincioglu, Eve. 2011. "It's Time to Deal with That Overflowing Inbox." MSNBC. Accessed January 29, 2015: http://www.nbcnews.com/id/41135478/ns/business-personal _finance/t/its-time-deal-overflowing-inbox/#.VFVFnvnF-So.

You Should Know

From Peter Shankman:

> You've got to be able to communicate in the appropriate form, and know the power of using the right words to get your message across. I received a letter from a young woman at Harvard who wrote, "I'd really like to come to New York and work 4U." I wrote back, "2 bad. U don't know how to write a real letter. You'll never work for me."

Peter Shankman is a social media entrepreneur, marketer, investor, blogger, and "adventurist." His most recent book is *Zombie Loyalists: Using Great Service to Create Rabid Fans.*

E-Magazines (See E-Publishing)

E-Newspapers (See E-Publishing)

E-Publishing

Before it became possible to post electronic text to the Internet or use computers to compose and design web pages, the term *publishing* was almost exclusively used to refer to the publishing industries and companies that specialized in turning the printed word into a book, newspaper, or magazine. This generally involved the skill and techniques of editors, copyeditors, proofreaders, and printers (meaning people in the printing trade). After the development of software that allowed people to compose work at their computer and post it on the Internet, the term *publishing* began to refer to self-posted works, too. So if someone *publishes* creative content on the Internet that act of posting text, graphics, music, video, or film can be referred to as *e-publishing* content.

Blogs and podcasts are often referred to as published works on the web, and new laws and policies have been developed to protect the rights of the person publishing that type of content. Therefore, the entire process and history of publishing, once transferred to electronic form, can now involve the legacy industries related to primarily text-based content, and self-published content. This move to *do-it-yourself* methods of creating and disseminating content has radically changed the business models of legacy companies and has brought about a number of challenges to ideas of traditional copyright, marketing, advertising, and distribution. The shift from legacy media to more current forms of e-publishing will constitute the focus of this entry. It should be noted, however, that each industry mentioned in this entry—books, scholarly publishing, magazines, newspapers, and greeting cards—all are subjects so vast that volumes have been written about the way each industry has responded to the migration to electronic platforms. What can be provided here is only a snapshot of each component of those large industries.

Compared to legacy forms of printed materials, electronic text-based forms of written materials are faster to produce, are easier to distribute, and can be updated quickly and inexpensively. In many ways, the shift from traditional forms of publishing to e-publishing has upset legacy industries radically—perhaps even more dramatically than the shift of the recording industry from records and CDs to streaming technology. And, since recorded music and e-publishing have changed already, both suggest ways we can expect to see other media forms, like film and television, change in the future.

One of the first shifts to e-publishing began through what was known as *desktop publishing* in the early 1980s, as computer manufacturers developed a series of software programs and technologies that allowed businesses and individuals to compose text on typewriters or computers, control fonts, layout, and design, and then print with the use of desktop printers. When the Apple Laser Writer emerged in 1985, the printed copy could not only look as though it were professionally printed by a printing company, but the quality of the text allowed the original copy to be photocopied many times and still remain of high quality. Later the same year PageMaker software was introduced by a company called Aldus for use in Apple computers, and, by 1987, PageMaker was made compatible with Windows programs. In 1994, Aldus and PageMaker were acquired by Adobe Systems.

Since that time there have been many improvements in new desktop publishing/e-publishing software and technology. Low-cost digitization technology allows traditional publishers or self-publishers to upload digital text directly from a computer for downloading elsewhere. Forms of e-publishing can even take place over mobile apps. A number of economic models have emerged to deal with this shift for anything from a personal letter to the written novel, and often the major controversy around e-publishing has to do with the loss of jobs in legacy industries and the very important questions concerning who is paid (or not) for their labor. For example, can an author publish a book without expecting to be paid compensation for the sale of the book? Can publishers who often sign authors to contracts afford to develop new talent, edit, produce the book, and market the book without any expectation of remuneration? Does the legal authority of copyright extend to those who self-publish?

In each case, legacy industries have struggled in different ways to maintain their operations, even if it means changing the way they do business. Because of the international nature of literature and the sale of books, there have been five dominant publishers of traditional (paper) books globally: Hachette, HarperCollins,

Macmillan, Penguin Random House, and Simon & Schuster. The same publishers have been active in the area of consumer e-books, but a number of newer enterprises have been introduced by online companies. Amazon's self-publishing site allows people to post their own creations online to be sold in electronic form that can be printed or distributed in e-form or in audio. Google Play has a self-publishing portal as does Yahoo! and Project Gutenberg, and many companies have been formed to help facilitate self-publishing. In each of these cases, the royalties paid to authors who self-publish are stated up front, and generally result in a 50–70 percent profit for the person who authors original work, while the rest of the cost of the product goes to any services in formatting or distributing the e-book.

Because so many types of e-publishing endeavors have affected major media industries, different legacy companies have adopted different economic and business models. A representative sample of them follows.

E-Books

Electronic books change the traditional models of the publishing industry, and a number of socioeconomic practices that have influenced everyone involved in the writing, manufacturing, distributing, and sales of books. Some bookstores have already gone out of business because of a shift in the way books are bought (whether physical books or e-books) and changing consumer habits. For example, a nationwide U.S. chain of superstores called Borders, which also had a subsidiary called Waldenbooks, closed in 2008. But the stores that have fared the worst are the independent bookstores, and what has commonly been referred to as "mom and pop bookstores." Like the independent or "mom and pop record stores," the loss of the smaller, more intimate bookstores made it more difficult for people to leaf through books and make decisions about what to buy from the categories of books sold in those stores.

One of the first experiments in creating a digital novella occurred with Stephen King's release of his 66-page story, *Riding the Bullet* in 2000. The digital "book" was sold for $2.50. Within the first 24 hours, the novella was downloaded 400,000 times, and by the end of the first two weeks, it had been downloaded 600,000 times (Thompson 2012, 314). This experience drove publishers of traditional books toward looking for new ways to distribute their book lists, but because there were competing ways of producing digital product and downloading it, the technology was not yet ready for mass distribution of digital text. What eventually drove the market was the development of e-readers, which did not catch on in the United States until 2007.

Though there are now a number of e-readers on the market, the technology has been more-or-less standardized to allow for a reliable download of digital content on each of the competing e-readers. Of course, e-print can be read on any electronic technology with a screen, like a computer or smartphone screen or tablet, but the portability factor of the technology and the ease of reading the text have propelled traditional publishers to look at e-print as an emerging market. What makes e-books more economical than a physical book is the ease of creating a digital copy, downloading it, and making it more portable on an e-reader, tablet, or smartphone. Many people miss the physical aspects of the traditional book, like the feel of the paper, the weight of the book, and the experience of the printed page. Additionally, it is much easier to share a physical book than an e-book (an aspect that libraries are concerned about), and a physical book does not require batteries!

One of the leaders in the distribution of e-books has been Amazon, a company that not only started business as an online bookstore, but has continued to support the e-book market through the development and marketing of the Kindle reader. Though Sony had released an e-reader in 2006, Amazon's Kindle, released in 2007, was sleek, attractive, and used e-ink technology rather than having the text backlit, the technological standard used by earlier e-readers. Within the first year of the Kindle's release (between 2007 and 2008), the number of e-books sold increased by 400 times (Thompson 2012, 318). By 2015, Amazon controlled about half of the distribution of popular books in the United States.

According to the Pew Research Center, e-book reading has been steadily increasing in the United States. In 2014, 28 percent of the adults had read an e-book, compared to 23 percent reporting the same behavior only a year prior. This increase was related to the increase of e-readers or tablets owned by 50 percent of American adults in 2014 (Pew Research Center 2013).

With the technology becoming more standardized and more e-readers and portable alternatives to books (like smartphones and tablets) becoming more popular, a part of the shifting business model of traditional publishers began to crumble. Until 2008, every publisher was establishing its own pricing models on e-books, and some start-ups, like Project Gutenberg, described below, began to furnish books for free. Amazon, which sold the Kindle for $399 when it was first launched, started to charge a flat rate of $9.99 for all *New York Times* bestsellers and new releases, which was a significant discount from the cost of a physical book sold at a bookstore for about $25. Amazon's reasoning was that like the model used by Apple and iTunes, the sale of the book (or in iTunes's case—music) was subsidized by the high cost of the e-reader. Assuming enough devices would be sold, Amazon could then establish itself as a dominant force in the marketing of e-print.

Traditional publishers began to be concerned about how this new economic model might evolve, and confusion over pricing continued over the next few years. What brought the controversy to a head was Apple's 2009 conversations with big publishers to develop content for what they were calling iBooks, an e-bookstore that would compete with Amazon, but would focus on the iPad reading experience (the Apple iPad was going to be launched in April 2010). Apple wanted to use the *agency model* that they used for iTunes and music, which would place the retailer in the position of taking a 30 percent commission on sales, and the retailer (in this case, Apple) would make a significant profit on the sale of an e-book as they acted as intermediary between the publisher and the consumer. What resulted, however, was a concerted effort of publishers to stop this process. Amazon retaliated by removing the buttons to purchase the books published by those companies that wanted greater control over the pricing system, making it impossible for books by some publishers to be purchased through Amazon, either in e-book or physical book form.

By 2010, Hachette, HarperCollins, Simon & Schuster, and Penguin had all adopted the agency model, but they continued to raise concerns about Amazon's practices that discriminated against publishers that would not be quiet and accept Amazon's pricing system. The following year, Random House adopted it, too, but what resulted was a major battle over the costs of e-books and the amount publishers would make in the evolving process of the e-book market.

In 2014, Amazon and Hachette engaged in a public dispute over the control of the cost of e-books that made publishers and distributors wary. Hachette's position was that by keeping the cost of e-book products on the popular market at $9.99, the publishers and authors were losing money. The publishers were joined by a list of about 1,500 authors who felt their royalties were being limited by the agency model, and The Authors Guild met with the U.S. Justice Department to investigate Amazon's business practices. The resolution to the problem was widely regarded as a "no win" situation for both the group of publishers led by Hachette, and Amazon, as each made concessions on the future pricing of e-books with concern to discounted titles. The end result was a wider range of prices that were tied more closely to the costs of publishing both physical and e-books, but protected the publishers and authors for the efforts toward their craft. Amazon responded by agreeing to continue to carry the works of publishers and not remove those purchase buttons from its service.

There have been a number of attempts to digitize books for a number of reasons. One of the largest projects so far is Project Gutenberg founded in 1971 by Michael S. Hart. When he began the project Hart was a student at the University of Illinois. He gained access to a mainframe computer and planned to digitize 10,000 of the books most consulted through the library, available to the public at little or no cost. The first document he digitized was the Declaration of Independence, and the majority of the books in the Project Gutenberg collection are those that have been in the public domain (i.e., not protected by copyright). By February 2015, Project Gutenberg had a collection of over 48,200 items.

Scholarly Books and Open Source Models

While commercial books still make up the greatest portion of the e-book market, academic and scholarly books also have migrated to a variety of forms including the traditional print book, to online journals and textbooks. In many ways digital publishing lends itself well to those subjects that change rapidly, but the economic models have changed more than just the publishing and marketing of books, they have influenced the ideas of intellectual property and the credibility of the author who writes for an electronic platform. And when it comes to textbooks, the idea of a digital textbook that vanishes once the course is over changes the way students relate to information and value its longevity.

In writing about university presses where much of the academic and scholarly writing has traditionally been centered, Ashley Dawson notes that scholarly publishing has become a "Darwinian world of frenetic competition and commodification" (Dawson 2012, 256). This means that the way a scholarly book is put together and what social capital it has for the author is rapidly changing. While once, a scholar would conduct research, write about it, and have editors, copyeditors, and outside jurors read the manuscript to verify facts, improve the language, and question any lapses or propositions, online scholarly publishing has become a business in which sometimes authors pay to have their work published online in books or journals.

Traditionally, the "publish or perish" form of evaluating a scholar's intellectual productivity was one of the major forms of measuring that person's commitment to scholarship and the academy. Tenure and promotion at research universities used the metrics of publication to judge whether a person's written work was valued by others. Today, however, many online journals have become mercenary in their quest to have academics and budding academics pay to have their scholarly manuscripts published online. These journals are often heavily scrutinized for their business models and sometimes dismissed by personnel committees evaluating a person for tenure or promotions, but the problem of publishing as a measure of scholarly importance is heavily debated in the academy.

Some university presses have moved to a more open source model in which the scholar can submit academic manuscripts, but then expects no payment for the production of a book. When it comes to textbooks, use of this model means that sometimes years of scholarly work results in no compensation for the author. Or, alternatively, it suggests a new model for collaboration and a more timely distribution of information that opens the topics up for discussion. Many academics prefer this model, but it still causes problems for the traditional measurement of academic intellectual output beyond the institution.

Electronic textbooks, though, are another matter. As more students have digital technologies that allow them to read academic work, e-publishing for classroom-related products can be quite enticing. Again, the author may not receive the same type of compensation they would have if they published a traditional paper textbook, but it is much easier to update information and provide links to other databases that can help a student navigate information on a variety of platforms. The trade-off, of course, is that when the digital copy of the textbook "disappears" (actually, access expires at the end of a term), students can't go back to that same source to reread information or catch up on what they hoped to read during the semester.

Magazines

From the early days of posting content online, a number of magazines have explored ways to monetize their products electronically. As was the case with newspapers, the use of paywalls were originally considered to be a way that magazine publishers could capitalize on electronic delivery and reduce the cost of printing, mailing, or distributing printed copies of their content.

The big change in the magazine industry has really revolved around the loss of general interest magazines that were a staple of American culture in the 1930s through 1950s. Since the start of the 1960s, the public's interest in general interest magazines has waned while the popularity of niche magazines has proliferated. A good number of those niche magazines have migrated exclusively to electronic platforms while others still produce print versions and often vary the content a bit when they publish online.

Consumer magazines often have maintained print versions more than trade magazines, but a good measurement of whether a magazine can publish in different formats has to do with the amount of advertising it carries, and the target audience for whom the publication is aimed.

Newspapers

Undoubtedly, traditional print newspapers have been the biggest victims of electronic print. In general, the traditional newspaper's reliance on advertising to offset approximately 80 percent of the cost of producing a newspaper was a part of the newspaper's decline, but newer forms of technology—particularly social media—have allowed information to circulate faster than possible with traditional news media. Additionally, bundling content, which newspapers did so effectively to reach different consumers and grab a variety of advertisers has changed with contemporary forms of news, entertainment, civic matters, and features attractive to niche audiences.

In many ways, traditional print newspapers were a major form of media in the twentieth century. How they evolve in the twenty-first century is still to be seen.

We have evidence that if traditional newspapers and newsgathering operations are to survive, they will have to change their business models, and many have begun to do that.

Some newspaper publishing powerhouses have already bone bankrupt, while others have tried to cut their news staffs by as much as half and have encouraged their news people to develop skills in multimedia storytelling. It is typical today for a newspaper journalist to also have a blog that can be linked to off of a newspaper's (or magazine's) website to provide additional information or write in a more informal tone for the typical audience member who uses that type of platform.

The printed versions of newspapers that have survived have often cut their number of pages, the number of stories they cover, and the number of features they offer (Star 2009). What may really be changing is the way people consume news and what they expect news to be. When online sites like Gawker and BuzzFeed flood the public with information and Tumblr and Twitter repost content to their users, the flow of information and the veracity of that information changes the traditional legitimacy of print. That doesn't necessarily mean that social media and social networks are not as good as a traditionally vetted newspaper when gatekeepers like editors and publishers watched carefully over the contents, but it does mean that the consumer needs to be aware of how this shift to electronic forms and a multiplicity of viewpoints has changed the way we make decisions about what is important or even accurate in contemporary news and information.

E-Cards

At one point in history, the greeting card industry was big business. Today, Americans buy about 6.5 billion greeting cards a year for an annual retail sales figure of somewhere between $7 and $8 billion. But shortly after the World Wide Web became available, online greeting cards emerged. The Electronic Postcard was created by Judith Donath at the MIT Media Lab in 1994, and though it first seemed that e-card activity started slowly, the growth has been steady ever since that time.

By 1996, commercial enterprises began offering cards. Awesome Cards, Blue Mountain cards, and Greetingcards.com were all operating by 2001, and by 2006 e-cards became more popular than traditional paper cards. In the United States, Hallmark and American Greetings have expanded their traditional paper market into the e-card business and with paper and e-cards combined, make up the largest producers of greeting cards in the United States (Singleton 2009). Overall, though, even with the addition of e-cards, most greeting card producers have not significantly increased their profits. Instead, e-cards have picked up where paper cards have fallen off. Most greeting card manufacturers are looking at the Chinese market where sending greeting cards has always been popular, and where the sheer size of the population promises great potential for e-card sales.

See also: Agency Model; Amazon; Copyright; Creative Commons; Digital Millennium Copyright Act (DMCA); E-Commerce; E-Reader; Tablet

Further Reading

Dawson, Ashley. 2012. "DIY Academy: Cognitive Capitalism, Humanist Scholarship, and the Digital Transformation." In *The Social Media Reader*, edited by Michael Mandiberg. New York: New York University Press, 257–274.

Kruger, Justin, Nicholas Epley, Jason Parker, and Zhi-Wen Ng. 2005. "Egocentrism Over E-mail: Can We Communicate as Well as We Think?" *Journal of Personality and Social Psychology*, 89: 925–936.

Pegoraro, Rob. 2010. "Amazon Charges Kindle Users for Free Project Gutenberg E-books." *Washington Post*. Accessed February 18, 2015: http://voices.washingtonpost.com /fasterforward/2010/11/amazon_charges_kindle_users_fo.html.

Pew Research Center. 2013. "E-Reading Rises as Device Ownership Jumps." Accessed February 18, 2015: http://www.pewinternet.org/files/old-media//Files/Reports/2014/PIP _E-reading_011614.pdf.

Singleton, Sharon. 2009. "E-cards Bite into Greeting Card Industry." *Toronto Sun*. Accessed April 30, 2015: http://www.torontosun.com/money/2009/12/22/12239986-qmi .html.

Star, Paul. 2009. "Goodbye to the Age of Newspapers (Hello to a New Era of Corruption)." *New Republic*. Accessed February 19, 2015: http://www.newrepublic.com/article /goodbye-the-age-newspapers-hello-new-era-corruption.

Thompson, Richard. 2012. *Merchants of Culture: The Publishing Business in the Twenty-First Century,* 2nd ed. London: Plume, 314–318.

E-Reader

Electronic readers are similar to tablets and smartphones in the sense that they can be used to read text on the electronic screen, but e-readers are often more commonly referred to as a classification of technology that specializes in presenting the printed word electronically, while tablets have more multifunctionality. A good number of e-readers are developed and sponsored by companies that also sell e-books and e-periodicals, and, since the early, or "first generation," e-readers became available, many of the same manufacturers have upgraded the e-readers to tablets, even though the names may sound similar to the earlier technologies. Each type of e-reader often has a relationship with the seller, so, for example, Amazon and the Kindle are highly compatible, and the Nook favors the Barnes and Noble business relationship. Overall, the popularity of the e-reader and the advanced technology that allowed the development of smaller laptops and tablets to evolve, all introduced new products to consumers quickly, and with more competitively priced models. E-readers generally have touch sensitive screens so that "pages" can be turned with a swipe of a finger, or by pushing a button that changes the page.

One of the most popular e-readers was the Kindle, released by Amazon in 2007, and sold for $399. The new device was so popular Amazon's stock was entirely depleted within five and a half hours. The name "Kindle" was chosen because it made reference to lighting a fire. In 2011, Amazon released the second generation e-reader as the Kindle Fire, which combined e-reader and tablet features capable of full-motion video and audio. In 2013, the new Kindle Fire HD, and Kindle Fire HDX debuted, each with twice the memory of the Kindle Fire and improved graphics and speed. Then, in 2014, Amazon dropped the name "Kindle" and introduced the fourth generation of their e-reader/tablet combination as the Fire HDX 8.9 and an improved Fire HD. All Kindle e-readers and their related models run on an Android operating system.

In 2009, the bookstore chain Barnes and Noble came out with its own Android-based e-reader, called the Nook, manufactured by Samsung. Nook models also went through different generations of development, but the Nook had additional features that were not included in the early Kindle models. For example, the Nook introduced Wi-Fi connectivity sooner than the Kindle did, and also allowed users to access a web browser, a dictionary, and games on the same e-reader. The Nook also allowed customers in any Barnes and Noble store to read books while they were in the store, for up to an hour.

In 2012, Microsoft invested $300 million for a partial ownership of Nook, but, by 2014, the partnership ended when Barnes and Noble purchased the option to retain ownership. But in the same year, the Nook partnership with Samsung Electronics resulted in two new models, the Samsung Galaxy Tab 4 Nook 7.0, and then the Samsung Galaxy Tab 4 Nook 10.1. The reason for the equipment upgrade and the refocusing of the business model involving the Samsung partnership was to enhance the use of e-readers (and the Nook models, in particular) for school reading programs.

Though all of the e-readers mentioned above operate on an Android operating system, Apple introduced its iOS-based iPad in 2010 and announced that it would also facilitate interaction with major publishers for the reading of e-books. The app is called iBooks, and electronic copies can be purchased through Apple's own iBookstore.

While there have been a number of e-readers that have been introduced to the market, there have also been some early examples that were not successful, like the early Rocket eBook that was developed in 1998, the Sony Librie (2004), and the Sony Reader (2006). The Kobo e-Reader, developed in Canada in 2010, was popular in some parts of the world, but in 2012 the Japanese conglomerate Rakuten bought the project, and since then has been developing the new Kobo as an app to be used on Windows 8 mobile phones. While all of these e-readers and the Kindle and Nook have been upgraded to new technology as it becomes available, the big differences have involved the readability of the screen, the power of the unit's processor, and the quality of the visual image (including pictures) on the screen.

There are several benefits to reading on an e-reader. The memory can store complete libraries at a time, and the lightweight portability of the unit is a handy feature for many people, especially when some books (hardcover, for the most part) can be heavy or awkward to carry around. But, at the same time, some people prefer the tactile nature of turning a paper page, or the physical experience of reading print on a paper page. Improved battery life has made the e-reader more functional over time, but there is always the possibility that the battery can die, just when you want to read the last chapter of an exciting thriller. As tablet computers get cheaper and smartphones increase the size of their screen and come down in cost, it will be interesting to see if e-readers survive the technological changes.

According to the Pew Research Center, e-readers have been most heavily adopted by adults rather than younger readers, but tablets have been adopted even more rapidly. The cost of the e-reader is a major factor for who is likely to buy a special device, especially when smartphones and other electronic technologies can also be used for reading. As of 2014, however, the Pew Research Center reported that the percentage of adults who read an e-book in 2014 was 28 percent, up from 23 percent at the end of 2012. The same study reported that 42 percent of adults owned tablet computers in 2014. According to the report, three in ten adults read an e-book in 2014. About seven out of ten read a book in print during the same year (Zickuhr and Rainie 2014). The evidence indicates that while e-readers are gaining in popularity, other devices including traditional books are being used, too.

While reading on an e-reader for pleasure is one type of reading, using e-readers for more scholarly purposes suggests other issues. Some critics have posited that e-reader use in schools might introduce a problem for the person's comprehension of what they've read. There have been many studies about reading an electronic image versus a print image on paper, and academic researchers seem to be divided on how well the electronic text is received by the reader's brain. Studies conducted before the development of e-readers generally concluded that people who read text on a computer screen or any other electronic screen often read slower than people whose eyes could scan a printed page more rapidly. The act of looking into an electronic screen can fatigue the eye, but, at the same time, most digital reading is of a different sort than paper-based text reading.

Perhaps some of the problems with electronic text has to do with what is available to be read. Most periodicals written to be online or in electronic form use a style of writing that is briefer than long-form text-based writing. At the same time, when we compare reading a novel or a text that is designed for long-form reading, the mind is ready for relaxation, rather than for facts and specific tone. In what is called the "physical landscape" of the page—whether it is on paper or electronic, the content should suit the form. As science writer Ferris Jabr wrote: "Most screens, e-readers, smartphones and tablets interfere with intuitive navigation of a text and inhibit people from mapping the journey in their minds . . . It is difficult to see any one passage in the context of the entire text" (Jabr 2013).

Another type of study reflects on the role of text (electronic or paper) and memory. In a study in 2003 at the University of Leicester in the United Kingdom, British college students were asked to read material on paper or electronically. Both groups scored equally well on comprehension but differed in how they remembered the information. The assessment was that those students who read the content on paper learned more thoroughly and more quickly and that they did not have to "search" their minds to remember the information. Other studies give credibility to the process of reading on an electronic screen that is physically more demanding than reading print on paper. The American Optometric Association has officially recognized what they call computer vision syndrome that affects about 70 percent of the people who work on computers for a long period of time. For these people, blurred vision, headaches, and eye strain are common.

See also: E-Publishing; Tablet

Further Reading

American Optometric Association, n.d. "Computer Vision Syndrome." Accessed March 7, 2015: http://www.aoa.org/patients-and-public/caring-for-your-vision/protecting-your-vision/computer-vision-syndrome?sso=y.

Jabr, Ferris. 2013. "Do e-Readers Inhibit Reading Comprehension?" *Scientific American.* Reprinted in *Salon.* Accessed March 7, 2015: http://www.salon.com/2013/04/14/do_e_readers_inhibit_reading_comprehension_partner/.

Zickuhr, Kathryn, and Lee Rainie. 2014. "E-Reading Rises as Device Ownership Jumps." Pew Research Center. Accessed March 7, 2015: http://www.pewinternet.org/2014/01/16/e-reading-rises-as-device-ownership-jumps/.

Etsy

In 1998, a small web service called Getcrafty was launched to capitalize on the growing creative economy and do-it-yourself (DIY) trends that were so popular at the time. The craft movement, as it was called, had a number of highly visible proponents who thought of handmade goods as an alternative to store-bought, and who wanted to keep handicrafts alive in an increasingly commercialized culture. In 2004, the founder of the site Jean Railla, hired 25-year-old Rob Kalin, fresh from New York University, to work with Etsy. He, along with Jared Tarbell, Chris Maguire, and Haim Schoppik, developed Etsy into an e-commerce site that also had strong moral and political values (Walker 2007).

Etsy is an e-commerce website focusing on handmade or vintage items and supplies, as well as unique factory-manufactured items, and was intended to act as an online craft fair for sellers to have a "personal storefront" on the Internet. According to Rob Kalin, the name was chosen because he wanted to build the brand from scratch, and after watching Frederico Fellini's film, *8 ½*, he heard the Italian term "etsi" so often, he thought it was catchy. In Italian, the word means "oy yes," and, in Latin, it means "and if" (Lammle 2011). Kalin's personal vision of etsy was that it could be a "cultural movement" that would be a response to the increasing power of big box retailers (Walker 2007). The motto for Etsy is "Do It Yourself."

Etsy uses a peer-to-peer method of e-commerce to market handmade items and vintage products that are defined as being at least 20 years old. Sellers list their goods for 20 cents per item. The company generates revenue primarily from three areas. The Marketplace revenue includes a fee of 3.5 percent of the sale value, plus a listing fee of 20 cents per item. The Seller Services area includes fees for services related to promoted listings, payment processing, and the purchase of shipping labels, and the Other category includes revenue from third-party payment processors (Walker 2012). About 90 percent of the crafters who list their items on Etsy are women.

While it may be one of the most successful craft sites, it is not the only one, perhaps in part because of the new e-commerce opportunities for marketing products or the ease with which online shopping has been accepted, online "mini malls" have proliferated as creative economy efforts have blossomed. Kalin's ideas of entrepreneurial activity and the building of community have kept Etsy at the forefront of online craft sales.

By 2012, Etsy was classified as a "B Corporation" meaning that it exhibited social and ecological consciousness in its choice of materials. By 2013, Etsy had 30 million registered users, and it was estimated that over $1 billion of transactions took place that year. The company has added a number of features that enhance the visual quality of the images, and it has added a "Shop Local" component to help people find goods that are made close to home.

See also: Creative Economy; Do-It-Yourself; E-Commerce

Further Reading

Lammle, Rob. 2011. "How Etsy, eBay, Reddit Got Their Names." Accessed December 26, 2015: http://www.cnn.com/2011/LIVING/04/22/website.name.origins.mf/.

Walker, Rob. 2007. "Handmade 2.0." *New York Times.* Accessed April 2, 2015: http://www.nytimes.com/2007/12/16/magazine/16Craftst.html?_r=3&oref=slogin&ref=magazine&pagewanted=all&.

Walker, Rob. 2012. "Can Etsy Go Pro without Losing Its Soul?" *Wired.* Accessed December 3, 2014: http://www.wired.com/2012/09/etsy-goes-pro/all/.

European Council for Nuclear Research (CERN)

The acronym CERN is derived from the French title of the organization, the *Conseil Européen pour la Recherche Nucléaire,* or, as translated, the European Council for Nuclear Research. CERN has a long history as a research laboratory specializing in information sharing and Internet technology research. While it operates the largest particle physics laboratory in the world, it deals with technologies that investigate the operations of the universe. Founded in 1954, the CERN laboratory is near Geneva, Switzerland. It was one of Europe's first joint ventures and has become famous for its development of the Hadron Particle Collider.

CERN was active in early Internet technology inventions and is perhaps best known as the place where the World Wide Web was "invented." The project was initially guided by Tim Berners-Lee in 1989. Robert Calliau joined the team in 1990, and the first website went online in 1991. In 1993, CERN announced that the World Wide Web would be free for anyone to use. A PDF copy of Berners-Lee's original proposal for the World Wide Web can be found at http://www.w3.org/History/1989/proposal.html

See also: Berners-Lee, Tim; Web 2.0; World Wide Web (WWW); World Wide Web Consortium (W3C)

Further Reading

Berners-Lee, Tim. 1989. "Information Management: A Proposal." World Wide Web Foundation. Accessed May 1, 2014: http://www.w3.org/History/1989/proposal.html.

Expedia

Travel has changed since the pre-Internet days, and travel sites like Expedia that allow customers to see comparisons of hotels, activities, social calendars and more, help consumers make better decisions about their travel plans. Whether for business or personal use, online travel sites and consulting services have truly revolutionized the travel industry and have forced many travel agencies to cut the size of their staff. According to the Questex Travel Group, traditional travel agencies now focus more on different types of services, and are responsible for 77 percent of all cruise bookings, 73 percent of package travel bookings, and 55 percent of airline travel bookings (Laverty 2015). While travel agencies have their own fare sites to consult, consumers tend to use online services to check for personal travel rather than business-related travel.

The business model that is used by online travel services is called *horizontal integration,* meaning that the relationships created within the service industry all have something to do with travel and often produce products that can further boost the profits of the host company. The idea behind online services for travel originated in 1996 when American Airlines formed a company called Sabre Holdings to handle reservations. Sabre then started Travelocity, which was later acquired (in 2015) by Expedia.

Expedia was one of the first online sites, founded in 1996 as the first online service of Microsoft. The company also runs a number of other, similar sites like Hotels.com, Hotwire.com, Trivago, Classic Vacations, and more. In 2001, the company was purchased by TicketMaster, which later changed its name, and then, in 2003, became the InterActiveCorp (IAC). In 2011, Expedia Inc. became its own company but maintained its portfolio of additional companies, all of which focus on travel services. In 2012, Expedia bought the majority stake in the search engine Trivago for a combined cash and stock deal that was worth approximately $630 million.

Expedia has continued to make further acquisitions and, in 2014, it announced that it would be expanding to the Asia-Pacific region through an acquisition of Wotif.com Holdings Ltd. In January 2015, Expedia acquired the online travel agency Travelocity from the tech firm Sabre Corporation for $280 million. Eight weeks later, it announced that it would also buy Orbitz for $1.3 billion, including Orbitz Worldwide, which owns the brands ebookers.com and cheaptickets.com.

Much of the competition for Expedia and the Expedia-owned brands comes from Priceline, a Norwalk, Connecticut, based company founded in 1997. In 2013, Priceline acquired Kayak.com, with the hope that Kayak would become a travel aggregator in the same way Expedia had.

The impact of online travel sites is critical to the success of the travel industry, which involves a wide range of different vendors, including transportation, lodging, restaurants, car rental companies, and tourism services. The travel industry reports that the amount of money spent by domestic and international travelers in 2013 totaled $621.4 billion and that spending on leisure travel alone generated $91.9 billion in tax revenue. About three-quarters of all domestic trips in the United States that year were for leisure purposes. Business travel in 2013 (domestic and international) totaled $266.5 billion (U.S. Travel Association 2015).

But as travel sites like Expedia expand and acquire other brands, they appear to be consolidating the online business into just a few competitors. This has led *Time* magazine's Money.com editor Brad Tuttle to write: "After all, when more travel search engines are in the hands of fewer and fewer corporate owners, there's obviously less true competition. Simply put, less competition = bad for consumers." Though there are several smaller online travel companies that provide comparative rates, like DealAngel, GuestMob, HotelTonight, and Tingo, the difference between many of these companies, large or small, is the point at which the consumer enters booking information and the point when each company expects payment.

See also: Airbnb; Do-It-Yourself (DIY); Prosumer

Further Reading

Laverty, Shiela. 2015. "Impact of Technology on the Travel Business." *Small Business Chronicle*. Accessed March 30, 2015: http://smallbusiness.chron.com/impact-technology-travel-agency-business-57750.html.

Tuttle, Brad. 2015. "What Expedia's Acquisition of Orbitz and Travelocity Means for Travelers." *Time* magazine, March 30, 2015: http://time.com/money/3707551/expedia-orbitz-impact-travelers/.

U.S. Travel Association. 2015. "Travel Facts and Statistics." Accessed March 30, 2015: https://www.ustravel.org/news/press-kit/travel-facts-and-statistics.

F

Facebook

At the end of 2014, Facebook was one of the world's most heavily consulted social networks with almost 1.3 billion users worldwide. On an average day, more than 800 million users around the world access the site. While Facebook can be accessed by computer or mobile phone, data provided by a research company reports that the average Facebook user accessing information on a mobile phone spends more time on Facebook than they spend on looking for all other information on the web (Madrigal 2014, 34). The ability of Facebook to distribute information among members of the network has resulted in what one journalist has referred to as Facebook's role as the "social spine" of the Internet (Madrigal 2014, 35).

The precursor of what we now know as Facebook was a Harvard-based site designed by Mark Zuckerberg that started functioning in October 2003, with the name *Facemash*. By February 2004, Zuckerberg and his Harvard friends, Eduardo Saverin, Andrew McCollum, Dustin Moskovitz, and Chris Hughes called the project "Thefacebook.com." Originally developed to link Harvard students on campus, the project was soon expanded to other Boston area college campuses and, later, to most universities in North America (both Canada and the United States). By the end of his sophomore year in 2004, Zuckerberg left Harvard to establish Facebook's headquarters in Palo Alto, California. The company began to grow nationally and expanded services to corporations and to younger users aged 13 or older with a valid e-mail address to sign up for the service.

The popularity of Facebook has been nothing short of phenomenal, based in part on its primary demographic—young people, who not only were acquiring personal digital technologies at an unprecedented rate in the 2000s, but who also found the ease of using social networks an effective way to shift all other forms of electronic communications to one way of distributing messages. One reason that Facebook has continued to grow, while so many other social networks have peaked and declined, is that Facebook has continued to change business practices and acquire apps that appeal to users. Facebook also was an early social network to migrate to a mobile platform and that, too, contributed to its success. Facebook's motto is "move fast and break things"—a philosophy that has served the company well.

Any start-up needs to have financial backing, and Facebook was no exception. At first, Zuckerberg and his friend Eduardo Saverin tried to raise money from venture capitalists but few thought there was much potential for this type of social network. The first major investor, Peter Thiel, provided $500,000, in 2004. By 2006, Facebook's financial picture was so grim that there was talk of its sale, but an initial offer of $750 million was turned down, with Zuckerberg hoping to reap at least $2 billion. Potential buyers included Viacom and MySpace. In 2007, Microsoft invested $240 million in Facebook, with the arrangement that it would be a third-party ad partner, but the two companies were never completely compatible. One of the problems was the competition in search strategies that Microsoft hoped to develop with its own search engine, Bing, but Bing was never as successful as Google. In 2012, Microsoft sold some of its stock in Facebook, and a year later, Facebook bought Microsoft's ad platform, Atlas. When Facebook made its entry into the stock market in 2012, it raised $16 billion, making it the biggest Internet stock offering in history. Since that time, other stock surges have propelled Facebook into a very profitable company.

Facebook now operates around the world and has offices in 34 different cities. In 2008, Sheryl Sandberg became Facebook's chief operating officer (COO) after several years as an executive at Google. The company continues to operate as a social network but has interests in developing apps, wearable technology, and exploring the mobile market. Already, the apps necessary to allow Facebook to be used on smartphones have increased Facebook's share of profits from mobile advertising.

While Facebook makes most of its revenue through advertising and is the second digital company in terms of ad revenue (Google is the first), the company has been acquiring apps and has been developing different search strategies. In 2013, Zuckerberg paid $85 million to acquire Parse, a start-up company that works to provide deep linking of apps, which would provide Facebook with an enormous amount of personal information about what users choose to add in the way of apps. In 2014, Facebook acquired a number of other web-based companies, like WhatsApp for which it paid $21.8 billion. This service already had 500 million users per month. Instagram was also acquired at the cost of $715 million, with 200 million users per month (Madrigal 2014, 35), and, the virtual reality wearable technology company, Oculus Virtual Reality, was purchased for $2 billion.

Facebook may be one of the most successful social networks when measured against others, but it has also had its share of criticism, not only for its privacy policy and the way it shares personal information, but for contributing to making a person who spends an inordinate amount of time online, lonely. In a 2012 article in the *Atlantic Monthly*, "Is Facebook Making Us Lonely?" Stephen Marche raised the question of social networks that connect us to others online, instead of face-to-face. Though not specifically critical of Facebook as a contributor to loneliness, Marche reminds us that at the same time Facebook (and other social networks) began to appear in American society, there was also a spurt in the "quantity and intensity of human loneliness" (Marche 2012). It may be impossible to accurately chart a positive correlation between social networks and the rise of loneliness, but the growth of an understanding of how society is changing related to our substitution of face-to-face communication with social networking leads many to believe that we should address the healthy use and socialization aspects of living in a more electronically connected environment, where it becomes easier to communicate online than in geographic spaces.

There are several predictions for Facebook's future. The Pew Internet and American Life report "Teens, Social Media and Privacy" reported that teens had a "waning enthusiasm" for Facebook. The authors write that between 2013 and 2014, Facebook's share of young users remained stable while other social networks saw dramatic increases in young users. But Facebook has become more popular with older adults. For the first time in Pew Research findings, more than half (56%) of Internet users aged 65 and older use Facebook. Overall, 71 percent of Internet users are on Facebook, a proportion that represents no change from August 2013 (Duggan et al. 2014).

Another prediction is that by 2019, Facebook will resemble Google more than it does today, because of its plan to deliver multifunctionality and a wide range of apps to users (Carr and Wilson 2014). Another scenario is that Facebook may not be able to compete with emerging social networks that guarantee much greater levels of privacy for users. Whether Facebook continues to develop services that capture the public's attention or not, it deserves to be considered one of the leading social networks, and one that has already made its impact on society known.

See also: Addiction; Cyberbullying; Hyperconnectivity; Identity; MySpace; Privacy

Further Reading

Carlson, Nicholas. 2010. "At Last—The Full Story of How Facebook Was Founded." *Business Insider.* Accessed December 1, 2014: http://www.businessinsider.com/how-facebook-was-founded-2010-3?op=1.

Carr, Austin, and Mark Wilson. 2014. "Facebook's Plan to Own Your Phone." *Fast Company Magazine.* Accessed February 11, 2015: http://www.fastcompany.com/3031237/facebook-everywhere.

Duggan, Maeve, Nicole B. Ellison, Cliff Lampe, Amanda Lenhart, and Mary Madden. 2014. "Social Media Update 2014." Pew Internet and American Life Project. Accessed January 22, 2015: http://www.pewinternet.org/2015/01/09/social-media-update-2014/.

Madden, Mary. 2013. "Teens Haven't Abandoned Facebook (Yet)." Pew Internet and American Life Project. Accessed January 22, 2015: http://www.pewinternet.org/2013/08/15/teens-havent-abandoned-facebook-yet/.

Marche, Stephen. 2012. "Is Facebook Making Us Lonely?" *Atlantic Monthly.* Accessed September 3, 2014: http://www.theatlantic.com/magazine/archive/2012/05/is-facebook-making-us-lonely/308930/.

Rosoff, Matt. 2014. "Facebook Dumps Microsoft." *Business Insider.* Accessed January 22, 2015: http://www.businessinsider.com/facebook-and-microsoft-seem-to-be-parting-ways-2014-12#ixzz3PZ8rNU2A.

Excerpts from the "Social Media Update 2014," Pew Research Center, January 9, 2015, Maeve Duggan, Nicole B. Ellison, Cliff Lampe, Amanda Lenhart, and Mary Madden

Facebook continues to be the most popular social media site, but its membership saw little change from 2013. The one notable exception is older adults: For the first time in Pew Research findings, more than half (56%) of internet users ages 65 and older use Facebook.

Facebook's large base of users continues to be very active. Fully 70% engage with the site daily (and 45% do so several times a day), a significant increase from the 63% who did so in 2013.

52% of online adults use multiple social media sites. Facebook acts as "home base"—it remains the most popular site for those who only use one, and has significant overlap with other platforms.

Source: Duggan, Maeve; Ellison, Nicole B.; Lampe, Cliff; Lenhart, Amanda; and Madden, Mary. "Social Media Update 2014." Pew Research Center, January 9, 2015. http://www.pewinternet.org/2015/01/09/social-media-update-2014/. Reprinted with permission from Pew Research Center.

Fanning, Shawn

At the age of 19, Shawn Fanning (1980–) started the original Napster, an MP3-based service that allowed peer-to-peer music file sharing in 1998. As a student at Northeastern University in Boston, Fanning shared the MP3 technology, and, quickly, students were sharing music with each other and amassing huge data files of music. The process also spread quickly to other college and high school students and, by 2000, almost 20 million people were using Napster (Knopper 2009, 135). Fanning was on the covers of *Time* magazine, *Fortune*, *Businessweek*, and *Industry Standard*.

Until Napster came along, the only legal method of sharing music was clarified in the Audio Home Recording Act of 1992, which stated that it was legal for one to make recordings of music that was purchased and lend them to other people, as long as it wasn't for commercial purposes. In 1984, the U.S. Supreme Court also provided a precedent that seemed perfect for Napster, the *Sony Corp. of America v. Universal City Studios* case (known as the Sony-Betamax Case) in which the court ruled that VCRs were legal and could record copyrighted television shows for their own use. Both of these precedents seemed to indicate that copying music was perfectly legal, as long as that music or video was not sold to someone else. Napster started out as a free download tool but the goal was to make it into a real business in partnership with the record labels.

Fanning figured out how to use the emerging MP3 technology to share music files. He originally figured out how to do it by thinking of the easy-to-use format of an Internet Relay Chat. He thought of setting up a central server where users could connect through log-in names, and view the titles of MP3 recordings they had on their computers. Through a search box, it was easy to locate music by artist or title. Fanning chose the name "Napster" because that was his Internet Relay Chat name. His uncle John Fanning helped him establish the business, with John Fanning receiving 70 percent of the profits and Shawn Fanning receiving 30 percent. A friend, Jordan Ritter, helped debug the code that Fanning had attempted to write in the C++ language. Another friend, Sean Parker lined up an investor and drew up a business plan that linked Napster users and sought to sell them concert tickets and band-related paraphernalia. Shawn Fanning and Sean Parker moved to San Mateo, California, rented an apartment together, and went into business.

Dan Dodge, the first vice president of product development recalled that, at first, Napster wanted to work with the major record labels, but it was too small to get meetings with the powerful record promoters and industry personnel. He wrote: "Napster went from being an unknown underground technology to the biggest threat the record labels had ever seen, all in the span of less than six months. At this point the record labels wanted us dead" (Dodge 2007, 113). Napster had a lot to offer: over 50 million users, many of whom were willing to pay $5 per month for a subscription, or $1 per download for digital music. Any record label or distributor willing to work with Napster could have earned a potential of $250 million a month or $3 billion within a year.

At the time, the members of the RIAA were selling CDs for approximately $17 retail. The retailers and distributors skimmed more than half of the price as their cut, and the manufacturers took another few dollars. Promotional costs took up most of the rest of the money, and the artists received very little—usually about $1 per CD. Napster's business model took advantage of niche sales, and therefore could streamline any advertising to the right people while still eliminating the many costs of album or CD manufacturing, artwork, or related costs.

Almost from the beginning, the Recording Industry Association of America (RIAA) raised concerns about the way the distribution of free music was cutting into its profits. In December 1999, the RIAA filed a copyright-infringement lawsuit against Napster in the U.S. District Court in San Francisco. The judge ruled in favor of the RIAA, stating that the record labels owned the copyrights to more than 70 percent of the music that was available on the Napster system. Napster was forced to remove all of that music, which basically shut down the entire service. By 2001, Napster was no longer in business and assets were sold to Rhapsody, an online music store.

Almost immediately, music companies began to look at using MP3 and peer-to-peer methods of exchange and tried to think of how the process could be monetized. Bertlesmann, a German multinational company, bought the majority of what was left of Napster for $60 million, and hired Fanning for $120,000 a year, promising him an additional $60,000 bonus. Bertlesmann's plan was to follow the Napster model but have all music go through a filter that contained copyrighted songs. Only those protected by copyright would be allowed to be transferred. But, unfortunately, the Bertlesmann management became nervous about the project and pulled the plug. By May 2002, Napster declared bankruptcy. The name and logo were acquired by another company, but the impact of Napster on the music industry has been enormous.

Shawn Fanning went on to start a number of other companies: Snocap, another online music venture; Rupture, a social networking service for gaming; and Path, a social networking service for photo sharing and messaging on mobile devices that allows users to access up to 50 contacts and Founders Fund, an organization that seeks innovations that benefit humanity.

Napster is important for several reasons: It provides an example of how freeware can be a threat to a legacy industry like the recorded music industry, and it shows the potential for peer-to-peer file sharing that circumvents traditional economic models and business practices. Later companies like Gnutella, Freenet, and Kazaa all grew because of the Napster experience.

See also: Freeware; MP3

Further Reading

Dodge, Dan. 2007. "How Napster Changed the World—A Look Back 7 Years Later." Dan Dodge on the Next Big Thing. Accessed March 30, 2015: http://dondodge.typepad.com /the_next_big_thing/2007/03/how_napster_cha.html.

Knopper, Steve. 2009. *Appetite for Self-Destruction: The Spectacular Crash of the Record Industry in the Digital Age.* New York: The Free Press, 113–148.

Federal Communications Commission (FCC)

The Federal Communications Commission (FCC) was established in 1934 as a component of the Communications Act of 1934. At the time, the FCC was charged with planning the use of the electromagnetic spectrum used for wireless (broadcast) technologies, and regulating their use. The dominant broadcast technology of the time was radio, which evolved from one-frequency only in the AM band (amplitude modulation) to a system of sharing call letters and distributing frequencies across the country. At the time of the Communications Act of 1934, the radio industry in the United States was highly profitable and had established strong working relationships with advertisers. Most of the advocates for the commercial aspects of broadcasting were the companies that had formed radio networks, like CBS, NBC Red, and NBC Blue (which became ABC), and the Mutual Broadcasting System (which was in operation from 1934 to 1999). Prior to the FCC, the Federal Radio Commission (FRC) had overseen the development of broadcasting from 1927, but the leadership reflected people from the industry, all of whom had a vested interest in developing the commercial aspects of broadcasting.

A number of educators, citizens, and politicians were concerned about the growing commercialization of the airwaves for advertising purposes and felt that more regulation was necessary to create a viable broadcast industry that would be accountable to the public in a more comprehensive way. Even the smaller broadcasters were concerned. Television was not far in the future and a number of smaller affiliate and independent radio stations voiced concerns about the future of local broadcasting if the networks maintained their growing control. The Communications Act of 1934 was a response to concerns about the future of broadcasting and the representation of a greater number of voices.

The first set of seven FCC commissioners took their seats in July of 1934. Contrary to the commissioners of the previous FRC, whose leadership represented major manufacturers, the new FCC rules stipulated that no more than four commissioners could be from one political party. Eventually the number of commissioners changed to five, with three commissioners (including the chair) from the president's political party, and the other two from the opposing political party.

When the FCC was established, the commission promised to act "in the public's interest," and deemed the airwaves the "property of the people."

In part because of the legacy of the FRC, and because the FCC was established to right the wrongs of the past, much of the commission's time was taken up with complaints about misleading advertising. In this respect, it sometimes reinforces decisions by the Federal Trade Commission (FTC) that is charged with issues of commerce related to products advertised. The FCC also had to contend with questions about what could be advertised, and what could not be advertised; a particularly important topic in the 1930s because prohibition had recently been repealed and many broadcasters wanted to air ads for alcoholic beverages.

Over the years, the FCC has tackled a number of important issues related to the use of public airwaves for commercial and noncommercial purposes, but the FCC does not have the ability to make laws. Rather, it explores critical issues and makes recommendations to Congress for the enactment of laws. The FCC does, however, have the mandate to explore critical topics related to the effective use of the communications and information industries.

At the time the FCC was established, wired communications did not fall into the organization's purview. Telephony, which at the time was all a wired form of distribution, was an example of the type of communications the FCC did not oversee. When cable television came about in the 1970s, it too was a wired form of communications so the FCC did not feel that it needed to be regulated. Of course, in the early days of the Internet, which was entirely wired (wireless forms had yet to be developed), the FCC relied on precedents of wired communications and left the Internet unregulated.

Today, though, the current FCC has to deal with the convergence technologies that have blurred the traditional categories of "wired" and "wireless." The Telecommunications Act of 1996 was an attempt to deal with the nature of digital information and the types of messages that often used both wired and wireless forms, including the use of broadcast satellites, but despite a number of amendments to the Telecom Act, the FCC has continued to take on projects that reflect the needs of "balance" between the commercial and public sectors of communications and information technologies. Among one of the most contentious issues was the FCC's position on *net neutrality,* which echoed the arguments of big broadcasters in the 1930s who wanted to control the distribution of information over wireless technologies. In the FCC ruling to support net neutrality in February 2015 (which passed on a 3 to 2 vote), the FCC supported the idea that the Internet should be open to all, and that the big telecommunications companies should not have the ability to pay for faster service for Internet delivery of their content.

See also: Legacy Media; Net Neutrality; Telecommunications Act of 1996

Further Reading

Barnouw, Erik. 1968. *The Golden Web: A History of Broadcasting in the United States 1933–1953*. New York: Oxford University Press, 23–36.

Federal Trade Commission (FTC)

The Federal Trade Commission (FTC) was created when President Woodrow Wilson signed the Federal Trade Commission Act into law on September 26, 1914. The FTC is the branch of the federal government that examines trade practices and acts as the federal arm of protecting consumers, while still promoting competition in industry. The FTC was set up to be an independent agency and it took over the former Bureau of Corporations, which had been created by the Commerce Department in 1903. Like the FCC, five commissioners are responsible for the operations of the agency.

While the FTC has three primary foci: Bureau of Consumer Protection, the Bureau of Competition, and the Bureau of Economics, the division most tied to media and communication technologies is the Bureau of Consumer Protection, which generally oversees advertising and deceptive practices. The bureau is responsible for the Do Not Call Registry, which allows consumers to list their phone numbers on the registry and block telemarketers from calling them directly. Similarly, the FTC has been involved in the oversight of the online advertising industry and its practice of behavioral targeting for some time. In 2011, the FTC proposed a "Do Not Track" mechanism to allow Internet users to opt-out of behavioral targeting.

With the growth of e-commerce, the FTC's Bureau of Competition has reviewed a number of cases that deal with antitrust laws. The division also reviews proposed mergers and examines agreements among competitors.

The Bureau of Economics focuses on issues pertaining to the economics of legislation and operations but also oversees the problem of identity theft. Anyone who suspects that their identity has been stolen can easily access the division online or call 1-877-ID-THEFT.

The FTC has produced an entertaining video available on YouTube that explains the origin of consumer culture in the United States and justifies the workings of the FTC (see https://www.youtube.com/watch?v=NssfPApe5iQ).

See also: Advertising; Children's Internet Protection Act (CIPA); Internet

Further Reading

"About What We Do." Federal Trade Commission. Accessed March 30, 2015: https://www.ftc.gov/about-ftc/our-history.

"A Brief History of the Birth of the Federal Trade Commission." 2009. Federal Trade Commission. Accessed March 30, 2015: https://www.youtube.com/watch?v=NssfPApe5iQ.

Flickr

Flickr is a file sharing company that specializes in photo sharing. The company was launched in 2004 by Ludicorp, a Vancouver-based company headed by Stewart Butterfield and Caterina Fake. The early version of the Flickr service had a chat room in which users could share pictures they had taken, but, by 2004, additional services were added to allow greater photo sharing.

Ludicorp (and Flickr) was acquired by Yahoo! in 2005, for somewhere between $22 and $25 million. But shortly after being acquired user interest in the service waned, with competition coming from Instagram, Facebook, and Google+. In 2008, Flickr allowed subscribers to post videos that were no longer than 90 seconds and 150 MB in size. The following year it accepted videos in High Definition (HD) format. In 2009, the company announced a relationship with Getty Images that allowed users to submit photographs to be used for stock purposes; if their images were accepted, the photographer received a modest payment. By 2010 the arrangement was made that photographers could charge for the use of their photography and be paid directly. What really changed Flickr's fortunes was a change in leadership at Yahoo!

In 2011, a new product manager at Yahoo! by the name of Markus Spiering took over the project, and when Marissa Mayer was appointed CEO of Yahoo!, more attention was paid to developing Flickr. The improved camera lens of the iPhone5 in 2012 helped steer interest back to Flickr. Soon after, roughly 3.5 million photos were being uploaded daily, and Flickr became used by more than 87 million users (Jeffries 2013).

One feature that had always separated Flickr from other photo sharing services was the active use of Creative Commons licensing, which it started using in 2004. This allowed users who wanted to upload their pictures a sense of authorship, but still honored the principles of freely sharing content, and required that attribution for the photograph be documented. In March 2015, Elon Musk, the CEO of SpaceX, a private space flight company, posted hundreds of pictures from space on Flickr that had been taken on his company's flights, and Flickr announced a number of new licensing schemes to users, all compatible with Creative Commons licensing. Flickr users could adjust the type of licensing and use features they wanted by changing the account settings in their Flickr account. Among the new features was the addition of Creative Commons Zero (CC0), which is the licensing feature with the least number of restrictions. The end result, as presumed, should increase interest in Flickr.

See also: Creative Commons; Freeware; Instagram; Mobile Phone Cameras

Further Reading

Geuss, Megan. 2015. "Flickr Offers New Public Domain Licensing in Wake of SpaceX Photo Release." *Ars Technica*. Accessed Marsh 31, 2015: http://arstechnica.com/busi ness/2015/03/flickr-offers-new-public-domain-licensing-in-wake-of-spacex-photo -release/.

Jeffries, Adrianne. 2013. "The Man Behind Flickr on Making the Service 'Awesome Again.'" The Verge. Accessed February 18, 2015: http://www.theverge.com/2013/3/20 /4121574/flickr-chief-markus-spiering-talks-photos-and-marissa-mayer.

Foursquare

Foursquare is a mobile app that allows users to create personal search experiences. The idea for the app began in 2008, and the company, Foursquare Inc., began operating in 2009. Cocreators Dennis Crowley and Naveen Selvadurai provided the slogan, "Foursquare helps you find places you'll love, anywhere in the world." When Foursquare was introduced at the South by Southwest (SXSW) Tech Conference in 2009, it was an immediate hit. From 2009 to 2011, the app was creating buzz and it seemed as though it had been designed to fit perfectly with the times; it connected people on a local level, it was mobile-based, and it was designed with social activity in mind.

Prior to starting Foursquare, Crowley had experience with one geolocation app that he had developed, while still an undergraduate, called Dodgeball. When he was accepted to New York University's ITP program in 2002 for graduate work, he met Alex Rainert who helped improve the code and together they built a text-based location sharing app modeled closely on Dodgeball. The service quickly became popular with students in the Manhattan area and spread to a number of other cities in a short time (Dudley 2015). Then, in 2004, while visiting a friend who was an intern at Google in Mountain View, California, Crowley had the opportunity to discuss the future of mobile devices and services, and Google acquired Dodgeball for an undisclosed sum. Google never did much with the app and it was allowed to wither. By 2009, it was dead.

Foursquare was specifically designed to run on a mobile platform. The app lets users "check in" to venues over their smartphones and share information about where they are, with whom, and where to meet up. Called a *geolocation/discovery* app, it evolved right around the same time as Yelp, and a number of other locally based apps that allowed people to connect to each other for purposes of getting together face-to-face. As tech blogger and entrepreneur Anil Dash said: "If you know where everybody is, where they're going, and what they're going to do when they get there, and you can't make money on that, you're a [expletive deleted] idiot"

(Dudley 2015). Users who participated in the Foursquare offerings could earn badges based upon the number of times they used the app and could earn rewards that were intended to incentivize engagement. Unfortunately, the badge and reward process seemed to make the app more attractive for younger users, and the older users began to lose interest.

Initially, it looked as though Foursquare would quickly become profitable. Local advertisers saw its benefit and flocked to advertise their services on the site, and often offered free drinks, food, or other enticements to people who used the app, but Foursquare wasn't ready with the internal infrastructure necessary to make the most of their relationships with their advertisers. The media became interested in Foursquare after it had surpassed a million users, and Crowley raised $50 million from venture capitalists Andreessen Horowitz and Union Square Ventures. By 2011, Foursquare had over 15 million users and 500,000 advertisers including Starbucks, but it was still struggling.

Both Facebook and Yahoo! made offers to buy the company, but Crowley and Selvadurai declined all offers. Internal tensions began to grow, and then suddenly, in 2012, Naveen Selvadurai departed the company, leaving Crowley with the responsibility of trying to compete with other geolocation apps and think of how Foursquare might be repositioned.

As CEO, Crowley secured $41 million in debt financing in April 2015, and separated the unpopular "check in" feature from the primary service. Badges and rewards were eliminated. The decision was made to split Foursquare into two services, a local recommendation service (restaurants, clubs, and the like), and the new "check-in" feature was renamed Swarm. Foursquare also attracted some high power advertisers like Uber and Path, which strengthened the company's advertiser base against its biggest competitor, Yelp. Still the company seemed to be failing until 2015 when Yahoo! began courting it as a possible acquisition with a buying price of $900 million as the reported offer (Dudley 2015). At the time of this writing, negotiations are currently under way.

See also: Advertising; Yelp

Further Reading

Carr, Austin. 2015. "Will Foursquare CEO Dennis Crowley Finally Get It Right?" Accessed April 23, 2015: http://www.fastcompany.com/3014821/will-foursquare-ceo-dennis-crowley-finally-get-it-right.

Dudley, Barry. 2015. "Why Foursquare Is a Must-Buy for Yahoo." The Drum. Accessed April 24, 2015: http://www.thedrum.com/opinion/2015/04/24/why-foursquare-must-buy-yahoo.

Freeware

From the early days of computer development and software development, the idea of *freeware* has captured the idea of a free and open Internet. Though hardware developers often charged for their technologies, software developers have often fallen into the category of making their work available to others for no charge. And, under a number of freeware practices, anyone has the right to make modifications to the original code, as long as they do not try to profit from the changes. While freeware constitutes an economic model, it also shows the marked changes from the economic models of the industrial revolution that were hierarchically structured. Freeware may be as much of an economic model as it is a concept that undergirds the foundation of new social values of sharing and collaboration. Ideas of the Creative Commons and open source models have used freeware as an example of what can be accomplished when traditional business arrangements are liberated and made freely available to all.

Freeware is an example of how our values toward proprietary ownership are changing. In his fascinating compilation of the innovators and innovations that influenced the information age, Walter Isaacson (2014) made the case that support of freely giving ideas away came from computer hobbyists who tweaked technologies until viable personal computers became possible, but software developments tended to favor a "for-profit" model. His approach to the topic of freeware shows that over the decades of the development of the tools of social media, competing economic models influenced what was developed, and by whom.

In the early days of computer and software development, some people strongly believed in the freeware model as the basis for collaboration and free exchange of information. Steve Wozniak originally gave schematic drawings of his early computer unit (which became Apple I) to anyone in the Homebrew Computer Club—an organization that was founded by computer enthusiasts who all valued the freeware model. Similarly, CERN made the World Wide Web free to users because it was considered so important to people that assessing a fee would be unfair. The Linux operating system created by Linus Torvalds was designed to be freely shared. The Internet was originally given to the public as a boon to communication and information sharing. It could be argued that e-commerce quickly changed the model, but the original intention of the Internet as a medium that can connect people and ideas is still well taken.

The term *freeware* sets free content apart from commercial sales of products. A former editor of *Wired* magazine, Chris Anderson has argued that free could be the new business model for digital information and earlier forms of remuneration for content that could be free could be easily replaced. He cites companies like YouTube, Massively Open Online Courses (MOOCS), e-mail, and wireless networks as examples of how we can now get things for free that we once had to pay for. He also reminds us that anyone who understands how free technologies and free services work thinks of paid services as ridiculous—and most of those people tend to be young (Anderson 2009, 4).

The idea of freeware is an example of the sharing economy in which people who have goods and services can make them available to others who need them, with no monetary exchange. The Free Software Foundation warns that there is no accepted definition of freeware and that it should be used with caution. The term has evolved over time and could mislead users into thinking that products are free, when, in reality, a payment structure of a nontraditional format might be used.

Another popular term that sometimes reflects the dichotomy between the traditional ownership of control and the newly emerging "hybrid" forms that we use is the term *remix,* indicating that convergence of some form takes place to disrupt the traditional media industry (Lessig 2008). As Lawrence Lessig writes in his book, *Remix: Making Art and Commerce Thrive in the Hybrid Economy,* new forms of media do not necessarily conform to old models. In particular, he discusses how copyright law was originally designed to control commerce and provide wages to creative personnel, but now, our hybrid technologies and services make copyright obsolete.

See also: Copyright; Creative Commons; Open Source; Sharing Economy

Further Reading

Anderson, Chris. 2009. *Free: The Future of a Radical Price.* New York: Hyperion.
Isaacson, Walter. 2014. *The Innovators.* New York: Simon & Schuster.
Lessig, Lawrence. 2008. *Remix: Making Art and Commerce Thrive in the Hybrid Economy.* New York: Penguin Press.

Friending

Friending is a complicated concept because it means different things to different people. Some people think of friends as a number, as in those who attempt to have as many Facebook friends as possible, but this type of friending does not rely on the intimacy that is usually shared by friends in real life. Others see social networks as a way to reconnect with old friend, or as communities in which they can make new friends. In online dating programs, friends may bond through emotional ties that are romantically involved. As we learn more about what people mean when they talk about friending, we realize that there are different definitions of the word and the concept of *friend* that come into play over a person's developmental experience.

The act of friending someone online turns the word "friend" from a noun into an adjective as well as a verb. When social networking is a catalyst that allows people to reach an individual or group, the people who get the messages are called *friends* even when there is no emotional attachment that one usually experiences when one deems a person a "friend." The adjectival use of the term was used by the social network *Friendster,* created in 2002 by Jonathan Abrams who applied the adjective to mean that friending occurred in the process of using the social network. It is interesting that the social network Friendster predated both MySpace and Facebook, but Facebook popularized the term by shifting the use of the term *friend* from a noun to a verb. At the 2006 meeting of the Association of Internet Researchers (AoIR), a scholarly group dedicated to all aspects of the social and technical uses of the Internet, David Fono and Kate Raynes-Goldie presented a paper on how the term evolved through the use of a blog called LiveJournal, which was in use in 1999. In their paper, they examined both the friending process and the defriending process and identified characteristics of online friends that were different than traditional concepts of personal face-to-face friendship.

In many ways, the term *friending* has, at its core, the sense of connecting to others. Sometimes the online friends one makes are ephemeral, and other times more long lasting. Communities often emerge from groups of friends who have a special purpose, and though those communities may be more short-lived than geographic communities, they serve a strong purpose for people who participate in them. Entire bodies of study have been given to the type of communities that focus on what the act of friending is in social networking and how the word is changing in contemporary society because of the increased use of social networks.

According to danah boyd (she uses lower case letters for her name) whose research has focused on teen use of social networks, many teens use friending features to build communities based on specific affiliations as well as having pride in the number of friends they have online. The expectations for intimacy with those unknown, or not-well-known, friends is lower than for those whom one might have in a special category of *friend.* boyd also writes about the decisions teens make and the rules they seem to operate by in creating a shared practice of friending on a social network. The importance of being liked and of having a quantitative measure of "like(s)" is a measure of one's popularity—rather than any measure of true emotional connection (boyd 2010, 78–115).

What online friending has in common with real-world friending is that the concept of what a friend is and what one hopes to find in a friend changes as one matures. What constitutes friendship changes over one's lifetime, and it appears that online friendships also fulfill different needs in one's life. For example, renewing old friendships from high school or a former neighborhood is a very desirable activity for older people who use social networks for finding old friends, as is carrying on new online friendships that are not burdened by geographic space.

One's idea of online friendship and the role a friend can play in a social network is often related to how much time someone spends on social networks. Internet addicts seem to lose the balance between thinking of online personas and real people more than people who are socialized in both the real world and the cyberworld. For Internet addicts, the "rules" that might be in place in real life become blurred with the "rules" of cyberspace.

For teens or adults, online *friending* has several potential problems. While it can help one's social anxiety (fear of dealing with people in a face-to-face situation), the online friends and friendships can sometimes be misleading, or, in very serious cases, can lead to unbalanced power relationships among individuals. The fear of pedophilia (adults who prey on children for sexual favors) is an unfortunate outcome of how friending can go awry. Cyberbullying and using online services like social networks for demeaning others is a dysfunction of the use of social networks and turns the idea of friending on its head.

See also: Addiction; Cyberbullying; Dating; Identity; Privacy

Further Reading

boyd, danah. 2010. "Friendship." In *Hanging Out, Messing Around, and Geeking Out: Kids Living and Learning with New Media*, edited by Mizuko Ito et al. Cambridge, MA: Massachusetts of Technology Press, 78–115.

Fono, David, and Kate Raynes-Goldie. 2006. "Hyperfriends and Beyond: Friendship and Social Norms on LiveJournal." In the *Internet Research Annual*, vol 4: Selected Papers, edited by Mia Consalvo and Carolyn Haythornthwaite. New York: Peter Lang.

Friendster

One of the original social networking sites, *Friendster* became the first social network to reach over one million members as early as 2002. The name was a combination of *friend* and *Napster*, which was an exciting peer-to-peer file sharing program that had recently been developed by Shawn Fanning. The founder of Friendster was Jonathan Abrams, a former engineer at Netscape, who reportedly said he started Friendster as a way to meet girls. Though Friendster became popular with three million users in its first few months, it predated MySpace, Facebook, and the boom in other social networks that have survived the number of social networks that have emerged since the early 2000s. In retrospect, though it is considered one of the early social networks, it also presents a company that suffered from its timing as it became a victim of the dot-com crash and the fact that it predated smartphones.

In 2003, Google offered to buy Friendster for $30 million, but many venture capitalists in the Silicon Valley area urged Abrams to decline the offer. MySpace and Tribe.net both emerged in 2003, and Google launched its own form of social networking in 2004 called Orkut.

Friendster had many technical problems that prevented people from easily logging on to the website. By the time the service became stable, MySpace and Facebook had each captured much of the social network market. In 2009, Friendster was acquired by MOL Global, an online payment company in Malaysia. It still operates in Asia but specializes in gaming. In 2010, Facebook bought Friendster's portfolio of social networking patents for $40 million.

See also: Facebook; MySpace; Social Networking

Further Reading

Fiegerman, Seth. 2014. "Friendster Founder Tells His Side of the Story, 10 Years After Facebook." Mashable.com. Accessed December 5, 2014: http://mashable.com/2014/02/03/jonathan-abrams-friendster-facebook.

Revlin, Gary. 2006. "Wallflower at the Web Party." *New York Times.* Accessed December 4, 2014: http://www.nytimes.com/2006/10/15/business/yourmoney/15friend.html?pagewanted=1&_r=2.

G

Gamergate (See Gaming)

Gaming

Games are inherently social, so it is not surprising that one of the first major forms of using social media and social networking had to do with the technologies and techniques of the online gaming industry. The social aspects of social media and social networking compliment online gaming and have given rise to a $21.53 billion gaming industry (Essential Facts 2014, 13). The history of online gaming reaches back to game consoles and dedicated handheld devices that culminated in today's laptop, table, and smartphone devices, and one of the most lucrative types of app to be developed today is one that fits the category of a gaming app.

The success of online gaming has also infiltrated education, business, and a host of other industries and much of the credit is due to who played games as the industry evolved in the early 2000s, and how creative opportunities became available to new Internet users. As game experts John C. Beck and Mitchell Wade wrote: "video games ultimately grew so pervasive among and exclusive to youth that they became the defining experience for an entire generation" (Beck and Wade 2004, 59). During the early days of the twenty-first century, approximately 92 percent of the American population between the ages of 2 to 17 had regular access to video games through a variety of technologies, software, and, at that time, the emerging app market (Beck and Wade 2004, 3). In those days, most games were designed for males and played by males. Today, however, gamers represent all generations, and different genders.

Gaming in all of its forms has become big business. According to the research firm NPD Group, game playing on mobile platforms increased 57 percent between 2012 and the end of 2014. That suggests that people playing games on their smartphones spend about three hours a day playing games on their phones. This has resulted in the mobile market becoming a $25 billion market (Grubb 2015). According to the Entertainment Software Association, 59 percent of Americans play video games. Of those gamers, 68 percent play on a console, 53 percent play on smartphones, and 41 percent play on a wireless device like a tablet or other digital technology (Essential Facts 2014).

The precursors to today's digital games were developed over several decades. Electronic games started to be developed in the 1950s, but they began to flourish in the 1970s with video games developed for arcades and bars, home consoles, and the emerging personal computer industries. Pioneers like Nolan Bushnell and Ted Dabney formed Atari Inc., a small company that developed games, and they had an immediate hit with their simple electronic game called *Pong* in 1972. *Pong* consisted of a black-and-white diagram of two lines and a ball that was bounced back and forth, simulating a ping-pong game. It became very popular with members of the "baby-boomer" generation. It was followed by games that were not much more complex, like *Space Invaders, Frogger,* and *Pac-Man.*

By 1988, Nintendo refined home playing machines and home consoles really began to attract attention. By 1990, Nintendo's *Super Mario Brothers 3* became the best-selling home-based game in history, with sales of a half-billion dollars. By 2005, names like Xbox and the Sony PlayStation were introducing single or multiple-player games for home use, and dedicated handheld devices like the Nintendo GameBoy made portable gaming possible.

When the Mosaic browser with its graphs capacity and the ability to connect to the new World Wide Web became available in 1993, Internet-based games began to be developed, but many of them were still conceptually simple because people needed to connect to the Internet with dial-up services. Only when broadband became more readily available in homes did the popularity of Internet-based gaming take off. Once the twenty-first century began, the number of home-based game genres exploded.

At the time, most gamers were males, and, almost immediately, questions about violence and video games began to surface. First-person shooter games garnered a great deal of attention, but, at the same time, issues of addiction, aggression, violence, social development, and a variety of stereotyping and sexual morality issues began to surface. Over the years, the gaming industry began to develop games specifically for girls, but many of the games have been criticized for pandering to stereotypes and not really allowing "girl games" to let players engage in the full experience most games offer.

But what also happened in the 2000s was that social networks became popular ways of sharing games with others, or playing games over those social networks. Many of these games were played by individuals of both genders, and sometimes players could assume gaming identities that blurred whether they were female or male. *FarmVille,* for example, is a game that can be distributed through Facebook in web-based and mobile platforms and can be played by anyone, anywhere. Many of these games emphasized collaborative decision making and social interaction, and often games allowed users to develop an avatar to represent a physical body in the imaginary world provided by the game.

Online gaming has given us a number of new acronyms and descriptions of the forms of game play. The generic grouping of these games is the massively multiplayer online game (MMOs) that represents online games that are designed to be a social experience. Multiuser domains, sometimes called multiuser dungeons (MUDs), are virtual spaces in which social interaction with other players online becomes a part of the experience. Massively multiplayer online role-playing games (MMORPGs) are more elaborate online fantasy worlds that generally include graphics, visual elements, and audio that is more complicated than in a regular MUD. Both MUDs and MMORPGs have much in common, but each form structures the type of social interaction in a slightly different way and there is a different set of visual and auditory cues for each.

MUDs often tend to be text based and players typically interact with each other by typing commands that resemble spoken language. Before the term MMORPG came about, the type of game that fit into the category was called a graphical MUD. Both types of games encourage role playing, and for this reason many scholars have examined the psychological states of the game players to better identify what type of gratification a gamer gets from the type of social interaction in an MMO.

One of the first MUDs was called MUD1, and it was developed in 1978 by Richard Bartle and Roy Trubshaw at the University of Essex, in England. The game was called Multi-User Dungeon and the term "dungeon" was used because of the popular board game Dungeons and Dragons, which became popular in the early 1970s. The name fit well with the medieval fantasy theme of the game genre. Bartle later identified four types of MUD players. Bartle wrote that some are "achievers" who are goal oriented, some are "explorers" who are discovery oriented, some are "socializers" who are socially oriented, and some are "killers" who are annoyance oriented and like to impose themselves upon others (Bartle 1996).

Psychologist Sherry Turkle has also studied gamers in MMOs and has written about the "parallel identities" that allow a person to act out an identity different from their real-world life, and possibly overcome personal problems (Turkle 1995, 186). She writes that, in MUDs [and by association, in MMORPGs], people sometimes blur the lines that separate their real-world existence from their online personas. While these parallel identities may be fine, they sometimes bridge into problematic areas when the person loses the ability to understand which "self" they are enacting. This often becomes a behavior problem when someone becomes addicted to gaming.

Virtual games, like *Second Life* or *The SIMS* also introduced more advanced ideas of virtual reality to game playing by using enhanced graphics to create a fantasy world in which players assumed other identities as well as a different sense of the environment. *Second Life* was developed by Linden Labs, an Internet company started by Philip Rosedale, who started the company with the money he had earned as chief technology officer at RealNetworks. The name of the company comes from the name of the street where the company first started, Linden Street.

As a game developer of virtual reality games, Linden Labs has experimented with a number of business models and ways to use virtual environments. For *Second Life*, they offered Linden Dollars, a form of cybercurrency that could be used not only to purchase virtual world products while one plays a virtual game but that for a time became transferable for real cash. As the official currency of *Second Life*, this form of cybercurrency has often been criticized for its volatility. *Second Life* simulations have also been applied elsewhere beyond the gaming world and have been used to create a virtual meeting space for businesses and social movements.

Online gaming is often criticized for the addictive nature of some games, violence, and for the sexism and misogyny in many games. Traditionally, men have dominated the design of games, and, as mentioned above, for many years males were thought to be the primary users of online games. In recent years, though, as more women have become active in gaming and in designing games, the sexist depictions of women have become a topic of major concern. In 2013 and 2014, the *gamergate* controversy resulted in a blurring of online and real-world criticism that saw many women—game designers, scholars, and game players—abused online and offline for their criticism of the male-dominated world. This became known as gamergate.

The gamergate controversy began in 2013 when game developer Zoe Quinn released a game called *Depression Quest*, an interactive game that allows players to portray a person suffering from depression. The game was designed to help people understand the problems that people with depression have and how they deal with them. The game is not meant to be entertaining or fun but, rather, to allow people to understand the emotional depths that people with depression go through. As a "game" it is an immersive experience rather than an experience that pits different combatants so that someone "wins."

By 2015, it became known that an anonymous poster on the site 4Chan had begun a campaign to threaten Quinn. The person wrote: "Next time she shows up at a conference we . . . give her a crippling injury that's never going to fully heal . . . a good solid injury to the knees. I'd say a brain damage, but we don't want to make it so she ends up too retarded to fear us" (Parkin 2014). Quinn had been "doxed," meaning that her personal details, like home address, phone numbers, bank information, etc., had been made public on the Internet. She began to get threatening e-mails, prank calls, harassing e-mail and Twitter messages, and she began to fear for her safety. Soon, the culture wars over gaming began.

Both game developer Brianna Wu and feminist cultural critic Anita Sarkeesian were also targeted and received misogynistic threats. Most of the attacks were launched over social media forms like reddit, 4chan, and 8chan and became represented with the Twitter hashtag #gamergate. The women were threatened with being doxed, rape, and, in Sarkeesian's case, death, in response to a university talk she was to have given. Sarkeesian had developed a YouTube video series called *Tropes vs. Women in Video Games,* for which she had mounted a Kickstarter campaign, and her work was seen as threatening to males who enjoyed the types of games she criticized.

The active blurring of the online world and the real world as evidenced by gamergate shows how some gamers negotiate (or do not negotiate) the space between the real world and the online world of gaming. Since a theme of this encyclopedia is the range of social media functions, this behavioral aspect of gaming and problems negotiating real and cyber worlds is troubling. Here, online games can become serious problems for those who can't control their behaviors and who prefer to live in the online world rather than the real world. Compulsive or addictive behavior is also a part of excessive use of online gaming. As a result, it is not surprising that so much criticism of social media comes from the examples that are all too apparent in gaming strategies and the big business of online games.

Any entry on gaming would be remiss if the range of games described did not include the types of traditional games that have become big business online. Online gambling, especially online poker, is extremely popular, and while online gaming was prohibited to operate within the United States (all casinos were located offshore) until 2013, only three states, Delaware, Nevada, and New Jersey, currently sponsor online poker and online gambling.

There are, however, a number on online casinos, sports betting sites, lotteries, and even bingo games that can be played online by individuals, for money, and most of these sites are operating legally. While data reflecting the amount of money that is exchanged on these sites is not generally available, the phenomenon alone shows that social media have extended well beyond the original dreams of the people and companies that developed the Internet and World Wide Web.

With several years of games to reflect on, and scholarly as well as market research examining games, gamers, and behavior, we now know much more about what people "get" when they play games. Not only might there be instant gratification, but the ability to "lose" oneself in the game has become a fascinating study of the real world versus the cyber, or online, world. Among the characteristics, Beck and Wade have identified the way games position the individual at the center of attention and reward the gamer's skill. In their examination of the way the gamer generation has absorbed what they have learned from games into their own attitudes and behaviors, they predict that gamers' view of the world influences the type of work that they do. With more work being done online, games might suggest a way to understand the behavior, attitudes, and reward system expected by gamers, even as real-world work becomes a part of their lives.

See also: Addiction; Anonymity; Avatar

Further Reading

Ahmed, Saeed, and Tony Marco. 2014. "Anita Sarkeesian Forced to Cancel Utah State Speech after Mass Shooting Threat." Accessed December 29, 2014: http://edition.cnn.com/2014/10/15/tech/utah-anita-sarkeesian-threat/index.html.

Bartle, Richard. 1996. "Hearts, Clubs, Diamonds, Spades: Players Who Suit MUDs." MUSE. Accessed April 27, 2015: http://www.mud.co.uk/richard/hcds.htm.

Beck, John C., and Mitchell Wade. 2004. *Got Game: How the Gamer Generation Is Reshaping Business Forever.* Boston, MA: Harvard Business School Press.

"Essential Facts about the Computer and Video Game Industry." 2014. Entertainment Software Industry 2014 Essential Sales, Demographic, and Usage Data. Accessed December 27, 2015: http://www.theesa.com/wp-content/uploads/2014/10/ESA_EF_2014.pdf.

Grubb, Jeff. 2015. "You're Spending More Time Playing Mobile Games Than Ever Before." *VentureBeat.* Accessed April 27, 2015: http://venturebeat.com/2015/01/27/youre-spending-more-time-playing-mobile-games-than-ever-before/.

Kaplan, Sarah. 2014. "With #GamerGate, the Video-Game Industry's Growing Pains Go Viral." *Washington Post.* Accessed December 29, 2014: http://www.washingtonpost.com/news/morning-mix/wp/2014/09/12/with-gamergate-the-video-game-industrys-growing-pains-go-viral/.

Parkin, Simon. 2014. "Zoe Quinn's Depression Quest." *The New Yorker.* Accessed May 6, 2015: http://www.newyorker.com/tech/elements/zoe-quinns-depression-quest.

Turkle, Sherry. 1995. *Life on the Screen: Identity in the Age of the Internet.* New York: Simon & Schuster, 186–187.

Gates, Bill

William Henry (Bill) Gates III (1955–), along with Paul Allen, founded Microsoft in 1975. By 1998, Microsoft Windows was running on approximately 95 percent of the personal computers running worldwide, and Gates had become the world's richest man.

Born in Seattle, Washington, Gates became interested in computer programming at the age of 12. After becoming interested in the Altair 8800 minicomputer that he had seen in a 1974 copy of *Popular Electronics*, he dropped out of Harvard and started a business with his high school friend, Paul Allen. Both realized they were more interested in software than hardware, so they focused on that aspect of the burgeoning computer wave.

Gates was introduced to early computing at the Lakeside school where, although only in seventh grade, he and some friends used the teletype terminal in the school's computer room that connected to a General Electric Mark II time-sharing computer system. The simple computer used BASIC code that had been developed at Dartmouth College in 1964. After becoming proficient in BASIC, he went on to teach himself Fortran and COBOL. By 1968, Gates and Allen had established the Lakeside Programming Group. In 1973, both were recruited to work for the Bonneville Power Administration that was looking for young talent to help program the company's electrical grid management system.

Soon, Gates moved on to Harvard University where he intended to major in math. He convinced Paul Allen to drop out of Washington State University, where he had been in attendance, and move to Cambridge. When the two saw the article about the Altair 8800 minicomputer in *Popular Electronics*, they decided to write software that would allow hobbyists to use the small computer. After first writing to the company that made the Altair 8800 but getting no response, they phoned the company and said they had written code in BASIC for the computer, and asked for the opportunity to show it to someone. When they were told that there was an interest in having a code that would work on the machine, they then started working on writing the code. After eight weeks of intense work, they had a code and Paul Allen flew to Albuquerque to demonstrate it. The company bought the program and offered Allen a job.

Between his sophomore and junior years at Harvard, Bill Gates went to Albuquerque and worked for a time. He and Allen had licensed their code to be used with the Altair computer for $30 per copy in royalties. They also started a company that they called Micro-Soft. Gates later returned to Harvard for two more semesters, but dropped out before his senior year. In 2007, Harvard awarded him with an honorary degree. In his acceptance speech he said: "I've been waiting for more than 30 years to say this, Dad, I always told you I'd come back and get my degree" (Malone 2007).

The business relationship between Gates and Allen was complicated. At first, Gates insisted that the profits be split 60–40; meaning he would receive 60 percent of the profit, and Allen, 40 percent. In two years, Gates proposed a new structure that would give him 64 percent, and Allen, 36 percent. In a short period of time, Gates became the energetic leader of Micro-Soft (later changed to Microsoft). Allen, an affable person, was not used to this type of confrontation and allowed the splits to occur, though, later in life, he wrote about the contentious relationship about money in his memoir, *Idea Man: A Memoir by the Cofounder of Microsoft* (2012).

When the Microsoft code became popular, computer enthusiasts assumed that it would be free, or accessible at a very low rate. Gates wrote an apocryphal letter to the enthusiasts asking for them to pay for the Altair BASIC code, but received very few payments. Instead, Gates and Allen decided to move their business to Seattle, where they set up headquarters. But Gates's reputation for his audacity and energetic protection of the company began to become legendary.

At Microsoft, Gates became known as a person who had an excellent business sense and used aggressive business tactics that were not always free of controversy. He was chief executive officer (CEO) and chief software architect. He retired in 2008, but has stayed on as chair and advisor on important development projects.

Gates married Melinda French in 1994, and together they began a charitable organization, the Bill and Melinda Gates Foundation, which, by 2013, was considered the world's wealthiest charitable foundation with assets valued at more than $34.6 billion. It is said that the foundation has an annual budget dedicated to world health care matters that is bigger than that of the World Health Organization (WHO). Among their many humanitarian projects, they have provided grants and aid to help eradicate disease in many parts of the world, especially Africa; supported efforts for girls to get education in developing countries; and funded projects to improve the quality of life for millions of people worldwide. In 2005, *Time* magazine named Bill and Melinda Gates, as well as Bono, as "Persons of the Year" for their philanthropic activities.

See also: Microsoft

Further Reading

Allen, Paul. 2012. *Idea Man: A Memoir by the Cofounder of Microsoft*. New York: Penguin.
Isaacson, Walter. 2014. *The Innovators*. New York: Simon & Schuster, 314–342.
Malone, Scott. 2007. "Dropout Bill Gates Returns to Harvard for Degree." Reuters News Service. Accessed April 20, 2015: http://www.reuters.com/article/2007/06/07/us-microsoft -gates-idUSN0730259120070607.
Toal, Robin. 2014. "Top Ten U.S. Charitable Foundations." FundsforNGOs. Accessed December 10, 2014: http://www.fundsforngos.org/foundation-funds-for-ngos/worlds-top -ten-wealthiest-charitable-foundations/.

Google

Google Inc. is a major multinational company that provides online search services for Internet users and develops user services. It has been a leader in making search strategies profitable through advertising. The company was started by Larry Page and Sergei Brin in 1996, both of whom were Stanford University graduate students at the time. The name comes from the mathematical term googol that would look like a unit of measurement with a "1" followed by 100 zeros. It seemed that the googol measurement would represent the amount of information the program could sift through, but when they tried to register the name "googol" it was taken. In their haste, they typed *Google* and the term was available. When Page and Brin realized their mistake, they tried to buy the domain name googol, but the owner didn't want to relinquish it. So, they stayed with Google, and the name began to grow on them.

The domain name *Google* was registered in 1997, and the company was incorporated in 1998, in Menlo Park, California. Today, though Google has major offices in various locations, the company headquarters are in a building complex called the Googleplex in Mountain View, California. In 2006, the *Merriam-Webster Collegiate Dictionary* and the *Oxford English Dictionary* each added Google as a verb, as in "to Google" meaning to use the Google search engine for information about something on the World Wide Web.

At Stanford, Page and Brin worked on a search engine they called BackRub, which searched through data in such a way that the popularity of searches could be tracked. Prior to BackRub, Page had developed a search strategy called "Page Rank." This became the idea behind Google's presentation of information, which lists the most popular sites at the top of its list and those less popular in descending order. By examining "backward" through data, they came up with a mode of searching that recognized the popularity of searches. Originally, they ran the new service on the Stanford server, but the large amounts of information caused the system to crash, and that was when the two decided to venture off campus as a start-up company.

Google has become one of the major success stories of companies that emerged during what became known as the *dot-com bubble* of the 1990s, and it now operates in over 150 languages. The company also has a number of data centers, including six in the United States, and in Chile, Finland, Ireland, Belgium, Singapore, and Taiwan.

When Page and Brin incorporated the company, they developed a company motto that stands to this day, "Don't be evil." They also wrote a mission statement in which they claimed that the company's purpose was "to organize the world's information and make it universally accessible and useful." Since 1999, the company has been headquartered in Palo Alto, California, in the heart of Silicon Valley.

Though much of Google's revenue now comes from its success with advertising, Page and Brin were initially opposed to the search engine carrying advertising. Still, they began the process of selling ads associated with search keywords in 2000. The keywords were sold on a process of advertisers bidding for the price, and the user clicking through to the ad. Originally, the bidding would start at five cents per click, some of which was returned to Google with the remainder going to the advertiser.

Prior to Google's acquisition of AdSense in 2003, the only way the service paid for ads was on a per-click basis, but, soon after the program was implemented, Google realized that some people were inflating the value of their advertising messages by repeatedly clicking on their own content. In 2009, Google acquired the AdWords system that allowed advertisers to create text ads for placement on the Google search engine and would relate to AdSense. This combined system allows advertisers to bid on placement of ads and then assesses revenue based upon placement. While the cost is not absolutely fixed, in general, 68 percent of the amount an advertiser pays for the placement of the ad is the revenue the content provider receives, and the rest is the commission made by Google for hosting the space.

According to market research published by comScore in 2014, Google is the dominant search engine in the United States with a market share of 65.6 percent ("comScore Releases March 2014 U.S. Search Engine Rankings" 2014). It is also a leader in online advertising, earning more than $50 billion a year, bringing in six times more revenue than Facebook, the second largest advertiser ("comScore Releases March 2014 Search Engine Rankings" 2014).

Google's search mechanism has allowed the company to develop models that connect words to concepts and words to advertisements, all while using big data analytics to track how people react to the ads they see on their screens. It can do this largely through the DoubleClick system that it acquired in 2007, which allows maximum identification of product with the reaction of the computer or mobile device user when they respond to an ad.

Historically, different advertising platforms have been measured according to the type of ratings system available at the time. So, for many years, television, for example, has relied on the Nielsen Ratings to help measure the potential audience. With search engines like Google, the combination of ad and direct consumer changes the measurement methods for online advertising, but, in 2014, Google went one step further. In 2014, Google acquired the online measurement firm, comScore, for an undisclosed sum. The combination of DoubleClick and comScore's analytics will provide a more contemporary form of measuring audience response in real time, meaning that advertisers will be able to see how an ad or campaign is working, and change strategies midstream if they are unhappy with the results. As reported in *USA Today,* "The deal, which has been in the works for almost a year, may affect billions of ads a day, changing the way agencies and big companies run and monitor campaigns. This is part of a broader push by Google to attract more big brands, which have traditionally spent most of their money on TV" (Barr 2014). With an estimated growth potential of capturing $31 billion a year in advertising by 2017, Google is well situated to dominate online advertising and to develop the type of ratings and analytic systems that can combine advertising on all platforms.

In addition to the acquisitions that have made Google a major force in advertising, the company has acquired a number of smaller companies and has developed several apps and content-based projects. In January 2014, ABC News reported that Google had been acquiring roughly one company every week for some time with over 160 acquisitions to date (Farnham 2014). Though the list of acquisitions is long, those that relate most directly to social networking are addressed in this section.

Google maps was launched in 2005, and, in 2006, Google purchased YouTube for $1.65 billion. Google made its Chrome web browser available for free in 2008. By January 2015, Chrome was the most popular web browser in the world with 51 percent of the world's laptop and desktop computers using it ("StatCounter Global Stats" 2015).

Google partnered with Android Inc., in 2009 to develop the Android mobile operating system and, in the same year, introduced Gmail, Google Calendar, Google Docs, and Google Talk. Google Ventures brought out Project Glass (Google Glass) in 2013, which started the company's investigations into wearable technology. Its largest acquisition so far has been the purchase of Motorola Mobility, a mobile device manufacturing company, for $12.5 billion, in 2011.

Google Ventures, the venture capital division of Google, has also been investing heavily in nonmedia companies and industries, dealing with clean energies, robotics, education, transportation, shopping, and medicine. In general, their investments total approximately $300 million annually.

Google+ (Google Plus)

In 2011, Google responded to criticisms of other social networks that were riddled with issues surrounding the personal privacy of their users. In response, Google introduced Google+ (spoken as Google Plus)—a social network purportedly more "private" for users than any other. It started its own social network in 2013. At the time, many social networks were being criticized for their violations of personal privacy. Facebook, in particular, was undergoing a number of changes in response to angry users who had been made aware of Facebook's selling of private information to third-party companies, like advertisers. So in response, Google publicized Google+ as a more secure social network and gave users a number of security features to control their own private information.

Google's plan, however, was to use Google+ to help integrate users' Google functions, like Google Docs, Google Glass, and other apps, so that users would be able to move seamlessly from one Google function to another. Despite initial interest in the social network, many users preferred to range from one system to another, and Google+ quickly peaked and then was heavily criticized for marginalizing other programs.

Google+ grew from the concept of Google Circles, and followed Google's other attempts at social networking with Orkut (2004), Google Friend Connect (2008–2012), and Google Buzz (2010–2011). All of these are attempts by Google to become a dominant force in social networks that are built on the concept of *friending* others for purposes of streamlining communication from person to person, and data mining the connections for more targeted advertising and communication efficacy. While the desire to bundle services is understandable, it is generally agreed that having a number of different services available, from which the consumer can pick and choose, actually makes for a more contented social media user.

According to Jeff Bercovici, a technology journalist for *Forbes* magazine (2014), Google's attempt to force users to use Google+ could eventually turn into a series of antitrust suits from companies that offer similar services, and Google (like all major multimedia companies) has been brought before the Federal Trade Commission by many companies already. The FTC has investigated some accusations, but not those related to Google+.

Google has aggressively started to examine its role as a manufacturer and distributor of wearable technologies. Among its first major developments was Google Glass, a product of Google Ventures. It is an example of wearable technology and suggests that a number of digital features will be available to us in the future, to be worn on our bodies rather than to be discrete physical technologies. Though called *Google Glass*, the technology resembles a pair of eyeglasses, with a small pane of glass at the corner of one eye, that is operated by voice command and a series of swipes along the earpiece and "computer" mounted on one earpiece. The unit can be combined with a computer to access directions, has simple navigational tools, and takes still pictures and short videos. Google's experiment with Google Glass was a step toward more wearable technology that we can expect to see in the near future.

Isabelle Olsson, the lead designer of Google Glass, reviewed hundreds of prototypes before coming up with Google Glass computer-equipped eyewear. When experiments began in 2010, testers used an augmented reality headset connected to a bag that included a touch pad and web cam. The first prototype looked more like a backpack than the light-weight eyewear that eventually debuted.

Google Glass eyewear was released on April 15, 2013, and sold for $1,500 to "Glass Explorers" who applied to buy the device and agreed to respond to Google's questions about their use of the glass. In May 2014, Google announced a one day sale of Google Glass in which anyone could purchase the device, regardless of application or agreement to communicate with Google on their use of the device.

To aid in the marketing of the eyewear, Google supported an online connection for those interested in Google Glass to show pictures that Google Glass owners had taken, videos, and experimental uses, such as movement through a cityscape, or for a piece of art. Interested owners could see online "albums" of what Google Glass could do, and occasional travelogues were posted.

While the visual images Google Glass produced were of high quality, video action could only be captured in six seconds. What seemed to concern the developers, though, were the range of criticisms people seemed to throw at the technology. Some reported a fear that the Glass would be able to see through other people's clothing, or invade privacy. Other common criticism was that the Google Glass itself was distracting to people who wore the glasses while driving, riding a bike, or even walking.

In January 2015, Google announced that it was going to end the chapter on the first commercial iteration of Google Glass, and it stopped the online support for creative activities using Google Glass. Though Google announced that it would continue developing wearable technology, the experiment in Google Glass was short-lived, but productive for the emerging field of *augmented reality*.

See also: Advertising; Brin, Sergei; Dot-Com Bubble; Page, Larry; Wearable Technology

Further Reading

Barr, Alistair. 2014. "Google Strikes Big Ad Measurement Deal with comScore." *USA Today.* Accessed March 31, 2015: http://www.usatoday.com/story/tech/2014/02/10/google-comscore-advertising-deal/5291189/.

Bercovici, Jeff. 2014. "Google Will Be Better Off Minus Google+." *Forbes.* Accessed March 1, 2015: http://www.forbes.com/sites/jeffbercovici/2014/04/25/google-will-be-better-off-minus-google/.

Cass, Stephen, and Charles Q. Choi. 2015. "Google Glass, HoloLens, and the Real Future of Augmented Reality." *IEEE Spectrum*, 52. Accessed March 1, 2015: http://spectrum.ieee.org/consumer-electronics/audiovideo/google-glass-hololens-and-the-real-future-of-augmented-reality.

"comScore Releases March 2014 U.S. Search Engine Rankings." 2014. Accessed December 12, 2014. https://www.comscore.com/Insights/Press-Releases/2014/4/comScore-Releases-March-2014-U.S.-Search-Engine-Rankings.

Farnham, Alan. 2014. "Google's Best and Worst Big Acquisitions." Accessed December 10, 2014: http://abcnews.go.com/Business/googles-best-worst-acquisitions/story?id=21526661.

Pimbblet, Kirstie-Ann. 2013. "How Google Glass Could Evolve Social Media." Social Media Today. Accessed December 10, 2014: http://www.socialmediatoday.com/content/how-google-glass-could-evolve-social-media.

"Should Digital Monopolies Be Broken Up?" 2014. *The Economist,* 413: 11.

"StatCounter Global Stats." 2015. StatCounter Analytics. Accessed April 27, 2015: http://gs.statcounter.com/#desktop-browser-ww-monthly-201501-201501-bar.

Gore, Al

Al (Albert) Arnold Gore Jr. (1948–) was a representative and senator from the state of Tennessee. Gore was originally elected to Congress at the age of 28 and served for 16 years. He then became vice president to President Bill Clinton from 1993 to 2001. A major advocate of telecommunications reform and improvements, Gore is credited with having coined the term "the information superhighway" to describe the Internet. The claim that he "invented" the Internet is a rumor and is not factually true. He ran for president in 2000 against George W. Bush and won the popular vote, though the close presidential race ended up being decided by the Supreme Court, which found in favor of Bush.

While in Congress, Gore was known as an *Atari Democrat*, meaning that he was drawn to technology and technological solutions to problems. The name "Atari" reflects a gaming console that was very popular during the 1970s and 1980s, which coincided with public interest and debate about the emerging Internet. In Congress he sponsored several bills that advanced the use of technology for security and defense purposes. As vice president, he became involved in the establishment of the National Information Infrastructure (NII). Gore sponsored the High-Performance Computing and Communications Act of 1991 (known as the Gore Bill or the Gore Act), which allocated money for high-performance computing and helped create the National Research and Educational Network (NREN). He strongly believed that the government should be actively involved in the development of the Internet and that it had a moral responsibility to make the Internet available to everyone. During the Clinton/Gore administration, the first official presidential and vice presidential websites were launched, and all federal agencies were required to use the technology. Gore also supported the use of the Internet for schools through his involvement with "Net Day" and stated that it was his mission to connect all classrooms in the country to the Internet by the year 2000. He was inducted into the Internet Hall of Fame in 2012.

After leaving the White House, he became a passionate advocate of defending the Earth from global climate change. His film, *An Inconvenient Truth*, earned him an Oscar in 2007 for "Best Documentary" and, the same year, Gore accepted a Nobel Prize for work on global warming as a coaward winner with the Intergovernmental Panel on Climate Change. His work after his political career earned him the title of "environmental activist."

Additionally, he has become a venture capitalist, investing in companies like Amazon.com and eBay, through the company he cofounded, Generation Investment. In 2005, he, along with Joel Hyatt, founded a liberal cable news channel called Current TV, aimed at a young audience. Current TV was sold to Al-Jazeera, an Arab news network, in 2013.

See also: Information Superhighway; Internet

Further Reading

Kessler, Glenn. 2013. "A Cautionary Tale for Politicians: Al Gore and the 'Invention' of the Internet." *Washington Post*. Accessed December 28, 2014: http://www.washington post.com/blogs/fact-checker/wp/2013/11/04/a-cautionary-tale-for-politicians-al-gore -and-the-invention-of-the-internet.

H

Hacker

Hacker is the term given to a person who is a computer expert and who is sometimes referred to as a computer addict who disrupts or vandalizes the normal processes of using computers. The people who first identified as technology enthusiasts at the Massachusetts Institute of Technology (MIT) who started a student-activity group called the Tech Model Railroad Club during the 1946–1947 school year focused on model trains and applied the word "hack" to indicate a person who applies ingenuity to bring about a clever result. Over time, hacker subculture has evolved that reifies hacker lifestyles and culture. According to psychologist Sherry Turkle, hackers take pride in being "outsiders" in the community and share a number of attributes, including a sense of being nerdy, self-centered, uncommunicative, and interested in ego and money. The hacker community is one in which knowledge of the hardware and software involved in computers and the Internet identifies an aspect of interpersonal identity and class. The identity often reflects someone who flouts conventions and rules, but over time hackers have come to be seen as malcontents who like to create problems for others, such as embedding viruses and worms in computer programs, or disrupting the daily routine of a computer program (Turkle 1984, 196–234).

In the early days of the public use of the Internet, many hackers seemed to engage in hacking just to see what would happen. Robert Tappan Morris is now a professor at MIT, but as an undergraduate at Cornell in 1988, he released what may have been the first computer worm that infected 6,000 Unix-based computers. He became the first person convicted under the 1986 Federal Computer Fraud and Abuse Act (Kushner 2014, 48).

Real-life hackers, like the self-proclaimed hacker Julian Assange who founded WikiLeaks, and the group that calls itself Anonymous, hack for political purposes, but hackers do what they do for a variety of reasons. For example, after Christmas, 2014, the hacktivist group Lizard Squad issued denial of service notices to users of both the PlayStation Network and Xbox Live, allegedly, as reported, "for laughs" and to expose the "incompetence" of the security teams at Microsoft and Sony.

The term *hacker* sometimes used to describe people who are more comfortable with computers than with other people and hacker culture has evolved to show the many dimensions of hacker life. In recent years the symbolic power of the hacker has been demonstrated in a number of popular culture venues. Movies like *The Matrix*, *Ghost in the Shell*, *Code Hunter*, *Tron*, *War Games*, *The Net*, and, of course, *Hackers*, blur science fiction and the hacker ethos, and often the popular culture hackers are represented as either "black hats" (hackers who are up to bad things) or "white hats" (who hack for the good of humanity). Books have been written about famous hackers, like Kevin Poulsen, who was the first hacker charged with espionage after allegedly stealing classified information from the Air Force. After being captured by the FBI and serving 51 months in prison for his crimes, the book *The Watchman: The Twisted Life and Crimes of Serial Hacker Kevin Poulsen* was published by Jonathan Littman (1997). Poulsen eventually gave up his hacking and became a journalist and editor for *Wired* magazine where he specializes in hackers and hacktivism. In 2011, Poulsen published his own book, *Kingpin: How One Hacker Took Over the Billion-Dollar Cybercrime Underground*.

In 2012, Kevin Mitnick published a book about his exploits as a hacker, *Ghost in the Wires: My Adventures as the World's Most Wanted Hacker*. Mitnick began his hacking career at age 15 by hacking the computer systems of major corporations. After he had served a five-year prison sentence for hacking major companies like IBM, Nokia, and Motorola (and more) in many states, Mitnick became a computer security consultant.

See also: Anonymous; Assange, Julian; Cyberwar; Snowden, Edward; Spyware; Surveillance

Further Reading

Kushner, David. 2014. "The Masked Avengers: How Anonymous Incited Online Vigilantism from Tunisia to Ferguson." *The New Yorker*, 90: 48.

Littman, Jonathan. 1997. *The Watchman: The Twisted Life and Crimes of Serial Hacker Kevin Poulsen*. New York: Little, Brown and Co.

Mitnick, Kevin, with William L Simon. 2012. *The Ghost in the Wires: My Adventures as the World's Most Wanted Hacker*. New York: Little, Brown and Co.

Poulsen, Kevin. 2011. *Kingpin: How One Hacker Took Over the Billion-Dollar Cybercrime Underground*. New York: Crown Publishing.

Turkle, Sherry. 1984. *The Second Self: Computers and the Human Spirit*. New York: Simon & Schuster, 196–238.

Hyperconnectivity

The term *hyperconnectivity* explains the relationship of people and things (content and technologies) that are digitally connected to each other through networks. Hyperconnectivity helps explain what it means to be inundated with technologies that extend our ability to communicate with others and to access a wide variety of forms of information. The term suggests that peoples' behaviors will be conditioned to the anywhere, anytime aspects of using technology to connect to others or to information in real time (in synchronous time).

Furthermore, the type of hyperconnectivity we can expect suggests that all of the technologies and people using them will communicate in a seamless, natural way with user-friendly technologies. This type of experience changes the way we think about ourselves and the world around us. The concept of hyperconnectivity helps us understand how reliant we have become on technology, and the energy infrastructure to support reliable communications interactivity.

Hyperconnectivity can affect our attention span, condition us to have expectations of others, contribute to our forgetting information quickly, and influence our sense of self and identity. It is estimated that by the year 2020 over 50 billion networked devices will be operational in the world, contributing even further to the technologically induced expectations for immediacy and self that we develop as human beings. The World Economic Forum, an independent organization that focuses on developing public and private partnerships predicts that hyperconnectivity will impact every aspect of the lives of those who use digital networks from health and education to transportation and business (Sherman 2014).

There is certainly a "down side" to hyperconnectivity in the sense that our brains can only process a certain amount of attention at any given time. According to Neil Postman, "We are a culture consuming itself with information, and many of us do not even wonder how to control the process . . . cultures may also suffer grievously from information glut, information without meaning, information without control mechanisms" (Postman 1992, 70). Nicholas Carr has written persuasively about the effect of too much online activity and our attention spans in *The Shallows: What the Internet Is Doing to Our Brains* 2010).

See also: Addiction; Digital

Further Reading

Carr, Nicholas. 2010. *The Shallows: What the Internet Is Doing to Our Brains.* New York: W. W. Norton and Co.

Postman, Neil. 1992. *Technopoly: The Surrender of Culture to Technology.* New York: Vintage Books.

Ranadive, Vivek. 2013. "Hyperconnectivity: The Future Is Now." *Forbes.* Accessed December 9, 2014: http://www.forbes.com/sites/vivekranadive/2013/02/19/hyperconnectivity-the-future-is-now/.

Sherman, Adam. 2014. "Hyperconnected World." World Economic Forum. Accessed December 9, 2014: http://www.weforum.org/projects/hyperconnected-world.

I

Identity

The Internet has fundamentally changed how people think of themselves and how they relate to one another. Social networks and online communities can extend the reach of real-world groups, but people can also form communities and close friendships with people they have never met in person. The concept of *identity* is a complicated one. Identity marks the way we think of ourselves, but on the Internet and in social networks, we do not always have to be truthful about who or what we are. In a famous *New Yorker* cartoon by Peter Steiner published July 5, 1993, one dog says to another, "On the Internet, nobody knows you're a dog." The cartoon became a popular meme that often explained how the Internet could be used to trick someone, or hide one's identity. At about the same time, one of the emerging social networks, MySpace, allowed users to *create* their own online identity that did not have to be an authentic identity, further giving credibility to the idea that the Internet could be used by people who were not who they really were.

The concept of identity on the Internet and particularly on social networks or social media goes much further than a person representing themselves in the most accurate way, or in the ways they use online media for purposes of self-expression. Some sites help people explore their identities through blogging, participating in communities that have self-actualizing principles, or experimenting to see that elements of their life are really important to them. Think, for example, of the way people define themselves on Facebook, or an online dating site. Chances are, if the social media user is engaging in online activities as an extension of one's self, his or her descriptions (and pictures) are probably accurate. But, at the same time, if people want to experiment with being someone of another race, gender, ethnicity, or even species, an avatar or a pseudoidentity is possible in some of those same sites as well as in gaming and role-playing venues. Online identities do not always have to be the same as a person's real identity, and therein lies some of the fascinating features of real world and online world dichotomies.

The term given to the identity/ies one creates online is called a *digital presence.* What this means is that people might describe themselves and manage their digital presence in different ways over social media depending on the type of identity they wish to express for that particular site or technology. For example, Facebook profiles generally show people at their best. This has led one researcher to surmise that because celebrities have become such powerful heroes in contemporary culture, Facebook actually allows everyone to be a celebrity, and those who use social media aspire toward celebrity status. "A part of their identity is defined by how many friends, or fans, they have" (Cirucci 2013, 47). In the same vein, when the same people play an online game like *World of Warcraft* (WOW), they can craft their avatar to be like themselves, or like someone else. "After creating an avatar in WOW, a gamer has many in-game options that continue to form the avatar's identity . . . the avatar undertakes and chooses the professions in which the avatar will excel" (Cirucci 2013, 47). These projections of self in two different online worlds show that one person can take on multiple "selves" when they immerse themselves into the culture of the site.

Sometimes, though, acting out a different identity online can be harmless. It can allow someone to feel what it's like to be someone else for a while, and as long as the intention isn't malicious, the freedom afforded by having a different identity online can give someone a different perspective. Issues of gender, race, and ethnicity can be supported online, but they can also raise questions of how people see their identity and describe themselves online. Psychologist Sherry Turkle has written that the Internet has allowed people to think of identity as "multiplicity." As she stated in *Life on the Screen: Identity in the Age of the Internet,* "On it, people are able to build a self by cycling through many selves" (Turkle 1995, 178). By this she meant that we can have one identity while talking to friends, a professional identity when talking to bosses or teachers, and a more playful self when involved in a chat room, or we can even be more overtly sexual while engaging in a site that is more "adult oriented."

While people may choose to use a false name (pseudonym) or describe themselves differently, or even choose an avatar to mask their real self, issues of identity go beyond representation of self to the world of privacy and security. Some people post significant amounts of personal information about themselves online that they think may be secure but can easily be stolen or sent to others. Because the places where we use social media or social networking are often private places like one's home or even bedroom—it is easy to think that we're engaging in personal communication that is meant for only the person to whom we're corresponding. But even sending a personal message on e-mail or Facebook can easily be forwarded to someone else. ISPs can typically trace online activity to a home address, which has made it possible for predators to target children and find out personal information, then confront the child at home when no adult is present. Posting pictures of your vacation in real time can be a signal to thieves that no one is home.

Identity theft is also a significant problem that has become a concern for individuals, law enforcement, and governments. Criminals can often gain a lot of information about a person by sending out messages as *spam* that look real but are designed to trick someone into giving up a lot of personal information. Sometimes the target is to find out someone's password or bank information but the possible number of ways criminals trick people into giving up personal information is growing. The U.S. Department of Justice has advice for people, who think or are sure they have been the targets of identity theft, on their website: http://www.justice.gov/criminal/fraud/websites/idtheft.html.

Increasingly, some parents are establishing digital presences for babies when they are born. Some parents register their babies for things like About.me pages, Instagram feeds, Twitter handles, Tumblr accounts, and e-mail accounts on Yahoo and Gmail, all within hours of their birth (Wood 2014). Some even post pictures of sonograms, giving the baby an ambiguous digital presence before they are born! But starting a digital presence for a newborn even before they have any sense of who they are comes with some theoretical problems: "Should you post photos of your children on sites that can be seen by anyone, or even on private profiles? If you give them Facebook accounts or email addresses, are you starting a data record for them before they're old enough to know any better? Are you signing your child up for targeted advertising at age zero?" (Wood 2014).

But in terms of traditional ideas of *identity* that call into question issues of race, ethnicity, class, and ability, online worlds provide users a chance to be someone who they are not. On some sites like gaming sites, there seem to be few problems with a person expressing themselves as they are, or as they would like to be. When we think of the capability of social media to allow us to explore from the relative safety of a non-face-to-face encounter, the choice of identity can be liberating.

For many though, getting lost in an alternative identity on a social media site can lead to problems. Accountability for one's actions, honesty, and the forthrightness expected of people engaging with others online is assumed, but obviously, not always what occurs. The psychological aspects of how people express themselves online with social media have filled volumes of books and journals dedicated to the understanding of a person who communicates over social media. At the same time, social media validates the idea of who and what some people are.

See also: Anonymity; Avatar; Blogs; Dating; Selfie

Further Reading

Cirucci, Angela M. 2013. "First Person Paparazzi: Why Social Media Should Be Studied More Like Video Games." *Telematics and Informatics,* 30: 47–59.

Turkle, Sherry. 1995. *Life on the Screen: Identity in the Age of the Internet*. New York: Simon & Schuster.

Wood, Molly. 2014. "How Young Is Too Young for a Digital Presence?" *New York Times*. Accessed May 2015: http://www.nytimes.com/2014/05/15/technology/personaltech/how -young-is-too-young-for-a-digital-presence.html?_r=0.

Federal Trade Commission: Clues That Someone Has Stolen Your Information

You see withdrawals from your bank account that you can't explain.

You don't get your bills or other mail.

Merchants refuse your checks.

Debt collectors call you about debts that aren't yours.

You find unfamiliar accounts or charges on your credit report.

Medical providers bill you for services you didn't use.

Your health plan rejects your legitimate medical claim because records show you've reached your benefits limit.

A health plan won't cover you because your medical records show a condition you don't have.

The IRS notifies you that more than one tax return was filed in your name.

You get notice that your information was compromised by a data breach where you do business or have an account.

Source: IdentityTheft.gov.

Information Age

The terms *information age, information society,* and *information revolution* all refer to the period in history characterized by computerization, digital information processing, and digital technologies. In contrast to the industrial revolution, which brought about the factory assembly line and made manufacturing the standard by which economies were measured, the information age relies on a *knowledge-based society* and a reliance on new business models and models of social organization. The key technology of the information age is the computer, and the key distribution system is the Internet (in either wired or wireless form). The primary repository of knowledge is the World Wide Web.

What constitutes *information* in the information age can be a number of things. Information may be thought of as quantifiable data that is transmitted in bits over systems. With this definition the mobile phone company can assess your information usage by quantifying how much time you spend talking, texting, or interacting with content, because the measure of information is how long you use your phone. This measurement of information as data can be quantified and, therefore, information is thought of as a commodity that can be bought, sold, and traded.

Information can also be defined as knowledge that has value for an individual; so news can be an important type of information in a democracy, or *Wikipedia* can be a valuable resource to someone who wants a general background of crowdsourced data. This type of information is much harder to reduce to a quantifiable measurement. The information (knowledge) one acquires may also have an immediate impact, but it may also be stored in the mind until a later time, making its impact more difficult to assess. In this definition, data that is rejected by an individual is not really information, because it is disregarded and there is no use-value.

Whatever the definition used, the *information age* is often characterized by the speed of the exchange of information as well as the social capital it has for the user; that is, the value of the information is established by the person who receives and uses (or chooses not to use) it. The economic models of the information age are a combination of those from earlier industries, but they also reflect a number of newer concepts like freeware and subsidized support. Examples of these are advertising, which represents the economic model that supported most legacy industries and is still used today, even for social media; freeware, which offers software and media content to consumers at no charge, and allows them to tinker with the content to produce something new, or a hybrid of something old along with a new treatment; and the subsidized model that is often used for apps. Some apps are offered for free, but either advanced versions of the app or a subscription for the app is sold to offset all of the free downloads that are available.

Because digital technologies have the capability of transmitting far more information than the human being can actually absorb or use, we often say that *information overload* occurs. This means that there is far too much information in circulation, and the human body cannot process everything. Sometimes the body feels as though it is bombarded with too much information and begins to shut down its information processing capability. The feeling you have when you are overwhelmed, and can't determine anymore whether the information is useful or not, is the physiological response to information overload. Some of this is attributed to the speed with which digital technology transfers messages, but another reason for information overload has to do with the content of technology.

Nicholas Carr, author of *The Shallows: What the Internet Is Doing to Our Brains*, writes persuasively about the effect of computers and too much information on the way he thinks. He agrees with Bruce Friedman, a blogger who wrote: "I now have almost totally lost the ability to read and absorb a longish article on the web or in print . . . Even a blog post of more than three or four paragraphs is too much to absorb. I skim it" (Carr 2010, 7). But even though some people seem to experience a physiological reaction to the amount of information to which they can be exposed in an information age, there are other problems, too. Information relativity and information anxiety are just two of the behavioral aspects often critiqued as negative effects of the information age.

Information relativity is the term given to information that often occurs in information overload. The person may be overwhelmed by the constant flow of information and therefore unable to identify what's important, or what is not. The sociologist Georg Simmel observed that when people are too overwhelmed by stimulation, they are unable to respond to a new situation. Similarly, psychologist George Armitage Miller observed that when individuals are faced with an abundance of information, they have to learn to break it down so that they can deal with the new information one issue at a time. Many make bad decisions when there are too many options to consider.

Information overload can also lead to a psychological state of anxiety referred to as *information anxiety*. When bombarded by the constant flow of messages over Twitter, Facebook, Instagram, etc., people have to develop a willingness to tell themselves that when they feel they're overwhelmed, they need to take a break from social media. These various psychological states are not germane to social media alone. Every form of media over time has challenged users to make sense of the content and the unique characteristics of the technology used. But in the world of social media and the unrelenting flow of information 24 hours a day, 7 days a week, day after day, some people begin to feel overwhelmed and unable to find a balance between technology always being on, and the body interacting with nature and the environment in a more natural state.

See also: Addiction; Digital; Hyperconnectivity

Further Reading

Carr, Nicholas. 2010. *The Shallows: What the Internet Is Doing to Our Brains.* New York: W. W. Norton and Co., 7.

Information Revolution (see Information Age)

Information Superhighway

The idea that the Internet and other media and communications systems are linked together for high-speed communications became known as the *information superhighway.* The term was popularized in the 1990s by Vice President Al Gore who took the lead for the Clinton administration to support development and public use of the Internet by all people.

Gore's father, also a senator from Tennessee, had been instrumental in passing government actions that helped develop the interstate highway program in the United States, and Al Jr. used the same metaphor to describe the way the Internet could connect people across the United States and create an infrastructure that would make the creative economy and the information age a reality.

The concept of a *superhighway* seemed to capture the imagination of the public, and, as journalists used the term, the idea of the Internet became more comfortable to the public. In 1986, while still a senator, Gore initiated a congressional study that looked at the creation of supercomputer centers, increasing bandwidth for better wireless connectivity, and opening the emerging Internet so that it could be used by more people. He followed up with hearings that led to the High Performance Computing Act of 1991, also known as the Gore Act, which allowed commercial networks to connect with the research network run by the National Science Foundation, the precursor to the Internet as we now know it.

When he was elected vice president in 1992, he sponsored the National Information Infrastructure Act of 1993 that further supported the emerging Internet and opened it up to private as well as government investment.

It is a myth that Gore once claimed to have created the Internet, though the myth has been perpetuated for many years. What really happened is that while Gore was campaigning for president in 1999, he was interviewed by CNN's Wolf Blitzer. When asked to list his qualifications, Gore said: "During my service in the United States Congress, I took the initiative in creating the Internet." Over the years, that phrase has been interpreted by many to mean that Gore claimed credit for creating the Internet (Isaacson 2014, 402–403).

The leadership Gore gave to the creation of bills to support the Internet helped clarify for Congress how important the Internet was to the country, and why it was important to be in the vanguard of creating reasonable policies in the public's interest for the growth and sustainability of the Internet. Therefore, Gore is largely responsible for helping seed the new economy and creating growth in the information sector. People still refer to the information superhighway as a metaphor for the speed of connectivity.

See also: Gore, Al; Information Age; Internet

Further Reading

Isaacson, Walter. 2014. *The Innovators.* New York: Simon & Schuster, 402–403.

Instagram

Instagram is a mobile online service that allows people to take pictures and short videos and post them on social networks. The service was created in 2010 by Kevin Systrom and Mike Krieger each of whom were students at Stanford University. Both met when they became participants in the prestigious Mayfield Fellows Program at Stanford. Instagram is a free service that allows users to share photos and videos on a number of social network platforms, like Facebook, Twitter, Tumblr, and Flickr. The name combines the terms *instant camera* and *telegram*. The company was acquired by Facebook in 2012 for approximately $1 billion in cash and stock. By 2013, Instagram was one of the most popular features on Facebook.

After graduation, Systrom started working at Google and then NextStop, a travel recommendation and gaming site that was acquired by Facebook in 2010. Inspired by the combination of features at NextStop, he started working on a website that became known as Burbn. This site allowed people to check in, make plans, and play social games. Krieger was an avid Burbn user, and when they began to collaborate, they decided to downscale the site and plan for one specific feature. They also made the important decision to move from a web-based program to an app. They decided to focus on photo sharing, and, shortly thereafter, Instagram was born. Instagram went live as an iPhone app on October 6, 2010, and was downloaded 100,000 times in the first week. Within a year, Instagram had 1 million users.

Today over 300 million people worldwide take and share Instagram photos and videos with the use of the Instagram app. Instagram photos are unique because they are easy to take and upload to a number of social networks, like Facebook, Twitter, Tumblr, Flipboard, or BuzzFeed. The pictures are presented in a square shape, and are created with the use of filters, that make the image look as though they were professionally produced, even though the pictures can be taken with consumer-grade cameras. The video feature shares videos of a maximum of 15 seconds.

Instragram was first marketed as an iPhone app in 2010 and did not expand to the Android system until 2014, but when it did enter the Android market, technological improvements allowed it to compress space and work even more easily. When the service started using hashtags in 2011, advertisers and celebrities started posting their own pictures and videos, and the public became even more interested. People using Instagram could follow their favorite performers through the pictures they posted, and advertisers could chart the popularity of their ads. Instagram's superior images and the buzz that the company had created interested a number of larger companies that made moves to acquire the start-up. Though other offers were made, Systrom and Krieger decided to accept an offer from Facebook, largely because the company promised that they would be able to maintain the Instagram division with greater autonomy.

Facebook acquired Instagram in 2012 for approximately $1 billion, although by the time the deal was concluded, the depressed share price of the company was closer to $700 million (Carr 2013). At the time most people accessed Facebook on their computer and the company was desiring greater presence on mobile devices to attract younger users. By capturing more of a mobile market, the potential for more advertising revenue was important. A temporary reputational setback occurred when Facebook's lawyers introduced a new "terms of service" section that allowed Facebook to use photos taken by people for advertising purposes. At the time, Facebook's lapse in protecting personal privacy was in the news and an uproar from the public ensued. Public opposition to the new terms resulted in Instagram retracting its decision, but not before many users switched to other photo and video sharing services like Pheed, and Flickr. Surprisingly, though, few people stopped using the service—they just used it less, for a while. When Facebook withdrew the clause, the number of Instagram subscribers began to grow again.

Instagram began allowing advertising in the United States in November 2013 and in the U.K. market in 2014. The revenue raised by ads supported Facebook, the parent company, while Facebook sought to look for a wider range of services to compete with other social networks and mobile apps. Instagram also positioned itself against Twitter as a short form news service. In, 2013, Instagram added the Direct feature that would allow users to send photos to other individuals, to compete with the mobile app, Snapchat.

Instagram has won several awards for its innovative approach to mobile apps, including the "Best Mobile App" for 2010 awarded by TechCrunch, "Best Locally Made App" at the San Francisco Weekly Web Awards (2011), and Apple named Instagram "Best App of the Year" in 2011. Today, some Instagram photos and videos have attained the reputation of being considered contemporary art. Perhaps Instagram's biggest competitor for still pictures is Flickr, now owned by Yahoo!. Another competitor is Snapchat. The short video service is similar to Vine, but Instagram has continued to develop a variety of additional apps to help produce high-quality pictures and short videos that have a professionally produced quality, despite being taken on consumer-grade cameras—often attached to smartphones or tablets.

See also: App; Flickr; Mobile Phone Cameras; Smartphone; Tablet

Further Reading

Carr, Austin. 2013. "How Instagram CEO Kevin Systrom Is Making Good on Facebook's Billion-Dollar Bet." *Fast Company* magazine. Accessed February 20, 2015: http://

www.fastcompany.com/3012565/how-instagram-ceo-kevin-systrom-is-making-good
-on-facebooks-billion-dollar-bet.

Tsukayama, Hayley. 2013. "Instagram Adding Ads Boosts Facebook's Outlook, Analysts Say." *Washington Post*. Accessed December 5, 2014: http://www.washingtonpost
.com/business/technology/instagram-adding-ads-boosts-facebooks-outlook-analysts
-say/2013/10/04/5bed98c4-2d10-11e3-8ade-a1f23cda135e_story.html.

International Telecommunications Union (ITU)

The International Telecommunications Union (ITU) is the United Nations' specialized agency for information and communication technologies (ICTs). Based
in Geneva, Switzerland, the organization has been in existence since 1865 when
it was called the International Telegraph Union. It became the International Telecommunications Union in 1947. The organization functions to allocate global radio
spectrum and satellites and develops standards that allow wired and wireless networks to work together seamlessly. The ITU is also committed to helping spread
the Internet to all countries of the world and making connections affordable for
people. With a belief in the fundamental right of people to communicate, the ITU
is primarily concerned with any telecommunications-related policies that impact
the people of nations of the world and that cross geographic boundaries.

The ITU has 173 member countries, and works with over 700 private entities and academic institutions. It has twelve regional offices around the world. It
holds regional and global meetings, and works on projects related to education,
health, cybersecurity, making technology available and affordable to all, and it has
become involved in the problems and challenges of climate change.

In recent years, the ITU has been accused of working too closely with the United
States to allow more Internet regulation to be controlled by the United States. In
2012, the European Parliament complained that the ITU was not the appropriate
body to have authority over the architecture and protocols of the Internet, and cited
the Internet Corporation for Assigned Names and Numbers (ICANN) as an organization based in the United States that was exerting too much power over the global
use of the Internet. The European Parliament requested that the ITU address new
agreements and craft guidelines to maintain more equality among nations using
the Internet, but this request was not honored.

On September 21, 2014, the ITU published a press release stating that only 40
percent of the world's population would have access to the Internet at the end of
2014, but it predicted that by 2017 half of the world will be connected to the Internet
(UN Broadband Commission 2014). Much of the predicted growth will be through
mobile communications, with a predicted increase of 7.6 billion people before
2017. This increase has been in part fueled by the popularity of broadband-enabled

social media applications, with 1.9 billion people active on social networks in 2014. At the end of 2014, there were 77 countries where over 50 percent of the population could access the Internet (UN Broadband Commission 2014).

See also: Digital Divide

Further Reading

"European Parliament Warns Against UN Internet Control." 2012. *BBC News*. Accessed April 27, 2015: http://www.bbc.com/news/technology-20445637.

"UN Broadband Commission Releases New Country-By-Country Data on State of Broadband Access Worldwide: Half the World Will Be Online by 2017." 2014. International Telecommunication Union Press Release, September 21, 2014. Accessed December 28, 2014: http://www.itu.int/net/pressoffice/press_releases/2014/46.aspx#.VKCJl14APA.

Internet

The Internet was developed to facilitate collaboration among researchers around the world. As a result, different countries experienced different approaches toward envisioning, funding, and supporting the infrastructure necessary to create and maintain such a massive undertaking. Internet development began in the United States during the 1960s. Some writers have justified the money and time spent on developing the Internet by rationalizing that the U.S. Department of Defense was concerned that an attack by the Soviet Union or nuclear war could cripple the country's communication network. What was needed was a redundant system, meaning that information could continue to flow and possibly be rerouted, even if one part of the system were destroyed. But while this reason provides a convenient rationale for the activities to support the concept of the Internet, other sources provide a more reasoned approach toward considering how and why the Internet came about. Since much of the research in the United States came from the defense industry, the desire to link Internet development to defense seems understandable, though much of the evidence indicates that the Internet was really more attuned to creating collaborative activities, which became a highly valued mode of operation in the burgeoning information age.

In 1962, a computer scientist working at the Advanced Research Projects Agency (ARPA) by the name of J. C. R. Licklider wrote a memo proposing a project called the Intergalactic Computer Network. The project he proposed involved the creation of a time-sharing network of computers that eventually became known as ARPANet and was the precursor to what we now know as the Internet. The agency he worked for became known as the U.S. Department of Defense Advanced Research Projects

Agency (DARPA). Licklider and two colleagues built a prototype of his idea, and, by 1969, the network was running. By 1974, the system was being described as "internetworking." By 1981, over 200 computers were linked to ARPANet. The U.S. military split the network into two parts with one part dedicated for military use and the other under the auspices of the National Science Foundation (NSF), an independent agency of the U.S. government. Eventually, the NSF incorporated its part of ARPANet into a network called the National Science Foundation Network (NSFNET) and this system eventually became known as the Internet.

The Internet was originally built to use the lines and connections of the telephone network, but technological advances in broadband and wireless services have made dial-up services seem slow and old fashioned. By 2013, only 3 percent of the population in the United States still used dial-up services to access the Internet at home. This can be contrasted to 2000, when a majority of homes had dial-up services, and only 3 percent of the homes in the United States had broadband access (Brenner 2013).

The Internet is a distribution system that has unique characteristics and has ushered in a clash of old media (legacy media) and new media uses. The Internet and the content it distributes over the World Wide Web has challenged traditional laws and policies nationally and internationally. As a distribution system it links billions of computers, mobile phones, and other devices to each other. As of 2015, a *World Internet Statistics* report showed that by the end of 2014 approximately 40 percent of the world's population could access the Internet through some form. According to the same source, 75 percent of the world's Internet users are in the top 20 industrialized nations, and the remaining 20–25 percent were in the other 178 countries of the world. Still, it is questionable whether the Internet should be regulated by a special agency that concerns itself with global information flow, or whether within the United States it should be classified as a basic utility, meaning that the cost of accessing the Internet should be regulated, either by the FCC or some other federal agency.

The Internet uses hardware that includes all of the computers, wires, and other physical structures and devices that make up the network. Software includes sets of rules called protocols that determine how the hardware sends, receives, and displays information. The protocols include Transmission Control Protocols (TCP) and Internet Protocols (IP), but other protocols have specialized purposes. For example, e-mail can be sent by either of two protocols—Internet Message Access Protocol (IMAP) or Post Office Protocol (POP). These protocols control how e-mails are sent, accessed, and displayed on people's computers. File Transfer Protocol (FTP) governs how files are downloaded from, or uploaded to, servers. The protocols determine how information flows from one Internet address to another. The data that make up the information is stored in packets that do not have to travel through the network on the same path, or in their original order. If parts of the network become overloaded, damaged, or blocked, the packets switch to another route. When the packets all arrive at their destination, they are reassembled into the complete file.

While computers had become common in businesses in the 1980s, they were primarily used for business-related word processing and internal financial purposes. As prices of computers began to drop in the 1980s and 1990s and became more user-friendly, computers began to be purchased by schools, small businesses, and for home use. Telephone companies and cable companies scrambled to become the Internet providers for the emerging use of computers, the web, and a number of start-up companies that were launched.

By the time the World Wide Web was developed and made available for free, home computers were more available and many content developers explored how the Internet and web could be used for a variety of purposes for home consumers. In 1993, a number of web browsers became available that also stimulated what would grow to become the dot-com bubble that took place late in the century. But until the Internet became more interactive in the 2000s, the Internet was limited in what it provided. A vast amount of information was stored in computers around the world, but the information was largely disorganized. People typically purchase access to the Internet's wires and transmitting equipment through an Internet service provider (ISP), many of which were telecommunication companies that were involved in other forms of telecommunications, like telephony or cable television. Now, however, every day the Internet transfers more data than all of the voiced phone calls and post office mail combined.

Web browsers became the gateway to organizing information on the Internet and facilitated the type of connections available on the World Wide Web. For a time, the Internet facilitated the type of communication that could have been accomplished in other ways. E-mail was a faster way of sending mail than through a post office, and listserves that are similar to electronic mailing lists could send information out to a large group of people at the same time. Emerging companies worked with web browsers, or many of the web browser companies, like AOL, Google, and Microsoft, experimented with different types of content. Three especially successful websites were launched in 1995—Amazon, Craigslist, and eBay, all of which helped establish online models for consumer use.

Shortly after 2000, technology improved and the interactive nature of the Internet became more popular. Web 2.0 allowed computer users to post their own content online, and blogs, videos, text files, and music files began to be shared. It took a few more years of improved technology before it became possible to transfer full video files that would not "hang" during transmission, but when this became possible, television and film migrated to the Internet, too.

In 2014 the Pew Research Internet Project conducted a study of 1,066 Internet users in the United States to determine what their attitudes toward the Internet were, with regard to accessing information. Among the findings, 87 percent of adults accessing the Internet (through computers and mobile phones) said that the Internet has improved their ability to learn new things. While 72 percent reported that they liked having so much information available, 26 percent felt overloaded with so much information. In general, however, the Pew study found that the Internet users they polled felt better informed about a number of things, including news, current events, friends, products, and civic matters (Purcell and Rainie, 2014).

The technical improvements facilitated interest in social networks that have similarities to the way we've interacted with others in the past (through face-to-face communication, or using e-mail instead of mail and instant messaging instead of a telephone call) but each social network has unique characteristics that can be used by people who choose to participate in them. Social networks stimulated interest of the younger population because communicating over a computer, or, later, mobile phone, could be done without parental knowledge or interference. Many social networks stimulated a sense of independence for young users that could be liberating, but could also be used dysfunctionally, as with cyberbullying.

While many of the entries in this encyclopedia discuss specific social networking sites and apps that facilitate use of social networks, a few criticisms of the Internet and how it has developed are important to keep in mind. A critic of the way the Internet is used and controlled by telecommunications companies, governments, and Internet Service Providers, Evgeny Morozov has written about the way the Internet promised a level of freedom to communicate while limits to freedom are masked by skillful politicians and governments that have learned to mislead the public through using social media and social networking. He warns that governments can feel pressure to try to regulate the Internet and web. He encourages governments to conduct studies of public opinion and seek agreement on what procedures might be best to create policies that are "acceptable, transparent, just, and democratic" (Morozov 2011, 218).

One particularly salient criticism of the Internet is how it structures our knowledge. Digital information on the Internet can exist for a very long time, but what about information that was stored in other forms before the Internet became available? And how thorough can an Internet search be when there are millions of web pages stored on the Internet?

Many people are familiar with what is called *link rot,* indicated by the error message "Page Not Found" that appears on a web page that is navigated to by an old or broken link. A similar problem for scholars is *Further Reading rot,* which takes place when documented facts and evidence no longer exist. In 2014, Harvard Law School conducted a study of legal Further Reading that had been originally in print form, but had been stored on the Internet in the form of electronic journals and Supreme Court opinions. What the study found was most disturbing. More than 70 percent of the URLs cited within the *Harvard Law Review* and other legal journals and 50 percent of the URLs referring to Supreme Court opinions were no longer linked to the original material. Similarly, researchers at the Los Alamos National Laboratory reported that three and a half million scholarly articles published between 1997 and 2012 dealing with science, technology, and medicine had link rot. One out of every five references were no longer accurate because of reference rot (Lepore 2015, 36).

For people who have grown up with the Internet, it is sometimes hard to realize that many of the events before the Internet have not been archived on the Internet, and even the early days of the Internet are not well documented. The Internet Archive (Archive.org), a nonprofit library in California, was created in 1996 to try to document the continual evolution of the Internet and save critical files relevant to websites that make up the Internet's history. The project was originally initiated by Brewster Kahle, a librarian and computer scientist, who started the project in his home. Individuals can submit information but the bulk of the data is collected automatically by web crawlers. The database now has its own building, and the motto is "Universal Access to All Knowledge."

Still, the amount of digital data that flows over the Internet every day is impossible to keep up with. "The average life of a Web page is about a hundred days," wrote Jill Lepore, a journalist with the *New Yorker* (Lepore 2015, 36). The Archive also has a repository for web pages called The Wayback Machine that has captured over 150 billion web pages. Despite these efforts, information that is stored on the Internet or web is likely to become a victim of drowning in the sea of information and being lost in the data flow.

See also: Broadband; Dark Net (Dark Web); Digital; World Wide Web (WWW)

Further Reading

Brenner, Joanna. 2013. "3% of Americans Use Dial-Up at Home," Pew Research Center. Accessed February 17, 2015: http://www.pewresearch.org/fact-tank/2013/08/21/3-of-americans-use-dial-up-at-home/.

"Brief History of the Internet." n.d. Internet Society. Accessed October 4, 2014: http://www.internetsociety.org/internet/what-internet/history-internet/brief-history-internet.

Internet Live Statistics. 2015. Accessed January 15, 2015: http://www.internetlivestats.com/internet-users/.

Lepore, Jill. 2015. "The Cobweb: Can the Internet Be Archived?" *New Yorker,* 89: 34–41.

Morozov, Evgeny. 2011. *The Net Delusion: The Dark Side of Internet Freedom*. Philadelphia: Public Affairs, 218.

Purcell, Kristin, and Lee Rainie. 2014. "Americans Feel Better Informed about the Internet." Pew Research Internet Project. Accessed December 10, 2014: http://www.pewinternet .org/2014/12/08/better-informed/.

From the High-Performance Computing Act of 1991 establishing the National Research and Education Network (precursor to the Internet)

The Network shall—

(1) be developed and deployed with the computer, telecommunications, and information industries;

(2) be designed, developed, and operated in collaboration with potential users in government, industry, and research institutions and educational institutions;

(3) be designed, developed, and operated in a manner which fosters and maintains competition and private sector investment . . . ;

(4) be designed, developed, and operated in a manner which promotes research and development . . . ;

(5) be designed and operated so as to ensure . . . copyright and other intellectual property rights, and . . . national security;

(6) have accounting mechanisms . . . [for] usage of copyrighted materials . . . ;

(7) ensure the interoperability of Federal and non-Federal computer networks . . . ;

(8) be developed by purchasing . . . services from vendors whenever feasible . . . ;

(9) support research and development of networking software and hardware; and

(10) serve as a test bed for . . . high-capacity and high-speed computing networks . . .

Source: https://www.nitrd.gov/congressional/laws/102-194.pdf.

Internet Corporation for Assigned Names and Numbers (ICANN)

The Internet Corporation for Assigned Names and Numbers (ICANN) helps administer many of the Internet's software protocols. Its purpose as a nonprofit organization is to help maintain the seemless nature of the Internet and prevent problems.

It serves as a registry for IP addresses and website domain names, making sure that no two devices share the same IP address. ICANN also ensures that no two organizations or individuals control the same website domain. When ICANN was incorporated in California on September 30, 1998, entrepreneur and philanthropist Esther Dyson became its founding chairwoman.

Through the U.S. Department of Commerce (DOC), ICANN represents the United States, but there has long been controversy over whether this is the best form of U.S. governance or not. In 2011, the FTC brought up concerns about ICANN's ability to protect consumers from illicit activities on the Internet, and the Association of National Advertisers brought charges against the organization concerning its control over commercial domain names. The Department of Commerce's arrangement with ICANN expires in 2015, at which time a new arrangement may be determined with the aid of the National Telecommunications Information Administration (NTIA).

Additionally, many countries of the world have questioned the control over Internet domain names by a company located in the United States. In 2012, the European Parliament petitioned the International Telecommunications Union (ITU) to draw up guidelines that would limit the power of an agency like ICANN to exert American control over the Internet. Though the United Nations was considered to be one agency that could represent all countries, no determination has yet been made at this time.

See also: Internet

Further Reading

"NTIA Announces Intent to Transition Key Internet Domain Name Functions." 2014. National Telecommunications Information Agency Office of Public Affairs. Accessed December 28, 2014. http://www.ntia.doc.gov/press-release/2014/ntia-announces-intent -transition-key-internet-domain-name-functions.

J

Jobs, Steve

As one of the founders of Apple Inc. (with Steve Wozniak), Steve Jobs (1955–2011) was one of the major entrepreneurs of the digital era. Though his talents lie primarily in design and product innovation, Jobs was known to be sometimes contentious and difficult. Still, he left his mark on major digital industries including personal computing, animated movies, and digital publishing. To many, he became known as the "father of the digital revolution."

Jobs was born in San Francisco and adopted by Paul and Clara Jobs. The family moved to Mountain Park, California, where Steve and his father tinkered with electronics in the garage. He met Steve Wozniak who had been a student at the same high school five years before Jobs, and the two electronics enthusiasts became friends. They were both fascinated by an article they had read in Esquire magazine about how "phone phreaks" had figured out a system to mimic the sound quality of circuit switching in the Bell Telephone System. They collaborated on what they called the Blue Box, used to circumvent the cost of calling on the Bell System, and sold a number of them for $150. As they tried to sell one of their illegal Blue Boxes at a pizza restaurant, they were held up at gunpoint. While that led to the end of making and selling Blue Boxes, the two had become fast friends and they realized they could work together.

But before they embarked on further adventures, Jobs briefly attended Reed College before dropping out and traveling to India. When he returned to Mountain Park, Wozniak had built a computer that eventually became known as the Apple I. In the partnership that would follow, Wozniak became the engineer, and Jobs began to develop his marketing know-how. Though Jobs had started working at Atari, an early video game company known for the game *Pong*, he maintained his friendship with Wozniak, and the two often played the new Atari games together when Wozniak would visit Jobs, who was working on the night shift.

Both Jobs and Wozniak became involved in what was known as the Homebrew Computer Club, and when Wozniak, who was working at Hewlett-Packard, brought the Apple I for the members to see, it became an instant hit. Jobs immediately set to marketing the Apple I and started selling the units, though Wozniak was constructing each one from scratch.

By 1976, the two began what they called the Apple Computer Company. Jobs became chairman and CEO, and Wozniak was the chief (and only) engineer. As Walter Isaacson wrote in *The Innovators*, a book dedicated to exploring the creative input of some of the most influential computer and Internet entrepreneurs, the "rise of Apple marked a decline of hobbyist culture" (2014, 353). What Isaacson meant is that the decisions Jobs and Wozniak made to market computer hardware shifted the attention from individuals who tinkered with computer technology to the creation of the large companies that had profit as their motive.

When the Apple II computer debuted, the little start-up company started to turn the heads of the larger computer companies, like IBM and Hewlett-Packard. Apple, with Jobs as the lead product designer, started to produce a variety of software and hardware combinations that were attractive and functional. Among the new products being turned out was the first mouse for computer navigation, the Apple Lisa computer, and, then, the Macintosh. Jobs also had a hand in the marketing of the LaserWriter.

Apple was growing, but by 1985 Jobs's intensity and drive resulted in a power struggle within the company that forced Jobs out. He went on to a number of computer companies and founded NeXT, a computer company that focused on higher education and business markets. In 1986, Jobs bought the computer graphics division of Lucasfilm, which then became known as Pixar Animation Studios, where he served as CEO until 2006.

In the meantime, Apple had started losing money. Jobs was asked to return as CEO, and then oversaw the development and marketing of a number of iconic Apple products, including the iMac, iTunes, iPod, iPhone, and iPad. By 2011, Apple had become the world's most valuable computer and multimedia company, with much of the credit being given to Jobs for turning around the company after many years of poor revenue returns.

In 2003, Jobs was diagnosed with a pancreas neuroendocrine tumor. In typical iconoclastic fashion, he worked with his doctors to craft an individualized plan of beating the disease. In 2011, Jobs took a medical leave from Apple, but his health forced him to resigned in August of that year. He died in October 2011.

See also: Apple; Wozniak, Steve

Further Reading

Isaacson, Walter. 2014. *The Innovators*. New York: Simon & Schuster, 353.

Isaacson, Walter. 2011. *Steve Jobs*. New York: Simon & Schuster.

Simon, William L., and Jeffrey S. Young. 2005. *iCon: Steve Jobs, The Greatest Second Act in the History of Business*. New York: John Wiley & Sons.

L

Legacy Media

The term given to media that existed before the Internet is *legacy media*. The term encompasses the industries, content, distribution forms, and economic models of those forms also referred to as "old" media. In the days in which legacy media dominated the culture, there was a unidirectional relationship between the producers of the media content and media consumers. The long history of the power of the printed word in the United States involving newspapers, books, and magazines are a part of legacy media. They, along with the large companies that grew to dominate radio and television networks, the establishment of the Recording Industry Association of America (RIAA) to represent the recorded music industry, the powerful Hollywood studios that combined their economic clout in the Motion Picture Association of America (MPAA), and the dominance of AT&T as the only viable telephone company in the United States all grew based upon the profit motive, and most of the profits made by the media companies came from advertising. Direct sales or subscription models were economic measures of some forms of media, but when advertising was factored into the equation, ratings became the currency for evaluating the size of an audience—particularly in radio and television.

The role of legacy media is so powerful in understanding the impact of today's social media—what they are, how they are funded, and what they say about how we think of connecting with others—that the move from legacy to "new" interactive media marks a major shift in how we establish our relationship to the world of work and leisure. The shift also marks a major economic milestone as we move from the dominance of "big" media to the importance of "small" media in our lives. As Alvin Toffler wrote in his influential book, *The Third Wave* (1980), the history of the world is a history of how we produce for our own consumption. The growth of the personal computer industry, semiconductor industry, the advent of the Internet and social media all contribute to what might now be called the *information age*, but these shifts have also given us ideas that support the *creative economy* and *e-commerce* and have helped us understand the dynamics of *social media* and *social networking*.

Legacy media were tightly wedded to the economic imperatives of the twentieth century. As economist Vaclav Smil wrote, the dominance of the manufacturing of goods in the United States during the period 1941–1973, and the reality of World War II and its aftermath, helped shift the national economy in the United States from the days of the factory assembly line into a new era dominated by a service-based economy driven by information. From 1941 to 1973 the United States attained the highest quality of living in the world, with the majority of jobs in the manufacturing sector that paid well and guaranteed long-term security to the employees. Throughout this period, the social, political, and economic systems reinforced each other, as typical of any era in history (Smil 2013, 110).

The legacy media of the time were no exception because they, too, were products of the twentieth century. Telephony had come to be dominated by the only monopoly allowed to exist in the media market, and that was because the telephone system created no content—instead, it was viewed as a utility that allowed other people to use its services, but not compete with information (content) providers. In the days when AT&T had a monopoly over telephony in the United States the organization was structured into four group: Bell Labs, where experiments and innovations were supported; AT&T Long Lines, the division that strung the phone wires and maintained the wired system; the Bell Companies, which were regional operating companies to handle the business aspects of billing and physically handling the transfer of telephone calls; and Western Electric, the manufacturer of the telephones used. AT&T was a *common carrier*, meaning that it had no input over the content of the telephone system, and handled every aspect of making telephones, renting them to users, maintaining the infrastructure for calls, handling billing, and every other aspect of wired telephones. Until the monopoly began to be challenged in the 1960s, and most certainly after deregulation in 1984, AT&T had no competition.

Other forms of media, however, did have competition of a sort, and often engaged in *vertical integration*, meaning that one company would own other companies that provided content, or fed the supply chain necessary for the maintenance of the organization. Legacy media were dominated by organizational structures that were large and expensive but that generally sent messages from a large, heterogeneous organization at considerable expense, to the public which was thought to be the "mass audience." But because of their power to reach and influence the entire population, the legacy broadcast industries also had an interest in protecting their own. Even after the deregulation of the media industries in 1984, the major companies that now could buy and sell smaller companies created a "landgrab" for media content and production facilities that would keep feeding the giant media machines. The effect of deregulation, which was intended to allow media

industries to operate by "marketplace rules"—meaning they would be self-moni-
toring—began to shift and focus on creating content that would appeal to both the
mass market as well as the underserved niche markets that complained that they
were not represented by the largely white, affluent media organizations.

As an example, Viacom shows how vertical integration works in practice, and
how the complicated set of mergers and acquisitions help make a major media corporation grow. Viacom was originally the syndication division of the Columbia Broadcasting System (CBS). It was formed in 1971 after the Federal Communications
Commission (FCC) forced CBS to spin off some cable television and syndication
operations. In 1999, Viacom acquired its former parent company, and, in 2005, the
company split into two divisions: Viacom and the CBS Corporation. While the CBS
Corporation focuses most heavily on content creation and distribution for broadcast
radio and television, Viacom concentrates on a wider range of media companies that
go beyond cable distribution of film and video content. The company owns a number
of print publishing companies, including Scribners, The Free Press, and Simon &
Schuster (to name a few). Viacom owns Paramount theme parks and Infinity/Out-
door, a major billboard and outdoor advertising company. The holdings extend to
radio companies and a range of media distribution companies, including the former
DVD/VHS rental giant, Blockbuster, which Viacom sold in 2011. Viacom also owns
a number of popular cable television networks all targeted to different audiences.
In the United States, it owns BET (Black Entertainment Television), CMT (Country
Music Television), Comedy Central, MTV, Nickelodeon, Spike, TV Land, and VH1
(to name a few). Viacom produces and distributes feature films through its motion-
picture division, Paramount Pictures Corporation, and is involved in digital content
production for games and Internet sites. The division, Viacom International, has
holdings in major countries around the world.

Between the deregulation of the media industries in 1984 and the start of
the twenty-first century, legacy media companies did what they knew best. They
remained dedicated to the economic models that had supported their growth, and
as they sought to find new audiences through different media, they bought up
smaller companies and filled the channels with the type of content they already
knew. An era of media consolidation grew. As Ben Bagdikian wrote about the
media in 2003: "Five global-dimension firms, operating with many of the characteristics of a cartel, own most of the newspapers, magazines, book publishers,
motion picture studios, and radio and television stations in the United States" (Bagdikian 2003, 3). These five dominant companies became so powerful that once the
Internet and World Wide Web came along, they fought any possible competition
from the smaller, more personal types of media that were emerging, and when they
did acknowledge their presence, they forced the new companies into old economic
models. Bagdikian wrote: "Ownership of media is now so integrated in political

orientation and business connections with all the largest industries in the American economy that they have become a coalition of power on an international scale" (Bagdikian 2003, 136).

As a result, the dominance of legacy media companies has influenced the policies and practices of newer media forms. The Internet, as an open conduit for information and collaboration is antithetical to legacy media practices. The World Wide Web with its vast array of information that flows across borders and includes virtually *anything* posted by individuals rather than companies alone, challenges traditional practices and policies. Most important, the ability of users to own, control, and produce content that can be posted to the Internet and exchanged without advertising or exchange of money sends fear into the hearts of the executives of legacy companies that have always operated on a profit motive.

Let us return for a moment to Viacom and how it has modified its holdings since the development of digital media and the spread of social media. Today Viacom also owns Paramount Home Entertainment Inc., a distributor of films on DVD and streaming content from the Internet. In 2006 Paramount acquired the film studio DreamWorks SKG. In 2006 and 2007, Viacom struck digital distribution deals with a number of large digital outlets that include Yahoo!, Microsoft, AOL, and the social networking site, Bebo. In addition, the company negotiated an agreement with the Chinese online-search leader Baidu to provide video over the Internet. But all of these developments grow from the content that Viacom was most familiar with, and continues to support the same economic models that legacy media have used for decades.

At the same time, employment statistics in the legacy industries tell another story of how these companies are faring during the shift to Internet delivery of media content in other forms that bypass the legacy companies. *Variety*, the trade publication of the entertainment industry reported in September 2014 that the "U.S. economy has seen a steady erosion of jobs in the motion picture and sound industries" (McNary 2014). For 2013 and 2014, the jobs in those sectors were reduced by 19 percent. Similarly, a number of studios and broadcasters have been reducing their number of employees. On September 4, 2014, Warner Brothers Entertainment announced that they were laying off 8,000 employees.

Ratings, the currency of legacy media, also tell of a coming decline in viewership. According to an analytics firm, MoffettNathanson, "The (ratings) declines at most of the cable networks were nothing short of staggering," in the third quarter of 2014. Combined, the major cable companies were down 8 percent in viewership, with only Fox surviving—probably because of the Simpsons marathon run on FXX (Littleton 2014).

Perhaps some of the most drastic reductions in staff have occurred at newspapers, as "the dramatic decline in newspaper ad revenues since 2000 has to be one of the most significant and profound . . . in the last decade, maybe in a generation," according to Mark Perry of the American Enterprise Institute and quoted by Jordan Weissmann (Weissmann 2014). With newspaper revenue down 50 percent between 2000 and 2015, the era of the major print newspaper in America may surely be winding down.

But before taking up a collection to shepherd legacy media through the current change of distribution and content creation, it is worth noting that social media, drawing from the advanced technologies of the Internet and wireless platforms is drawing on content that was produced years ago as well as embracing the new content from regular people as well as from distributors that are looking for new ways to deliver content. What is changing most are the models that relied on ratings for negotiating the cost of an advertising campaign, and the number of audience members necessary to make a show a "hit." When it comes to news and information many of the sites that try to get news out to people faster (like Twitter) may not be fully vetted, but that, too, is the social cost of relying on instant technology rather than the expensive news bureaus that fact-checked and verified information. And, it should be noted—advertising is still a major form of paying for content online. Even YouTube assesses users 45 percent of the revenue that is made when advertising supports a show or content clip. Niche audiences may be smaller, but the cost of advertising is less and the direct contact with an interested consumer may result in more revenue for a smaller market.

Much of today's media come from user experiences with social media that spanned gaming, podcasting, blogging, e-print (including e-books and e-magazines,) websites, e-news, and streaming technologies. Every legacy media form has had to contend with the role social networking plays in distributing content. For example, webisodes are considered new media but YouTube and other distribution forms have been attempting to be "publishers" or "broadcasters" to bridge old regulations that largely protected the rights of the publisher or broadcaster, but become less clear in the application of new forms, such as digital media. For example, issues of copyright traditionally protected the original creator of information in legacy media. Now, newer models of controlling, but sharing, content involve new structures like the Creative Commons licenses and freeware.

See also: E-Commerce; E-Publishing; Niche Marketing; Streaming Media; Webisode

Further Reading

Bagdikian, Ben. 2003. *The New Media Monopoly*, 5th ed. Boston: Beacon Press.

Littleton, Cynthia. 2014. "Cable under Fire: Plunge in Ratings Could Spell Trouble for Top Nets," *Variety*, November 4, 2014. Accessed November 10, 2014: http://variety.com /2014/tv/news/cable-network-ratings-1201346782/.

McNary, Dave. 2014. "Showbiz, Music Industry Jobs Drop 19% in Two Years." *Variety*. Accessed September 11, 2014: http://variety.com/2014/artisans/news/government-issues -bleak-jobs-report-for-movie-sound-industries.

Smil, Vaclav. 2013. *Made in the USA: The Rise and Retreat of American Manufacturing*. Cambridge, MA: MIT Press, 110.

Toffler, Alvin. 1980. *The Third Wave*. New York: Bantam.

Weissmann, Jordan. 2014. "The Decline of Newspapers Hits a Stunning Milestone." Slate. com. Accessed April 22, 2015: http://www.slate.com/blogs/moneybox/2014/04/28 /decline_of_newspapers_hits_a_milestone_print_revenue_is_lowest_since_1950 .html.

Excerpts from the "State of the News Media 2015," Pew Research Group, April 29, 2015, by Amy Mitchell

Financially, the newspaper industry continues to be hard-hit. Newspaper ad revenue declined another 4% year over year, to $19.9 billion—less than half of what it was a decade ago . . . three different companies in 2014 spun off more than 100 newspaper properties.

At the network level, ABC and CBS revenue grew while that of NBC declined. ABC Evening News revenues, based on data from Kantar Media, have now nearly caught up to NBC's. In cable, the NBCUniversal property MSNBC also fared worst. Its total revenue was down 1% for the year, due mainly to a 5% decline in ad revenue, according to projections from SNL Kagan. CNN's revenue was projected to rise 3%, while Fox News revenue was projected to rise 6%, and was the only one of the three channels to report an increase in profit (10%).

Source: Mitchell, Amy. "State of the News Media 2015." Pew Research Group, April 29, 2015. http://www.journalism.org/2015/04/29/state-of-the-news-media -2015/. Reprinted with permission from Pew Research Center.

LinkedIn

LinkedIn is a business-oriented social networking service. Founded in December 2002 and launched on May 5, 2003, it was originally intended to be used for professional networking, but over the years it has started to resemble a number of other social networks that not only serve to connect people, but also allow users to define their own profiles. The company was founded by Reid Hoffman, Allen Blue, Konstantin Guericke, Eric Ly, and Jean-Luc Vaillant, all of whom worked at either PayPal or Socialnet.com.

When the company started, the founders realized that most social networks were targeted to be used by young people. LinkedIn was specifically designed for use by working people for professional development. Despite a relatively slow start, LinkedIn grew steadily and finally posted its first profit in 2006. The company also started a number of new features to combine job listings with its "recommendation" engine, and first involved the launch of LinkedIn Jobs, which allowed hiring managers to assess LinkedIn users who were on the job market in relationship to their colleagues, references, and reputation. This helped set LinkedIn apart from its main job listing competitors, Monster, HotJobs, and CareerBuilder.

Today LinkedIn generates its revenue through three sources: premium subscriptions, advertising sales, and job listings. Most of its revenue comes from the Talent Solutions business unit targeted for job recruiters, which makes up 57 percent of the organization's total revenue.

As of 2015, LinkedIn had over 300,000 users in more than 200 different countries. Mobile apps appeared in 2008. But perhaps one of the biggest questions about this company is whether or not LinkedIn can help someone find a job. According to Business Insider, the answer is "yes." Approximately 94 percent of job recruiters regularly look at LinkedIn profiles, and, in a 2013 survey, 77 percent of those people who had profiles on LinkedIn said that the site helped them research people and companies (Hiranya Fernando 2014). However, surprisingly little data suggests how many people actually do get jobs because of their LinkedIn profiles.

LinkedIn has been criticized for changing its business model to make it more difficult for job seekers to actually make connections with potential employers. Originally, LinkedIn's services were free to job seekers, but a shift in the business model changed the way job seekers and recruiters might connect. The company started charging employers to post jobs and gain access to resumes, and job seekers were asked to pay for "premium" services (Collamer 2013). One of those services restricted to premium members only was the ability to send up to 10 special messages to job recruiters. The result is that the site began to function more as a job board than a connection-maker. According to the employment industry watchdog firm CareerXroads, job boards are less effective than other means of making employment connections. In the 10 years in which job boards and companies like LinkedIn, Monster.com, and CareerBuilder.com grew rapidly, only 2.5 percent of hires were actually made once counting all of the job boards combined (Collamer 2013).

The $29.95 monthly fee for the "Job Seeker Premium" category does move applicants up to the level of "featured applicant," despite their qualifications. More importantly, people who don't have the wherewithal to pay for premium services are further marginalized by the current practices and business model.

See also: Social Networking

Further Reading

Collamer, Nancy. 2013. "Has LinkedIn Crossed an Ethical Line?" Huffington Post. Accessed January 8, 2015: http://www.huffingtonpost.com/2013/09/06/linkedin-ethics_n_3865859.html.

Fernando, Hiranya. 2014. "A Step-by-Step Guide to Getting a Job through LinkedIn." Business Insider. Accessed April 24, 2015: http://www.businessinsider.com/getting-a-job-through-linkedin-2014-3#ixzz3YGEDdwxD.

M

Malware

Malware—harmful software programs—can quickly infect thousands of connected computers and mobile devices like tablets and smartphones with viruses, worms, bots, or other forms of harmful programs. Malware is a type of software that is used to intentionally harm the user of digital technology. The most common form of malware is a program that impersonates another human being, and when a person clicks on that file or message, the infection works its way through the software and sends duplicate information out to anyone in the user's mail program. Social networks are one of the fastest ways to spread malware from one person's devices to another person's devices.

Though some malware is created by hackers for the pleasure of disrupting effective computer use, a much larger problem is in the way cybercriminals remotely control computers infected by malware, and how they use the information they gain for identity theft, or personal profit (such as obtaining a person's passwords or bank account or financial information). Another form of spreading malware is in the use of pirated (unauthorized or poorly duplicated) software. It is estimated that more than 50 percent of pirated software contains malware that affects a user's computer. In 2014, the intentional use of malware to create havoc or steal personal information was assumed to be worth approximately $315 billion worldwide. The exact cost of malware-related problems is unknown because often malware goes undetected for a long time. Some people use malware-infected programs for years without knowing it, and it is virtually impossible to identify the spread of malware-infected programs. Based on the $315 billion estimated cost, companies and individuals would have to spend approximately $25 billion in security measures to track and/or fix malware attacks (Robinson 2014).

Filters and antivirus software can protect against malware to some extent, and modern web browsers have built-in security settings, but the best way to control malware is to be a smart computer user and not open or download suspicious-looking files. In a recent study, consumers were asked about their biggest fears regarding security threats and 60 percent named loss of data or personal information as their biggest fears. But in the same study, 43 percent of the respondents reported that they don't routinely install security updates (Robinson 2014).

Smartphones are an even greater security risk than computers because apps often have malware attached to them, and they serve to spread malware even more easily than through a computer's mail system. The number of problems related to malware and smartphones have multiplied over recent years from relatively simple apps that cause problems to sophisticated code that taps peoples' smartphones for profit. This is particularly problematic with the potential for digital currency being transferred over smartphones, and the necessary security measures now needed to protect fraudulent use of electronic transfer of currency.

Because smartphones are created to be able to function with so many third-party devices, they are particularly vulnerable to malware attacks. Android phones are more likely to spread malware than iOS phones, but no smartphone is impenetrable. Furthermore, all mobile phones have GPS tracking devices that allow for sharing the user's location. Anyone who takes pictures or videos shows their surroundings, and that too can be triangulated to find a person's location relatively easily.

Apps are often developed so quickly that they are often not subject to security tests that would ensure their resistance to malware (Suarez-Tangil et al. 2013, 2–3). This has given rise to the idea of *grayware,* which reflects software that is originally not intended to be malicious, but that can be used for malicious purposes once put into place.

See also: Bots; Cookies; Cyberwar; Phishing; Privacy; Spam; Spyware; Surveillance

Further Reading

Robinson, Ted. 2014. "Breaches, Malware to Cost $491 Billion in 2014, Study Says." *SC Magazine.* Accessed October 3, 2014: http://www.scmagazine.com/breaches-malware-to-cost-491-billion-in-2014-study-says/article/339167/.

Suarez-Tangil, Guillermo, Juan E. Tapiador, Pedro Peris-Lopez, and Arturo Ribagorda. 2013. "Evolution, Detection and Analysis of Malware for Smart Devices." *IEEE Communications,* 16: 961–987.

Federal Trade Commission Advice: Protect Your Computer

The good news, there's a lot you can do to protect yourself and your computer. One of the most important steps you can take, install security software from a reliable company and set it to update automatically . . . Don't buy security software in response to unexpected calls or messages, especially if they say they scanned your computer and found malware. Scammers send messages like these to trick you into buying worthless software, or worse, downloading malware.

Use a pop up blocker, and don't click on links and popups. Don't click on links or open attachments in emails unless you know what they are, even if the emails seem to be from friends or family.

Download software only from websites you know and trust. Free stuff may sound appealing, but free downloads can hide malware.

If you suspect malware, stop doing things that require passwords or personal info, such as online shopping or banking.

Source: http://www.consumer.ftc.gov/media/video-0056-protect-your-computer-malware.

Massive Open Online Courses (MOOCs)

As a development in distance learning, massive open online courses (MOOCs) have a lot to do with changing economic models of education and ideas about the sharing economy. Distance education is not new, but the number of new ideas that have contributed to different ways of delivering information and education are many. In the early days of radio some courses allowed students who were registered in classes through schools to learn by classes taught using the radio. This helped many people in locations that had few schools available, and the method of course delivery could benefit learners of all ages. In some parts of the world courses are still taught over short-wave, AM and FM, radio waves to people in locations where schools are not available. Flipped classrooms, where in-class activities are focused on collaboration and discussion while lecture material is delivered outside of the classroom by video, podcast, or online tools are in various states of experimentation and acceptance. But the recent wave of educational reform that looked to the MOOC as a solution to the cost of education has had a more controversial history.

The idea for a MOOC has its roots in a course taught by Stephen Downes, senior research officer at the National Research Council of Canada, and Professor George Siemens, who was then teaching at the University of Manitoba. The 2008 course cotaught by Downes and Siemens was called "Connectivism and Connective Knowledge" and had 25 tuition-paying students at the University of Manitoba, as well as over 2,200 online students from the general public who paid nothing. Course content was available through an RSS feed and students could use blog posts and threaded discussions in Moodle and hold virtual meetings in the virtual community furnished by *Second Life.*

The term *MOOC* came about when Professor Dave Cormier, who was working on the "Connectivism and Connective Knowledge" course at the University of Prince Edward Island, had a conversation with a colleague, Bryan Alexander, director of research at the National Institute for Technology in Liberal Education. The movement has come to be known as the Open Educational Resource (OER) movement.

Since then, many universities around the world have developed MOOCs as a cost-effective way of delivering courses to students. Some companies have been formed to develop and deliver MOOCs over their own platforms, like Coursera, edX, and Udacity in the United States, and FutureLearn in the United Kingdom. Both nonprofit and for-profit models have been developed.

In 2011, Stanford University began by offering three courses, one of which attracted 160,000 enrollments. The popularity of MOOCs was at its height in 2012, a number of problems have emerged since that time. Some experimental programs have facilitated MOOCs, such as the free textbook program facilitated by Chegg, an online textbook-rental company that has worked with Coursera to furnish inexpensive, online textbooks that disappear once the course is over.

One problem is the rate of completion for a course on a MOOC. In 2014, a research fellow at Harvard University conducted a study of the 80,000 people taking nine courses at Harvard through one of the MOOC programs. While only 13.3 percent of the students actually finished their courses, he found that 19.5 percent had initially intended to complete the course, but didn't. He also found that 5.4 percent of those who started the MOOC course never intended to finish it (Kolowich 2014).

MOOCs may provide unique learning experiences for people who can't afford to take time off to go to school and carry a full academic load, but they have also been blamed for dumbing down curricular matter to keep students engaged. But many of the courses designed to be run on the MOOC platforms turned out to be entertainment with little pedagogical substance, and some were too mired in the one-way form of lectures on video that they failed to interest students with static, passive experiences. Many of the MOOCs reach over 100,000 people but use video lectures and old-style threaded discussion lists.

When new ideas become mired in old models of delivery, or the real qualities of engagement, communication, and connection are sacrificed for financial profit, the new initiative is likely to fail. At this point, those MOOCs that have learned how to emphasize the collaborative nature of the Internet and web have provided valuable lessons, but others have not fared as well. If MOOCs are to become more viable methods of instruction and education, greater attention to the human dimensions of education using technology need to be addressed.

See also: E-Publishing

Further Reading

Kolowich, Steve. 2014. "Rethinking Low Completion Rates in MOOCs." *Chronicle of Higher Education.* Accessed January 2, 2015: http://chronicle.com/blogs/wiredcampus/rethinking-low-completion-rates-in-moocs/55211.

Parr, Chris. 2013. "Mooc Creators Criticize [sic] Courses' Lack of Creativity." Times Higher Education. Accessed January 2, 2015: http://www.timeshighereducation.co.uk/news/mooc-creators-criticise-courses-lack-of-creativity/2008180.fullarticle.

Massively Multiplayer Online Role-Playing Games (MMORPGs) (See Gaming)

Mayer, Marissa

Marissa Mayer (1975–) is the chief executive officer (CEO) of Yahoo!, having attained her current position in July 2012. Yahoo! (the exclamation mark is part of the official title of the company) is a multinational Internet corporation founded in 1994. It currently has over 700 million users worldwide. Mayer's successes are largely attributed to the aggressive position she has taken on acquiring smaller companies, such as Flickr, Tumblr, and other small companies. In her first two years as CEO, she acquired 37 start-up companies, which resulted in attracting top talent for the Yahoo! executive team. Her business model for Yahoo! is to focus on the company's growth in core content, social, gaming, video, and conference calls. Among some of her most successful projects are Yahoo!'s mail and weather apps. She has also been credited with reviving Yahoo!'s position in the information technology market after several years of lower than expected earnings.

Mayer grew up in Wausau, Wisconsin, and received her BS in symbolic systems with honors at Stanford University. She received an MS degree from Stanford in computer science with a specialization in artificial intelligence. She had internships at SRI International (a research and development firm) in Menlo Park, California, and the UBS research lab (a financial services company) in Zurich,

Switzerland. She was the first woman engineer hired at Google in 1999, and was also its twentieth employee. At Google she held many positions spanning diverse projects such as Google Search and Google Maps, to the design of the Google Toolbar, iGoogle, and Gmail. She also had creative control over the design of the simple search homepage.

While there are so few women in leadership roles in the tech industry, Mayer has attracted a surprising amount of attention and criticism. In the words of Nicholas Carlson, "To a public casually interested in her career, Mayer's working life before Yahoo—spent entirely at Google—is remembered as one success after another. It wasn't" (Carlson 2015, 21). Still, Mayer's accomplishments at Google and Yahoo! Have given her the added pressure of being a figurehead for all women in the tech industry. In 2014, *Fortune* magazine ranked her number 32 of the World's 100 Most Powerful Women, and number 1 in the list of the top business stars under the age of 40.

Mayer's tenure at Yahoo! Has been marked by her aggressive acquisition of other companies, and the successful migration to a more mobile platform. Before Mayer assumed the position of CEO, Yahoo! had acquired 24 percent of the Chinese online marketing firm, Alibaba. When Alibaba went public in September 2014, Yahoo!'s share of the profits were in the range of $20 billion (La Monica 2014). With this added value, Mayer has acquired even more app-based firms and the mobile users of Yahoo! have climbed to over 430 million in the first quarter of 2014, a 30 percent increase from the 2013. Within two years of leading Yahoo!, Mayer had increased the value of the company to $33 billion, double what it was when she assumed leadership in 2012.

See also: Yahoo!

Further Reading

Carlson, Nicholas. 2015. *Marissa Mayer and the Fight to Save Yahoo!* New York: Hachette Book Group, 21.
"50 Most Powerful Women: Global Edition." 2014. *Fortune*, 169: 16.
La Monica, Paul R. 2014. "Put Up or Shut Up Time for Marissa Mayer." CNN.com. Accessed October 1, 2014: http://money.cnn.com/2014/09/02/investing/yahoo-alibaba-ipo-marissa-mayer/.

Meme

A *meme* is a unit of expression that has cultural meaning. Memes are often ideas, jingles, catch-phrases, or images that spread from person to person. The term comes from the Greek word *mimeme* which means "to imitate." In 1976, biologist Richard Dawkins popularized the term in a book that compared memes to biological genes that replicate as they spread. Calling memes "the DNA of culture,"

Dawkins's concept of meme could be explained as basic ideas or expressions of culture that were repeated through word of mouth, or through forms of media (Dawkins 1976, 189–201). Today, we often think of Internet memes as those catchy phrases, ideas, or images that spread over the Internet and become part of popular culture. The number of hits a meme receives is a measure of how fast the meme goes viral, meaning that it has replicated, like a virus throughout society (or the world). Dawkins also warned that memes are subject to changing as they go from person to person. Using the metaphor of "the survival of the fittest" Dawkins's biological approach to memes shows that the longer memes are around, the more they evolve as they take on cultural meaning.

Many writers have interpreted the word to mean that culture can be expressed in small units of information. Some explain that memes replicate shared cultural ideas in the minds of the people who pay attention to them. The study of mimetics became popular in the 1990s as people became interested in the way ideas evolve over time, from person to person.

Internet memes include jokes and videos. They also include more serious ideas, such as political attacks. Memes typically spread through e-mails, social networks, blogs, and other websites. The way memes spread somewhat resembles the spread of viruses among human hosts. If enough people pass on a meme to others, the message is said to "go viral."

In marketing, memes are related to the idea of word of mouth, sometimes called "buzz." Some marketers create viral marketing campaigns to promote products by spreading memes. In some cases, people may not even realize they are taking part in viral marketing. Memes can also be thought of as "short-cuts" to ways of thinking about social issues and what is of importance in a culture.

See also: Trending; Viral

Further Reading

Davison, Patrick. 2014. "The Language of Internet Memes." In *The Social Media Reader,* edited by Michael Mandiberg. New York: New York University Press, 120–134.
Dawkins, Richard. 1976. *The Selfish Gene.* Oxford, UK: Oxford University Press, 189–201.

Memorializing

The online world has come to be known as a place for connection to others, and perhaps one of the most emotional uses of online spaces, particularly on blogs, is for memorial pages, or sites where people can express grief and be soothed by the words of others who post comforting thoughts in an act of memorializing a person, place, or thing. *Memorializing* often conjures images of remembering those who have passed on, but online memorials often capture the emotions and feelings of a community or group of people who have collectively experienced an event—such as the Ferguson, Missouri, memorializing of the actions of police against Michael Brown in August 2015, or the brutal shooting of 26 individuals, 20 of whom were children, in what became known as the "Newtown Massacre" in 2013. In extreme cases like these, online memorials can reach beyond the geographic boundaries of the location where the tragedy happened and connect people who can grieve, express emotion, and offer support to others.

In almost every culture, death is accompanied by some form of collective grieving, or, sometimes, celebration of the person who has passed from the earthly life to something other. When this happens, communities often form to help regularize the process and the shared commitment of the group in honor of the one who has passed. It is not surprising, then, that social networks, in particular, have become a way of extending those communities far beyond geographic borders.

What makes online space attractive to those who want to share grief or remember loved ones is the range that can extend beyond a local space. But what adds to the problem of memorializing online is the nature of digital information. The rush of digital information over multiple platforms of information distribution is often blamed for shortening our attention spans and allowing us to forget information, but the act of online memorializing features issues of connecting to loved ones and participating in communities of grief and remembrance.

In 1995, Michael Kibbee was dying of Hodgkin's disease. He launched the World Wide Cemetery Website (http://cemetery.org/) to include short profiles of those who passed on, and allowed photos, videos, and comments to be left by mourners. Though Kibbee died in 1997, the site still exists and has continued to add thousands of dignified memorials to the site.

Other sites have emerged, too, with perhaps not so constant dignity. Facebook's RIP pages are a mix of serious notices, about the deaths of people, with nonrelated content, such as an announcement about the television show *The Walking Dead* or silly quotes about "feeling" dead. Perhaps the mixed intentions displayed on social media sites have contributed to the growth in moderated, professional memorial sites, which now abound. Some sites focus on members of the military, some of victims of suicide, and others on victims of violent crime—all linking the notice of death to others who may have never known the deceased, but who are interested in following the information about the subject's demise.

Some websites focus on the aspects of communal mourning in particular. In Hong Kong, a shortage of usable burial space on the island prompted the creation in 2010 of a government-run cyber graveyard called Memorial.gov.hk. Similarly, Eterni. me, a start-up company launched in 2014 by Marius Ursache, a student who proposed the idea at the Martin Trust Center for MIT Entrepreneurship, has introduced a "virtual you" site that allows friends and relatives to communicate with a person long after they are dead, by allowing the person to structure what the site looks like themselves. The site draws on the use of an artificial intelligence avatar that takes the place of the deceased and simulates a conversation with those who log on to the site. Eterni.me helps users "curate your legacy for the future" (Chayka 2014).

While online memorials and sharing information about commemorations over social media has generated a number of professional sites as well as dedicated spaces on social networks, memorializing remains a very personal type of communication. A growing problem, however, is the nature of personal profiles posted by an individual alive that remain online after the person passes on. Facebook and MySpace have policies on deleting a user's digital presence if a friend or family member produces a death certificate, and most social networks will link death announcements to the content posted by individuals who create accounts while still living, but there is also another category of online "death" that is now becoming relatively popular.

Sometimes people choose to take some time away from their social profiles or digital identities and create a temporary "digital absence." Killing a profile online is referred to as "webicide." The retreat from such a space is sometimes called a "digital death" and when a person chooses to withdraw from their online profiles we see how the desire for permanency on social networks clashes with the rights of the individual to withdraw. Many online companies have policies that make it difficult to delete information because of the fear that someone else might do the deleting. Facebook users have to make a specific request, while Twitter users can select an option of "delete account" on their profile settings.

See also: Blogs; Identity; Right to Be Forgotten

Further Reading

Chayka, Kyle. 2014. "After Death, Don't Mourn, Digitize with Sites Like Eterni.me." *Newsweek*. Accessed February 27, 2015: http://www.newsweek.com/2014/08/29/after -death-dont-mourn-digitize-sites-eternime-264892.html.

Thomas-Jones, Angela. 2010. *The Host in the Machine: Examining the Digital in the Social*. Oxford, UK: Chandos, 123–131.

Microsoft

The Microsoft Corporation was founded by Bill Gates and Paul Allen in Albuquerque in 1975. Over the years it has grown into a multinational corporation that manufactures and sells computer software and consumer electronics and develops personal computers and related services. Among its most well-known products are the Microsoft Windows line of operating systems for computers, and the Microsoft Office suite of software products.

Though one of the biggest names in computer software, Microsoft has had its ups and downs with successes and failures in product development. But it is also known for the legal troubles it has had in the United States and Europe, and, more recently, for the philanthropic activities of one of its founders, Bill Gates.

Gates and Allen first met in high school and remained friends, even though Allen was a bit older than Gates. At the Lakeside School, the private high school the two attended, they would often work together in a "computer laboratory" that was a room with a fax machine and some related hardware. They figured out how to hack the school's computer, but, in the school, this type of behavior was considered an application of scientific principles, and instead of expulsion, they were offered unlimited computer time in exchange for helping to improve the computer's performance.

Allen graduated high school first and attended Washington State University, but dropped out after two years in order to work as a programmer for Honeywell in Boston. By this time, Gates had entered Harvard, but spent a good deal of time with Allen. After Allen read an article about the Altair 8800 microprocessor in a *Popular Electronics* magazine, he approached Gates and the two enthusiastically saw some of the possibilities of using the Altair for a greater number of purposes. The two contacted Ed Roberts, the designer of the Altair 8800 and co-owner of Micro Instrumentation and Telemetry Systems (MITS) in Albuquerque, New Mexico, and asked if Roberts would be interested in seeing the program they developed for the Altair. They were told they could come and show their product, and, at that point, Gates got busy writing a program for the system. Within eight weeks, Allen was on a plane to Albuquerque, where he pitched the idea.

MITS liked the idea and agreed to distribute the product under the name of the Altair BASIC. This inspired Gates and Allen to start their own company, and, in 1975, after Gates had sent a letter to Allen calling the partnership Micro-soft, they agreed to use the name for their new company. In 1978, they decided to move the company back to Seattle, and, in 1981, the company incorporated in the state of Washington and became Microsoft Inc. Bill Gates was the president of the Company and the chairman of the board, and Paul Allen was the executive vice president.

The number of technological and software developments followed, including the release of the 1983 Microsoft Windows program that used a graphical user interface and had a system that could process multiple messages on different screens, called "windows." Their software was sold to IBM computers, and, from that point, the company took off with their line of "personal computers." That same year they also introduced the Microsoft Mouse. The key to the technology was the Microsoft

Disk Operating System, known as MS-DOS, which Gates wrote for IBM in 1981, in a deal that made MS-DOS exclusive to IBM machines. Gates held the patent on the software, and that made him a very rich man. By 1983, when Microsoft Windows became available on IBM machines, Gates was a millionaire at age 31.

Microsoft moved its headquarters to Redmond, Washington, in February 1986, and on March 13 the company went public. By 1998, Microsoft's profits were about twice as large as General Motors, which at the time was the biggest company in the world. In that same year, Apple sued Microsoft for copyright infringement having to do with rights to the graphical user interface (GUI) both were using. While the court proceedings were occurring, Microsoft continued to develop software that became extremely popular. In 1989 the Office suite of software that created a multifunctioning computer with word processing and a mail program was released, as was a new line of business presentation software, and more. Both Office and Windows became dominant programs in their respective areas. When the relationship between Microsoft and IBM began to deteriorate in 1991, Microsoft began to focus more on computer networking and accessing the World Wide Web. By 1995, they released the Windows 95 version of their software and began bundling Internet Explorer into their packages. By 2001, Microsoft introduced their first gaming unit, the Xbox system, which posed competition for Sony's PlayStation 2. For a while Microsoft withdrew the Xbox until further developments could help it compete with Sony and the other emerging game technologies that were flooding the market, and, in 2005, it released a new, improved Xbox 360 gaming console, which was a success.

Microsoft was producing software and was seemingly an engine of growth for the new information economy and e-commerce, but a series of legal issues began to besiege the organization. In hindsight, many of the problems occurred because there were no firm legal precedents to guide the development of such a new industry. Microsoft's rapid growth attracted attention to whether the company was trying to become a monopoly on computer software. All former legal cases involved matters of antitrust and anticompetitive practices, but it was not clear whether a software developer and manufacturer fit neatly into the annals of previous trade investigations.

In 1989 when Apple sued Microsoft, the FTC and Department of Justice investigated Microsoft's business dealings and the problem was resolved in 1994 when a consent decree was agreed upon allowing both Microsoft and Apple to use the GUI interface in question. But by 1997, a more serious legal threat occurred, described by Ken Auletta as "one of the largest civil antitrust investigations in U.S. history" (Auletta 2001, xix).

Microsoft was accused of aggressive business tactics that, if left unchecked, could have benefited the company's move to be a monopoly. This time, many other computer manufacturers and web browser companies had an interest in the outcome of whether Microsoft was guilty of violating the terms of the 1994 consent decree. *United States v. Microsoft Corporation* 253 F.3d 34 (D.C. Cir. 2001) was the "largest antitrust trial since the 1911 Standard Oil case" and it was held as Microsoft's Windows and Internet Explorer served about 90 percent of the computers available in the United States (Auletta 2001, xiii). In 2001, the Department of Justice reached an agreement with Microsoft, and the case was settled. Microsoft was required to share its interfaces with third-party companies and some of the business dealings were to be monitored for five years to make sure the company was complying with the agreed upon terms. But what was most notable about this case was that the U.S. government became integrally involved in the burgeoning software business, justifying the integral relationship of a private company and a government at the time the economy was shifting from industrial and service jobs to a more information-related focus.

As the company entered the new century, Gates stepped down from being the CEO and Steve Ballmer, an old college friend and employee of the company since 1980 took over the job of chief. Allen had to resign because of an illness, and Gates took the title of chief software architect. Soon after, Ballmer found himself having to deal with the antitrust suit brought by the European Union against Microsoft. In 2004, the European Union found Microsoft guilty in a highly publicized antitrust case largely because the Internet Explorer web browser came bundled in software and customers had no choice to but use Internet Explorer, if they had a computer in which the software had been bundled (Curtis 2014).

By the time Microsoft released its next version of Windows called Windows Vista in January 2007, Microsoft was fully operating but a number of competitors had joined the field. Consumer satisfaction of Vista's functionality were less than stellar. Though the program was supposedly a more secure software, less prone to glitches and bugs, consumers found the new interface frustrating. And, at the same time, the European Union imposed another fine $1.4 billion for Microsoft's lack of compliance with the March 2004 judgment.

Microsoft then started to expand its offerings into other technologies, and, in 2007, it came out with the Windows Mobile phone, a smartphone that used an interface similar to the Windows Office computer design. For a while, it seemed that Apple was taking the lead, and Microsoft was struggling to keep up. Microsoft opened its first retail store in Scottsdale, Arizona, in 2009. Microsoft developed a line of products integrating Microsoft software that they hoped would compete with some of the other technologies, but were not quite as successful. The Surface Tablet was developed in reaction to Apple iPad, and was released in 2012. Though the tablet went through other iterations, it received mixed reviews. The Zune MP3 recorder was released but was not as successful as the iPod; and attempts to develop a mobile phone failed.

In 2012, Microsoft posted its first quarterly loss ever, with a net loss of $492 million. In 2013, Ballmer announced that the company would reorganize into four new divisions that specialized on operating systems, apps, cloud services, and devices. In 2014, Ballmer stepped down and was succeeded by Satya Nadella, who previously led Microsoft's Cloud and Enterprise division, while Bill Gates took on the title of technology advisor.

When Nadella became CEO, he began to take the company in a new direction. Many people thought he would be an excellent leader, and thought that his longevity in the organization would be good for the stability of the culture within the organization. Under Nadella's leadership, the organization has once again been reorganized and Microsoft has expanded its interests into new areas of exploration such as wearable technology and gaming that uses Microsoft software (Nadella acquired *Minecraft*'s parent company, Mojang, for $2.5 billion).

See also: Gates, Bill

Further Reading

Auletta, Ken. 2001. *World War 3.0: Microsoft and Its Enemies.* New York: Random House, xiii–xix.

Brinkley, Joel. 2000. "U.S. vs. Microsoft: The Overview; U.S. Judge Says Microsoft Violated Antitrust Laws with Predatory Behavior." *New York Times.* Accessed April 2, 2015: http://www.nytimes.com/2000/04/04/business/us-vs-microsoft-overview-us-judge-says -microsoft-violated-antitrust-laws-with.html.

Chan, Sharon Pian. 2011. "Long Antitrust Saga Ends for Microsoft." *Seattle Times.* Accessed April 27, 2015: http://www.seattletimes.com/business/microsoft/long-antitrust -saga-ends-for-microsoft/.

Curtis, Sophie. 2014. "Bill Gates: A History at Microsoft." *The Telegraph.* Accessed November 11, 2014: http://www.telegraph.co.uk/technology/bill-gates/10616991/Bill -Gates-a-history-at-Microsoft.html.

Mobile Phone Cameras

While mobile phones and smartphones have a number of functions, mobile phone cameras have evolved dramatically. Apple's first attempt to add a camera to a mobile phone was in 1995, though the technology was still too primitive to be effective. The first mobile phone to effectively use a camera was created in Japan in 2000 on the J-phone model. In North America, Sanyo debuted its first mobile phone with a camera in 2004. Since then new improvements in lenses, storage, and apps that facilitate picture quality and curation have evolved. Many of the patents leading to today's mobile phone cameras go back to 1956 when portable cameras became popular, but since that time mobile phone cameras have become better than many low-end stand-alone cameras. The technology has also evolved so that there are a number of options for picture taking, such as pushing buttons, or using swipe technology on touch screens. Since 2006, mobile phones and smartphones have regularly bundled photo features on their units, and along with photo sharing apps, there have been revolutions in photo creativity and curation, personal privacy, newsgathering, and surveillance.

Mobile phone cameras are an example of "Moore's Law" that claims the information processing units in digital technologies are doubling in capacity approximately every 18 months. As a result, mobile phone cameras have developed quickly, and costs have come down dramatically. There are many manufacturers of mobile camera phones and the list seems to grow every year, but major manufacturers include Toshiba, ST Micro, OmniVision, Aptina, Sharp, Nokia, Sanyo, Samsung, Motorola, Siemens, Sony Mobile, and LG Electronics. Many of these manufacturers experimented with cameras on some of their phone models, but most were in the early stages of development. By 2015, cameras on mobile phones had become so sophisticated that one of the films shown at the Sundance Film Festival that year was entirely shot on a mobile phone. The film, called *Tangerine*, was shot on an iPhone 5S using an $8 app called the Filmic Pro, a Steadicam (for camera stability), and a set of lens adaptors for the big screen (Newton 2015).

Like the use of a smartphone to record a feature film, cameras on phones have provided opportunities for many to participate in photography (still and moving images), and in photo curation. While early mobile phone photographers usually had to use e-mail programs to send their images to another computer for storage or visual manipulation, today's smartphones have many more connectivity options. Improvements in cameras have given birth to a number of artistic endeavors that rival traditional photography, and mobile phone art exhibits have been held in major cities around the world. Some scholars have viewed the increased attention to the role of the mobile phone camera as an artistic medium and have written about the new visual aesthetic allowed by smartphones with cameras and the creative ways they have been used (Goggin 2006).

A number of apps have allowed photo sharing for any number of reasons, including the desire to connect with friends and family, share images that have special meaning for the photographer and possibly the receiver of the image, and to capture spontaneous moments. Instagram and Flickr are among the most downloaded apps, but more than 10,000 photo apps are available at a variety of prices and with a number of specialized features.

Mobile phone cameras also make it possible to take pictures in very intimate settings, or for the purpose of sending selfies or sexts directly to others, though perhaps there are a range of moral questions that might be asked of those who send sexts—wanted or unwanted—to others. This encyclopedia includes entries for both of those photo uses, so they will not be explored in depth at this point, but it is important to realize that without the mobile phone camera, these types of photo uses would be much more difficult to take and send. They also reflect the personalized use of the mobile phone to bypass traditional photo processing programs that would easily be seen by others.

Some have said that the mobile phone camera is changing the sense of people's personal privacy, and when it comes to selfies and sexting, that idea gains much credence. But, at the same time, mobile phone cameras are often banned in public places where covert taking of pictures can violate the privacy of others. Most commonly, gyms and locker rooms restrict the use of mobile phones, particularly for the reason that it is so easy to snap a picture of someone in a state of undress that could violate their personal privacy. Theaters ban the use of mobile phone photography (and all photography) for the safety of actors on stage who are distracted by flashes or the sound of cameras clicking images, and because the use of mobile phones distracts other patrons. Government buildings often restrict the use of mobile phones, particularly because of the photo features that can snap sensitive information, and museums often restrict the flash features of mobile phone cameras because the intense light can destroy the quality of paintings that require climate and lighting control for preservation.

Though the personal use of mobile phone cameras can indeed facilitate our own choices about personal images and the way we want to share them or not (Hanson 2007, 49–52), mobile phone cameras have already proven to be critical tools for citizen journalism and surveillance. On many occasions, news events have been documented by a person using the camera features of their phone, such as the July 7, 2005, "London Bombings" in which terrorists planted three bombs on London Underground trains and one on a London bus. The first images to be transmitted of the devastation came from mobile phone cameras and were immediately streamed to the press and to the public. Since then, there have been a number of important events that have been captured on mobile phone cameras, and those images have often turned the tide of public sentiment once they have been released to the press.

The term *citizen journalism* has often been used to describe the role of an average person who takes an image or reports on real events that become newsworthy. In 2007, Mayor Bloomberg of New York City encouraged the public to document any event they thought questionable and send those mobile phone images to the police. Even though the request of a mayor may seem to legitimize the use of the mobile phone camera, there are many who say that when citizens record events, the context and the whole story is not immediately apparent. Still, the power of those recorded images are important in establishing trust within communities and in expressing a particular point of view.

The ability to capture images with a mobile phone camera has provided the world with extraordinary images, such as the 2006 execution of Iraqi dictator Saddam Hussein, the beheadings of journalists in 2014 and 2015, and the conflicts between police and a number of unarmed black men in the United States throughout 2014 and 2015. In each one of these extreme situations, lawmakers, the public, and the communities that form around specific points of view are important factors in helping to illuminate events and spread information that becomes a part of social life.

Finally, the role of the mobile phone camera and its function in surveillance is worth mention. Not only do mobile phones emit GPS tracking information, which is one way of thinking of the privacy one has compared to the privacy one gives up when using a mobile phone, but the camera features of the phone are often overlooked in terms of documenting where someone is and what they may be doing. The presence of video cameras in banks, elevators, and public buildings is commonplace today, but the unobtrusive nature of the camera on a mobile phone increases the type of surveillance of the environment that seems to be a part of living in a more technologized world where privacy becomes an even more elusive concept.

With cameras on mobile phones and the prediction that by 2020 most Internet access will be through mobile platforms, we should well ask what the eventual impact of the mobile phone camera will be on our sense of privacy, personal creativity, concept of news and the role of citizen journalism, and on the type of surveillance we might expect.

See also: Mobile Phone; Privacy; Selfie; Sexting; Smartphone; Surveillance

Further Reading

Goggin, Gerard. 2006. *Cell Phone Culture: Mobile Technology in Everyday Life*. New York: Routledge.

Hanson, Jarice. 2007. *24/7: How Cell Phones and the Internet Change the Way We Live, Work, and Play*. Westport, CT: Praeger, 49–52.

Newton, Casey. 2015. "How One of the Best Films at Sundance Was Shot Using an iPhone 5S." The Verge. Accessed March 26, 2015: http://www.theverge.com/2015/1/28/7925 023/sundance-film-festival-2015-tangerine-iphone-5s.

The movie *Tangerine*, the first Sundance Film Festival Film Shot on an iPhone, debuted at the 2015 Sundance Film Festival in Park City, Utah.

One of the most visually striking components of the film is its look, which is grainy yet also highly saturated, creating a sense of tension within the images. [Director Sean] Baker and Director of Photography Radium Cheung actually shot the film on iPhones. Baker explained, "The iPhone 5S had recently come out with its better camera . . . We realized it could be good for shooting with first-time actors because it wouldn't intimidate them and the extras that we were grabbing off the street . . . But I wanted to still make this film extremely cinematic, so we shot with anamorphic lenses. They were actually prototypes from a company called Moondog Labs, which provided us with prototype anamorphic adapters for the iPhone. Nobody else had shot like this . . . They really were great for what we were doing, as they turn the phone camera into real anamorphic capturing devices. This gave the picture a much more classical film look. We were so lucky that the prototypes were made just in time and were available to us!"

Source: From the press release for *Tangerine*, courtesy of Magnolia Films.

Mobile Phones (Cellular Telephones)

Mobile phones are wireless devices that transmit and receive messages through radio signals that reach antennas that send the signals to base stations that connect to other phones, or to other base stations. To send a message beyond the geographic region where the base station is located, messages are transferred through various areas of coverage called "cells" until they reach their destination. Early mobile phones sent signals in analog waves, but today's phones use digital signals, which allow phones to have multiple functions, making phones capable of transmitting voice, text, and data, including video and games. Many phones also have additional features like cameras, GPS, and storage capacity for digital material like music, films, phone numbers, and calendars. Some phones with advanced computer capability are called smartphones, but in general, small, handheld phones are referred to as mobile, or cellular phones. The term "mobile" is more commonly used globally, while in the United States the term *cell phone* is more widely used. For purposes of this encyclopedia, the term *mobile* will be used.

Mobile phones combine the technologies of telephone systems and radio transmission. Each phone has a transmitter and receiver inside the unit. When a caller makes a call or sends a text, the message is sent in wireless form to an antenna usually mounted on a steel tower. The tower is connected by cables to a mobile telephone switching office (MTSO) that either sends the signal to a local telephone company, or retransmits the signal to another area of coverage called a "cell," until the receiving phone gets the message. If the caller is moving, the network automatically passes the call from one cell to the next without interruption. This is the derivation of the term *cell phone* as used in the United States and some other countries. This transfer of a call from cell to cell is called handoff or handover. The term *roaming* is used to describe the process of the phone's transmitter sending signals to find the next antenna so the message continues without a break in action. Some phones with advanced computer capability are called smartphones (addressed as a separate entry in this book).

The world's first commercial mobile system went into operation in Japan in 1979 and was entirely analog-based, meaning the type of electronic signals used were analog waves, rather than digital waves. The first analog mobile phone in the United States was produced by Motorola in 1983, and by the early 1990s, the "second generation" of cell phones using digital transmission were available. Today a combination of 3G (third generation) and 4G (fourth generation) systems are in use, both in the United States and elsewhere. Each "generation" indicates the level of sophistication of the phone and the way messages are transmitted over the wireless system. Since the second generation, all mobile phones operate with digital signals.

The number of mobile phones now exceeds the number of wired phones in existence in the United States, and, as of 2011, there were more mobile phones in America than there were people (meaning some people had multiple phones). According to studies by the Pew Research Center, as of 2014, 90 percent of American adults had a mobile phone ("Mobile Technology Fact Sheet" n.d.) and by 2015 nearly two-thirds (64%) of American adults had a smartphone (Smith 2015).

Mobile phones have operating systems that include powerful processors to make graphics and memory features useful. These features add high-resolution touchscreens and the functionality of handling different types of media files, from simple telephone and text storage to full-motion video, Internet connectivity, and more. Apple introduced the iPhone operating system in 2007, and Google introduced the Android operating system in 2008. While there are other operating systems in existence, the iPhone and Android systems are currently the most popular in the United States, and Android is the most used operating system in the world.

Most mobile telephones are battery-powered, and small enough to keep in a pocket or purse. There are a range of phones and calling plans to fit lifestyle or income level. Some phones have limited features, like those that are preprogrammed to only reach a limited number of other phone numbers, or those with big number buttons for the visually impaired. Prepaid plans are available to allow callers to use phones while keeping track of the amount of money they pay for service. Some phones have GPS features, or are capable of using satellite systems to distribute signals beyond national boundaries, a useful feature for global travelers.

Mobile phones have made telephony available to people in other countries of the world where traditional wired systems of telephone service were too expensive to introduce and maintain, but even though mobile platforms are expected to rise, a number of barriers for people in developing nations still exist. Not only is there the expense of buying or renting a phone, but the cost of electricity for charging batteries may be too high, or the service may be intermittent. Still, the International Telecommunications Union (ITU) produces statistics for telecommunications use around the world, and a publication of the ITU reports that mobile use is increasing at a double-digit rate. As of 2014, 32 percent of the people of the world had mobile-broadband subscriptions. In 2014, mobile broadband penetration levels were highest in Europe (64%) and the Americas (59%), followed by the Commonwealth of Independent States (CIS) (49%), the Arab States (25%), Asia-Pacific (23%) and Africa (19%) ("ICT Facts and Figures" 2014, 3).

See also: Android; Apple iOS; Smartphone; Tablet

Further Reading

Hanson, Jarice. 2007. *24/7: How Cell Phones and the Internet Change the Way We Live, Work, and Play.* Westport, CT: Praeger.

"ICT Facts and Figures." 2014. International Telecommunications Union (ITU). Accessed April 27, 2015: http://www.itu.int/en/ITUD/Statistics/Documents/facts/ICTFactsFigures 2014-e.pdf : 3.

"Mobile Technology Fact Sheet." n.d. Pew Research Center. Accessed March 26, 2015: http://www.pewinternet.org/fact-sheets/mobile-technology-fact-sheet/.

Smith, Aaron. 2015. "U.S. Smartphone Use in 2015." Pew Research Center. Accessed April 27, 2015: http://www.pewinternet.org/2015/04/01/us-smartphone-use-in-2015/.

"Worldwide Smartphone Shipments Edge Past 300 Million Units in the Second Quarter; Android and iOS Devices Account for 96% of the Global Market." International Data Corporation (IDC). Accessed October 2, 2014: http://www.idc.com/getdoc.jsp?containerId=prUS25037214.

Woyke, Elizabeth. 2014. *The Smartphone: Anatomy of an Industry.* New York and London: The New Press.

MP3

MP3 is the abbreviation of MPEG-1 or MPEG-2 Audio Layer III, which is an audio coding format for digital audio. It allows a user to make a duplicate of an original audio file, with no appreciable loss of sound quality. MP3 technologies can also facilitate storage of digital files and have become common methods of compressing digital information for transfer and playback on audio players. The original MP3 technologies were confined to audio engineers who used the technology largely for voice compression. Only later was MP3 technology used for music compression that allowed for the development of the iPod and other digital technologies that allow for the streaming of music. But it is MP3 technology that is largely responsible for the shakeup in the traditional recorded music industry, the proliferation of portable music players and mobile phone music services now available, and the streaming of media content.

Though many electronics companies were experimenting with MP3 technologies and taking out patents on component improvements, many engineers credit a German graduate student, Karlheinz Brandenburg, with one of the pivotal moments in digital music compression that began in the early 1980s at the University of Erlangen-Nuremberg. One of Brandenburg's professors urged him to work on the problem of how to transmit music over an Integrated Services Digital Network (ISDN) phone line, and Brandenburg began working on his PhD dissertation in audio compression.

At the time, the ISDN was the most up-to-date set of communication standards for digital transmission of media content over the traditional circuits of the public telephone networks. To his credit, Brandenburg realized that transmitting media content over the ISDN line was not just a technical matter. He realized that he also needed to understand how people perceive the quality of music. He used a Suzanne Vega song, *Tom's Diner,* as his test product, and he attempted a number of methods to compress the signal without losing audio quality. In recounting the story of the process, Brandenburg recalled how tricky it was to try to sort out the intellectual property rights behind inventions that involve numerous organizations and people (Ewing 2007). Among the major companies that were also experimenting with MP3 technology at the time were Alcatel-Lucent, Microsoft, Bell Labs, and others, but their experiments were not limited to audio alone. Instead, they were focusing on how to compress video and audio for use over the telephone lines. But perhaps Brandenburg's contributions did most to understand the need for a high-quality system that replicated original sound quality, and his developments translated to the use of the Internet for distribution.

In 1997, an entrepreneur by the name of Michael Robertson created MP3.com, a website that could be used to find free music on the Internet. The company he started bought 45,000 CDs and loaded them into an internal server for unlimited use by customers (Knopper 2009, 119) and was quickly sued by the RIAA and forced to shut down. Around the same time, Shawn Fanning had the idea in his Northeastern University dorm room that Internet Relay Chats (IRCs) could be modeled to use MP3 technology to share music. He planned to set up a central server that would allow users to connect and share the digital music they had stored on their own computer hard drives. By 1999, he was working on developing a code that allowed peer-to-peer file sharing for the purpose of sharing music, and he called his nascent company Napster. Though Napster was challenged by the RIAA and forced to shut down, so much attention had been given to the downloading and distribution of music that the MP3 technology and the experiments that surrounded the transfer of digital music forced the recorded music industry to radically change its business model.

MP3 technology allowed many companies to compete for the emerging digital music market. Apple used MP3 to develop its iPod media player and the iTunes download service. Other companies also used MP3 to develop their own digital music players, such as Nullsoft's audio player Winamp, developed, in 1977, and the first solid-state digital audio player, MPMan, developed by SaeHan Information Systems in Seoul, South Korea, in 1998.

Today, MP3 technology is used for a wide variety of audio devices. Smartphones use it, computers use it, and audio systems in cars use it. Recorded audio books on CD are often created with the use of MP3 files, and practically any audio signal over the Internet can ostensibly use the technology to transfer audio. Over time the technology has become so successful that it can compress a digital audio signal into a package nearly 1,000 percent smaller than the original, noncompressed sound signal, and it can do so without any loss of sound quality. MP3 technology is largely responsible for the development of streaming services, both audio and video.

See also: Fanning, Shawn; Legacy Media; Streaming Media

Further Reading

Ewing, Jack. 2007. "How MP3 Was Born." *Bloomberg Businessweek.* Accessed March 26, 2015: http://www.bloomberg.com/bw/stories/2007-03-05/how-mp3-was-bornbusiness week-business-news-stock-market-and-financial-advice.

Knopper, Steve. 2009. *Appetite for Self-Destruction: The Spectacular Crash of the Record Industry in the Digital Age.* New York: Free Press, 119.

Multiuser Dungeons (MUDs) (See Gaming)

MySpace

MySpace is a social network that has a very different history than most other social networks. While it was modeled on Friendster.com and other emerging social networks, its founders, Chris DeWolfe and Tom Anderson, had a very different goal for MySpace that was rooted in a Hollywood-style business model and favored advertising from the very beginning. As marketers, they knew that the most important thing to do was develop a group of users who would become loyal to the site, so that products could be marketed to them through pop-ups. They chose the most likely audience members as users and gave them tools and features to keep them coming back to MySpace.

DeWolfe had been working in an Internet company that specialized in sending spam for a company called ResponseBase, and Anderson ran a pornography website. Together, they worked for an Internet company called eUniverse, which became MySpace's parent company. MySpace's programming language allowed users to customize their profiles with choices of wallpaper and backgrounds and this appealed to a number of teen females. DeWolfe and Anderson knew that the newest adopters of social networks were teenage girls. The "accident" of allowing users to modify their profiles turned out to be MySpace's biggest advantage. The open architecture that allowed the user so much control over the site was popular with users, though it often created a number of bugs and quirks for MySpace itself.

DeWolfe and Anderson launched MySpace in Beverly Hills, California, in 2003, just as broadband had penetrated 25 percent of the homes in the United States, and the younger generation was learning how to download music and create mashups and remixes. DeWolfe and Anderson allowed individuals who became members to create their own identities online, without divulging who they were (which was required by other social networks). They also allowed a process of "friending" people that allowed users to click on a button that stated "Add to Friends." The person who received the message that they were being asked to be a friend could respond with a "yes" or "no." As a result, many users attempted to accumulate as many friends as possible, making the acquisition of the number of "friends"—either real or not—a symbolic badge of honor. Anderson recruited some popular social network names to come to MySpace, and publicity from that raised the profile of the company as those popular bloggers brought their own friends to the new space.

While MySpace was growing, eUniverse was having financial problems. By January 2004, MySpace was getting close to having one million members. The site decided to offer musicians online marketing by setting up profiles on the space and offering new musical options to users. Though the Recording Industry Association of America (RIAA) was in the process of suing AOL for sponsoring the website mp3.com on which independent musicians could stream their music, MySpace used a different music player technology and allowed bands to have sites with their real band names. MySpace also became a place for game sharing, particularly multiuser games like *Mafia Wars* and *FarmVille*.

Anderson also realized that sex sells, and he collaborated with others to promote MySpace with a series of parties in cities across the United States where girls were brought to parties to meet men and possibly "friend" them. The girls who worked for the parties and those who came to participate in the parties were often photographed in sexy positions, many of which showed bare skin. Some became MySpace celebrities, with "friends" constantly checking for newly posted pictures, often provocative. Lurkers—people who didn't have their own profiles on MySpace but wanted to voyeuristically view the sites of others, became a huge portion of the MySpace membership. By the end of 2004, MySpace opened its website to the larger world, and dropped its membership requirement so that anyone could view member files, and the number of lurkers seemed to decrease, but the number of pages visited skyrocketed.

In 2005, DeWolfe discussed selling MySpace to Mark Zuckerberg of Facebook, but Zuckerberg's offer of $75 million was rejected. In the same year, Rupert Murdoch, the head of News Corp. and media mogul, purchased MySpace for $580 million. The purchase was Murdoch's first venture into the Internet world of media, and he was interested in the advertising potential of the site. With media interests all over the world, Murdoch had intended to bring a version of MySpace first to England, and then elsewhere in the world.

But MySpace's popularity and the salacious business of pop up ads, sex, and a link to questionable content received a great amount of attention. In 2006, Connecticut Attorney General Richard Blumenthal began a formal inquiry into childrens' access to pornography and questionable content on MySpace. MySpace was unable to develop an effective spam filter to control access, and MySpace began to be known as a social network that crashed a lot and had material that most people wouldn't want their children or little brothers or sisters to see. The site was known for crashing and passing on viruses, vandalism, and phishing scams, and advertisers became wary of the way the public was talking about MySpace.

By 2008, MySpace had 41.4 billion pages and 75 million visitors, nearly twice that of Facebook, and it was the leading social network in the world until April of that year, when Facebook began to overtake it. In hindsight, many believe that MySpace remained committed to music and entertainment and that made it seem "old fashioned" while Facebook and Twitter began to launch new features that attracted new users.

MySpace activity began to dwindle, and, by March 2011, the market research firm comScore reported that MySpace had lost over 10 million users in the first two months of 2011. News Corp. put the site up for sale, and on June 29, 2011, MySpace announced that it had been acquired by Specific Media for an undisclosed amount, though CNN reported that the selling price was $35 million (Segall 2011). Other terms of the sale were not specified. One of the partners in Specific Media is the musician Justin Timberlake.

In 2012, Timberlake tweeted a link to a video that introduced the "new MySpace" that had been redesigned and relaunched to focus on musicians and their fans. In 2013, new MySpace went live, along with a new mobile app that allowed for streaming radio stations and programs that were curated by artists. Focusing more on niche audiences, the new iteration sought to strengthen the ties among performers, music, fans, and music sharing sites. The new platform was redesigned so that artists could manage their "digital presence" from any given location. Many of the features from the previous iteration of MySpace were discontinued, such as the blogs, private messages, photo site, and games. By October 1, 2013, MySpace had 36 million users, and, by 2015, the number had grown to 50.6 million users (Shields 2015). The reason for the rebound was a program for more targeted advertising and the addition of original content.

There are still over a billion registered users globally, and, though MySpace may not have the number of return visitors other social networks have, MySpace is still a viable social network.

See also: Facebook; Social Networking

Further Reading

Angwin, Julia. 2009. *Stealing MySpace: The Battle to Control the Most Popular Website in America.* New York: Random House.

Segall, Laurie. 2011. "News Corp. Sells Myspace to Specific Media." CNN Money. Accessed April 21, 2015: oney.cnn.com/2011/06/29/technology/myspace_layoffs/index.htm?hpt=te_bn2.

Shields, Mike. 2015. "MySpace Still Reaches 50 Million People Each Month." *Wall Street Journal.* Accessed April 21, 2015: http://blogs.wsj.com/cmo/2015/01/14/myspace-still-reaches-50-million-people-each-month/.

Vascellaro, Jessica E., Emily Steel, and Russell Adams. 2011. "Newscorp Sells MySpace for a Song." *Wall Street Journal.* Accessed December 26, 2014: http://www.wsj.com/articles/SB100014205270230584004576415932273770852.

N

Netflix

Netflix was originally conceived of by Marc Randolph and Reed Hastings in Scotts Valley, California, in 1997. By 1999, the company started developing a subscription base and loaned single DVDs through the mail to subscribers. The company has built its reputation on the business model of flat-fee unlimited rentals without due dates, late fees, shipping and handling fees, or per title rental fees. As streaming technologies improved, the company shifted to a newer method of delivery through direct streaming to one's home computer, smartphone, or console. Presently, the company has subscribers in more than 40 countries in North and South America, parts of Europe, and the Caribbean and has plans to do business in even more countries on more continents. Though it would be difficult to document, it could be said that Netflix is one of the major contributors to the way people watch television through *binge watching*, as opposed to *appointment viewing*, the traditional model of watching broadcast television at the time when it is originally broadcast. *Binge viewing* allows media consumers to watch episode after episode, and control how many episodes they view at any given time.

While Netflix was one of the most successful dot-coms to emerge out of the dot-com bubble, its acquisition of Starz Entertainment in 2008, which provided original programming for the streaming market globally, became one of Netflix's success stories. However, not all of Netflix's activities have been successful. In 2000, Netflix was offered for acquisition by Blockbuster, the largest brick-and-mortar video rental company in the United States, for $50 million. Blockbuster chose not to acquire the company, and it may never be known whether Netflix might have saved Blockbuster from bankruptcy in 2010.

Netflix's biggest problems occurred in 2011, when Reed Hastings announced a plan to restructure Netflix's DVD rental service and identified it as a subsidiary company called Qwikster. The separation of the DVD rentals through the mail and the streaming service would each have a different pricing structure. The only difference in the two services is that Qwikster would also carry home video games for rent in addition to the DVDs. The cost of the streaming service was to have been $7.99 per month, which was considerably more expensive than the rental by mail. Subscribers were outraged by the action and many cancelled their subscriptions. Within a month, Netflix backpedaled, and dropped the two-tier plan, but only after losing 800,000 subscribers.

More recently, Netflix has become involved in producing original content for the company. At first, original programming was confined to television productions, including the highly successful *House of Cards*, which debuted in its first season in 2011. In 2014, Netflix announced that it would exclusively control the streaming of Adam Sandler's next four movies. In April 2015, Netflix announced it would be raising the cost of its subscription to $8.99 per month.

See also: Legacy Media; Streaming Media

Further Reading

Wallenstein, Andrew. 2014. "What Netflix's Sandler Stunner Means for Movies." *Variety.* Accessed October 2, 2014: http://variety.com/2014/digital/news/what-netflixs-sandler -stunner-means-for-movies-1201319579/.

Net Neutrality

In one of the most contentious battles between public interest groups, businesses, and the Federal Communications Commission (FCC), complicated by issues that spanned the chairmanships of four different FCC chairs between 2003 and 2015, *net neutrality* was finally approved by the FCC on February 26, 2015. Net neutrality is the idea that all pieces of data that move through the Internet should be treated equally. The action was prompted by big telecom providers like Comcast that preferred a tiered system of payment for access to the "channels" of the Internet. What this means is that big companies could essentially get the rights to use the most popular bandwidth of the Internet, and smaller companies would be relegated to the less popular, less reliable bandwidth. Because the major Internet delivery services had invested over $30 billion in developing an infrastructure to support content delivery, the fight was sometimes likened to a "David and Goliath" scenario with the public as the small Davids, and the major Internet service providers standing in as Goliath. Between 2013 and 2015, the citizen actions and public awareness of the problem of Internet governance became so large, that FCC Chair Tom Wheeler actually reversed his opinion and became an advocate for net neutrality.

Most people access the Internet through an Internet Service Provider (ISP) that charges a fee for Internet access. But ISPs can potentially increase their profits by controlling the amount of data they allow people to download and charging some users more for better connections. The term *net neutrality* was first used by Columbia media law professor Tim Wu in 2003 to liken the Internet to a *common carrier*, a form of telecommunications delivery that keeps the carrier of information (the network) open and free from making decisions about what content will be carried and what will not be carried. Common carrier status prohibits discriminating or refusing service to customers based on the type of goods they transmit over the system. The term common carrier was often used in the early days of telephony when the wired telephone system was a delivery system of other people's content.

In 2013, after being heavily lobbied by the telecommunications industries, the FCC took the position that it would be advantageous to allow telecommunications companies that use the Internet for their businesses to be given priority treatment, meaning that they would have the most reliable delivery system for their products. On May 15, 2013, FCC Chairman Tom Wheeler released a plan for the Internet that would let ISPs charge content companies for "fast lane" priority delivery, which would result in creating a slower tier of service for smaller, or less powerful, companies. Citizen action groups and outspoken advocates began to raise public awareness of the problem of keeping the Internet available to all content providers, big and small, and battled the FCC for years to prevent such a ruling.

The Free Press, one of the major opponents to the FCC plan, is a political action organization dedicated to maintaining openness and accountability on the Internet as well as advocating for Freedom of the Press, and fighting media consolidation. The position of The Free Press was that if the FCC's rules went into effect, only the major telecommunications giants, like AT&T, Comcast, and Verizon, would have access to fast Internet delivery, and small companies without big budgets would be relegated to slower traffic, thereby marginalizing them and creating another avenue for the powerful media giants to overcome the small companies. This position was supported by other Internet advocates, like the Electronic Frontier Foundation and the American Civil Liberties Union. Internet advocates like Vint Cerf and Tim Berners-Lee also advocated to keep the Internet free from tiered financing systems.

Supporters of net neutrality worried that telecommunications companies would also seek to control the type of data people can access. For example, an ISP might limit access to data from a rival company or from a service that is critical of that service provider. Supporters of net neutrality argued that the Internet's unique position as an open communications medium must be safeguarded. The telecommunications companies and opponents of net neutrality charged that upholding the idea would require intrusive government regulation and hamper technological innovation.

One of the pivotal moments for the public awareness of net neutrality came during John Oliver's weekly HBO comedy news show called *Last Week Tonight* aired on June 1, 2014. In a 13-minute segment on net neutrality, Oliver urged viewers to take advantage of the FCC's initial open commenting period concerning net neutrality that was scheduled to run from May 15 to June 27. The result was the sending of over 47,000 comments that crashed the FCC comments section and prompted the FCC to explain why they experienced a crash by releasing Twitter messages saying that "technical difficulties" had affected its commenting servers.

Finally, on February 26, 2015, FCC Chair Thomas Wheeler announced that the FCC would back net neutrality. In his blog on the FCC website, Wheeler wrote: "Thank you to the over four million Americans who participated in the Open Internet proceeding. Thanks to them, this decision on Internet openness was itself the most open proceeding in the history of the FCC . . . Consumers now know that lawful content will not be blocked or their service throttled" (Wheeler 2015).

See also: Broadband; Legacy Media; Telecommunications Act of 1996

Further Reading

Aamoth, Doug. 2014. "John Oliver's Net Neutrality Rant Crashes FCC Servers." *Time*. Accessed March 26, 2015: http://time.com/2817567/john-oliver-net-neutrality-fcc/.

Crawford, Susan. 2013. *Captive Audience: The Telecom Industry and Monopoly Power in the New Gilded Age.* New Haven: Yale University Press, 56–63.

Wheeler, Tom. 2015. "Good News for Consumers, Innovators and Financial Markets." FCC Chair's Blog. FCC.gov. Accessed March 26, 2015: http://www.fcc.gov/blog/good -news-consumers-innovators-and-financial-markets.

Edited selections from FCC Chair Tom Wheeler's Statement on Net Neutrality, March 12, 2015

The Open Internet Order: Preserving and Protecting the Internet for All Americans An Open Internet means consumers can go where they want, when they want. It means innovators can develop products and services without asking for permission.

Separating Fact from Fiction

Myth: This is utility-style regulation.
Fact: There is no "utility-style" regulation.

(Continued)

Myth: The FCC plans to set broadband rates and regulate retail prices in response to consumer complaints.

Fact: The Order doesn't regulate retail broadband rates.

Myth: This will increase consumers' broadband bills and/or raise taxes.

Fact: The Order doesn't impose new taxes or fees or otherwise increase prices.

Myth: This is a plan to regulate the Internet and let the government take over the Internet.

Fact: The Order doesn't regulate Internet content, applications or services or how the Internet operates, its routing or its addressing. The Order does not regulate the Internet.

Source: Wheeler, Tom. FCC *Open Internet Order—Preserving and Protecting the Internet for All Americans.* Federal Communications Commission, March 12, 2015. http://www.fcc.gov/document/fcc-open-internet-order-separating-fact-fiction.

Netscape

Netscape Communications (formerly Netscape Communications Corporation) is commonly known as *Netscape*. In its formative years, Netscape was the most well-used web browser, carrying approximately 90 percent of all Internet traffic. The company was founded in 1994, by Marc Andreessen and Jim Clark.

The code used to create the browser had been created by Andreessen and a colleague of his, Eric Bina, who developed the code while they worked at the University of Illinois Urbana-Champaign's National Center for Supercomputing Applications. The project they worked on was called Mosaic, and at the time Mosaic was a superior web browser compared to the other emerging browsers at the time, Prodigy and CompuServe. Mosaic had been the first web browser to work with multiple Internet protocols and was the first browser to allow users to connect to the World Wide Web. Mosaic was released to the public in 1983, and, by 1984, Andreessen and Clark had set up the Mosaic Communications Corporation in Mountain View, California.

The University of Illinois was understandably unhappy with the co-opting of the Mosaic name, so the company changed its name to Netscape Communications and called its web browser Netscape Navigator. At the time of Netscape's domination in the field of web browsers, it was one of the few that would work on any computer, while many of the other emerging browsers were bundled with software that came with the computer, such as Microsoft's Internet Explorer.

America Online (AOL) acquired Netscape in 1998, and, in 2000, Time Warner acquired AOL. When this merger occurred, the decision was made to break up Netscape. After a series of assigning parts of the company to different units within AOL, the Netscape Browser was reconceptualized to look more like the newer and highly successful Mozilla Firefox browser, produced by the Mozilla Foundation, that had been created in 2003. From 2005 to 2007, the Netscape Browser was still available but carried only a fraction of the Internet traffic that it once had transferred, due to the number of browsers that had become available in the market for competition. AOL continued to support Netscape Navigator until 2008, but then recommended that users switch to other browsers, like Flock or Firefox, both of which used the same type of technology as Netscape Navigator.

The AOL and Time Warner merger in 2000 was the largest media merger to take place up until that date. The speculation that fueled the $350 billion merger was the result of the potential of the Internet to influence the change in traditional media companies and the way they would deliver content to homes, but the speculation was premature. In retrospect, the resulting chaos of the AOL/Time Warner merger and failure of many Internet start-ups in 2000 came to be known as the "dot-com crash" that began in March 2000.

See also: America Online Inc. (AOL); Browser

Further Reading

Arango, Tim. 2010. "How the AOL–Time Warner Merger Went So Wrong." *New York Times*. Accessed December 1, 2014: http://www.nytimes.com/2010/01/11/business/media/11merger.html?pagewanted=all&_r=0.

Lashinsky, Adam. 2005. "Remembering Netscape: The Birth of the Web." CNNMoney.com. Accessed December 1, 2014: http://web.archive.org/web/20060427112146/http://money.cnn.com/magazines/fortune/fortune_archive/2005/07/25/8266639/index.htm.

Network Theory

With a history grounded in media theory, information theory, engineering, and mathematics, *network theory* is the study of human and technological interface and the dynamics of control, communication, and feedback that perpetuate an activity or change its course based upon the constantly dynamic tensions among internal forces of the system. Related to the study of cybernetics that focuses on the interrelationship of human beings and machines, network theory is evolving to mean more than the surface charting of information flow among people and machines; it is becoming a phrase that also explains how and what transpires when social networks use technologies for human purposes. Network theory helps explain the balance between the humanistic and the scientific aspects of communication, and, in terms of social media, it helps us understand how and why some uses of social media are successful, while some are not.

Physicist Albert-Laszlo Barabasi described characteristics of network theory as helping us understand how popularity breeds more popularity, such as that which we see in trending, the diffusion of Twitter messages, or when something goes viral. Additionally, the element of time helps us understand how long it takes messages to spread. We often see this in action when we look at how social media or social networks are used for social or political mobilization, but we can also see how it affects trending, the distribution of memes, and the ways content goes viral.

There are a number of related theoretical contributions that help us understand what really occurs in network theory, or social network theory. The *diffusion of innovations* is a theoretical perspective that helps explain how information or news travels from the originator of the information throughout the population. Diffusion studies help us understand the role of markets in the exchange of money or goods to establish social or economic value. One of the leading theorists of diffusion of innovations was Everett M. Rogers, who also described *social diffusion*, a term he applied to describe the human impact on how long it takes and in what way(s) messages spread whenever there is a new innovation.

See also: Cybernetics; Meme; Trending; Viral

Further Reading

Barabasi, Albert-Laszlo. 2002. *Linked: How Everything Is Connected to Everything Else and What It Means for Business, Science, and Everyday Life.* London: Penguin.
Rogers, Everett M. 2003. *Diffusion of Innovations*, 5th ed. New York: Free Press.

Niche Marketing

In contrast to *mass marketing*, meaning that messages (usually advertising or public relations) are aimed at the widest range of audience members possible, *niche* marketing focuses more specifically on demographic variables like age, race, gender, and lifestyle to identify the particular characteristics of an audience. Legacy media that focused on mass market approaches for reaching audiences was different than the strategies used online, where smaller groups of more like-minded people are likely to share content. The concept is particularly powerful when considering how advertising over social networks or apps can appeal to niche audiences that share the same characteristics for a more direct link to those most likely to be attracted by the ad or product.

Niche marketing is a more efficient way to think about what types of images appeal to people who share characteristics. Often, those people spread what they like to their friends over social media. The economic benefit of niche marketing is that the targeted ad can be more effective because it serves a smaller group, but that it gets a higher percentage of responses from that group than an ad distributed to a wide range of people, most of whom disregard that ad.

In his influential book, *The Long Tail: Why the Future of Business Is Selling Less of More*, Chris Anderson profiles how niche markets emerge in response to how the Internet structures access to content. He writes: "What the Internet has done is allow businesses to weave together those types of improvements in a way that amplifies their power and extends their reach" (Anderson 2006, 41). By that, he means that the longevity of product availability on the Internet and World Wide Web prolongs the time line of a product's marketability because it allows people more time to become aware of the product. The longevity of the online marketplace gives consumers a much longer time in which they can become aware of and purchase a product. Music, books, and other media content are almost ideal for the nurturing of niche markets and result in the success of a host of new genres and styles that appeal to some people, even though they may not appeal to everyone. Therefore, cultivating the niche market can effectively use people's online connections to others through social media and social networks to connect products with like-minded friends.

Advertising that spreads through social media and social networks is much less expensive that traditional advertising, but potentially more effective. Niche marketing and the idea of niche audiences are typical by-products of a shift to a lifestyle that relies more on e-commerce and a multiplicity of economic models.

See also: Advertising; Legacy Media; Trending; Viral

Further Reading

Anderson, Chris. 2006. *The Long Tail: Why the Future of Business Is Selling Less of More.* New York: Hyperion, 41.

O

Occupy Movement

Between 2009 and 2011, a number of activities around the world began to focus on the oppression of people while dictators, power brokers, and the rich controlled most of the world's resources. The Arab Spring had recently proven that youth could mobilize for political action, and many credited social networks and social media for helping organize protests and spread the word about plans for civil disobedience. The *Occupy Movement* was in part a reaction to the Arab Spring and other actions around the globe. The purpose of the movement was to bring attention to the great disparities in local and global wealth, with only 1 percent of the population controlling the majority of wealth, and the 99 percent majority reacting to such a great disparity. Noted professor and public intellectual Cornel West called the Occupy Movement a "democratic awakening" (Democracy Now 2011).

One of the most well-known protests in the United States was the Occupy Wall Street event that began in Zuccotti Park, New York City, on September 17, 2011, and lasted until November 15–16 when police raided the park and evicted protestors. The occupation of the park may have formally ended that night, but the Occupy Movement continues to gain support from people in communities around the world. What is most striking about the Occupy Movement, as well as others that occurred within this time period, is the use of social networking and social media to organize and facilitate the protestors' mobilization and political discourse.

In what has been called "participatory democracy," the Occupy Movement, like the Arab Spring, used contemporary technology and communications to help connect with supporters. Facebook and Meetup were popular social media that let people know where actions were going to take place, and Twitter became one of the primary forms of getting information out to the press and to others. Some supportive groups from around the world set up websites and e-mail lists that have continued to support the initial efforts of the movement.

Even though the Occupy Movement still has a presence on social media, the occupation of parks and public places has considerably diminished. The Turkish sociologist Zeynep Tufekci noted that "digital tools make it much easier to build up movements quickly and the greatly lower coordination cost. This seems like a good thing at first but it often results in an unanticipated weakness . . . [But] it's much easier to pull off spectacular events with digital technologies than to knit together lasting organisations [sic]" (Gitlin 2014).

See also: Arab Spring; Facebook; Political Fund-Raising; Twitter

Further Reading

Democracy Now! 2011. Cornel West on Occupy Wall Street: It's the Makings of a U.S. Autumn Responding to the Arab Spring. Interview with Amy Goodman. Accessed December 1, 2014: http://www.democracynow.org/blog/2011/9/29/cornel_west_on_occupy_wall_street _its_the_makings_of_a_us_autumn_responding_to_the_arab_spring.

Gitlin, Todd. 2014. "Where Are the Occupy Protesters Now?" *The Guardian.* Accessed April 28, 2015: http://www.theguardian.com/cities/2014/jun/17/where-occupy-protesters -now-social-media.

Open Source

Open source is the term given to the type of code that is made freely available or that extends the opportunity to contribute to the creation of or knowledge about a product. Collaboration, discussion, and cooperation are the key components that make open source projects work most effectively. The Internet was designed to be an open source technology meaning that different people could modify the basic architecture and function, and the World Wide Web was intended to be used openly, with users modifying the code as it spread through society and through the world. The Linux computer was also designed as an open source technology that allowed anyone to tinker with the technology. But *open source* ideas have influenced new economic models, social organization, and notions of ownership and proprietary information. With these technical, economic, and social interpretations so freely used today, *open source* tends to be a somewhat slippery term.

The trend to support open source activity has its roots in the American counterculture of the 1960s when young people began to resent the authority of government and corporate entities, and demanded more accountability from decision makers and influential agents. While the 1960s might have set the social tone for a major change in the relationships between marketers and the public, government and the governed, and producers and consumers of information, the Internet and social media made the transition to more open models of accountability and access more of a reality.

Some claim that the open source ideas stem from the interests of hobbyists in the 1960s who were a part of the counterculture. Many of the people who were instrumental in tinkering with circuit boards and semiconductors were hobbyists who shared ideas and modified each other's designs. The Homebrew Computer Club in Silicon Valley that hosted hobbyists and computer enthusiasts met from March 5, 1975, to December 1986, and, collaboratively, they worked on computer components and software that they hoped would make computers more accessible to everyone. Even before the Homebrew Computer Club, the members of the Tech Model Railroad Club (TMRC) at MIT would gather to figure out how things worked, and tinkered with making them better. Though getting together to talk about and tinker with model railroads was a bit of an excuse, the group developed collaborative ways of talking about and solving technology problems. Years later, at a Hackers' Conference in 1984, Stewart Brand was credited with originating the phrase that "information wants to be free" based on the statement made by Steven Levy in his book *Hackers: Heroes of the Computer Revolution* that "information should be free" (Levy 1984, 28–29). Brand's phrase came to represent the open source movement.

Open source ideas are particularly well suited to social media. Wikipedia, for example, is a collaborative open source encyclopedia that asks for volunteers to post information. There is an element of trust that they will not only have the appropriate knowledge to make a contribution to the site, but there is also a system of checks and balances to weed out inaccurate or inappropriate content. The idea is similar to *crowdsourcing* in which the ideas of many improve content and ultimately result in the most accurate information. Even the idea of *wikis*—online spaces where collaboration and discussion can occur—are forms of open source discursive spaces.

Siva Vaidhyanathan (2014, 24–31) has written on the concept of open source and claims that open source activities are closer to the way humans have always operated throughout history. Traditional copyrighted materials that were originally intended to be proprietary and that reward authors or inventors for their creative activities become a challenge for open source activities, but new licenses like GNU licensing and the Creative Commons licenses allow for much more collaboration on projects, without the economic imperative hanging over the heads of those who tinker with other peoples' ideas.

Open source projects come in all types and sizes, but what all uses of open system have in common is that they change traditional "top down" bureaucratic behaviors toward more participatory, user-generated means. As Micah Sifry has noted with regard to the use of open source software that is used for political purposes, from everything from political fund-raising to the existence of an organization like WikiLeaks, "the Internet rewards open methods, but not closed ones" (Sifry 2011, 58). Similarly, Don Tapscott and Anthony D. Williams wrote in their book *Wikinomics*, "as a growing number of firms see the benefits of mass collaboration, this new way of organizing will eventually replace the traditional corporate structures as the economy's primary engine of wealth creation" (Tapscott and Williams 2006, 1–2).

Open source technology and philosophy has also influenced the way governments—particularly democratic governments—view their responsibility to their publics. In 2006, the Federal Accountability and Transparency Act, sponsored by then senator Barack Obama and Senator Tom Coburn, became a federal database for people looking for information on grants and contracts issued by the government. This "open-government" activity was an effort to make government more accountable to the public and changed the relationship of the governed and the governing bodies. As this type of connection to constituents has grown, some scholars and pundits have referred to it as the growth of e-democracy, or e-government.

Generally, open source refers to a computer program in which the source code is available to the general public for use and/or modification from its original design. Open source code is meant to be a collaborative effort, where programmers improve upon the source code and share the changes within the community. Typically this is not the case, and code is merely released to the public under some license. Others can then download, modify, and publish their version (fork) back to the community. Today you find more forked versions, than teams with large membership.

A main principle of open source software development is peer production, and peer-to-peer file sharing is an example of how the Internet and World Wide Web can facilitate online collaboration and information exchange. In 1996, while anticipating the passage of the Telecommunications Act of 1996, John Perry Barlow, founder of the Electronic Frontier Foundation, authored a *Declaration of the Independence of Cyberspace* that he posted online. In the *Declaration* he wrote: "Cyberspace consists of transactions, relationships, and thought itself, arrayed like a standing wave in the web of our communications. Ours is a world that is both everywhere and nowhere, but it is not where bodies live. We are creating a world that all may enter without privilege or prejudice accorded by race, economic power, military force, or station of birth. We are creating a world where anyone, anywhere may express his or her beliefs, no matter how singular, without fear of being coerced into silence or conformity" (Barlow 1996). Many of these ideas seemed to embody the essence and the future of open source ideas and are represented in the projects the Electronic Frontier Foundation embraces.

Today, open source projects and open source ideas abound. In January 2015, *Wired* magazine featured some of the "hottest" open source projects under development. They include: Storj, a cloud-based storage system that helps people maintain their privacy; IPFS, also known by its full name, "InterPlanetary File System," that creates a censorship-resistant alternative to the web and is inspired by peer-to-peer technologies like BitTorrent; and Kubernetes, a Google project that allows people to use Linux "containers to improve online applications" (Finley 2015).

See also: Copyright; Creative Commons

Further Reading

Barlow, John Perry. 1996. "A Declaration of Independence in Cyberspace." Electronic Frontier Foundation (EFF). Accessed February 13, 2015: https://homes.eff.org/~barlow/Declaration-Final.html.

Finley, Klint. 2015. "These Are the Hottest New Open Source Projects Right Now." *Wired*. Accessed April 28, 2015: http://www.wired.com/2015/01/black-duck-rookies/.

Levy, Steven. 2010. *Hackers: Heroes of the Computer Revolution*. Sebastopol, CA: O'Reilly Media, 28–29.

Sifry, Micah L. 2011. *WikiLeaks and the Age of Transparency*. Berkeley, CA: Counterpoint, 58.

Tapscott, Don, and Anthony D. Williams. 2006. *Wikinomics: How Mass Collaboration Changes Everything*. New York: Penguin, 125.

Vaidhyanathan, Siva. 2014. "Open Source as Culture/Culture as Open Source" In *The Social Media Reader*, edited by Michael Mandiberg. New York: New York University Press, 24–31.

P

Page, Larry

Lawrence (Larry) Page (1973–) is an American computer scientist who, along with Sergei Brin, founded Google Inc. He was born in East Lansing, Michigan, to parents who were both computer scientists. Page attended Stanford University where he joined the Human-Computer Interaction Group, where researchers focused on how machines and humans communicated. He became an advocate of what was called user-centered design that situated the human being as the primary control agent of the computer interaction.

When Page began looking for a dissertation topic for his degree, he became fascinated by how researchers cite other research in their notes and bibliography. He woke one night with the thought that if the whole web could be downloaded, it might be a manageable project to just keep the links and create a program to connect to related links.

In 1996, Page and Brin combined their interests in hyperlink curation and data mining and created a search engine called BackRub that counted links leading to each web page it found. The logic was that the pages with many incoming links were probably the most important and most relevant. This method has been very successful in helping Google users see how information is structured, with the information that receives the most "hits" structured at the top of the list of links. The amount of information overwhelmed the Stanford computers, so, in 1998, the two raised $1 million in capital from friends and family and started Google in a garage owned by one of their friends. Page's contribution to Google was the idea that the popularity of websites could be an indication of the usefulness of information to users, while Brin was an expert at data mining.

Until 2001, Page and Brin were copresidents of Google, but Page also led product development. In 2011, he became Google's chief executive officer (CEO). By 2014, Page was listed as number 17 on *Forbes* magazine's list of the wealthiest individuals and he was *Fortune's* Businessperson of the Year.

Page and Brin continue to develop new projects in artificial intelligence, robotics, and delivery drones. Google has expanded its venture unit and has been working on driverless cars. Google bought the automated home company Nest for $3.2 billion and it has invested heavily in Calico, an independent biotech firm that is working on antiaging processes.

Personally, Page has invested in philanthropy and renewable energy projects and Tesla Motors, an electric car manufacturer.

See also: Brin, Sergei; Google

Further Reading

Isaacson, Walter. 2014. *The Innovators*. New York: Simon & Schuster, 462.
"The World's Billionaires." 2014. *Forbes*. Accessed April 21, 2015: http://www.forbes.com /pictures/mel45hdjl/17-larry-page/.

Pandora

Of the many digital music programs, Pandora is distinguished in that it links a listener's listening behavior to other tunes that the listener is likely to enjoy. Pandora Media Inc. was formed in 2000 by Will Glaser, Jon Kraft, and Tim Westergren to deliver music directly to consumers through a streaming service similar to Internet radio. Pandora caters to listeners who "like" or "dislike" music by hitting a button that gives a little icon that indicates "thumbs up" or "thumbs down." If the listener "likes" the music, the algorithm matches the collection of "liked" music and streams additional music to that person that is similar to what they have "liked."

Pandora is a variation of Internet radio (broadcast, or terrestrial, radio on the AM or FM frequencies that are also delivered over the Internet) and functions like traditional terrestrial radio, though ads are grouped into blocks rather than disbursed throughout the playlist. There is also no radio personality to fill time with local news or babble. But unlike terrestrial radio, Pandora serves a narrower audience and can collect information on listeners by age, sex, zip code, and musical taste. A free service, it has become the top station in 14 of the 15 U.S. markets that include both broadcast and online radio services. Pandora earns $45.97 per 1,000 hours streamed, according to its 2015 public earnings statement (Porter 2015).

Pandora calls its collection of music the Music Genome Project and has the rights to over 1.5 million tracks to send to its registered users, which number more than 76 million. Pandora clusters ads in spots of 15 to 30 seconds every 20 minutes to help pay for its service, but the consumer must participate in the "thumbs up," "thumbs down" features of the service (indicating likes or dislikes) to receive the ads.

In 2014 the company partnered with Merlin, a consortium of independent record labels, to pay musicians a smaller royalty than if they used the traditional Library of Congress royalty rating for delivering streamed music to a consumer. This has concerned its larger competitors like Beats Music, Google Play, Grooveshark, iHeartRadio, iTunes Radio, Last.fm, Sony Music, Rhapsody, Rdio, Slacker, Spotify, and Xbox Music (Sydell 2014). This action was swiftly criticized by musical artists, but, other than the action of JayZ, who started his own music streaming service with the financial support of some of the major recording stars, little attention has been paid to Pandora's new finance model (see Streaming for JayZ's streaming music company).

Internet radio is a significantly smaller market than the on-demand music market, of which Spotify is a leader. According to data from Paul Lamere, who discussed the role of alternate music services at the 2014 South by Southwest Festival, 93 percent of Americans listen to music in some form, but a much smaller percentage actually pay for what they hear (Porter 2015).

See also: Legacy Media; Streaming Media

Further Reading

Peckham, Matt. 2014. "Streaming Music Services Compared by Price, Quality, Catalog Size and More." *Time.* Accessed November 27, 2014: http://time.com/30081/13-streaming -music-services-compared-by-price-quality-catalog-size-and-more/.

Porter, David. 2015. "Spotify vs. Pandora: Which Market Is Bigger?" *Forbes.* Accessed April 24, 2015: http://www.forbes.com/sites/davidporter/2015/04/24/spotify-vs-pandora -which-market-is-bigger/.

Sydell, Laura. 2014. "Pandora's New Deal: Different Pay, Different Play." NPR's *Morning Edition.* Accessed November 29, 2014: http://www.npr.org/2014/11/26/366339553 pandoras-new-deal-different-pay-different-pay.

PayPal

PayPal is an online payment system that was founded in 1998 by Max Levchin and Peter Thiel who met at the Stanford University Department of Engineering-Economic Systems and Operations Research. The 23-year-old Levchin had already started three different companies, and he had an idea for the fourth, but he needed to find money. Thiel was working in finance and was intrigued by Levchin's idea for the newest company that would involve an encrypted payment system that could use the Palm Pilot personal digital assistant—a forerunner to a mobile phone. The two established a company named *Confinity* that they registered in 1999. While the initial seed money was not difficult to raise (Thiel was able to convince Nokia Ventures to offer $3 million), he and Levchin realized that the potential for the business went well beyond Palm Pilots to other forms of secure person-to-person payments.

The same year, Confinity merged with another online payment company called X.com, which had been founded by the 24-year-old South African–born Elon Musk, who had graduated from the University of Pennsylvania with degrees in physics and economics and had attended the Wharton School. Musk had moved to California to begin a PhD in physics at Stanford, but left the program to develop his own interests in Internet business, renewable energy, and space studies.

By early 2000, eBay users were contacting Thiel and Levchin and asking for permission to use the service for their own transactions. eBay had been trying to start its own payment system but had not yet found the right business model, and after trying a number of banks and other emerging online systems, the company's management settled on a system called Billpoint that was guaranteed by the Wells Fargo Bank.

By 2001, the name Confinity was changed to PayPal. The service was free for both buyers and sellers, and Thiel developed a plan to publicize the new service by encouraging everyone who signed up to refer a friend and they would receive $5. By the end of 1999, 12,000 users had registered. This viral campaign was largely responsible for making PayPal the recognized name it has become, and along with that came both positive and negative attention. PayPal began to emerge as a leader in the increasingly crowded field of online payment systems, but it also attracted people who used it to commit fraud. PayPal had become targeted by Russian and Nigerian Internet crime rings and had been hit with $8.9 million in unauthorized credit card charges (Cohen 2002, 230). Despite the negative publicity that came with the fraudulent use of the system, by early 2002, PayPal went public, and by midyear, the company was sold to eBay for approximately $1.5 billion.

By 2014, PayPal was operating in 203 markets and had 152 million active, registered accounts. Financial transactions can be made in 26 international currencies. PayPal's revenue has continued to grow and is responsible for more than 41 percent of eBay's total revenue and 36 percent of its total profits.

At present, PayPal is targeting the digital wallet and electronic funds transfer business with a vengeance and, with its experience and the credibility it has gained in financial markets despite the occasional abuse, is likely to be successful in the creation of e-currency independent from governments and central banks. What seems to be a hurdle, however, is whether it can continue to grow as an offshoot of eBay, or whether it will have to separate as an independent company, or merge with another for its survival in a field that has competition from Amazon, Bitcoin, and other digital currencies.

See also: eBay

Further Reading

Bertoni, Steve. 2014. "Can PayPal Beat Apple, Google, Amazon and Icahn in the Wallet Wars?" *Forbes*. Accessed March 4, 2015: http://www.forbes.com/sites/stevenbertoni /2014/02/12/can-paypal-beat-apple-google-amazon-and-icahn-in-the-wallet-wars/.
Cohen, Adam. 2002. *The Perfect Store: Inside eBay*. Boston: Little, Brown and Co.

Paywalls

Paywalls are systems that block access to a company's service or their information until the service has been paid for. Hard paywalls restrict all access to information, but soft paywalls allow some information to be accessed for free, even though unlimited services can be accessed if the consumer pays for the service or takes out a subscription.

Paywalls were initially introduced by the newspaper industry that was losing revenue from the sale of paper newspapers as more news and information became available online. Most major news organizations attempted to reinvent their businesses by putting news and information online, but the challenge was to figure out how to finance their news gathering and dissemination costs without the same type of advertising, point-of-purchase, or subscriptions that they had used so successfully for years in the newspaper and magazine industries. The perceived necessity for paywalls was to protect the newspaper and magazine industries as digital information became easier to access, while publishers explored the viability of electronic print for the survival of their industry. While it was often said that 80 percent of the revenue of a traditional paper newspaper came from advertising, the model of online advertising was significantly lower than print advertising, and sales of paper newspapers and cancellations of subscriptions devastated many newspapers—driving some to stop publishing paper forms altogether.

Magazines had a somewhat easier transition to the online world because the industry adapted to focus more on niche audiences than on mass audiences, but once-important general interest arbiters of national culture like *Time, Newsweek,* and *U.S. News and World Report* have all had to adjust to a smaller subscription audience for paper magazines, and all have developed additional information to better use the online format of delivery for their general interest content.

When newspapers and magazines went online, many used the paywall system to encourage people to pay for the service. Sometimes they would use soft paywalls that allowed access to a certain number of articles for free before requiring payment, and some limited access to only a certain number of articles each month. Often online print companies will provide an abstract to help the consumer see if they want to purchase the article or take out a subscription.

While paywalls have been most often employed for e-print, other services have explored using paywalls, too. Paywalls have been suggested as possible economic models to pay for the distribution of e-mail and access to some other media forms like radio and television programs.

See also: E-Publishing; Legacy Media

Further Reading

Rosen, Rebecca J. 2011. "Can a Paywall Stop Newspaper Subscribers from Canceling?" *The Atlantic Monthly.* Accessed December 3, 2014: http://www.theatlantic.com/technology /archive/2011/09/can-a-paywall-stop-newspaper-subscribers-from-canceling/244932/.

Peer-to-Peer (P2P)

Once part of the vision of the World Wide Web, *peer-to-peer* (P2P) file sharing allows computers to link together so that digital information can flow from one computer to another. While P2P services were once exploited by entrepreneurs for sharing music and other collaborative projects, the term has now been expanded to include a range of activities that focus on the *connecting* and *sharing* aspects of online (and social) action.

Digital information can be easily transmitted over airwaves (by streaming) or networks, and stored on devices in other locations. While P2P file sharing is still evolving, there have been several technological breakthroughs, while issues of copyright, ownership, and payment for authorized content are still challenges to the act of P2P sharing. Most of the types of content shared over P2P services include music, books, other digitized print matter, and, increasingly, television programs and films.

The first generation of P2P systems were Napster and eDonkey2000, both of which used central server models of transferring information. Later, Kazaa, Gnutella, and Gnutella2 facilitated direct contact from one computer user to another. The third generation of file sharing networks are called darknets and include services like Freenet and BitTorrent. BitTorrent is a bit different than the earlier forms of peer-to-peer file sharing. Instead of linking information over a network, every file (called a torrent) allows the protocol to send batches of files to another computer. As in the case of Pirate Bay, the Swedish company that used BitTorrent to transfer files, not all features of using the BitTorrent protocol are free from controversy.

There are a number of different viewpoints that support the idea of P2P activity. Yochai Benkler wrote that "peer-to-peer file-sharing networks are an example of a highly efficient system for storing and accessing data in a computer network" (Benkler 2006, 84). If made to work efficiently and circumvent problems of a system that is liable to be open to hackers or cybercriminals, P2P networks could indeed be used for collaboration and the transfer of massive files of data.

However, one of the problems with P2P file sharing is that it can easily be used to violate copyright, and for that reason the Recording Industry Association of America (RIAA) and the Motion Picture Association of America (MPAA) have both lobbied to prevent more widespread use of P2P technology that could further harm their industries.

But the P2P metaphor has been used in other ways. Peer-to-peer lending has become a much less formal way for consumers to get loans from lending companies other than banks. Surprisingly, it was the economic financial crisis in 2008 that spurred interest in this new form of lending. The largest company involved in this type of service is the San Francisco-based Lending Club, founded in 2007 for the purpose of using the Internet to match investors with projects. Most of the loans go to individuals who are trying to pay down credit card debt or who need short-term loans for specific projects related to their homes or businesses. The result is a type of "e-Harmony for borrowers" (Cohan 2014, 24). The microloans requested and the amount of money loaned is usually far less than a major bank would consider, but what is important is that the *sharing* aspect of the P2P ethic is being used for social activities that reflect a change in the way traditional money lending and banking has been done.

P2P lending has eliminated the need for brick-and-mortar banks and uses the information accessed over the Internet to function. As the Lending Club's biggest investor said at a meeting of people who were interested in the P2P lending concept, marketplace lending would change banking the way Amazon changed retail (Cohan 2014, 24–27).

See also: E-Commerce; Fanning, Shawn; MP3; Piracy; Sharing Economy

Further Reading

Benkler, Yochai. 2006. *The Wealth of Network: How Social Production Transforms Markets and Freedom.* New Haven, CT: Yale University Press, 84.
Cohan, William D. 2014. "Bypassing the Bankers." *The Atlantic Monthly,* 314: 24–27.

Phishing

Phishing is a criminal technique used to gain personal information about Internet users. Phishers "fish" for such information as passwords, social security numbers, and bank account numbers by tricking users into giving up information, and they hope the computer user takes the "bait." Or, they may plant a virus or form of malware that invades a person's computer to access private information.

Usually phishing schemes try to trick a person into giving up their login and password combinations by pretending to be someone known to the computer user. A typical attempt might be a message that resembles something your own bank would send that requests that you confirm your login and password and often includes a threat if you don't do this immediately.

Social media are particularly vulnerable to phishing scams. Phishing often looks very much like a real message, and that tends to trick a number of people. In fact, according to one study of phishing, 70 percent of the phishing attacks on social networks were successful (Jagatic et al. 2007, 96). Perhaps one reason social networks are primed for phishing schemes is that many people expect to get information that is shared from friends, not from people who are not in their network.

Unauthorized mobile apps are often phishing schemes, so educated consumers should look for apps that are sold on legitimate sites, and, even then, question content that seems to ask for personal information too quickly. Data shows that mobile users are three times more likely to fall for a phishing scam than someone using a computer or other digital device. While the reason for this increase is purely speculative, it may be that the immediacy of using a mobile phone encourages a person to respond to input very quickly, without thinking of consequences.

In the United States, the Federal Trade Commission (FTC) is responsible for prosecuting phishers, and has occasionally worked with the FBI and, on the international side, with Interpol to track down phishers and phishing schemes. In the United States, Senator Patrick Leahy introduced the Anti-Phishing Act of 2005 to Congress, but the law was not passed. Still, some of the features of the bill are still being discussed in Congress, such as assessing fines of up to $250,000 for perpetrating a phishing scheme, and the possibility of prison time.

In the first six months of 2014, Trend Micro, an industry group that tracks computer fraud, counted more than 123,700 unique phishing attacks that affected 756 different institutions. The most commonly attacked company was Apple (Vijayan 2014).

See also: Bots; Cookies; Malware; Privacy

Further Reading

Jagatic, Tom, Nathaniel Johnson, Markus Jakobsson, and Filippo Menczer. 2007. "Social Phishing." *Communications of the ACM*, 50: 94–100.

Vijayan, Jai. 2014. "Hackers Devise New Simplified Phishing Method." *InformationWeek*. Accessed January 3, 2015: http://www.darkreading.com/attacks-breaches/hackers-devise-new-simplified-phishing-method/d/d-id/1317242.

Pinterest

Pinterest is an app designed by Paul Sciarra, Evan Sharp, and Ben Silbermann in 2009. Pinners (those who use the app) can arrange things that interest them on virtual corkboards leading to what some people have called "the ultimate creative act." Called a "virtual discovery, collection and storage tool," pinners contribute images and content to Pinterest to be shared with others, and they can also use the material submitted by other users. With this function, people curate topics and present material in such a way as to stimulate inspiration in the way groups of things come together. The app attracts those individuals who like to participate in craft projects, commemoration of special events, and collectibles.

Among the content one could expect to find on Pinterest are food and craft ideas, fitness ideas, guides to technology, inspirational quotes, fashion, humor, and travel. Among U.S. users, about 70–80 percent of the Pinterest users are women, but, in other parts of the world, gender usage is far more varied. The project is now funded by venture capitalists who hope to see the app grow in the area of style trending.

Pinterest also allows businesses to promote their companies online in what might be termed a "virtual storefront." Some brand studies have shown that Pinterest is more effective at driving sales than other forms of social media, but this type of consumer use is not without problems. One of the major controversies with Pinterest is that the company has claimed that they own the copyright for everything posted online, but, so far, this controversy has not been adjudicated.

As of 2014, the mobile component of the app made up about 75 percent of the business, and features introduced in April 2013 allowed users to tap their screens for added functionality and use the Guided Search discovery tool for organizing material (Fortini 2014, 94).

See also: App; Creative Economy; Friending

Further Reading

Fortini, Amanda. 2014. "The Inspiration Factory: How Pinterest Fosters Creativity." *Wired*, 21: 94–99.

Silver, Hayley, with Eileen Tan and Cory Mitchell. 2012. "Pinterest vs. Facebook: Which Social Sharing Site Wins at Shopping Engagement?" Bizrate Insights. Accessed October 2, 2014: http://www.bizrateinsights.com/blog/2012/10/15/online-consumer-pulse -pinterest-vs-facebook-which-social-sharing-site-wins-at-shopping-engagement/.

Piracy

One of the benefits of digital media is that duplicated content looks and sounds as good as the original. Unauthorized duplication of digital content is illegal, but many justify pirating on the grounds that it is easy, and today's technologies make it simple to avoid thinking about copyright issues and who has the right to profit on unauthorized content. The term given to people who duplicate, distribute, or knowingly engage in accepting unauthorized content are called software pirates, and the action they take is called *piracy*.

Films, videos, games, computer software, and music make up the bulk of pirated content because they can so easily be compressed by a number of technologies, and then recorded or streamed to someone who can see or listen to the content on a digital platform. Governments have taken steps to crack down on widespread piracy, and different companies have taken steps to try to make it hard for pirates, but the lure of the money can be very appealing for those people who become pirates. In the United States and around the world, the "War on Piracy" began in the late 1990s as unauthorized digital content began to be shared, traded, and sold.

Governments around the world have tried to deal with their own problems of media piracy with varying levels of success. The World Intellectual Property Organization (WIPO) has established a number of guidelines for the protection of intellectual property, but different nations with different cultural values often interpret copyright and unauthorized duplication somewhat differently. In the United States, the Digital Millennium Copyright Act (DMCA) was passed in 1998 to establish culpability for authorized and unauthorized digital duplication, and in the European Union, the E-Commerce Directive passed in 2000 similarly provides protection for intermediaries, like Internet service providers (ISPs), from becoming responsible for the content that flows over its channels.

Streaming services and peer-to-peer file sharing are major problems that contribute to media piracy. Some of the companies that have been sued for unauthorized duplication of intellectual property (i.e., violating copyright) include Napster, Grokster, eMule, SoulSeek, BitTorrent, and Limewire. These services might not host or transmit content, but they could be considered, as ISPs are, to contribute to the actions of illegal activities over their systems. But because they are intermediaries that are dedicated to the exchange of certain types of content, they are not exempt from the DMCA or related policies that protect ISPs.

Piracy is both a legal and a moral problem in the sense that laws may specify penalties for piracy, but technologies that make it easy to steal content or remarket it are always juxtaposed against what might be thought of as a high cost of legally buying something. Individuals who engage in piracy for their own personal reasons often do so because either they are collectors who may never even watch or listen to what they steal, or they may be people who can't afford the content they want. The laws still pertain to these individuals, but the authorities have little incentive to seek out and prosecute individuals who steal content for their own use. The real problem of piracy has to do with whether or not a profit is being made from the sale of content.

In 2009, a *Los Angeles Daily News* article cited a loss figure of "roughly $20 billion a year" for Hollywood studios that were learning that many of their films were being shown without authorization in China, Russia, India, and Canada (Strauss 2009). In one example, Disney's film *Wall-E* was released in movie theaters in the United States, and, within 10 days, an unauthorized version of *Wall-E* was released in the Ukraine with copies online in five different languages. Along with these pirated copies, taken by the use of a camcorder in the movie theater, and with unauthorized DVD sales, it would be hard to estimate the actual financial impact, though it is fair say that it was a sizable loss of revenue for Disney.

The Recording Industry Association of America (RIAA) estimates that digital music theft has been a major factor contributing to the decline in recorded music sales, and many jobs have been lost to the impact of music piracy. According to the RIAA, ever since Napster appeared, "music sales in the U.S. have dropped 53 percent, from $14.6 billion to $7.0 billion in 2013; during the period from 2004 to 2009 approximately 30 billion songs were illegally downloaded on file-sharing network" and that "only 37 percent of music acquired by U.S. consumers in 2009 was paid for" (Scope of the Problem 2015).

One of the most controversial piracy actions came from a group in Sweden that brazenly called themselves The Pirate Bay (commonly abbreviated TPB). The Pirates started their project in 2003 using BitTorrent protocol to facilitate peer-to-peer file sharing among its members. The Pirate Bay had amassed a vast catalog of audio books, music, films, television programs, games, and pornography that it shared for free. The site was paid for through advertising and donations.

One of the first challenges to The Pirate Bay came from the Motion Picture Association of America (MPAA), the major industry association and lobbying group funded by the motion picture industry. The MPAA and its associates filed charges against The Pirate Bay for copyright violation. Though Sweden has more liberal copyright laws than many countries, The Pirate Bay was raided by Swedish police in 2006 and shut down for three days. In 2009, three of the founders of the organization were sentenced to prison for copyright violation and assessed a fine, but the court decision was held up on appeal and subsequently modified.

In 2009, a Swedish advertising company called Global Gaming Factory X AB announced their intention to buy the site. Despite a number of take-downs and legal issues, The Pirate Bay continued to function until 2014, at which time it disappeared from the Internet, along with its Facebook page. It reappeared a year later on January 31, 2015.

In the United States, there have been two major campaigns to curb piracy. The first was the Stop Online Piracy Act (SOPA) introduced in the House of Representatives by Representative Lamar S. Smith in October 2011. It was complemented by the Senate's Protect IP Act (PIPA). Both bills were heavily supported by the MPAA, the largest lobbying group in Washington D.C., to allegedly curb the piracy of Hollywood films. The purpose of these bills was to make it harder for websites to sell or distribute pirated copyrighted material such as movies and music as well as other physical goods such as counterfeit purses and watches. Many people thought that the intention of SOPA and PIPA was noble but criticized the way they were written. Passage of the acts would have expanded criminal laws to include unauthorized streaming of copyrighted content and would have suggested imprisonment of those who violated the law, even for their own use, rather than for selling or profiting from transfer of the content. The law, if enacted, would also prevent companies like Visa, MasterCard, and PayPal from transmitting funds to the site and could potentially make these organizations the point of intervention for legal authorities.

Attention to the bills generated a number of estimates for the financial cost of piracy. Kal Raustiala and Chris Sprigman of the *Freakonomics* website reported that the figures discussed in the Senate and House of Representatives—declaring that piracy cost the U.S. economy between $200 billion and $250 billion per year and was responsible for the loss of 750,000 jobs—were wildly out of sync with reality (Raustiala and Sprigman 2012). They also reported that the $58 billion reported as the U.S. share of the cost of piracy as reported by the Institute for Policy Innovation (IPI) were also rife with statistical errors. In their estimation, the real cost of piracy in the United States and elsewhere could not adequately be measured or accounted for because the disparities in measuring jobs and in how and where people spend their money are just too complicated to adequately report.

The problem with SOPA and PIPA was that much of the unauthorized duplication comes from other countries, therefore enforcing the law would be very difficult. Open source sites realized that a change in the law would probably force them to shut down, since so much of their material is remixed, reposted, or posted by everyday social media users who don't know the legal ramifications of what they post. *Wikipedia* and some other sites chose to go dark for 24 hours to protest the possible passage of SOPA and PIPA, and organizations like the Electronic Frontier Foundation (EFF) and The Free Press organized actions to protest the passage of the acts. In the end, public pressure prevented the bills from passing.

Since the "War on Piracy," many of the relevant industries have come up with ways to deal with the ease of unauthorized content that violates copyright and that often falls prey to pirates. Encryption methods are one way to attempt to control duplication, but, at the same time, many new distribution forms have accompanied lower costs. In Europe, film companies have tried to combat movie pirates by pricing films very low so that people can afford them on demand, but this has led to block booking of groups of films so that one big name film may come to the market with a number of films of lesser quality. The film companies protect their interests, but the market becomes flooded with mediocre and less desirable content. The attempts to find ways to prevent piracy through different economic incentives in no way indicates that piracy is no longer a problem, but, rather, it has entered a new phase.

Paul Tassi, a contributor to *Forbes* magazine has cited a number of changes in industries that have come about, in part, by the reaction to piracy, but that have changed the availability of content to consumers. He writes that Netflix, for example, has changed the availability of film and television and that Netflix and other streaming services have made it easier to find content that is legal. In the realm of music, streaming services like iTunes, Spotify, and Pandora have figured out how to sell products inexpensively, and Amazon has made it cheap to own e-books (Tassi 2014). Though the War on Piracy has wound down, it hasn't come to a halt.

A controversial new policy in Australia makes ISPs responsible for monitoring content downloads. If piracy is suspected, the ISP is supposed to issue a warning to the user. ISPs may become responsible for blocking sites like The Pirate Bay, and the ISPs are required to notify authorities if someone receives multiple "take down" notices because of suspected piracy. These actions are currently being debated, and, depending on the outcome, other nations may follow Australia's lead or introduce other methods to curb piracy.

See also: Copyright; Creative Commons; Digital; Digital Millennium Copyright Act (DMCA); Legacy Media; Streaming Media

Further Reading

Raustiala, Kal, and Chris Sprigman. 2012. "How Much Do Music and Movie Piracy Really Hurt the U.S. Economy?" Freakonomics.com. Accessed April 30, 2012: http://freakonomics.com/2012/01/12/how-much-do-music-and-movie-piracy-really-hurt-the-u-s-economy/.

"Scope of the Problem." 2015. Statement of the RIAA. Accessed April 2, 2015: https://www.riaa.com/physicalpiracy.php?content_selector=piracy-online-scope-of-the-problem.

Strauss, Bob. 2009. "Film Piracy Heads North of Border." *Los Angeles Times*. Accessed April 2, 2015: http://www.dailynews.com/20090407/film-piracy-heads-north-of-border.

Tassi, Bill. 2014. "Whatever Happened to the War on Piracy?" *Forbes*. Accessed April 2, 2015: http://www.forbes.com/sites/insertcoin/2014/01/24/whatever-happened-to-the-war-on-piracy/.

Podcast

Podcasts are an example of how radio and listening devices have evolved over the years. They also show that when a new form of media evolves, the previous forms don't go away, though they may change. Podcasting, like *webisodes* for video content and *streaming* media for both audio and video, show that new distribution forms add options for consumers. They also present themselves as opportunities for advertisers, software, and hardware developers and suggest new creative approaches to connecting audiences with media content. While many podcasts are sold upon a subscription basis, many can be accessed with apps available at any number of app distributors. Because so many of them are distributed on a subscription basis, the number of subscribers tell distributors and advertisers a lot about who listens to what. The concept of a *podcast* has changed since the term was first used in 2000.

While radio was originally envisioned as a point-to-point form of communication for the Navy so that communication could take place with ships at sea, it didn't take long to find the commercial viability in the medium that emphasized sound and sound effects. From individual stations experimenting with content to the linking of networks (in the original sense of the word, that meant connecting radio stations), radio became a dominant medium for immediacy in the first half of the twentieth century. By the time television was introduced to the American public in the mid-twentieth century, radio's prominence as a national medium changed to that of a more locally based medium. Even the addition of FM radio in 1967 and the developing youth market it targeted changed in the 1970s when digital media players came out and began to change listeners' options. By the time the Internet became available and streaming technologies changed how people listened to radio, the recorded music industry began to change and radio became more popular for all-talk, or all-news formats. Advertising for radio has become increasingly locally driven for local programs, but podcasts have taken on the national and international audience who listens over different types of digital technologies and often binge listen instead of tuning to whatever is playing on the radio at a given time.

The origin of the word, *podcast*, is somewhat elusive, but it is generally agreed that the "pod" component of the word comes from "portable online delivery," and "cast" comes from "broadcast." The idea is attributed to Dave Winer, a software developer who came up with the idea of how to create a podcast with the emerging MP3 compression technology that was becoming popular in the early 2000s, but disc jockey Adam Curry of MTV became the first public figure to make use of the technology for commercial purposes (Hanson and Baldwin 2007, 125).

When Apple introduced its iPod in 2001, a host of terms seized the opportunity to make podcasts seem as different from radio as possible. People spoke of *podmercials* to define advertising that was used in podcasts and parents were informed of content that was *podsafe*, meaning that content was suitable for children. In 2005, *podcast* was the word of the year as named by the *New Oxford American Dictionary*.

When podcasts first appeared they were forms of small-format audio content that could be played on a digital media player or computer. Anyone with low-cost consumer audio recording equipment could create a podcast, and it seemed that college and high school students took the opportunity to create podcasts because they didn't need a broadcast license to distribute content. The technology needed to create a podcast is MP3 compression software that transfers a recorded message to digital waves and compresses the signal so that the message takes very little bandwidth to send the message. Since 2004, a number of freeware services have become available over the Internet for people who want to post their own podcasts. At first glance, podcasts and podcast technology seem to fit into the category of public access media, but it can also be viewed as a type of do-it-yourself media. The portability of iPods, smartphones, and laptop computers has contributed to the success of podcasting, especially as the cost of creating a podcast has come down, and freeware exists that can be downloaded from the Internet to allow almost anyone with the patience to learn the system to become a podcaster.

Before long, a number of podcasting genres began to appear online. There were podcasts about sports, literature, comedy, politics, and just plain conversation—often crude, and sometimes disturbing—since podcasting was not regulated by any agency like the FCC. Since podcasting cost so little to produce, amateurs flocked to the form, and even mainstream media experimented with trying to reach potential audiences through podcasts. *Fortune* magazine, the *Economist*, *New York Times*, *C-Span*, and even the White House created podcasts. Bridge Ratings Media Research estimated that by the end of 2005, about 5 million people had heard at least one podcast, and the Podcast Directory (http://www.podcastdirectory.com/) had been developed to help people find podcasts that would interest them from all around the globe (Hanson and Baldwin 2007, 126–127).

But by 2009 or 2010, the general interest in podcasts began to shift, perhaps due to the growing success of YouTube as well as the ability to stream audio and video over a number of digital technologies, including mobile phones. National Public Radio's (NPR) programs *This American Life* and *RadioLab* were available as podcasts as well as broadcast programs, and they retained interest, but many of the smaller, amateur podcasts began to dry up.

Then, something seemed to shift as advertisers began to understand the role of niche audiences and the way podcasts could reach people who had similar interests. Since 2012, podcasts have had a rebirth, but this time it appears that part of the success is the serial nature of podcasting and the way audiences have shifted from "appointment media" (paying attention to media when it is originally aired) and binge consumption (listening or viewing sequentially to a number of episodes). New software makers have launched apps that make podcasts available, and third-party apps have become easier to negotiate and use. Third-party apps can be stand-alone programs or they can be small plug-ins that add functionality to an existing parent program. Podcasting has had a rebirth, and the options for listener choice have once again begun to grow. In 2013, Apple announced one billionth podcast subscription had been accessed on the iTunes store.

In addition to better software for creating and downloading podcasts, many professional producers have found that podcasts are relatively inexpensive to produce, and when the niche audience is considered, the advertising effectiveness of podcasting for a niche audience is a practical business decision. Podcasts are cheaper to produce than a radio show and because it is possible to trace the number of podcasts downloaded, the traditional CPM (cost per thousand) is between $20 and $45. Podcasts with single hosts can be even cheaper to produce.

Another reason for the success of podcasting is today's automobile that is outfitted with better audio components to play smartphone apps over Bluetooth connectivity or through USB auxiliary plugs. Google and Apple have introduced connected-car platforms that allow a person to access music or podcasts over their car audio systems, and, with 44 percent of all radio listening done in a car, the "mobile" market (meaning cars) has great potential for allowing a consumer to listen to what they want to hear in their automobiles. In one estimate, 50 percent of all cars sold in 2015 could be connected to the Internet, and it is assumed that all cars will be Internet-capable by 2025 (Roose 2014).

In 2014, five professionally produced podcast networks debuted and listeners responded favorably. What these podcasts had in common was that they took the ideas of long-form journalism and created ongoing stories that appealed to those people who continually tuned in to either binge-listen or catch up on stories they felt to be compelling. National Public Radio's podcast *Serial* became one of the top podcasts. The show focuses on the story of Adnan Syed, a high school student in Chicago who was convicted of murdering his girlfriend. In true nonfiction form, the episodes each focus on approaching the story from a different perspective, much the way the television series *True Detective* did. But, in this case, the producers did not release the entire series at one time. Instead, each week a new episode was prepared and unfolded. As critic Conor Friedersdorf wrote in the *The Atlantic Monthly* (2014), "If the rest of the inaugural season's episodes were released together, like *House of Cards*, I'd consume them in one sitting, foregoing sunshine, sleep, and human contact until all episodes were exhausted. That's how I binge-watched much of *The Wire*, *The Sopranos*, and *Breaking Bad*. At the time, I never imagined I'd ever binge-listen to radio."

See also: Legacy Media; Streaming Media; Webisode

Further Reading

Friedersdorf, Conor. 2014. "Podcasts So Good You Want to Binge-Listen." *The Atlantic Monthly.* Accessed January 20, 2015: http://www.theatlantic.com/entertainment/archive/2014/10/podcasts-so-good-you-want-to-binge-listen/382055/.

Hanson, Jarice, and Bryan Baldwin. 2007. "Mobile Culture: Podcasting as Public Media." In *Displacing Place: Mobile Communication in the Twenty-First Century,* edited by Sharon Kleinman. New York: Peter Lang, 123–139.

Palser, Barb. 2006. "Hype or the Real Deal?" *American Journalism Review.* Accessed February 1, 2015: http://ajarchive.org/Article.asp?id=4060.

Roose, Kevin. 2014. "What's Behind the Great Podcast Renaissance?" *New York Magazine.* Accessed January 20, 2015: http://nymag.com/daily/intelligencer/2014/10/whats-behind-the-great-podcast-renaissance.html.

Political Fund-Raising

Politicians and political action committees have learned how to use the important networking features of social media to raise funds. The first use of social networking to support a candidate occurred on April 23, 2003, when a blogger named Jeff Tiedrich, working on the Howard Dean presidential campaign, posted a message on the website SmirkingChimp.com. Tiedrich had started the site that he named satirically after President George W. Bush. Another blogger working on the Dean campaign, Mathew Gross, posted a message on behalf of Dean, asking people to send in questions, which he then (Dean) would read and to which he would respond. Within an hour, about 30 messages came in, and people began to take notice of how the Internet could be used to mount a grassroots campaign.

The Dean campaign also used the Internet to organize volunteers to go door-to-door, host meetings, and write personal letters to likely voters. With the help of a social network called Meetup, the Dean staffers were able to initially reach 3,000 people, and those people recruited others. In the third quarter of 2003, Dean raised nearly $15 million in contributions that often ranged from just a few dollars to more substantial sums. By mid-November 2003, Meetup had 140,000 members supporting Dean, and the attention attracted the Service Employees International Union and the American Federation of State, County, and Municipal Employees, two of the countries more influential labor groups. In a conversation with Gary Wolf, a journalist writing for *Wired* magazine, Dean said: "A lot of the people on the Net have given up on traditional politics precisely because it was about television and the ballot box, and they had no way to shout back," he says. "What we've given people is a way to shout back, and we listen—they don't even have to shout anymore" (Wolf 2004).

Even a year after the Dean campaign started to use the Internet for social organizing and fund-raising, most donors to presidential candidates contributed an average of about $2,000 each, and those contributions came from one-quarter of 1 percent of the population. Dean raised money from 600,000 people with the average donation around $80, and in so doing raised Dean's campaign coffer higher than any other potential candidate. From this point on, social media became critical for political fund-raising and had the added benefit of helping candidates whose teams understood how the Internet could be used for political purposes gain public support.

When Barack Obama ran for president in 2008, his team strategically used the Internet for fund-raising and political awareness, so well that he won the Democratic nomination despite a highly strategic campaign by Hillary Clinton. In February 2008, Obama raised $55 million, $45 million of which was raised online. According to the Campaign Finance Institute, 30 percent of Obama's fund-raising during the primary elections came in small donations over the Internet. A significant percentage (49%) of the donations were less than $200 each. Many of the donations were given by people who then returned to give more online, and in the end $745 million was raised, most of which came in the form of online donations.

In the reelection campaign of 2012, Obama once again relied heavily on small donations. The big change in political fund-raising, however, came from the use of volunteers in the field who could also use an app that could connect mobile phones to direct electronic payments through a device called the Square Reader that allowed credit cards to be swiped through the device that was connected to a mobile phone. In September 2012, Obama's reelection campaign set a new fund-raising record bringing in more than $150 million that month alone.

Today almost every politician raises funds, in part, through the use of social networks, and many companies make their fund-raising campaigns available to candidates and individuals. Some of the *crowdsourced* funding sites like Kickstarter or Indiegogo are used by politicians as much as they are used by individuals who hope to raise money for their own start-up venture, but some organizations like Trailblazer (Trailblaz.com) focus specifically on fund-raising for politicians.

Fund-raising, like using social media for any political purpose, turns the traditional behavior of "top-down" activity to that of "bottom-up," or grassroots-style behavior. In many ways it empowers individuals who may not have a lot of political power themselves, or a lot of money, to become involved and invested in the ideas of political leaders and in their chance for success. Therefore, the democratizing effect of political fund-raising is one that draws on the power of communication over the Internet, and reflects the social, political, and economic changes that have evolved since the establishment of the Internet, World Wide Web, and Web 2.0. In 2001, only about one-quarter of the political candidates running for office had campaign websites. In 2015, it would be hard to find a politician who did not have a campaign site.

See also: Crowdfunding; Crowdsourcing

Further Reading

Gainous, Jason, and Kevin M. Wagner. 2014. *Tweeting to Power: The Social Media Revolution in American Politics.* New York: Oxford University Press.
Sifry, Micha L. 2011. *WikiLeaks and the Age of Transparency.* Berkeley, CA: Counterpoint, 48–49.
Wolf, Gary. 2004. "How the Internet Invented Howard Dean." *Wired*, 12: 38.

Pornography

While *pornography*—the depiction of sexual activity for the purpose of sexual arousal—is not new, social networks and social media has allowed the adult entertainment industry and the related pornography industry to become more pervasive and even more lucrative. Pornography is different from erotica, with the former focusing on depictions of physical acts, and the latter with aspirations of being more artistically oriented. Early images of pornography were found in statues and painted on walls, showing that there is an ancient origin to graphic depictions of sexual acts and sexually suggestive content. Print media excelled at both the pictorial and textual forms of printed pornography, but to obtain it a person would have to go to a store to buy it, risking being seen by others. Pornographic films were often showed in XXX (triple X) "art" theaters, where, again, a person could be seen buying a ticket or coming out of the theater.

The widespread availability of pornography during the Civil War (1861–1865) resulted in an antipornography movement spearheaded by a moral crusader, Anthony Comstock. The United States passed a federal law in 1873 called "The Comstock Law," which made it illegal to use the U.S. Post Office to send erotica, contraceptives, sex toys, or any information about these types of products, including remedies for self-abortion.

The Internet was a boon to pornography. In the campy theatrical production of *Avenue Q*, a parody of Sesame Street, Muppet Trekkie Monster (a version of Cookie Monster) and Kate Monster sing a song titled *The Internet Is for Porn*. While the show ran on Broadway from 2003 to 2009, and then moved off-Broadway where it still runs today, the humor is in realizing that the Internet allowed pornography to reach anybody, wherever they could access the Internet.

The actual profits in the pornography industry are hard to ascertain because the industry keeps these figures closely guarded. It is difficult to accurately assess how large the online pornography industry is, because there are so many avenues for the creation and dissemination of porn, and the industry spans many different countries. A good portion of the pornography industry is underground—meaning that it does not publicize its activities or make its profits known. Pornography is legal in some countries, but not in others. For example, many of the adult entertainment companies are found in the United States, Brazil, and the Netherlands, but the top pornography producing countries include China, South Korea, Japan, and the United States. In general, though, according to toptenreviews.com, over $3,000 is spent every second of every day on world pornography consumption.

Even though present figures are hard to obtain, sometimes, in retrospect, it is easier to gather data to reflect the growth of the industry. In his book, *Obscene Profits: Entrepreneurs in the Cyber Age*, Frederick S. Lane III noted that as the twenty-first century began, adult websites accounted for $1–2 billion a year in money spent online; $5 billion was spent on adult videos, and $150 million was spent on pay-per-view services in hotels. The pornography industry in general received between $2 and 10 billion in revenue, while some estimates indicated that the general amount was closer to $15–20 billion (Lane 2000, xiv–xv.) These statistics are just an indicator of what type of money was changing hands in the early days of the Internet.

A more recent figure as reported by the Adult Video Network and verified by Kirk Doran, an economics professor, is that, by 2006, revenue from online subscriptions and sales of pornography were approximately $2.8 billion (Doran 2008). With the estimated growth and distribution options afforded by new technologies, by 2015, it was believed that the pornography industry was generating more revenue than Netflix, Google, eBay, Yahoo, Amazon, Microsoft, and Apple, combined.

Since the public started to use the Internet in the 1990s, pornography can be found on websites, through peer-to-peer file sharing, or in newsgroups. The World Wide Web is a major distributor of pornography, and much of it is generated in countries with more liberal sex laws, but sent free, or through paid services, over the Internet where people are less worried about being seen while they engage in viewing pornography. The personal space of the home, or through personal technologies, has helped the online pornography industry grow by leaps and bounds.

Of course, there are many objections to pornography online, but most of them have to do with the availability of images that one does not want to see, but that come to a computer or phone through spamming or some other form of hacking. If we separate the issues of pornography that some people choose to seek and pay for as opposed to pornography that floods screens without the user wanting the images, the issues become somewhat easier to address.

The most significant problem with unwanted pornography online has to do with children's access to mature content. Whether a child seeks content or is presented with possibly disturbing images is a topic for which every parent is concerned. The short-lived Communications Decency Act (CDA) was an attempt to make the senders of pornography responsible for luring children to pornography sites, and later attempts to regulate child access to pornography came through the Child Online Protection Act (COPA), the Children's Online Privacy Protection Act (COPPA), and the Children's Internet Protection Act (CIPA) all were attempts to create legislation to control children's use of online services. They reflect the fears and concerns that parents and lawmakers have when it comes to children accessing questionable content, and the problem of protecting children while still allowing adults to experience a level of freedom of speech that prevents censorship.

Exploitation of women is of great concern to many, and there are several advocacy groups that say that women are often exploited for sex or degraded by being represented in pornography. The adult entertainment industry, sex industry, or sex workers industries are different approaches to the role of gender and issues of possible coercion versus choice for anyone who becomes involved in the types of controversial portrayals of sex and sexual imagery.

According to *Los Angeles Times* political commentator David Horsey, a 2014 study published in the *Archives of Sexual Behavior* reviewed a survey of 487 American males of college age who reported that "the more pornography a man watches, the more likely he was to use it during sex, request particular pornographic sex acts of his partner, deliberately conjure images of pornography during sex to maintain arousal, and have concerns over his own sexual performance and body image. Further, higher pornography use was negatively associated with enjoying sexually intimate behaviors with a partner" (Horsey 2014).

See also: Addiction; Child Online Protection Act (COPA); Children's Internet Protection Act (CIPA); Communications Decency Act (CDA); Cyberbullying; Dark Net; Privacy; Sexting

Further Reading

Doran, Kirk. 2008. "Industry Size, Measurement, and Social Costs." Presentation at Princeton University, December 11–13. Accessed January 2, 2015: http://www.social costsofpornography.com/Doran_Industry_Size_Measurement_Social_Costs.Pdf.

Douthat, Ross. 2008. "Is Pornography Adultery?" *The Atlantic Monthly*. Accessed November 12, 2014: http://www.theatlantic.com/magazine/archive/2008/10/is-pornography -adultery/306989/.

"Federal Laws Concerning the Sexual Exploitation of Children." 2015. National Center for Missing and Exploited Children, U.S. Government. Accessed January 2, 2015: http:// www.missingkids.com/LegalResources/Exploitation/FederalLaw.

Horsey, David. 2014. "Internet Porn Is an Experiment in Dehumanization." *Los Angeles Times*. Accessed January 2, 2015: http://www.latimes.com/opinion/topoftheticket/la-na -tt-internet-porn-20141215-story.html.

Lane, Frederick S. III. 2000. *Obscene Profits: Entrepreneurs in the Cyber Age*. London: Routledge, xiv–iv.

Wallace, Benjamin. 2011. "The Geek Kinds of Smut." *New York Magazine*. Accessed May 11, 2015: http://nymag.com/news/features/70985/index2.html.

Privacy

From personal practices involving the way we use social media to the growing areas of data mining, hacking, and cybercrime that can affect a person's personal privacy, the social media revolution brings a host of potential problems. Many of the laws that exist to protect personal privacy are tested by some of the newer uses of social media technologies and social networking that haven't successfully capitalized on the unique characteristics of using personal technologies in public places, or using messages intended for one person to be easily spread to an entire network. Privacy issues involve understanding the forms of media we use to communicate, our personal sense of the value of privacy that influences our behaviors, and the growth of businesses that think of data as a commodity to be bought and sold. With these three elements, it's not surprising that we often find that our personal privacy is invaded, sometimes without our even knowing it.

The range of issues that bring the term "privacy" to mind also involve a number of concerns. While the Pew Research Center has periodically polled Americans to assess their views on personal privacy, the most recent studies show that people are becoming increasingly concerned about privacy issues. "When Americans are asked what comes to mind when they hear the word 'privacy,' there are patterns to their answers . . . when responses are grouped into themes, the largest block of answers ties to concepts of security, safety, and protection. For many others, notions of secrecy and keeping things 'hidden' are top of mind when thinking about privacy" (Madden 2014). The leaks of information about the National Security Agency (NSA) by Edward Snowden in 2013 prompted many to think about the role of the government and monitoring personal e-mails and phone calls (wired and mobile) and alerted citizens to the type of information that is gathered about us, and by whom. The 2014 Pew study reported that 81 percent of those people surveyed feel "not very" or "not at all secure" using social media sites when they want to share private information with another trusted person or organization; 68 percent feel insecure using chat or instant messages for private information; 58 percent feel insecure sending private info by text; 57 percent feel insecure sending private information via e-mail; and 46 percent feel "not very" or "not at all secure" sharing private information over their mobile phone (Madden 2014).

Episodes like the Snowden affair have contributed to changing attitudes about privacy and whether privacy can be assured or not, but often assumptions about privacy and our use of technology get us into trouble. For example, most people think that they "own" their e-mail and whatever media content they legitimately purchase, even though they store it on cloud-based services. While personal e-mail messages through an Internet service provider are supposed to be the property of the person who signs up for the service, employers who provide those Internet services actually own the content of anything that goes over the system they pay for. Students are often shocked to find that a university has tagged them for downloading massive amounts of music, films, or pornography, and the student often has to pay a fine for violating the university's rules. Likewise, employers who make Internet services available to employees have the right to monitor the employee's use of the computers and servers paid for by the company. Similarly, when someone stores music from the iTunes Store on the iTunes cloud system, the person no longer has access to that music if something happens to disrupt the connection to the cloud or the cloud service crashes.

At the same time, the nature of the portable technologies we use for digital information transfer give us an illusion of privacy. Social media builds on the characteristics of letting people connect to each other or follow news, celebrities, the stock market, or any range of information access that social media facilitate. But when we post information online, we have no control over where other people send it or for what purposes they might use it. We often work with laptops and mobile devices in private places, and even when we use them in public places we tend to think that because we are thinking about personal communication, the public has no interest in what we're doing on those technologies. But anyone who has ever overheard a very private mobile phone conversation understands how private information that is transmitted in a public place blurs someone's privacy—either the user, the person with whom they are communicating, or sometimes even that of the bystander. Similarly, if you've ever caught a glimpse of what people watch on mobile phone screens, laptops, or tablets being used in public places—even if the sound is monitored by the person's headphones—it should be obvious that what we notice about a person's use of their own technologies tells us something about them, and blurs the idea of private communication.

One of the most attractive features of social networks is that they allow users to participate in online communities as well as communicate directly with one person at a time, but the ability to use technologies and social networks in public places comes with a social cost and an economic cost. From the technological issues of storing personal information that can easily be tracked and traded through cookies or peer-to-peer networks, and simple technical processes such as forwarding messages to people for whom they were unintended, privacy issues have blossomed since the birth of social networking. While every official social network has a privacy policy, sometimes things don't operate as seamlessly as one might imagine. As the Internet has become the engine of a number of industries in the "information age," data has become a valuable commodity. Big data companies have been formed that mine data and profit by the intelligence that data reports. In an article titled: "I'm Being Followed: How Google—and 104 Other Companies—Are Tracking Me on the Web," journalist Alexis C. Madrigal wrote about using a Mozilla tool called *Collusion* to find out how many companies were tracking his online behavior: "Even if you're generally familiar with the idea of data collection for targeted advertising, the number and variety of these data collectors will probably astonish you. Allow me to introduce the list of companies that tracked my movements on the Internet in one recent 36-hour period of standard web surfing: Acerno. Adara Media. Adblade. Adbrite. ADC Onion. Adchemy. ADiFY. AdMeld. Adtech. Aggregate Knowledge. AlmondNet. Aperture. AppNexus. Atlas. Audience Science. And that's just the As. My complete list includes 105 companies, and there are dozens more than that in existence" (Madrigal 2012). Even after going to a site to register to "opt out" of being tracked, Madrigal found that the same companies were still monitoring his Internet usage. In 2010 the Digital Advertising Alliance (DAA) set out regulatory guidelines to help self-regulation of the behavioral advertising business. Backed by the FTC, the new principles offered a list of "best practices" for those companies that mined data from Internet users. These guidelines suggest that people be informed that they can request "do not track" services, but there is little way to enforce whether they are implemented are not. These guidelines have been somewhat effective, but they have not solved the problem of the way many social media companies manage data that results in a violation of privacy.

For example, such companies as Google and Facebook often employed opt-out privacy policies. Such policies meant that unless people specified that their information be kept private, the companies made it public. But Google publishes photographs of people's houses and streets on its Google Maps service, which comes from a different service than those that are linked through data miners or shared over different social networks.

As indicated in the entry for cybercrime in this encyclopedia, privacy violations have the potential to be used for identity theft and, therefore, violate even the terms of privacy agreed upon when a person signs up for an Internet service. Facebook's security department has admitted that over 600,000 accounts are usually compromised every day (Goodman 2015, 87).

One part of the problem is that people often don't do enough to protect their own information. About 75 percent of people who use social networks use the same password for multiple Internet sites (Goodman 2015, 87) and, usually, those passwords reflect their own birthdays, names of pets, or some combination of a nickname or address. Similarly, organized crime is responsible for 85 percent of the break-ins of many social networks like LinkedIn, Snapchat, Google, Twitter, and Yahoo! (Goodman, 2015, 88). "Best practices" for individuals suggests that they change their passwords every six months or so, and that they create passwords 10 characters long (hint: song titles without spaces often provide good passwords that are memorable for the user!).

While privacy matters are becoming part of today's discourse surrounding the responsible use of social media, everyone bears some responsibility to be informed, thoughtful, and aware of what happens when we use social media. Until effective laws are developed and implemented, and the people who violate those laws are caught and prosecuted, we can expect to see the good features of the Internet and web's welcoming components juxtaposed against the darker features of systems that allow us to easily transfer personal information.

See also: Anonymity; Cybercrime; Data Mining; Hacker; Right to Be Forgotten

Further Reading

Goodman, Marc. 2015. *Future Crimes*. New York: Doubleday, 87–88.

Madden, Mary. 2014. "Public Perceptions of Privacy and Security in the Post-Snowden Era." Pew Research Center. Accessed April 28, 2015: http://www.pewinternet.org/2014/11/12/public-privacy-perceptions/.

Madrigal, Alexis C. 2012. "I'm Being Followed: How Google—and 104 Other Companies—Are Tracking Me on the Web." *The Atlantic Monthly*. Accessed April 28, 2015: http://www.theatlantic.com/technology/archive/2012/02/im-being-followed-how-google-151-and-104-other-companies-151-are-tracking-me-on-the-web/253758/.

> **Fourth Amendment**
>
> The Fourth Amendment to the U.S. Constitution reads:
>
> The right of the people to be secure in their persons, houses, papers, and effects, against unreasonable searches and seizures, shall not be violated, and no Warrants shall issue, but upon probable cause, supported by Oath or affirmation, and particularly describing the place to be searched, and the persons or things to be seized.
>
> *Source:* Fourth Amendment to the U.S. Constitution. http://www.gpo.gov/fdsys /pkg/GPO-CONAN-1992/pdf/GPO-CONAN-1992-10-5.pdf.

Prosumer

A *prosumer* is a person who both produces and consumes something—usually in terms of media. Another definition of the term considers professional and consumer indicating that the person is engaged in an activity that had formerly been conducted by a professional in an area, such as a professional filmmaker, while the prosumer records a video to post on YouTube. The idea of *prosumerism* is linked to the idea that people can do projects themselves, and that they don't have to be satisfied with mass produced goods or information.

In the 1980 book, *The Third Wave*, futurist Alvin Toffler used the term to describe how in the future technology would make it easier for us to be self-sufficient. We could grow our own food for our own consumption, or, we could be a part of the do-it-yourself, "DIY," culture to avoid big industry, and scale down activities to a local level. His vision was in contrast to the growing mass media and mass culture that had dominated American society in the middle of the twentieth century and the standardization of products that emerged at that time.

Since then, the word *prosumer* has also been attached to inexpensive technologies that a regular consumer can buy and use. The "cam-corder" a relatively low cost camera that also recorded video would be an example of a prosumer device, as would a mobile phone with a camera that could upload pictures or videos to an app, online service, or social network.

When the Internet became available, a number of online start-ups helped consumers become prosumers. The travel industry was revolutionized by online travel companies that allowed consumers to book their own flights, check in online, compare airline fares, hotel rates, and more. MP3 technology made it possible to bypass traditional record distribution companies and change the entire business model of the music industry.

In their popular book, *Wikinomics*, Don Tapscott and Anthony D. Williams discussed the growing number of businesses, services, and websites that allowed consumers to contribute to the development of the project, and called those people *prosumers*. For example, they discuss the growth of the popular video game *Second Life* and write: "Second Life is no typical 'product' and it's not even a typical video game. It's created almost entirely by its customers—you could say the 'consumers' are also the producers, or the 'prosumers'" (Tapscott and Williams 2006, 125).

See also: Creative Economy; E-Commerce; Sharing Economy

Further Reading

Tapscott, Don, and Anthony D. Williams. 2006. *Wikinomics: How Mass Collaboration Changes Everything.* New York: Penguin, 125.

Toffler, Alvin. 1980. *The Third Wave.* New York: Bantam.

R

Reddit

Reddit is a social networking service and news website that structures what is important based upon community taste and active involvement of users. Different users can submit information and community members can vote the content either "up" or "down." Reddit's web page calls the service the "Internet's Front Page" because it helps people sift through the massive amount of information on the Internet to group relevant sites together. The name is a reference to the statement "I read it on." The site functions very much like an electronic bulletin board.

Sites like reddit (the actual site uses the lower case "r") and Digg are useful not only because they help people with specific interests find what they are looking for on the Internet, but because they often cut through the clutter of the constant flow of information on the Internet and help mark articles for others to view or to ignore. The website is known for its diverse content and the way it relies on users to provide the content. The subject areas are broadly identified and further divided into subreddits.

Reddit has received many accolades for the way it introduces people to important topics in a nonthreatening but educational way. Ana Swanson wrote of one such example when she described a thread that was titled: "Disabled people of reddit, what is something we do that we think helps, but it really doesn't?" (Swanson 2015). In the postings, disabled people vented about the things they hear that annoy them, and offered helpful ways to help people rephrase information that would be more acceptable. Swanson wrote: "The Internet community reddit has become a destination for all kinds of arcane topics, including cats dressed up as lobsters, creepy things found at garage sales, and people riding invisible bicycles. But once in a while, the forum also hosts a conversation that connects people with different life experiences in mind-opening ways" (Swanson 2015). This example shows how reddit can actually be a socially compassionate, helpful tool to bring information into the lives of people who might not know about it, but who can be strengthened through their ability to connect with others and learn through social media.

The service was founded by two roommates at the University of Virginia, Steve Huffman and Alexis Ohanian when both were in their sophomore year. The service was acquired by one of the major magazine publishers in the world, Condé Nast Publications in 2006. The service operates independently and is based in San Francisco, California. In 2014, the entertainers Snoop Dogg and Jared Leto, and a group of investors, contributed $50 million. The site can be accessed for free but in 2010 a new feature was added. Reddit Gold was offered for $3.99 a month or $29.99 for a year.

At the end of 2014, reddit had 174 million users, and, in 2015, the web analytics firm Alexa (a division of Amazon) ranked reddit as the tenth most visited site in the United States, and the twenty-fourth globally.

See also: App; Social Media; Trending

Further Reading

Lessig, Lawrence. 2008. *Remix: Making Art and Commerce Thrive in the Hybrid Economy.* New York: Penguin Press, 59.

Swanson, Ana. 2015. "A Powerful reddit Thread Reveals What It's Like to Be Disabled." *The Washington Post.* Accessed April 24, 2015: http://www.washingtonpost.com /blogs/wonkblog/wp/2015/04/24/a-powerful-reddit-thread-reveals-what-its-like-to-be -disabled/.

Right to Be Forgotten

Though it may sound illogical, the life span of digital information can be both temporary and permanent. It is temporary in the sense that the attention span of readers may be fleeting or that some digital information can be deleted with the touch of a button, but permanent in the sense that official information and the archives of Internet content may live on, well beyond the statute of limitations that would be expected in many real-world situations. For example, when a person dies, who has the credentials to end that person's Facebook profile? And, when it comes to inaccurate or misleading information, who should have the right to say what, about themselves, should be available to others on the Internet? What happens when incorrect information lives on, and the people most affected by it are powerless to correct that information? Also important, what responsibility do big companies like Google, Facebook, or any repository of information have in correcting or deleting incorrect information that could be injurious to a person's reputation? The *Right to Be Forgotten* is an action that has been given significant attention in Europe, and it is expected to be addressed by concerned citizens in other parts of the world.

In 2010, a Spanish citizen lodged a complaint against a Spanish newspaper and Google, because a notice to repossess his home appeared on Google's search results page. The individual had been in the Spanish courts to resolve a problem he had years earlier about the payment on his home, and the problem had been solved, but the "life span" of the information on the archive of the newspaper remained online, and therefore portrayed an inaccurate picture of his financial position. He requested that the newspaper remove or alter the content in their online database and that Google Spain and Google Inc. be required to remove his personal information.

The court referred the case to the Court of Justice of the European Union (EU) asking whether the EU's 1995 Data Protection Directive applied to big search engines like Google, and whether the Google server, which resided in the United States could be compelled to follow the European rules. In May 2014, The EU Court of Justice ruled that a person who wants their personal information removed from any online search has the right to request that information be taken down from the web. They specified that the material should be related to private individuals, and not those who are in the news, and they placed the burden of proof on the individual asking for the action to show that the information is "inadequate, irrelevant or no longer relevant" (Toobin 2014).

The action by the EU has major implications for multinational organizations, like Google, Facebook, and other social networks and social media in general. Google is perhaps the most heavily affected, and, since the beginning of 2015, Google had received 182,604 requests for link-removal under the Right to Be Forgotten legislation. Google had denied 59.5 percent of the links that were requested. This compares to 4,565 links removed by Facebook ("Gone, But Hardly Forgotten" 2015, 11).

The type of information that has been removed runs the gamut from the Spanish citizen who had real estate assets seized for nonpayment, to a German story about a rape, and a story about a Norwegian mass murderer that categorized his 1,500-page "war-plan" ("Gone, But Hardly Forgotten" 2015).

Though the EU's ruling currently affects only the countries within the EU, many people expect to see similar legislation emerging in other countries (including the United States) in the next few years.

See also: Privacy

Further Reading

"Gone, But Hardly Forgotten." 2015. *Columbia Journalism Review*, Editorial, 53: 11.

Toobin, Jeffrey. 2014. "The Solace of Oblivion." *The New Yorker*. Accessed April 26, 2015. http://www.newyorker.com/magazine/2014/09/29/solace-oblivion.

Excerpts from the Factsheet on the "Right to Be Forgotten" Ruling

How will the Right to Be Forgotten work in practice? Who can ask for a deletion of personal data and how?

For example, John Smith will be allowed to request Google to delete all search links to webpages containing his data, when one enters the search query "John Smith" in the Google search box.

Google will then have to assess the deletion request on a case-by-case basis and to apply the criteria mentioned in EU law and the European Court's judgment. These criteria relate to the accuracy, adequacy, relevance—including time passed—and proportionality of the links, in relation to the purposes of the data processing.

The request may for example be turned down . . . In such cases, John Smith still has the option to complain to national data protection supervisory authorities or to national courts. Public authorities will be the ultimate arbiters of the application of the Right to Be Forgotten.

Source: Factsheet on the "Right to Be Forgotten" Ruling (C-131/12). European Commission. http://ec.europa.eu/justice/data-protection/files/factsheets/factsheet_data_protection_en.pdf.

S

Samsung

Samsung is a multinational firm that has grown from a small export company founded in 1938 in Taegu, South Korea, to become a world leader in electronics manufacturing and sales. The founder of the company was 26-year-old Lee Byung-chul, a college dropout and the son of a wealthy Korean landowning family. At first, Lee used his inheritance to open a rice mill, but that business failed, and he turned his attention to building a small fish-and-produce exporting business that he named Samsung (Korean for "three stars"). Lee expanded the business with a sugar-refining company, a wool-textile subsidiary, and a couple of insurance businesses. In 1969, he added Samsung-Sanyo Electronics, which manufactured television sets (Eichenwald 2014). It now includes shipbuilding, construction, life insurance, advertising, and even a theme park in Korea called Everland. But by far the most profitable division is now Samsung Electronics. Samsung's smartphone business is so successful, it accounts for two-thirds of the company's total profits (Woyke 2014, 61).

When the Electronics division was started in 1969, Samsung manufactured a wide range of household technologies including washing machines, refrigerators, television sets, and other home-based technologies. In addition to manufacturing technologies the company became active in improving the design for computer chips and improving digital technologies. By 2009, it had become the largest Information Technology (IT) company in the world.

In recent years Samsung has won praise for their innovative design of mobile telephones and tablet technologies. By 2011 it had become the largest manufacturer of mobile phones for the world. In the United States, the Galaxy mobile phone series has become the major competitor to Apple's iPhone. One of the features that makes Galaxy smartphones the best-selling phones in the world is the use of the Android operating system, which is the most commonly used worldwide and allows for a greater number of interconnections, like apps developed from a wide variety of software systems.

Samsung's success has contributed to South Korea's reputation as a nation known for innovative electronics and effective export of technologies. The country's capital, Seoul, is referred to as "the Miracle on the Han River" because of the effectiveness of the Korean electronics firms and the economic boom they have brought to the region in the period between the 1960s and the present.

See also: Apple; Mobile Phone; Smartphone

Further Reading

Eichenwald, Kurt. 2014. "The Great Smartphone War." *Vanity Fair*, June 2014. Accessed April 26, 2015: http://www.vanityfair.com/news/business/2014/06/apple-samsung-smartphone-patent-war.

Woyke, Elizabeth. 2014. *The Smartphone: Anatomy of an Industry.* New York: The New Press, 61.

Second Life (See Gaming)

Selfie

A selfie is a picture that a person takes of themself. Facilitated by cameras on mobile smartphones, and other digital devices like laptops and tablets, the subject holds the camera at arm's length (or less) to include him/herself as the subject (or one subject) of the picture. Digital editing and photo manipulation can be used before posting the selfie on a social network. The 2014 *Oxford English Dictionary* named *selfie* the "word of the year" for 2013 because of the popularity of the phenomenon.

The selfie is a natural outgrowth of self-portraiture. Photography aided self-portraits and the earliest known photographic self-portraits date from 1839, when daguerreotype pioneer Robert Cornelius took a picture of himself outside his family's store. In the 1970s, Andy Warhol used Polaroid instant cameras to record his own likeness, starting a phenomenon that was popular throughout the 1970s.

Though self-portraits are not a new phenomenon, using digital technologies and social networks to distribute them is fairly recent. Improved mobile phone cameras and a number of apps that make a selfie easy to take and to post have helped make selfies popular. Social networks like Flickr started showing selfies in 2004, but the idea of taking a self-portrait with digital technology became much easier once the iPhone 4, with a front-facing camera, made it much easier to take a selfie without distortion. The photo-based messaging service Snapchat processes over 350 million selfies each day, and Instagram contains over 90 million selfies.

A crowdfunded project in 2010 using Kickstarter raised $90,000 to develop and sell a small Bluetooth shutter release for smartphones and tablets that made it even easier to take a selfie.

Celebrities have effectively used selfies for self-promotion. Justin Bieber and Kim Kardashian, both celebrities that owe much of their popularity to their ability to promote themselves, are among the many who have posted selfies online and on their Twitter feeds but politicians have found them useful promotional tools, too, to make the politician seem more likable to the public. Depending on the platform used to post a selfie, the number of "likes" a person gets can be thought of as a measure of popularity. Author John Paul Titlow has described selfie-sharing as "a high school popularity contest on digital steroids" (Day 2013).

Many people expressed a wide range of opinions about selfies. Some claim they might be a reflection of our media-saturated environment. Others claim that the selfie has become the ultimate symbol of the narcissistic age in which we live. Still others feel that comfort with the technology has allowed people to just express a silly or fun side of their personality in a more public way. Sharing these images on Facebook, Instagram, or Twitter has an impact, though receivers may not have the same understanding of why the sender posted the selfie. Whatever the reason a person may have for taking and sharing a selfie—there is probably a psychological interpretation of how and why that particular person did it.

The selfie phenomenon has attracted the attention of scholars who often regard selfies as a unique form of self-expression. Dr. Mariann Hardey, a lecturer at Durham University (U.K.), wrote: "The selfie is revolutionising [sic] how we gather autobiographical information about ourselves and our friends . . . It's about continuously rewriting yourself. It's an extension of our natural construction of self. It's about presenting yourself in the best way . . . [similar to] when women put on makeup or men who bodybuild to look a certain way: it's an aspect of performance that's about knowing yourself and being vulnerable" (Day 2013).

Sometimes the intention of a selfie is for a personal use that demonstrates the intimate nature of social media. Because mobile phones can be used in the privacy of one's most intimate settings, people may feel comfortable taking pictures of themselves that they would never want someone else to take. *Sexting* is a form of taking a selfie that is sexually provocative in nature; perhaps with the subject nude, or a part of his or her anatomy showing. Sexts are usually intended for viewing by one other person, rather than posting to the masses, but there are entire porn sites devoted to the "amateur" naked selfie, and even the pouty mouth, sucked in cheeks, and provocative head tilt favored by many women who take selfies can reflect a certain amount of pornography-inspired selfie style.

See also: Identity; Mobile Phone Cameras; Privacy; Sexting

Further Reading

Day, Elizabeth. 2013. "How Selfies Became a Global Phenomenon." *The Guardian.* Accessed October 2, 2014: http://www.theguardian.com/technology/2013/jul/14/how -selfies-became-a-global-phenomenon.

Wortham, Jenna. 2010. "My Selfie, Myself." *New York Times, Sunday Review.* Accessed October 2, 2014: http://www.nytimes.com/2013/10/20/sunday-review/my-selfie-myself .html?pagewanted=all&_r=0.

Sexting

Sexting is the act of sending a nude or sexually provocative picture over a mobile phone or the Internet. Most sexting takes place over mobile phones and is related in part to the ease of using a mobile phone camera in a private place. While there can be many reasons individuals choose to send a nude or provocative picture to someone else, sexting shows not only how we often use technology in very personal ways, but it also shows how easy it is to forward a message meant for one person on to an entire group of people. When a person knows who is receiving the sext a certain amount of intimacy between or among the sender and recipient(s) can be assumed, but often sexts are forwarded to others by the original recipient. When that happens, a number of problems might arise. While there can be social and moral consequences to sexting, most of the controversy surrounding the subject deals with teens sexting each other, or messages that cross into the boundary of child pornography.

Because mobile phones in particular are personal technologies, there are very few legal guidelines to limit what one person does with their own mobile phone and how the content of the message is accepted by the intended receiver of that message. But when it comes to teens who are experimenting with what may seem like testing sexual boundaries, the consequences of sexting become more complicated. For the most part, the biggest problems occur when messages are shared with others, and the sender of the sext is humiliated or embarrassed by the mass distribution of a sext. Photo messaging services like Instagram or Snapchat can become disseminators of messages meant to be personal and aimed to an individual but that often become collections of similar types of images.

In the cover story to an *Atlantic Monthly* article on why teens sext, journalist Hanna Rosin profiled several teens who sent and received sexts and discussed the problems for those individuals, parents, and law enforcement personnel who are often called in to deal with the problems of sexting among teens. While Rosin reports that the most common reason teens say they sext is that "their boyfriend of girlfriend wanted the picture" and that most experience no major consequences for engaging in the behavior. However, Rosin also cites a study by Professor Elizabeth

Englander indicating that about 70 percent of the girls reported feeling that they were under some pressure to send a sext, while 12 percent reported that they felt very pressured to send a sext. The "pressured sexters" were much more likely to feel bad about their actions, and often felt less assured about "their place in the social hierarchy after sending a sext" (Rosin 2014, 73–74). Furthermore, it is more likely that those images taken as a result of pressure are often those that are more likely to be shared with others, rather than by the one person who requested that the picture be taken.

While there are a number of studies that have conflicting reports about the problem of sexting among teens, most acknowledge that sexting is a popular activity for teens in particular because they are trying to come to terms with sexuality and their own value of individualism and control over their own body. For these reasons, law enforcement is often uncomfortable seizing the mobile phone of a person who sends or collects sexts, because what might be a youthful indiscretion has the potential to create a permanent record of possible sexual deviance. While some states have very explicit laws about how to classify sexts (particularly among age groups that have not yet reached majority), some states are more heavy-handed than others. For example, some states classify visual images of nude individuals who are under the legal age of majority as child pornography, and possession of this type of content is illegal and a criminal offense.

The laws regarding teen sexting are sometimes complicated. Florida is one state that has passed laws specifically relating to minors who transmit sexts. A first offender might have to pay a fine, complete community service, or attend a class on the implications of sexting, but a second offense is classified as a misdemeanor, and a third offense is a felony. In Virginia, though, anyone who takes a picture and distributes it, or anyone who has a sext stored on their phone, could be arrested on a felony charge.

But while sexting is particularly troubling when it comes to teens, the act of sending and receiving sexts is by no means the purview of teens alone. The Pew Research Center conducted a study of technology and couples' relationships and found that 9 percent of adult mobile phone owners have sent a sext of themselves to someone else; 20 percent have received a sext of someone they know on their mobile phone; and 3 percent have shared a sext they have received with others (Lenhart and Duggan 2014).

Often, people who sext (whether teens or adults) are carried away by the personal use of mobile phones or the idea of sending an image over the Internet to a specific person and they forget how easy it is for that message to be intercepted or forwarded to others. In 2011, U.S. Representative Anthony Weiner of New York was forced to resign from Congress because of sexts he took of himself and shared over his Twitter account. Though he first denied that he sent the messages, and actually used the pseudonym "Carlos Danger," he finally confessed that he had shared the explicit images with six different women over a three-year period. The humiliation and negative attention forced him to resign from public office.

See also: Cyberbullying; Mobile Phone Cameras; Pornography

Further Reading

Lenhart, Amanda, and Maeve Duggan. 2014. "Couples, the Internet, and Social Media." Pew Research Center. Accessed March 16, 2015: http://www.pewinternet.org/2014/02/11/couples-the-internet-and-social-media/.
Rosin, Hanna. 2014. "Why Kids Sext." *The Atlantic Monthly*, 314: 65–77.

Sharing Economy

The growth in e-commerce has produced a number of new economic models. Some of the new models are still taking shape and being formed, but many of the older, familiar economic models are still in existence, too. Traditional ideas of the "ownership economy," in which people purchase goods and services for their own consumption alone, are undergoing some of the most comprehensive changes, and, yet, the idea of sharing is as old as time. Today, the *sharing economy* offers an alternative to the older economic models, but, at the same time, it is founded on principles that have historic roots. Sharing goods and services doesn't always result in a flow of money, but the principles of sharing establish relationships that cut across economic and social contexts. If a number of the values held by today's millennials continue, we may see that the new paradigm where on-demand access to products and services, rather than ownership, sets the tone for the future economy.

The Internet, social networks, and the different ways of collaborating to get things done is a part of what has been called the *sharing economy*. The act of participating in the sharing economy is also akin to *prosumerism*, or producing and consuming as an individual action rather than as a part of a large corporate system of supply and demand. Valuing communal ideas or the exchange of goods or services has been likened to the first step in a more collaborative form of social interaction, and a healthier economy that values information collaboration and often results in improved ideas.

The elements of the sharing economy are conceptually simple but the economic impact may be profound. Yochai Benkler describes sharable goods as those that make a sustainable social practice feasible. By that, he means that the sharing economy challenges traditional market economics and creates value for goods that are, in return, valued by people. Benkler also identifies the types of sharing that can go on as integral to an *information*-based economy, affecting information, culture, education, computation, and communication sectors. Additionally, he cites the movement toward *freeware* as a typical example of the type of sharing that can go on in an advanced economy (Benkler 2004).

Also known as the *mesh economy*, the principle of sharing is built on *collaborative consumption* and relies on information sharing—often through social networks—that combines elements of trust, reputation, performance, and repetition. For example, after selling her start-up photo-sharing company Ofoto to Eastman Kodak in 2010, Lisa Gansky wrote a best-selling book called *The Mesh: Why the Future of Business Is Sharing*, in which she likened the sharing economy principles with what she called the Mesh economy. She identified over a thousand ventures that spanned projects that allowed the sharing of clothing manufacture, education, energy, finance, food and wine, gardening, health and fitness, real estate, vacations, and more (Gansky 2010). The basic idea behind the sharing economy, or the mesh economy, is that "renting" multiple times is more profitable than owning. In the sharing economy, the industrial model is changed so that individuals control their properties, but work together collaboratively in a network for participation in something bigger.

A number of apps and services on the Internet are based on ideas of the sharing economy, but some companies still use "ownership economy" principles to allow the owner of goods to rent those products to others for a fee. The estimated value of the goods is computed based on the original cost of the item, wear and tear, and the estimated needs of others. So, for example, party planning stores, those that rent out garden implements when needed, and even the leased-car market are all examples of traditional companies that use older economic models to allow people to use services and goods when they need them. But some of the newer services, like Airbnb and Uber are a much larger step into the sharing economy because they bypass the traditional models and use social media to be the "mediator" of transactions. Instead of a physical store or location to house the goods, all transactions take place over the Internet with the help of websites and apps.

The value of information is also important in the sharing economy even though a specific financial figure can't easily be ascribed to the exchange of information. For this reason, crowdsourcing is an excellent example of the sharing economy, even though sharing ideas might conflict with traditional notions of copyright or the ownership of ideas. Even elements of providing recommendations and sharing experiences on sites like Trip Advisor or Yelp can be thought of as components of a sharing economy, and they reference the collaborative nature of freely giving one's knowledge and experience to others.

In 2013, *Forbes* magazine journalist Tomio Geron evaluated the growth of the sharing economy and estimated that the migration to a greater number of sharing experiences would be fundamental to changing economic balances in the future. Citing over one hundred examples of goods, services, and products that where shared, Geron predicted that the future of the sharing economy would someday rival traditional industrial models that have been prevalent for decades (Geron 2013, 58). Similarly, a division of the firm Price Waterhouse Coopers in the United Kingdom produced a report predicting that the five largest components of the sharing economy, which they identified as peer-to-peer lending services, online staffing for jobs, accommodations, car sharing, and music and video streaming, will alter traditional industries and be worth $335 billion of the world's economy by 2025 ("The Sharing Economy" 2015).

Thomas L. Friedman, author of the influential book *The World Is Flat: A Brief History of the Twenty-First Century*, wrote an article in the *New York Times*, in which he stated that economists are having trouble measuring the impact of the sharing economy (Friedman 2013, SR1). One of the fundamental questions he poses is whether the sharing economy creates new value or just replaces existing businesses. But, he reminds us, the sharing economy is also built on trust, and, therefore, the success of the sharing economy is also a harbinger of a society in which we place increased emphasis on social relationships and the bonds that occur when goods and services are exchanged.

See also: Airbnb; Creative Economy; Crowdsourcing; Freeware; Uber

Further Reading

Benkler, Yochai. 2004. "Sharing Nicely: On Shareable Goods and the Emergence of Sharing as a Modality of Economic Production." *Yale Law Review*, 114: 273–359.

Friedman, Thomas L. 2005. *The World Is Flat: A Brief History of the Twenty-First Century*. New York: Farrar, Straus and Giroux.

Friedman, Thomas L. 2013. "Welcome to the Sharing Economy." *New York Times, Sunday Review,* July 20: SR1.

Gansky, Lisa. 2010. *The Mesh: Why the Future of Business Is Sharing*. New York: Penguin.

Geron, Tomio. 2013. "Airbnb and the Unstoppable Rise of the Share Economy." *Forbes*, 191: 58–62.

"The Sharing Economy—Sizing the Revenue Opportunity." 2015. PwC (UK). Accessed April 27, 2015: http://www.pwc.co.uk/issues/megatrends/collisions/sharingeconomy/the -sharing-economy-sizing-the-revenue-opportunity.jhtml.

Silicon Valley

The area known as *Silicon Valley* refers to the southern part of the San Francisco Bay area in Northern California where many of the world's largest technology corporations either started or now have business headquarters. The name has been attributed to Ralph Vaerst, a local entrepreneur who used the term in a 1971 news article for a weekly trade newspaper called *Electronic News*. The term *silicon* reflected the material used to make computer semiconductors.

Within the region, Stanford University has played a significant role in the research and development of a number of computer-related technologies and software development. With a long history in promoting start-up businesses, Stanford has contributed to an entrepreneurial spirit in the valley. With a very educated workforce and as a center for venture capitalists who hope to profit from the intellectual activity in the area, Silicon Valley has attracted computer enthusiasts, business people, and creative people who enjoy the culture of the area. In many ways, Silicon Valley can claim to be the social and intellectual hub of the computer industry.

A number of successful public/private partnerships have developed in the Bay area, including those initiated by Bell Telephone Laboratories, Shockley Semiconductor, Fairchild Semiconductor, and Xerox PARC. Stanford University's Research Institute (SRI) was one of the original nodes to become a part of ARPANET, the predecessor to the Internet.

While Silicon Valley was the top research area at the time of the dot-com bubble, it also survived the dot-com crash very well. In 2006, *The Wall Street Journal* ran a story on the top research and development areas in the world, and found that 12 of the 20 "most inventive" towns in the United States were in California, and 10 of those were in Silicon Valley.

See also: Apple; Google; Yahoo!

Further Reading

Albergotti, Reed. 2006. "The Most Inventive Towns in America." *Wall Street Journal.* Accessed October 28, 2014: http://online.wsj.com/news/articles/SB11535218834631 4087?mg=reno64-wsj&url=http%3A%2F%2Fonline.wsj.com%2Farticle%2FSB11 535218 8346314087.html.

Lécuyer, Christophe. 2005. "What Do Universities Really Owe Industry? The Case of Solid State Electronics at Stanford." *Minerva: A Review of Science, Learning & Policy,* 43: 51–71.

Smart Mob

In 2002, Howard Rheingold published a book called *Smart Mobs: The Next Social Revolution,* in which he wrote about how groups of people can work intelligently together to connect with others and perform social coordination tasks. The concept drew from how technologies could enable people to communicate for a specific purpose, whether for fun, organizing, or mobilizing people to action.

Some people confuse *flash mobs* with *smart mobs*, and some use the terms synonymously. While they are related, there is a difference between the two concepts. Flash mobs are groups of people who appear in a physical place to do something unusual, to catch attention of the public and the media, or who make a political or social statement by their coordinated actions in that physical space. It could be said that flash mobs often occur for a cultural purpose. Sometimes flash mobs are created to make people stop and think about something else other than their typical day. Flash mobs often involve symphony orchestras, dances, art installations, and collective actions that appear spontaneous at first, but make people smile because of the unexpected nature of the event. The flash mob event appears to just happen, even though it is apparent that coordination was necessary to make the event become successful.

A smart mob is a group of people that organize and communicate efficiently to perform a task that tends to have more of a political motive. They often rely on social media and social networks to help spread the message and organize the activities related to that action. In almost any political action today, social media are used to spread information and coordinate activities. The Arab Spring and the Occupy Movements are examples of how smart mobs can function at a time of crisis and while people are under duress.

See also: Arab Spring; Collective Intelligence; Crowdfunding; Crowdsourcing; Occupy Movement

Further Reading

Rheingold, Howard. 2002. *Smart Mobs: The Next Social Revolution.* Cambridge, MA: Perseus Books.

Smartphone

There is no specific technical definition of what makes a mobile phone a smartphone, but perhaps the defining feature of a smartphone is its ability to connect to the Internet and web. The term started to be used by the public in 2007, shortly after the debut of the highly publicized Apple iPhone, but different telephone companies and manufacturers used the term to describe mobile phones and personal digital devices (PDAs) as early as 1997, touting the e-mail and calendar features of those technologies as "smart" features. Today the term *smartphone* is generally used to describe a mobile phone that functions more like a handheld computer and has PDA functions, a media player, digital camera, GPS navigation unit, and the capacity to load apps into its memory. Most smartphones now have touchscreens, but a touchscreen is not one of the defining features of a smartphone. But, most important, telecommunications companies and smartphone manufacturers are banking on the fact that the smartphone will someday replace the laptop computer as the most common technology to combine computing, advertising, shopping, and Internet connectivity.

The global market for the smartphone industry is large and lucrative, which has resulted in manufacturing competitors constantly making improvements and aggressively seeking to add new features. The smartphone market is assumed to be much larger than the PC market and the advertising potential is twice that of computer-based Internet advertising. Profit margins are much higher than other technology products. While there are a number of smartphones being manufactured by different companies today, Apple and Google together have about 94 percent of the global smartphone market (Woyke 2014, 62), and Apple and Samsung are the largest manufacturers of smartphone devices.

With smartphones seemingly so prevalent today, it may be surprising to think that the United States was relatively slow to adopt smartphones. The reasons have much to do with the slow roll-out of mobile telephony in the United States, which was in part due to the number of traditional wired phones that existed at the time, but there were also other factors that influenced the diffusion of the smartphone. First, there was a great deal of competition at the time from smartphone manufacturers who were producing PDAs and other digital devices, like early tablets, and second, telecommunications firms were slow to upgrade their wireless infrastructures to support the additional needed frequencies to make smartphones work seamlessly. Finally, in the United States the cost of mobile phones and contract services were relatively high, which kept a number of consumers placated with their traditional wired phones and their simpler mobile phones.

Like earlier mobile phones, much of the early research and development in mobile telephony took place in the United States at Bell Labs and Motorola, while a number of smaller companies were working on developing technology, too. Comparatively, more research was conducted elsewhere and the lead in developing smartphones came from other countries, like Finland, Japan, and Korea.

Finland's Nokia, a multinational information technology company, developed the first device that could be called a mobile smartphone in 1995 with the Nokia 9000 Communicator. The unit had a QWERTY keyboard, a 4.5 inch screen, and weighed 0.9 pounds. At the time, Nokia didn't refer to the Communicator as a smartphone, but, by 1996, Nokia was shipping the popular phone to other European countries where traditional wired telephony was not as ubiquitous, and calling plan costs were kept lower that in the United States.

In 2000, the Swedish-based Ericsson company launched another version of a smartphone called the R380, which had a touchscreen and used a technical standard called wireless application protocol (WAP) that allowed web pages to be loaded faster, and the phone was called a *smartphone*. Like other mobile phones, the standardization of using a global system for mobile communication (GSM) in Europe allowed greater interoperability of the smartphones with the infrastructure for communications.

Meanwhile, in the United States the FCC was dealing with the problem of how to allocate airwaves for increased mobile phone traffic, and different manufacturers were experimenting with other forms of smartphones. Palm Computing developed the Pilot 5000, and an offshoot of Palm, called Handspring, developed advanced PDAs called Visor, which was a precursor to an American-made smartphone. In Canada, Research in Motion (RIM) developed the BlackBerry 5810 in 2002, which claimed the right to be called the first North American–made smartphone.

By 2009, RIM and BlackBerry had about 20 percent of the global smartphone market, and it was the best-selling brand in the United States. Soon after, Handspring developed a competitor for the U.S. smartphone market called the Treo, which used the flip-phone design.

The operating system of a smartphone is an important feature for users because the popularity of the operating systems indicate the range of functions the phone might have. While phones that use Android operating systems are the most popular, Apple's iOS system also has its share of users. BlackBerry has its own operating system, and a host of others have smaller shares of U.S. business. Globally, a number of other operating systems are popular in various countries, but still, by the end of 2014, Android systems led in global operating systems, with 84.7 percent, and iOS with 11.7 percent. WindowsPhone operating systems had only 2.5 percent of the global market, and BlackBerry, only 0.05 percent ("Smartphone OS Market Share, Q2 2014" n.d.).

While smartphones continue to be adopted in industrialized as well as developing countries, the cost of smartphones is becoming increasingly problematic. Not only are the phones themselves expensive, but the data plans marketed to make them work are excessively high compared to the actual use. In the United States alone, smartphones are a $90 billion market, and, globally, a $400 billion market (Woyke 2014, 144). However, even in developing countries smartphones may be the only means of communication over the Internet. In many of these countries, no traditional wired phone infrastructure existed, but the wireless forms can be used more easily. In some countries, sharing phones or small businesses set up to allow members of the community to rent a mobile phone for a phone call are popular. In Bangladesh, for example, the "Bangladeshi Phone Ladies" have formed an entire sector of the economy by buying phones with money from microloans, and then renting them out to people who need to make a call.

While the cost of service in the United States may remain high for some time, a number of new smartphone manufacturers from around the world have begun to compete for the growing mobile market. At the January 2015 Consumer Electronics show in Las Vegas, a number of new smartphones were demonstrated, from the high-end Italian Tonino Lamborghini 88 Tauri, priced at $6,000 to lower priced smartphones made in China, Korea, and Japan that will sell for $100–$400. While there are manufacturers in all major areas of the world, Asian dominance in smartphones is on the rise. Xiaomi, a Chinese company, has grown explosively with customers around the world, and it now threatens to sell more phones than Samsung over the next few years, largely because it has targeted both China and India, the two countries with the largest populations. Equally important was the announcement that mobile devices will be able to run with computer chips that measure speed in teraflops—a measurement that can best be described as having the capacity of processing a trillion operations per second.

The cost of operating smartphones varies throughout the world, but there are generally two types of payment systems. In the United States, most plans are postpaid, meaning that individuals are charged a flat rate for the number of minutes they use, but if they go over that amount, the costs escalate. In many parts of the world, the favored payment plan is prepayment, in which the customer pays for the number of calls they make prior to using the phone, and then recharge the payment plan according to what they feel they still need once the minutes available have expired. Carriers often lock a person's mobile phone so that it can access only that carrier's equipment, therefore giving the carrier the ability to monitor how much the smartphone is used, and for what reasons. Because these carriers are profit-driven, they've developed payment plans guaranteed to maximize their profits.

Interestingly, though disturbingly however, the cost of using a smartphone can be very misleading. According to a mobile analytics firm Validas, a typical American subscriber pays a carrier about $200 a year for excess messages and data. This computes to about $52.8 billion a year in wireless waste. Globally, the estimate is that $926 billion are wasted by people paying for more service than they actually use (Woyke 2014, 141). Another analytics firm, Alekstra, places the cost of wasted service plans even higher, suggesting that in the United States $70 billion are wasted on unused minutes (Woyke 2014, 142).

According to the Nielsen company, as of 2014, 71 percent of the U.S. population owned a smartphone, and people with smartphones spanned all age groups. Millennials, aged 18–24 owned 86 percent; those 25–34 owned 86.2 percent; 35–44 owned 80.7 percent; 45–54 owned 70.8 percent; 55–64 owned 61.1 percent; and those over 65 owned 46.3 percent ("Mobile Millennials" 2014).

The Pew Research Center reports that 19 percent of American smartphone users rely to some degree on a smartphone for accessing the Internet, either because they lack broadband at home, or because they have few options for Internet access other than their mobile phone (Smith 2015).

There are many problems with smartphones beyond the cost of service. From the perspective of privacy, apps are enormously problematic in terms of app developers and service providers selling people's personal information. The type of information sold involves where a person is using the app (geographic location), the type of phone used (a simple computation traced to the user's number), and the length of time someone interacts with a particular app or service. Sometimes app developers have multiple buyers for this type of data. The companies that market the game *Angry Birds* and the feature that allows someone to use the phone for a flashlight, *Brightest Flashlight,* have been found to sell users' personal data to as many as seven different mobile ad companies.

See also: Mobile Phone; Mobile Phone Cameras

Further Reading

"Mobile Millennials." 2014. Nielsen. Accessed April 27, 2015: http://www.nielsen.com/us/en/insights/news/2014/mobile-millennials-over-85-percent-of-generation-y-owns-smartphones.html.

"Smartphone OS Market Share, Q2 2014." n.d. International Data Communication. Accessed October 28, 2014: http://www.idc.com/prodserv/smartphone-os-market-share.jsp.

Smith, Aaron. 2015. "U.S. Smartphone Use in 2015." Pew Research Center. Accessed April 27, 2015: http://www.pewinternet.org/2015/04/01/us-smartphone-use-in-2015/.

Woyke, Elizabeth. 2014. *The Smartphone: Anatomy of an Industry.* New York and London: The New Press.

Smartphone Use

Smartphones are used for much more than calling, texting, or basic internet browsing. Users are turning to these mobile devices as they navigate a wide range of life events:

62% of smartphone owners have used their phone in the past year to look up information about a health condition.

57% have used their phone to do online banking.

44% have used their phone to look up real estate listings or other information about a place to live.

43% to look up information about a job.

40% to look up government services or information.

(Continued)

30% to take a class or get educational content.

18% to submit a job application.

Source: Smith, Aaron. *U.S. Smartphone Use in 2015.* Pew Research Group, April 1, 2015. http://www.pewinternet.org/2015/04/01/us-smartphone-use-in-2015/. Reprinted with permission from Pew Research Center.

Snowden, Edward

Known as one of the most prominent "whistle-blowers" in recent history, Edward Snowden (1983–) is an American who leaked classified information from the National Security Agency (NSA). Having leaked over a hundred-thousand documents, he is alternately being hailed as a hero for freedom of speech and a traitor to his government.

Snowden is a U.S. citizen who claimed to be incensed over the attack on the World Trade Towers in New York City on September 11, 2001 (Bamford 2014, 88). At that point he decided to join the Army's special forces unit, but after being accepted and in training for the physical fitness component of the unit, he broke both legs and was discharged a few months later. After the Army he got a job as a security guard at a facility that required he get a high-level security clearance, which he did without incident. He was later offered a job at the CIA where he was in the global communications division, dealing with computer issues. He was trained by the CIA at a secret school for intelligence experts, and after training completion, was assigned to a unit investigating the banking industry, and housed in Geneva, Switzerland. There, he witnessed many of the compromises CIA agents were faced with in the course of their duties. He also met many spies who were deeply opposed to the U.S. policies in Iraq and the Middle East.

In 2010, Snowden moved to the National Security Agency (NSA) and worked as a technical expert in Japan. In 2011, he was relocated to Maryland where he worked with Dell computers, a CIA subcontractor, as the lead technologist to solve technical problems for the CIA. In 2012, he was sent to Hawaii where he found out that the CIA was passing private communications and metadata to Israeli intelligence in the form of e-mails and phone calls of millions of Arab and Palestinian Americans who had relatives in Palestine. He also learned that the CIA was spying on the pornography consumption of people who were considered political radicals.

Snowden moved on to work with another NSA contractor in 2013, Booz Allen Hamilton, where he was in charge of intercepting cyberattacks domestically and internationally. Part of his job was planting malware into systems around the world and stealing information. He also dealt with intelligence from China that involved the NSA's hacking into university, hospital, and civilian infrastructures. He also was in charge of investigating a cyberwarfare program code-named Monster-Mind—a program that would attack potentially dangerous malware that Snowden determined to be a potentially dangerous in terms of accidentally starting a war. Though he shared his concerns with other NSA employees, his own personal code of ethics was brought to the boiling point, and he decided to do something drastic. He said, "It's not really hard to take that step—not only do I believe in something, I believe in it enough that I'm willing to set my own life on fire and burn it to the ground" (Bamford 2014, 89).

Within months, he had loaded much of the material he had been working on onto thumb drives, and he left for Hong Kong, where he met with journalist Glenn Greenwald and filmmaker Laura Poitras. He released the information about the NSA's secret dealings that he believed violated appropriate protocol, and the news of the leaks went viral. Nine days later, he publicly revealed his identity.

On June 14, 2013, the U.S. Department of Justice charged Snowden with two counts of violating the Espionage Act and theft of government property and the U.S. Department of State revoked his passport. According to Russian President Vladimir Putin, Snowden also met with Russian diplomats while in Hong Kong and arranged for asylum in Russia, where he has remained since that time.

Some people call Snowden a patriot, while others call him a traitor. Some reporters who have clandestinely met with him often cite the hero and villain activities in the same stories, some people and public programs have honored him for his bravery in making these abuses of privacy known to the world. Glenn Greenwald wrote about his fateful meeting with Snowden in Hong Kong in May 2013, and wrote a book titled *No Place to Hide: Edward Snowden, the NSA, and the U.S. Surveillance State*, published in 2014. Greenwald's feeling is that Snowden is a hero and a patriot for his commitment to showing how the United States has abused the surveillance system through NSA operations. In fall 2014, Laura Poitras released a documentary about Snowden and the NSA called *CitizenFour* based upon the information he shared with her and Glenn Greenwald in Hong Kong. The documentary won an Oscar in 2015.

Snowden, like the hackers of Anonymous and WikiLeaks show that in the digital age, it is relatively easy for an individual to influence world events when acting as a counterpoint to traditional media that relies on gatekeepers to vet information. Clay Shirky, writing in the *Columbia Journalism Review*, cited Snowden as a harbinger of the future of political journalism in which the power of the "leaker" points to the failure of the mainstream press to serve the public. The result is a skeptical public that responds to the power of an individual rather than the controls of the press or the government (Shirky 2015, 45–46).

In September 2014, Snowden received the "Right Livelihood Honorary Award," considered the alternative to the Nobel Prize, both conferred by Sweden.

See also: Anonymous; WikiLeaks

Further Reading

Bamford, James. 2014. "The Most Wanted Man in the World." *Wired*, 22: 88–95.

Greenwald, Glenn. 2014. *No Place to Hide: Edward Snowden, the NSA, and the U.S. Surveillance State.* New York: Henry Holt.

Shirky, Clay. 2015 (March/April). "Revolt of the Clerks." *Columbia Journalism Review*, 45–49.

"World News: Edward Snowden: Winning Sweden's Alternative Nobel Prize Is Vindication." 2014. *The Guardian.* Accessed September 26, 2015: http://www.theguardian.com/world/video/2014/sep/25/edward-snowden-sweden-alternative-nobel-prize-video.

Social Media

There are different interpretations of what some people mean with they refer to *social media*. One way to look at the phenomenon is that all forms of media are inherently social to some degree, or they would not be "mediating" messages between senders and receivers of messages. More specifically, there are three ways of looking at the characteristics that make up what we usually mean when we refer to social media: (1) The technical aspects of social media including the hardware, like smartphones or laptops; (2) the content that includes the programs that make social networking possible with identifiable names like Facebook or Pinterest (sometimes described as the software); and (3) the features of Web 2.0 that allow the Internet to be used as a means of interactive (two-way) communication that has had the greatest impact on other media industries. From the economic perspective, social media have resulted in a variety of new economic models, many of which are hybrids from legacy forms of media as well as some entirely new ways of thinking about how social media are paid for, and by whom. From the social perspective there are a range of ways of looking at the impact and importance of social media ranging from the way one thinks about democracy and political governance to sharing intimacies with those who are emotionally close to you. But whatever variation on a definition people choose to emphasize, social media have become integral components for the way we communicate today and for the way we see ourselves relating to others and in relationships with others.

With social media making an impact on our lives from technological, content, industry-oriented, economic, and social perspectives, we should realize that they are not responsible for all of the changes in our society and in the world. They may be critical factors, but all exist alongside the media forms that preceded social media, and all are used in environments in which we have a physical presence that has been shaped by socialization factors, and an online presence, some of which we have control over and some of which are created and shaped by others, and then presented to us. If there are unique characteristics that cut across all forms of social media, they are most likely those of time and space, but, even then, all forms of media have used those characteristics in their unique ways.

Instead, what social media do is speed up our sense of time, and change our sense of space faster than any previous form of media humans have ever had. Steve Wozniak, cofounder of Apple Inc., believes that social media have created an environment in which things seem to happen faster and faster, and that the biggest problem we have today is trying to deal with how quickly change occurs (Wozniak 2015). It is the *speed of change* that he sees as the defining feature of social media, and his assertion suggests that even our sense of place (i.e., geographic boundaries) is changing rapidly. The Internet and cyberspace allow us to be in one physical space and, at the same time, in another space that is hard to fathom, as we send and receive messages from around the world from our homes or workplaces. And, because we can connect with others from virtually anywhere, anytime, those small portable technologies that we often use for social media continually present us with different situations that blur traditional concepts of space, and traditional concepts of public and private behaviors and communication contexts.

Many of those communicative contexts are outlined in the entries in this encyclopedia, but to address the phenomenon of social media, it might be useful to break down the categories that present specific points of entry for us as we analyze the impact of social media and contemporary life. As identified in the entries in this encyclopedia, social media have the ability to help us *friend* others, *follow* others, *text* others (meaning that the forms we use to connect to others are unique to social media), and *connect* to others. In each one of these communication contexts, social media facilitate the human interactions while increasing the use of technologies of communication that function as tools to shape human interaction.

The industries that use social media to deliver their content have changed and continue to change. Some have become powerhouses for information access and transfer, and others have been short-lived, or acquired by larger companies and forced to change. But all of these industries have developed new economic models for effective delivery of content. We've come a long way since the Internet was developed with the purpose of allowing us to collaborate online from distances and the initial idea that the World Wide Web would allow scientists and educators to share knowledge. While these features still exist, the commercial aspects of social media industries have attracted the lion's share of attention and have created the widest range of economic models for funding commercial services.

Social changes have accompanied our use of social media and have allowed us to develop a new vocabulary and a way of thinking about our place in the world and what we feel is important. New values have been introduced because of the speed of change afforded by social media, and older concepts of what was meant by "democracy," "privacy," "security," and "identity" have all begun to enter our discourse to see if, or how, our lives are changing because of social media.

Social media are also used in businesses and professional life as well as for personal use involving information flow and entertainment. Because social media so often include portable technologies like mobile phones, cameras, or laptops, they are often assumed to be used in very personal ways, sometimes causing a problem for intimacy and inappropriate self-disclosure in public places. One criticism, or trade-off (depending on your point of view), is that participating in social media means that your body and mind respond to an always "on" lifestyle. As danah boyd (she prefers lowercase letters for her name) describes the social media lifestyle, "It's about living in a world where being networked to people and information wherever and whenever you need it is just assumed" (boyd 2014, 72). This feature is in marked contrast to the separation that had previously existed about work and home life, work and leisure, and the way we have become familiar with a number of social practices, like shopping, where we are when we want to be entertained, and what we know about the surveillance of the environment (either from news, or from the changing nature of what it means to know about the relationships of individuals and their communities or governments). The public/private use of social media is often the focus of criticism of how people blur their public and private senses of self, and perhaps these aspects are often some of the most heavily criticized features of the social media phenomenon.

Social media have the potential to allow a different type of community to develop that is not place-based, but rather, more ephemeral, or even considered to be an "imaginary" place. This aspect of using personal technologies, and especially portable technology, is deeply connected to how people use social media, where they use it, and what the form of social media and social interaction then becomes in terms of meaningful communication for that user. In many ways social media are an outgrowth of communication and information industries that have changed the way they function so that they cater to individual use, rather than use by large, heterogeneous, anonymous audiences, often the target markets for mass media. In addition to a strong interest by legacy forms of mass media, like radio, television, print, film, and the earlier music industry, to deliver the same content to as many people as possible, social media allow for much greater individuality in the makeup of the audience. Some social media is person-to-person, while some use a protocol that open up communication channels (often called one of the democratizing effects of social media) for many.

Social media are often criticized for targeting individuals as consumers to the degree that users have choices, but end up choosing messages that are most aligned with their previously held values. Therefore, criticism of social media and the press often devolves into the situation in which people choose only that information that they want, and often, this leads to knowing less, rather than exploring a variety of viewpoints before making up one's mind.

Social media also can be abused, as in the case of cyberbullying, in which we see individuals use forms of social media to harass, bully, or degrade someone. Even when media allow communities to form for civic purposes, we know that social media can also be used to deceive or control people. Similarly, the more we use the Internet for financial transactions, the more we risk being victims of cyber-crimes from hackers or thieves.

See also: Cyberbullying; Cybercrime; Cyberspace; Friending; Identity; Privacy

Further Reading

boyd, danah. 2014. "Participating in the Always-On Lifestyle." In *The Social Media Reader*, edited by Michael Mandiberg. New York: New York University Press, 71–76.

Hanson, Jarice. 2007. *24/7: How Cell Phones and the Internet Change the Way We Live, Work, and Play.* Westport, CT: Praeger.

Hunsinger, Jeremy, and Theresa Senft, eds. *The Social Media Handbook.* New York: Routledge.

Wozniak, Steve. 2015. "A Conversation with Steve Wozniak." Springfield Public Forum, Springfield, MA, May 1.

Excerpts from the "Social Media Update 2014," Pew Research Center, January 9, 2015

About half (49%) of Instagram users and 17% of Pinterest users engage with their respective platforms daily, although neither of these represent a significant change from 2013. Some 36% of Twitter users visit the site daily, but this actually represents a 10-point decrease from the 46% who did so in 2013. While the 13% of LinkedIn users who engage with the platform daily is unchanged from 2013, the proportion of users who use the site weekly or less often increased significantly—that is, more users log on less frequently.

Fully 52% of online adults use two or more social media sites, a significant increase from the 42% who did so in 2013.

(Continued)

Social Networking

The term *social networking*, like social media, is subject to a few different descriptions and there is no one absolute definition. The term generally refers to the personal connections people make to each other over media that connect to the Internet (through wired or wireless means). Web 2.0 allows for the interactive nature of communication over social networks. But perhaps unique to social networking is the reality that we can communicate with others over technologies that know no geographic bounds. Social networking has the power to connect us and truly represents what it means to be in a *global village*.

Social networks pay a debt to the work of people like Norbert Wiener, who provided the concept of *cybernetics* to help conceptualize the way systems and their structures operate; the amount of control exerted over those systems; and the feedback the system receives so that it can monitor the effectiveness of the system. The root word *cyber* when applied to *cyberspace* gives us a sense of where those social networks exist in comparison to the real world. Because cyberspace is a unique concept, we can think of the way the systems that operate in cyberspace influence our concepts of space (real vs. virtual) and time (synchronous vs. asynchronous, real vs. virtual).

Wiener's work, along with the many innovators and organizations that have conducted research into how social networks operate, has given rise to a number of theories about how humans and machines work together in a cybernetic system. With the Internet providing a distribution form that allows us to transcend time and space, and the World Wide Web making Web 2.0 possible for allowing messages to be sent back and forth, interactively and seamlessly, we have the structure available to facilitate the flow of a wide range of information. Even though we should be cognizant of the digital divide and the inequality of the people of the world to use technologies that allow us to socially network to others, we can think of social networking as the most powerful means of communicating to and with individuals and masses around the world.

Like social media, social networks influence the way people friend, follow, text (communicate), and connect to others, but they also do more. Social networks fundamentally shift the way people interact when the physical body is not present. They are continually evolving and changing, so while they are often thought of as facilitating the way we connect with others, it is also important to realize that social networks can potentially change the way people also interact in face-to-face situations because the habits and expectations we form through social media and social networks are often blurred with the type of communication we use in face-to-face communication. For example, people's sense of what friends are can be influenced by the way they think of online friends and real-world, face-to-face encounters with friends. A sense of a person's popularity can be influenced by the number of "likes" or "dislikes" they receive when posting something in an online format. And, most important, a person's sense of identity or digital presence can moderate the way a person migrates from an online (virtual) space to a real-world space.

Furthermore, social networks can change the way people think about a whole host of forms of communication from personal interaction to participating in society. Intention in sending or responding to messages on social networks becomes complicated by behaviors that are not always particularly well thought out. Twitter may be a good platform for spreading jokes, memes, and pointed observations, but the short messaging service is less effective when engaging in dialogue is necessary. Even elements of participation may be unequal, or less than one might imagine, when they participate on a social network. For example, most of the people who log on to social networks are lurkers, rather than participants. A lurker is a member of an online community who observes, but doesn't actively participate in interaction online. While it may be impossible to accurately identify how many members who read social networks are lurkers rather than active posters, a general rule of thumb is that on the Internet, only 1 percent of the members actively post online, 10 percent might interact with the posted information, but 89 percent of the traffic will be made up of lurkers (Arthur 2006).

Honesty on social networks is also a subject that receives a lot of attention, from the person who hides anonymously to rant, bully, or subject someone to harm, to the person who posts an old picture on a dating site, hoping to look a little better than they might in reality. The psychological dimensions of honesty and presentation of self on a social network is complicated and best covered elsewhere in this book, but it is appropriate to note that social networks are a conduit for information, but individuals are responsible for what they post online.

Social networks often become specially focused communities that have the benefit of extending beyond traditional geographic boundaries. People on social networks like Facebook, LinkedIn, or MySpace can connect with other people on the network by friending or following them—that is, by asking them to become friends or followers—and friends can see each other's profiles that include whatever personal information the poster wants to share. Blogs, comments, photos, videos, and music identify the host, but sometimes the messages created for one set of "friends" may not be appropriate for others, like potential employers or even older family members. People with similar interests often participate in online communities that can also be called social networks. Some networks are organized around sports, celebrity gossip, health information, or other topics.

One of the benefits of social networks is that they can operate either synchronously (in real time) or asynchronously (over time). Synchronous communication takes place in a live, often back-and-forth exchange and most closely resembles the time in thought and action as face-to-face conversation, even though the individuals participating in the communication may not be able to see each other while communicating. In asynchronous communication, participants receive and respond to messages at their leisure. For example, people often leave posts on social networks and then wait for others to read and respond. The result is a "conversation" spread over a longer time.

When it comes to political uses of social networks, gender, age, and racial gaps have been noticed in the literature on who uses social networks for political purposes. More women participate on social networks than men, and younger people and minorities are also more likely than others to use social networks.

Social capital is the idea that social networks provide value to those who participate because of a number of benefits that can come from connecting to others through the networks. In a Harvard University Saguaro Seminar on Civic Engagement in America, the value of social capital was found to have four major themes that are unique to social networks. Social networks *facilitate information flow* that helps us learn about the ideas of others. This can be very important for political and civic engagement, but it has a utilitarian purpose for helping us feel connected to others, too. There are *norms of reciprocity* that also evolve on social networks that facilitate a sense of belonging to a community. *Collective action* can often come about when people feel truly connected to each other for a specific purpose, like raising awareness of a fund-raiser to benefit autistic children, and getting people to participate. Finally, as identified in the Harvard Saguaro Seminar, solidarity and a broader sense of identity can be facilitated by social networks that help change people from having an "I" mentality to a "we" mentality (Saguaro Seminar, 2015).

This idea is particularly important at a time in history when, as author Robert Putnam wrote in *Bowling Alone*, social conditions have made us become increasingly disconnected from family, friends, neighbors, and our democratic structures (Putnam 2000). Whereas once upon a time a person would be born, live, and die within a short range of their birth family, our real world challenges have come to incorporate a loss of geographic or physical connection to primary social groups, like family. Increasingly the migration of individuals to other places and the creation of different affinity groups can lead us to feel more like nomads than as active community members who participate in civic actions for the good of everyone in the community. Families break up, reform, and create different relationships. The social stigma of divorce, once so present in American culture in the early twentieth century, is no longer the problem it once was. The equality of civil rights, whether race, ethnicity, or class oriented, have been joined by the civil rights that have allowed same-sex marriages in different states, and a growing understanding and acceptance of the trans community. But as we see the changes emerging in the social structures that form, reinforce, and change social values, we can also feel less "connected" to the past, and the values of our parents and grandparents. Social networks may be the answer to how we may ultimately reconnect to others as well as to the structures that make it possible to thrive in a more globalized world.

When we think of social networks as replacing the type of social engagement in more traditional social structures, we start to ask a number of new questions. Do we lose part of what it means to be a member of a larger society when most of our interactions are online? What should we know about the world to be able to make more informed decisions about what we do?

One of the most fundamental questions of our current, media-saturated environment is whether social networks can fill the loss of traditional social engagement. Many scholars address this topic from the perspective of social involvement in civic matters in a democracy, and ask whether social networks can replace what has been lost in America today when so few who are eligible to vote actually go to the polls. The most recent record of voting in a presidential race was in 2012 when 61.8 percent of the eligible voting population actually cast a vote. This can be contrasted to 2010, a congressional election year, when only 45.5 percent of the population voted (Data Web 2012). But certainly, voting is not the only measurement of civic involvement.

Examples of using social networking for political mobilization are apparent in the Arab Spring and Occupy Movements, but the use of social networks for direct connection to politicians and to federal agencies are also examples of political activity. Most politicians have Twitter feeds and a digital presence on social media with the hope of spreading their news and information to constituents and those who might be unsure of their position on a matter. Political fund-raising has been revolutionized by the use of social networks, which have been valuable tools to reach audiences.

But along with the use of social networks to support campaigns, the relationship of news and the public, vital to a healthy democracy, has been a concern of many. As so many legacy companies change their practices to reach niche audiences and online consumers, the role of journalism has changed, too.

One of the biggest issues in this category has to do with the loss of the professional standards of those big media companies that had formerly dominated news and information that affected what we know, and how we know it. Social media presents us with a vast range of points of view through news sources, links to more information, and even the ability to post comments (in many cases), but those benefits are somewhat ameliorated by the partisan positions of the writers. The authenticity and veracity of news undergoes less scrutiny in online news services, and, while information can be delivered quickly, it is not always delivered thoroughly.

Social networks can be updated constantly, and information can change, but whether that information is valid or not is of critical concern for the person who sees it and takes for granted that it is truthful. Similarly, the loss of major forms of newspapers once considered "official" records of events, like the *New York Times* or the *Washington Post*, have changed in status. While the print versions of these two newspaper have traditionally featured news on the front page, many online services tend to feature gossip and entertainment content. As online sources become more available, the major newspapers of record have lost some of their importance.

According to the 2015 Pew Research Group's annual *State of the News Media* report, "39 of the top 50 digital news websites have more traffic to their sites and associated applications coming from mobile devices than from desktop computers" (Mitchell 2015). Drawing from data reported by comScore, an analytics firm, these data reflect that people who use computers (desktop and laptop) tend to spend more time on the sites they consume, while mobile consumers spend less time on news sites.

If we consider how and why most people use social networks, we can shed light on some of these social issues and make some reasonable assumptions about how and in what way(s) social networks help a person negotiate information about their worlds that influences their sense of self within that world. While sweeping statements may provide summary points, they should not be taken as a reflection of every aspect of using social networks.

When social networks are viewed with the idea of connecting people to things they care about, we see the mediating factors of people in shaping what we know. Perhaps using social networks for news and information brings someone into a position of seeking viewpoints they share, and there may be some negative impact of that as people screen out diverse viewpoints, but we can't assume that always happens. If we look at the sheer amount of information available on the web, we can be optimistic about the wealth of information to which many of us have access. At the same time we need to be aware that not everyone participates on social networks, and they may have a different viewpoint of the relationship of media and the environment.

While social networks do fundamentally allow us to connect to others for purposes of friending and following, the way we use social networks influences the range of information to which we may expose ourselves. News and participation in a political environment are possible, but not necessarily inevitable. With more people using social networks for entertainment and the more amusing aspects of connecting to others, we need to wonder whether the promise of the Internet and World Wide Web are really becoming true.

But we can be sure of one thing. Social networks will change and evolve over time. At any moment we can see a snapshot of present-day reality, but realize that social media and social networks are still in their adolescence. We have a long way to go before they reach maturity.

See also: Anonymity; Arab Spring; Blogs; Digital Divide; Identity; Occupy Movement; Privacy

Further Reading

Arthur, Charles. 2006. "What Is the 1% Rule?" *The Guardian*. Accessed January 8, 2015: http://www.theguardian.com/technology/2006/jul/20/guardianweeklytechnology section2.

"Data Web: Voting and Registration." 2012. U.S. Census Bureau. Accessed May 6, 2015: http://thedataweb.rm.census.gov/TheDataWeb_HotReport2/voting/voting.hrml.

Fallows, James. 2010. "How to Save the News." *The Atlantic Monthly*, 305: 44–56.

Gainous, Jason, and Kevin M. Wagner. 2014. *Tweeting to Power: The Social Media Revolution in American Politics*. Oxford and New York: Oxford University Press, 44–45.

Mitchell, Amy. 2015. "State of the News Media 2015." Pew Research Center. Accessed May 6, 2015: http://www.journalism.org/2015/04/29/state-of-the-news-media-2015/.

Putnam, Robert D. 2000. *Bowling Alone: The Collapse and Revival of American Community*. New York: Simon & Schuster.

Saguaro Seminar on Civic Engagement in America. n.d. Harvard University Kennedy School. Accessed January 8, 2015: http://www.hks.harvard.edu/programs/saguaro/about /the-original-saguaro-seminar-meetings.

Spam

Spam is a term given to unwanted information distributed over the Internet. It is also called *unsolicited* information on the Internet. The first use of e-mail to send what later came to be considered "spam" was sent in 1994 by lawyers Laurence Canter and Martha Siegel, who used bulk postings over Usenet to clients with the purpose of promoting their law practice that focused on immigration issues. The word *spam* comes from a 1970s British comedy show, called *Monty Python's Flying Circus*. In a sketch, two people are in a restaurant where the menu includes the canned meat "Spam" with every item.

Once the Internet became available to the public and commercial spammers became active, the problem of spam started to attract attention. Individuals could send spam, or flood someone's mailbox just by hitting "send" for one message over and over, but the bigger problem came from the professional spammers who used computers to generate multiple messages sent out over networks that they hacked. In 2008, Facebook won an $873 million judgment against a professional spammer that had been the largest penalty up until that time, but spammers were (and are) hard to track down and locate. Many of them used bots to send thousands of messages within fractions of seconds.

One of the most notorious spammers was Sanford Wallace, who brazenly called himself the "Spam King" and "Spamford." Wallace lived in New Hampshire but hacked peoples' personal e-mail accounts around the country to send advertisements to their lists of friends, without the host knowing about it. He then received a portion of the per-click revenue when people opened those messages. Like many spammers, he targeted those sites that had the best networks of people with like-minded interests, and social networks became his primary vehicle to reach his audience. In 2008, MySpace took him to court and won a $230 million judgment against him that caused him to file for bankruptcy. Then, in October 2009, Facebook sued Wallace and won a $711 million judgment against him for hacking personal accounts. This time he was sentenced to prison. In that same year, Ferris Research, an organization that tracked spammers and online activity, estimated that the loss to companies that had been hacked by professional spammers was in the area of $130 billion worldwide (Fletcher 2009). These costs reflected the expenses companies had to find and track down spammers and take legal actions against them.

Spam problems abounded because the Internet was originally set up with open architecture. Because it was thought that the Internet would be used for collaboration, little thought was given to possible abuses of using the system. Before professional filters and new security settings were installed on computers, it was estimated that about 90 million spam e-mails were sent every day and about 85 percent of the messages coming to an e-mail mailbox were spam (Fletcher 2009). Most of those messages came from commercial spammers who had the technology to simultaneously send out multiple messages; a considerable number of those spam messages were for pornography sites.

In the United States the problem of spam became so great that Congress held hearings to figure out what to do about it. The acronym CAN-SPAM derives from the bill's full name: Controlling the Assault of Non-Solicited Pornography and Marketing Act of 2003. The CAN-SPAM Act of 2003, signed into law by President George W. Bush established the United States' first national standards for the sending of commercial e-mail. The Federal Trade Commission (FTC) was charged with enforcing the provisions of the act.

The CAN-SPAM Act is occasionally referred to by critics as the "You-Can-Spam" Act because the bill failed to prohibit many types of e-mail spam, and the wording was so ambiguous it was difficult to understand who was really responsible for sending spam messages. The act also made no mention of requiring e-mailers to get permission before they sent marketing messages to other people. It did, however, set up a complaint division at the FTC so that people could notify the FTC of spam that they were receiving. By 2005, the FTC reported that the number of spam messages had begun to fall off, but most people felt that consumers had taken active steps to set up filters and firewalls on their computers that screened some of the spam directly into their "junk" folders.

Since the passage of the CAN-SPAM Act in the United States, the problem hasn't lessened—in fact, it has worsened. Today there are major spam centers around the world in countries like Russia, China, India, and Canada, where computers send out over 650,000 messages every hour, equaling more than a billion a day.

Professional spammers can harvest e-mail addresses in a number of ways. Software can scrub regular general newsgroups online and extract e-mail addresses, or they can program spambots to search for the "@" sign to extract an e-mail address. Some sites called "squeeze pages" ask people to type in their e-mail address to receive more information about something, and these addresses can be replicated for spammers. Some traders sell CDs full of e-mail addresses to professional spammers.

In his excellent cultural history of spam called *Spam: A Shadow History of the Internet*, Finn Bruntun parallels the development of spam with the Internet's becoming open to the public and the start of e-commerce. In his introduction he demonstrates the range of people who perpetuate spam as a problem. "Spam is not a force of nature but the product of particular populations distributed throughout all the world's countries: programmers, con artists, cops, lawyers, bots and their botmasters, scientists, pill merchants, social media entrepreneurs, hackers, identity thieves, sysadmins, victims, pornographers, do-it-yourself vigilantes, government officials and stock touts" (Bruntun 2013, xiv–xv).

See also: Bots; E-Mail; Malware

Further Reading

Bruntun, Finn. 2013. *Spam: A Shadow History of the Internet.* Cambridge, MA: MIT Press, xiv–xv.

Fletcher, Dan. 2009. "A Brief History of Spam." *Time.* Accessed April 21, 2015: http://content.time.com/time/business/article/0,8599,1933796,00.html.

"Rise and Fall of Online Advertising." n.d. 1st Web Designer. Accessed March 23, 2015: http://www.1stwebdesigner.com/online-advertising-history/.

**Excerpts from the "FTC'S CAN-SPAM Act:
A Compliance Guide for Business"**

Despite its name, the CAN-SPAM Act doesn't apply just to bulk email. It covers all commercial messages, which the law defines as "any electronic mail message the primary purpose of which is the commercial advertisement or promotion of a commercial product or service," including email that promotes content on commercial websites.

Each separate email in violation of the CAN-SPAM Act is subject to penalties of up to $16,000, so non-compliance can be costly.

Don't use false or misleading header information.

Don't use deceptive subject lines. The subject line must accurately reflect the content of the message.

Identify the message as an ad.

Tell recipients where you're located.

Tell recipients how to opt out of receiving future email from you.

Honor opt-out requests promptly.

Monitor what others are doing on your behalf.

Source: CAN-SPAM Act: A Compliance Guide for Business. Federal Trade Commission, September 2009. https://www.ftc.gov/tips-advice/business-center /guidance/can-spam-act-compliance-guide-business.

Spyware

Search engines, online stores, and other websites also collect information about their users. *Spyware* is special type of software that gathers information about people's Internet and web browsing habits. Most spyware is legally installed without a user's knowledge. Even though the term seems to suggest political espionage, the typical spyware really deals more with the consumer's right of privacy and their control over their computer and mobile platforms. Some people even consider cookies a form of spyware, but, generally, the term is reserved for the range of programs and tools that monitor a person's use of their own technology for purposes of finding out about that person's behaviors. Generally, spyware is legal, though it may be unethical or morally questionable. Some examples of how spyware can be used help differentiate spyware from adware or malware.

In 2010, the Lower Merion School District in southeastern Pennsylvania furnished students with MacBook laptops that had web cameras that could be activated at the school. When students used their laptops at home, the webcam sent pictures back to the school and school personnel could see the environment in which the student was using the computer. In one case, a student was called in for what was believed to be his taking pills, when in reality he was eating candy (Cringely 2010). Once students and parents found out about the school's use of the webcams, they realized that all sorts of personal privacy could be invaded by the use of the cameras. When a class-action suit against the district was filed on behalf of the 2,400 students who received the school-sponsored laptops, the school responded by saying that the webcams were only activated to track lost or stolen laptops, but they agreed they should have told students and parents about it. The school district had the right to install the spyware, but they did not have the right to abuse it, and they had an ethical responsibility to inform students and parents that the spyware was part of the computer package. After the FBI and local police investigated, the project was scrapped.

Spyware is now a commercial app sold for monitoring mobile phones, especially in situations where parents may want to know what their children are really doing when they are away from home, or perhaps, more commonly, when a spouse thinks their partner is cheating on them. Employers who give their employees company-sponsored mobile phones may want to monitor the employee's behavior, too. Mobile phone spyware, which is completely legal, can be purchased for as little as $15 or for several hundred dollars. As Chris Wysopal, cofounder of Veracode, a software security company, said: "Not only can you look at a person's e-mail or listen to their calls, in some cases you can also just turn on the microphone [on a smart phone] and listen to what the person is doing any time you want" (Ramirez 2010). Though different states and municipalities are just coming to terms with spyware on mobile platforms now, the number of commercial vendors have begun to grow. A person must have legal access to a smartphone to install a piece of spyware, so families that use mobile phones as family property can legally use it, and employers who furnish a company phone to an employee can use it. Installation of the app takes only a few minutes, and it can be monitored on a remote site.

While the tools that fit the classic definition of spyware are legal, they are often confused with adware, which is also legal, and malware, which is not. When Google uses one of its adware systems to track a user's buying behavior and then sells that data to a marketing company, it uses personal information that the user might not know about, but the adware is legal because the customer agreed in the "terms of service" to allow Google to sell that information to a third party. The big problem, of course, is that consumers rarely read the "terms of service" information required when signing up for a service.

Malware, on the other hand, is not legal and often is used to disrupt a person's normal use of their technology. As the name implies, malware is launched with a malicious intent to spy on someone's behavior without their knowledge or infect their machines with viruses or worms that destroy content.

Quite often the terms *spyware*, *adware*, and *malware* are used interchangeably, but that use is factually incorrect and can lead to important misunderstandings.

See also: Advertising; Malware; Privacy

Further Reading

Cringely, Robert X. 2010. "When Schools Spy on Their Students, Bad Things Happen." *PC World*. Accessed April 21, 2015: http://www.pcworld.com/article/190019/school_spying_webcams.html.

Ramirez, Jessica. 2010. "Spyware on Your Cell Phone?" *Newsweek*. Accessed April 21, 2015: http://www.newsweek.com/spyware-your-cell-phone-73569.

Streaming Media

Streaming media is the term that describes how content is sent over the Internet through wired or wireless means, to be received over a television, computer, smartphone, or digital media player (in general). *Streaming* technology compresses a signal and transfers it so that it can be transmitted over a wireless form and used in real time or saved to a hard drive or other storage technology. The *media* part of the term reflects both the technologies that send and receive the stream, as well as the type of industry to which it refers. *Streaming audio* generally refers to the music industry or to podcasts, but Netflix is a company that streams film or television content to our television sets (if they are compatible), computers, or other digital devices. E-books and audio books can also be streamed to any digital technology. There are literally hundreds of different streaming companies that specialize in streaming one form of content or another.

Today, streaming media can present consumers with real-time access to live sporting events, concerts, plays, and other forms of entertainment, or prerecorded content. Some content can be stored and then digitally transferred to other personal devices. For example, if you stream music from a bona fide online music store, you can have it loaded to your smartphone, but later, transfer it to an iPod or computer. The consumer products necessary to receive streamed content have to be sophisticated enough to handle the amount of content, so streaming video, for example, can't be shown on a regular television set, though it can be seen on an

Internet-compatible television, or hooked up through a computer or digital device to capture and recompose the streamed content so that it can be viewed.

There can be many reasons a person would prefer to stream content rather than buy a CD or other software in addition to the lower cost streaming technologies offer. People can create playlists that are much more personalized to their own tastes. They can use features to stop and rewind simultaneously as the content is being streamed. But perhaps the biggest reason is that the costs to all of the "middle level" personnel in the supply chain is lower; streamed media has no cover art, dust jacket, or distribution to a store or through an intermediary. Therefore it is simply faster and cheaper to use than buying or renting the physical objects of media forms.

While most people think of streaming technologies as consumer products, streaming has also changed the nature of businesses and industries. Movie theaters have shifted from using traditional celluloid-based film to showing "movies" through the ease of streaming product from a distributor. Educators often use streaming content for massively open online courses (MOOCs) or to access live presentations elsewhere. Many businesses are shifting to streaming conferences and meetings because it is much cheaper than sending an entire staff to another location for a presentation or meeting in real time. But, for many, it is the home-based form of streaming that is most well known and that presents an alternative to the distribution of every other form of media content.

The technology used in streaming media has a long history, but most of the industries that have begun to use streaming media are much newer, since it took a long time for the components necessary to stream media to work efficiently—particularly in terms of sending video signals that don't freeze or visually break up during transmission and reception. But the history of streaming involves the cost of technology and issues of copyright—both issues that are still very much with us today.

The precursor to streaming media was the process of multiplexing—sending multiple analog signals over a wired system of communication. The process was patented by George Owen Squier, a major general in the U.S. Army signal corps who experimented with sending audio over wires between 1910 and 1920. Many electronics companies were working on the same problem, but in 1922 a company called the North American Company bought Squier's patent and started a company called Wired Radio, which in 1934 was renamed Muzak. The company began going after commercial clients who would play background music in stores, elevators, and other places and quickly became so popular that by 1937, Warner Brothers bought the company especially for the purpose of sending movie music over the system with the hope of encouraging listeners to come see their movies (Baumgarten 2010). After World War II, Warner Brothers sold the business.

The Muzak Company eventually fell on hard times and was franchised to a number of different owners. The new owners experimented with a number of business models, and, for a while, the music of Muzak was a satellite distribution service. But while Muzak was changing ownership and distribution forms, a number of newer technologies were being developed that simplified wireless distribution of signals and improved reception devices.

The transistor, developed in 1947 at Bell Labs, was a semiconductor that allowed radios to operate without wires, and made wireless portable radio a reality. The transistor was also the key technology that ultimately gave rise to integrated circuits and computer chips. But in the late 1940s, radio programs were already popular, and inexpensive portable radios helped spread the popularity of audio at the same time television was starting to be introduced into the American home.

By the 1970s streaming technology had improved to the point where it could be used more easily by professionals, but inexpensive receiving technologies did not come about for typical home consumers until the late 1990s and early 2000s. Early adopters used MP3 technologies (like Napster) to transfer music files in the late 1990s, but problems with *buffering* (loading a batch of signals at once, and then waiting for the next batch to load) prevented many people from really feeling that the streaming content was as reliable as prerecorded content. Once the iPod emerged in 2001, audio streaming technology had improved greatly for the consumer, and, after that, it didn't take long for streaming video technologies to emerge, too.

The problem of streaming video was harder to solve than streaming audio, because the signal requires more bandwidth. In 1995, Microsoft developed the ActiveMovie media player that could be used for streaming media that could be connected to a computer. In 1999, Microsoft released Windows Media Player 6.4, and, in the same year, Apple introduced its QuickTime 4 application for computers. But what really improved streaming services was the 2002 development of Adobe Flash, which made it possible to download video content, and suddenly, it seemed that a new distribution form for short-form video (like YouTube) was the new wave of the future.

Throughout the 2000s, streaming technologies improved greatly and streaming services began to attract niche audiences. A number of online music streaming companies started in the early 2000s, and Netflix started to stream full movies and television shows in 2007. Streaming music sales that started in the late 1990s began to overtake traditional music distribution by CD, much to the frustration of the Recording Industry Association of America (RIAA). By 2013, there were over 118.1 billion music streams (Masnick et al. 2014).

In 2008, Hulu began to stream some content from its group of investors, NBCUniversal Television, Fox Broadcasting, and Disney. For a short time Hulu was also supported by Providence Equity Partners, but this investor sold its 10 percent share in 2012. Hulu was started as an experiment in streaming television shows, clips, movies, and more by the companies that wanted to learn more about the potential audience for streamed content. Some services were supported by advertising and free to consumers, or at least free for a trial subscription, but the Hulu Plus service that included some games and sporting events is subscription-based. Hulu has also entered the original content arena, and produces a number of talk format and scripted programs.

In addition to the major shift in the music industry, other industries now routinely use streaming for the delivery of their products. Social media and social networking have contributed to the growth of streaming services by including live chats, online surveys, and more and make it much easier for friends to send links to content to other friends. Additionally, a growing number of companies have started to use streaming for the delivery of what might have traditionally been the domain of legacy television companies (broadcast and cable). Today, even companies that specialized in other types of business are exploring the possibility of new delivery systems for video content.

Now producers can upload full series of television programs to the Internet and advertisers have been able to use the nonstandard times to insert more advertising. No longer do the number of programs in a season conform to traditional legacy broadcast seasons. As a result, traditional television is now as likely to change as the traditional radio, film, and recorded music industries have.

YouTube has diversified into thousands of different "channels" that can be bought by companies, and Amazon, Netflix, and other media companies have started to explore using the Internet for entire series of shows. *Binge* watching, in which a person can view each episode in a series sequentially without having to wait a week until it has been broadcast, has challenged traditional *appointment* television (watching at a certain time every week). Webisodes, which were a bridge from one time videos online to short series, have cultivated viewers for the migration to watching online, whenever desired.

There are some new business models that have emerged in Web TV (online streaming of television content). According to Aymar Jean Christian, writing for the Media Industries Project at the Carsey-Wolf Center at the University of California, Santa Barbara, four types of Web TV networks are now in operation: (1) corporate, subscription networks; (2) corporate, ad-supported networks; (3) multichannel networks (like YouTube, for example), and (4) independent networks (Christian 2015). Each of these emerging networks has a different model of funding, and each targets different types of audiences.

Even legacy television broadcasters and cable operators have announced new streaming initiatives. HBO was among the first to announce that it would change its business model to break away from exclusive delivery to homes over cable services and would allow people to subscribe to a streaming service in 2015. NBC announced their new subscription service to viewers in 2015 for approximately $2.50–3.50 a month, complete with original shows created for the service.

One reason for the shift to streaming technologies has to do with the high cost of cable subscriptions and a growing belief particularly among young people that media content should be free. Though it has taken 40 years to migrate from the first music streaming to today's burgeoning video streaming market, technological improvements that make digital technologies more friendly, new consumer behaviors, and the idea that Internet delivery can still fuel advertising has pushed earlier companies toward more streaming models.

As each of the media industries explores different distribution methods relying on the Internet, we can expect to see new services emerge. Sometimes those services will blend economic models from legacy media as well as streaming technologies. A new streaming music service was announced in March 2015 by the rapper Jay Z, who, along with other major recording artists, launched a new service called Tidal that does just that. Each of the major artists signed on to Tidal will receive 3 percent equity in the company and will ultimately receive more compensation than that afforded by other streaming companies like iTunes, Google Play, or any other streaming music services. Tidal blends older economic models that pay established musical performers more, but also uses the much less expensive distribution system of streaming over the Internet to reach audiences based on a subscription model. When Tidal was initially launched, it had over 540,000 paid subscribers, but it was looking forward at the potential 7.7 million paying subscribers for music content (Gervino and Hampp 2015).

Streaming has many benefits. The cost of technologies for streaming are much lower than traditional delivery services such as physical disks, and people can personalize their viewer choices and playlists. With home technologies capable of streaming and sharing information, traditional companies have had to revise their business models to take into account consumer behavior.

At the same time, streaming can create a host of problems. Copyright is very difficult to control when digital content can be streamed from one device to another. Cloud-based storage systems sometimes fail, or they can tip off authorities about large caches of unauthorized (pirated) content.

Streaming media content may develop a number of additional models in the future, and it is likely that some blending of economic models from legacy media and the benefits of lower cost or free distribution will remain a part of the media environment.

See also: Cloud; Legacy Media; MP3; Piracy; Podcast

Further Reading

Baumgarten, Luke. 2012. "Elevator Going Down: The Story of Muzak." Red Bull Music Academy. Accessed April 1, 2015: http://www.redbullmusicacademy.com/magazine/history-of-muzak.

Christian, Ayhmar Jean. 2015. "Web TV Networks Challenge Linear Business Models." Media Industry Project, Carsey-Wolf Center, University of California at Santa Barbara. Accessed March 18, 2015: http://www.carseywolf.ucsb.edu/mip/article/web-tv-networks-challenge-linear-business-models.

Gervino, Tony, and Andrew Hampp. 2015. "Jay Z on Competing with Jimmy Iovine: 'I Don't Have to Lose . . . For You Guys to Win,'" *Billboard Magazine*. Accessed May 4, 2015: http://www.billboard.com/articles/business/6516945/jay-z-jimmy-iovine-streaming-tidal.

Masnick, Michael, Michael Ho, Joyce Hung, and Leigh Beadon. 2014. "The Sky Is Rising. Floor 64" (Report). Accessed April 2, 2015: https://www.ccianet.org/wpcontent/uploads/2014/10/Sky-Is-Rising-2014.pdf.

Ozer, Jan. 2011. "What Is Streaming?" Streaming Media.com. Accessed April 2, 2015: http://www.streamingmedia.com/Articles/ReadArticle.aspx?ArticleID=74052.

Porter, David. 2015. "Spotify vs. Pandora: Which Market Is Bigger?" *Forbes*. Accessed April 24, 2015: http://www.forbes.com/sites/davidporter/2015/04/24/spotify-vs-pandora-which-market-is-bigger/.

Surveillance

The idea of *surveillance* can have both positive and negative connotations. Some surveillance activities are conducted for safety and security, such as the cameras in public places that are intended to oversee public safety in urban areas, or that monitor activity in stores, schools, or airports, to watch for shoplifters, or the presence of unauthorized individuals. Few people have problems with those uses of technology to surveil an environment, but often the negative interpretation is used to describe how our civil liberties are being infringed upon by technology or people who work for government or business who eavesdrop on our privacy.

The Fourth Amendment to the U.S. Constitution states that "the right of the people to be secure in their persons, houses, papers, and effects, against unreasonable searches and seizures, shall not be violated, and no warrants shall issue, but upon probable cause, supported by oath or affirmation, and particularly describing the place to be searched, and the persons or things to be seized." However, the use of electronic media and social networks in particular that are used in both private and public places blurs the distinction that so clearly represented a sense of place in the 1700s.

Surveillance often brings to mind the relationship of government and the people, as evidenced by Edward Snowden's leaks concerning the National Security

Agency's (NSA) monitoring of phone calls and Internet use by some citizens suspected of terrorism. Surveillance without the knowledge of those being surveilled always points to the relationship of power between those being monitored and those doing the monitoring. But the more unobtrusive forms of surveillance can be just as powerful in shaping the dynamics of the information society.

Advertising and the types of technologies used to monitor a person's use of social media can be thought of as just as frightening as government surveillance of one's activities. The sense that the technologies we use can easily be monitored by others—whether for profit or for purposes of sharing one's identity without the individual's knowledge—creates an environment in which social values begin to change.

A typical reaction to the unauthorized or unknown aspects of the way technology can identify individuals is the position that "as long as I'm not doing anything wrong, what difference does it make?" But over time, we have seen how attitudes toward surveillance are changing. The Pew Internet and American Life Project surveyed 475 adults between November 26, 2014, and January 3, 2015, and found that 87 percent had heard something about the Snowden/NSA leaks, and a good number (30%) have taken steps to change their online behavior on social media. Of this group, 17 percent changed their social media privacy settings; 15 percent have chosen to use social media less often; 15 percent have avoided using some apps; and 13 percent have uninstalled apps. Additionally, 14 percent said they have changed their behavior to speak more in person instead of communicating online or on the phone, and 13 percent have avoided using certain terms when they use online communications (Rainie and Madden 2015).

Even though the events concerning Snowden and government surveillance of private activities are on the public's mind, we should also ask about the impact of changing attitudes about surveillance once the Snowden episode is well behind us, and, even more importantly, on shaping the attitudes of young children as they get older.

Many children today grow up with simple forms of surveillance. Sonograms, baby monitors, and cameras in child care facilities are common for prenatal to toddler stages, and in all of these categories it is easy to see how the benefits of surveilling's one's child can alleviate concerns of parents—but when those children grow up with an increase in the types of technologies that monitor actions, a normalization of the panoptic power (surveillance power) of technology abounds. What makes this more difficult for children and adults is the way we use social media in private and public places. The Fourth Amendment gave us protection within our homes, but what happens when we use technologies in the home to connect to a broader system that is controlled by Internet service providers (ISPs) and companies that value our personal information?

There are no easy answers for these questions, other than the simple assertion that we need to keep talking about the power of social media to infringe on our personal use of technology. In a way, the ability to be *followed* when that action is unwanted comes along part and parcel with the information society and our increased use of social media.

See also: Advertising; Bots; Cookies; Cybercrime; Data Mining; Privacy; Snowden, Edward; Spyware

Further Reading

Greenwald, Glenn. 2014. *No Place to Hide: Edward Snowden, the NSA, and the U.S. Surveillance State.* New York: Henry Holt.

Rainie, Lee, and Mary Madden. 2015. "Americans' Privacy Strategies Post-Snowden." Pew Research Center. Accessed May 4, 2015: http://www.pewinternet.org/2015/03/16/americans-privacy-strategies-post-snowden/.

Excerpts from the White House Press Release on the Cybersecurity Summit, February 13, 2015

As a nation, the United States has become highly digitally dependent . . . But this dependency also creates risks that threaten national security, private enterprises and individual rights. It is a threat not just here in the United States, but one that everyone, everywhere who is connected to cyberspace faces . . .

This Summit comes at a crucial point . . . cyber threats to individuals, businesses, critical infrastructure and national security have grown more diffuse, acute, and destructive. Despite improvements in network defense, cyber threats are evolving faster than the defenses that counter them. Malicious actors ranging from sophisticated nation states to common criminals to hacktivists take advantage of the anonymity, reach, and broad range of effects that cyberspace offers.

Source: Fact Sheet: White House Summit on Cybersecurity and Consumer Protection. The White House Office of the Press Secretary, February 13, 2015. https://www.whitehouse.gov/the-press-office/2015/02/13/fact-sheet-white-house-summit-cybersecurity-and-consumer-protection.

T

Tablet

Tablets are computers that have a display, circuitry, and battery all in one unit. They may not have the same functionality as a laptop, but they often allow for some of the functions that laptops or other personal computers have. Some tablets are used primarily for reading electronic text and are similar to e-readers, but more sophisticated tablets may have cameras, microphones, and a variety of data packages that allow downloads of e-books, music, games, apps, and movies. Most tablets use either touchscreen surfaces or styluses, and some allow a digital keyboard to appear for typing purposes. One of the first marketing campaigns for early models of tablets focused on the ability of the technology to transfer handwritten information (using a special stylus) for conversion to text.

One of the earliest images of a tablet computer appeared in Stanley Kubrick's 1968 film, *2001: A Space Odyssey* based on the story by Arthur C. Clarke. In that story, the *NewsPad* bore a remarkable resemblance to what we now recognize as a tablet computer. The original *Star Trek* television series that began in 1966 featured a number of computer-operated technologies that have become realities. One of those technologies was the Personal Access Display Device (PADD) that looked remarkably like the Apple iPad that was not introduced until 2010. But even though the idea of tablet computers was introduced to many through science fiction, the technologies were provocative because they looked like something that could become a reality in the future—and they did.

One of the contributors to making a tablet computer possible was Alan Kay who saw the potential for using a small computer-like technology for educational purposes that he thought would change the nature of education for children of all ages. When Kay was a graduate student in 1972, he wrote a proposal that outlined a prototype laptop that used a graphical user interface (GUI) and windowing features that he called a Dynabook. While the Dynabook combined a keyboard and screen, the cost of manufacturing it was too high for the project to be viable (approximately

$6,000 per unit), but the ideas behind the Dynabook gave other innovators ideas that contributed to the eventual growth of the tablet market.

As previously mentioned, some of the early tablets required a stylus to write on the screen and the sensors under the screen converted handwriting into digital information. The Linus Write-Top was introduced in 1987. This was followed by the 1989 release of the GridPad, produced by Palm Computing, a company that developed personal digital assistants (PDAs) and other electronic organizers. Apple introduced the Newton MessagePad in 1993, but it too was limited in function. In 1997, Palm came out with a better PDA called the Palm Pilot, which also had a keyboard in addition to the stylus, enabling users to type messages on the screen. This feature propelled the rest of the tablet developers to look into better ways to make the devices more user-friendly and, in the process, the handwriting translation feature of the tablet was deemed too problematic to be really useful. The Microsoft tablet was introduced in 2000 and was the first to really resemble today's tablet, and this was followed by the Windows XP tablet in 2002.

Apple finally introduced its iPad in 2010, with a sleek case and a greater number of functions than any previous tablet. By this time, swipe technology was working well and customers who had become brand-conscious with the iPod and iPhone welcomed the new addition to the tablet market. From this point on, the potential of the tablet to someday replace the laptop became part of popular culture.

With the new iPad, the improved Microsoft XP tablet, and a number of other competitors from Samsung and the Kindle, tablets began infiltrating the market in 2010. Even the relatively high cost of tablets, ranging from $600 to $800 did not seem to dissuade many from purchasing them. E-Readers had been around for a while but none had the information capacity of a tablet, and the battery life of tablets generally lasted longer than many of the early e-readers. What the tablet did was combine many of the features of a computer and a mobile phone. The size of the image on the screen along with swipe features made it a comfortable device for consumers, and added features such as cameras and picture storage made the tablet appealing to those who liked the ability to use it for e-reading, Internet access, and picture storage.

The 2013 holiday season resulted in a number of tablet and e-reader sales. By 2014, the number of Americans ages 16 and older who owned tablets had grown to 42 percent of the American public, and the share of those who had e-readers like Kindles or Nooks had grown to 32 percent. According to a 2014 study by the Pew Research Group, about half of adults in the United States owned either a tablet or an e-reader at the beginning of 2014 (Zickuhr and Rainie 2014).

One of the most remarkable features about tablets is that they have come down in cost. Prices now start at about $200 and models can be found at a number of different price points. This relatively low cost has created a resurgence in looking at tablets as an alternative to laptops in schools, medical facilities, government, restaurants, and more. They have been so quickly adopted in large organizations that many see the growth of the tablet as the wave of the future, and some have even remarked that laptops will soon become obsolete (Moscaritolo 2010). Interestingly, however, a poll by the research firm Poll Position reported that younger respondents (aged 18–29 years old) were less likely to predict the demise of the laptop, while 50 percent of the respondents between the ages of 30–64 felt that tablets would someday replace laptops (Moscaritolo 2010).

Tablets have also been found to be very useful in helping some people with developmental disabilities improve their communication. Autism researchers have found that tablets have appealing features for people with autism, because images can be swiped and typing is not necessary.

See also: Apple (iPad); E-Reader

Further Reading

Clarke, Arthur C. 1968. *2001: A Space Odyssey.* New York: Penguin Putnam.

Moscaritolo, Angela. 2010. "Will Tablets Make Laptops Obsolete?" *PC World.* Accessed April 23, 2015: http://www.pcmag.com/article2/0,2817,2398731,00.asp.

Zickuhr, Kathryn, and Lee Rainie. 2014. "E-Reading Rises as Device Ownership Jumps." Pew Research Center. Accessed March 7, 2015: http://www.pewinternet.org /2014/01/16/e-reading-rises-as-device-ownership-jumps/.

Telecommunications Act of 1996

All forms of communication within the United States are entrusted, in part, to federal agencies to monitor and, when necessary, regulate practices in the interest of the population. The Telecommunications Act of 1996 (referred to as the Telecom Act) was the first major overhaul of United States telecommunications law in more than 60 years, significantly changing the Communications Act of 1934, the prior legislation covering communications technologies in the United States. It was called for because many technologies, including the Internet and all digital technology (including mobile phones), had not yet been widely available when the earlier act was enforced in 1934. Even though many of the technologies in use in 1996 were in development and prototype stages in 1934, it was impossible to envision whether radio, television, telephony, and digital media would ever be successful and technologies as complex as the Internet and World Wide Web could hardly have been thought to have been possible. Though the Telecom Act of 1996 has been amended many times, it is still the primary policy document for telecommunications in the United States.

The Telecom Act has many components, but, most notably, amendments have dealt with the role of the Internet and the increased use of wireless signals for many of today's communications technologies. When it was enacted, the act's stated objective was to open markets to competition by removing regulatory barriers to entry, but a criticism of the act is that by lifting restrictions and weakening the power of the Federal Communications Commission (FCC), the telecommunications industries raised prices, bought up small companies, and, through mergers and acquisitions, actually limited the number of opportunities for companies to compete in telecommunications industries.

The Internet has been one of the most rapidly changing technologies for which the Telecom Act is the arbiter. Over the years, the FCC struggled with the appropriate way to classify the Internet. Should it be considered a utility? Should it be regulated by the FCC, since there were so many aspects to Internet use that combined public use, commercial use, and government use? Large companies like AT&T and Comcast lobbied hard to prevent the FCC from creating more regulations for the Internet, claiming that it would restrict their ability to operate. AT&T alone spent almost $6 million in the first three months of 2010 lobbying the FCC to create regulations only if they benefited the telecommunications sector (Crawford 2013, 61).

Eventually, the issue of *net neutrality* became the wedge issue that pitted the large companies against a growing movement of concerned citizens that put pressure on the FCC to keep the Internet "open" to all, but that decision almost didn't happen. In May 2014, FCC Chair Tom Wheeler released a plan that would have allowed major telecoms like AT&T, Comcast, and Verizon to pay more for faster Internet service lanes for their customers. The customers, though, knew that this would result in higher costs to them and feared that, in addition to greater cost, any "tiered service" would result in smaller companies becoming marginalized on the Internet. Public pressure coerced Wheeler to reverse his position, and, on February 4, 2015, he announced that he would support net neutrality rules, keeping the Internet "open" to both small and large companies. The other commissioners voted 3–2 to endorse Wheeler's proposal on February 26, 2015. Net neutrality rules went into effect in June 2015.

While the Telecom Act was the first federal legislation to suggest guidelines for Internet use and access, many people feel that it was not as forward thinking as it could have been and, therefore, has become a burden to the FCC and the public, because difficult decisions about developing technologies and those that use the Internet are not clearly defined. When conflicts occur that are adjudicated in courts, often those courts side with the telecommunications industries because of precedents and the wording in the act. Legal scholar Susan Crawford has criticized the implementation of the Telecommunications Act of 1996 by likening it to a "regulatory pendulum" that seems to swing back and forth as different interests and different technologies are debated. Still, until a new telecommunications law is drafted and put before the public and Congress, the Telecommunications Act of 1996 is the preeminent document to which legal authorities turn in disputes over the regulation of all legacy and digital technologies and their distribution forms.

See also: Federal Communications Commission (FCC); Net Neutrality

Further Reading

Crawford, Susan. 2013. *Captive Audience: The Telecom Industry and Monopoly Power in the New Gilded Age.* New Haven and London: Yale University Press, 49–63.

Texting

Texting is the term given to the sending and receiving of short messages over digital technologies, and usually has the connotation of alphanumeric communications over mobile phones, though some people refer to e-mail on computers as a variation of texting. In general, text messages must be sent to people who have a specific address (e-mail or mobile phone address). The practice is similar to writing (typing) a message to someone, but the messages can be sent to individuals or to groups of people.

Much has been written about how texting has changed the way people communicate and the type of etiquette (or netiquette) that takes place in the act of texting, or using electronic technologies. The field of computer-mediated communication (CMC) often explores the aspects of interpersonal relationships tied to how people communicate online as well as what they communicate. CMC often addresses the intention of the sender of a message and how effectively that message is received without distorting the sender's original intention. While texting does not necessarily have to take place in real time (synchronous time), the messages exchanged have the appearance of being sent immediately and, of course, in instant messaging, the immediacy of the text is part of the purpose of sending and receiving the text messages.

Mobile phones became sophisticated enough to send and receive texts in 1992 through a process originally called short messaging service (SMS). Early texting made use of the phone's 9-digit keypad in a rather complicated manner, with the sender of a message having to push the number 2 (for example) one time for "A," twice for "B" and three times for "C," etc., but in the early 2000s, full keyboards became widely available, making texting easier. The BlackBerry was one of the first mobile phones to effectively use this type of QWERTY keyboard, and since the keyboard was too small for regular touch typing, the use of thumb typing evolved and helped the BlackBerry become a popular mobile phone.

In different countries or regions of the world, the telephone companies charge users for using texts and voiced messages in different ways. Texts take up less bandwidth to send and receive, and billing procedures that charge people by the minute rather than the bandwidth used have been criticized for encouraging texting rather than voiced messages. This is the way most mobile phone companies charge subscription rates in the United States, which has led some critics to report on the excessive cost of mobile telephony, with telecommunications firms making profits that are exponentially higher than the cost of the transmission of the messages—even with a reasonable profit assured for shareholders.

The technologies used to create texts are tied to the range of communicative ability the message sender has. People often assume that a text message will be received and answered immediately and are sometimes frustrated when a receiver of a message doesn't respond quickly. Almost from the beginning of texting, people have used shorthand and the technical characteristics to help make creating a text faster, and, sometimes, more creative. Shorthand abbreviations like LOL (laugh out loud) or CU (for "see you") are ways to adapt language to a text-based form, and for people sending texts on devices that require you pay for service from the time you start the message until the time you send it, shorthand can speed the process and shave a few precious seconds off of the charges.

But texting has also expanded into a language beyond full words and shorthand abbreviations. Emoticons are shorthand messages that represent an image, using the characters available on a typewriter or a mobile phone keypad that often represent an emotion. The term comes from the blending of the words "emotion" and "icon." Combinations of colons, commas, and other punctuation symbols can be combined to create a symbolic image that communicates a sender's intention. Some emoticons look like this: ;-) or :-(.

Similar images can be created by *emojis,* which were created in the late 1990s by the Japanese company NTT DoCoMo. The name references the words "e" and "moji," which roughly translates to mean a pictograph. Emojis are pictures that can be inserted into a text message, but only if the communicator's software has the capability of sending and receiving the images. Sometimes an emoji sent on an Android system might show up on an Apple iOS device looking a bit different than the sender intended for it to look.

Because of the way texting has constituted a new written "language" for communication, some critics have worried about the eventual impact of texting on spoken and written English. Some critics of texting claim that texts change our relationship to words. Texting may combine some of the elements of speech, but the lack of social cues, pronunciation, vocal inflection, and vocal tone have given some critics the idea that texting is a "lesser" form of communication. In some ways, the shorthand of using texts is considered to be rude, or an even incomplete form of communication that establishes a response to a message, rather than a conversation (one-way vs. two-way dialogue).

In an extensive study of the literature on children and adults who text, British and Australian scholars Clare Wood, Nenagh Kemp, and Beverly Plester (2014) determined that texting has no appreciable effect on the ability of someone to learn proper spelling, conversation, or literacy skills, but they also cite evidence that texting has become the preferred mode of communication rather than talking, in several countries (Wood, Kemp, and Plester 2014, 4–5). When that occurs, we must ask what effect this change in communication is having on communication effectiveness, technological literacy, and the meaning of messages.

What has become more prevalent in our culture is the way texting has introduced different communication behaviors for people. Some behaviors in texting are considered rude, such as *flaming*, to send rude, hostile, or aggressive messages. Similarly, when a person sends a message in all capital letters, it is usually construed to be a message that is "yelling" at the recipient. But some behaviors can be particularly annoying, such as when people exchange messages that are answered incompletely. For example, a person could send a message saying, "Do you want to go to a movie tonight? Which one? Should we ask Joe to come too?" only to get a reply that tersely says "Sure." When this happens, texting becomes much more like responding to a message than really communicating over the medium (Hanson 2007, 39–41).

When texting became popular in the United States, teens were the first group to seize upon the opportunity to communicate with friends without the prying eyes (or ears) of parents or other family members. In a Pew Research study in 2012, texting was determined to be the dominant daily mode of communication for teens. While the number of texts sent by teens in 2009 was 50, the number rose to 60 by 2011. Overall, 75 percent of teens were active texters (Lenhart 2012).

By 2013 the discourse about how much people texted and where shifted to the problem of people who text in cars. The National Highway Traffic Safety Administration reported that in 2012 driver distraction caused by texting was the cause of 18 percent of all fatal crashes. A Federal Communications Commission (FCC) report provided the following statistics: 40 percent of teens in the United States said they were in cars when the driver was using a mobile phone; text messaging created a risk 23 times more than when people are not distracted while driving, and 11 percent of drivers aged 18 to 20 had been in an automobile accident and admitted sending or receiving texts when they crashed (The Dangers of Texting while Driving 2015).

See also: E-Reader; Mobile Phone; Smartphone; Tablet

Further Reading

"The Dangers of Texting while Driving." 2014. FCC Report. Accessed April 29, 2015: http://www.fcc.gov/guides/texting-while-driving.

Hanson, Jarice. 2007. *24/7: How Cell Phones and the Internet Change the Way We Live, Work, and Play.* Westport, CT: Praeger, 39–41.

Lenhart, Amanda. 2012. "Teens, Smartphones & Texting." Pew Research Center. Accessed March 29, 2015: http://www.pewinternet.org/2012/03/19/teens-smartphones-texting/.

Wood, Clare, Nenagh Kemp, and Beverly Plester. 2014. *Text Messaging and Literacy—The Evidence.* London and New York: Routledge.

Woyke, Elizabeth. 2014. *The Smartphone: Anatomy of an Industry.* New York and London: The New Press.

Some Texting Abbreviations

ebcac: error between chair and computer

kthxbai: okay, thanks, by

rofl: rolling on floor laughing

bbl: be back later

idk: I don't know

noob: newbie

tl;dr: too long, didn't read

tg2bt: too good to be true

a3: anytime, anyplace, anywhere

acorn: a completely obsessive, really nutty person

anfscd: and now for something completely different

3D Printing

Because of new techniques and new technologies, the ability to duplicate a three-dimensional (3D) object is a reality that would surprise many. But the ability to make a 3D product in a matter of seconds would make both a science fiction fan and a contemporary manufacturer ecstatic. The fundamental principle of 3D printing is digitally obtaining the dimensions of an item and deconstructing the product's mathematical code so that it can be recombined elsewhere with height, width, and depth. Most media forms (other than sculpture) are in two dimensions, meaning that there is height and width, but the surface looks flat. With 3D printing, special scanners and printers can reproduce a model of something by adding the third dimension of depth. 3D printing has great potential to use crowdsourcing and social media to identify and design products that could appeal to either individuals or small or large groups of consumers. As a result, 3D printing can have an impact on social marketing, the sharing economy, and the creative economy. It is believed that 3D printing will contribute a wide range of new products in the do-it-yourself (DIY) and creative economy initiatives, and Creative Commons licenses may have a major impact on what products can be duplicated and which ones are protected by traditional copyright law. But what is creating the potential for a whole new model of innovation and manufacturing is the 3D printer, which some have called the "gateway" technology for innovation and product manufacturing.

In addition to the cost benefit of using 3D printing for manufacturing products, the process of creating 3D products is also potentially revolutionary. Many of the products that are now being made have raised money through crowdfunding, and many of the ideas have used crowdsourcing to refine ideas for new products. Incubator spaces have started to emerge to take advantage of the unique set of circumstances that allow people to think effectively and create projects with new technologies and techniques. *Maker Labs* are examples of how ideas can be generated in a certain place, and with the low-cost resources of technologies like 3D printing, the ideas of several people together can be a catalyst for new products and uses. Increasingly, schools, libraries, and community centers are creating Maker Labs or *Maker Spaces* to encourage innovation and collaboration. Also called the *Maker Movement*, the emerging subculture has been likened to a "new industrial revolution" for the twenty-first century (Swan 2014). But this type of sharing of ideas and product development is not rooted in geographic space alone. Many of the ideas that are loosely called "makers" projects that use new technologies like 3D printing take place over social networks as concepts of *collective intelligence*.

In the United States, more than 200 groups have registered their online spaces with "makerspace.com" and the concept is not limited to the United States. According to Noelle Swan, writing for the *Christian Science Monitor* on July 6, 2014: "A few hundred [of these groups] have sprouted all over the world from Northern Ireland to Bhutan, and all are connected virtually through a digital video bridge." Even the United Nations has been looking at establishing the equivalent of maker spaces in refugee camps where children and adults have few opportunities for formal education, but where they can collaborate to develop skills and share ideas (Swan 2014).

The revolutionary potential of using 3D printing to change traditional models of manufacturing and the economics behind the ideas of product research, development, manufacturing, and distribution may not yet be fully understood, but from the economic perspective, change seems inevitable. The possibility of using relatively low-cost duplicators to create models and produce content on demand (meaning according to order, rather than manufacturing multiple products to sit in a warehouse until they are purchased) has extraordinary potential to change the way products are manufactured in the future. By changing the traditional manufacturing model, 3D printing can be used to create new prototypes at less cost than traditional research and development in laboratories or warehouses, produces less material waste, and reduces transportation costs for distribution, and, products can be adjusted for individual needs or to individual specifications. In his 2013 State of the Union Address, President Obama called attention to the way 3D printing had the potential to revolutionize the way manufacturing would be done in the future.

Building a 3D model is also called *additive manufacturing* (AM). The 3D printer adds layers of material so that the product takes shape. Because 3D printing is so new, most of the products created through 3D printing involve novelties and artifacts, but successful 3D models of ears, hands, and other body parts have also been developed to replace body parts damaged by birth defects, war, disease, or accident. While these models do not function as an organ with living tissue and nerve might function, the 3D printing process gives hope to eventually constructing working body parts to prolong one's independence and functionality.

While there has been interest in creating 3D simulations for many years, progress in creating a digital modeling process began in 1981 in Japan. By 1985, Chuck Hull of 3D Systems Corporation improved upon the Japanese technique and effectively created 3D simulations using stereolithography, lasers, and a product called a photopolymer (a plastic that can absorb the outline, or image of a product). Though manufacturers have been experimenting with how 3D printing can create objects, like replacement parts for cars, refrigerators, and other items that would normally be made somewhere and then shipped to the person who needed it, 3D printers can often do the job faster and in one place. The cost of the machines has been prohibitively high until recently, but now, professional grade and consumer grade machines have become more ubiquitous.

Costs for both professional and consumer printers have come down since the 1980s, and it is possible for a home consumer to buy a basic 3D copier for approximately $400, with many major office supply chains stocking them. Professional 3D copiers start in the $5,000 range and escalate into the million dollar range, depending upon the features included. At this point the future of using 3D printing to have an impact on the retail world is speculative, but it has been suggested that among the uses that could be seen in the future are a range of personalizing of brand-name products. In this type of cocreating of a product, a popular brand could be customized according to the consumer's desires. For example, a person could walk into a retail clothing store and create a custom purse on the spot. Or a child might customize accessories for a doll, or action hero toy. A traveler who forgets something at home might be able to order a product at an airport, and it would be ready when they arrive at their destination airport to pick it up.

Some commercial experiments so far have included the ability to personalize items and components. A company that manufactures components for mobile phones, SoundCloud, has worked with the 3D printing company Shapeways to comanufacture an iPhone case by allowing a fan to choose a favorite song and have a personalized 3D case created by having the sound waves printed on the back. The Creators Project, an online collaboration of people who experiment with technology (started by the Intel Corporation) has come up with the ability to create a person's Facebook profile into a 3D sculpture based upon what the person lists on their profile.

See also: Copyright; Creative Commons; Creative Economy; Crowdfunding; Crowdsourcing; Digital; Do-It-Yourself

Further Reading

Carmy, Carine. 2014. "The Next Leap in Social: 3D Printing." *Ad Age.* Accessed October 4, 2014: http://adage.com/article/digitalnext/3d-printing-leap-social-media/240561/.
Swan, Noelle. 2014. "The 'Maker Movement' Creates D.I.Y. Revolution." *Christian Science Monitor.* Accessed March 29, 2015: http://www.csmonitor.com/Technology/2014/0706 /The-maker-movement-creates-D.I.Y.-revolution.

Trending

The term *trending* reflects the popularity of an idea or artifact and how quickly it spreads through a particular social network or form of media. It is a measure of how many people are interested in a topic, picture, phrase, app, or any other issue that is spread with the help of social media. Most social media sites have a section that indicates what is *trending* so that users can see the popularity (or lack of popularity) of articles, videos, tweets, or other topical issues. Trending on the web means that messages are being generated over social media and that people are noticing that information flow. Trending topics are a measure of popular interest at any given time, based upon the amount of information that is generated with keywords and/or ideas.

Trends are determined by an algorithm that is used by a particular social media form. For example, Twitter trends are determined by who the user follows and by location. On Twitter, trends can be found on the home, notifications, discover, or profile pages when using a computer. On a mobile app, Twitter displays a trends area on the discover timeline. A hashtag is a clue to the type of message sent.

Social media analytics companies chart the trends and publish the results to measure the topics that are trending in society. For example, according to the online version of the *Boston Globe*, the topic of the deadly disease Ebola began getting media coverage in March 2014, but the trending figures didn't start to skyrocket until the end of September. Citing research from analytics firm Crimson Hexagon, 4.2 million global tweets were sent between August 31 to September 30, 2014, that used the word "Ebola" or the hashtag #ebola. By September, most of the people in the world had become aware of the presence and the problems associated with the disease (Rice 2014). This type of public opinion awareness is one of the special characteristics afforded by social media and social networking.

The term is also commonly used by companies that use social media, like eBay, that reflects the trending price of something, meaning the average price.

See also: Advertising; Meme; Twitter

Further Reading

Rice, Chelsea. 2014. "OMG! Ebola Is Trending! Wait, What Does That Actually Mean?" Boston.com. Accessed January 1, 2015: http://www.boston.com/health/2014/10/09/omg -ebola-trending-wait-what-does-that-actually-mean/sUM8k7DBqKiD9wgeQ2eloI/story .html.

Tumblr

The microblogging social network service Tumblr was founded in 2007 by David Karp, an entrepreneur who wanted to make a site that was easy for people to use. Tumblr is a site that allows people to express themselves through multimedia posts, short-form blogs, and other content. As one critic summed up the site: "Tumblr lowered the bar to creating a beautiful, dynamic website and raised the payoff in the form of positive social reinforcement" (Bercovici 2013). Users can follow other users' blogs, post their own privately, or publicly, and reblog (send blogs to others) with ease. Though Tumblr was acquired by Yahoo! in 2013 for approximately $1.1 billion, it deserves to have its own entry in this encyclopedia because of the popularity and success of the site.

Tumblr combines features of blogging and social networking. Karp's design featured a "dashboard" interface that allows people to navigate through the site. In 2013, Tumblr claimed to have more than 100 million blogs on its site and an audience of 44 million people in the United States and 134 million around the world. When Yahoo! acquired the site, it did so to increase its presence among the young followers that frequently used or at least checked Tumblr. Within two years, traffic to the site doubled and Tumblr became profitable.

It was the appeal to youth that made Tumblr an attractive property for Yahoo!, and the loyal following it had has boosted Yahoo!'s revenue. When Karp initially started the site, he had no intention of advertising, but he soon realized that if he advertised differently than other social networking sites, he could make money and do something that was unique to Tumblr. The result is an ad-based model that incorporates ads by clustering most of them in the dashboard.

One reason for Tumblr's success had to do with the effects of Hurricane Sandy that flooded data centers in New York, making it impossible for news services like the Huffington Post, Gawker, and BuzzFeed to produce content. A majority of the users of those sites gravitated to Tumblr as a temporary publishing platform (Bercovici 2013). When many saw how simple, but elegant, Tumblr's use of graphics was, they began to post their own content.

The success of the site has much to do with the way Karp has been able to use the characteristics of blogging and social networking for a young audience that thinks nothing of mixing news and humor. Tumblr looks as though it is a list of posts, but the visual quality of the moving graphic, photography, songs, and inside jokes have given it a unique appeal. The site often juxtaposes images for comic effect, like the cartoonist's impressions of Darth Vader that blend into a flow of hamsters that look like President Obama (Bercovici 2013). Tumblr users have become a community in the sense that they have started their own vocabulary to tag pictures, like GPOY, meaning a Gratuitous Picture of Yourself.

One concern that advertisers have is the amount of content that sometimes scares advertisers away from a site. Pornography represents a fraction of content on the site but the wide range of subjects often reflect topics that can be considered questionable. Tumblr has been criticized for not policing the occasional pornography that is posted, and for allowing users to post antisocial or potentially harmful content online. When a British 15 year old died after being hit by a train in St. Pancras station in London in 2014, her mother reported that the girl had spent months accessing blogs about self-harm and suicide on Tumblr (Hern 2014). The user policy of Tumblr banned blogs that encourage self-harm, but like most social networks, it acts to delete that type of content only when someone complains or brings it to their attention.

See also: Blogs; Cyberbullying; Yahoo!

Further Reading

Bercovici, Jeff. 2013 "Tumblr: David Karp's $800 Million Art Project." *Forbes.* Accessed April 29, 2015: http://www.forbes.com/sites/jeffbercovici/2013/01/02/tumblr-david-karps -800-million-art-project/.

De la Merced, Michael J., Nick Bilton, and Nicole Perlroth. 2013. "Seeking Flair, Yahoo Agrees to Buy Tumblr." *New York Times,* May 19: A1.

Hern, Alex. 2014. "Social Networks to Face Government Grilling Over Suicide Content." *The Guardian*. Accessed November 16, 2015: http://www.theguardian.com/technology /2014/jan/27/social-networks-to-face-government-grilling-over-suicide-promotion.

Twitter

Twitter was founded by venture capitalists Jack Dorsey, Noah Glass, Biz Stone, and Evan Williams in 2006. Originally, the idea of the messaging system combined a number of former technologies, like GPS, police-scanning radio technology, and other citizen communication services. What makes it an important form of social media is that it is easy to send and receive messages, especially over smartphones. Twitter is an example of short messaging service (SMS), and the temporary nature of the tweet—the message sent, gives the impression of real-time interaction. Twitter has been used between and among friends, with celebrities, and with politicians and retail establishments that hope to establish their brand with the greater public in a low-cost way. While some people argue that Twitter is just a digital form of sending one-way "blasts" of information or data, others extol its virtue as a unique communication form. As our media landscape grows to encompass social media as well as legacy media, an important consideration is whether short messaging services like Twitter really influence the way the public thinks and behaves.

At first, the team that created Twitter was not sure of how Twitter would be used, and by whom. When Twitter was first released in 2006, it prompted users to respond by asking a simple question, "What are you doing?" The answer to this question could provide valuable information to analytics firms that thought Twitter might become an ideal advertising medium for point-of-purchase products. In November 2009, that short question was made even shorter by restating it as, "What's happening?" From that point on, Twitter has had seemingly an explosive growth and use as a real-time information network, but while it has made an impact in breaking news, it has also capitalized on celebrity culture and the relationship between people in the media and their followers.

In a *Los Angeles Times* article in which he recalled how Twitter took form, Jack Dorsey discussed how the LiveJournal blog gave him the idea for instant messaging over a mobile phone. At first, he tried using his BlackBerry phone, and he wrote a program that would allow him to send messages to a list of friends who could then reply to the message to tell him what they were doing (all of the friends at the time were BlackBerry users). Just a year earlier (2005) the SMS-type messages were becoming popular, but the technology of the mobile platform restricted messages to 160 characters before the message was split into two. Twenty characters were necessary for the user's name and address, but 140 characters were available for the sending of the message. At first, Dorsey and his partners called the service *Status*, but that name lacked the snap that they hoped to find. One of the partners suggested the name "twitch" because that was the feeling of the mobile phone in your pocket when it was set to vibrate, but after looking in the dictionary for a synonym, the group came up with the name *Twitter*, which was defined as "a short burst of inconsequential information" as well as "chirps from birds" (Sarno 2009). Immediately, the name and the concept it symbolized were accepted. The logo that the group chose is a little bird, which is instantly recognizable to Twitter users.

Twitter allows only 140 characters to be sent in any tweet, which makes working with the format of the message interesting. The reason for the limitation is that SMS necessarily impose a limit of 160 characters, and Twitter wanted to leave 20 characters for the user name. The brevity of the message has created new styles and genres of communication. There have been Twitter haikus, Twitter fiction, and Twitter poetry that has emerged to explore the short-form messaging characteristics, but the medium itself has also been criticized for being limited and not-providing full, in-depth information at times when more information may be better than short-form.

Like all social media, users tend to be representative of a certain age, ethnicity, and class. Though people of all ages use Twitter, the typical user is between 18 and 34 years old, has a university degree (or is currently in school), and has no children. About three-quarters of the Twitter users access the Internet over wireless devices like laptops and mobile phones, and users can generate their own tweets as well as post retweets of other content. It didn't take long for the service to catch on, and by the 2007 South by Southwest conference (SXSW) in Austin, Texas, Twitter had become a communication phenomenon for those who wanted to send their comments to others to tell them what they were seeing and hearing.

By 2014, Twitter had more than 500 million users worldwide, with more than half of them regular, active users, though there is conflicting data on this last point. According to the respected Pew Research Center, in 2014, about 23 percent of the adults in the United States used Twitter on a daily basis, and adult men over the age of 50 were a significant part of the growing user base (Duggan et al. 2014), but the social media analytics firm Venture Beat reported a 19 percent use of Twitter in which only 7 percent of the audience actively tweeted or retweeted, with most activity by lurkers (Ferenstein 2015). About 85 percent of Twitter sites are supported by advertising revenue.

Twitter is overwhelmingly used more for entertainment than for news or politics, though having a presence on Twitter is important for anyone in the public spotlight. As a public relations medium it is unparalleled in terms of the low cost of the use and the way information goes viral through retweets, and the analytics it generates results in the ability to see what's trending at any given time. Among the first celebrities to use Twitter were Tom Petty, Brittany Spears, and Ashton Kutcher, and the first politician to use Twitter was Barack Obama.

For the celebrities, Twitter helps develop a fan base and give the illusion to the fans that the celebrities are sending direct messages to them and that they care about the responses of their fans. While these approaches might be true, many celebrities have been found to use staff members to send and receive tweets, rather than send them themselves. And, like other social networks, it has been known to create celebrities.

In January 2013, Twitter launched a video app called Vine that lets people record, edit, and share very short (six second or less) videos. The purchase of the video app cost the company a reported $30 million but the videos can be shared through Vine's own social network and shared on other services like Twitter or Facebook. At first, the app was made available for free on iOS devices, and, later in the same year, an Android app was released.

But if Vine is an example of an emerging medium, it also sheds light on how fleeting any social network can be. As Marcus Johns, a "Viner" with 4 million followers said in an article in *Rolling Stone*: "Your grandmother's on YouTube—it's not cool," "Vine is the thing now. Kids in our ADD generation want to express an idea and move on to the next thing" (Kushner 2014).

The *Rolling Stone* article portrayed the romance and breakup of Jessi Smiles (real name, Jessica Vazquez) with 3 million followers on Vine, and Curtis Lepore, a top 10 Viner who also had 10,000 followers on Instagram. The article illuminates their romance and breakup, but it also explains what happens to a person when they become a social network celebrity. As Smiles said: "It happened very fast. When you're on Vine, you become a brand. Everyone is a brand. I'm a brand, and there's nothing you can do about that." For Smiles and Lepore, though, their public romance ended badly. Both were Vine's first superstars, falling in love online, and becoming so popular with followers that advertising money supporting their feeds came rolling in. "But once they met in the real world, things went horribly wrong," reported David Kushner (2014). When the two agreed to meet for the first time in Washington Square Park, about 2,000 fans showed up. But a few weeks after their public meet-up, Smiles pressed charges against Lepore alleging rape.

When it comes to the political arena, there has been much controversy over whether social media, and Twitter in particular, contributes to a more democratic society by bypassing big media and allowing users a more direct form of communication from sender to receiver. Some claim tweets and retweets are an important form of political information dissemination, while others criticize them for advancing a politician's public relations activity.

Politicians have been quick to seize the use of Twitter for political purposes. And, like celebrities, while it may be impossible to know whether a politician is actually tweeting themselves, the medium has become a quick messaging service to get out a point of view, or to establish a personal relationship with whomever subscribes to the politician's Twitter account. Many people assume that Twitter is a highly influential form of communication, but studies that investigate the real impact of Twitter's communicative potential in political life are only starting to emerge.

During President Obama's nomination acceptance speech for the 2012 presidential election at the Democratic National Convention, over 50,000 tweets were sent per minute, and in three days, over 10 million tweets were sent (Gainous and Wagner 2014, 6).

In their book on *Politics and the Twitter Revolution*, John H. Parmelee and Shannon L. Bichard (2012) present data that shows who uses political tweets, and who pays attention to them. While the authors take the perspective that, in the realm of political communication, Twitter followers tend to be from an older and more professional demographic than groups who use other forms of social media, they discuss the issues of followers' political ideologies, demographics, and the relative influence of Twitter vis-à-vis traditional media and interpersonal sources of information. They also warn that there is little research to date on whether Twitter actually influences political beliefs. They conclude that even though Twitter essentially operates as one-way communication from political leaders to the public, the relationships between political leaders and their followers is quite powerful.

Twitter has been cited as one of the key technologies that helped organize activists during the Arab Spring, but while anecdotal evidence shows that hundreds of thousands of tweets were sent and received, there is no way to know how many of them were sent by activists, sympathizers, or people who were loyal to the regimes that were under siege (Morozov 2011, 15).

However, when the public and police were caught in the chaos of the Boston Bombing incident in 2013, the mainstream press could not keep up with the information being transmitted over social media. Twitter, in particular, became a tool for citizen sharing of information on the search for the two suspects who left bombs at the finish line of the Boston Marathon, killing three people and critically wounding dozens more. From the initial use of Twitter by the Boston Police who distributed information about the suspects, information about sightings of the pair, to the tweets that reported: "Suspect in custody. Officers sweeping the area. Stand by for further info. (Boston Police Department, 8:45 pm)" and "CAPTURED!!! The hunt is over. The search is done. The terror is over. And justice has won. Suspect in custody. (Boston Police Department 8:58 pm)," Twitter served as a fast link to official information from the Bureau of Public Information (Keller 2013).

Twitter has been criticized for contributing to *information overload* and has been blamed for contributing to people thinking that what is current is also "news." The concept of *information relativity* is also a significant issue and Twitter has been criticized for allowing an appearance of instant messaging as synonymous with news, though so many messages constitute a declaration of an event rather than the type of news that actually contributes to knowing something of significance that affects a person's knowledge of the environment that may have social or political consequences.

Many people use Twitter as though it were their own stream-of-consciousness writing. Knowing when someone goes to buy lunch, do their laundry, or other mundane information can sour subscribers from wanting to pay attention to a person's tweets. The mindless ephemera of the constant flow of messages can be off-putting for many and is often the reason some people decide to give up their Twitter accounts. But as a monitor of public awareness, Twitter is one of the fastest, most low-cost means of tapping the collective shoulders of users and allowing them to know what's happening.

See also: Arab Spring; Blogs; Occupy Movement; Social Media; Social Networking; Trending; Viral; YouTube

Further Reading

Duggan, Maeve, Nicole B. Ellison, Cliff Lampe, Amanda Lenhart, and Mary Madden. 2014. "Social Media Update, 2014." Pew Research Center. Accessed January 22, 2015: http://www.pewinternet.org/2015/01/09/social-media-update-2014/.

Ferenstein, Gregory. 2015. "Here's How Many People Check Facebook, Twitter, and Instagram Daily." Venture Beat. Accessed May 5, 2015: http://venturebeat.com/2015/01/09/heres-how-many-people-check-facebook-twitter-and-instagram-daily-in-2-graphs/.

Gainous, Jason, and Kevin M. Wagner. 2014. *Tweeting to Power: The Social Media Revolution in American Politics*. New York: Oxford University Press, 6.

Keller, Jared. 2013. "How Boston Police Won the Twitter Wars during the Marathon Bomber Hunt." *BloombergBusiness*. Accessed October 24, 2015: http://www.bloomberg.com/bw/articles/2013-04-26/how-boston-police-won-the-twitter-wars-during-bomber-hunt.

Kushner, David. 2014. "The Six Seconds between Love and Hate: A Vine Romance Gone Wrong." *Rolling Stone*. Accessed May 5, 2015: http://www.rollingstone.com/culture/news/the-six-seconds-between-love-and-hate-a-vine-romance-gone-wrong-20140521#ixzz3ZH3ykzV4.

Morozov, Evgeny. 2011. *The Net Delusion: The Dark Side of Internet Freedom*. New York: Perseus.

Parmelee, John H., and Shannon L. Bichard. 2012. *Politics and the Twitter Revolution: How Tweets Influence the Relationship between Political Leaders and the Public*. Lanham, MD: Lexington Books.

Sarno, David. 2009. "Twitter Creator Jack Dorsey Illuminates the Site's Founding Document, Part I." *Los Angeles Times*. Accessed January 6, 2015: http://latimesblogs.latimes.com/technology/2009/02/twitter-creator.html.

U

Uber

Uber is a car sharing service introduced by Garrett Camp and Travis Kalanick, in 2009, and officially launched using a mobile app for iPhone and Android phones in the San Francisco, California, area in 2010. Originally called UberCab by Kalanick and Camp, the service was welcomed by many customers, while established taxi and limo services began to complain about the way it was contributing to competition. Users access an Uber car and driver with the use of an app that shows them where available cars are in the area and allows them to request a ride to a desired location. The company promises a pickup within five minutes. Beginning in 2012, Uber expanded internationally and, by 2014, the car sharing service was available in 60 cities on 6 continents. It is estimated that the profit of the company grew approximately 20 percent every month throughout 2014.

As a prime example of the sharing economy Uber allows rates for cars to be established, but concedes that dynamic pricing (also known as surge pricing) can occur at certain times—meaning that in peak times of need, or time of day, the cost of using an Uber car can be higher when the cars and rides are in greater demand. Uber pricing is usually similar to the cost of a taxi ride, but money is collected by Uber and not the driver; there is also no meter in the vehicle. The price of the trip is established before the ride, and passengers pay by swiping a credit card in the vehicle.

Uber began in the San Francisco area and expanded quickly throughout Silicon Valley as a way of providing car services for those in the information industries. Soon after it began, the company attracted venture capital from a number of investors including Benchmark Capital, Goldman Sachs, Menlo Ventures, and Bezos Expeditions (the venture capital branch of Jeff Bezos's Amazon empire). In August 2013, Google's venture capital group valued Uber at $3.5 billion, and invested $258 million in the company—the largest amount Google ever invested in a start-up firm, to that date (Wilhelm and Tsotsis 2013). In 2013, *USA Today* named Uber its tech company of the year.

While Uber has been restricted from operating in some cities and locations—largely because of the power of the local taxi and transportation service outrage and the resulting loss of revenue to the city in taxes—Uber has also experienced a range of other problems as well. The number of cities that have filed class-action suits against the company continue to grow, but other serious complaints and lawsuits have also resulted. In 2013, an Uber driver hit and killed a six-year-old girl and injured the child's mother and brother. The family filed a wrongful death claim against the company, claiming that the driver was using his mobile phone app at the time and not paying attention to the pedestrians in the area. There have been cases in the United States and in India, where women passengers have allegedly been raped by Uber drivers. In California, a lawsuit was filed in 2014 by the National Federation of the Blind, claiming that Uber discriminated against blind riders and forbid guide dogs access to the cars. In 2014, Parisian cab drivers attacked an Uber car driver's car near Charles de Gaulle Airport, and, in the same year, taxis in a number of European cities blocked roads to protest alternative car services, like Uber.

Uber's business practices have also been highly criticized. In a Salon article on August 31, 2014, staff writer Andrew Leonard wrote a scathing article titled "Why Uber Must Be Stopped," claiming that Uber was "the closest thing we've got today to the living, breathing essence of unrestrained capitalism" (Leonard 2014).

See also: Sharing Economy

Further Reading

Leonard, Andrew. 2014. "Why Uber Must Be Stopped." Salon. Accessed March 17, 2015: http://www.salon.com/2014/08/31/why_uber_must_be_stopped/.

Wilhelm, Alex, and Alexia Tsotsis. 2013. "Google Ventures Puts $258M into Uber, Its Largest Deal Ever." TechCrunch. Accessed October 29, 2014: http://techcrunch.com/2013/08/22/google-ventures-puts-258m-into-uber-its-largest-deal-ever/.

Wohlsen, Marcus. 2014. "Uber in Overdrive: What the Car Service Will Do with Big Money from Google." *Wired*, 22: 49–54.

V

Viral

A virus spreads rapidly, so when something on the Internet experiences rapid dissemination, the term "going viral" refers to the speed with which a message (meme, idea, or concept) spreads through society—or through the social group that constitutes the interest group that understands the meaning of the message in terms of its cultural impact. Comparing messages and ideas that spread virally is related to the biological concept of a virus that spreads from one organism to another.

Behind the metaphor of the virus, as it is transmitted and shared throughout a social group or society, is the work of biologist Richard Dawkins, who wrote the influential book *The Selfish Gene* in 1976. In that book, he identified the concept of the meme that is a form of "cultural transmission . . . analogous to genetic transmission" (Dawkins 1976, 189). Several authors have expanded upon Dawkins's metaphor and have extended it to mean that information that is exchanged rapidly over the Internet can be viral. In some early applications of the word it stood for how information that might formerly have been transmitted in "face to face" communication can be mediated by technology, and, therefore, sent virally over forms of social media—often from friend to friend, connecting people with content.

Scholars Henry Jenkins, Sam Ford, and Joshua Green have analyzed the traditional applications of the word viral with regard to the way information spreads through social media because of the nature of the relationships that are at stake. They have criticized some of the uses of the term because it "is at once too encompassing and too limiting, creating false assumptions about how culture operates and distorted understandings of the power relations between producers and audiences" (Jenkins, Ford, and Green 2013, 20). The term they suggest as more flexible is the term "spreadable" as in "spreadable media" that avoids metaphors of "infection" and "contamination" that gives an inordinate amount of power to the industries and corporations that control media content, and too little credit to audiences who participate in the making of shared meaning (Jenkins, Ford, and Green 2013, 21).

See also: Advertising; Arab Spring; Information Age; Meme; Occupy Movement; Social Networking

Further Reading

Dawkins, Richard. 1976. *The Selfish Gene*. New York: Oxford University Press.
Jenkins, Henry, Sam Ford, and Joshua Green. 2013. *Spreadable Media: Creating Value and Meaning in a Networked Culture*. New York: New York University Press.

Virtual Reality

While we seem to understand the qualities of what is typically called real life (RL) because we have a number of physical cues to inform our senses of height, width, and depth that we encounter every day, virtual reality is an immersive experience, meaning that technologies simulate real life through artificial means. Some of the most common virtual reality experiences we typically have come through gaming and devices that extend one or more of our senses. So, for example, Oculus Rift is a gaming device that has a headset that allows the wearer to see another "world" emerge through the manipulation of the user's senses. Games like *Second Life* create virtual environments that also use virtual reality to simulate an environment in which some images resemble real life, while others, like avatars, are representational images within the virtual environment.

Even though concepts of virtual reality have been introduced to us through science fiction film and literature, today's gaming industries have exploited research and development to make some levels of virtual reality possible for the typical consumer. But virtual reality is no longer confined to the "pretend" worlds of fiction and gaming. Today's virtual reality technologies are real and are being applied to a much wider range of activities.

While virtual reality was more of an idea than a reality in the twentieth century, the term broadly described a number of what were considered "alternate environments." Much of the research that resulted in implementing virtual reality environments came from other forms of media. Film had pioneered the creation of 3D images on a large screen in the 1950s. Dolby sound, created by compressing six different streams of sound to be run with 35mm film, debuted in 1994 and made the sound quality of a movie seem to be coming from different directions. Experiments had even been made in "smell-o-vision" in the 1960s. By 2002, the Canadian company IMAX (short for ImageMaximum) had created a larger-than-traditional film format that required a specially designed screen that employed the peripheral vision of the film viewer and manipulated the person's visual sense by simulating a more 3D-like film experience. But while all of these advancements related to manipulating an audience members sensory experience, they were complemented by developments in virtual reality in other fields as well.

Many companies and universities were doing research on space travel, magnetic imaging for health care, and Internet research. A good number of them saw the connection to ideas of cyberspace as a metaphor for understanding how the human being could interact with technology in cyberspace. When the Internet and the concept of cyberspace came along, the meshing of ideas that had emerged through popular culture and hard science finally seemed to become a reality. Since then, virtual reality has become a serious subject for the studies of the body and understanding how the physical body of a person acts in a metaphorical space. The ideas of Norbert Wiener and cybernetics, and the provocative ideas of artificial intelligence and robotics, began to influence the way we think about what virtual reality was and how it could be used.

Some of the ideas behind virtual reality and the impact of technology on the body were seeded by the work of Marshall McLuhan, a Canadian scholar, who, in the 1960s, coined the provocative phrase: "the medium is the message" (McLuhan 1964, 19), only to change the emphasis on the words later so that the statement read: "the medium is the *massage*" (McLuhan and Fiore 1967, 1). What McLuhan meant was that all forms of media influence our balance of senses.

In one of his most well-known works, *Understanding Media: The Extensions of Man*, (1964) he wrote: "We have extended our central nervous system itself in a global embrace, abolishing both space and time as far as our planet is concerned. Rapidly, we approach the final phase of the extension of man—technological simulation of consciousness" (McLuhan 1964, 19). The more stimulating an artificial environment, the more our senses react by allowing the environment to wash over us. The less stimulating a form of medium, the more our senses have to fill in what is not included. Therefore, going to an IMAX movie would be less sensory involving than listening to the radio, where the audio messages prompted us to imagine more of what was going on in our minds. Many scholars took the ideas of McLuhan and went further with the concept of what happens to the body when we use media. These ideas were further developed by others who took the basic idea of media, and the mediated form of experience when using technology, to develop contemporary ideas about the relationship of virtual reality and the body (Heim 1991, 59–80). And, as we learn more about the way the brain functions to create a sensory balance in our lives (Hepler 2012), the ability to apply virtual reality technologies and concepts has begun to revolutionize a number of aspects of the information society.

Aspects of cybernetics that Wiener discussed in the 1940s that focus on the relationship of human beings and machines in a system that measures communication, control, and feedback to alter one's senses through virtual reality has provided a provocative metaphor for many of today's technologies that allow us to register a physical presence in cyberspace. Virtual reality technologies have been used to create simulations to train police, the military, medical personnel, and other critical care workers, when real-world training would be too dangerous or costly.

Through virtual reality programs it is now possible to have virtual organizational meetings, training sessions, and virtual reality classrooms. The virtual reality industry has exploded and has moved from the state of being a metaphor for something other than the real-world, to a fully fledged research area that combined computer science, communications, mathematics, and kinesthetics.

See also: Android; Cybernetics; Network Theory; 3D Printing; Wiener, Norbert

Further Reading

Heim, Michael. 1991. "The Erotic Ontology of Cyberspace." In *Cyberspace: First Steps*, edited by Michael Benedikt. Cambridge, MA: MIT Press, 59–80.

Hepler, John C. 2012. "The Impact of Transformational Technology: Does Changing the Medium Change the Message?" Paper presented at the Mid-Atlantic Popular & American Culture Association, Pittsburgh, Pennsylvania, April 30.

McLuhan, Marshall. 1964. *Understanding Media: The Extensions of Man.* New York: Signet Books, 19.

McLuhan, Marshall, and Quentin Fiore. 1967. *The Medium Is the Massage: An Inventory of Effects.* New York: Bantam Books.

Virus (see Malware)

W

Wearable Technology

With smaller, more powerful technologies being developed on what seems like a daily basis, it hasn't taken long to create an entire range of wearable technology that has the potential to change where and how we use them. Though experiments and expensive prototypes have been around for 20 years or more, wearable technology has been primarily popular with cyber enthusiasts while the general public has retained a passing interest. Today, however, wearable technology has become more available to the average consumer and is having an effect on fashion. The 2015 International Consumer Electronics Show in Las Vegas highlighted a number of "wearables" and products leading to what has been referred to as the "Internet of Things" (IoT). What these technologies have in common is that they allow us to connect to the Internet wirelessly, for new applications and older, reimagined, purposes.

Google's Google Glass was an experiment in computing with a pair of eyeglasses, and as discussed in the Google entry in this encyclopedia, the company went through many iterations of development before Google decided to stop supporting the project, even though what the company learned about Google Glass will undoubtedly shape many of the future products developed by Google Ventures. But, in terms of wearable technology, Google Glass was only one of the first projects marketed to the public.

Gamers have long been interested in the immersive characteristics afforded by wearables, and one of the first virtual reality headsets made available to the public was the Oculus Rift, sold to consumers in 2015. When Oculus VR, the independent company that developed the Rift for gaming purposes began to develop its headset in 2012, it raised $2.4 million within the first two years. At the Consumer Electronics Show in 2015, several companies debuted their wearable products including Microsoft's HoloLens Augmented Reality headset, and the Osterhaut Design Group's eyewear that delivers graphics to the user's central frame of vision, unlike the Google Glass positioning of the visual information unit in the upper corner of one lens. Epson introduced smart glasses too, called the Moverio BT-200, with a potential for making their glasses simulate 3D images.

Some wearables have already hit the market and have found dedicated users. Fitbit activity trackers come in a range of sizes, styles, and models, and (depending on price) have the ability to track a person's physical activity, caloric input and output, heart rate, and more. But while Fitbit is one of the most successful activity trackers, there are a number of other products that do essentially the same thing. Between April 2013 and March 2014, approximately 3.3 million fitness bands and activity trackers were sold in the United States (Thompson 2014, 26).

Most of the wearables today connect through smartphones, and some analysts have predicted that the wearable market will grow faster than the smartphone market did, largely because wearables can piggyback on smartphone access to the Internet, rather than having to go through the long process of connecting disparate systems, as mobile phones and smartphones did. Research has shown that the time a consumer is willing to wait for accessing data is approximately two seconds before interest in using the device begins to wane (Wasik 2014, 95), but wearable technology has now met that goal and can potentially move toward having the device "know" what the consumer wants before activating the device. It does this through understanding the consumer's behavior, and "anticipating" a typical search for information.

In 2015, a number of wristwatches emerged, like the Apple Watch (with models retailing from $350 to $17,000) that connects to the user's other Apple products, and the Samsung Galaxy Gear Watch (approximately $300) that has a camera, calendar, and microphone to make phone calls.

While some of the major multimedia companies like Google or Samsung have company divisions that raise the venture capital to develop wearables, many of the smaller start-ups that have invested in wearables have raised funding through crowdfunding on the Internet. Two Kickstarter projects have resulted in the NFC Ring, a piece of jewelry that has a near-field-communication chip in it that allows the ring to lock doors, but also access touchless payment networks that are already used in many places throughout the United Kingdom and Europe. The other device is the Embrace+ (pronounced Embrace Plus) that notifies users of information from their smartphones that signals messages based on colors. Different colors flash to let users know that a particular person is trying to reach them, even when they can't answer their phones at that moment.

Wearables have also had a major impact on psychology and emotional health. Many of these types of technologies are called haptic technologies, and communicate directly through the wearer's skin through vibrations, or by providing a buzz or vibration that allows the wearer to monitor behavior. For example, the Jawbone

UP is a bracelet that senses activity and the wearer's physical state and produces feedback on exercise, diet, and sleep. Posture sensors can communicate with a person to make sure they sit or stand up straight, and some technologies that have actually been available for some time tap a person's arm when it is time to take medication or warn a person when they are exerting too much activity (Morris and Aguilera 2012, 625).

See also: Gaming; Virtual Reality

Further Reading

Morris, Margaret E., and Adrian Aguilera. 2012. "Mobile, Social, and Wearable Computing and the Evolution of Psychological Practice." *Professional Psychological Research,* 43: 622–626.

Thompson, Clive. 2014. "Good Vibrations: Tech That Talks through Your Skin." *Wired,* 22: 26.

Wasik, Bill. 2014. "Try It On." *Wired,* 22: 90–99.

Web 2.0

While there are several variations on definitions of Web 2.0, it is generally agreed that the term came from O'Reilly Media's Web 2.0 Conference, held in 2004. Media writer Tim O'Reilly described Web 2.0 as an upgraded level of the web that has the potential for many interactive functions that facilitate and enable participation by individuals in web content creation and sharing through social networks, or in other ways. The term has also become a brand for a type of content that flows over the web.

The term signals a shift from the earlier web, or Web 1.0, in which much of the information was "one-way" information, with significantly less opportunity for the user to contribute to, and create, messages themselves. The designations have to do with the sophistication of the way in which the web is used, and the ongoing development of the architecture of the World Wide Web.

The movement to a Web 2.0 concept reflects the larger reality that the web, Internet, software development, and growing area of e-commerce all developed individually, though symbiotically. Hardware manufacturers were protecting their new developments and raising funds to support more traditional manufacturing of hardware systems, but software developers were working on freeware and on raising venture capital to support new projects. Many legacy companies were trying to import their old models based on raising advertising revenue, while some of the new efforts at creating systems to facilitate collaborative work shifted traditional ideas of copyright and payment for systems into new models of shared beliefs and a different measurement of economic value. In some ways, the development of Web 2.0 brought together two clashing visions of the Internet and web. While Tim Berners-Lee wanted the World Wide Web to remain open and free to users, entrepreneurs like Mark Andreessen and Netscape looked for models of payment for services. Legacy print companies shifted their newspapers and magazines to the Internet and hoped that people would be willing to pay for the service to protect the print industries. Web 2.0 marked a time in history when people who were concerned about the future of online activity and commerce realized that multiple economic models were likely to exist for some time.

At the first Web 2.0 conference, O'Reilly and John Battelle identified the defining features of Web 2.0. They include: (1) An acknowledgment that the web is a platform. If the term Web 1.0 had been used, it would have defined the simpler web, such as that used by Netscape, which did not have the dynamic features offered by Microsoft and therefore presented information in a less interactive manner; (2) Web 2.0 fosters the idea of collective intelligence, or the ideas of many; (3) O'Reilly and Battelle posited that data drives the web; (4) the timing of software releases has ended; (5) programmable models have become lightweight; (6) software extends to multiple forms of media; (7) users may have a "rich-user" experience; and (8) both development and business models are changing.

In summary, Web 2.0 facilitated ideas of collaboration and exchange of information, and acknowledged that the interactive features of online communication would employ multiple economic models that would affect legacy media as well as the new producer/user models that were emerging through social media and social networks.

See also: Berners-Lee, Tim; European Council for Nuclear Research (CERN); World Wide Web (WWW)

Further Reading

O'Reilly, Tim. 2014. "What Is Web 2.0? Design Patterns and Business Models for the Next Generation of Software." In *The Social Media Reader*, edited by Michael Mandiberg. New York: New York University Press, 32–52.

Webisode

The term *webisode* is derived from a specific type of content tied to the growing popularity of Internet television. While the idea of users generating video content to post on the web comes from terms such as "vlogs" or "vlogging" (video blogging) to accompany individual blogs online, the term webisode has grown to encompass all forms of user-generated, and corporate-generated, video content posted to the Internet and/or web. Essentially, a webisode is a short form of video content intended to be viewed over the Internet. While some people call a one-time short video on the web a webisode, the more specific identification deals with short, episodic, scripted series content.

Webisodes are a form of creative content with hybrid characteristics reflecting the shift from television viewing by means of broadcast or cable, to Internet delivery—through computers to Internet-ready televisions, direct to laptops, or even to mobile phones. In the process the "connection" a viewer makes to the content on their personal devices is just as compelling an idea of connected viewing as the migration from one distribution form to another. Whereas many of the ideas behind webisodes come from traditional television and film genres, both webisode content and viewer engagement provide different relationships between and among producers, viewers, and viewership.

The short history of Internet and web delivery of television provides a few clues about how webisodes are contributing to entertainment and information choice for consumers, and how the distribution medium of the Internet changes viewer relationships with content. In 1995, the advertising agency Fattal and Collins financed an Internet-based fictional series set in a California beach house called *The Spot*. Viewers could correspond with the fictional characters in the show through blogs and e-mails and influence the way the narrative of the series evolved. Advertising was primarily dealt with through banner ads and product placement. Within a few short years, other production companies and cable networks began to experiment with the same type of content that encouraged viewer involvement and direct access to a level of "participation" to influence storyline and action.

By 2005, creative personnel were producing online webisodes, but were also experimenting with webisodes that could be delivered to the small screen of mobile phones. As streaming technologies became more available the veritable floodgates of professionally produced content competed against the posting of original user-generated content on YouTube (launched in October 2006), and it became increasingly difficult to tell who or what was responsible for some of the content online. Perhaps one of the first truly viral hits was *lonelygirl15*, which captured viewers actively and emotionally. When, in 2006, *lonelygirl15* was outed as a fictional series, viewers were outraged by the hoax, but the power of the Internet to reach viewers with engaging episodic series had come of age and become an alternative to traditional entertainment. The viral success lonelygirl15 at the initial cost of $150 per episode and spin-offs from around the world showed there was money to be made in this low-cost production form and prompted *The New York Times* to quote one person behind-the-scenes, who said of the production team: "They were like the new Marshall McLuhan" (Heffernan and Zeller 2006).

While there were many successful series produced throughout the years, one of the most notable webisodes was produced by Joss Whedon, known as a television industry insider with the highly successful series, *Buffy the Vampire Slayer.* Produced in 2008 during the 2007–2008 Hollywood Writers Guild strike, Whedon and his friends, including Felicia Day, who herself was having success with her new web game–based webisode, *The Guild*, produced *Dr. Horrible's Sing-Along Blog*, a three-part web series that netted $2.6 million even before being released on DVD. *"Dr. Horrible"* was even given an Emmy in 2009 by the Television Academy of Arts and Sciences. The critical and monetary success that followed drove both big Hollywood content providers to seriously consider webisodes a viable distribution medium. The self-referential nature of webisodes that embraced both the interactive components of fan-responses and low-cost production values possible through low-cost video production techniques and Internet delivery drove producers—big and small—to the Internet as an alternative to traditional Hollywood distribution. By 2009, the industry had validated this new content and distribution system by establishing the International Academy of Web Television, charged with honoring primarily the Hollywood insider-produced content through the annual Streamy Awards.

See also: Blogs; Podcast; Prosumer; Streaming Media

Further Reading

Heffernan, Virginia, and Tom Zeller Jr. 2006. "The Lonelygirl That Really Wasn't." *New York Times.* Accessed October 12, 2014: http://www.nytimes.com/2006/09/13/technology/13lonely.html.

Hustveldt, Mark. 2008. "Dr. Horrible Could Bank 2.6 Million Even Before DVDs." TubeFilter. Accessed September 21, 2012: http://www.tubefilter.com/2008/07/23/dr-horrible-could-bank-26-million-even-before-dvds-2/.

Wiener, Norbert

Mathematician and philosopher Norbert Wiener (1894–1964) conducted research on electronic systems and authored the influential 1948 book, *Cybernetics: Or Control and Communication in the Animal and the Machine.* His work led to advances in electronic engineering, electronic communication, and control systems that led to advanced study of robotics and information systems. Known as "the father of the information age," Wiener was a child prodigy who entered college at the age of 11 and graduated from Harvard at age 18.

The concept of "feedback," so critical in information and communications study, was instrumental to the eventual development of the computer, information theory, and network theory. The list of scholars who were influenced by his ideas are many and varied. John von Neumann cited his influence in the development of the computer. Mathematician Claude Shannon used his ideas to develop the mathematical theory of communication as well as advanced information theory. Gregory Bateson and Margaret Mead, both anthropologists, applied cybernetics and feedback concepts to the role of human communication.

Though Wiener died in 1964, his legacy lives on, and his work is once again being celebrated. As we move toward more realistic visions of humans and machines working together, either through wearable technology, robotics, or the study of artificial intelligence, his ideas have once again become attractive to technologists and humanists who see how forward thinking his research really was. In 2014 the Institute of Electrical and Electronics Engineers (IEEE) celebrated his work with a conference on "Norbert Wiener in the 21st Century" dedicated to scholarly work on the ideas that he proposed more than half a century ago.

See also: Cybernetics; Network Theory

Further Reading

Conway, Flo, and Jim Siegelman. 2006. *Dark Hero of the Information Age: In Search of Norbert Wiener, the Father of Cybernetics.* New York: Basic Books.
Wiener, Norbert. 1948. *Cybernetics: Or, Control and Communication in the Animal and the Machine.* New York: Wiley.

WikiLeaks

WikiLeaks was founded in 2006 by Australian Julian Assange as an online, nonprofit journalistic organization that uses the Internet to distribute news leaks and classified information from a variety of anonymous sources such as governments and corporations. According to the WikiLeaks website, the organization claims: "We are of assistance to peoples of all countries who wish to reveal unethical behavior in their governments and institutions. We aim for maximum political impact." Because official websites can be traced, WikiLeaks relies on a host of mirror sites (those that repeat a site when the original site generates too much traffic for a single server to support).

While WikiLeaks could be classified as a site where "citizen journalists" have access to post information that makes governments' and organizations' activities transparent, the organization is often referred to as a "whistle-blower" organization that gets media and the public to focus on issues that are of concern to the public, though they may be buried or protected by the activities of governments or organizations that do not want the information to be publicly available. The organization reflects a level of freedom of information that is unprecedented. What makes the function of the organization possible is the way people use technology and social networks to spread information.

When WikiLeaks first appeared, the organization claimed to be headquartered in Iceland and sponsored by the Sunlight Foundation, a group dedicated to encourage bloggers and citizens to investigate their government representatives and provide forums for people who cared about democracy. Though Sunlight officially started operating in 2006, a few citizen-activist groups predated it, with many of the same goals. For example, in 2004, Joshua Tauberer, a linguistics graduate student, developed the site GovTrack.us to access the work of the U.S. Congress. Tauberer culled internal congressional memos and updates, distilled information from them, and posted them for the public's use. Even before that, a group of citizens in the U.K. in 2003 developed a site called mySociety.org that focused on helping people use the Internet more efficiently and provided information for how people could become more civically active. These types of sites have often been referred to as "open source politics."

WikiLeaks has moved from country to country over time, and the website has been sponsored by different organizations, but because no one in the group actually gets paid (except perhaps a few of the major participants, including Julian Assange), the costs of operation remain low, and the organization is supported by public donations through bank transfers and PayPal. In 2011, WikiLeaks began accepting donations in Bitcoins.

Many of the initial WikiLeaks leaks focused on what the organization felt were injustices in the governments in Africa and Europe, but, in 2010, a number of stories and documents were published that directly affected the U.S. government. WikiLeaks published a video from an airstrike over Baghdad in which the U.S. military killed Iraqi citizens and journalists. The video became known as the *Collateral Murder* video, and brought worldwide attention to the activities of WikiLeaks, and to the founder, Julian Assange. After Assange appeared on the Comedy Central TV show *The Colbert Report*, the *Collateral Murder* video went viral and, within days, the organization had received $150,000 in donations.

The *Collateral Murder* video was leaked along with 250,000 diplomatic cables and reports that became known as the Iraq War logs and Afghan War logs by an Army intelligence analyst Bradley Manning who has since changed his name to Chelsea Manning and lives as a transwoman. Manning leaked the classified information to WikiLeaks. Manning also leaked information about the Guantanamo

Prison system to the *New York Times* and *The Guardian*, a major British publication that exposed the inhumane treatment of many of those prisoners. In July 2013, Manning was dishonorably discharged from the Army, convicted of violations of the Espionage Act and sentenced to 35 years in prison. She is currently in the Fort Leavenworth military prison in Kansas.

WikiLeaks continues to operate and has become even more powerful over time because it exposed the type of control of information earlier governments held, and the changing social relations brought about by the power of social media and the Internet as a distribution tool. Public opinion about WikiLeaks and other anonymous whistle-blower sites continues, but opinions often run the range from thinking of these sites as powerful tools for freedom of speech and government accountability to the governed, to collectivities of people who are engaged in espionage.

It seems that every politician has her or his opinion of WikiLeaks, but perhaps the evolution and reality of living with open tools for information flow can be summed up by the change of opinion articulated by Vice President Joe Biden. In 2010, Biden called Julian Assange a "high-tech terrorist," but later that year he told MSNBC's Andrea Mitchell that the leaks were not terribly damaging. He said, "Look some of the cables are embarrassing . . . but nothing that I'm aware of that goes to the essence of the relationship that would allow another nation to say 'they lied to me, we don't trust them'" (Sifry 2011, 155). While Biden's remarks may reflect different contexts, it does seem that WikiLeaks has had the type of political impact that few organizations survive—until the power of online communications and the distributed information of social networks came into effect.

Therefore, we expect many controversies to emerge because of WikiLeaks and the work of whistle-blowers, but at the same time the fundamental purpose of the group does have impact on transparency of government and on global diplomatic relations. The act of participating in leaking secret documents can be viewed as patriotic, by some, and traitorous by others. Sometimes rewards come from places with different values, and the acts of participation are seen in a new light. For example, Manning was awarded a "Whistleblowerpreis" (Whistle-blower Prize) by the German Section of the International Association of Lawyers against Nuclear Arms and the Federation of German Scientists and the Sean MacBride Peace Prize by the International Peace Bureau. In 2014 both Manning and Edward Snowden were nominated for the Nobel Peace Prize by the Icelandic and Swedish Pirate Party because both were seen to have "inspired change and encouraged public debate and policy changes that contributed to a more stable and peaceful world."

See also: Assange, Julian; Snowden, Edward

Further Reading

"Pirate Party Members Nominate Snowden, Manning for Nobel Peace Prize." 2014. RT .com. Accessed January 5, 2015: http://rt.com/news/snowden-manning-nobel-pirate-633/.

Sifry, Micah L. 2011. *WikiLeaks and the Age of Transparency*. Berkeley, CA: Counterpoint.

Wikipedia

In 2001, Jimmy Wales and Larry Sanger began an impressive project to make a user-generated encyclopedia available free on the Internet. They based the name of the encyclopedia on the Hawaiian word "wiki" meaning "quick," combined with "encyclopedia" and came up with *Wikipedia*. While there are many other wikis available on the World Wide Web, *Wikipedia* is one of the most popular sites on the Internet, and, as of 2014, was receiving almost 500 million visitors each month (Alexa Research 2015). The *New York Times* reported in 2014 that *Wikipedia* was the fifth most popular website in the world, following Google, Facebook, Yahoo!, and Microsoft.

Jimmy Wales had been a futures trader in Chicago who had earned a considerable salary. With the start of the dot-com bubble in the late 1990s, he began to create web sites, including *Bomis*, a search engine that focused on salacious photographs with a blog about people involved in the adult entertainment industry (including pornography). Based upon the success of *Bomis*, Wales and his partner, Larry Sanger, decided to create a user-generated site called *Nupedia*, which was the predecessor to *Wikipedia*. The big difference between the two sites is that while *Nupedia* was an utter disaster, *Wikipedia* has become one of the most heavily consulted websites in the world.

Wales and Sanger initially started *Nupedia* in March of 2000. The approach to creating the *Nupedia* encyclopedia involved contacting academics and scientists to write the entries. Participants who were asked to write had to send copies of their degrees to the organization to be deemed credible. Then, there was a seven-stage process of editing, fact-checking, and peer review. "After 18 months and $250,000 we had 12 articles," reported Sanger (Bruns 2008, 104).

Wales and Sanger had learned that the peer-review process used for submissions by experts to *Nupedia* was time consuming, cumbersome, expensive, and at the rate of article vetting, their project would stretch on forever. They decided to rebrand the project and use the more open-access wiki form. *Nupedia* was dissolved and rebranded as *Wikipedia* in 2001.

At first, the open source *Wikipedia* was popular, but some people tried to exploit its "openness." On his show *The Colbert Report* comedian Stephen Colbert urged his audience to find the *Wikipedia* entry on elephants and create an entry that stated their population had tripled in the last six months. So many members of his viewing audience took his challenge and logged on to *Wikipedia* to vandalize about 20 articles on elephants that the site was locked. Then a *Wikipedia* administrator blocked Colbert from the website, reportedly to verify his identity. Colbert talked about the action on his show and demonstrated one of the problems with open source websites, but, at the same time, he drove many new users to *Wikipedia*.

Over the years, *Wikipedia* has allowed those who post and edit entries to help define the rules of participating on *Wikipedia*. Anyone who wants to contribute has to agree to the terms. The result is that the quality of the articles has continually improved and the way the site identifies questionable facts has given consumers a tag to help them know how much they can trust that entry. The organization has become more rigorous in accepting online content and more rigorous in vetting that information, including disclaimers that indicate when the veracity of a statement of concept has not been proven.

Wikipedia has been criticized for allowing people without reasonable authority to post information, resulting in the contents not always being accurate or well written. But over time, the organization has worked to control the editing and formatting that is necessary to make an entry more reliable. In 2005, the science journal *Nature* examined 42 scientific entries on *Wikipedia* and compared them to the same entries in the *Encyclopedia Britannica*. The reviewers concluded that *Wikipedia* entries had approximately four inaccuracies, while the *Encyclopedia Britannica* had about three (Giles 2005, 900–901).

Wikipedia has also added a number of features over the years and has developed 288 language editions of the encyclopedia. The largest, the English *Wikipedia*, has over 4.8 million articles. According to the Alexa Research website rankings, in 2015, *Wikipedia* was the sixth most heavily consulted website in the world, and English *Wikipedia* receives approximately 63 percent of the traffic (Alexa Research 2015).

The success of *Wikipedia* prompted Jimmy Wales to start the Wikimedia Foundation (WMF) to handle all of the intellectual property rights and domain names for wiki products in 2003. The WMF is a nonprofit and charitable organization headquartered in San Francisco, California. Its purpose is to make educational content available to everyone in the world, and it provides wiki-based projects free of charge. In addition to *Wikipedia*, other major wiki projects are Wiktionary, Wikiquote, Wikibooks, Wikisource, Wikimedia Commons, Wikispecies, Wikinews, Wikiversity, Wikidata, Wikivoyage, Wikimedia Incubator, and Meta-Wiki. All wiki projects are collaboratively developed using MediaWiki software that is available through a Creative Commons license.

See also: Open Source

Further Reading

Alexa Research. 2015. "How Popular Is Wikipedia?" Accessed April 29, 2015: http://www
.alexa.com/siteinfo/wikipedia.org.

Bruns, Axel. 2008. *Blogs, Wikipedia, Second Life, and Beyond: From Production to Pro-dusage*. New York: Peter Lang.

Giles, Jim. 2005. "Special Report: Internet Encyclopaedias Go Head to Head." *Nature*, 438: 900–901.

Neate, Rupert. 2008. "Wikipedia Founder Jimmy Wales Goes Bananas." *The Telegraph*. Accessed December 5, 2014: http://www.telegraph.co.uk/finance/newsbysector/media technologyandtelecoms/3399843/Wikipedia-founder-Jimmy-Wales-goes-bananas.html.

World Wide Web (WWW)

The World Wide Web is perhaps the most recognizable portion of the Internet. The web is not the same thing as the Internet, but many people use the terms synonymously. If the web did not exist, people could still use the Internet to e-mail each other and exchange files, but it might be easiest to describe the difference between the two as identifying the Internet as the conduit through which information flows, and the World Wide Web as the network that connects websites that contain information. The Internet is made up of connections and processors, but the World Wide Web exists only in code.

The World Wide Web was developed in 1989 at the European Organization for Nuclear Research (known as CERN) through the efforts of Tim Berners-Lee. As a major research lab for particle physics and the study of the cosmos, CERN often had scientists who participated in experiments for extended periods of time, but then returned to their laboratories around the world. Berners-Lee understood the necessity of allowing these scientists to continue to connect to each other and share data, and with that in mind he began to look at how the emerging distribution of the Internet might be used to help them connect and share data. From the beginning, Berners-Lee had an egalitarian mission in mind for the web. It would be free to users, and it would be used for the purposes of bringing opportunities for collaboration and information sharing to the public for the betterment of society.

By 1990, Berners-Lee was joined by Robert Cailliau, and together they specified three protocols that eventually made the World Wide Web possible. First was the development of HyperText Markup Language (HTML). This publishing format allowed different documents to be accessed and linked together. Second, the Uniform Resource Identifier (URI) was developed to help function as an address unique to each resource on the web. The URI eventually became known as the

Uniform Resource *Locator* (URL). Finally, Hypertext Transfer Protocol (HTTP) allowed for access to linked resources from any location on the web.

Web browsers are the intermediary technologies that allow people to access and interact with web pages. Popular web browsers include Chrome, Firefox, Internet Explorer, and Safari, but, worldwide, a number of web browsers are in existence. Many computers, smartphones, and other devices come with browsers already installed. Other programs—for example, certain applications or "apps" on smartphones—can also access and display web content in a more limited fashion.

Websites are collections of individual web pages. A domain name is somewhat like a street name. Each house on the street corresponds to a URL address. An organization's website has a home page along with potentially thousands of links to other web pages for related content. Domain names are abbreviations that often give an idea to users about the type of communication being transferred over the web. The ".com" in a typical URL is called a top-level domain and the .com (dot com) actually represents a *commercial* service, not a *communication*, as is often assumed. Other top-level domains include ".gov" for the U.S. government; ".ca" for Canadian websites; ".au" for Australian sites; and ".edu" for universities and educational institutions.

With the web having celebrated its twenty-fifth birthday in 2014, many pundits have taken the opportunity to look back and see whether the web actually fulfilled its egalitarian mission. Citing cybercrime and the rise of cyberbullying and antisocial activities on the Internet, some say the web has lost its way. Others claim that it is not too late, and that the benefits of the web and the Internet clearly outweigh the potential problems.

Tim Berners-Lee used the opportunity to record a video that celebrated the web, but also called for increased use of the web to spread civil rights (see http://www .usnews.com/news/articles/2014/03/12/happy-25th-birthday-world-wide-web).

See also: Berners-Lee, Tim; Browser; European Council for Nuclear Research (CERN); Internet Corporation for Assigned Names and Numbers (ICANN)

Further Reading

Jeffries, Stuart. 2014. "How the Web Lost Its Way—And Its Founding Principles." *The Guardian*. Accessed March 30, 2015: http://www.theguardian.com/technology/2014 /aug/24/internet-lost-its-way-tim-berners-lee-world-wide-web.

Risen, Tom. 2014. "Happy 25th Birthday World Wide Web." *U.S. News and World Report*. Accessed April 20, 2015: http://www.usnews.com/news/articles/2014/03/12/happy-25th -birthday-world-wide-web.

World Wide Web Consortium (W3C)

In 1994, Tim Berners-Lee founded the World Wide Web Consortium (W3C) at the Massachusetts Institute of Technology (MIT) with the purpose of facilitating dialogue among companies that contributed to developing improvements to the World Wide Web. The W3C decided that its standards should be based on royalty-free technology, so that anyone could adopt the web and contribute to its growth and improvement. Strongly committed to a free and open Internet, and backing net neutrality, Berners-Lee and the W3C are dedicated to making the web more affordable for people all over the world.

The W3C is led by Tim Berners-Lee and CEO Jeffrey Jaffe. Members include individuals and organizations that sign membership agreements, and most have a vested interest in web technologies and products or hope to contribute to web development themselves through additional research and experimentation. Current membership includes a number of research universities around the world, global manufacturing and research companies, and government agencies.

The organization runs several working groups that focus on different aspects of improving the web, such as dealing with privacy issues, improvements in HTML, open standards, cybercurrencies, and other related matters of improving web functionality for the people of the world. Papers are published in different languages, and topics are continually updated. Each working group and paper are posted to be available for comment from anyone who wishes to register an opinion or position.

See also: Berners-Lee, Tim; European Council for Nuclear Research (CERN)

Further Reading

World Wide Web Consortium (W3C). 2014. Accessed September 23, 2014: http://www.w3.org/Consortium/.

Wozniak, Steve

Along with Steve Jobs, Steve (Stephen) Wozniak (1950–) started the Apple Computer Company. Known as "Woz" he met Steve Jobs while the two were still in high school. Wozniak is generally regarded as the genius behind the Apple computer having single-handedly designed the hardware, circuit board designs, and operating system for the Apple I.

Before the development of Apple, Jobs and Wozniak were known as pranksters. Both had read an article in an *Esquire* magazine about "phone phreaks"— people who had figured out how to get free calls on a Bell Telephone System phone by mimicking the sound of the circuits and causing connections to be made. The two collaborated on what they called the Blue Box, which essentially allowed people to make free calls. Even though the box was illegal, they built and sold about 100 of them for $40 each. As part of the testing, Wozniak called the Vatican and pretended he was Henry Kissinger and said it was imperative that he speak to the Pope. The call went through, but a clever Vatican official figured out it was a prank, and declined to wake the Pope. Still, Wozniak and Jobs had a great laugh and were encouraged by the success of the Blue Box.

Finally, while trying to sell one of the boxes, both were held at gunpoint in the illicit deal. This stopped their adventure in marketing a free call work-around technology, and, for a while, each buckled down to their own jobs. Steve Jobs was working at Atari, and Steve Wozniak worked at Hewlett-Packard (HP). Wozniak initially developed plans for a personal computer while at HP, though his job was to work on improvements for the HP calculator. He offered the specifications for the computer that was a fully functioning circuit board, monitor, and keyboard to the company, but it was not interested in developing a new line of hardware at the time. This design became known as the Apple I computer, and through Jobs's initiatives and Wozniak's tinkering with the hardware, the new computer started to attract attention. When the two discussed this design at what was known as the "Homebrew Computer Club"—a group of computer enthusiasts in the Palo Alto, California, area, interest in the design began to attract more attention. Even before Apple I was marketed, Wozniak was developing what would become Apple II, with improved circuit design, the ability to use color graphics, and packaged into a fully integrated consumer product.

In 1981, Wozniak was in a small plane crash and suffered amnesia and a number of non-life-threatening injuries. He limited his work at Apple, and chose to end his full-time employment with Apple in 1987. He now receives an annual stipend from Apple and is a stock holder in the company. Since leaving the company officially, he has engaged in a number of start-up technology firms and has become a philanthropist as well as a teacher. He donated funds to create the "Woz Lab" at the University of Colorado at Boulder, and he was a major contributor to the Children's Discovery Museum of San Jose, which named the street in front of the museum "Woz Way" in his honor.

He has been awarded a number of honors, including the Grace Murray Hopper Award (1979), and the National Medal of Technology (with Steve Jobs) in 1985. In 2000, he was inducted into the National Inventors Hall of Fame, and in 2011 he received the Isaac Asimov Science Award from the American Humanist Association. He has also received numerous honorary doctorates from universities around the world.

See also: Apple; Jobs, Steve

Further Reading

Isaacson, Walter. 2011. *Steve Jobs*. New York: Simon & Schuster, 23–29.

Wozniak, Steve, with Gina Smith. 2006. *iWoz: Computer Geek to Cult Icon: How I Invented the Personal Computer, Co-Founded Apple, and Had Fun Doing It*. New York: Norton.

Y

Yahoo!

Yahoo! is a search engine founded in 1995 and a division of Yahoo! Inc. At the beginning of 2014, Yahoo Search was the second largest search director on the web, but it was eclipsed by the larger, more dominant Google search engine. By February 2015, it had dropped to the third largest search engine in the United States, handling 12.8 percent of the search queries. Google had 64.5 percent of the searches, and Bing, 19.8 percent (comScore 2015).

Yahoo! was founded by Jerry Yang and David Filo, both electrical engineering students at Stanford. Yang and Filo were early adopters of the emerging Internet and World Wide Web and they were familiar with the early web browser, MOSAIC. They created a website called "Jerry and David's Guide to the World Wide Web," which provided a directory to other sites, and organized their site by categories such as business, education, entertainment, etc., all with dozens of other subcategories. What made the directory unique is that all entries were made by hand, until the proliferation of the information on the Internet became so vast, that they hired a web crawler to organize the listings.

At first they were running the site on the Stanford University server and were getting around 50,000 hits a day (Carlson 2015, 31); the university was not pleased with the amount of use Yang and Filo were generating. They sat down one night and decided to start their own company, and they wanted a catchy name. By going through the dictionary they chose the word Yahoo to stand for "Yet another Hierarchical Officious Oracle," and they put an exclamation point at the end of the acronym. In January 1994, they officially named the organization Yahoo! and, by 1995, they incorporated the business and created the domain name "yahoo.com."

Yahoo! is unique among search engines because it started early, compared to others. According to Nicholas Carlson, in the 1990s, for many, "Yahoo was the Internet." The problem, according to Carlson, was that Yang and Filo really didn't have a plan to have Yahoo! become a business. The company grew rapidly and, by

1998, it was the most popular starting point for web users. It also was the first Internet company to branch out into other types of content. It was the first company to carry news as part of its service, and it established a relationship with the Reuters news service to supply that news. It also started carrying ads in 1995 and was a part of the online advertising juggernaut. It began making a number of acquisitions and profited greatly during the dot-com bubble, with stock prices closing at $118.75 a share at the beginning of January 2000. But then the bubble burst, and within a year, stock prices were down to a mere $8.11 by September 2001 (Carlson 2015, 31–37).

In 2000, Yahoo! began using Google as the search engine, and over the next four years, it developed Yahoo Search, which went live in 2004. From that point they started to incorporate features that had been successful on other browsers. Google's Gmail was generating buzz, so in 2007, Yahoo! changed their e-mail service to provide unlimited storage, but still, the business did not bounce back after the dot-com crash.

In February 2008, the Microsoft Corporation made a bid to acquire Yahoo! for $44.6 billion, but Yahoo! rejected the bid, claiming that it undervalued the company and a sale would not be in the best interest of the stockholders. The following years were not particularly easy for Yahoo!, but Yahoo! knew something else was in the works that could change the future fortune of the company.

Yahoo! had started exploring the market in China in 1999 with the launch of a platform for e-mail and instant messaging, and a translated version of U.S. news into two Chinese languages. The Chinese market for the services grew to 40 million by 2002, but Yahoo! was one of the only social media companies to be able to crack the market.

The China division of Yahoo! knew of the private company in the south of China founded by Jack Ma called Alibaba, an online retail establishment very much like Amazon. In 2004, Alibaba had generated more than $4 billion in gross merchandise sales through its platform and it had established two start-up business lines, Alipay, a new payment system designed to work like PayPal; and Taobao, an auctions site (Decker 2014). The prospect of working with a company that had already made inroads into the large Chinese population attracted Yahoo! and, by 2005, Yahoo! invested $1 billion is Alibaba, which earned Yahoo! 40 percent of the Alibaba business.

Cultural problems made the establishment of social networking sites like Facebook and Twitter difficult for the Chinese market because the government blocked such sites, but Yahoo!'s limited use made the company more palatable for government officials. What also helped was that Yang and Ma seemed to share a cultural affinity for social media, and that led to the most successful inroad of any U.S. Internet company in China.

On July 16, 2012, Marissa Mayer was appointed president and CEO of Yahoo!, and the public's attention once again turned to Yahoo! with its young, attractive

CEO. While Mayer did contribute to a number of departmental reorganizations within the company, her tenure has been marked most by the acquisitions she has made, and the revenue created when Yahoo! announced that it was selling a portion of its stake in Alibaba. It would retain 23 percent rather than the original 40 percent, and the result was that Yahoo! ended up with $4.3 billion after taxes and fees (Letzing and Mozur 2012).

Under Mayer's leadership, Yahoo! has acquired a number of high-profile companies. She has indicated that she hopes to take the company toward a more mobile market, so many of the apps she has acquired for the company have attracted attention to Yahoo!'s other services. In 2013, Yahoo! acquired Tumblr for $1.1 billion. By mid-July 2013, the acquisition of Tumblr resulted in greater traffic to the Yahoo! site than Google's site, but that rush to use Tumblr did not help sustain return customers, and, by 2015, Yahoo!'s prominence was once again showing signs of fading.

On March 12, 2014, Yahoo officially announced its partnership with Yelp Inc., which it hoped would help boost its local search results to better compete with services like Google. When Yahoo! acquired the video ad company BrightRoll in 2014, it looked as though it was positioning itself for much more aggressive advertising.

See also: Mayer, Marissa; Tumblr

Further Reading

Carlson, Nicholas. 2015. *Marissa Mayer and the Fight to Save Yahoo!* New York: Hachette Book Group, 31–37.

"comScore Releases February 2015 U.S. Desktop Search Engine Rankings." 2015. comScore. Accessed April 29, 2015: http://www.comscore.com/Insights/Market-Rankings /comScore-Releases-February-2015-US-Desktop-Search-Engine-Rankings.

Decker, Sue. 2014. "An Insider's Account of the Yahoo-Alibaba Deal." *Harvard Business Review*, August 6, 2014. Accessed April 29, 2015: https://hbr.org/2014/08/an -insiders-account-of-the-yahoo-alibaba-deal/.

Letzing, John, and Paul Mozur. 2012. "Yahoo Closes Alibaba Deal, Will Dole Out $3.65 Billion." *Wall Street Journal*. Accessed April 29, 2015: http://www.wsj.com/articles /SB10000872396390443816804578004290541336274.

Yelp

Yelp is a company based in San Francisco, California, that develops and hosts crowdsourced reviews about local businesses. Started in 2004 by Jeremy Stoppelman and Russell Simmons, the website, which is available online and through mobile devices, provides customer reviews to people who are seeking information about retail establishments like restaurants and businesses and gives information such as the company's hours, location, and telephone number. As Stoppleman has said, the purpose of the site "is connecting people with great local businesses."

The founders of Yelp formerly worked at PayPal, and the $1 million seed money to start Yelp was provided by one of PayPal's cofounders, Max Levchin. After a rocky start in 2004, the company redesigned its site, and, in 2005, immediately started attracting attention.

Though the company did not become profitable until 2012, it has become a leader in online advertising. In fact, Yelp is really in the business of advertising local businesses. Local businesses pay Yelp to include their establishments on the site, and customers browse Yelp offerings that are also ad supported. What makes it very different from just a regular advertising site is that people can contribute reviews and suggest referrals, and they can make reservations through the "Open Table" feature on the site. Through *crowdsourcing*, Yelp has become an influential app that has attracted the attention of much larger Internet giants, like Facebook and Google.

While Yelp has a web app, its users are increasingly using mobile phones, and though the mobile ad market is not as profitable as web ads yet, many people are banking on the fact that Yelp will be one of the future leaders in promoting local businesses and making money while gathering information from the app's users. By 2014, Yelp had 135 million monthly visitors and gathered 71 million reviews worldwide. Revenue that year was already up 63 percent from the previous year (Chafkin 2013). What makes Yelp so likely to become profitable is that people who use the app are really looking for the goods and services listed on the site, so the click through rate (the measure of efficiency in linking a consumer with a company) is built into the design of the feature. And, because Yelp's features are local, the site capitalizes on what Sheryl Sandberg, COO of Facebook, calls "the holy grail of the Internet" (Chafkin 2013).

Between 2009 and 2012, Yelp expanded the business in Europe and Asia. It was courted by Google as a possible acquisition, but the two parties never agreed upon terms, and once Yelp began to offer stock options in 2012, it started to record a profit. By 2013, Yelp saw $46.1 million in net revenue in the first quarter alone.

Yelp, like other review sites, has been criticized for allowing bogus reviews to be posted on its site. In most cases, the types of reviews are posted anonymously, and readers sometimes question whether the company advertised is just hyping its own product at the expense of the trust elements that really contribute to making reviews fair and impartial. In court proceedings, Yelp has conceded that about 25 percent of their reviews seem suspicious ("Spotting the Fakes among the Five-Star Reviews" 2015). Though Yelp has about 10 percent of its employees dedicated to looking for bogus reviews, searching for them and proving they are not authentic is time consuming and expensive ("Spotting the Fakes among the Five-Star Reviews"

2015). Like other companies that tout the collaborative aspects of online communication, the matter of authenticity of reviews is part of the business's reputation.

See also: App

Further Reading

Chafkin, Max. 2013. "Not Just Another Web 2.0 Company, Yelp Basks in Its Star Power." *Fast Company Magazine.* Accessed February 23, 2015: http://www.fastcompany.com /3002950/not-just-another-web-20-company-yelp-basks-its-star-power.
"Spotting the Fakes among the Five-Star Reviews." 2015. PBS Newshour (transcript). Accessed April 22, 2015: http://www.pbs.org/newshour/bb/spotting-fakes-among-five -star-reviews/.

YouTube

YouTube was created by three former employees of PayPay in 2005 in Silicon Valley, Chad Hurley, Steven Chen, and Jawed Karim. Though there are different stories about how they came up with the idea, one of the most pervasive stories is that the idea was inspired by the famous Janet Jackson "wardrobe malfunction" that took place at the 2004 Super Bowl half-time show during which Justin Timberlake pulled a part of Jackson's costume, revealing a nipple. The three reasoned that even though there was no way to see the event again, there was so much press about it and the Federal Communications Commission (FCC) had made such a big deal about the decency infraction, there must be a market for people who would want to see video clips over and over again.

Another story is that the three were inspired by Flickr, the photo-sharing site, and thought that there might be great interest in people seeing other peoples' short videos. What the three creators did with YouTube was put together an easy to use website where people could upload and share short videos. Other companies were also doing this, but YouTube didn't limit the number you could post and they provided URLs and HTML code that allowed people to embed their videos on the website. In short, YouTube worked more effectively than other sites available at the time. But still, YouTube was not considered an "overnight" hit.

In April 2005, as the three creators experimented with posting content on the first YouTube site. Karim uploaded the first video to YouTube—an 18-second clip of himself standing in front of the elephant enclosure at the San Diego Zoo. By the time YouTube went live in the beta stage (experimental), most of the videos had been taken by the three founders and their friends. Chen had recorded a few videos with his cat, Stinky. But as "exciting" as these videos may sound, the public wasn't paying much attention to YouTube or this new art form. The three posted ads on craigslist for "good looking babes" who they were willing to pay to help advertise YouTube, but no one responded. Then, Karim sent an e-mail to Chen and Hurley suggesting that viewers would probably like music videos and sketches from *Saturday Night Live.*

YouTube's first success was a sketch from the television show *Saturday Night Live* that was posted in December 2005, and within the first week was viewed 1.2 million times. The "Lazy Sunday" sketch, with Andy Samberg and Chris Parnell talking about eating cupcakes and going to see a matinee of *The Chronicles of Narnia,* finally drew considerable attention to YouTube even though NBCUniversal complained that the sketch, along with other clips, violated the Digital Millennium Copyright Act (DMCA). NBCUniversal's request forced them to take down the video, but, by the time they did, it had been seen more than five million times (Seabrook 2012, 24).

The cultural significance of YouTube is one of the most fascinating features of the site. As an example of the type of social network that challenges previous economic models, YouTube represents ideas of "do-it-yourself" cultural content, as well as participatory, and sharing cultural models (Burgess and Green 2009, 15). It has introduced a number of memes to popular culture, like GrumpyCat, Lonelygirl15, and Gangnam style, but it has also become one of the most well-known sites for people to create their own content and "publish" it on the web. For those reasons, it has also become a financial powerhouse. In November 2006, Google bought the service for $1.65 billion, and, by 2008, YouTube was one of the most visited websites, globally. Today, it boasts an audience of one billion people. Over 300 hours of video are uploaded every minute, and the ad revenue from YouTube's mobile platform has increased by 100 percent (Statistics 2015).

YouTube has gone from a single channel into a multichannel organization that extends beyond short, user-generated one-time videos to the creation of entire web series (some of which are called webisodes). Collections of original material financially supported by mainstream media content producers has found YouTube to be one of the best ways of reaching audiences—particularly young audiences. Many YouTubers (as they are called) who have produced content that has attracted subscribers have found advertisers that support their efforts, and many star YouTubers have made a considerable amount of money on their channels. The online website *BusinessInsider* posted the top 20 YouTubers in 2014 who earned over $1 million from their channels, and ranked Swedish YouTuber Felix Arvid Ulf Kjelberg as number one, earning between $825,000 and $8.47 million annually, after YouTube's 45 percent cut of the advertising revenue. Describing him as a "foul-mouthed Swedish video game commentator," the number one YouTuber in the world has approximately 3.69 billion viewers around the world (Jacobs 2014).

The average YouTuber watches YouTube content for only about 15 minutes a day, but YouTube has plans to keep the average viewer connected for a longer time. Since 2005, YouTube has been exploring streaming video that would allow the site to be the platform for television and film viewing as well as for uploaded user content. Unlike broadcast or cable television, YouTube has an infinite number of channels that can be created. In 2012, Shishir Mehrotra, YouTube's vice president of product management said: "The benchmark for what makes mass-market television has changed. Cable has run out of space. If you're going to broadcast content to everybody whether or not they watch it, you can only afford to broadcast a few hundred channels. But if you move to a world where you can broadcast on demand to only whoever wants it, now you can support millions of channels" (Honan 2012). The goal is to have YouTube become the major platform for watching all television, and to do that it started with niche programming to cultivate a loyal group of dedicated YouTube watchers.

Early in 2011, YouTube began cultivating creative personnel who might develop programming for a variety of YouTube channels. Backed by Google, a number of those channels have become popular, but overall, the experiment was judged as having limited success. YouTube offered several million dollars in funding to be used as development money. Once the advances were earned back, YouTube shared ad revenues with the creators. YouTube maintained an exclusive right to use the content for a year, but the creators retained ownership of their intellectual property. But what was most valuable to the organization in the process of expanding the number of channels and funding original content was an understanding of who watches, and what they watch. That understanding of niche audiences may be the key to YouTube's possible success in the future as a source for television content that can be accessed on any form over the web. As Shishir Mehrotra explained: "Advertising will be done at the level of the audience rather than at the level of the show. Content is no longer proxy for an audience—we know who the audience is. We know what your preferences are, the types of shows you like to watch" (Seabrook 2012, 26).

YouTube has plans to introduce original half-hour scripted content to their audience, based upon a subscription model of measuring viewership. At the 2015 National Association of Television Programming Executives (NATPE) conference, Alex Carloss, YouTube's executive in charge of future programming initiatives, announced that new content will not be restricted to half-hour formats, and that longer programs were being considered.

See also: Meme; Mobile Phone Cameras; Niche Marketing; Prosumer; Webisode

Further Reading

Burgess, Jean, and Joshua Green. 2009. *YouTube: Online Video and Participatory Culture.* Malden, MA: Polity.

Honan, Matt. 2012. "YouTube Re-Imagined: 505,347,842 Channels on Every Single Screen" *Wired.* Accessed April 20, 2015: http://www.wired.com/2012/08/500-million -youtube-channels/.

Jacobs, Harrison. 2014. "We Ranked YouTube's Biggest Stars by How Much Money They Make." Business Insider. Accessed March 29, 2015: http://www.businessinsider.com .au/richest-youtube-stars-2014-3#20-evantubehd-1.

Seabrook, John. 2012. "Streaming Dreams: YouTube Turns Pro." *The New Yorker,* 86: 24–30.

Statistics 2015. "YouTube." Accessed April 20, 2015: https://www.youtube.com/yt/press /statistics.html.

Z

Zuckerberg, Mark

Mark Elliot Zuckerberg (1984–), an American computer programmer, cofounded the popular social networking website Facebook. Though the concept of social networking was the result of a few computer enthusiasts, Zuckerberg is most often associated as the "developer" of the Facebook site, having written the original code that made Facebook viable. By the time he was in his mid-20s, he became one of the richest people in the world, though his official salary from Facebook is $1 a year. However, because of stock options and Facebook's growth, Zuckerberg's net worth in 2014 was about $33.1 billion. In 2014, he ranked number 16 in *Forbes* magazine's ranking of the world's billionaires (Borison 2014).

Zuckerberg was born in White Plains, New York, and began studies at Harvard University in 2002. At the time, Harvard student residence houses had online photographs of their residents that were called "facebooks" to help residents in the house recognize and connect with each other. Zuckerberg developed a website called Facemash that used the photographs without the students' permission and the site was soon shut down after students and the administration objected to the unauthorized use of residents' pictures and information.

In February 2004, Zuckerberg launched thefacebook.com with the original intent that it be used only by Harvard students. But soon, Zuckerberg and a few of his friends extended the service to other university campuses and, later, to high schools.

By June 2004, Facebook officially incorporated as a private business. Zuckerberg left Harvard and moved to Palo Alto, California, where he became the company's chief executive officer (CEO). After a shaky financial start during which time Zuckerberg considered selling the business, Facebook became a profitable business, largely because of advertising revenues. Over time, Zuckerberg began to acquire a number of different start-ups that further attracted users and offered a wider range of apps that could be connected through one's Facebook account. As his personal fortune grew, he also donated to, and supported, a variety of educational causes.

A 2010 film called *The Social Network* based on the book *The Accidental Billionaires* by Ben Mezrich (2009) portrayed Zuckerberg and the founding of Facebook in an unflattering way. Facebook employees and other people who knew Zuckerberg have challenged its accuracy.

See also: Facebook; Social Networking

Further Reading

Borison, Rebecca. 2014. "The Fabulous Life of Mark Zuckerberg." Business Insider. Accessed April 20, 2015: http://www.businessinsider.com/the-fabulous-life-of-mark-zuckerberg-2014-7.

Mezrich, Ben. 2009. *The Accidental Billionaires*. New York: Random House.

Bibliography

Aamoth, Doug. 2014. "John Oliver's Net Neutrality Rant Crashes FCC Servers." *Time*. Accessed March 26, 2015: http://time.com/2817567/john-oliver-net -neutrality-fcc/.

"About What We Do." Federal Trade Commission. Accessed March 30, 2015: https://www.ftc.gov/about-ftc/our-history.

Abramson, Jill. 2015. "The Public Interest: Defying the White House, from the Pentagon Papers to Snowden." *Columbia Journalism Review* 53: 14–16.

"A Brief History of the Birth of the Federal Trade Commission." 2009. Federal Trade Commission (FTC). Accessed March 30, 2015: https://www.youtube.com /watch?v=NssfPApe5iQ.

Ahmed, Saeed, and Tony Marco. 2014. "Anita Sarkeesian Forced to Cancel Utah State Speech after Mass Shooting Threat." CNN.com. Accessed December 29, 2014: http://edition.cnn.com/2014/10/15/tech/utah-anita-sarkeesian-threat/index.html.

Albergotti, Reed. 2006. "The Most Inventive Towns in America." *Wall Street Journal*. Accessed October 28, 2014: http://online.wsj.com/news/articles/SB115 352188346314087?mg=reno64-wsj&url=http%3A%2F%2Fonline.wsj.com%2F article%2FSB115352188346314087.html.

Alexa Research. 2015. "How Popular Is Wikipedia?" Accessed April 29, 2015: http://www.alexa.com/siteinfo/wikipedia.org.

Alexander, Alison, and Jarice Hanson, eds. 2016. *Taking Sides: Clashing Views on Controversial Issues in Media and Society,* 14th ed. Dubuque, IA: McGraw-Hill.

Allen, Paul. 2012. *Idea Man: A Memoir by the Cofounder of Microsoft*. New York: Penguin.

"A Look at Comcast's Changes over the Decades." 2011. *Seattle Times*. Accessed April 2, 2015: http://www.seattletimes.com/business/a-look-at-comcasts-changes -over-the-decades/.

Amazon.com, Inc. 2014. "Annual Report Form 10-K." U.S. Securities and Exchange Commission. Accessed November 8, 2014: http://sec.gov/Archives/edgar/data /1018724/000101872414000006/0001018724-14-0000006-index.htm.

Anderson, Chris. 2006. *The Long Tail: Why the Future of Business Is Selling Less of More*. New York: Hyperion.

Anderson, Chris. 2009. *Free: The Future of a Radical Price*. New York: Hyperion.

Angwin, Julia. 2009. *Stealing MySpace: The Battle to Control the Most Popular Website in America*. New York: Random House.

"Anonymous Hacks, Outs Missouri KKK." 2014. *Toronto Sun*. Accessed December 3, 2014: http://www.torontosun.com/2014/11/17/anonymous-hacks-outs-missouri-kkk.

Ante, Spencer E. 2012. "Kevin Rose: Digg Failed Because 'Social Media Grew Up.'" *Wall Street Journal*. Accessed February 26, 2015: http://blogs.wsj.com/digits/2012/07/13/kevin-roses-exit-interview-digg-failed-because-social-media-grew-up/.

"Apple Posts the Biggest Quarterly Profit in History." 2015. BBC News. Accessed April 7, 2015: http://www.bbc.com/news/business-31012410.

Arango, Tim. 2010. "How the AOL–Time Warner Merger Went So Wrong." *New York Times*. Accessed December 1, 2014: http://www.nytimes.com/2010/01/11/business/media/11merger.html?pagewanted=all&_r=.

Arnold, Chris. 2015. "15 Years after the Dot-Com Bust, a Nasdaq Record." NPR's *All Things Considered*. Accessed March 24, 2015: http://www.npr.org/blogs/thetwo-way/2015/04/23/397113284/15-years-after-the-dot-com-bust-nasdaq-closes-at-new-record.

Arthur, Charles. 2006. "What Is the 1% Rule?" *The Guardian*. Accessed January 8, 2015: http://www.theguardian.com/technology/2006/jul/20/guardianweekly technologysection2.

Arthur, Charles. 2012. *Digital Wars: Apple, Google, Microsoft & the Battle for the Internet*. London and Philadelphia: Kogan Page, Inc.

Assange, Julian. 2014. *When Google Met WikiLeaks*. O/R Books.

Au, Wagner James. 2008. *The Making of Second Life*. New York: HarperCollins.

Auletta, Ken. 2001. *World War 3.0: Microsoft and Its Enemies*. New York: Random House.

Auletta, Ken. 2011. "You've Got News: Can Tim Armstrong Save AOL?" *The New Yorker*. Accessed December 3, 2014: http://www.newyorker.com/magazine/2011/01/24/youve-got-news.

Bagdikian, Ben. 2003. *The New Media Monopoly*, 5th ed. Boston: Beacon Press.

Bamford, James. 2014. "The Most Wanted Man in the World." *Wired*, 22: 88–95.

Barabasi, Albert-Laszlo. 2002. *Linked: How Everything Is Connected to Everything Else and What It Means for Business, Science, and Everyday Life*. London: Penguin.

Barlow, John Perry. 1996. "A Declaration of Independence in Cyberspace." Electronic Frontier Foundation (EFF). Accessed February 13, 2015: https://homes.eff.org/~barlow/Declaration-Final.html.

Barnett, Chance. 2013. "Top 10 Crowdfunding Sites for Fundraising." *Forbes.* Accessed December 3, 2014: http://www.forbes.com/sites/chancebarnett/2013 /05/08/top-10-crowdfunding-sites-for-fundraising/.

Barnouw, Erik. 1968. *The Golden Web: A History of Broadcasting in the United States 1933–1953.* New York: Oxford University Press, 23–36.

Barr, Alistair. 2014. "Google Strikes Big Ad Measurement Deal with com-Score." *USA Today.* Accessed March 31, 2015: http://www.usatoday.com/story /tech/2014/02/10/google-comscore-advertising-deal/5291189/.

Bartle, Richard. 1996. "Hearts, Clubs, Diamonds, Spades: Players Who Suit MUDs." MUSE. Accessed April 27, 2015: http://www.mud.co.uk/richard/hcds .htm.

Bartlett, Jamie. 2014. *The Dark Net.* Brooklyn, NY, and London: William Heinemann, 175–179.

Bartlett, Jamie. (Interview) 2015. "Infiltrating 'The Dark Net,' Where Criminals, Trolls and Extremists Reign." NPR's *All Tech Considered.* Accessed June 4, 2015: http://www.npr.org/sections/alltechconsidered/2015/06/03/411476653/infiltrating -the-dark-net-where-criminals-trolls-and-extremists-reign.

Bateson, Gregory. 1972. *Steps to an Ecology of Mind: Collected Essays in Anthropology, Psychiatry, Evolution, and Epistemology.* San Francisco: Chandler Publishing.

Baumgarten, Luke. 2012. "Elevator Going Down: The Story of Muzak." Red Bull Music Academy. Accessed April 1, 2015: http://www.redbullmusicacademy.com /magazine/history-of-muzak.

Baym, Nancy K. 2010. *Personal Connections in the Digital Age.* Malden, MA: Polity Press.

Beck, John C., and Mitchell Wade. 2004. *Got Game: How the Gamer Generation Is Reshaping Business Forever.* Boston, MA: Harvard Business School Press.

Benkler, Yochai. 2004. "Sharing Nicely: On Shareable Goods and the Emergence of Sharing as a Modality of Economic Production." *Yale Law Review,* 114: 273–359.

Benkler, Yochai. 2006. *The Wealth of Network: How Social Production Transforms Markets and Freedom.* New Haven, CT: Yale University Press.

Bennett, Philip, and, Moises Naim. 2015. "21st Century Censorship." *Columbia Journalism Review,* 53: 22–28.

Bercovici, Jeff. 2013. "Tumblr: David Karp's $800 Million Art Project." *Forbes,* January 2. Accessed April 29, 2015: http://www.forbes.com/sites/jeffbercovici /2013/01/02/tumblr-david-karps-800-million-art-project/.

Bercovici, Jeff. 2014. "Google Will Be Better Off Minus Google+." *Forbes.* Accessed March 1, 2015: http://www.forbes.com/sites/jeffbercovici/2014/04/25 /google-will-be-better-off-minus-google/.

Berger, Arthur Asa. 2015. *Ads, Fads, and Consumer Culture: Advertising's Impact on American Character and Society,* 5th ed. Lanham, MD: Rowman & Littlefield.

Bernays, Edward. 1928. *Propaganda*. New York: H. Liveright.

Berners-Lee, Tim. 1989. "Information Management: A Proposal." World Wide Web Foundation. Accessed May 1, 2014: http://www.w3.org/History/1989/proposal.html.

Bertoni, Steve. 2014. "Can PayPal Beat Apple, Google, Amazon and Icahn in the Wallet Wars?" *Forbes*. Accessed March 4, 2015: http://www.forbes.com/sites /stevenbertoni/2014/02/12/can-paypal-beat-apple-google-amazon-and-icahn-in-the -wallet-wars/.

Bogart, Nichole. 2015. "What Is Yik Yak? The Latest App to Cause Concern at Canadian Schools." *Global News*. Accessed January 22, 2015: http://globalnews .ca/news/1785227/what-is-yik-yak-the-latest-app-to-cause-concern-at-canadian -schools/.

Boorstin, Julia. 2010. "The Big Business of Online Dating." CNBC.com. Accessed February 27, 2015: http://www.cnbc.com/id/35370922.

Borison, Rebecca. 2014. "The Fabulous Life of Mark Zuckerberg." Business Insider. Accessed April 20, 2015: http://www.businessinsider.com/the-fabulous -life-of-mark-zuckerberg-2014-7.

boyd, danah. 2014. "Participating in the Always-On Lifestyle." In *The Social Media Reader*, edited by Michael Mandiberg. New York: New York University Press, 71–76.

Brabham, Daren. 2008. "Crowdsourcing as a Model for Problem Solving: An Introduction and Cases." *Convergence: The International Journal of Research into New Media Technologies*, 14: 75–90.

Brandt, Richard L. 2011. *One Click: Jeff Bezos and the Rise of Amazon.com*. New York: Penguin.

Brenner, Joanna. 2013. "3% of Americans Use Dial-Up at Home." Pew Research Center. Accessed February 17, 2015: http://www.pewresearch.org/fact-tank/2013 /08/21/3-of-americans-use-dial-up-at-home/.

"Brief History of the Internet." n.d. Internet Society. Accessed October 4, 2014: http://www.internetsociety.org/internet/what-internet/history-internet/brief -history-internet.

Brinkley, Joel. 2000. "U.S. vs. Microsoft: The Overview; U.S. Judge Says Micro- soft Violated Antitrust Laws with Predatory Behavior." *New York Times*, April 4. Accessed April 2, 2015: http://www.nytimes.com/2000/04/04/business/us-vs -microsoft-overview-us-judge-says-microsoft-violated-antitrust-laws-with.html.

Broderick, Daniel. 2014. "Crowdfunding's Untapped Potential in Emerging Mar- kets." *Forbes*, August 5. Accessed March 31, 2015: http://www.forbes.com/sites /hsbc/2014/08/05/crowdfundings-untapped-potential-in-emerging-markets/.

Bruns, Axel. 2008. *Blogs, Wikipedia, Second Life, and Beyond: From Production to Produsage*. New York: Peter Lang.

Bruntun, Finn. 2013. *Spam: A Shadow History of the Internet*. Cambridge, MA: MIT Press, xiv–xv.

Bryant, Matt. 2014. "iOS 8 Review: The Real Advances Here Are Yet to Come." The Next Web. Accessed January 8, 2015: http://thenextweb.com/apple/2014/09/17 /ios-8-review/1.

Burgess, Jean, and Joshua Green. 2009. *YouTube*: *Online Video and Participatory Culture*. Cambridge, UK: Polity.

Burnett, Robert, and David P. Marshall. 2003. *Web Theory: An Introduction*. London and New York: Routledge.

Carlson, Nicholas. 2010. "At Last—The Full Story of How Facebook Was Founded." *Business Insider*. Accessed December 1, 2014: http://www.businessinsider.com /how-facebook-was-founded-2010-3?op=1.

Carlson, Nicholas. 2015. *Marissa Mayer and the Fight to Save Yahoo!* New York: Hachette Book Group.

Carmy, Carine. 2013. "The Next Leap in Social: 3D Printing." *Ad Age*. Accessed October 4, 2014: http://adage.com/article/digitalnext/3d-printing-leap-social-media /240561/.

Carr, Austin. 2013. "How Instagram CEO Kevin Systrom Is Making Good on Facebook's Billion-Dollar Bet." *Fast Company Magazine*. Accessed February 20, 2015: http://www.fastcompany.com/3012565/how-instagram-ceo-kevin-systrom -is-making-good-on-facebooks-billion-dollar-bet.

Carr, Austin, and Mark Wilson. 2014. "Facebook's Plan to Own Your Phone." *Fast Company Magazine*, Accessed February 11, 2015: http://www.fastcompany.com/ 3031237/facebook-everywhere.

Carr, Nicholas. 2010. *The Shallows: What the Internet Is Doing to Our Brains*. New York: W. W. Norton and Co.

Cass, Stephen, and Charles Q. Choi. 2015. "Google Glass, HoloLens, and the Real Future of Augmented Reality." *IEEE Spectrum*, 52. Accessed March 1, 2015: http://spectrum.ieee.org/consumer-electronics/audiovideo/google-glass-hololens -and-the-real-future-of-augmented-reality.

Castrataro, Daniela. 2011. "A Social History of Crowdfunding." Social Media Week. Accessed March 31, 2015: http://socialmediaweek.org/blog/2011/12/a -social-history-of-crowdfunding/f-crowdfunding/.

Chafkin, Max. 2013. "Not Just Another Web 2.0 Company, Yelp Basks in Its Star Power." *Fast Company Magazine*. Accessed February 23, 2015: http://www.fast company.com/3002950/not-just-another-web-20-company-yelp-basks-its-star -power.

Chan, Sharon Pian. 2011. "Long Antitrust Saga Ends for Microsoft." *Seattle Times*, May 11. Accessed April 27, 2015: http://www.seattletimes.com/business/ microsoft/long-antitrust-saga-ends-for-microsoft/.

Charles, Aaron. 2015. "How Can Craigslist Be Free?" *Houston Chronicle*. Accessed April 9, 2015: http://smallbusiness.chron.com/can-craigslist-free-64147 .html.

Chayka, Kyle. 2014. "After Death, Don't Mourn, Digitize with Sites Like Eterni. me" *Newsweek*. Accessed February 27, 2015: http://www.newsweek.com/2014/ 08/29/after-death-dont-mourn-digitize-sites-eternime-264892.html.

Chen, Adrian. 2014. "Unseen." *Wired*, 22: 109–117.

Children's Internet Protection Act. 2015. Federal Communications Commission. Accessed March 26, 2015: http://www.fcc.gov/guides/childrens-internet -protection-act.

Christian, Ayhmar Jean. 2015. "Web TV Networks Challenge Linear Business Models." Media Industry Project, Carsey-Wolf Center, University of California at Santa Barbara. Accessed March 18, 2015: http://www.carseywolf.ucsb.edu /mip/article/web-tv-networks-challenge-linear-business-models.

Cirucci, Angela M. 2013. "First Person Paparazzi: Why Social Media Should Be Studied More Like Video Games." *Telematics and Informatics*, 30: 47–59.

Clarke, Arthur C. 1968. *2001: A Space Odyssey*. New York: Penguin Putnam.

Cohan, William D. 2014. "Bypassing the Bankers." *The Atlantic Monthly*, 314: 24–27.

Cohen, Adam. 2002. *The Perfect Store: Inside eBay*. Boston: Little, Brown and Co.

Coleman, Gabriella. 2014. *Hacker, Hoaxer, Whistleblower, Spy: The Many Faces of Anonymous*. London: Verso.

Coll, Steve. 1986. *The Deal of the Century: The Break-Up of AT&T*. New York: Athenaeum.

Collamer, Nancy. 2013. "Has LinkedIn Crossed an Ethical Line?" Huffington Post. Accessed January 8, 2015: http://www.huffingtonpost.com/2013/09/06/linkedin -ethics_n_3865859.html.

Colvin, Geoff. 2014. "In the Future, Will There Be Any Work Left for People?" *Fortune*, 169: 193–202.

"Competition among U.S. Broadband Providers." 2014. U.S. Department of Commerce, Economic and Statistics Administration. Accessed April 8, 2015: https:// www.ncta.com/sites/prod/files/BroadbandCompetition-800.png.

"comScore Releases February 2015 U.S. Desktop Search Engine Rankings." 2015. comScore. Accessed April 29, 2015: http://www.comscore.com/Insights/Market -Rankings/comScore-Releases-February-2015-US-Desktop-Search-Engine -Rankings.

"comScore Releases March 2014 U.S. Search Engine Rankings." 2014. Accessed March 31, 2015: https://www.comscore.com/Insights/PressReleases/2014/4/com Score-Releases-March-2014-U.S.-Search-Engine-Rankings.

Conway, Flo, and, Jim Siegelman. 2006. *Dark Hero of the Information Age: In Search of Norbert Wiener, The Father of Cybernetics*. New York: Basic Books.

Copps, Michael J. 2011. "Dissenting Statement of Commissioner Michael J. Copps Re: Applications of Comcast Corporation, General Electric Company and NBC Universal, Inc. For Consent to Assign Licenses and Transfer Control of

Licensees, MB Docket 10-56, FCC 11-4." FCC. Medendtenbank.db.edu: 1–3. Accessed February 28, 2015: http://www.mediadb.eu/fileadmin/downloads/PDF -Artikel/Copps_Statement.pdf.

Cox, Kate. 2014. "Why Isn't America Freaking Out about AT&T/DirecTV Merger—And Should We Be?" *The Consumerist*. Accessed April 6, 2015: http://consumerist.com/2014/09/05/why-isnt-america-freaking-out-about-attdirectv -merger-and-should-we-be/.

Crawford, Susan. 2013. *Captive Audience: The Telecom Industry and Monopoly Power in the New Gilded Age*. New Haven: Yale University Press.

Cringely, Robert X. 2010. "When Schools Spy on Their Students, Bad Things Happen." *PC World*. Accessed April 21, 2015: http://www.pcworld.com/article /190019/school_spying_webcams.html.

Curtis, Sophie. 2014. "Bill Gates: A History at Microsoft" *The Telegraph*. Accessed November 11, 2014: http://www.telegraph.co.uk/technology/bill-gates/10616991 /Bill-Gates-a-history-at-Microsoft.html.

"The Dangers of Texting While Driving." 2014. FCC Report. December 8. Accessed April 29, 2015: http://www.fcc.gov/guides/texting-while-driving.

"Data Web: Voting and Registration." 2012. U.S. Census Bureau. Accessed May 6, 2015: http://thedataweb.rm.census.gov/TheDataWeb_HotReport2/voting/voting .hrml.

Davison, Patrick. 2014. "The Language of Internet Memes," In *The Social Media Reader*, edited by Michael Mandiberg. New York: New York University Press, 120–134.

Dawkins, Richard. 1976. *The Selfish Gene*. New York: Oxford University Press.

Dawson, Ashley. 2012. "DIY Academy: Cognitive Capitalism, Humanist Scholarship, and the Digital Transformation." In *The Social Media Reader*, edited by Michael Mandiberg. New York: New York University Press, 257–274.

Day, Elizabeth. 2013. "How Selfies Became a Global Phenomenon." *The Guardian*. Accessed April 25, 2015: http://www.theguardian.com/technology/2013/jul/ 14/how-selfies-became-a-global-phenomenon.

Decker, Sue. 2014. "An Insider's Account of the Yahoo-Alibaba Deal." *Harvard Business Review*. Accessed April 29, 2015: https://hbr.org/2014/08/an -insiders-account-of-the-yahoo-alibaba-deal/.

De la Merced, Michael J., Nick Bilton, and Nicole Perlroth. 2013. "Seeking Flair, Yahoo Agrees to Buy Tumblr." *New York Times*, May 19: A1.

Democracy Now! 2011. Cornel West on Occupy Wall Street: It's the Makings of a U.S. Autumn Responding to the Arab Spring. Interview with Amy Goodman, September 29. Accessed December 1, 2014: http://www.democracynow.org /blog/2011/9/29/cornel_west_on_occupy_wall_street_its_the_makings_of_a_ us_autumn_responding_to_the_arab_spring.

Deresiewicz, William, 2015. "The Death of the Artist and the Birth of the Creative Entrepreneur." *The Atlantic Monthly*, 315: 92–97.

Dodge, Dan. 2007. "How Napster Changed the World—A Look Back 7 Years Later." Dan Dodge on the Next Big Thing. (Blog). Accessed March 30, 2015: http://dondodge.typepad.com/the_next_big_thing/2007/03/how_napster_cha .html.

Doran, Kirk. 2008. "Industry Size, Measurement, and Social Costs." Presentation at Princeton University, December 11–13. Accessed January 2, 2015: http://www.socialcostsofpornography.com/Doran_Industry_Size_Measurement _Social_Costs.Pdf.

Douthat, Ross. 2008. "Is Pornography Adultery?" *The Atlantic Monthly*, October. Accessed November 12, 2014: http://www.theatlantic.com/magazine/archive/2008/10/is-pornography-adultery/306989/.

Dubbin, Rob. 2013. "The Rise of Twitter Bots." *The New Yorker*. Accessed April 8, 2015: http://www.newyorker.com/tech/elements/the-rise-of-twitter-bots.

Dudley, Barry. 2015. "Why Foursquare Is a Must-Buy for Yahoo." The Drum. Accessed April 24, 2015: http://www.thedrum.com/opinion/2015/04/24/why-foursquare-must-buy-yahoo.

Duggan, Maeve, Nicole B. Ellison, Cliff Lampe, Amanda Lenhart, and Mary Madden. 2014 "Social Media Update, 2014." Pew Internet and American Life Project. Accessed January 22, 2015: http://www.pewinternet.org/2015/01/09/social -media-update-2014/.

Edwards, Jim. 2013. "Where Are They Now? The Kings of the '90s Dot-Com Bubble." Business Insider. Accessed February 26, 2015: http://www.business insider.com/where-are-they-now-the-kings-of-the-90s-dot-com-bubble-2013 -10?op=1#ixzz3SrIyY4uD.

Eichenwald, Kurt. 2014. "The Great Smartphone War." *Vanity Fair*. Accessed April 26, 2015: http://www.vanityfair.com/news/business/2014/06/apple-samsung -smartphone-patent-war.

Elgin, Ben. 2005. "Google Buys Android for Its Mobile Arsenal." *Bloomberg Businessweek*. Accessed April 6, 2015: http://www.webcitation.org/5wk7sIvVb.

Enright, Allison. 2015. "U.S. Annual E-Retail Sales Surpass $300 Billion for the First Time." Internet Retailer. Accessed April 30, 2015: https://www.interne-tretailer.com/2015/02/17/us-annual-e-retail-sales-surpass-300-billion-first-time.

"Essential Facts about the Computer and Video Game Industry." 2014. Entertainment Software Industry 2014 Essential Sales, Demographic, and Usage Data. Accessed December 27, 2015: http://www.theesa.com/wp-content/uploads/2014/10/ESA_ EF_2014.pdf.

"European Parliament Warns Against UN Internet Control." *BBC News*. 2012. Accessed April 27, 2015: http://www.bbc.com/news/technology-20445637.

Ewing, Jack. 2007. "How MP3 Was Born." *Bloomberg Businessweek.* Accessed March 26, 2015: http://www.bloomberg.com/bw/stories/2007-03-05/how-mp3 -was-bornbusinessweek-business-news-stock-market-and-financial-advice.

"Falling Through the Net: A Survey of the 'Have Nots' in Rural and Urban America." 1995. National Telecommunications & Information Administration, U.S. Department of Commerce. Accessed April 6, 2015: http://www.ntia.doc.gov /ntiahome/fallingthru.html.

Fallows, James. 2010. "How to Save the News." *The Atlantic Monthly*, 305: 44–56.

Fallows, James. 2014. "How You'll Get Organized." *The Atlantic Monthly*, 314: 30–32.

Farnham, Alan. 2014. "Google's Best and Worst Big Acquisitions." January 15. Accessed December 10, 2014: http://abcnews.go.com/Business/googles-best -worst-acquisitions/story?id=21526661.

"Federal Laws Concerning the Sexual Exploitation of Children." 2015. National Center for Missing and Exploited Children, U.S. Government. Accessed January 2, 2015: http://www.missingkids.com/LegalResources/Exploitation/FederalLaw.

Federal Trade Commission, 2015. "Complying with COPPA: Frequently Asked Questions." Accessed March 26, 2015: https://www.ftc.gov/tips-advice/business -center/guidance/complying-coppa-frequently-asked-questions#COPPA Enforcement.

Ferenstein, Gregory. 2015. "Here's How Many People Check Facebook, Twitter, and Instagram Daily." Venture Beat. Accessed May 5, 2015: http://venturebeat .com/2015/01/09/heres-how-many-people-check-facebook-twitter-and-instagram -daily-in-2-graphs/.

Fernando, Hiranya. 2014. "A Step-By-Step Guide to Getting a Job through LinkedIn." Business Insider. Accessed April 24, 2015: http://www.businessinsider .com/getting-a-job-through-linkedin-2014-3#ixzz3YGEDdwxD.

Fiegerman, Seth. 2014. "Friendster Founder Tells His Side of the Story, 10 Years After Facebook." Mashable.com. Accessed December 5, 2014: http://mashable .com/2014/02/03/jonathan-abrams-friendster-facebook/.

"50 Most Powerful Women: Global Edition." 2014. *Fortune*, 169: 16.

Finkle, Eli. 2015. "In Defense of Tinder." *New York Times,* February 8: SR9.

Finley, Klint. 2015. "These Are the Hottest New Open Source Projects Right Now." *Wired.* Accessed April 28, 2015: http://www.wired.com/2015/01/black-duck -rookies/.

Fisher, Marc. 2014. "Who Cares If It's True?" *Columbia Journalism Review,* 53: 26–32.

Fletcher, Dan. 2009. "A Brief History of Spam." *Time.* Accessed April 21, 2015: http://content.time.com/time/business/article/0,8599,1933796,00.html.

Flew, Terry. 2005. "Creative Economy" In *Creative Industries*, edited by John Hartley. Malden, MA: Blackwell Publishing, 350.

Florida, Richard. 2011. *The Rise of the Creative Class Revisited*, revised and expanded. New York: Basic Books.

Fono, David, and Kate Raynes-Goldie. 2006. "Hyperfriends and Beyond: Friendship and Social Norms on LiveJournal." In the *Internet Research Annual*, vol 4: Selected Papers, edited by Mia Consalvo and Carolyn Haythornthwaite. New York: Peter Lang.

Fortini, Amanda. 2014. "The Inspiration Factory: How Pinterest Fosters Creativity." *Wired*, 21: 94–99.

Friedersdorf, Conor. 2014. "Podcasts So Good You Want to Binge-Listen." *The Atlantic Monthly*, October 29. Accessed January 20, 2015: http://www.theatlantic.com /entertainment/archive/2014/10/podcasts-so-good-you-want-to-binge-listen/382055/.

Friedman, Thomas L. 2005. *The World Is Flat: A Brief History of the Twenty-First Century*. New York: Farrar, Straus and Giroux.

Friedman, Thomas L. 2013. "Welcome to the Sharing Economy." *New York Times, Sunday Review*. July 20: SR1.

Fuchs, Christian. 2014. *Social Media: A Critical Introduction*. London: Sage, 4.

Gainous, Jason, and Kevin M. Wagner. 2014. *Tweeting to Power: The Social Media Revolution in American Politics*. New York: Oxford University Press.

Gansky, Lisa. 2010. *The Mesh: Why the Future of Business Is Sharing*. New York: Penguin.

Geier, Ben. 2015. "What Did We Learn from the Dotcom Stock Bubble of 2000?" *Time*. Accessed April 19, 2015: http://time.com/3741681/2000-dotcom-stock-bust/.

Genes, Raimund. 2015. "What the Next Government's Cyber-Security Policy Should Look Like." *SC Magazine*. Accessed May 21, 2015: http://www.scmagazineuk.com /what-the-next-governments-cyber-security-policy-should-look-like/article/413600/.

Geron, Tomio. 2013. "Airbnb and the Unstoppable Rise of the Share Economy." *Forbes*, 191: 58–64.

Gervino, Tony, and Andrew Hampp. 2015. "Jay Z on Competing with Jimmy Iovine: 'I Don't Have to Lose . . . for You Guys to Win.'" *Billboard Magazine*. Accessed May 4, 2015: http://www.billboard.com/articles/business/6516945/jay -z-jimmy-iovine-streaming-tidal.

Geuss, Megan. 2015. "Flickr Offers New Public Domain Licensing in Wake of SpaceX Photo Release." *Ars Technica*. Accessed March 31, 2015: http:// arstechnica.com/business/2015/03/flickr-offers-new-public-domain-licensing -in-wake-of-spacex-photo-release/.

Gibbs, Samuel. 2013. "Sir Tim Berners-Lee and Google Lead Coalition for Cheaper Internet." *The Guardian*. Accessed September 19, 2014: http://www.theguardian .com/technology/2013/oct/07/google-berners-lee-alliance-broadband?africa? CMP=EMCNEWEML6619I2&et_cid=51918&et_rid=7107573&Linkid=http% 3a%2f%2fwww.theguardian.com%2ftechnology%2f2013%2foct%2f07%2fgoo gle-berners-lee-alliance-broadband-africa.

Gibson, William. 1984. *Neuromancer.* New York: Berkley Publishing Group.

Giles, Jim. 2005. "Special Report: Internet Encyclopaedias Go Head to Head." *Nature*, 438: 900–901.

Gillette, Felix. 2014. "Department of Blogging Extinction; Technorati Rankings Are Dead," *Businessweek.* Accessed November 3, 2014: http://www.business week.com/articles/2014-06-24/department-of-blogging-extinction-technorati -rankings-are-dead.

Gitlin, Todd. 2014. "Where Are the Occupy Protesters Now?" *The Guardian.* Accessed April 28, 2015: http://www.theguardian.com/cities/2014/jun/17 /where-occupy-protesters-now-social-media.

Gjelten, Tom. 2013. "Cyberattacks, Terrorism Top U.S. Security Threat Report." NPR's *All Things Considered.* Accessed April 24, 2015: http://www.npr.org /2013/03/12/174135800/cyber-attacks-terrorism-top-u-s-security-threat-report.

Gladwell, Malcolm. 2010. "Small Change: Why the Revolution Will Not Be Tweeted." *The New Yorker*, 86: 30.

Goggin, Gerard. 2006. *Cell Phone Culture: Mobile Technology in Everyday Life.* New York: Routledge.

Goldstein, Gordon M. 2014. "The End of the Internet?" *The Atlantic Monthly,* 314: 24–28.

"Gone, But Hardly Forgotten." *Columbia Journalism Review,* 53: 11.

Goodman, Marc. 2015. *Future Crimes.* New York: Doubleday, 16–17, 87–88.

Google. 2014. "Investor Relations." Accessed September 25, 2014: http://investor .Google.com/earnings/2014/Q1_google_earnings.html.

Graslie, Serri. 2015. "Pick Up Your Smartphone Less Often. You Might Think Better." NPR's *All Tech Considered.* Accessed February 10, 2015: http://www.npr .org/blogs/alltechconsidered/2015/02/09/384945981/pick-up-your-smartphone -less-often-you-might-think-better.

Greenwald, Glenn. 2014. *No Place to Hide: Edward Snowden, the NSA, and the U.S. Surveillance State.* New York: Henry Holt.

Griswold, Alison. 2014. "What Makes BuzzFeed Worth $850 Million?" Slate. Accessed April 11, 2015: http://www.slate.com/blogs/moneybox/2014/08/11/buzzfeed _raises_50_million_jonah_peretti_is_building_a_viral_media_empire.html.

Groth, Aimee. 2011. "This Is What 'Computer Dating' Looked Like in the 1960s," Business Insider. Accessed March 1, 2015: http://www.businessinsider.com /first-online-dating-site-2011-7.

Grubb, Jeff. 2015. "You're Spending More Time Playing Mobile Games Than Ever Before." *VentureBeat.* Accessed April 27, 2015: http://venturebeat.com/2015/01/27 /youre-spending-more-time-playing-mobile-games-than-ever-before/.

Ha, Anthony. 2014. "AOL's Q4 Revenue Grows to $679M but Earnings per Share of $0.43 Fall Short of Estimates." TechCrunch. Accessed September 3, 2014: http:// techcrunch.com/2014/02/06/aol-q4-earnings-2/.

Hanson, Jarice. 2007. *24/7: How Cell Phones and the Internet Change the Way We Live, Work, and Play.* Westport, CT: Praeger.

Hanson, Jarice. 1994. *Connections: Technologies of Communication.* New York: HarperCollins.

Hanson, Jarice. 2013. "The New Minority: The Willfully Unconnected." In *The Unconnected: Social Justice, Participation, and Engagement in the Information Society,* edited by Paul M. A. Baker, Jarice Hanson, and Jeremy Hunsinger. New York: Peter Lang, 223–240.

Hanson, Jarice. 1987. *Video Theory: Applications, Impact, and Theory.* Thousand Oaks, CA: Sage.

Hanson, Jarice, and Bryan Baldwin. 2007. "Mobile Culture: Podcasting as Public Media," In *Displacing Place: Mobile Communication in the Twenty-First Century,* edited by Sharon Kleinman. New York: Peter Lang, 123–139.

Hargittai, Ezster. 2002. "Second Level Digital Divide: Differences in People's Online Skills." First Monday. Accessed April 1, 2015: http://www.firstmonday.org/ issues/issue7_4/hargittai/.

Harris, Alex. 2008. "Child Online Protection Act Still Unconstitutional." The Center for Internet and Society, Stanford Law School. Accessed March 26, 2015: http://cyberlaw.stanford.edu/blog/2008/11/child-online-protection-act-still-unconstitutional.

Hartley, John, 2005. "Creative Industries." In *Creative Industries,* edited by John Hartley. Malden, MA: Blackwell Publishing, 5.

Hastings, Michael. 2012. "Julian Assange: The Rolling Stone Interview." *Rolling Stone,* 1142: 50–60.

Heffernan, Virginia, and Tom Zeller Jr. 2006. "The Lonelygirl That Really Wasn't." *New York Times.* Accessed October 12, 2012: http://www.nytimes.com/2006/09/13/technology/13lonely.html.

Heim, Michael. 1991. "The Erotic Ontology of Cyberspace." In *Cyberspace: First Steps,* edited by Michael Benedikt. Cambridge, MA: MIT Press, 59–80.

Helft, Miguel. 2014. "Where Google Ventures Is Pinning." *Fortune,* 169: 76–79.

Helft, Miguel, and Claire Cain Millerjan. 2011. "1986 Privacy Law Is Outrun by the Web." *New York Times,* January 9. Accessed March 30, 2015: http://www.nytimes.com/2011/01/10/technology/10privacy.html?hp&_r=0.

Hempel, Jessi. 2014. "Marissa's Moment of Truth." *Fortune,* 169: 80–86.

Hepler, John C. 2012. "The Impact of Transformational Technology: Does Changing the Medium Change the Message?" Paper presented at the Mid-Atlantic Popular & American Culture Association, Pittsburgh, PA. April 30, 2012.

Hern, Alex. 2014. "Social Networks to Face Government Grilling Over Suicide Content." *The Guardian.* Accessed November 16, 2015: http://www.theguardian.com/technology/2014/jan/27/social-networks-to-face-government-grilling-over-suicide-promotion.

Hicks, Josh. 2014. "Identity Theft Cost the IRS 5 Billion Last Year. Here's What Congress Can Do about It." *The Washington Post*. Accessed April 13, 2015: http://www.washingtonpost.com/blogs/federal-eye/wp/2014/09/23/identity-theft -cost-the-irs-5-billion-last-year-heres-what-congress-can-do-about-it/.

Hintz, Arne. 2013. "Dimensions of Modern Freedom Expression: WikiLeaks, Policy Hacking, and Digital Freedoms." In *Beyond WikiLeaks: Implications for the Future of Communications, Journalism, and Society*, edited by Benedetta Brevini, Arne Hintz, and Patrick McCurdy. New York: Palgrave Macmillan, 146–165.

Holiday, Ryan. 2014. "Fake Traffic Means Real Paydays." Observer. Accessed October 3, 2014: https://observer.com/2014/01/fake-traffic-means-real-paydays/.

Holwerda, Thom. 2011. "The History of 'App' and the Demise of the Programmer." *OSNews*. Accessed October 2, 2014: http://www.osnews.com/story/24882 /The_Histhttp://www.osnews.com/story/24882/The_History_of_App_and_the _Demise_of_the_Programmer.

Honan, Matt. 2012. "YouTube Re-Imagined: 505,347,842 Channels on Every Single Screen." *Wired*. Accessed April 20, 2015: http://www.wired.com/2012/08 /500-million-youtube-channels/.

Horsey, David. 2014. "Internet Porn Is an Experiment in Dehumanization." *Los Angeles Times*. Accessed January 2, 2015: http://www.latimes.com/opinion/top oftheticket/la-na-tt-internet-porn-20141215-story.html.

Howe, Jeff. 2006. "The Rise of Crowdsourcing." *Wired*. Accessed December 3, 2014: http://archive.wired.com/wired/archive/14.06/crowds.html.

Hunsinger, Jeremy, and Theresa Senft, eds. 2014. *The Social Media Handbook*. New York: Routledge.

Hustveldt, Mark. 2008. "Dr. Horrible Could Bank 2.6 Million Even Before DVDs." TubeFilter. Accessed September 1, 2012: http://www.tubefilter.com/2008/07/23 /dr-horrible-could-bank-26-million-even-before-dvds-2/.

"ICT Facts and Figures." 2014. International Telecommunications Union (ITU), April 3. Accessed April 27, 2015: http://www.itu.int/en/ITU-D/Statistics/Documents /facts/ICTFactsFigures2014-e.pdf.

"Innovators under 35." 1999. *MIT Technology Review*. Accessed May 21, 2015: http://www2.technologyreview.com/tr35/profile.aspx?TRID=518.

International Data Communication. 2014. "Smartphone OS Market Share, Q2 2014." Accessed October 28, 2014: http://www.idc.com/prodserv/smartphone-os -market-share.jsp.

Internet Advertising Bureau (IAB). 2014. "At $11.6 Billion in Q1 2014, Internet Advertising Revenues Hit All-Time First Quarter High." Accessed October 29, 2014: http://www.iab.net/about_the_iab/recent_press_releases/press_release_archive /press_release/pr-061214#sthash.pCBKfT0Q.dpuf.

"Internet Users in the World by Geographical Region." 2015. Internet World Statistics. Accessed April 1, 2015: http://www.internetworldstats.com/stats.htm.

Isaacson, Walter. 2011. *Steve Jobs*. New York: Simon & Schuster.

Isaacson, Walter. 2014. *The Innovators*. New York: Simon & Schuster.

Ito, Mizuko, et al., eds. 2010. *Hanging Out, Messing Around, and Geeking Out*. Cambridge, MA: MIT Press.

Jabr, Ferris. 2013. "Do e-Readers Inhibit Reading Comprehension?" *Scientific American*. Reprinted in *Salon*. Accessed March 7, 2015: http://www.salon.com/2013/04/14/do_e_readers_inhibit_reading_comprehension_partner/.

Jackson, Maggie. 2009. *Distracted: The Erosion of Attention and the Coming Dark Age*. Amherst, NY: Prometheus.

Jacobs, Harrison. 2014. "We Ranked YouTube's Biggest Stars by How Much Money They Make." *Business Insider*. Accessed March 29, 2015: http://www.businessinsider.com.au/richest-youtube-stars-2014-3#20-evantubehd-1.

Jagatic, Tom, Nathaniel Johnson, Markus Jakobsson, and Filippo Menczer. 2007. "Social Phishing." *Communications of the ACM*, 50: 94–100.

Jeffers, Dave. 2013. "Bots, Both Good and Evil, Dominate the Internet." *PC World*. Accessed October 3, 2014: http://www.pcworld.com/article/2080300/bots-both-good-and-evil-dominate-the-internet.html.

Jeffries, Adrianne. 2013. "The Man behind Flickr on Making the Service 'Awesome Again.'" *The Verge*. Accessed February 18, 2015: http://www.theverge.com/2013/3/20/4121574/flickr-chief-markus-spiering-talks-photos-and-marissa-mayer.

Jeffries, Stuart. 2014. "How the Web Lost Its Way—And Its Founding Principles." *The Guardian*. Accessed March 30, 2015: http://www.theguardian.com/technology/2014/aug/24/internet-lost-its-way-tim-berners-lee-world-wide-web.

Jenkins, Henry. 2006. *Convergence Culture: Where Old and New Media Collide*. New York: New York University Press.

Jenkins, Henry, Sam Ford, and Joshua Green. 2013. *Spreadable Media: Creating Value and Meaning in a Networked Culture*. New York: New York University Press.

Johnson, Tom. 2000. "That's AOL Folks: Internet Leader and Entertainment Firm to Join Forces: New Company Worth $350B." *CNN Money*. Accessed March 22, 2015: http://money.cnn.com/2000/01/10/deals/aol_warner/.

Kaplan, Sarah. 2014. "With #GamerGate, the Video-game Industry's Growing Pains Go Viral." *The Washington Post*. Accessed December 29, 2014: http://www.washingtonpost.com/news/morning-mix/wp/2014/09/12/with-gamergate-the-video-game-industrys-growing-pains-go-viral/.

Kelleher, Kevin. 2014. "5 Lessons from Survivors of the Dotcom Crash." *Fortune*. Accessed February 26, 2015: http://fortune.com/2014/01/03/5-lessons-from-survivors-of-the-dotcom-crash/.

Keller, Jared. 2013. "How Boston Police Won the Twitter Wars during the Marathon Bomber Hunt." *BloombergBusiness.* Accessed October 24, 2015: http://www.bloomberg.com/bw/articles/2013-04-26/how-boston-police-won-the-twitter-wars-during-bomber-hunt.

Kendall, Jake, and, Roger Voorhies. 2014. "How Cell Phones Can Spur Development." *Foreign Affairs,* 93: 9.

Kennedy, Pagan. 2013. "William Gibson's Future Is Now." *New York Times Book Review.* Accessed April 19, 2015: http://www.nytimes.com/2012/01/15/books/review/distrust-that-particular-flavor-by-william-gibson-book-review.html?pagewanted=all.

Kessler, Glenn. 2013. "A Cautionary Tale for Politicians: Al Gore and the 'Invention' of the Internet." *The Washington Post.* Accessed December 28, 2015. http://www.washingtonpost.com/blogs/fact-checker/wp/2013/11/04/a-cautionary-tale-for-politicians-al-gore-and-the-invention-of-the-internet/.

Klein, Alec. 2003. *Stealing Time: Steve Case, Jerry Levin, and the Collapse of AOL Time Warner.* New York: Simon & Schuster.

Knopper, Steve. 2009. *Appetite for Self-Destruction: The Spectacular Crash of the Record Industry in the Digital Age.* New York: The Free Press.

Kolowich, Steve. 2014. "Rethinking Low Completion Rates in MOOCs." *Chronicle of Higher Education.* Accessed January 2, 2015: http://chronicle.com/blogs/wiredcampus/rethinking-low-completion-rates-in-moocs/55211.

Kordell, Nicole. 2011. "FTC Will Propose Broader Children's Online Privacy Safeguards." *National Law Review,* 123 (2). December 22. Accessed December 18, 2014: http://www.natlawreview.com/article/ftc-will-propose-broader-children-s-online-privacy-safeguards.

Kot, Greg. 2009. *Ripped: How the Wired Generation Revolutionized Music.* New York: Scribner.

Kruger, Justin, Nicholas Epley, Jason Parker, and Zhi-Wen Ng. 2005. "Egocentrism Over E-mail: Can We Communicate as Well as We Think?" *Journal of Personality and Social Psychology,* 89: 925–936.

Krupnick, Matt. 2011. "Freedom Fighters or Vandals? No Consensus on Anonymous." *Oakland Tribune,* August 15. Accessed September 23, 2014: http://www.mercurynews.com/top-stories/ci_18686764.

Kushner, David. 2014. "The Masked Avengers: How Anonymous Incited Online Vigilantism from Tunisia to Ferguson." *The New Yorker,* 90: 48.

Kushner, David. 2014. "The Six Seconds between Love and Hate: A Vine Romance Gone Wrong." *Rolling Stone.* Accessed May 5, 2015: http://www.rollingstone.com/culture/news/the-six-seconds-between-love-and-hate-a-vine-romance-gone-wrong-20140521#ixzz3ZH3ykzV4.

Lammle, Rob. 2011. "How Etsy, eBay, Reddit Got Their Names." Accessed December 26, 2015. http://www.cnn.com/2011/LIVING/04/22/website.name.origins.mf/.

La Monica, Paul R. 2014. "Put Up or Shut Up Time for Marissa Mayer." CNN.com. Accessed October 1, 2014: http://money.cnn.com/2014/09/02/investing/yahoo -alibaba-ipo-marissa-mayer/.

Lane, Frederick S. III. 2000. *Obscene Profits: Entrepreneurs in the Cyber Age.* London: Routledge.

Lashinsky, Adam. 2005. "Remembering Netscape: The Birth of the Web." *CNNMoney. com.* Accessed December 1, 2014: http://web.archive.org/web/20060427112146 /http://money.cnn.com/magazines/fortune/fortune_archive/2005/07/25/8266639 /index.htm.

Launder, William, Christopher S. Steward, and Joann S. Lublin. 2013. "Bezos Buys Washington Post for $250 Million." *Wall Street Journal.* Accessed September 19, 2014: http://online.wsj.com/news/articles/SB10001424127887324653004578 650390383666794.

Laverty, Shiela. 2015. "Impact of Technology on the Travel Business." *Small Business Chronicle.* Accessed March 30, 2015: http://smallbusiness.chron.com /impact-technology-travel-agency-business-57750.html.

Lécuyer, Christophe. 2005. "What Do Universities Really Owe Industry? The Case of Solid State Electronics at Stanford." *Minerva: A Review of Science, Learning & Policy,* 43: 51–71.

Lee, Edmund. 2011. "Sen. Rockefeller: Get Ready for a Real Do-Not-Track Bill for Online Advertising." *Advertising Age.* Accessed April 1, 2015: http://adage.com /article/digital/sen-rockefeller-ready-a-real-track-bill/227426/.

Lee, Newton. 2013. *Facebook Nation: Total Information Awareness.* New York: Springer.

Leisring, Penny A. 2009. "Stalking Made Easy: How Information and Communi- cation Technologies Are Influencing the Way People Monitor and Harass One Another." In *The Culture of Efficiency*, edited by Sharon Kleinman. New York: Peter Lang, 230–244.

Lenhart, Amanda. 2007. "Cyberbullying." Pew Internet Research Project. Accessed October 29, 2014: http://www.pewinternet.org/2007/06/27/cyberbullying/.

Lenhart, Amanda. 2012. "Teens, Smartphones & Texting." Pew Research Center. Accessed March 29, 2015: http://www.pewinternet.org/2012/03/19/teens-smart phones-texting/.

Lenhart, Amanda, and Maeve Duggan. 2014. "Couples, the Internet, and Social Media." Pew Research Center. Accessed March 16, 2015: http://www.pewinternet .org/2014/02/11/couples-the-internet-and-social-media/.

Leonard, Andrew. 2014. "Why Uber Must Be Stopped." *Salon.* Accessed March 17, 2015: http://www.salon.com/2014/08/31/why_uber_must_be_stopped/.

Lepore, Jill. 2015. "The Cobweb: Can the Internet Be Archived?" *New Yorker,* 89: 34–41.

Lessig, Lawrence. 2008. *Remix: Making Art and Commerce Thrive in the Hybrid Economy.* New York: Penguin Press.

Letzing, John, and Paul Mozur. 2012. "Yahoo Closes Alibaba Deal, Will Dole Out $3.65 Billion." *Wall Street Journal.* Accessed April 29, 2015: http://www.wsj.com/articles/SB10000872396390044381680457800429054133 6274.

Levy, Ari. 2012. "Ad-Supported Software Reaches Specialized Audience." *San Francisco Chronicle.* Accessed May 11, 2014: http://www.sfgate.com/business/article/Ad-supported-software-reaches-specialized-audience-3501806.php.

Lévy, Pierre. 1997. *Collective Intelligence: Mankind's Emerging World in Cyberspace.* Translated by Robert Bonnano. Cambridge, MA: Helix Books.

Levy, Steven. 2010. *Hackers: Heroes of the Computer Revolution.* Sebastopol, CA: O'Reilly Media.

Lindenberger, Michael A. 2010. "Craigslist Comes Clean: No More 'Adult Services,' Ever." *Time.* Accessed January 8, 2015: http://content.time.com/time/nation/article/0,8599,2019499,00.html.

Lindstrom, Martin. 2002. *Clicks, Bricks & Brands*, rev. ed. South Yarra Victoria, Australia: Kogan Page.

Littleton, Cynthia. 2014. "Cable under Fire: Plunge in Ratings Could Spell Trouble for Top Nets." *Variety.* Accessed November 10, 2014: http://variety.com/2014/tv/news/cable-network-ratings-1201346782/.

Littleton, Cynthia. 2015. "Comcast CEO on Ending Time Warner Cable Deal: 'Today, We Move On.'" *Variety.* Accessed April 24, 2015: http://variety.com/2015/biz/news/comcast-ceo-time-warner-cable-cablevision-1201479107/.

Littman, Jonathan. 1997. *The Watchman: The Twisted Life and Crimes of Serial Hacker Kevin Poulsen.* New York: Little, Brown and Co.

Mackay, Robert. 2010. "'Operation Payback' Attacks Target MasterCard and PayPal Sites to Avenge WikiLeaks." *New York Times.* Accessed January 25, 2015: http://thelede.blogs.nytimes.com/2010/12/08/operation-payback-targets-mastercard-and-paypal-sites-to-avenge-wikileaks/.

Madden, Mary. 2014. "Public Perceptions of Privacy and Security in the Post-Snowden Era." Pew Research Center. Accessed April 28, 2015: http://www.pewinternet.org/2014/11/12/public-privacy-perceptions/.

Madden, Mary. 2013. "Teens Haven't Abandoned Facebook (Yet)." Pew Internet and American Life Project. Accessed January 22, 2015: http://www.pewinternet.org/2013/08/15/teens-havent-abandoned-facebook-yet/.

Madrigal, Alexis C. 2012. "I'm Being Followed: How Google—and 104 Other Companies—Are Tracking Me on the Web." *The Atlantic Monthly.* Accessed April 29, 2015: http://www.theatlantic.com/technology/archive/2012/02/im-being-followed-how-google-151-and-104-other-companies-151-are-tracking-me-on-the-web/253758/.

Madrigal, Alexis C. 2014a. "Email Is Still the Best Thing on the Internet." *Atlantic Monthly*, August 14. Accessed April 30, 2015: http://www.theatlantic.com /technology/archive/2014/08/why-email-will-never-die/375973/.

Madrigal, Alexis C. 2014b. "The Fall of Facebook." *The Atlantic Monthly*, 314: 34–35, 39.

Malone, Scott. 2007. "Dropout Bill Gates Returns to Harvard for Degree." Reuters News Service. Accessed April 20, 2015: http://www.reuters.com /article/2007/06/07/us-microsoft-gates-idUSN0730259120070607.

Mamiit, Aaron. 2014. "Sony Pictures Cyber Attack May Cost $100 Million, Says Expert." *Tech Times*. Accessed April 20, 2015: http://www.techtimes.com /articles/21869/20141210/sony-pictures-cyber-attack-may-cost-100-million-says -expert.htm.

Mandiberg, Michael, ed. 2012. *The Social Media Reader*. New York: New York University Press.

Mann, Adam. 2013. "Google's Chief Internet Evangelist on Creating the Interplanetary Internet." *Wired*. Accessed March 2, 2015: http://www.wired.com/2013/05 /vint-cerf-interplanetary-internet/.

Marche, Stephen. 2012. "Is Facebook Making Us Lonely?" *The Atlantic Monthly*. Accessed September 3, 2014: http://www.theatlantic.com/magazine /archive/2012/05/is-facebook-making-us-lonely/308930/.

Masnick, Michael, Michael Ho, Joyce Hung, and Leigh Beadon. 2014. "The Sky Is Rising. Floor 64" (Report). Accessed April 2, 2015: https://www.ccianet.org /wp-content/uploads/2014/10/Sky-Is-Rising-2014.pdf.

McLuhan, Marshall. 1964. *Understanding Media: The Extensions of Man*. New York: Signet Books, 19.

McLuhan, Marshall, and Quentin Fiore. 1967. *The Medium Is the Massage: An Inventory of Effects*. New York: Bantam Books.

McNary, Dave. 2014. "Showbiz, Music Industry Jobs Drop 19% in Two Years." *Variety*. Accessed September 11, 2015: http://variety.com/2014/artisans/news /government-issues-bleak-jobs-report-for-movieound-industries.

McPhail, Thomas L., ed. 2009. *Development Communication: Reframing the Role of the Media*. Malden, MA: Wiley-Blackwell, 125.

Mell, Peter, and Timothy Grance. 2011. "The NIST Definition of Cloud Computing: Recommendations of the National Institute of Standards and Technology." Special Publication 800-145. U.S. Department of Commerce. Accessed February 25, 2015: http://csrc.nist.gov/publications/nistpubs/800-145/SP800-145.pdf.

Mezrich, Ben. 2009. *The Accidental Billionaires*. New York: Random House.

Mitchell, Amy. 2015. "State of the News Media 2015." Pew Research Center. Accessed May 6, 2015: http://www.journalism.org/2015/04/29/state-of-the-news -media-2015/.

Mitnick, Kevin, with William L Simon. 2012. *The Ghost in the Wires: My Adventures as the World's Most Wanted Hacker.* New York: Little, Brown and Co.

"Mobile Advertising Spending Worldwide from 2010 to 2017 (in Billion U.S. Dollars)." 2015. *Statistica.* Accessed April 5, 2015: http://www.statista.com /statistics/280640/mobile-advertising-spending-worldwide/.

"Mobile Millennials." 2014. Nielsen. Accessed April 27, 2015: http://www.nielsen .com/us/en/insights/news/2014/mobile-millennials-over-85-percent-of-generation -y-owns-smartphones.html.

"Mobile Technology Fact Sheet." n.d. Pew Research Center. Accessed March 26, 2015: http://www.pewinternet.org/fact-sheets/mobile-technology-fact-sheet/.

Morozov, Evgeny. 2011. *The Net Delusion: The Dark Side of Internet Freedom.* New York: Public Affairs.

Morris, Margaret E., and Adrian Aguilera. 2012. "Mobile, Social, and Wearable Computing and the Evolution of Psychological Practice." *Professional Psychological Research,* 43: 622–626.

Moscaritolo, Angela. 2010. "Will Tablets Make Laptops Obsolete?" *PC World.* Accessed April 23, 2015: http://www.pcmag.com/article2/0,2817,2398731,00.asp.

Moyer, Justin. 2014. "The Surprisingly Political Origins of 'Cyber Monday.'" *The Washington Post.* Accessed December 9, 2014: http://www.washingtonpost.com/ blogs/wonkblog/wp/2014/12/01/the-surprisingly-political-origins-of-cyber-monday/.

Neate, Rupert. 2008. "Wikipedia Founder Jimmy Wales Goes Bananas." *The Telegraph,* November 7. Accessed December 5, 2014: http://www.telegraph .co.uk/finance/newsbysector/mediatechnologyandtelecoms/3399843/Wikipedia -founder-Jimmy-Wales-goes-bananas.html.

"Net Losses: Estimating the Economic Impact of Cyber Crime." 2014. *McAfee Center for Strategic and International Studies.* June. Accessed April 20, 2015: http://www .mcafee.com/us/resources/reports/rp-economic-impact-cybercrime2.pdf.

"Net Sales Revenue of Amazon from 2004 to 2014 (in Billion U.S. Dollars)." 2015. Statistica. Accessed April 6, 2015: http://www.statista.com/statistics/266282 /annual-net-revenue-of-amazoncom/.

Newton, Casey. 2015. "How One of the Best Films at Sundance Was Shot Using an iPhone 5S." *The Verge.* Accessed March 26, 2015: http://www.theverge .com/2015/1/28/7925023/sundance-film-festival-2015-tangerine-iphone-5s.

"NTIA Announces Intent to Transition Key Internet Domain Name Functions." 2014. National Telecommunications Information Agency Office of Public Affairs. Accessed December 28, 2014: http://www.ntia.doc.gov/press-release /2014/ntia-announces-intent-transition-key-internet-domain-name-functions.

O'Reilly, Tim. 2014. "What Is Web 2.0? Design Patterns and Business Models for the Next Generation of Software." In *The Social Media Reader,* edited by Michael Mandiberg. New York: New York University Press, 32–52.

Ostrom, Elinor. 1990. *Governing the Commons: The Evolution of Institutions for Collective Action*. Cambridge, UK: Cambridge University Press.

Ozer, Jan. 2011. "What Is Streaming?" StreamingMedia.com. Accessed April 2, 2015: http://www.streamingmedia.com/Articles/ReadArticle.aspx?ArticleID=74052.

Palser, Barb. 2006. "Hype or the Real Deal?" *American Journalism Review*, 44. Accessed February 1, 2015: http://ajrarchive.org/Article.asp?id=4060.

Parkin, Simon. 2014. "Zoe Quinn's Depression Quest." *The New Yorker*. Accessed May 6, 2015: http://www.newyorker.com/tech/elements/zoe-quinns-depression-quest.

Parmelee, John H., and Shannon L. Bichard. 2012. *Politics and the Twitter Revolution: How Tweets Influence the Relationship between Political Leaders and the Public*. Lanham, MD: Lexington Books.

Parr, Chris. 2013. "Mooc Creators Criticize Courses' Lack of Creativity." *Times Higher Education*. Accessed January 2, 2015: http://www.timeshighereducation.co.uk/news/mooc-creators-criticise-courses-lack-of-creativity/2008180.fullarticle.

Paumgarten, Nick. 2011. "Looking for Someone." *The New Yorker*. Accessed March 2, 2015: http://www.newyorker.com/magazine/2011/07/04/looking-for-someone.

Peckham, Matt. 2014. "Streaming Music Services Compared by Price, Quality, Catalog Size and More." *Time*. Accessed November 27, 2014: http://time.com/30081/13-streaming-music-services-compared-by-price-quality-catalog-size-and-more/.

Pegoraro, Rob. 2010. "Amazon Charges Kindle Users for Free Project Gutenberg E-books." *Washington Post*. Accessed February 18, 2015: http://voices.washingtonpost.com/fasterforward/2010/11/amazon_charges_kindle_users_fo.html.

Pew Research Center. 2013. "E-Reading Rises as Device Ownership Jumps." Accessed February 18, 2015: http://www.pewinternet.org/files/old-media//Files/Reports/2014/PIP_E-reading_011614.pdf.

Pimbblet, Kirstie-Ann. 2013. "How Google Glass Could Evolve Social Media." *Social Media Today*. Accessed December 10, 2014: http://www.socialmediatoday.com/content/how-google-glass-could-evolve-social-media.

"Pirate Party Members Nominate Snowden, Manning for Nobel Peace Prize." 2014. RT.com. Accessed January 5, 2015: http://rt.com/news/snowden-manning-nobel-pirate-633/.

Pogue, David. 2010. "Looking at the iPad from Two Angles." *New York Times*. Accessed April 7, 2015: http://www.nytimes.com/2010/04/01/technology/personaltech/01pogue.html?pagewanted=all&partner=rss&emc=rss&_r=0.

Porter, David. 2015. "Spotify vs Pandora: Which Market Is Bigger?" *Forbes*. Accessed April 24, 2015: http://www.forbes.com/sites/davidporter/2015/04/24/spotify-vs-pandora-which-market-is-bigger/.

Postman, Neil. 1992. *Technopoly: The Surrender of Culture to Technology*. New York: Vintage Books.

Poulsen, Kevin. 2011. *Kingpin: How One Hacker Took Over the Billion-Dollar Cybercrime Underground.* New York: Crown Publishing.

Primack, Dan. 2014. "Why Venture Capitalists Are Right to Be Crazy about Bitcoin." *Fortune*, 169: 40.

Purcell, Kristin, and Lee Rainie. 2014. "Americans Feel Better Informed about the Internet." Pew Research Internet Project. Accessed December 10, 2014: http://www.pewinternet.org/2014/12/08/better-informed/.

Putnam, Robert D. 2000. *Bowling Alone: The Collapse and Revival of American Community.* New York: Simon & Schuster.

Radicati, Sara, and Justin Levenstein. 2013. "Email Statistics Report, 2013–2017." The Radicati Group, Inc. Accessed April 30, 2015: http://www.radicati.com /wp/wp-content/uploads/2013/04/Email-Statistics-Report-2013-2017-Executive -Summary.pdf.

Rainie, Lee, and Mary Madden. 2015. "Americans' Privacy Strategies Post-Snowden." Pew Research Center. Accessed May 4, 2015: http://www.pewinternet .org/2015/03/16/americans-privacy-strategies-post-snowden/.

Rainie, Lee, and Aaron Smith. 2013. "Tablet and E-reader Ownership Update." Pew Research Center Report. Accessed March 26, 2015: http://www.pewinternet .org/2013/10/18/tablet-and-e-reader-ownership-update/.

Ramirez, Jessica. 2010. "Spyware on Your Cell Phone?" *Newsweek.* Accessed April 21, 2015: http://www.newsweek.com/spyware-your-cell-phone-73569.

Ranadive, Vivek. 2013. "Hyperconnectivity: The Future Is Now." *Forbes.* Accessed December 9, 2014: http://www.forbes.com/sites/vivekranadive/2013/02/19/hyper connectivity-the-future-is-now/.

Raustiala, Kal, and Chris Sprigman. 2012. "How Much Do Music and Movie Piracy Really Hurt the U.S. Economy?" *Freakonomics.com.* Accessed April 30, 2012: http://freakonomics.com/2012/01/12/how-much-do-music-and-movie -piracy-really-hurt-the-u-s-economy/.

Reilly, Richard Byrne. 2014. "The Cookie Is Dead. Here's How Facebook, Google, and Apple Are Tracking You Now." *Venture Beat.* Accessed April 1, 2015: http:// venturebeat.com/2014/10/06/the-cookie-is-dead-heres-how-facebook-google -and-apple-are-tracking-you-now/.

Reno v. American Civil Liberties Union et al. 1997. U.S. Supreme Court No. 96-511 521 U.S. 844 (argued March 19, 1997; decided June 26, 1997). Accessed March 26, 2015: https://scholar.google.com/scholar_case?case=1557224836887427725 &q=reno+v.+aclu&hl=en&as_sdt=40000006&as_vis=1.

Revlin, Gary. 2006. "Wallflower at the Web Party." *New York Times.* Accessed December 4, 2014: http://www.nytimes.com/2006/10/15/business/yourmoney /15friend.html?pagewanted=1&_r=2.

Reza, Pantha Rahman. 2015. "The Mobile Money Revolution Is Transforming Bangladesh." Translated by Pantha Rahman Reza. *Global Voices Online.* Accessed

February 3, 2015: http://globalvoicesonline.org/2015/01/08/the-mobile-money -revolution-is-transforming-bangladesh/.

Rheingold, Howard. 2002. *Smart Mobs: The Next Social Revolution*. Cambridge, MA: Perseus Books.

Rice, Chelsea, 2014. "OMG! Ebola Is Trending! Wait, What Does That Actually Mean?" *Boston.com*. Accessed January 1, 2015: http://www.boston.com /health/2014/10/09/omg-ebola-trending-wait-what-does-that-actually-mean /sUM8k7DBqKiD9wgeQ2eloI/story.html.

"Rise and Fall of Online Advertising." n.d. *1st Web Designer*. Accessed March 23, 2015: http://www.1stwebdesigner.com/online-advertising-history/.

Risen, Tom. 2014. "Happy 25th Birthday World Wide Web." *U.S. News and World Report*. Accessed April 20, 2015: http://www.usnews.com/news/articles /2014/03/12/happy-25th-birthday-world-wide-web.

Robinson, Ted. 2014. "Breaches, Malware to Cost $491 Billion in 2014, Study Says." *SC Magazine*. Accessed October 3, 2014: http://www.scmagazine.com /breaches-malware-to-cost-491-billion-in-2014-study-says/article/339167/.

Rogers, Everett M. 2003. *Diffusion of Innovations*, 5th ed. New York: Free Press.

Roose, Kevin. 2014. "What's Behind the Great Podcast Renaissance?" *New York Magazine*. Accessed January 20, 2015: http://nymag.com/daily/intelligencer/2014 /10/whats-behind-the-great-podcast-renaissance.html.

Rosen, Rebecca J. 2011. "Can a Paywall Stop Newspaper Subscribers from Canceling?" *The Atlantic Monthly*, September 12. Accessed December 3, 2014: http://www.theatlantic.com/technology/archive/2011/09/can-a-paywall-stop-news paper-subscribers-from-canceling/244932/.

Rosenberg, Alyssa. 2013. "Why The Federal Government Is Going after Bitcoin, but Amazon Coins Are Safe." *ThinkProgress*. Accessed September 19, 2014: http:// thinkprogress.org/alyssa/2013/05/15/2017091/why-the-federal-government -is-going-after-bitcoin-but-amazon-coins-are-safe/.

Rosin, Hanna. 2014. "Why Kids Sext." *The Atlantic Monthly*, 314: 65–77.

Rosoff, Matt. 2014. "Facebook Dumps Microsoft." *Business Insider*. Accessed January 22, 2015: http://www.businessinsider.com/facebook-and-microsoft-seem -to-be-parting-ways-2014-12#ixzz3PZ8rNU2A.

Rothkopf, David. 2014. "Disconnected." *Foreign Policy* 205: 79–80.

Ruiz, Rebecca. 2015. "Jackpots for Local TV Stations in F.C.C. Auction of Airwaves." *New York Times*. Accessed April 28, 2015: http://www.nytimes.com /2015/04/17/technology/local-broadcasters-could-reap-billions-in-airwaves-auction .html?_r=0.

Rushe, Dominic, and Paul Lewis. 2014. "How the 'Safest Place on the Internet' Tracks Its Users." *The Guardian*. Accessed January 22, 2015: http://www.theguardian .com/world/2014/oct/16/-sp-whispers-secret-safest-place-internet-tracks-users.

Rustiala, Kal, and Chris Sprigman. 2012. "How Much Do Music and Movie Piracy Really Hurt the U.S. Economy?" *Freakenomics.com*. Accessed April 30, 2015: http://freakonomics.com/2012/01/12/how-much-do-music-and-movie-piracy -really-hurt-the-u-s-economy/.

Sandoval, Greg. 2009. "RealNetworks Loses Critical Ruling in RealDVD Case." *CNet*. Accessed December 18, 2014: http://www.cnet.com/news/realnetworks-loses -critical-ruling-in-realdvd-case/.

Sanger, David E., and Nicole Perlroth. 2014. "U.S. Said to Find North Korea Ordered Cyberattack on Sony." *New York Times*. Accessed January 20, 2015: ww.nytimes.com/2014/12/18/world/asia/us-links-north-korea-to-sony-hacking .html?_r=1.

Sarno, David. 2009. "Twitter Creator Jack Dorsey Illuminates the Site's Founding Document. Part I." *Los Angeles Times*. Accessed January 6, 2015: http://latimes blogs.latimes.com/technology/2009/02/twitter-creator.html.

Schneier, Bruce. 2015. *Data and Goliath: The Hidden Battles to Collect Your Data and Control Your World*. New York: W. W. Norton and Co.

Schneier, Bruce. 2015. "In Our Modern Surveillance State Everyone Can Be Exposed." *Christian Science Monitor*. Accessed March 17, 2015: http://www .csmonitor.com/WorldPasscode/Passcode-Voices/2015/0311/In-our-modern -surveillance-state-everyone-can-be-exposed.

"Scope of the Problem." 2015. *Statement of the RIAA*. Accessed April 2, 2015: https://www.riaa.com/physicalpiracy.php?content_selector=piracy-online -scope-of-the-problem.

Seabrook, John. 2012. "Streaming Dreams: YouTube Turns Pro." *The New Yorker*, 86: 24–30.

Segall, Laurie. 2011. "News Corp. Sells Myspace to Specific Media." *CNN Money*. Accessed April 21, 2015: http://www.money.cnn.com/2011/06/29/technology /myspace_layoffs/index.htm?hpt=te_bn2.

Saguaro Seminar on Civic Engagement in America. 2015. Harvard University, Kennedy School. Accessed January 8, 2015: http://www.hks.harvard.edu/programs /saguaro/about/the-original-saguaro-seminar-meetings.

"The Sharing Economy—Sizing the Revenue Opportunity." 2015. PwC (UK). Accessed April 27, 2015: http://www.pwc.co.uk/issues/megatrends/collisions /sharingeconomy/the-sharing-economy-sizing-the-revenue-opportunity.jhtml.

Sherman, Adam. "Hyperconnected World." *World Economic Forum*. Accessed December 9, 2014: http://www.weforum.org/projects/hyperconnected-world.

Shields, Mike. 2015. "MySpace Still Reaches 50 Million People Each Month." *Wall Street Journal*. Accessed April 21, 2015: http://blogs.wsj.com/cmo/2015/01/14 /myspace-still-reaches-50-million-people-each-month/.

Shirky, Clay. 2011. "The Political Power of Social Media." *Foreign Affairs*, 90: 1.

Shirky, Clay. 2015 (March/April). "Revolt of the Clerks." *Columbia Journalism Review*, 45–49.

Shontell, Alyson. 2012. "Inside BuzzFeed: The Story of How Jonah Peretti Built the Web's Most Beloved New Media Brand." *Business Insider.* Accessed April 8, 2015: http://www.businessinsider.com/buzzfeed-jonah-peretti-interview-2012-12?page=2.

"Should Digital Monopolies Be Broken Up?" 2014. *The Economist*, 413: 11.

Sifry, Micah L. 2011. *WikiLeaks and the Age of Transparency.* Berkeley, CA: Counterpoint, 48–50.

Silva, Sean. 2014. "Bitcoin, Litecoin, Dogecoin and Other Cryptocurrencies Now Taxable Income." *Bloomberg.* Accessed September 20, 2014: http://www.bna.com/bitcoin-litecoin-dogecoin-b17179890404/.

Silver, Hayley, with Eileen Tan and Cory Mitchell. 2012. "Pinterest vs. Facebook: Which Social Sharing Site Wins at Shopping Engagement?" *Bizrate Insights.* Accessed October 2, 2014: http://www.bizrateinsights.com/blog/2012/10/15/online-consumer-pulse-pinterest-vs-facebook-which-social-sharing-site-wins-at-shopping-engagement/.

Simon, William L., and Jeffrey S. Young. 2005. *iCon: Steve Jobs, The Greatest Second Act in the History of Business.* New York: John Wiley & Sons.

Singh, Maanvi. 2015. "Apps Can Speed the Search for Love, but Nothing Beats a Real Date." National Public Radio. Accessed March 25, 2015: http://www.npr.org/blogs/health/2015/02/12/385745267/apps-can-speed-the-search-for-love-but-nothing-beats-a-real-date.

Singleton, Sharon. 2009. "E-Cards Bite into Greeting Card Industry." *Toronto Sun.* Accessed April 30, 2015: http://www.torontosun.com/money/2009/12/22/12239986-qmi.html.

"Smartphone OS Market Share, Q2 2014." n.d. *International Data Communication.* Accessed October 28, 2014: http://www.idc.com/prodserv/smartphone-os-market-share.jsp.

Smil, Vaclav. 2013. *Made in the USA: The Rise and Retreat of American Manufacturing.* Cambridge, MA: MIT Press, 110.

Smith, Aaron. 2010. "Trends in Broadband Adoption." Pew Research Center. Accessed December 5, 2014: http://www.pewinternet.org/2010/08/11/trends-in-broadband-adoption/.

Smith, Aaron, and Maeve Duggan. 2013. "Online Dating and Relationships." Pew Research Center. Accessed March 25, 2015: http://www.pewinternet.org/2013/10/21/online-dating-relationships/.

Smith, Aaron. 2015. "U.S. Smartphone Use in 2015." Pew Research Center. Accessed April 27, http://www.pewinternet.org/2015/04/01/us-smartphone-use-in-2015/2015.

Smith, Dave. 2014. "Why Hacker Gang 'Lizard Squad' Took Down Xbox Live and PlayStation Network." *Business Insider.* Accessed January 20, 2015: http://www.businessinsider.com/why-hacker-gang-lizard-squad-took-down-xbox-live-and-playstation-network-2014-12#ixzz3PO7Fd6xq.

Spangler, Todd. 2015. "NBC to Launch Comedy Internet-Subscription Service in 2015." *Variety.* Accessed March 3, 2015: http://variety.com/2015/digital/news/nbc-to-launch-comedy-internet-subscription-service-with-tonight-show-snl-episodes-report-1201445426/.

"Spotting the Fakes among the Five-Star Reviews." 2015. PBS Newshour (transcript). Accessed April 22, 2015: http://www.pbs.org/newshour/bb/spotting-fakes-among-five-star-reviews/.

Star, Paul. 2009. "Goodbye to the Age of Newspapers (Hello to a New Era of Corruption)." *New Republic,* March 4. Accessed February 19, 2015: http://www.newrepublic.com/article/goodbye-the-age-newspapers-hello-new-era-corruption.

"StatCounter Global Stats." 2015. *StatCounter Analytics.* Accessed April 27, 2015: http://gs.statcounter.com/#desktop-browser-ww-monthly-201501-201501-bar.

"State of the Media 2012." 2012. Pew Research Center. Accessed November 11, 2014: http://www.stateofthemedia.org/2013/overview-5/ and http://www.stateofthemedia.org/2012/mobile-devices-and-news-consumption-some-good-signs-for-journalism/what-facebook-and-twitter-mean-for-news/.

Steel, Emily. 2009. "AOL–Time Warner Divorce Is Official." *Wall Street Journal.* Accessed March 22, 2015: http://www.wsj.com/articles/SB10001424052748704825504574586393655471238.

Stokes, Robert. 2012. "Virtual Money Laundering: The Case of Bitcoin." *Information & Communication Technology Law,* 21: 221–236.

Stone, Brad. 2013. "Can Marissa Mayer Save Yahoo!?" *Bloomberg Businessweek.* Accessed November 12, 2014: http://www.businessweek.com/articles/2013-08-01/can-marissa-mayer-save-yahoo.

Strauss, Bob. 2009. "Film Piracy Heads North of Border." *Los Angeles Times.* Accessed April 2, 2015: http://www.dailynews.com/20090407/film-piracy-heads-north-of-border.

Streitfeld, David. 2014. "In Latest Volley against Amazon, Hachette's Writers Target Its Board." *New York Times.* Accessed September 24, 2014: http://www.nytimes.com/2014/09/15/technology/in-latest-volley-against-amazon-hachettes-writers-target-its-board.html?_r=0.

Suarez-Tangil, Guillermo, Juan E. Tapiador, Pedro Peris-Lopez, and Arturo Ribagorda. 2013. "Evolution, Detection and Analysis of Malware for Smart Devices." *IEEE Communications,* 16: 961–987.

Surowiecki, James. 2004. *The Wisdom of Crowds: Why the Many Are Smarter Than the Few and How Collective Wisdom Shapes Business, Economies, Societies and Nations*. New York: Anchor Books.

Swan, Noelle. 2014. "The 'Maker Movement' Creates D.I.Y. Revolution." *Christian Science Monitor*. Accessed March 29, 2015: http://www.csmonitor.com/Technology/2014/0706/The-maker-movement-creates-D.I.Y.-revolution.

Swanson, Ana. 2015. "A Powerful reddit Thread Reveals What It's Like to Be Disabled." *The Washington Post*. Accessed April 24, 2015: http://www.washingtonpost.com/blogs/wonkblog/wp/2015/04/24/a-powerful-reddit-thread-reveals-what-its-like-to-be-disabled/.

Sydell, Laura. 2014. "Pandora's New Deal: Different Pay, Different Play." NPR's *Morning Edition*. Accessed November 29, 2014: http://www.npr.org/2014/11/26/366339553pandoras-new-deal-different-pay-different-pay.

Sydell, Laura. 2015. "With Downloads in Decline, Can iTunes Adapt?" NPR's *Morning Edition*. Accessed January 7, 2015: http://www.npr.org/blogs/therecord/2015/01/06/375173595/with-downloads-in-decline-can-itunes-adapt.

Tahmincioglu, Eve. 2011. "It's Time to Deal with That Overflowing Inbox." MSNBC. Accessed January 29, 2015: http://www.nbcnews.com/id/41135478/ns/business-personal_finance/t/its-time-deal-overflowing-inbox/#.VFVFnvnF-So.

Tapscott, Don, and Anthony D. Williams. 2006. *Wikinomics: How Mass Collaboration Changes Everything*. New York: Penguin, 125.

Tassi, Bill. 2014. "Whatever Happened to the War on Piracy?" *Forbes*. Accessed April 2, 2015: http://www.forbes.com/sites/insertcoin/2014/01/24/whatever-happened-to-the-war-on-piracy/.

Thomas-Jones, Angela. 2010. *The Host in the Machine: Examining the Digital in the Social*. Oxford, UK: Chandos.

Thompson, Clive. 2014. "Good Vibrations: Tech That Talks through Your Skin." *Wired*, 22: 26.

Thompson, Derek. 2013. "The Riddle of Amazon." *The Atlantic Monthly*, 313: 26–31.

Thompson, Derek. 2014. "The Shazam Effect." *The Atlantic Monthly*, 314: 67–69+72.

Thompson, John B. 2012. *Merchants of Culture: The Publishing Business in the Twenty-First Century*, 2nd ed. London: Plume.

Thorpe, Devin. 2015. "Omidyar Network Pairs Grants with Investments to Solve Problems." *Forbes*. Accessed February 24, 2015: http://www.forbes.com/sites/devinthorpe/2015/01/22/omidyar-network-pairs-grants-with-investments-to-solve-problems/.

Timberg, Scott. 2015. *Culture Crash: The Killing of the Creative Class*. New Haven: Yale University Press.

Toal, Robin. 2014. "Top Ten U.S. Charitable Foundations." *FundsforNGOs*. Accessed December 10, 2014: http://www.fundsforngos.org/foundation-funds-for-ngos/worlds-top-ten-wealthiest-charitable-foundations/.

Toffler, Alvin. 1980. *The Third Wave*. New York: Bantam.

Toobin, Jeffrey. 2014. "The Solace of Oblivion." *The New Yorker*. Accessed April 26, 2015: http://www.newyorker.com/magazine/2014/09/29/solace-oblivion.

"Total US Ad Spending See Largest Increase Since 2004." 2014. *e-Marketer*. Accessed March 23, 2015: http://www.emarketer.com/Article/Total-US-Ad-Spending-See-Largest-Increase-Since-2004/1010982#sthash.nJimcAYo.dpuf.

Tsukayama, Hayley. 2013. "Instagram Adding Ads Boosts Facebook's Outlook, Analysts Say." *Washington Post*. Accessed December 5, 2013: http://www.washingtonpost.com/business/technology/instagram-adding-ads-boosts-facebooks-outlook-analysts-say/2013/10/04/5bed98c4-2d10-11e3-8ade-a1f23cda135e_story.html.

Turkle, Sherry. 1984. *The Second Self: Computers and the Human Spirit*. New York: Simon & Schuster.

Turkle, Sherry. 1995. *Life on the Screen: Identity in the Age of the Internet*. New York: Simon & Schuster.

Turkle, Sherry. 2012. *Alone Together: Why We Expect More from Technology and Less from Each Other*. New York: Basic Books.

Tuttle, Brad. 2015. "What Expedia's Acquisition of Orbitz and Travelocity Means for Travelers." *Time*. Accessed March 30, 2015: http://time.com/money/3707551/expedia-orbitz-impact-travelers/.

"UN Broadband Commission Releases New Country-by-Country Data on State of Broadband Access Worldwide: Half the World Will Be Online by 2017." 2014. International Telecommunication Union Press Release, September 21. Accessed December 28, 2014: http://www.itu.int/net/pressoffice/press_releases/2014/46.aspx#.VKCJl14APA.

"United States of America." 2014. Internet Usage and Broadband Usage Report. Accessed December 5, 2014: http://www.internetworldstats.com/am/us.htm.

U.S. Immigration and Customs Enforcement. 2014. "Cyber Crimes Center." U.S. Government, Department of Homeland Security. Accessed October 29, 2014: http://www.ice.gov/cyber-crimes.

U.S. Travel Association. 2015. "Travel Facts and Statistics." Accessed March 30, 2015: https://www.ustravel.org/news/press-kit/travel-facts-and-statistics.

Vaidhyanathan, Siva. 2014. "Open Source as Culture/Culture as Open Source." In *The Social Media Reader*, edited by Michael Mandiberg. New York: New York University Press, 24–31.

Vascellaro, Jessica E., Emily Steel, and Russell Adams. 2011. "Newscorp Sells MySpace for a Song." *Wall Street Journal*. Accessed December 26, 2014: http://www.wsj.com/articles/SB10001424052702304584004576415932273770852.

Vasel, Kathryn. 2014. "When Did Black Friday Start?" CNN. Accessed December 9, 2014: http://money.cnn.com/2014/11/28/news/black-friday-history/.

"Ventures Puts $258M into Uber, Its Largest Deal Ever." 2013. *TechCrunch*. Accessed October 29, 2014: http://techcrunch.com/2013/08/22/google-ventures-puts-258m-into-uber-its-largest-deal-ever/.

Vijayan, Jai. 2014. "Hackers Devise New Simplified Phishing Method." *Information Week*. Accessed January 3, 2015: http://www.darkreading.com/attacks-breaches/hackers-devise-new-simplified-phishing-method/d/d-id/1317242.

Von Lohmann, Fred. 2010. "Unintended Consequences: Twelve Years under the DMCA." *Electronic Frontier Foundation*. Accessed December 18, 2014: https://www.eff.org/files/eff-unintended-consequences-12-years_0.pdf.

Wahaba, Phil. 2014. "Cyber-Monday Sales Pass 2 Billion." *Fortune*. Accessed December 9, 2014: http://fortune.com/2014/12/02/cyber-monday-sales-pass-2-billion/.

Walker, Rob. 2007. "Handmade 2.0." *New York Times*. Accessed April 2, 2015: http://www.nytimes.com/2007/12/16/magazine/16Crafts-t.html?_r=3&oref=slogin&ref=magazine&pagewanted=all&.

Walker, Rob. 2012. "Can Etsy Go Pro without Losing Its Soul?" *Wired*. Accessed December 3, 2014: http://www.wired.com/2012/09/etsy-goes-pro/all/.

Wallace, Benjamin. 2011. "The Geek Kings of Smut." *New York Magazine*. Accessed May 11, 2015: http://nymag.com/news/features/70985/index2.html.

Wallenstein, Andrew. 2014. "What Netflix's Sandler Stunner Means for Movies." *Variety*. Accessed October 2, 2014: http://variety.com/2014/digital/news/what-netflixs-sandler-stunner-means-for-movies-1201319579/.

Walter, Joseph, and Spencer E Ante. 2012. "Once a Social Media Star, Digg Sells for $500,000." *Wall Street Journal*. Accessed February 26, 2015: http://www.wsj.com/articles/SB10001424052702304373804577523181002565776.

Wasik, Bill. 2014. "Try It On." *Wired,* 22: 90–99.

Weiss, Philip. 2014. "A Guy Named Craig." *New York Magazine*. Accessed February 25, 2015: http://nymag.com/nymetro/news/media/internet/15500/.

Weissmann, Jordan. 2014. "The Decline of Newspapers Hits a Stunning Milestone." *Slate.com*. Accessed April 22, 2015: http://www.slate.com/blogs/moneybox/2014/04/28/decline_of_newspapers_hits_a_milestone_print_revenue_is_lowest_since_1950.html.

Wheeler, Tom. 2015. "Good News for Consumers, Innovators and Financial Markets." FCC Chair's Blog, FCC.gov, February 26. Accessed March 26, 2015: http://www.fcc.gov/blog/good-news-consumers-innovators-and-financial-markets.

Wheeler, Tom. 2015. FCC Open Internet Order—Preserving and Protecting the Internet for All Americans. Federal Communications Commission, March 12. Accessed March 25, 2015. http://www.fcc.gov/document/fcc-open-internet-order-separating-fact-fiction.

Wiener, Norbert. 1948. *Cybernetics: Or, Control and Communication in the Animal and the Machine*. New York: Wiley.

Wilhelm, Alex, and Alexia Tsotsis. 2013. "Google Ventures Puts $258M into Uber, Its Largest Deal Ever." *TechCrunch.* Accessed October 29, 2014: http://techcrunch.com/2013/08/22/google-ventures-puts-258m-into-uber-its-largest-deal-ever/.

Wingfield, Nick. 2011. "Apple Adds Do-Not-Track Tool to New Browser." *Wall Street Journal.* Accessed October 3, 2014: http://www.wsj.com/articles/SB10001424052748703551304576261272308358858.

Wohlsen, Marcus. 2014. "Uber in Overdrive: What the Car Service Will Do with Big Money from Google." *Wired,* 22: 49–54.

Wolf, Gary. 2004. "How the Internet Invented Howard Dean." *Wired,* 12: 38.

Wolfe, Kristin Roeschenthaler. 2014. *Blogging: How Our Private Thoughts Went Public.* Lanham, MD: Lexington Books.

Wolman, David. 2013. "How to Save Bitcoin: Let's Take ECash Mainstream." *Wired,* 21: 39–42.

Wood, Clare, Nenagh Kemp, and Beverly Plester. 2014. *Text Messaging and Literacy—The Evidence.* London and New York: Routledge.

Wood, Molly. 2014. "How Young Is Too Young for a Digital Presence?" *New York Times.* Accessed May 1, 2015: http://www.nytimes.com/2014/05/15/technology/personaltech/how-young-is-too-young-for-a-digital-presence.html?_r=0.

"World News: Edward Snowden: Winning Sweden's Alternative Nobel Prize Is Vindication." 2014. *The Guardian.* Accessed September 26, 2015: http://www.theguardian.com/world/video/2014/sep/25/edward-snowden-sweden-alternative-nobel-prize-video.

"The World's Billionaires." 2014. *Forbes.* Accessed April 21, 2015: http://www.forbes.com/pictures/mel45hdjl/17-larry-page/.

"Worldwide Smartphone Shipments Edge Past 300 Million Units in the Second Quarter: Android and iOS Devices Account for 96% of the Global Market." 2014. International Data Corporation (IDC). Accessed October 2, 2014: http://www.idc.com/getdoc.jsp?containerId=prUS25037214.

Wortham, Jenna. 2010. "My Selfie, Myself." *New York Times, Sunday Review.* Accessed October 2, 2014: http://www.nytimes.com/2013/10/20/sunday-review/my-selfie-myself.html?pagewanted=all&_r=0.

Woyke, Elizabeth. 2014. *The Smartphone: Anatomy of an Industry.* New York and London: The New Press.

Wozniak, Steve. 2015. "A Conversation with Steve Wozniak." Springfield Public Forum, Springfield, MA, May 1.

Wozniak, Steve, with Gina Smith. 2006. *iWoz: Computer Geek to Cult Icon: How I Invented the Personal Computer, Co-Founded Apple, and Had Fun Doing It.* New York: Norton.

Yarrow, Jay. 2013. "Android Activations Hit 1 Billion." *Business Insider,* September 4. Accessed December 3, 2014: http://www.businessinsider.com/chart-of-the-day-android-activations-hit-1-billion-2013-9#ixzz3KqjT0wuK.

Young, Kimberly. 2010. *Internet Addiction: A Handbook and Guide to Evaluation and Treatment*. Hoboken, NJ: John Wiley and Sons.

Zickuhr, Kathryn, and Lee Rainie. 2014. "E-Reading Rises as Device Ownership Jumps." Pew Research Center. Accessed March 7, 2015: http://www.pewinternet.org/2014/01/16/e-reading-rises-as-device-ownership-jumps/.

Zittrain, Jonathan. 2008. *The Future of the Internet and How to Stop It*. New Haven, CT, and London: Yale University Press.

Index

Page numbers in **bold** indicate main entries in the encyclopedia.

About the Author

JARICE HANSON, PhD, is a professor in the Department of Communication at the University of Massachusetts, Amherst. She is the author of Praeger's *24/7: How Cell Phones and the Internet Change the Way We Live, Work, and Play* as well as *Connections: Technologies of Communication* and *Understanding Video: Applications, Impact and Theory*. She is also coauthor, editor, or coeditor of 27 books, including the successful textbook series, *Taking Sides: Controversial Issues in Media and Society*, now in its fourteenth edition. Hanson has been recognized as a distinguished lecturer at the University of Massachusetts, where she has also received the Distinguished Teaching Award in the College of Social and Behavioral Sciences. She held the Verizon Chair in Telecommunications at Temple University.